HIS WAY
THE UNAUTHORIZED BIOGRAPHY
OF FRANK SINATRA

- The whole story of his childhood, which is far different than the one he invented.

- His beginnings as a skinny kid crooner who caused a bobby sox craze.

- His relationships with Harry James and Tommy Dorsey.

- His climb to the top as a singer and movie star— and the scandal, violence and moodswings that followed.

- His trail of broken marriages to Nancy Sinatra, Ava Gardner and Mia Farrow.

- His on-going womanizing with the famous and unknown.

- The inside story of the rise and fall of the Rat Pack.

- His friendships with powerful Mafia figures.

- His public and private displays of verbal and physical abuse, both with and without his notorious bodyguards.

- His wildly lavish displays of generosity toward friends and charities.

- His vast influence that extends into the White House, today more than ever.

- The magnetism that still draws huge audiences worldwide.

THE NO-HOLDS-BARRED INSIDE LOOK
AT THE MAN, THE LEGEND, AND THE LIFE
OF FRANK SINATRA

KITTY
KELLEY

HIS
WAY

THE UNAUTHORIZED
BIOGRAPHY OF
FRANK SINATRA

BANTAM BOOKS
TORONTO • NEW YORK • LONDON • SYDNEY • AUCKLAND

HIS WAY: THE UNAUTHORIZED BIOGRAPHY OF FRANK SINATRA

A Bantam Book

Bantam hardcover edition / October 1986
8 printings through November 1986
Bantam paperback edition / September 1987

Library of Congress Cataloging-in-Publication Data
Kelley, Kitty.
  His way.

  Bibliography: p. 541
  Includes index.
  1. Sinatra, Frank, 1915–   2. Singers—United
States—Biography.   I. Title.
ML420.S565K4 1986   784.5'0092'4 [B]   85-48264
                    ISBN 0-553-26879-1

To Stanley Tretick,
whose tireless efforts on behalf of this book
disprove his theory that photographers are a shiftless lot.

"Reputation is what men and women think of us;
Character is what God and angels know of us."

—Thomas Paine

AUTHOR'S NOTE

I tried several times to interview Frank Sinatra for this book. Over a period of four years, I sent him several letters but received no response. I began calling and writing his publicist, Lee Solters. Again, no response. I then made several phone calls to Mr. Sinatra's lawyer, Milton Rudin, and sent him several letters. On August 26, 1983, Mr. Rudin wrote me, saying he "would be willing to arrange an appointment" in his law office in Los Angeles. Apparently, he changed his mind.

On September 21, 1983, Frank Sinatra sued to stop this book from being published before a word was ever written. He filed suit in California seeking two million dollars in punitive damages from me for presuming to write without his authorization. He claimed that he and he alone, or someone he anointed, could write his life story, but no one else was allowed to do so. As he stated in his complaint: "Sinatra has, on numerous occasions, informed his friends and publicly stated that at such time as he decides is appropriate, he will 'set the record straight' as to many aspects of his life."

He further claimed that I was misrepresenting myself as his official biographer to get "inside knowledge of the private aspects or events of [his] life." Asserting that I was misappropriating his name and likeness for commercial purposes, he asked the court to issue an injunction.

Fortunately a national coalition of writers' groups rose up

to protest this action, claiming that Frank Sinatra's lawsuit against me was an assault upon all writers' constitutionally protected freedom of expression and should be dismissed on its face. In a joint statement they said: "The apparent goal behind Sinatra's filing of this suit is to scare Ms. Kelley away from her investigation and, ultimately, to force her to scrap the book. Abuses of the judicial system such as these pose a serious threat to all writers."

Calling Sinatra's lawsuit "a chilling example of how a powerful public figure using money and influence can orchestrate what the public shall know about him," the coalition focused public attention on the rights guaranteed to all Americans under the First Amendment, even those people not approved of by Mr. Sinatra.

For one year, Sinatra pursued his lawsuit. His allegations proved groundless, and on September 19, 1984, he dropped the matter.

The writers groups applauded his action. "The court's dismissal of this meritless suit—at the request of Mr. Sinatra—is a victory for all writers and the public," stated their press release. "It reaffirms the right of the public to be informed about the lives of influential public persons whether or not they approve of the writer and his or her approach."

This coalition, which included the Reporters Committee for Freedom of the Press, Sigma Delta Chi (Society of Professional Journalists), the Newspaper Guild, PEN, the American Society of Journalists and Authors, the National Writers Union, the Council of Writers Organizations, and Washington Independent Writers, mobilized quickly and effectively to offer their support. Without them, I could never have written this book.

I am also grateful for the editorial support I received from the New York *Daily News* and the *Baltimore Sun* as well as Jules Feiffer's brilliant cartoon in *The Village Voice*. Joseph Foote and Ronald Goldfarb in *The Washington Post*, Liz Smith in the New York *Daily News*, and William Safire in *The New York Times* wrote eloquently that censorship, no matter how you dress it up, is constitutionally impermissible. Such distinguished commentary deploring Mr. Sinatra's attempt at prior restraint emphasized how important the press considers its right to cover public figures without restriction. As the *Baltimore Sun* stated: "If all the public can learn of the person is what the person himself wants it to learn, then ours will

become a very closed and ignorant society, unable to correct
its ills, quite unlike what the drafters and subsequent generations of defenders of the free-speech First Amendment had in
mind."

During this time I received the good counsel of several
lawyers, including my father, William V. Kelley, his law
partner, Duane Swinton, and his former associate, Irene
Ringwood, of Witherspoon, Kelley, Davenport & Toole in
Spokane, Washington; my personal attorney, Benjamin L.
Zelenko of Landis, Cohen, Rauh and Zelenko in Washington, D.C.; and my California attorneys, William W. Vaughn
and Robert C. Vanderet of O'Melveny & Myers in Los
Angeles.

To research my subject as thoroughly as possible, I began
by trying to read everything ever written about Frank Sinatra,
an enormous task considering a career that spans over forty
years. Heather Perram, my research assistant, spent months
gathering books, magazine articles, and newspaper clippings,
which she diligently filed and cross-referenced. Later, Patti
Pancoe helped index the 857 interviews I conducted, while
Maya Picado tried to give my office some semblance of order.

Librarians across the country contributed their skills, and
I am especially grateful to William Hifner of *The Washington
Post*, Sunday Orme Fellows, formerly of *The New York Times*,
Joe Wright of the *Miami News*, John Hodgson and Fred Schmidt
of the New York *Daily News*, Homer Martin of the *Bergen
County Record*, Marcy Marchi of *Playboy*, Judy Gerritts of the
San Francisco Chronicle, Tom Lutgen, Nancy McKinney, Joyce
Pinney, and Cecily Surace of the *Los Angeles Times*, Kay
Shepard of the *Los Angeles Herald Examiner*, Vera Busanelli of
the *Paterson News* and *Hudson Dispatch* (New Jersey), Judy
Marriott of the *Chicago Tribune*, June Paramore of the *Las Vegas
Sun*, Glenda Harris of the *Las Vegas Review-Journal*, Nan Stod-
dard of the *St. Louis Post Dispatch*, Merle Thomason of *Women's
Wear Daily*, Cecelia Weaver of the *Sacramento Bee*, Woody
Wilson of *Variety*, Beryl Costello of the Brockton, Mass.,
Enterprise, Andy Eppolito of *Newsday*, Lucy Forcucci of the
Palm Springs Public Library (Reference Room), Arlene Nevens
of the Great Neck (New York) Library, Joyce Miller and
Jeanne Smith of the Information Office of the Library of
Congress, Virginia C. Lopiccolo of the College of Journalism
of the University of South Carolina, and Joan Doherty of the
New Jersey Room in the Jersey City Public Library.

I also received excellent research help from Simon Nathan and Heidi Stock in New York; Jerry MacKenzie, Michael May, and Louis Raino in New Jersey; Gloria N. Christopher in Minnesota; Miki Jameson in California; Jamie Raskin and Thomas F. Timberman at Harvard University in Cambridge, Massachusetts, and Brandon Brodkin in Chicago.

Editors, writers, and reporters across the country contributed help and advice throughout the project, and I'm most grateful to Nathan Adams of *Reader's Digest;* Jennifer Allen; Hollis Alpert; Larry Ashmead of Harper & Row; Lissa August of *Time* magazine in Washington; Jim Bellows of ABC-TV; Lowell Bergman of CBS-TV; Winnie Bonelli of the *Hudson Dispatch;* Myram Borders of the *Reno Gazette Journal;* Patricia Bosworth; Arlene Bouras of *Playboy;* William Brashler; Norma Lee Browning; Herb Caen of the *San Francisco Chronicle;* Barney Calame of the *Wall Street Journal;* Tony Capaccio, a Jack Anderson staff associate; Ben Cate, senior correspondent of *Time* magazine; Charles Champlin of the *Los Angeles Times;* Garry Clifford, Washington bureau chief of *People;* Robert Carl Cohen; Patsy Collins of KING-TV (Seattle); Morton Cooper; Bill Davidson and the late Muriel Davidson; Ned Day of KLAS-TV in Las Vegas; Al Delugach of the *Los Angeles Times;* Digby Diehl of the *Los Angeles Herald Examiner;* Mary Ann Dolan, executive editor of the *Los Angeles Herald Examiner;* Jim Drinkhall of the *Wall Street Journal;* Harlan Ellison; Mike Ewing; Larry Fields of the *Philadelphia Daily News;* Roland Flamini of *Time* magazine (Beirut); the late Ketti Fringe; Tom Frisbie of the *Chicago Sun-Times;* Nicholas Gage; Jeff Gerth of *The New York Times;* Vera Glaser of the *Washingtonian;* Norman Glubok of CBS News; Albert Goldman; Fred Laurence Guiles; Joyce Haber; Jim Harrington of the *Brockton Enterprise* (Mass.); Pete Hamill; Seymour Hersh; Paul L. Hoch; A. E. Hotchner; Beverly Jackson of the *Santa Barbara News-Press;* Jody Jacobs, former society editor of the *Los Angeles Times;* Orr Kelly of *U.S. News & World Report;* Arthur Knight; Larry Leamer; Barney Leason; Bettijane Levine of the *Los Angeles Times;* Peter Maas; Scott Malone; Waits May of *Time* magazine in Washington; Arthur Marx; Peter McKay of the *London Daily Mail;* Marianne Means of Hearst newspapers; Hank Messick; Dan Moldea; Roy Newquist; Phil Nobile of *Forum;* Mel Opotowsky and Jerry Uhrammer of the *Press-Enterprise* (Riverside, Calif.); Tom Pryor of *Variety;* St. Clair Pugh; Peter Ross Range; Barbara Raskin; Wendall

Rawls; Rex Reed; Thomas C. Renner of *Newsday;* David Richards, drama critic of *The Washington Post;* John Riley; Jerome D. Rowland, formerly with the *Chicago American;* Mann Rubin; Murray Schumach; Vernon Scott of United Press International; Barbara Seaman; Art Seidenbaum of the *Los Angeles Times;* Martin Short; Nancy Siracusa of the *Hudson Dispatch;* Martha Smilgis of *People* magazine (Los Angeles bureau chief); Martin Smith of the *Sacramento Bee;* Malvina Stephenson of Knight-Ridder; Anthony Summers; Basil Talbott, Jr., of the *Chicago Sun-Times;* Gay Talese; Jack Tobin of *Sports Illustrated;* Wallace Turner of *The New York Times;* Denny Walsh of the *Sacramento Bee;* Wayne Warga; Benton J. (Jack) Willner, Jr., formerly with the *Chicago Daily News;* Paul Witteman of *Time* magazine (San Francisco bureau chief); and Maurice Zolotow.

I'm especially grateful to those writers who gave me their unpublished interviews for this book. My thanks to Ovid Demaris for his interview with Bobby Garcia; to David Horowitz for his interview with Milt Ebbins; to Bill Martin for his interview with Budd Granoff; and to Michael Thornton for his interviews with Ava Gardner. I'm also very grateful to Dick Partee for the hundreds of tapes he gave me of Frank Sinatra's "tea breaks"—the intervals during his performances when he addresses personal remarks to his audience.

My thanks also to the presidential libraries of Franklin D. Roosevelt, John F. Kennedy, and Lyndon B. Johnson, as well as the archivists of Hubert Humphrey's papers at the Minnesota Historical Society. The oral histories at Columbia University and the University of Nevada-Reno in Las Vegas were most helpful, as was the assistance I received from the Mugar Memorial Library at Boston University. The information provided by the American Film Institute and the Margaret Hedrick Library of the Motion Picture Academy of Arts and Sciences in Los Angeles, the Harry Ransom Humanities Research Center at the University of Texas in Austin, and the Performing Arts Research Center of the New York Public Library was invaluable. I'm grateful to the staff at the University of Southern California for providing access to the Warner Bros. collection, to the Special Collections Office at the University of California at Los Angeles for the Stanley Kramer papers, and to Herbert Nusbaum, legal counsel of MGM/UA, for giving me access to the studio's legal files. Patrick F. Healy, executive director of the Chicago Crime Commission, was most helpful, as were Virgil Peterson, former executive director of the Chicago Crime Commission; David Schippers, former chief of the organized crime and racketeering section, U.S. District Attorney's Office in Chicago; Terrance A. Norton, assistant director, Better Government Association, Chicago; and Joe A. Nunez of the U.S. District Court, Los Angeles. My thanks also to the family of Thomas Thompson— his brother Larry, his former wife, Joyce, and his two sons Kirk and Scott—for giving me unrestricted access to Tommy's papers.

Backed by extensive research, I began my interviews in Hoboken, New Jersey, where Frank Sinatra was born and raised. I tried to locate people who had known him and his family, and could speak with authority about his childhood. I made several trips to the area and talked to neighbors, friends, and classmates. I'm grateful to Anthony DePalma for his orientation to the mile-square city, to playwright Louis LaRusso, who lives in Hoboken and wrote *Lamppost Reunion*, and to all who shared their recollections, including Vinnie Amato, Bob Anthony, Mary Caiezza, Steve Capiello, Connie Cappadona, Minnie Cardinale, Anne Cardino, Rose Bucino Carrier, Fran Capone Ciriello, Doris Corrado, Josephine DeAngelis, Sister Mary Consilia Dondero, O.S.F., Ed Fitzsimmons, Laurence Florio, Frank and Minnie Garrick, Ellen Gates, Agnes Carney Hannigan, James Lanzetti, Joseph Lanzo, Joe "Gigi" Lissa, Eileen Clancy Lorenzo, Mike Losito, Tony Macagnano, Jerry Malloy, Johnny Marotta, Mike "Don" Milo, John Pascale, Tony "Skelley" Petrazelli, Joseph Romano, Joan Crocco Schook, Marion Brush Schreiber, Adam Sciarea, Richard Shirak, Fred "Tamby" Tamburro, Jimmy Trombetta, Frank "The Barber" Viggiano, Dominick Vitolo.

Others in New Jersey who were helpful include Al Algiro, Grace Barentis, Jean Cronan, Danny Figarelli, J. Owen Grundy, Judge Roger Hauser, Sam Lafaso, Elaine Lopez, Dolly Molla, Jimmy Roselli, Lud Shebazian, Thomas F. X. Smith, Bill Tonelli, Irv Wagen, Adeline Yacenda.

My sources made the most important contribution to this book. Some were too afraid of reprisals from Frank Sinatra to speak on the record; others, because of their positions in the entertainment industry, law enforcement, and the White House, cannot be thanked by name, but I'm grateful to all of them for their help. Only by interviewing as many people as possible, and some several times, with a tape recorder running, did I come to know my subject. Not every interview could be used in the book, but I appreciate the time and consideration of everyone who cooperated, including several of Frank Sinatra's relatives, who so generously shared their recollections.

My thanks to: Jay Allen, Steve Allen, Mrs. Ted Allen, Louise Anderson, Joe Armstrong, Charlotte Austin, Pat Babineau, Seth Baker, Rona Barrett, Ben Barton, Arthur Bell, Kevin Bellows, Sandra Grant Bennett, Nancy Berg, Mr. Blackwell, G. Robert Blakey, Neil Blincow, Bob Block, Rosalie Garavente Blumberg, Joan Benny Blumofe, Peter Borsari, Jean Israel Brody, Dick Brooks, Edmund G. "Pat" Brown, Vanessa Brown, Buck Buchwach, Jessica Burstein, Jim Byron, Sammy Cahn, Tita Cahn, Joe Canzeri, Irene Carmi, Randy Carmichael, Hoagy Carmichael, Jr., Anna Carroll, Paul Chandler, Isolde Chapin, Eleanor Churchin, Blair Clark, Mrs. Lee J. Cobb, Victor LaCroix Collins, David Patrick Columbia, Richard Condon, Bill Connell, Carol Conners, Ruth Conte, Pat Cooper, Paul Corbin, Tony Costa, Ronnie Cowan, Jean Cronan, Joan Crosby, Pat Cuda, John Daly, Peter Darmanin, Norma Ebberhart Dauphin, Shelly Davis, Lorna Dawkins, Arlene Demarco, Sally Denton, Iris de Reyes, Armand S. Deutsch, Joan Dew, Brad Dexter, Dennis Diamond, Phyllis Diamond, Maria DiMartini, John Dinges, Stanley Donen, William Dozier, Henry Dressel, Lenny Dunne, Fred Dutton, Les Edgley, George Eels, Larry Eisenberg, Corinne Entratter, Richard Epstein, Louis Estevez, Laura Eustace, Norman Evans, Phil Evans, Alice Everett, Dan and Katherine (Judith) Exner, Irving Fein, Michael Feinstein, Dennis Ferrara, Anita Colby Flagler, Heather and Tom Foley, Sue Foster, Franklin Fox, John Frankenhiemer, George Franklin, Emily Friedrich, Fred Froewiss, Katherine Foster Galloway, Joe Garafolo, Betty Garrett, Elio Gasperetti, Sondra Giles, Dizzy Gillespie, Edith Mayer Goetz, Vic Gold, Jerry Goldsmith, Harry Goodman, Harry Gossett, Currie Grant, Eleanor Roth Grasso, Kathryn Grayson, Johnny Green, Stephen Green, Shecky Greene, Elizabeth Greenschpoon, Mrs. Romy Greenson, Leo Guild, Richard Gully, Mel Haber of the Ingleside Inn in Palm Springs, Connie Haines, Corky Hale, Tom Hanlon, William Harnevious, Larry Harris, Robin "Curly" Harris, Joan Cohn Harvey, John Hearst, William Randolph Hearst, Jr., James P. Hoffa, Jr., Sam Holt, Karen Homewood, Allen Horowitz, William G. Hundley, Joe Hyams, George Jacobs, Marcia

Jacobs, Eddie Jaffe, Kitty Kallen, Joanne Kane, Lee Kendall, Maggie Kilgore, Nick Kostopolous, Joel Kozol, Kris Kristofferson, Helyne Landres, Jules Levine, Christine and Joe Laitin, Richard Lamparski, Lor-Ann Land, Abe Lastfogel, Tom Lauria, Esther Burns Lauter, the late Peter Lawford, Dr. Gordon Letterman, Marvin Lewis, Sr., Perry Lieber, Muriel Lipsey, Debra Davis Lipson, Kurt Ludtke, Sid Luft, Judy Lynch, Dick Lyneis.

Bob Maheu, Jim Mahoney, Gratsiella Maiellano, Peter Malatesta, Albert Maltz, Sylvia Blut Mann, Irving Mansfield, Maurice Manson, Rita Maritt, Betty Marshall, Jack Martin, Marion Marx, Gloria Massingill, Jackie Mason, Eugene J. McCarthy, Phyllis McGuire, Marvin "The Wizard" McIntyre, Barbara Barondess McLean, Arthur Michaud, John J. Miller, Mitch Miller, John Mitchell, Ellen Moesch, Bill Moran, Chuck Moses, Jim Murray, Muriel and Joseph Nellis, Gerry Nettleton, Charlotte Newcorn, Tracy Noble, Rudy Pacht, George Pappas, Betty Burns Paps, Jacqueline Park, Ben Pearson, Celia Pickell, Milt Pickman, Aldo Poncato, Beans Ponedel, Dave Powers, Doug Prestine, Ed Pucci, Anthony Quinn, Nancy Siedman Rapapport, Dan Rapoport, Matt Reese, Ed Reid, Sue Reilly, Nancy Clark Reynolds, the late Nelson Riddle, Kenny Roberts, Kendis Rochlin, William Roemer, Bahman Rooin, N. Joseph Ross, Barbara Ann Rowan, Barbara Rudd, China and Mort Sahl, Jeannie Sakol, Ralph Salerno, Tommy Sands, Yvonne Sangiacomo, Nadine Sauer, Frank Saunders, Chuck Scardina, Madeline Schapp, Barbara Schick, Mrs. Edward Schisser, Arthur Schurgin, Dr. Maxine Schurter, Carolyn See, John Seigenthaler, Mary Lou Watts Setylmayer, Nick Sevano, Artie Shaw, Julie and Bob Sherman, Norman Sherman, Joseph Shimon, Donna Shor, Mike Shore, Jo-Carroll Silvers, Phil Silvers, Antoinette Spatolla Sinatra, Frank Anthony Sinatra, Frank Sinatra, Jr., Marilyn Sinatra, Robert Slatzer, Pearl Similly, Glen Spencer, Penina Spiegel, Sam Spiegel, Arlene Stern, Raymond Strait, Elaine Stritch, the late David Susskind, Lee Sylvester, Johanna Tani, Daniel Taradash, Josephine Tingley, Mel Tormé, Fred Tredy, Maureen Tretick, Renee Valente, Rudy Vallee, Ted Van Dyke, Bethel Van Tassel, Michael Viner, Olga von Loewenstein, Karen Von Unge, Walter Wager, Eli Wallach, Mary Wallner, Bob Warren, Steven Weisman, Michael Whalen, Suzanne Wickham, Dr. Joan Willens, William Reid Woodfield, Yabo Yablonsky, Mickey Ziffern, Sybilla Zinsser, Tony Zoppi.

My special thanks to Mervin Block, who is the best friend and mentor a writer can have. From the beginning he helped to shape this book, which he later edited, trying to impose grammar, punctuation, and correct spelling. In the four years I worked on the book, he battled bureaucracy in several cities to scour court records and retrieve secret documents. He pored over microfilm, persuaded reluctant people to talk, and opened slammed doors. All with unflagging persistence and rollicking good humor. By example, he taught me to shun mediocrity, to strive for excellence.

There would have been no book without the efforts of my agent, Lynn Nesbit of I.C.M., Wayne S. Kabak, General Counsel of Josephson International, Inc., and Jeanne Bernkopf, an editing genius.

And finally, my love and my thanks to my husband, Mike Edgley, whose solid support lifts the wings I fly on.

Kitty Kelley
February 1986

1

On the night of December 22, 1938, two constables from Hackensack, New Jersey, headed for the Rustic Cabin in Englewood Cliffs to arrest Frank Sinatra.

Armed with a warrant charging adultery, the two officers walked into the dim little roadhouse looking for the skinny singer who waited tables and sang with Harold Arden's band over the radio line to WNEW in New York.

They waited until Frank finished his midnight broadcast and then sent word that they wanted to give him a Christmas present from one of his admirers. Falling for the ruse, Sinatra walked over to their table, where the criminal court officers arrested him and took him off to the courthouse. After posting five hundred dollars bail, he was released on his own recognizance.

The next day a Hoboken newspaper carried a story head-lined: SONGBIRD HELD IN MORALS CHARGE, but no one in Hoboken paid much attention. They were accustomed to seeing the Sinatra name in print for getting into trouble with the law. Frank's uncle Dominick, a boxer known as Champ Sieger, had been charged with malicious mischief; his uncle Gus had been arrested several times for running numbers; his other uncle, Babe, had been charged with participating in a murder and had been sent to prison. His father, Marty, was once charged with receiving stolen goods, and his mother, Dolly, was regularly in and out of courthouses for performing illegal abortions. And Frank himself had been arrested just a month before on a seduction charge.

Frank's relationship with the woman who pressed criminal charges against him had begun earlier that year, when Antoinette Della Penta Francke, a pretty twenty-five-year-old who had long been separated from her husband, went to the Rustic Cabin.

"He got on the platform to sing and I turned to face him," she said. "I was sucking a lemon from my Scotch, and he got mad at me. He came to the table afterwards and said, 'Look, young lady. Do you know you almost ruined my song? You suck a lemon and you make me go dry.'

" 'I'm going to give you a lemon in your sour face,' I joked to him. He asked me to dance and then he said, 'Can I take you out next week?' He was playing two against the middle with me and Nancy Barbato, but I didn't know it for a long time. We went together quite a few months, but then, because of his mother, he dropped me. He made me die of humiliation over something. To this day, I think about it."

Toni Francke was from Lodi, New Jersey, an Italian blue-collar town of tiny clapboard houses, several of which had plaster shrines to the Blessed Virgin Mary on their front porches. Dolly Sinatra, who prized her uptown location in Hoboken, was enraged that her son had reached into such a poor area for a girlfriend.

"After dating Frank awhile," Toni said, "I learned how to drive, and sometimes I'd pick him up in my car. Dolly would come out and holler at me, 'Who are you waiting for?'

" 'I'm waiting for Frank,' I'd say.

" 'You are after his money and you are nothing but cheap trash from Lodi,' she'd say.

"Then Frank would come down. He'd feel real embarrassed. He'd put his head down and get in the car, but Dolly would start screaming at him. He used to cry in my car because she didn't want him to be a singer. She said he was a bum. 'Go to college. Go to college,' she'd yell. 'You would not go to school.' 'You want to sing.' 'You bring home bad girlfriends.' She kept it up all the time, always nagging and screaming at him.

"I asked him how he could stand all that hollering. Frank said that she yelled at him all the time. Even when he went for a walk with his dad, she'd scream out the door. 'Where youse going? Don't start making him drink beer like you do, do you hear me?' Frank loved his father then. He really did. He used to say to me, 'I'd give Ma anything if she'd just leave my old man alone.'

"I said to him, 'Frank, why don't you open your mouth to your mother?'

" 'I don't like to say anything,' he said. 'She's my mother.'

"He loved her but he didn't, if you know what I mean."

Despite his mother's strenuous objections, Frank kept going to Lodi. After a few months of steady dating, Toni and her parents invited the Sinatras to dinner.

"Frank told me that Dolly yelled, 'What do you mean I have to go down there?' You see, she felt she was better than us."

Dolly finally relented and went with her husband and her son to the Della Penta home. Frank was looking forward to introducing his father to Toni, but he was worried about his mother kicking up a scene. He didn't have long to wait.

Tension pulsated on both sides of the front door when the Sinatras arrived and rang the bell. Mr. Della Penta answered, and Dolly walked in first, followed by Marty and Frank. Toni stepped forward and said hello. "You look so nice," she said. "You have such a nice dress on." As Dolly was looking around the house, Toni took their coats and hung them up. Here's how she recalls the occasion:

Frank went into the living room, sat down, and asked Toni to sit beside him. His parents sat down as well. Mrs. Della Penta said she was going into the kitchen to check on dinner. Frank popped up to help her.

"That's more than he does for me," said Dolly. "I'm sorry I had a boy. I should have had a girl."

"You get what God gives you," said Toni's father.

"How many children do you have anyway, Mr. Della Penta?"

He said that he had two daughters and one son, which seemed excessive to Dolly. "My, that's a big family, isn't it," she said.

"Big?" said Toni. "It's a pleasure. At least you are never alone."

"If God wanted me to have more kids, I would've had them," Dolly said.

Frank walked into the room. "Did you say God, Ma? I haven't seen you go to church in quite a while."

They had barely sat down to dinner when Dolly turned to

Mr. Della Penta and said, "Don't you think these kids are kind of young to be going around together?"

Frank looked at him and said, "I care for your daughter."

"It's only puppy play," said Dolly.

"Mom, I'm a twenty-two-year-old man," said Frank. "Besides, you got married young."

Dolly persisted. "I don't want these kids to get married. Frankie has to go to school first."

"I quit school, and you know it," said Frank.

"You what?" said Toni, who thought Frank was a high-school graduate. "When did you quit?"

"Now you know," said Frank. "You don't have to read it in the papers with Ma around, do you?"

"I don't want Toni to go with him," said Dolly. "They're too young. She'll keep Frankie from being a big singer. I want him to be a star."

Mr. Della Penta looked at Marty, who had not said a word. "Are you against this too?"

Turning to Dolly, Marty said, "I've had it. She's a fine girl. Just because she has Italian grandparents, does that mean she is so bad? Your parents did not like the idea of me, but you did it anyway, so why can't Frankie do what he wants?"

"Shut your goddamned mouth," said Dolly.

"Yeah, if someone's not Irish, you don't want me to have anything to do with them," said Frank.

Rose Della Penta left the room, and Toni's brother turned to Dolly. "Your son came after my sister," he said. "She didn't go after Frank."

"I don't care," said Dolly. "I don't want them going around together anymore."

Mr. Della Penta went into the kitchen to join his wife. Frank turned to his mother. "You should not have come. You're making Mr. and Mrs. Della Penta feel bad," he said.

Toni got up from the table to serve dessert. "Would you care for some fruit?"

"Oh, no," said Dolly. "I'm on a diet." Then she asked to go to the bathroom. Toni showed her where it was, saying, "Watch yourself coming down the steps."

"Oh, I can watch myself, don't you ever worry about that, young lady," said Dolly.

The dinner ended with Frank's telling his parents to go home without him because Toni would drive him back later.

"You have to get your rest, Frankie," said his mother. "You can't stay out late."

"Don't worry, Ma. I'll be home later."

"I don't like that. What time will you be back? I worry. I don't sleep right."

Marty looked at her and said, "You do okay. I'm the one who gets up at night."

Dolly never called to thank the Della Pentas for the macaroni dinner, nor did she ever invite them to Hoboken to have dinner at her house on Garden Street.

Frank told Toni not to take his mother's insults personally. "It's not just you," he said. "It's any girl I go with. No matter who the girl is, my mother always has something to say."

In the summer of 1938, Frank asked Toni to go steady and gave her a small diamond ring. A few days later, she said, he proposed in his car, saying, "I got to make more money, but I'm going to marry you, Toni."

He teased her because she wouldn't go to bed with him, saying that other girls treated their boyfriends better than she treated him.

"I'm not that type," Toni recalls.

"What have you got to lose?"

"What do you mean? If you marry me, okay, but otherwise you can't touch me until you marry me."

"Why, you made of gold or something?"

After a few nights of such sparring, Toni softened, convinced she would eventually get a divorce and marry Frank. She said she had known him a long time and felt good about him.

"Frank didn't seem like he had been to bed with anyone before," she said later. "He was kind of shy. He wasn't all that good because he was so thin. But he was very gentle with me. He did not grab me the first night. He could have but he didn't. We had gone to a big hotel outside of town with a bunch of other couples. We never slept together at my house. We always went to hotels, and Frank registered us as Mr. and Mrs. Sinatra. He sang to me in bed."

Within six weeks, Toni was pregnant. When she broke the news to Frank, he did not say anything for the longest time. Then he said, "Well, I'll have to marry you."

"Don't do me no favors, Frank."

She said that there were no fights or arguments over her

pregnancy and that Frank did not suggest an abortion. But Dolly bore down so hard on him for continuing to see Toni that the anxiety contributed to her miscarriage in her third month.

"When I told Frank, he was real sweet. 'Gee, I'm sorry,' he said. 'I'll do anything to take care of you.' Later, he said he would marry me anyway. But his mother kept up her screaming about us, and after a while Frank started to get real snippy. He told me that I was standing in the way of him being a big singer and he didn't come around anymore."

Toni called Frank one night at the Rustic Cabin. Nancy Barbato answered the phone and announced, "He's my boyfriend and I want to know why you want to talk to him."

Toni was so angry that she jumped into her car and drove to the Rustic Cabin. Frank saw her walk in and quickly got off the bandstand and walked the other way. She grabbed him.

"I told him that I was going to make such a scene in that place that he would probably get fired. Then Nancy Barbato tried to grab me to help him, but I screamed at her. 'Get your hands off me.'

" 'What is this? Another whore?' Nancy asked.

" 'Get away from me or I'll hit you,' I yelled. Then I tore her dress. Frank had been standing there without saying a word. Finally he spoke up.

" 'Is that necessary?' he said.

" 'If you didn't want to see me anymore, why didn't you let me know?' I said.

" 'No,' he said. 'I want to see you.'

" 'You what?' screamed Nancy.

" 'Will you get the hell out of here,' Frank said to her."

Taking Toni by the hand, Frank led her into the lounge. "That's where he said, 'I have to marry Nancy. Otherwise her father will kill me. She's pregnant.' "

"So what?" said Toni. "I was pregnant and you didn't break your neck for me."

"Yeah, but my mother. . . ."

"Never mind about your mother."

"You were a fighter, but Nancy won't stand up to her."

Toni stormed out of the Rustic Cabin and drove home, wondering how she would ever tell her friends in Lodi that Frank wasn't going to marry her.

Determined to punish him for publicly embarrassing her,

she swore out a warrant for his arrest on a morals charge, stating that on November second and ninth, 1938, Frank Sinatra, "being then and there a single man over the age of eighteen years, under the promise of marriage, did then and there have sexual intercourse with the said complainant who was then and there a single female of good repute for chastity whereby she became pregnant."

Frank's first arrest was on November 27, 1938. He was taken to the Bergen County jail and held for sixteen hours. The news made the papers, and Dolly called Toni Francke in tears.

"If you cared for him, you would not have done this," she said.

"Frank was going out with Nancy the whole time he was going with me," said Toni.

"Not that I know of," said Dolly. That was a lie.

"He made a fool out of me."

"Please get him out of jail."

"I'll get him out when I'm good and ready," said Toni, slamming the receiver down.

Dolly called back begging for her son's release and even offered Toni money, but she got nowhere. In desperation, Dolly sent Marty to Lodi to talk to Toni's family.

"Marty came to my father's house, and he was shaking," she said. "He walked real slow and quiet, like he was a beaten man. Dolly made that man so low. He said, 'Frank should respect his mother but when he doesn't, she takes it out on me.' You never embarrass an Italian man and make him low like that. As soon as I saw him I felt bad. He looked like a hobo at the door begging for something to eat. He didn't even ask for help right away, but his face said it all. He was stunned when I let him in. He thought I was going to swear at him. My father came out and said, 'You look bad. You want a shot of liquor?'

" 'Yeah,' said Marty. 'Today I feel tired.' "

The two men talked for a couple of hours, and then Toni's father asked her to get Frank out of jail. "Why?" she asked. "So he can go to another party with Nancy Barbato?" Mr. Della Penta shrugged his shoulders and Marty lowered his head without saying a word. His hangdog expression made Toni feel so guilty that she changed her mind and decided to let Frank out after she visited him in jail. She called her brother-in-law, the assistant sheriff, who took her to Frank's cell.

"You going to take me out?" he asked when he saw her.

"No," said Toni. "I just brought you a sandwich."

"I can't take it no more," said Frank, starting to cry.

"I don't see your girlfriend around here to help you."

"Please, Toni. Don't do this to me," he said, sobbing.

"You embarrassed me, Frank. You humiliated me. What makes your mother, an abortionist, think she is better than me? You have to apologize to me and your mother has to apologize."

Dolly was willing to promise anything to get her son out of jail, so Toni signed the papers withdrawing her charges against Frank.

Three weeks later, no one had yet apologized to her. When Frank did not call, Toni was convinced that it was his mother's fault, so she drove to Hoboken "to have it out with that awful Dolly."

"I went to her house on Garden Street and said, 'Who the hell do you think you are? Your lousy son is so thin. Don't you ever feed him or don't he want to stay home with you long enough to eat?' She got so mad she threw me down the cellar. But I wasn't scared. The next-door neighbors heard all the screaming, and Frank's aunts recognized my car in the front of the house and came over yelling at Dolly not to hurt me."

Within minutes, the police arrived, as did Toni's grandfather, Anthony Della Penta.

"This nut is keeping my granddaughter in the cellar," the old man said.

The police asked Dolly why she had Toni locked up. "She's running with my son and I don't like it. She's caused a big disturbance here and I want her arrested like she arrested my son," said Dolly.

Detective Sergeant John Reynolds arrested Toni, who was given a suspended sentence for disorderly conduct. The next day, December 22, 1938, Toni swore out her second warrant for Frank's arrest, this time charging him with adultery.

But before Frank's hearing, Toni's grandfather persuaded her to drop the charges and forget Frank's songs of love. He had looked up Dolly's arrest record and did not want to be related to her even by marriage. "How bad you need a boyfriend to have one with a mother who kills babies?" he asked her.

"It took me fourteen years to get married again after Frank," she said many years later. "I don't hate him for what he did to me. He was in a hole at the time and had to do what his mother said. It was really her fault. She ran his life."

Dolly Sinatra also ran part of Hoboken, a mile-square city of seventy thousand people, which had long since lost its luster as a resort for New York's monied socialites. From the turn of the century on, the lush landscape had been devoured by concrete foundries and wooden tenements to accommodate the waves of immigrants who had come in search of a dream.

The Germans had arrived first and in time had become prosperous merchants who lived in mansions high on the hill of Castle Point, overlooking the Hudson River. Their lawns stretched to the banks of the river, where their view spanned the skyline of Manhattan. They sent their daughters away to finishing schools while their sons stayed home to attend the Stevens Institute of Technology, the oldest college of mechanical engineering in the country.

Next had come the Irish, who nestled snugly in the middle of town, where they were welcomed by the Catholic church and soon dominated the police force and the fire department.

At the bottom of the heap were the Italians, who lived on the west side of town, packed into five-story wooden tenements. Little Italy was the dirty downtown area west of Willow Avenue, where the air smelled of the garlic and hunks of provolone hung in the front windows of groceries alongside strings of spicy sausage and garlands of red peppers. Old Sicilian women wearing black dresses, black stockings, and black shawls walked to and from church on the narrow cobblestone streets. Scorned by the uptown Irish and Germans, who barred them from their clubs and churches, the Italians were disparagingly referred to as Wops because so many had arrived from the old country without papers. Immigration officials had stamped their cards accordingly—W.O.P.—and the abbreviation soon became a term of derision.

Within Little Italy there was a further division: The northern Italians dismissed their countrymen from the south as peasants. And it was this class distinction that affected the coupling of Natalie Della Garavante from Genoa and Anthony Martin Sinatra, a Sicilian from Catania.

When nineteen-year-old Natalie, considered so adorable

as a child that they called her Dolly, first began dating the twenty-two-year-old boxer with tattoos all over his arms, John and Rosa Garavante began to worry—especially when she crept out of the house every night wearing her brothers' clothes so that she could watch Marty fight. Women were not allowed to attend boxing matches in those days, but Dolly refused to stay away. So she pulled on her brothers' trousers, shirts, and boots, stuffed her strawberry-blond hair into a poor-boy's cap, stuck a cigar into her mouth, and marched into a gymnasium with her two brothers, who were also fighters.

While Marty Sinatra seemed nice enough, he certainly wasn't anything special, and Dolly's parents were heartsick when their exceedingly gregarious daughter decided she wanted to marry the quiet, asthmatic boxer. The son of a boiler-maker, Marty could neither read nor write, and he'd never held a steady job, but because of his mother's small grocery store he never went hungry. To the Garavantes, though, he exemplified the southern Italians' attitude which held that learning was for a cultural life that peasants could never aspire to. "Do not make your child better than you are," runs a Sicilian proverb.

Dolly, pretty and spirited, was the daughter of a lithographer's stonecutter, and she had had an elementary education that put her light years beyond her would-be fiancé. Her proud Genoese parents pleaded with her not to marry this Sicilian who wasn't even a good boxer and had little chance of ever making a successful life for himself, but Dolly wouldn't listen. She felt that her driving ambition more than compensated for Marty's lack of direction and that his weaknesses softened her toughness. In a last attempt at dissuading her, the Garavantes refused to give their daughter a wedding. But Dolly remained undaunted. On February 14, 1914, she and Marty headed for City Hall in Jersey City.

The young couple told the clerk they were born in Jersey City rather than admit they were from "the other side"—or "over the line," as immigrants referred to their motherland. Giving his full name as Tony Sinatra, the bridegroom said his occupation was athlete. He didn't mention that he had to fight under the Irish name of Marty O'Brien to be permitted in the ring, since even the gymnasiums closed their doors to Italians in those days. With their Hoboken friends Anna

Caruso and Harry Marotta standing up for them, Natalie Garavante married Martin Sinatra against her parents' wishes.

The young couple started housekeeping in a four-story eight-family building at 415 Monroe Street in Hoboken. The water was cold, and the bathroom was in the hallway. Even so, Dolly and Marty were the envy of their immigrant neighbors who were living in one-room hovels crammed with beds, and whose toilets were in the backyard.

Monroe Street was the heart of Little Italy, and few immigrants dared to venture out of their enclave. Most could not speak English well and they feared people in authority, especially policemen in uniform, who, they believed, could send them back to Ellis Island. Their swarthy complexions, dark hair, and brown eyes coupled with their broken English made them immediately recognizable to the uptown Irish, whom they sought to avoid.

Most Italians would never be so bold as to cross the dividing line of Willow Avenue into Irish territory, but Dolly Sinatra refused to be deprived of anything her betters had. And her blond hair and blue eyes enabled her to pass. She would introduce herself as Mrs. O'Brien, thereby making herself acceptable to the Irish. She was determined to become uptown, and she dreamed constantly of better days, even though Marty, a plain man who loved baseball and boxing, did not share her aspirations. He boxed regularly but not well; he was never a champion like Dolly's brother Dominick. Marty spoke only when necessary; she talked all the time. He was quiet; her raucous laughter shook the ceiling plaster. He preferred staying downtown in the pool halls and bars of Little Italy, where he could eat ravioli and drink homemade wine with the rest of the men, but Dolly wanted to wear Hoboken like a ribbon in her hair.

She had an amazing facility with languages. She spoke all the dialects heard in Little Italy as well as she spoke English. This made her someone her immigrant neighbors could turn to when they had problems understanding the rules and regulations of the new world. She was also the person in Little Italy to whom Irish politicians could go when they needed Italian votes. And so she became a natural for the position of leader of the third ward in the ninth district, a position never before held by an immigrant woman.

Dolly was a woman of such gall that men had to recognize

her as their equal. If they didn't, she told them off in words that from a man would have started a brawl.

"The mouth on that woman would make a longshoreman blush," said Steve Capiello, a former mayor of Hoboken, who knew Dolly when he was growing up. "Her favorite expression was 'son of a bitch bastard.' She'd curse your mother to hell without even blinking."

"Dolly had the roughest language of any female I've ever known," said Doris Corrado, a Hoboken librarian. "One time, she walked into a party from pouring-down rain and the first thing she said when she got in the door was, 'Holy Jesus! It's raining sweet peas and horseshit out there.' She was a devil! Her mouth dripped with honey one minute and the next it was 'Fuck this' and 'Fuck that.' "

The vile language added to Dolly's tough reputation. Immigrants in Little Italy knew that she would never be intimidated by Irish policemen, Irish priests, or Irish politicians. So they naturally turned to her whenever they needed someone to plead their case to the public officials.

Her door always open, Dolly came to know those in the downtown area on a first-name basis. People flocked to her home for spaghetti and linguine. Fun-loving, she danced the tarantella at weddings. When someone died, she swooped into the wake to comfort the bereaved with a platter of sausages and homemade pasta. During the holidays she made *crispeddi*, the sugar-coated fried dough pastry that the Italians loved, and distributed it to everyone on her block.

A year after she married Marty, Dolly became pregnant. Both families were excited by the prospect of a grandchild, the first to be born in America to either the Garavantes or the Sinatras. And so the Garavantes became more tolerant of their Sicilian son-in-law.

The child would come into the world with four uncles and two aunts on his mother's side, one uncle and one aunt on his father's side, and two sets of grandparents, all living within two blocks of one another. Later, there would be almost a dozen cousins. And the generations would live together in daily contact. For the family was the primary source of support.

The baby arrived in the Sinatras' Monroe Street apartment on December 12, 1915. It was a breech birth and an excruciating delivery for the twenty-year-old mother, who was never able to bear children again. As a result of the doctor's forceps, the baby—a thirteen-and-a-half-pound boy—

emerged with a punctured eardrum, a lacerated ear, and deep facial wounds on the left side of his face and neck.

Because of the baby's birth injuries, the baptism was delayed for several months. When it did take place, downtown Hoboken was shocked by the *compari* (godparents) the Sinatras had selected. Traditionally, Italian couples chose their maid of honor and best man to be godparents of their firstborn, but Dolly boldly ignored the custom.

Taking her first step uptown, she selected for her son an Irish godfather, Frank Garrick, circulation manager of *The Jersey Observer*. Garrick and Marty were very good friends: they played baseball together, drank together. But it was the fact that Garrick's uncle, Thomas Garrick, was a Hoboken police captain that appealed to Dolly. She knew that the gloss reflected from that association would give her child more standing than any Italian godfather could ever bestow.

On April 2, 1916, Martin Sinatra carried the four-month-old boy who was to be his namesake into St. Francis Church and handed him to his godmother, Anna Gatto, a good friend of Dolly's, for the christening.

"We were standing in the front hall of the church, where the font is," Frank Garrick recalled many years later. "The priest came in and asked my name, and I said, 'Francis.' He then started the baptism, saying, 'I baptize thee in the name of the Father and the Son and the Holy Ghost.' I knew the boy was to be named after his dad, so I didn't pay much attention. Afterward, when we were walking out of the church, Marty turned to me and said, 'Guess what the kid's name is?'

" 'Martin,' I said.

" 'Nope. It's now Francis. The priest forgot and named him after you instead of me.'

"I never heard the priest say Francis, but Marty did, only he never said a word. Marty wouldn't, of course, and Dolly wasn't there. She was at home in bed still recovering from the birth. If she'd been there, she would have thundered and raised hell all over the place."

Dolly never challenged the absentminded cleric. She accepted his mistake as a good omen, a way of further cementing the relationship between her Italian son and his Irish godfather. Already Francis Albert Sinatra had a fighting edge in Hoboken.

2

On April 2, 1917, President Woodrow Wilson called for a declaration of war against Germany. Immediately, he made Hoboken a principal port of embarkation for American troops and ordered all two hundred thirty-seven waterfront saloons closed, making the city the first in the nation to experience federal prohibition.

The Germans who had ruled the town for so many years found themselves ostracized after German spies were discovered placing a time bomb aboard a steamship carrying sugar from New York to France. Throughout America, Germans became suspect, but wartime hysteria over imagined German espionage was especially high in Hoboken. German newspapers were banned and German beer gardens closed. The German part of the city was put under martial law, and military police rounded up "enemy aliens" and shipped them off to Ellis Island without even the semblance of a hearing. Panic swept through the German community, and thousands fled after being told to vacate their luxury apartments or face arrest.

The Irish now ascended to the ruling class, but the city became more Italian in character as thousands of immigrants moved into the downtown area. Their natural distrust of authority became heightened when the President insisted that everyone in the United States subscribe to "the simple and loyal motto: America for Americans." A few days later, the chairman of the Iowa Council of Defense received national attention with his announcement, "We are going to love every foreigner who really becomes an American, and all others we are going to ship back home."

Fearing deportation, the immigrants in Little Italy rarely ventured off their own blocks and seldom went uptown for anything. Some even tried to stop speaking Italian except in their own homes, and encouraged their children to learn English and become "Americanized."

Around that time, Dolly Sinatra was summoned to the mayor's office where, in addition to her duties as ward heeler, she was given the title of official interpreter to the municipal court. This meant that she was paid to accompany the immigrants whenever they had to appear before a judge.

"She told wonderful stories about taking the immigrants to get their citizenship papers," recalled her niece, Rosalie Garavante. "She had one Italian who was a fruit peddler, and when the judge asked him how many stars were in the American flag, the man said, 'How many-a-bananas in a buncha?' The judge looked puzzled, and before Dolly could say anything, the little man looked up at the judge and said, 'Say, your honor. You sticka your business. I sticka mine.' " Dolly immediately stepped forward to cajole the judge into granting the fruit vendor his citizenship papers.

That meant one more vote that Dolly could deliver for the Democratic machine of New Jersey's Hudson County, a corrupt political organization run by Mayor Frank "I am the boss" Hague of Jersey City. Dolly's political activities put such great demands on her time that she turned her baby over to her mother's care while she attended to her duties. Her main function was to open the way for the poor people in her neighborhood to get help from City Hall. In return, they were expected to vote the way she told them to on Election Day.

Dolly knew that if she delivered enough votes, she would eventually get patronage that she could use to provide employment for her family and friends. But as considerable as her influence was becoming, it was not yet enough to shield her family from punishment for their crimes.

"The whole family had run-ins with the police at some time or other, but Babe was the real bad boy of the family," said Rose Bucino Carrier, a Hoboken neighbor who baby-sat for young Frank when she was twelve years old. "Babe was the youngest of all the Garavantes and the only one born in this country, but he was the one who got in the most trouble."

In 1921, Babe was arrested on a charge of murder in connection with the killing of a driver of a Railway Express Company truck. While he was not charged with the shooting, Babe was identified by a witness as the driver of the getaway car carrying the five men who had attempted the robbery. He was arrested a few hours later and held in the county jail without bail because he was thought to know the identity and whereabouts of his five friends, who were eventually captured.

Even before the news of the murder charge was published in *The Jersey Observer*, people were whispering that Dolly's brother was going to be locked up forever or sent to the gallows. Dolly left Frankie with her mother and went to court every day of the trial. Pretending to be Babe's wife, she walked into the courtroom holding a baby she had borrowed just for the occasion. Babe was not married at the time, nor did he have any children, but Dolly wanted to do all she could to engender sympathy for her brother. She wept loudly and cried out that the baby needed his father to take care of him.

The judge was unimpressed by Dolly's tears. He sentenced Babe to ten to fifteen years at hard labor, fined him one thousand dollars, and ordered him to share the costs of the trial with the other defendants.

Outside the courtroom, Dolly called the judge a "son of a bitch bastard" and shed real tears when she saw the bailiffs hauling Babe off in handcuffs. She called to him, promising to visit every week, and she kept the promise over the more than ten years her brother was in prison.

The costs of Babe's defense almost bankrupted the Garavante family. None of them was making much money, but everyone contributed something to pay the lawyer. Dolly's share came mostly from her earnings as a midwife.

Until the turn of the century, most babies in the United States were delivered by midwives. They were not qualified as physicians but were trained to assist women in childbirth.

Dolly began her work as a midwife shortly after Frank was born by accompanying several doctors on home-birth calls. Soon she learned enough from watching them to do it herself.

Dolly's black bag became a familiar sight in Hoboken even when she was not helping with a birth.

"I remember when Dolly took up midwifery," said Rose Carrier. "She used it as an excuse to get out of the house at night when there was a party she wanted to go to. She'd take her black bag with her whether she was going on a call or not. It was the excuse she gave Marty to get out, and he never knew the difference."

Dolly's son was frequently seen dressed up like a little girl. "I wanted a girl so I bought a lot of pink clothes," she said many years later. "When Frankie was born, I didn't care. I dressed him in pink anyway. Later I had my mother make him Little Lord Fauntleroy suits."

Every day before leaving for City Hall to make her rounds, Dolly took Frankie to the two-family house on Madison Street that her mother shared with Dolly's sister and brother-in-law, Josephine and Frank Monaco.

Dolly made no secret of the fact that she disliked her older sister, Josie, who was pretty, petite, and refined, in direct contrast to the loudly profane Dolly. Rosa Garavante, a sweet elderly woman, ignored the rivalry between her two daughters and concentrated her loving attention on her grandson, Frankie, nursing him through all his childhood diseases. She prayed fervently when he had to have a mastoid operation, which left a massive scar behind his left ear and caused him partial deafness. Despite the ugly gash and the permanent loss of hearing, Grandmother Garavante felt her prayers had been answered when Frankie did not develop meningitis, as often happened when the mastoid bone was not drained in time. She worried about his catching tuberculosis, which had been the chief cause of death throughout the world during her childhood and which still claimed the lives of thousands of children subjected to crowded living and inadequate diets. So every time Frankie coughed, his grandmother fed him, and soon he grew fat on Rosa Garavante's pasta. But he was not a happy child.

"I used to see Frankie sitting forlornly on his tricycle on the sidewalk outside his house, waiting quietly for his parents to come home," said Thomas Fowler, a Monroe Street neighbor.

"I remember Frankie as a very lonely child—no brothers or sisters and no little friends to play with. He was quiet and shy," said Beatrice Sadler, a family friend.

"I'll never forget that kid leaning against his grandmother's front door, staring into space," recalled another.

When Frank started elementary school, he went to his grandmother's house every day for lunch. "Afterwards, he would hang around here until Dolly came home at night," his Aunt Josie said.

Dolly was not so lenient and loving with Frankie as his grandmother was.

"Dolly really made him toe the line," said Rose Carrier, who baby-sat for Frank on the weekends. "I remember when he said 'the bad word' once. It came out when Dolly least expected it, and she was so shocked that she grabbed him and dragged him to the sink to wash his mouth out with soap. Frank screamed and yelled, but Dolly didn't care. She jammed that soap right in his mouth. Even though she used that kind of language all the time, she wanted to teach her son not to say bad words, especially that one."

On Saturdays, after Dolly turned her household over to Rose's care, she went to work in the backroom of Cochone's Ice Cream Parlor as a chocolate dipper.

"That was the only soda store in Hoboken," Rose said. "It was owned by a Greek, and I had to take Frankie there every Saturday afternoon because Dolly wanted to see him. We watched her dipping almonds and niggertoes in chocolate. I guess I shouldn't call them niggertoes anymore, but that's what we called them way back then. They were Brazil nuts, and Dolly would dip them in chocolate and put them on a tray to chill. She hand-dipped everything with two fingers. It was a production line.

"After I took Frankie in there, we would go to the movies to see the Pearl White serials. Dolly didn't pay me much, but she always gave me lots of candy. She'd just take it right off the tray and give it to me and Frankie.

"Frankie liked going to the movies, but the poor kid didn't have much choice in the matter because that's where I was going and he had to be with me. The movie houses didn't have any air-conditioning in those days, so when it got hot, they'd leave the side doors open and me and Frankie would sneak under the screen door and not pay the nickel admission price. We spent it on popcorn instead."

Dolly had taken the weekend job as a chocolate dipper because Marty was out of work. After breaking both wrists boxing, he retired from the ring in 1926 and took a job on the docks as a boilermaker, but because of his racking asthma attacks, he was laid off.

"When Marty was out of work, I would go to Grandma Sinatra's grocery store on Jackson Street every week with a list from Dolly, and Marty's mom would send over a week's worth of food for them," said Rose Carrier. "It was hard because Marty's cousin, Vincent Mazolla, had come from Italy. They called him Chit-U, but I don't know why. He didn't have any people except for Dolly and Marty, so he lived with them on Monroe Street, and he didn't have a job either."

Once Dolly had firmly established her base of power and could be counted on to deliver six hundred votes from the third ward at election time, she wasted no time in using her influence. Beginning with Chit-U, she marched him down to the docks and demanded that he be hired as a steward's assistant.

"She made Chit-U hand her his pay every week," said Doris Corrado, "but he didn't seem to mind because he always said, 'She good to me. She give me money for shoes when I need it.' Then Dolly took out a life insurance policy on Chit-U and made herself the beneficiary."

Next, Dolly headed for City Hall and banged on the mayor's door, telling his assistant, James J. Rutherford, that she wanted her husband to be appointed to the Hoboken fire department.

"But Dolly, we don't have an opening," he said.

"*Make* an opening," she demanded.

On August 1, 1927, Marty Sinatra was appointed to the Hoboken fire department. Because of his wife's political connections, he was spared the embarrassment of taking a written test.

Having established her husband in the Irish-dominated fire department, in a position which paid two thousand a year and provided a pension, Dolly was now ready to make her move uptown. She found a three-bedroom apartment at 703 Park Avenue. Only ten blocks from their Monroe Street tenement, the Sinatras' new home might as well have been a thousand miles away, for it was completely removed from the noisy street vendors of Little Italy and much closer to the Hudson River in the part of town reserved for those with money and power.

Dolly outfitted herself splendidly for this move and bought loads of new clothes for twelve-year-old Frankie, who had become extremely thin following an emergency appendectomy. She insisted that her husband dress up as well. Throwing out his worn overalls, she sent him off with one of the neighbor boys to buy some gabardine pants.

"I still remember when Dolly made my brother take Marty shopping for those pants," said Doris Corrado. "He kept saying, 'I want "gardenia" pants.'

"I also remember the traveling merchants who would come to our doors selling Chantilly lace and chenille bedspreads and organdy doilies, things like that. Dolly would buy and buy and buy, and then never pay. She was always a dollar down and a dollar when you catch me. One lady who sold her loads of stuff came to collect but Dolly hid and sent Chit-U, the general mop, to answer the door." (Doris coined the description "general mop" for Chit-U, because, as Dolly's gofer, he not only ran her errands and fetched her beer but mopped her floors and cleaned her house.) "Chit-U said, 'No here. She no here.' So the lady came to my mother's house and called Dolly on the phone. Dolly answered. 'Oh, what a surprise,' she said. 'I just walked in the door.' The lady yelled at her. 'Stay there. I'm coming over for my money.' But when she got to the apartment, Dolly was gone and 'the mop' was hiding."

No one else living on Park Avenue had "gardenia" pants or Chantilly lace or an only child with a closet full of new clothes, so the Sinatras, or O'Briens, as they frequently called themselves, appeared prosperous to their new neighbors.

"Frank's people was rich," recalled Tony Macagnano, a boyhood friend from the Park Avenue Athletic Club. "I was a poor guy. My dad died in 1925. My sister died of tuberculosis the same year. We had five kids, which was the average number."

"I used to play with Frankie when we was kids," said Adam Sciaria, another childhood friend from Hoboken. "His uncles were always coming around and giving him candy and picking him up. They weren't married then, so they really spoiled Frankie. They were fighters, so no one laid a hand on him. They always gave him money. He was flush. I was one of thirteen kids, and we was beggars."

"Being an only child made all the difference," said Bob Anthony, a Hoboken neighbor who grew up with Frank. "Frank had more. He didn't have to share with brothers or sisters. He even had his own bedroom. None of the rest of us had half of what he had. He wore brand-new black-and-whites that his mother bought him, while the rest of us wore old oxfords that were hand-me-downs. He even had his own charge account at Geismer's department store. He had so many pairs of fancy pants from that store that we called him 'Slacksy O'Brien.' No question about it. Frank was the richest kid on the block."

"He was the best-dressed kid in the neighborhood and he always had the newest toys and gadgets," said Rose Carrier. "He had bicycle after bicycle, and later on his folks would take him on vacations to the Catskills or maybe to the shore in Long Branch for two or three weeks each summer. That was unheard of for anyone in Little Italy."

But those vacations were not so happy for Frank as his envious Hoboken friends imagined.

"I remember in 1929 when my folks and I went with the Sinatras on a summer vacation to the Catskill Mountains in Cairo, New York," said Kathryn Buhan, a Hoboken neighbor. "Frankie, who was thirteen then, seemed happy. His parents had been much too busy for him in Hoboken, and he thought that now they'd spend some time with him. But one morning, both our parents set off on a driving trip, leaving Frankie and me at the boardinghouse where we were staying. Frankie threw an awful tantrum.

"The boardinghouse owner tried to calm him down, but Frankie ran upstairs and locked himself in the bathroom, screaming bloody murder.

"A few hours later, I had to visit the bathroom, but Frankie wouldn't let me in. I pounded on the door. But he wouldn't come out until his parents came back."

Kathryn Buhan also remembers photographs from that vacation that show Frankie holding a doll in every shot. "He was kind of a mama's boy," she said. "A little bit of a sissy."

On another vacation, Frank was so embarrassed by his mother's antics that he went to his room and wouldn't come out for hours.

"Frankie had to do whatever Dolly said, and she would do anything to get a laugh," said Joan Crocco Schook, who ran Mae's Shoppe in Hoboken and knew both Dolly and Frank well. "One day she dressed up as a baby in a bonnet with a bottle and a frilly dress and made Frankie push her down the boardwalk in Long Branch in a big cart that was supposed to be a baby carriage. He was so humiliated, he wouldn't come around for hours afterward."

The kids on the block were the best excuse Frank had to get out of the house, and his mother liked to see him play with the neighborhood boys. She always gave him extra money to treat his friends to ice cream and sodas. When they started a club called the Turk's Palace, which was half secret handshakes and half baseball, they needed uniforms. Dolly bought them the flashy orange and black outfits they picked out with a half moon and dagger on the back, thereby ensuring that Frank was made manager of the team as well as pitcher.

Reflecting on Frank's childhood largesse many years later, some of the boys felt they had been bought, while others appreciated the generosity of a frail little boy trying to make friends.

"He used to buy friendship from the other kids," said schoolmate Joe Romano. "Frank always had money, and he would share it with anybody who'd promise to be his friend."

"If we were going to the movies and I couldn't afford it, I was never left out," said Tony Mac. "Frankie always paid for me. He treated me like a brother."

In return, Tony Mac and some of the other boys from the Park Avenue Athletic Club became Frank's protectors.

"Frank wasn't much of an athlete, and even though his dad and his uncles tried to teach him how to box, he couldn't fight at all. I guess he was just too little," Tony Mac recalled.

"He was a mischievous guy, but he couldn't defend himself when he got in trouble. He was a real good kid and never gave anyone any trouble. Just mischief, like when we used to go to the movies. If a bald-headed guy was sitting in front of us, Frank would throw his popcorn box at him and hit him in the head. That's the kind of trouble Frank got into as a kid.

"Other times, Frank and me would be walking along and Frank would tap a guy on the shoulder, jump back, and point to me as if I'd done it. The guy would start chasing us, but we'd always get away. Getting chased was a big deal in those days."

"Tony Mac always had to save Frank from his scraps," said Agnes Carney Hannigan, who grew up in the Irish section of Hoboken. "Frank couldn't fight at all. He was an arrogant kid, though, and would go looking for trouble. Then he couldn't defend himself, so Tony would have to do it for him."

By this time, people in Hoboken were listening to the radio for accounts of Babe Ruth's home runs and Jack

Dempsey's boxing triumphs. The most thrilling event of the time had been Charles Lindbergh's dramatic nonstop solo flight across the Atlantic from New York to Paris in May 1927. "Lucky Lindy" had become every American boy's hero, and youngsters throughout the country dreamed of becoming pilots and built models of Lindbergh's plane, *The Spirit of St. Louis.* In Hoboken the theater chain owners held contests to see who could build the best model Piper Cub.

"Billy Roemer always came in first in those contests because he was the most mechanical of all the boys," said Agnes Hannigan. "But one year Frank wanted to win the prize, so Billy, who was his best friend, built his plane for him and let him take first place, which was an airplane ride over New York City."

Thrilled with his rigged victory, Frank ran home to tell his mother, who recalled several years later: "He came in all excited and said, 'You be sure to look up, Mama. I'll wave to you.' And, do you know, I was just as ignorant about flying as he was. I went outdoors and craned my neck, expecting that I'd be able to see him."

After school, Frank spent most of his time at Billy Roemer's apartment at Sixth and Park, where he soon developed his first crush. Billy's sister, Marie, was six months older than Frank. A pretty, blond German girl, and extremely precocious, she was not very impressed with her young Italian admirer. So Frank turned to Lee Bartletta for help. Lee was a Hoboken friend whose parents were very close to Dolly and Marty.

"I was a bit older and inclined to feel like Frank's big sister, so he asked me how to win Marie's attention," she said. "I tried to help him out to the best of my sixteen-year-old knowledge. When we got around Marie to the extent that she accepted a birthstone ring he bought her for St. Valentine's Day, you'd have thought she had handed Frank the world on a silver platter just by agreeing to go steady."

Frank followed the birthstone ring with a crystal bead necklace and earrings, two pairs of shoes, four sweaters, a swimming suit, a purse, and, for her sixteenth birthday, a sheer black negligee.

Marie's sweet-sixteen party was so important to Frank that he bought a three-piece sharkskin suit, which cost him twenty-nine dollars, and he told everyone to "dress sharp" for the occasion.

"One of the crowd, Jimmy 'Doo Doo' Shannon, didn't have any clothes for the party, so Frank bought him an outfit," said Tony Mac. "For himself, Frankie was sharp. But this was ridiculous. He bought Jimmy loud, checkered pants and black-and-white shoes that were so pointed, the kid had to take them off and walk to the party in his bare feet."

"I'll never forget seeing those two come down the street," said Dan Hannigan, a Hoboken pal who later married Agnes Carney. "By the time they reached Sixth and Washington, those pinching shoes had become unbearable. So there was Frankie, looking miserable and embarrassed, and our other friend in those silly checkerboard pants, was limping along, carrying his shiny new shoes. You never saw two sadder guys."

"Frank would have dressed his dog in high heels if it would've made Marie happy," said one of his friends.

"It's true," said Agnes Hannigan. "Frank gave Marie everything. He was just crazy about her, but she wasn't all that interested in him because he didn't seem to be going anyplace. He wasn't very smart in school, and he never worked any jobs like the other guys, so we didn't think that he would ever amount to much."

3

In Hudson County, Prohibition was a law to be flouted. Jersey City's Mayor Frank Hague pleased his hard-drinking constituents by refusing to enforce the Eighteenth Amendment prohibiting the sale of alcoholic beverages. "It's a matter of giving the people what they want," he said.

Dolly Sinatra saw at once that the illicit liquor trade promised great profit, and she wasted no time getting involved. Convinced that a saloon would make her rich, she borrowed money from her mother so that she and Marty could open a tavern at Fourth and Jefferson. They called it "Marty O'Brien's," but it was in Dolly's name because firemen could not own or operate saloons.

The ethnic caste system ruled the children as strongly as the parents.

"If you were Irish, you had no friends in Guinea Town, which is what we called the area west of Willow Avenue where the Italians lived," said Agnes Carney Hannigan. "Our Lady of Grace Church would not even take them, and my father would have killed me if I had ever brought home an Italian boyfriend. Tony Mac and Ross Esposito and Frank Sinatra were the only Italians ever allowed in our home, and they were acceptable only because they came from Park Avenue and not down there on Madison or Monroe. They would never have gotten in our house if they'd lived down there. In those days we treated the Italians like we treat the Puerto Ricans today."

Dolly had gotten her family onto Park Avenue, and now she dreamed of owning her own home and having an uptown address. She was also determined to send her boy to the Stevens Institute to study engineering. With enough money she could make Frankie the first college graduate in the family. And the money would come from the profits of the saloon.

"Anytime we saw a drunk in the streets, we'd say that he was part of the MOB, meaning Marty O'Brien's pub," said Tony Mac. "Us kids didn't go around there a lot. We were a little afraid of Marty. He was a grouchy guy with a mad kisser on him. But he never said anything to hurt us. Dolly would have knocked him dead if he did. She was great, always laughing and joking and hollering, but Marty never said very much. Just grunted a lot."

Even as youngsters, Tony Mac and the rest of Frank's Italian friends understood that Dolly dominated the Sinatra family. That made the Sinatras very different from their own families, where the fathers were feared and respected and the mothers automatically assumed secondary roles.

"Marty was just a mouse," said Doris Corrado. "Just a mouse."

"He was a weak man," said former mayor Steve Capiello. "Not physically weak but weak in the sense that he could never stand up to Dolly. Never."

Fortunately, Marty Sinatra seemed perfectly content to let his wife be the boss. "He's a quiet man," said his brother-in-law, Frank Monaco. "Dolly was always the brains of the family. She was the go-getter. There never was any conflict, though. Marty just agreed with Dolly."

Ignoring the local law that women could not be in a bar, Dolly became Marty's barmaid. She also disregarded the statute prohibiting minors from the premises and frequently entertained Frank and his friends. Many years later, Frank would entertain people with stories of how he used to sit on top of the piano in his father's saloon and sing.

"I still remember Dolly yelling at me from the saloon when I was on my way home from school one day," recalled Nick Sevano, who was born and raised in Hoboken, and who knew Dolly from the time he was a little boy, because, as he said, "Everybody in Hoboken knew Dolly Sinatra."

"Dolly poked her head out the door and hollered, 'Come over here, you little son of a bitch. I want you to take some of these sausages home for your family's dinner.' I came from a lot of kids, and we didn't have much. Dolly knew that and helped out once in a while. Anytime we were in trouble or needed something, we always went to her. We looked to her for confidence and leadership. She was so powerful that she could march into City Hall and demand jobs for us. One summer, she stomped in with a bunch of us kids and said, 'Give these little bastards a job,' and, by God, we were put to work. Our own fathers couldn't do that, but Dolly Sinatra could. She was tougher than most men."

Unquestionably, Dolly had become the one person in Hoboken to turn to when in trouble, and at times that meant more than simply providing food and jobs for people. As the local midwife, she was also called upon to perform abortions.

"If an Italian girl got pregnant, her family would disown her," said Tony Mac. "Completely disown her. There was no forgiveness in the family if that happened. It was the worst dishonor that could befall an Italian Catholic family in those days. Dolly saved a girl's family embarrassment by doing an abortion. By doing her operations, she saw to it that many of these young girls could go on with their lives and not be disowned by their families."

Not everyone looked as kindly on Dolly for her illegal operations, especially in a community of churchgoing immigrants who considered abortion murder. Not only was it against the law of the land but, in their eyes, it was a sacrilege, for it violated God's law as well.

Still, once the word circulated that Dolly Sinatra would perform an abortion for twenty-five to fifty dollars, she soon found herself with a steady business. Doctors afraid of losing their licenses by performing the illegal operation themselves frequently referred patients to her, and she traveled regularly to Jersey City, Lodi, Weehawken, Union City, and Paterson with her little black bag.

"She even set up a table in her house," said Anna Spatolla Sinatra, who married Frank's first cousin. "I had to go to her three times. She had me come to the house and lie down on that table in the basement. Then she brought out a long wire—not a coat hanger—with special medication on the end of it. Afterwards, she told me to take Lysol douches three times a day and quinine pills. Lord, those quinine pills made my ears ring. They were the worst part."

For many years, Dolly performed these operations secretly, but when she was arrested in 1937, her abortion business became public knowledge. The abortion business, along with her running a saloon during Prohibition and dealing with bootleggers, did not enhance Dolly's respectability in certain circles, and some of the churchgoing people in Hoboken took it out on her son by refusing to let their children play with him.

"Frank felt it too," said Tony Mac. "He never talked about it, but he heard people calling his mother a rabbit-catcher and a baby-killer. I think that's the reason that once he finally got out of Hoboken, he never came back."

Ignoring the scandal she created, Dolly was unconcerned by the talk behind her back. She continued to do all she could to help her son make friends by giving him money daily for treats and allowing him to buy whatever he wanted at any store. Although she always went out to political parties on Saturday nights, she let Frank bring his friends in for dancing and always left them plenty of cake and cream soda.

"The Sinatras were always open-handed and hospitable," said Lee Bartletta. "We knew that anytime we asked, Dolly would let us gather in their home for an evening."

After Rosa Garavante died, Frank's grandfather came to live with them and would act as the chaperon for these parties. "We'd sit and listen to the radio," Lee said. "Rudy Vallee, Russ Columbo, and Bing Crosby were our idols. And we'd dance—the Charleston, the black bottom, the lindy hop. Frankie's radio was something special. It looked like a small grand piano."

The invitation to an Italian wedding was too tantalizing for Frank's Irish friends to resist, so when his cousin, Frank Anthony Sinatra, married Anna Spatolla, Frank was the best man, Marie Roemer was a bridesmaid, and the gang from Park Avenue was invited to the festivities.

"The wedding was in an Italian house downtown," said Agnes Hannigan. "It was so unusual for us to be going down there, and to be going to an Italian wedding was unheard of. We had never seen one before. There was so much noise you couldn't hear, and so much dancing and thumping, you would have thought the floors would sink into the ground."

Dolly provided their most memorable party in the summer of 1931, when she gave Frankie and his gang tickets to a political rally at Rye Beach for Lee's father, Frank Bartletta, who was running for mayor of Hoboken. As part of the Hague machine, Dolly owed her allegiance to the Irish incumbent, Bernard McFeeley, but when her good friend Bartletta decided to run, she supported him secretly despite the fact that he was a Republican. He was an Italian, and that was more important to Dolly than his political affiliation.

Since she and Marty could not publicly endorse Bartletta, they bought tickets to his rally and gave them to Frankie to give to his friends.

"It was a political party, and firemen could not go because McFeeley would have fired them on the spot," said Agnes Hannigan. "Dolly gave the tickets to Frankie and then sent a taxi to pick all of us up. She also sent along a huge picnic basket and a big bottle of wine. She even provided a porter to carry it all for us. It was really something."

Dolly tried to help Frankie in his courtship of Marie Roemer, whom he took to his junior high school graduation dance after buying both of them splendid new outfits. For that occasion, Frank had his own Tin Lizzie, a green 1929 Chrysler without a top that he and his gang had bought for twenty dollars. Still, Marie was not too impressed.

"She was so much more sophisticated than Frankie that she finally dropped him and started going with an older man who had a big black Cadillac and took her into New York City a lot," said Agnes Hannigan. "She later married him, and on her wedding day she wore a white lace dress with a black orchid and a black lace hat. That's how sophisticated Marie was! She was just too mature for Frankie. She was more a companion for Dolly. Besides, Frank didn't seem to be going anyplace. He didn't have a job and he wasn't doing well in school."

Frank was graduated from David E. Rue Junior High in 1931 and entered A. J. Demarest High School, where he lasted only forty-seven days. He later admitted being expelled for "general rowdiness."

"Frankie showed no real talent for anything," said Arthur Stover, the high school principal. "It was possible for a student to leave school before sixteen in those days, provided he had permission from an authorized person. I had that authority."

"He was a lazy boy," said Macy Hagerty, Frank's math

teacher. "He had absolutely no ambition at all when it came to school . . . and he was so thin!"

Frank's expulsion from school put an end to his formal education as well as to his mother's dream of his becoming a civil engineer or a doctor. With no education and no skills, he now seemed destined for a lifetime of menial labor in odd jobs. Dolly was enraged when she found out about all the classes that Frank had cut, but he didn't care. He told her that he would rather play pool all day in the Cat's Meow than sit in a boring classroom.

Dolly screamed at him. "If you think you're going to be a goddamned loafer, you're crazy." She insisted that he get a job, but Frank said that he didn't know where to look.

"Call your godfather," Dolly said. "Make him give you a job on *The Jersey Observer*."

The next day Dolly phoned Frank Garrick herself, saying, "Can you help Frankie?"

Garrick, the circulation manager, hired his godson to work on the delivery truck, bundling the newspapers before they were dropped off for paper boys to distribute. "I think he got paid twelve dollars a week," recalled Garrick, who soon regretted ever making the gesture.

"A few weeks after Frankie started work, one of the boys who was a sportswriter was killed in an auto crash and Dolly heard about it. You know Dolly. Push, push, push. She was always aiming to go higher and higher. She told Frankie to go see his godfather, that I'd get him that job. So he came in the day after the boy was killed, but I wasn't in the office. Frank went on into Editorial anyway and sat down at the dead boy's desk and acted as if he had the job. He filled the glue pots and sharpened pencils and started looking through the guy's notebooks. When the editor asked him what he was doing in there, Frank said he was the new sportswriter who had come to take the dead boy's place. He said that I had sent him in.

"When I got in later, the editor called me and said, 'Did you send that young Italian kid in here?' I didn't know what he was talking about until I looked into Editorial and saw Frankie sitting at the guy's desk all dressed up. 'No,' I said. 'I didn't send him in.'

" 'Well, he says you did,' said the editor. 'I think it's pretty bold of him to just barge in here like this on the day of the guy's funeral and try to take his job. You'd better let him go.'

"So, I had no choice," said Frank Garrick. "I went over to Frankie and said, 'Why'd you do this, Frankie? This isn't right. If you'd come to me in the first place, I could have gotten you the job. Now my hands are tied. I have to let you go.'

"Oh, the temper and the words and the filthy names he called me," said Frank Garrick. "You have no idea of what that temper was like in those days. Murderous. Like he was going to kill me. He flared up something terrible, cursing and swearing and so vulgar. The words he used were hateful, awful. He called me every terrible name in the book and then he stormed out. He never said another word to me until fifty years later, after his mother died. She wrote me off, too, and even though we lived in the same town, she never said another word to me for the rest of her life."

When Frank ran home to tell Dolly what his godfather had done to him, his mother took his side because she saw no impropriety in what he had done. After all, he was simply trying to get ahead, which is what one is supposed to do in life. Instead of asking Frank to apologize to his godfather, she took up the cudgel herself and sustained the feud for a lifetime. As she said many years later, "My son is like me. You cross him and he never forgets."

4

The 1930s were hungry years for most of America; the Great Depression crippled the country and the people. Cities and towns alike became bloated with the luckless, the jobless, the homeless. Men sold apples on street corners while women holding babies with swollen bellies waited in long lines for dry bread and watery soup.

In 1932 desperate voters swept the Republicans out of office and made Franklin D. Roosevelt president in hopes that he would do something to get the country moving again. But they had to wait until the new year and the inauguration to find out about the New Deal. In the meantime, there was a sad Christmas for the more than forty million people who had fallen into poverty.

Insulated by a father with a steady job and a mother with several, Frank Sinatra escaped the ravages of the worst economic disaster the country had ever known. His Christmas in Hoboken that year was merry indeed. To the amazement of their poor friends and neighbors, the Sinatras were moving into their first home at 841 Garden Street, a four-story wooden house that cost $13,400—an astronomical sum in the middle of the Depression, when the price of a modern six-room bungalow in Detroit with a two-car garage was only $2,800, and a Spanish stucco with seven rooms in Beverly Hills cost $5,000. The only comparable price was for a twelve-room

Italian villa in Westchester County, which cost $17,000 in 1932.

The house on Garden Street was a multiple-family unit, and Dolly intended to take in tenants, including her brother, Babe, when he got out of prison. With Marty's salary as a fireman, the profits they had received when they decided to sell the saloon, Chit-U's salary, Dolly's political job, and her thriving midwife and abortion business, they were able to make a sizable down payment and move in time for Frank to throw a New Year's Eve party, which Dolly reported to the newspaper's society page.

"[A] New Year's Eve party was given at the home of Mr. and Mrs. M. Sinatra of upper Garden Street in honor of their son, Frank. Dancing was enjoyed. Vocal selections were given by Miss Marie Roemer and Miss Mary Scott, accompanied by Frank Sinatra," the item read.

Frank's friends, most of whom lived in small, rented apartments, were wide-eyed to be partying in a house that not only had central heating but a bathroom as well. "And not just a toilet, but a bathtub too," said Tony Mac. "Everybody else we knew had to wash in a tub in the middle of the floor."

The girls were dazzled by Dolly's decor, especially the gold birdbath with the gold gilded angels holding red plastic roses that graced the entranceway.

"The house was full of what our parents called Guinea furniture, but we thought it was all wonderful," said Agnes Hannigan. "Dolly had the best of everything, let me tell you. I remember her massive dining room set that looked like a banquet table, and the glass on top of that table, which was at least four inches thick. The same on the buffet. I had never seen that before and thought it was quite glamorous. She also had a small baby grand piano, and on it was draped a Spanish shawl. On top of that she had her radio, and on top of the radio was a baby picture of Frankie, nude on a rug with his bottom up in the air.

"In her bedroom, she had a chaise longue, and next to it was a high pedestal that held a gold and white French phone. I was only fifteen years old at the time, but I thought that that was really something right out of the movies."

Dolly Sinatra's Garden Street home became her showplace, and she kept it scrupulously clean. In fact, cleanliness became an obsession with Dolly, who often hired neighborhood boys to sweep and dust and wash windows. She bequeathed this compulsion to her son, who in later years became just as fixated. He showered three times a day, constantly washed his hands, refused to handle dirty money, and carried nothing but new bills in his pocket. His intolerance of dirty ashtrays was reminiscent of his mother's chasing his father with a washcloth whenever he smoked cigars in the house—and finally making him go outside to smoke them.

The house-proud Genoese immigrant of the first generation believed that cleanliness was next to godliness. By the second generation, psychiatrists interpreted this mania for cleaning, especially constant hand washing, as a person's attempt to cleanse himself of real or imagined guilt, or to remove the mire of a sullied past. It would seem that Dolly cleaned to establish her position, while her son possibly wanted to purge himself of a past that made him feel dirty.

"He hid his face once when I got mad and called his mom an abortionist," said Toni Francke. "He was mortified by her baby-killing."

The shame that Frank carried over his mother's abortion business intensified when he moved to Garden Street.

"That was where the real trouble started," said Marion Brush Schreiber, Frank's pretty, red-haired neighbor who became his Garden Street girlfriend. "Dolly did an abortion there in her basement on a girl who almost died. The girl had to be rushed to the hospital and was in critical condition when she arrived. She barely survived. Dolly was arrested and had to stand trial. She was put on probation for five years and had to go down to the probation office every week to sign in. I remember how mad she'd get every time she had to go. She'd say it was a 'goddamn inconvenience' and that she had better things to do. She wasn't a bit embarrassed about it, but the Irish Catholic neighborhood we lived in was scandalized. What she did was considered worse than murder. It was awful hard on Frank."

Despite probation, Dolly kept her table in the basement as she continued to perform her illegal operations for those who sought her out. She was arrested several other times. She had to go to court each time, but probably because of her political connections she was never sent to prison, despite being convicted of a felony.

"My mother was shocked by Dolly and her abortion business, but it didn't bother me," Marion said. "I was three years younger than Frank and still in high school when we met. He came to one of the Saturday night dances on the roof of Joseph Brandt Junior High and introduced himself as a neighbor. The next day he came to get me and said, 'Come and meet my mother.' We spent most of our time taking long walks together and necking or driving in his car. That was when gas cost thirteen cents a gallon.

"Sometimes we went to the Fabian Theater in Hoboken. Frank always wore a white hat with a gold anchor like a Navy captain's hat. His whole life was music and singing, and he thought Bing Crosby was the greatest thing in the world."

Dolly loved to sing and managed to do so at political beer parties every Saturday night. According to one of Frank's Italian Hoboken friends, "We all sang. You can still stop any five guys here and get a harmony group going."

But Frank seemed especially inspired by Bing Crosby movies. He decided he wanted to be a singer just like Bing, started smoking a pipe like Crosby's and wearing the decorated Navy hat because Crosby always wore a hat. Dolly did not encourage him. In fact, when she saw Crosby's picture on Frank's bedroom wall, she threw a shoe at her son and called him a bum.

"After I met Dolly," Marion said, "I would go over to see her every day after school and on the weekends too. She drank beer constantly and was always rushing the growler down to the gin mill. It was a big beer barrel can with a handle and lid that she would push to the corner bar to be filled with beer. She'd put butter on the edge of the rim so that she would not get so much foam, and then sip all day. She drank beer all the time but never seemed to get drunk.

"Before Frankie and I went out on Saturday nights, I would do Dolly's hair for her parties. Saturday night was her time to howl. Marty would go off with the men and drink downtown in Little Italy, and Dolly would go out with her best friend, Rose Vaughn, all dressed up and wearing a spectacular hat with birds of paradise floating on gold shimmering roses that fell over the ear. She and Rose would hit every political meeting in town, drink beer, and sing "When Irish Eyes Are Smiling" until their lungs almost burst. After three hours, Dolly's birds of paradise would be flying around her knees, and she and Rose would have to take a cab home. Frank, who was a very quiet guy, sometimes got embarrassed by all her carryings-on.

"Frank wanted a college education desperately, but he couldn't get through high school. University studies would have been too much for him. He couldn't read very well. But he still wanted to be like those boys up on the hill from Stevens Tech, and so he dressed the role and looked like Joe College. If you didn't know he was a high school dropout, you'd think he was Harvard or Yale from the great clothes he wore.

"He didn't have a job at the time, but he loved hanging around musicians, so I suggested that he get an orchestra together for our Wednesday night school dances. He'd just started singing [in public] a little bit [at about age 17], and in exchange for hiring the musicians he'd get to sing a few numbers with the band. I'd take money at the door, and when we got enough, we all went to the Village Inn in New York so that Frank could sing with the orchestra there. We'd go in and ask the manager beforehand to let Frankie sing. We said that's the only way we would come in, and so he usually said yes.

"Frank did such a great job for our school dances on Wednesdays that he wanted to take the orchestra to Our Lady of Grace for their Friday night dances, but the Irish Catholics wouldn't let him in because of the scandals involving his mother. They would have nothing to do with him. When he found this out, he went into one of his terrible moods. He'd get real sullen and sour, and you couldn't get a word out of him. There were no tantrums; just an ugly silence that could sometimes last for hours. He also got headaches all the time."

Dolly felt so bad about the church's refusing to let Frank arrange the orchestra because of her abortion business that she bought him a sixty-five-dollar portable public address system so that he would have an easier time booking musicians.

"That PA system had a mike and speakers and a case covered with sparkling stuff," said Tony Mac. "Those things were rare in those days, so when Frankie would let a band use his PA, the leader would usually let him sing—for free, of course."

Dolly also gave her son money to buy orchestrations, which helped him as much as the public address system. "I always liked to sing and I liked to be around bands and to have a part of the band glamour," Frank said a few years later. "I couldn't play an instrument and I didn't care about learning to play one. So I tried to figure out a way in which I could be sure of being a part of a band. . . . I started collecting orchestrations. Bands needed them. I had them. If the local orchestras wanted to use my arrangements—and they always did, because I had a large and up-to-the-minute collection—they had to take Singer Sinatra too.

"Nobody was cheated. The bands needed what they rented from me, and I got what I wanted too. While I wasn't the best singer in the world, they weren't the best bands in the country either."

He sang the songs of the time, ones he had heard on the radio. But people in Hoboken agreed with him that he wasn't the best singer in the world. And his ukulele-playing—an instrument his uncle, Champ Sieger, gave him—was no better. Whenever he went to Cockeyed Henry's and pestered the older men with his singing and playing, they threw him out. Even Frank's friends were unimpressed. Adeline Yacenda refused to let him sing at her wedding. "He was that bad," she said.

Tony Mac told him to get out of the business. "I heard him on WAAT and the next time I saw him, I said, 'You'd better quit. Boy, you were terrible.' "

"Frank was always asking for work," said Don Milo, who had his own orchestra. "He was a real pusher like his mom. He never let up. I lived across the street from him and he was always coming over and ringing the bell wanting me to hire him, but I used Ozzie Osborn instead because he was a much better singer than Frankie. I'd use Frankie only when Dolly told me to."

By 1935, when Frank was twenty years old, still living at home and without a steady job, his mother finally acknowledged that singing was all he cared about. So she set out to find him work by calling Joseph Samperi, the owner of the Union Club at 600 Hudson Street in Hoboken.

"Why don't you give Frankie a job?" she asked. "You've got a nice place here. You ought to have a boy like Frankie singing for you."

No Italian in Hoboken was going to say no to Dolly Sinatra, so Frank was hired for a couple of months.

"We could afford to pay him forty dollars a week for a five-night week, but we couldn't put in a radio wire," said Samperi. "We weren't big enough for that kind of thing."

Following his Union Club gig, Frank began hustling one-night stands at the Italian social clubs in Hoboken. He also drove a local trio called The Three Flashes to Englewood Cliffs and watched them perform with Harold Arden's orchestra at the Rustic Cabin.

"Frank hung around us like we were gods or something," recalled Fred Tamburro, the trio's baritone. "We took him along for one simple reason. Frankie-boy had a car. He used to chauffeur us around. Then, one night, a guy came up to us and said he wanted us to make some movie shorts for Major Bowes. When Frank got wind of it, he begged us to let him in on the act."

The Three Flashes had no intention of upgrading their driver, so they turned Frank down. He told his mother what had happened. The next day, she went to see Tamburro, known as "Tamby," one of eight children living on Adams Street in the heart of Little Italy, where Dolly Sinatra was the immigrants' lifeline to the new world. By that afternoon, Frank was part of the group.

"Sinatra's mother, who was a big wheel in Hoboken, started pestering us to take him along," said James "Skelly" Petrozelli, another of The Three Flashes.

"There was nothing I could do about it," said Tamby many years later.

The movie shorts—*The Night Club* and *The Minstrel*—took seven days to film, and every day Frank drove Don Milo and his band, who were, as they frequently did, playing with The Three Flashes, to the Biograph Studios on Tremont Avenue in the Bronx. "It was a minstrel show and Frank, who was twenty years old, was paid ten dollars a day to wear a top hat and make up in blackface with big, wide white lips," said Don Milo. "He acted as a waiter in one of the shorts, and in the other The Three Flashes sang to him in blackface. Every morning at five A.M., before we left for a day of filming, Dolly got up and made us all a big breakfast. Then Frank drove us to the Bronx over the George Washington Bridge, which had just opened."

"The way Frankie flipped about appearing in blackface, you'd think he was already a star," said Tamby. "All he had was a walk-on. He kept haunting the theaters here asking when they were going to play his pictures—HIS pictures!"

The movie shorts, entitled *Major Bowes Theater of the Air*, were shown in Radio City Music Hall in October 1935, but before their release Major Bowes summoned the boys for an audition for his amateur hour, which was broadcast nationally every week.

Again Dolly made sure that Frank was included in the group, and The Three Flashes became The Hoboken Four. Don Milo told them to sing the Mills Brothers' arrangement of "Shine."

"I also told them to dress with class," he said, which meant white suits, black ties, and black hankies.

The boys did as they were told, and Major Bowes was impressed enough to schedule them as contestants on his show, which was broadcast from the stage of the Capitol Theater in New York City on September 8, 1935.

That evening, Major Bowes introduced them as The Hoboken Four, "singing and dancing fools." In response to an offstage question about his description, he said, "I don't know. I guess 'cause they're so happy."

Tamby then introduced himself and Skelly and Pat Principe (Patty Prince), telling Major Bowes where each one worked. He ignored Sinatra.

"What about that one?" Bowes asked, pointing to Frank.

"Oh, he never worked a day in his life," said Tamby, and the audience laughed.

The applause meter scored highest for the singing and dancing fools of Hoboken, who Major Bowes said had "walked right into the hearts of their audience." He immediately signed them to contracts—fifty dollars a week, plus meals—with the Major Bowes Number Five tour unit to play the country. The boys were to sing at every stop along the way. Traveling by bus and by train, The Hoboken Four joined sixteen other acts, including mouth organists, bell ringers, jug players, yodelers, and tap dancers. Tamby later described them all as "hillbillies and cowboys."

"We were sponsored by a coffee company [Chase and Sanborn]," said Skelly. "We used to have to play the grocery stores in all the cities where we stopped, and they made us sign our autographs on the company's coffee cans."

At first, the boys were thrilled by their new celebrity, but soon the novelty of performing on the road began to wear thin. In a letter to his mother from Vancouver, Frank wrote, "Still going strong on this tour, but there's no place like Hoboken." Dolly immediately called *The Jersey Observer*'s society page and told the editor what Frank had written. "Dolly was always calling the newspapers to get her name in for something," said photographer Irv Wegen. "Then she'd call me to come and take a picture." Inordinately proud of her son, Dolly made sure that news of The Hoboken Four was published regularly.

"We were the rowdies of the lot," said Skelly. "Me and Prince were the clowns, Fred was the fighter, and Frank was the serious one. That's the reason he got where he did.

"They tried to keep us like baseball players, making us go to bed before eleven o'clock, and all that. But we'd sneak out and get caught, or we were always late for the shows."

"They wanted to fire us at least twenty times," said Tamby.

One such time was in San Diego, when the group was singing "Shine" and Frank, Skelly, and Patty Prince started giggling. Tamby, the boss, slugged anyone who got out of line and threatened to kill him if they didn't stop. Convulsed now and unable to sing, the trio ran offstage, leaving Tamby alone. He apologized to the audience as Major Bowes brought the curtain down. The four performers went into their dressing room and waited for the Major to come in and fire them. Tamby was furious and lunged at Frank, yelling, "Are you crazy?" Frank, still giggling, said, "I can't help it. You can't keep me from laughing onstage. That's my sense of humor."

"Well, here's my sense of humor," screamed Tamby, smashing his huge fist into Frank's face and knocking him off a wardrobe trunk into a heap on the floor.

"After I hit him, it took us nearly an hour to wake him up," said Tamby, "but when he came to, I said, 'Frank, now you know my sense of humor.' "

Frank picked himself off the floor, glared at Tamby, and walked out of the room.

As the lead singer of The Hoboken Four, Frank stood out as the best in the group. He soon became the star of the entire traveling unit, getting a lot of attention from Major Bowes and the other executives running the tour. Every time he growled in a song or crooned a solo, the girls besieged him backstage, which made Tamby and Skelly extremely jealous.

"They would be asked to sign an autograph or two, but Frank was practically torn apart," said Patty Prince many years later. "He'd have to fight off the nicest women you've ever seen.

"That's when Tamby and Skelly started getting in the habit of beating Frank every once in a while, whenever they got mad at something and had to take it out on someone. It happened often enough so that you could call it abuse. They abused Frank, and it happened most often when Frank went off with some woman after the show and these two no-talents had to go to their rooms alone.

"Sometimes it got pretty bad for Frank. After all, he was a skinny little guy and the two picking on him were older and bigger, truck drivers back home, and Frank couldn't fight back. Once, we were sitting in a diner, stretched in a line along the counter. Frank leaned over and whispered to me, 'Why don't you beat me, too, and make it unanimous?' I shrugged him off. I felt real bad about it . . . but what could I have done back then?"

It was still only 1935 when, unwilling to take the beatings any longer, Frank left the tour in Columbus, Ohio, and returned to Hoboken, while Tamby, Skelly, and Patty Prince continued with Major Bowes as The Hoboken Trio. Dolly didn't call the newspaper when Frank returned home, but she told her friends that he was coming back because he was homesick and missed Nancy Barbato, his new girlfriend from Jersey City.

The previous summer he had gone to Long Branch, New Jersey, to stay with his aunt, Josephine Monaco. During that time, Frank had worked as an occasional chauffeur for the Cardinale family of Hoboken, driving the car for the younger children.

"Frank used to drive us crazy playing the ukulele on the porch all the time," said his aunt. "He would sit there and play, kind of lonesome. Then one day I noticed him talking to a pretty little dark-haired girl who was living across the street for the summer. She was Nancy Barbato, the daughter of Mike Barbato, a plasterer from Jersey City."

When Dolly and Marty arrived for a weekend that summer, Josie told them that Frankie had a girlfriend. Marty was indifferent. Dolly, ever pragmatic, said, "He doesn't have a penny." But she asked whom her son was seeing.

Josie pointed to the attractive young girl sitting on the porch across the street. "Well, she seems like a nice child," said Dolly, dismissing the eighteen-year-old girl as harmless.

That summer, Frank wrote to Marion Brush, his Garden Street girlfriend, and sent her a picture of himself, but by then both of them knew their relationship had no future.

"Frankie was the one with the crush, not me," said

Marion. "After the boyfriend-girlfriend business wore off, we became very good friends. I never even thought of marrying him or getting seriously involved because I knew that he didn't have any money, and as a singer he would be on the road and have a loaf of bread one day and be starving the next. Besides, my mother was the type to instill in me the need for a college education, and I was leaving that fall for Jersey City State Teachers College.

"When Frank came home at the end of that summer, he brought Nancy Barbato to Hoboken and introduced me. She was a nice little Italian girl from Jersey City, but the way Dolly was carrying on, you'd have thought she was a duchess or something. She was not your typical poor little Italian girl. Her dad was a plasterer and her five sisters were married to accountants and lawyers, which Dolly just lapped up. Marrying up like that was so important to her. Nancy certainly was not rich, but she was well off in comparison to Frank, which is why Dolly fussed all over her so."

Not only had Nancy Barbato's sisters married well, but her family lived in a freestanding wooden house with a porch. That porch signified a comfortable life-style to Dolly, and certainly one far removed from Hoboken's Little Italy. The Barbatos did not have to take in tenants as Dolly did. Within one generation, Nancy's father, Mike, had made enough money to move his family of six daughters and one son into a house with a front porch, which was the kind of worldly success that Dolly respected.

Still, girlfriends worried her. Very much aware of the trouble that adolescent boys could cause, Dolly had been on the alert ever since Frank was fourteen years old. One night, he had stayed out too late with Marie Roemer, and Dolly had sent her husband in a cab to Marie's house to bring Frankie home after instructing Marty to smack his son a few times so that he'd get the message.

When Frank was still seeing Marion Brush, he had grabbed her by the hand one night to lead her upstairs to his bedroom to show her something. Dolly would not let the youngsters out of her sight.

"She was dirty-minded," said Marion. "She stood at the bottom of the stairs glaring at us as if we were going to do something terrible in Frank's room. She didn't trust him at all. She didn't say anything, but she looked scared to death when we walked up those stairs. She stood at the bottom, watching to see if we were going to go in his room and close the door. God only knows what she would have done then."

And it wasn't only Frank Dolly was watching.

"I still remember what happened to Chit-U when he met a woman in the neighborhood and took her out for a few drinks, wanting to get to know her better," Marion said. "Dolly found out about it and stormed up to the rooming house where the poor soul lived and started screaming at her to stay away from Chit-U. I thought that rooming house would come down brick by brick. That was the end of Chit-U's relationship with the woman, but it was more that he was spending his money on her for drinks rather than doing anything sexually with her. After all, Dolly wouldn't have Chit-U drinking money away with some woman when he could be giving it to *her*. She was very grasping that way, and in the end Chit-U never married. He lived with Dolly all his life and did her cleaning."

Though Dolly still didn't take Frank's singing seriously, she didn't want anything to stand in his way, especially a hurried marriage or an unnecessary baby. She had seen some of the women whom Frankie had met since he had started singing and she didn't like them, especially the ones she called "cheap trash," who wrote him love notes.

"She showed me a few of the letters," said Marion Brush, "but Frank never knew because Dolly threw them away."

When Frank had begun seeing Nancy Barbato, Dolly was naturally suspicious. But after scrutiny, she had decided that this quiet little girl who came from a devout Catholic family and was so devoted to her son would not pose any problems. Nancy understood how much singing meant to Frankie.

Since leaving The Hoboken Four, Frank had been singing at every Italian wedding and Irish political rally in town. He sang at the ladies' auxiliaries and at Elks Club meetings for two dollars a night. He sang in Hoboken social clubs like The Cat's Meow and The Comedy Club and on local radio stations like WAAT in Jersey City at no charge. He haunted music companies in New York trying to get auditions. He badgered song pluggers for professional copies of sheet music. He hounded radio stations for air time. He followed musicians and begged to carry their instruments so he could get into the hall free and, once inside, sing with the orchestra.

At one point, he thought he might have a better chance for success if he changed his name when he sang outside of

Hoboken, so he appeared as Frankie Trent. The name change lasted as long as it took Dolly to find out about it. If he was going to accomplish anything in life and bring honor to his parents, he had better, by God, do it with the family name— either O'Brien or Sinatra, preferably Sinatra.

Around this time, Frank went to a New York vocal coach, John Quinlan, for forty-five-minute voice lessons costing one dollar, but the lessons seemed to be as much diction as music. "He talked different," Tamby said. "He didn't talk Hoboken anymore. He sounded like some Englishman or something. I asked him about it, and he told me he took lessons from some professor or something."

Impressed with Frank's range, the vocal coach said: "He has far more voice than people think he has. He can vocalize to a B flat on top in full voice, and he doesn't need a mike either. Frank is over-particular and fussy about his work. But he has a great brain—for what he is doing. He has his faults. We all have." The relationship ended a few years later when Quinlan suffered a heart attack and could not accompany Sinatra to California. "I guess Frank didn't understand," he said. "He hasn't spoken to me since."

Years later Sinatra said, "I never had a vocal lesson—a real one—except to work with a coach a few times on vocal calisthenics to help the throat grow and add a couple of notes on the top and spread the bottom."

In 1938, Frank heard about an opening at the Rustic Cabin, a small-time roadhouse along Route 9W above the Jersey Palisades. The owner, Harry Nichols, was looking for a singing waiter who would act as master of ceremonies and introduce the dance selections of Harold Arden's band. The pay was only fifteen dollars a week, but the roadhouse had a wire—direct radio line—to WNEW in New York City, and once a week the band and the singer were heard on the *Saturday Dance Parade* broadcast. What better way to be heard by a big-time band leader? Frank immediately arranged for an audition. The problem was Harold Arden, who remembered Frank from the days he chauffeured The Three Flashes. He hadn't liked him then, and he didn't like him any better after his audition.

Dejected, Frank went home and told his mother about the opening.

"But the bandleader doesn't like me," he said.

"That's just fine," said Dolly. "I won't have you staying out until all hours, singing in one of those night clubs."

"Frankie just looked at me," Dolly told a reporter a few years later, "and he didn't say a word. He took his dog, Girlie, in his arms and he went up to his room. Then I heard him sobbing."

To have her son in tears was too much for Mama Sinatra.

"I stood it for a couple of hours, and I suppose I realized then, for the first time, what singing really meant to Frankie," she said. "So I got on the phone and I called Harry Steeper, who was mayor of North Bergen, president of the New Jersey musicians' union, and an assistant to James 'Little Caesar' Petrillo, president of the American Federation of Musicians. As fellow politicians, we used to do favors for one another. I said, 'What can we do? Frankie wants to sing at the Rustic Cabin and the bandleader doesn't like him.' I told him what happened and I asked him to see to it that Frankie got another tryout, and this time, I said, see to it that he gets the job.

"Well, Harry had heard Frankie sing, and he must have noticed the start of that quality which Frankie later learned to bring out so effectively. So Harry said he'd fix that—that I was to tell Frankie he was as good as hired. That's how it happened. So many people claim to have started Frankie professionally, but the truth is it was actually Harry Steeper."

From the minute Frank started at the Rustic Cabin, he felt that he was destined for success.

"He told me and my brother that he was going to be so big that no one could ever touch him," said Fran Capone Ciriello of Hoboken. " 'Yeah, sure, Frankie. Sure you are,' we'd say. No one thought he'd ever make it, except for him, that is."

Even Dolly was dubious. "His salary was only fifteen dollars a week, and I used to give him practically twice that so he could pick up the tabs for his friends when they dropped in," she said. "When he got a five-dollar raise, I told him, 'This isn't getting me anywhere. It would be cheaper for me to keep you at home.' 'Mama,' he said, 'it's going to roll in someday. I'm going to be big time.' He always believed that. But I said, 'Yeah, it's going to roll in and you're going to roll out.' "

"I worked a lot of club dates with Frank," said Sam Lefaso, a Jersey City musician. "He was such a nuisance, hogging the mike all the time and singing every chorus when he was only supposed to do an occasional vocal. Finally, we started taking the mike away from him. We ridiculed him because he just wasn't that good. Even though he was singing at the Rustic Cabin, he didn't seem to have any talent. No style whatsoever. Until he started going to a vocal coach, he was singing in a tight, high voice and sounded awful.

"But when we'd tell him how bad he was, he'd get furious and start cursing and swearing at us. 'Son of a bitch,' he'd yell. 'You bastards wait. You just wait. One of these days, you're going to pay to hear me sing. You just wait.'"

While Frank yelled at the musicians, Dolly yelled even louder at Frank when he started dating Toni Francke.

After Toni dropped her charges against Frank, Dolly decided that he should marry Nancy Barbato as soon as possible. Despite the newspaper publicity about his arrests, Dolly knew that Nancy was very much in love with him and wanted to marry Frank as much as Dolly now wanted her to. She felt that her son was too vulnerable to women like Toni. She wanted him to be married and settled down.

Frank was not enthusiastic about getting married. After the uproar with Toni, he had told Nancy that he didn't want any woman getting in the way of his ambition. "I'm going to the top," he said, "and I don't want anyone dragging on my neck."

Nancy promised never to get in his way, and the wedding was set for February 4, 1939.

Dolly asked him what he was going to give Nancy for an engagement present inasmuch as he had no money. It had cost fifteen hundred dollars to get him out of jail after the first arrest and five hundred after the second arrest. Frank said that maybe he could save up for something. Dolly said that would take years. "Well," he said, "maybe I could give her your diamond ring." Dolly sputtered for a few moments about how she had just finished making payments on the ring and that it was so expensive, but in the end she handed it over.

"The only reason Frank married Nancy is because Dolly made him do it," said Marion Brush Schreiber. "She really pushed him into that one fast."

Toni Francke was convinced that they were forced to marry. After all, Frank had told her Nancy was pregnant. Some of Nancy's friends suspected as much when they received the abrupt announcement in January of the February wedding. And so they were quite surprised when Nancy did not give birth to her first child until sixteen months after the wedding. They did not know how hard Dolly was pushing to get her son married before another Toni Francke came along.

"When Nancy told me she was getting married in February, I was quite taken aback," said Adeline Yacenda. "She and Frankie had been sweetheart kids together and he used to pick Nancy and me up from school in Jersey City. We were good friends then and I knew they hadn't planned on getting married so soon at all. That wedding was very, very sudden. I guess it was on account of Frank getting caught going out of a lady's bedroom window. Poor Nancy. It was a nice wedding, though, but not big. It was so sudden, I don't know how they got it planned as quickly as they did."

Dolly insisted on giving her future daughter-in-law a bridal shower in her home in Hoboken.

"None of Dolly's Hoboken friends was invited except for me, and I didn't know a soul in the place," said Marion Brush Schreiber. "It was just Nancy and her friends and family. All her sisters and their successful husbands were there, and all the husbands were big, strapping guys at least six-two. Poor Frank looked like a baby around those guys. He had just turned twenty-three, but he seemed like a pathetic kid."

"I remember Dolly's shower for Nancy because Frank showed us his nice clothes afterwards," said Adeline Yacenda. "He opened his closet for everyone.

"He had a terrific personality in those days and could win anyone over. Nancy was very much in love with him. But he did not have an education, which meant a lot at that time. I did not know anyone who didn't go to school. We knew that he didn't even go to high school and that he was not educated. As I said, education was important to all of us. But . . . Frank dressed very well."

Because the Barbatos were such devout Catholics, the wedding took place at Our Lady of Sorrows Church in Jersey City with Monsignor Monteleone presiding over a nuptial mass and a double-ring ceremony. The bride wore a long white dress, which was made at home, and walked down the aisle on the arm of her father. "I still remember Nancy coming down that aisle and crying her eyes out," said Adeline Yacenda. "I always wondered why."

"It was a small wedding. After all, most of us didn't have two nickels to make a dime back then," said Nancy's friend Andrea Gizza. "But it was nice. . . . The reception was in Nancy's family's house over on Arlington Avenue. There must have been about fifty people at the reception. There was wine and sandwiches and Italian cookie trays. Frank was nervous. I think it was the first wedding he didn't sing at."

Noticeably absent among the wedding guests were any of the Sinatras' Hoboken friends, with the exception of Marion Brush Schreiber. None of Frank's childhood friends from Little Italy or Park Avenue was there. Nor was his godfather, Frank Garrick, invited. That feud was not to be forgotten even to celebrate a godson's married future.

"I don't think Nancy wanted to have much to do with people from Hoboken," said Marion Brush Schreiber. "When I was leaving the reception at her house, I went up to the bedroom to get my coat, and Frank followed me. We had become such good friends by then. I wished him all the luck and happiness in the world and he kissed me. I'll never forget him that day. He looked like the saddest man I'd ever seen."

After a four-day honeymoon that was spent mostly driving to and from North Carolina, Frank and Nancy moved into a three-room Jersey City apartment, which they rented for forty-two dollars a month. Their combined monthly income at the time was two hundred dollars: Nancy earned twenty-five dollars a week as a secretary for American Type Founders in Elizabeth, New Jersey, and Frank, who had received a raise at the Rustic Cabin, was making twenty-five dollars a week as a singing waiter. Together they earned more than Marty Sinatra brought home as a fireman.

With 9.4 million Americans unemployed that year, Frank's and Nancy's combined salaries could buy a lot, and Nancy stretched the money as far as she could. She scrubbed her own floors, and she shopped carefully for food every week, always looking for bargains. Grocery prices ranged from five cents for a one-pound can of pork and beans, and seven cents for a package of Pillsbury pancake flour, to thirty-three cents for a dozen eggs and thirty-four cents for a pound of butter. A bottle of Pepsi-Cola cost five cents; a fifth of Scotch three dollars and twenty-nine cents.

After food and rent, most of their money supported Frank's mania for clothes so he would always be well-dressed when he performed. He needed to dress rich to feel important, and admitted that new clothes bolstered his ego.

"Every time I felt insecure I used to go out and get ten

more suits," he said. In 1939, his clothes addiction ran to $35 Woodside suits, $12.50 Johnston & Murphy shoes, and $2.50 broadcloth shirts. He insisted on all-silk bow ties for $2.50 and silk hose for sixty-five cents a pair. Frank spent whatever he wanted on clothes, charging them when he was broke. He once bounced a check to his tailor, Louis Stoll, who lived in their apartment building, but made good the next month.

Still, his excessive spending terrified Nancy, who was so frugal she deprived herself of any extravagances. She sewed her own dresses and suits, and bought only an occasional jabot blouse for $3.50. Everything else she put toward Frank's wardrobe.

"She used to sew a lot for Frank so he'd look nice when he went on auditions and jobs," said her friend Andrea Gizza. "She'd make him things like scarves and socks. Once, when he needed a new tie to match an outfit he was wearing on a job, she even cut up a dress of hers and made him a tie out of the material. Another time—it was his birthday—she didn't have much to give him so she took an old glove of his and stuffed a quarter into each of the fingers. She said he cried when he opened the gift and said, 'Honey, someday we're going to be rich, you'll see.'

"But Nancy didn't care about being rich. She wanted nice things, sure. But above all she wanted to have a nice family and settle down to a nice normal life. Or at least near-normal, since she was married to a singer."

But Frank continued to spend money whether he had it or not.

"I remember visiting Nancy on Audubon Avenue after she and Frank got married," said Adeline Yacenda. "Frank was away a lot. One day Nancy brought out this beautiful bag that Frank had bought her for thirty-five dollars. You have no idea of how expensive that was in those days. Nancy held the purse like a sacred relic, and I was absolutely wide-eyed. 'You better tell him to hang on to his money,' I said. 'That kind of money won't come along that often.' "

Nancy was so grateful to be Mrs. Frank Sinatra that she did anything she could to make him happy. She cooked his favorite meals—spaghetti and lemon pie. She tolerated the odd hours that he kept as he raced from one radio station to the next begging to sing free simply to be heard. She waited patiently for him to come home from the Rustic Cabin every night. She encouraged him constantly, saying he was going to be a bigger star than Bing Crosby. And she tried to get along with her mother-in-law, which required great effort on her part because she did not like Dolly and bitterly resented her hold over Frank. Dolly insisted on her son's visiting her in Hoboken at least once a week, and he dutifully did as he was told. Usually, he went by himself.

"Frank visited his mother often after he was married because she demanded it," said Nick Sevano, Frank's Hoboken friend. "If he didn't come to see her, she'd go looking for him in New York!"

Nancy was thoroughly humiliated by her mother-in-law's abortion business, which had become even more publicized after she and Frank returned from their honeymoon. On February 27, 1939, Dolly was arraigned in Hudson Special Sessions Court for performing yet another illegal operation. She pleaded *non vult* (does not wish to contest) before Judge Lewis B. Eastmead. The story was published in Hudson County newspapers, and Nancy confided her shame to her friend Adeline. "I had only met Dolly once at the bridal shower, but after listening to Nancy I sure didn't want to meet her again or get to know her in any way," Adeline said.

Nancy saw little of her husband during the week; she went to work early in the morning and came home around dinnertime. That's when Frank was getting ready to go to the Rustic Cabin, where he stayed until early morning. Many days when she arrived, he wouldn't be home, having spent the day in New York, before going to work in Englewood Cliffs.

Nancy soon grew resentful of the hours her husband spent away from home with his men friends like Hank Sanicola, a former boxer and now a song plugger from the Bronx, who played the piano for Frank on all his singing dates.

"Hank was the only guy Frank ever feared, or at least did not double-cross," said Nick Sevano. "He knew that Hank feared nobody, and I mean nobody! He was a rough guy, Hank was. He was Frank's muscle man for years. That's why Frank kept him on his side."

Frank was not at all athletic. He was too frail and too thin to hold his own in the ring like the father and uncles he looked up to. Even his childhood friends had to do his fighting for him. But he grew up admiring brute strength, and Hank Sanicola treated him like a kid brother from the beginning.

"I was always his right arm, the strong right arm," he said. "I know how to fight. I was an amateur fighter. I used to step in and hit guys when they started ganging up on Frank in bars. . . . We were both of Sicilian origin, both Italians, so we became good friends. When Frank wasn't working, I would arrange a club date for him and go along to accompany him. We knew, both of us, that it was only a question of time until somebody bought Frank."

That somebody was Harry James, a fiery trumpeter who had left Benny Goodman's band to start his own, and who was looking for a singer when he heard Frank on the radio. The next night he went to the Rustic Cabin to see the singer in person. At first, Frank didn't believe that Harry James had come to the small-time roadhouse, and Harry James did not believe that the singer he'd heard on the radio was simply a waiter.

"This very thin guy with swept-back greasy hair had been waiting tables," he recalled. "Suddenly he took off his apron and climbed onto the stage. He'd sung only eight bars when I felt the hairs on the back of my neck rising. I knew he was destined to be a great vocalist."

In June 1939, James, whose band was only four months old, offered Frank a two-year contract as the featured male vocalist for seventy-five dollars a week. Frank accepted immediately without mentioning that he had already auditioned with Jack Miles, trombonist with Guy Lombardo, who was forming his own band, and had started practice workouts with Bob Chester, also starting his own band.

"All I could think of was 'Lock the doors! Board up the windows! Don't let this guy out!' " Frank said later. "I had hold of his arm so tight, his fingers went numb."

Harry James had already hired a female vocalist, Marie Antoinette Yvonne Jamais, and changed her name to Connie Haines. Now he said "Frank Sinatra" might sound too Italian and suggested that Frank become "Frankie Satin."

When Frank told his mother, Dolly raised her hefty fist and bellowed, "I'll give him 'Frankie Satin' with a shot to knock him cold. Your name is Sinatra, and it's going to stay Sinatra. So tell him to fuck off with this 'Frankie Satin' crap."

The next day, Frank phoned James and said if he wanted the voice, he'd have to take the name with it.

That same June, Frank made his first appearance with Harry James and his Music Makers at the Hippodrome Theater in Baltimore, where he sang "Wishing" and "My Love for You." Then the band headed for the Roseland Ballroom in New York City, where it played most of the summer, breaking for a three-week stint at the Steel Pier in Atlantic City, New Jersey.

After three months, Frank complained to Harry James that the music critics were ignoring him. He said he wasn't getting the recognition he deserved. He had made only a few recordings with the band, and one of them, "All or Nothing at All," sold a dismal eight thousand copies. (Four years later, a reissue of that same record would sell more than a million.) And the recordings he had made received little air time because of the radio ban on all ASCAP (American Society of Composers, Authors, and Publishers) music. In an effort to counter the Musician's Union's demands for royalties for bands and orchestras whose records were played on the radio, ASCAP banned radio performance of any song licensed by that society—and ASCAP controlled most U.S. music. The ban lasted until 1944.

Frank was also frustrated that Harry's band wasn't streaking toward the great success he thought he was due. Restless and dissatisfied, he considered quitting, but Hank Sanicola persuaded him to hang on for a few more months. In September 1939, George T. Simon of *Metronome* went to Roseland to hear the band, and as he was leaving he was approached by the band's road manager, Jerry Barrett.

"Please give the new boy singer a good write-up because he wants it more than anybody I've ever seen, and we want to keep him happy," said Barrett.

In his review, Simon raved about Harry James and "his sensational, intense style," complimented the drummer Ralph Hawkins, saluted Dave Matthews on the saxophone, and praised the arrangements of Andy Gibson. Then he mentioned the "pleasing vocals of Frank Sinatra, whose easy phrasing is especially commendable."

That wasn't good enough for Frank. He needed raves to get where he was going. Pleasing vocals and commendable phrasing would never catapult him to stardom.

And yet in 1939 the voice that would become one of the most exceptional in popular music was untrained. Frank sang uncertainly, hesitantly, and without the self-confidence he later exuded. His voice was pitched two tones higher than normal. Yet, even then, he displayed a natural way of phrasing that was distinctive and extremely musical.

By now, his repertoire included "My Buddy," "Willow Weep for Me," "It's Funny to Everyone but Me," "Here Comes the Night," "On a Little Street in Singapore," "Ciribiribin," and "Every Day of My Life."

The next month the band played the Hotel Sherman in Chicago, where *Billboard* mentioned the twenty-four-year-old vocalist who sang "the torchy ballads in a pleasing way in good voice. [His] only blemish is that he touches the songs with a little too much pash, which is not all convincing. . . ." Frank was incensed, and Harry James, who was voted the number-one trumpeter in the nation by *Downbeat*, was astounded by his arrogance.

A few nights later, a reporter asked the bandleader about the skinny little singer who slicked his hair back in a big pompadour and acted like a matinee idol at the microphone.

"Not so loud," said Harry James. "The kid's name is Sinatra. He considers himself the greatest vocalist in the business. Get that! No one ever heard of him. He's never had a hit record. He looks like a wet rag. But he says he is the greatest. If he hears you compliment him, he'll demand a raise tonight. . . ."

The public response to Harry James and his Music Makers was improving, but only slightly. The most dedicated swing fans preferred the established bands of Benny Goodman, Artie Shaw, Tommy Dorsey, Bob Crosby, Glenn Miller, Count Basie, Jimmy Dorsey, Duke Ellington, and Jimmie Lunceford. Harry's fledgling band was discouraged until they landed a choice booking at the Palomar Ballroom in Hollywood; then their spirits soared. "We felt sure that a successful engagement at the Palomar was all we needed to put us up on top," said Frank.

By the time the band bus had reached Denver, though, their spirits had plummeted. The Palomar had burned to the ground. Harry James wired his agent at MCA and was quickly booked into Victor Hugo's in Beverly Hills, an establishment more used to the sweet sounds of Guy Lombardo. The owner was flabbergasted when he first heard the hard-driving beat of Harry James and his swinging sidemen.

"He kept telling us we were playing too loud," said Harry. "And so he wouldn't pay us. We were struggling pretty good and nobody had any money, so Frank would invite us up to his place, and Nancy would cook spaghetti for everyone." Nancy had given up her job because she was pregnant and was traveling with Frank.

A few nights later as Frank stood at the microphone singing "All or Nothing at All," the manager rushed to the stage waving his hands and yelling, "Stop! No more! Enough!"

"We were thrown out—right in the middle of that song," said Frank. "They didn't even let us get through it. The manager came up and waved his hands for us to stop. He said Harry's trumpet-playing was too loud for the joint. He said my singing was just plain lousy. He said the two of us couldn't draw flies as an attraction—and I guess he was right. The room was empty as a barn."

The owner figured that he should charge Harry for emptying his establishment, so he refused to pay the band. With no money, Frank sent his wife back to New Jersey. Then he and the band headed for Chicago for another booking in the Sherman House Hotel. Every big band in the area was in town that week at the command of the musicians' czar, James Petrillo, to perform for the annual Christmas benefit party sponsored by Chicago's Mayor Edward J. Kelly.

After the benefit, Frank was slipped a note from Tommy Dorsey that said, "Meet me in my suite at the Palmer House." Frank knew that the famous bandleader was looking for someone to replace Jack Leonard, who in 1939 was considered the best band vocalist. Leonard was thinking of leaving Dorsey to go on his own, and that's all the temperamental bandleader had needed to hear before looking for another singer.

Frank was convinced that with Tommy Dorsey he would become a star. Backed by that orchestra, he would never have to worry about bookings or getting thrown out of places like Victor Hugo's. He knew that the critics would have to write about him, and recordings and radio shows would follow. There would be one-nighters all over the country in the best ballrooms and biggest theaters. But Frank worried that Dorsey might remember him from an earlier disastrous audition.

As Frank himself recalled it: "I'd sung in front of Dorsey once a few years before I'd joined him. Or rather I *hadn't* sung! It was an audition, and I had the words on the paper there in front of me and was just going to sing when the door opened and someone near me said, 'Hey, that's Tommy Dorsey.' He was like a god, you know. We were all in awe of him in the music business. Anyway, I just cut out completely—

dead. The words were there in front of me, but I could only mouth air. Not a sound came out. It was terrible."

Hurrying to the hotel now, Frank waited hours for Tommy Dorsey. Finally the "Sentimental Gentleman of Swing" arrived wearing wire-rimmed glasses. A direct, blunt man, his first words were: "Yes, I remember that day when you couldn't get out those words." Undaunted, Frank laughed, and this time he didn't mouth air. In a smooth baritone he sang "Marie," which was Jack Leonard's signature song and one of Dorsey's biggest hits. The bandleader offered him $125 a week, provided he could get out of his contract with Harry James. Frank accepted on the spot.

Returning to his hotel, he went to James's room. "He was reading," recalled Frank. "I walked into the room. I walked out again. I must've done that four times. Then I walked around in circles. Finally, Harry put down his magazine. 'What's bothering you? Seven-year itch?' So I told him. I'd've been happier opening a vein."

Harry called his business manager and asked for Frank's contract, which still had seventeen months to run.

"When he had it, he sat there and tore it into little pieces," said Frank. "He did that just because I had a better offer. No getting sore, no talking about letting him down, then or later."

Frank stayed on with Harry James long enough to break in a new singer by the name of Dick Haymes. On Sinatra's last night with the band, Harry wished him well and Frank introduced Haymes to the audience. Afterward, he walked with the band to the bus.

"The bus pulled out with the rest of the boys at about half past midnight," recalled Frank. "I'd said good-bye to them all and it was snowing. There was nobody around, and I stood alone in the snow with just my suitcase and watched the taillights disappear. Then the tears started, and I tried to run after the bus."

A few days later, he began rehearsing with the Dorsey band, convinced that he was at last on his way to becoming a star. He even arrived with one of the trappings—an entourage that consisted of Hank Sanicola, his piano player and protector, and Nick Sevano, the young man from Hoboken who had become his general factotum.

Nick had worked for De Santo tailors in Hoboken and had helped Frank get his clothes made there.

"I started by helping Frank dress," Nick said. "He always liked my sharp pinstriped suits and my silk ties, so I started helping him pick out his clothes. When I quit my job, I became his valet, secretary, gofer—everything. I lived with Frank and Nancy on the weekends on Audubon Avenue in Jersey City and I traveled with Frank on the road. I had to do everything for him—screen all his calls, buy his ties, design his clothes, deliver his records to disc jockeys, run his errands. You name it, I did it.

"Frank became a star within a few months of starting with Dorsey when he recorded 'I'll Never Smile Again.' That's the song that launched him, and became number one on the hit parade for weeks. After that, Tommy put Frank's name above everyone—above Connie Haines, above Jo Stafford and The Pied Pipers, and above all the other musicians, including Buddy Rich, who hated Frank because of it."

A brilliant and dynamic drummer, Rich did not like the new singer, who was as cocksure about his talent as Buddy was of his own. Equally arrogant, both men had violent tempers, which erupted when the band played the Meadowbrook in New Jersey. By that time, Frank had persuaded Tommy Dorsey to include his picture at the bottom of the band's publicity poster. Buddy Rich saw the poster and exploded. If anyone deserved to be featured, he said, it was he and not some lousy singer with jug ears. Dorsey did not budge. Buddy retaliated by speeding up his tempo whenever Frank sang his slow ballads, and soon Frank was complaining that Buddy's drums messed up his vocals. Their fights escalated, sometimes terrifying members of the band who happened to be present.

Jo Stafford saw one such incident backstage at the Astor Hotel in New York. "Buddy called Frank a name," she said, "and Frank grabbed a heavy glass pitcher filled with water and ice and threw it at Buddy's head. Buddy ducked. If he hadn't, he probably would have been killed or seriously hurt. The pitcher hit the wall so hard that pieces of glass were embedded in the plaster."

San Francisco columnist Herb Caen recalled going backstage at the Golden Gate Theater one night and seeing the drummer trying to skewer the singer.

"Buddy was trying to ram Frank against the wall with his cymbal—the high F cymbal that you play with your foot—and Sinatra was screaming and swinging at him," he said.

"Finally, Tommy broke it up with the help of a couple guys in the band."

Frank did not tolerate anyone's interfering with his singing. At one point, he refused to share the microphone with Connie Haines, Dorsey's female vocalist, because the little southerner attracted too much attention.

"When Frank wouldn't let me sing on the same mike, I'd look at some guy in uniform in the audience and sing to him instead," said Connie Haines. "The guys loved it and started hollering and screaming for me, which really made Frank mad. He was ready to kill me. Between choruses, I'd step out to do the boogie or the lindy, and Frank would always belittle me. 'Do your thing, cornball,' he'd say. He didn't like me because I was from down south and wasn't New York sophisticated like he thought he was. Finally, he told Tommy to fire me, but Tommy fired him instead, and for two weeks we worked with the guy who played Doc [Milburn Stone] on *Gunsmoke.* Then Frank apologized, and Tommy let him come back."

Frank's compulsion for cleanliness showed itself when he traveled with the Dorsey band. The musicians called him "Lady Macbeth" because he was always showering and changing his clothes.

Dorsey knew that he had a spectacular singer in Sinatra, whose soft ballads carried intimate messages of love that made women swoon. Frank in turn idolized Tommy, making him the godfather of his daughter, Nancy Sandra, born June 7, 1940. He imitated the flashy way the bandleader dressed. He threw the same kind of temper tantrums. He copied his mannerisms. Tommy was demanding, a perfectionist, and so Frank became one, too. He spent money as openly as Tommy and took women as easily. The bandleader had a passion for toy trains, so Frank adopted the same hobby. Soon he even began to sound like Tommy Dorsey.

"I used to sit up there on the bandstand with the other singers," he said. "They'd be looking all around the dance hall or whatever it was we were playing in, and I'd be looking at Tommy Dorsey's back. I never took my eyes off his back. He'd stand there playing his trombone, and I'd swear the son of a bitch was not breathing. I couldn't even see his jacket move—nothing. Finally, he gets finished playing 'Sleepy Lagoon' one night and he turns to me and says, 'Jesus Christ, you mean you still haven't figured it out yet?' "

"He knew I'd been watching him all the time, but he would never let me know. Then that night he explained to me how he would sneak short breaths out of the corners of his mouth at certain points in the arrangement. I do the same thing in a song."

Having taught Frank his technique for seamless phrasing, Dorsey advised him to listen to Bing Crosby's singing. "I used to tell him over and over, there is only one singer you ought to listen to, and his name is Crosby. All that matters to him is the words, and that is the only thing that ought to matter to you too."

Frank listened to Tommy Dorsey, who had become his mentor, his guide, his hero. "He became almost a father to me," he said. On the road, he sat up with him playing cards until five in the morning because Dorsey could not sleep. "He had less sleep than any man I've ever known," said Frank many years later. "I'd fall off to bed around then, but around nine-thirty A.M. a hand would shake me and it'd be Tommy saying, 'Hey pally—how about some golf?' So I'd totter out onto the golf course."

Nevertheless, Frank was no longer star-struck. If Dorsey was late to a rehearsal, Frank acted as substitute orchestra leader. "When Dorsey arrived, Sinatra would fix him with a glare of 'Where the fuck you been?'" said lyricist Sammy Cahn. "Dorsey would apologize that he'd been tied up in this and that, and Sinatra'd say something quaint like 'Bullshit.'"

Tommy was a fan of Dolly Sinatra. Nick Sevano said, "Tommy adored Frank's mom and her cooking, so we were always dragging the band to Hoboken for one of Dolly's Italian dinners." Sevano had been one of the many babies delivered by Mrs. Sinatra. Now in his work with Frank, he soon became the conduit between the overbearing mother and her elusive son.

"Dolly would get mad at me if I didn't call her every day to keep her informed of what was going on," said Nick. "I even had to call her when we were on the road because Frank didn't have the time. Boy, if I didn't call, she'd chew me out the next time I talked to her. 'You bastard, where have you and that son of a bitch son of mine been? Why didn't you call me, ya fucking bum?' she'd say. I still remember sitting in her living room on Garden Street just after we had come home from California with Dorsey's band and Frank had not been in touch with her for over a week. God, did she give him hell. 'You bastard, you too good to call your own mother?' she shouted. I always took her side, of course. 'Jesus, Frank,' I'd say. 'Why didn't you call her?' Frank would lower his head and say, 'I couldn't. I was on the road.' Then she'd really light into him. Frank would sit there and take it because he respected her. After she got the last word and blasted us both by yelling and screaming, cursing and swearing, she'd say, 'Okay, you bastards. Into the kitchen. I've made some linguine.' ''

Besides pacifying Mama Sinatra, Nick Sevano frequently had to run interference between Frank and his wife. Once little Nancy was born—mother and daughter would be forever defined by size—big Nancy developed an uneasy alliance with Dolly out of sheer necessity. Frequently, she had to turn to her two-fisted mother-in-law to bring her husband home at night. Now that the baby was born, Nancy was no longer traveling with Frank.

"Nancy was always interrogating me," said Nick Sevano. "She'd corner me and say, 'Where were you last night? Who were you with? Why were you out so late? I called the hotel all night and there was no answer in your room. Why not? Was Frank with another woman?' God, I'd have to think fast at times. I'd always lie and cover for Frank, saying that we were with another band member in his room rehearsing or something. Then Frank would take me aside and ask me what Nancy had said. 'Does she know? What did you tell her?'

"Sometimes Nancy would come right out and confront him about other women, crying and carrying on, but Frank would just ignore her. When she really started sobbing, he'd walk out of the room. 'Let's go, Nick,' he'd say, and we'd leave Nancy in tears and head for New York. I'd feel awful about it, but there was nothing I could do. That's the way Frank is.

"Then Nancy would call Dolly and bring the old lady into the act. Dolly didn't mess around, let me tell you. She had the guts of a bandit. She'd collar Frank and say, 'What are you doing with those broads? You know you're a married man. You have a family now. You can't be acting like a bum.' Frank would deny everything, of course, and say the girls were just friends. 'They hang around the band,' he'd say. He always had that excuse, but he dreaded those confrontations with his mother. She could be real tough on him. She had that Italian way of keeping her family together, no matter what. She was the one who pushed for that marriage with Nancy. She brought it together, and now she was going to keep it from coming apart. You don't have to like your daughter-in-law as long as you do what's right by the family and make your son do what's right. That's the way Dolly felt about things in those days."

Most of Frank's friends knew that the marriage was over for him within the first year. He made no pretense about his interest in other women and even talked openly about his marital problems.

"It must have been sometime in 1940 . . . he was a restless soul even then," said Sammy Cahn. "He told me how unhappy he was being a married man. I gave him the George Raft syndrome. 'George Raft has been married all his life. Put it this way—you're on the road all the time, you at least can go home to clean sheets.' He kind of understood that."

The first major rupture in the marriage occurred in October 1940, when Frank went to Hollywood with the Dorsey band to open the Palladium, a lavish new dance palace. With the Dorsey band as the star attraction, prices were raised from the usual one dollar to five dollars a person, which included "a deluxe dinner." After playing nights at the Palladium, Tommy and the band worked all day at Paramount studios making *Las Vegas Nights*, their first feature film. Frank appeared on screen as the anonymous band vocalist singing "I'll Never Smile Again."

"We got paid as extras," said the clarinetist, Johnny Mince. "Frank, The Pied Pipers, Buddy Rich . . . I think it was about fifteen dollars a day. Shortly after we got to the studio the band would be asleep all around the set. There just wasn't that much to do."

By the second or third day, Frank had met Alora Gooding, a beautiful blond starlet. Within a week, they were staying together.

"This was Frank's first big love away from home," said Nick Sevano. "In fact, she was the first big love of his life after he married Nancy. He was crazy about her, really in love with her. She was his first brush with glamour, and he was mad for her. The affair lasted a few years, and Frank even tried to leave Nancy because of it, but Dolly put the pressure on and wouldn't let him get a divorce.

"Although it was an unheard-of thing to do in 1940, Frank and Alora lived together when he was in California. She stayed with him at the Hollywood Plaza, which is where the band was staying."

Back in Jersey City taking care of their new baby, Nancy Sinatra had no idea of what was going on. She called Frank frequently, but usually ended up talking to Nick Sevano or Hank Sanicola, who tried to allay her fears with all sorts of creative stories about how tired and bored everyone was working at night and filming all day. By the time Frank returned home, he was besotted with Alora Gooding and carried her picture in his wallet. His wife soon found it.

"Sometimes I wondered if Frank did that kind of thing on purpose just to get caught," Nick Sevano said. "When Nancy confronted him with the photograph and demanded to know who the beautiful blonde was, he said, 'Oh, that. She's just a fan, a kid who was hanging around the band and wanted me to have her picture.' I couldn't believe it when he said that. Nancy wasn't stupid, but what could she do?"

A procession of women followed Alora Gooding, including a sixteen-year-old named Rita Maritt, who said she was fresh from a convent school when the twenty-five-year-old singer first seduced her.

"I remember when he took me to bed and told me stories about his childhood—how he would have to steal milk bottles to get the money to feed his family," she recalled. "He said that when he was a little boy, he would stand on the street corners in Hoboken singing songs to people, who threw coins at him."

Between the touch of Hollywood glamour and the teenager was a Long Island debutante who looked like Katharine Hepburn in *The Philadelphia Story*. She lived on an estate in Great Neck with nine acres fronting on Manhasset Bay and separate quarters for the maids and butlers. Her father was an oil baron, and she and her prep school friends loved the big bands. Every week they climbed into their shiny new cars to seek out the swinging sounds of Glenn Miller at the Glen Island Casino or Benny Goodman in the Manhattan Room.

"That's how I first met Frank," said Mary Lou Watts. "I'd gone with a date to hear Tommy Dorsey at the Astor Roof, and I went up to say hello to the trumpeter, Bunny Berrigan. He introduced me to Frank, and we became very good friends."

Frank was immediately beguiled by this Episcopalian princess from America's upper class. "She was some kind of untouchable thing to him," said Nick Sevano. "He couldn't reach that high, not where he came from. With a high-falutin family like hers, he was definitely from the wrong side of the tracks. They did not acknowledge him, of course, but that didn't make any difference to Frank. He called Mary Lou constantly and saw her all the time. He cared a great deal for her."

Mary Lou attended the Mount Vernon School for Girls in Washington, D.C., which she described as a private finishing school of sorts that taught one hundred and fifty young women how to be ladies.

"It was comparable to the first year of junior college, and a very strict establishment," she said. "We had to write down who we were going out with, and when we had dates, who came to see us. We had to introduce them to everybody, and bring them into one of the small living rooms to sit down. The doors to these rooms had to be open at all times. When Frank visited me, I always signed him in as Frank Steel because I didn't want the other girls mooning around. I knew they'd go in and look in the book and come out screaming and shrieking and all that kind of stuff if they saw his name.

"One weekend he came on a Sunday night and he was going to go to chapel with me. Afterwards, we were sitting in one of the little rooms, and some girls walked by who had just come from a prom in Chapel Hill, North Carolina, where the Dorsey band had played. I could see them looking in and going 'Oh' and 'Ah'; then they ran up the stairs, and fifteen minutes later, three quarters of the school was standing on this great winding staircase staring down at us. One of the girls was so excited that she told the teacher on duty that Frank Sinatra was sitting in the room. The teacher ran to the book and saw that I had signed in a man named Frank Steel, so she told the girls that they were wrong. 'That's Frank Steel,' she said. But the girls started squealing and told her it was Frank Sinatra and they had just come from hearing him sing at a prom.

"She said, 'Miss Watts, come in here this minute. The girls tell me that they have just come from Chapel Hill, where they saw the gentleman that you are entertaining. They say that his name is not Frank Steel but Frank Sinatra.'

"You have no idea of the trouble I got into as a result of

that! I was campused for weeks, and the school wrote a letter to my mother asking if she realized that I was going out with Frank Sinatra. The school was shocked and incensed. Not because Frank was a married man, which I didn't know at first, or because he was eight years older than me, but because he was a singer! Well-bred young women simply didn't go out with show-business people. They were declassé and beneath the consideration of ladies. My mother was wonderful about it. She wrote me back and said that she trusted me completely, and, by the way, who is Frank Sinatra? She'd never heard of him."

After Mary Lou was graduated from Mount Vernon and living at home again, Mrs. Watts soon became acquainted with Frank, for he started calling her daughter at three o'clock in the morning. Those early morning phone calls rang on the phone in her bedroom, and Mrs. Watts had to get up and walk down the hall to her daughter's room to tell her she was wanted on the telephone.

"At that hour of the morning, I'd know that it was Frank and that he'd just gotten off the bandstand and finished work for the evening," said Mary Lou. "My mother would shake her head. 'I simply don't understand anybody who works at this hour of the night,' she'd say."

Entranced by the big bands, Mary Lou Watts enjoyed socializing with Frank. "We'd sit around and talk about the band," she said. "Frank hated Buddy Rich, who was uncouth and common, and he couldn't stand Connie Haines either. I don't know why. You didn't ask. If he didn't like them, you didn't like them either, and that was it. If he didn't talk to them, you didn't talk to them.

"After he got off work, we'd go out to fun places like Jack White's Club 18 and to Harlem to hear Billie Holiday sing. He took me to publicity benefits and to a lot of recording sessions. I remember, they'd rehearse in the worst places, and they'd practice a long time before they ever recorded one song."

By now, Mary Lou was engaged to the man who became her husband. Nick Sevano said he spent many hours consoling her fiancé when he'd cry to Nick about Mary Lou's being out with Frank.

But she had her fiancé with her when she decided to help the unschooled singer from Hoboken by introducing him to café society. They took him to the Stork Club, where he met their friends. "Maybe we taught him how to eat," she said. "He learned, and he was always nice to everyone." She felt rewarded for her efforts.

"Frank sang beautifully, but he spoke with 'deze, dem, and doze' diction," she said. "He had a terrible New Jersey accent, but it didn't show in his singing. It's like the Japanese who sing English and sound just like us. If you can string it out into syllables, it will sound right, and that's what Frank did, I guess. I always knew that he was going to be a great success someday because he was absolutely determined to become a star. He had amazing confidence in himself. He was torn about leaving Tommy Dorsey, though, and kept asking me if he should do it. It was a terrible decision for him."

In May 1941, Frank, age twenty-five, was named the top band vocalist by *Billboard*, and girls started swooning. Every time they did, Dorsey had his musicians stop the music and swoon right back at them. "This inspired the girls to go one better," said the bandleader, "and the madness kept growing until pretty soon it reached fantastic proportions."

Tommy couldn't believe how moved women were by the frail singer with the face of a debauched faun. "I used to stand there on the bandstand so amazed I'd almost forget to take my solos," he said. "You could almost feel the excitement comin' up out of the crowds when that kid stood up to sing. Remember, he was no matinee idol. He was a skinny kid with big ears. And yet what he did to women was something awful."

By the end of the year, Frank had displaced Bing Crosby at the top of the *Downbeat* poll, a position that Crosby had held for six years.

"That's when he really started pushing Tommy," said Nick Sevano, remembering how Frank clamored to record some solo songs. Dorsey finally agreed, and on January 19, 1942, with Axel Stordahl as arranger and conductor, Frank held his first recording session, singing "Night and Day," "The Night We Called It a Day," "The Song Is You," and "Lamplighter's Serenade."

"Frank rehearsed day and night for that project," said Connie Haines. "We were playing the Hollywood Palladium at the time and rehearsing there. They put the record on the loudspeaker, and Frank's voice began to fill the Palladium.

We all knew it was a hit. Frank knew it, too, because he said, 'Hey, Bing, old man. Move over. Here I come.' ''

The next afternoon, Frank sat in his room at the Hollywood Plaza with Stordahl, playing the two sides of the record over and over on his portable machine. "He just couldn't believe his ears," said the conductor. "He was so excited, you almost believed he had never recorded before. I think this was a turning point in his career. I think he began to see what he might do on his own."

That evening, Frank told Sammy Cahn that he had to leave Dorsey and go on his own because he was going to be the best singer in the world. He had worried so much in the last few months about making the move that he'd lost his appetite and barely weighed a hundred pounds.

"He was almost tubercular," Nick Sevano recalled. "He was seeing all kinds of doctors, but he was so nervous that he couldn't eat. He never finished a meal. He'd order fifteen different things but then he'd just pick, eat two bites of a steak, a forkful of pasta, and that would be it. He'd always get in deep depressive moods, but now he started talking a lot about death and dying. He'd tell me that he didn't think he would live very long. 'I get the feeling that I'm going to die soon,' he'd say. That's why he filled his days with so much activity. He always had to be moving and constantly doing something.

"He knew the time had come to move on and was just trying to 'guts' up to it. I thought he was crazy myself. So did Hank. Tommy had given him such prominence with the band that Frank had become a star with Dorsey. He was making about thirteen thousand a year. He'd already been in two movies, *Las Vegas Nights* and *Ship Ahoy*, and made over eighty recordings. I thought he was nuts to throw all that away, but Frank was determined to go on his own. 'I gotta do it, I gotta do it,' he kept telling me. 'And I gotta do it before Bob Eberly does it.' He drove Tommy up the wall telling him he didn't want to be known as 'Dorsey's boy' all his life. Hank and I were worried at first, but Frank would scream at us and say, 'I'm going to be big, real big, bigger than Bing Crosby, bigger than anybody. I'll leave the rest of those singers in the dust.' So we fell in line. We started by staying up all night calling Frank Cooper, an agent at GAC [General Amusement Corporation], to represent him. Manie Sacks, head of Columbia Records, had taken a liking to Frank, and he was kind of guiding us. He'd already promised Frank a recording contract and then recommended Cooper at GAC to represent him. Later, he got Frank a spot on CBS and helped us find a press agent."

Dorsey held his band close to him and took it as a personal affront if someone wanted to leave. "When a kid in the band said, 'I'm giving you two weeks' notice,' Tommy wouldn't look at him for the whole two weeks," Frank said. "In fact, he would never talk to the guy again. I knew this, so when I started thinking about leaving, I said to him one day, 'I'm giving you a year's notice.' He looked at me and said, 'What?' He didn't believe me. He thought I was kidding. That was in 1942. Six months later I asked him if he wanted me to look for another singer. He got the message then, and for the next six months he never spoke to me."

"Tommy held on to Frank so fiercely," said Nick Sevano. "He cherished him like a son. When he realized that Frank was finally serious, he called me, crying, 'Please, Nick, talk him out of it. Please talk him out of it.'

"But you couldn't talk Frank out of anything. Ever. He was a driven man in those days. He was relentless, so ambitious. He was like a Mack truck going one hundred miles an hour without brakes. He had me working around the clock. 'Call Frank Cooper. Do it now. Don't wait until tomorrow,' he'd say. 'Send my publicity photos to Walter Winchell.' 'Get my records to the Lucky Strike *Hit Parade*.' 'Call Columbia Records and tell them I'll be singing such and such.' Frank knew so much about promotion and how to hype himself. He learned it from Tommy. He was wining and dining disc jockeys when no one else was paying any attention to them. He knew that was the way to get his records played on the radio. He bought drinks for reporters all the time and took columnists out to dinner and was always buying them presents or sending them flowers. He never once let up—not for a minute.

"We'd be walking out of the theater at two in the morning after working all day and he'd say to me, 'Did you talk to So-and-So? You didn't call, did you?' 'Yeah, yeah,' I'd say, 'I'm on it.' Of course, I'd have forgotten all about it, but Frank didn't."

Once he had a recording commitment from Manie Sacks, Frank wanted to make his move. He asked Axel Stordahl to go with him to do his arrangements. After seven years with

Dorsey, Stordahl was reluctant to leave, but Frank agreed to pay him $650 a month, five times what Dorsey paid him. As angry as he was about his taking Stordahl, Dorsey still offered to advance Frank $17,000 if he would sign a contract pledging Dorsey 33 1/3 percent of his gross earnings over $100 a week for the next ten years. The contract also called for Frank to pay an additional ten percent to Leonard K. Vannerson, Dorsey's personal manager, as a commission for bringing Frank to the attention of Columbia Records.

Frank needed the advance because he no longer would have a steady salary. He had to hire men and he wanted to buy a new house for his wife and baby daughter. Besides, he always needed money because he spent so heavily. So, in August 1942, he signed eagerly.

But a year later, he was sorry. He had given Dorsey only one thousand dollars under the contract, and now was refusing to pay anything further. He complained bitterly to the press about the financial hammerlock Tommy had on him, and his fans started boycotting Dorsey's performances.

"You can quote Sinatra as saying that he believes it is wrong for anybody to own a piece of him and collect on it when that owner is doing nothing for Sinatra," Frank told the *New York Herald-Tribune*. "Sinatra will fight this foreclosure or whatever it is to the last ditch."

"It all sounds like a black-market meat-slicing affair to us," said an editorial in *Metronome*.

Piqued at being portrayed as something short of an extortionist, Tommy sued. "I thought the lug would think the price too high," he said. "I didn't want him to quit, but he did. I never tried to collect, but when he gave out with interviews about how I had him all cut up, it made me sore."

In August 1943 Frank's lawyer, Henry Jaffe, flew to Los Angeles to meet with Dorsey's lawyer, N. Joseph Ross, to try to settle the matter. In the end, MCA, the agency representing Dorsey and courting Sinatra, made Dorsey a $60,000 offer that he accepted. To obtain Frank as a client, the agency paid Dorsey $35,000 while Sinatra paid $25,000, which he borrowed from Manie Sacks as an advance against his royalties from Columbia Records. MCA agreed that until 1948 it would split its commissions on Sinatra with GAC, the agency that Frank had signed with when he left the Dorsey band.

Afterward, everyone seemed satisfied with the arrangement. MCA had Frank as a new client, and GAC was well compensated for giving him up. Frank told the press that he was delighted to own himself once again, and Tommy told friends that he had made "a hell of a deal."

"I saw Dorsey that afternoon, and he was in a great mood," said Arthur Michaud, who had managed Dorsey and would soon manage him again. " 'I just turned Frank Sinatra over to MCA for sixty thousand dollars,' he told me.

" 'You got the money?' I asked him.

" 'Yeah.'

" 'Dope. You should've taken twenty thousand with two and a half percent for seven years or three and a third of his earnings. That's the deal you should have made.'

"Tommy thought for a minute and said, 'You're right. Those bastards at MCA gave me bad advice.' Dorsey and I were close, close friends and he would've told me if the buy-out had been anything else. That's why I never believed that stupid Mafia story."

Michaud was referring to the fact that as time passed, the story of MCA's simple buy-out had changed to a far more ominous one, which held that Willie Moretti, the *padrino* of New Jersey who was to become Frank's good friend and neighbor when Frank moved to Hasbrouck Heights, had gone to Dorsey's dressing room and demanded that he release the singer—using as persuasive argument a revolver he rammed down Dorsey's throat. Supposedly, Dorsey thereupon sold Sinatra for one dollar.

"That's crap," said Nick Sevano. "It was a simple buy-out by MCA. Frank was involved with the racket boys later but not on the Dorsey deal."

Tommy Dorsey's attorney swore that his client had never been subjected to Mafia intimidation. "Oh, God, no," N. Joseph Ross said. "Absolutely not. It's not true. I remember after we got a settlement I called Tommy and woke him up. He was very happy with the outcome. No, there was no gun put down his throat. Ever."

But Frank was never to forget the terms of the original break with Dorsey. And he was reminded of it all over again in 1951 when he read an article in *American Mercury* magazine about his associations with gangsters in which Dorsey talked of the contract dispute with Frank. The bandleader said that after a breakdown in negotiations he was visited by three businesslike men who told him out of the sides of their mouths to "sign or else." Five years passed before Frank spoke to Dorsey again.

In August 1956, fourteen years after that agreement was signed, Frank accepted a week's engagement with the Dorsey brothers at the Paramount, where his film *Johnny Concho* was the screen attraction. Three months later, Tommy Dorsey died suddenly after choking in his sleep. His widow never received any kind of condolence from Frank Sinatra. There was no letter, no telephone call, no flowers, no acknowledgment of any kind. Nor would Frank join Dorsey's friends and former band members in the one-hour television show called *A Tribute to Tommy Dorsey*. Connie Haines sang "Will You Still Be Mine," and Jo Stafford, with Paul Weston conducting, sang the first song she had ever recorded with the Dorsey band. Even Jack Leonard returned to sing "Marie," but there was no song by Sinatra.

He had never forgiven the bandleader, especially after Tommy gave an interview to a newspaper reporter in which he characterized Frank as "brittle." When asked what he thought of the singer, Dorsey had said, "He's the most fascinating man in the world, but don't stick your hand in the cage."

Rancor continued to fester within Frank. More than three decades after the contract break with Dorsey, Frank's grudge seemed even stronger than it had been. At a concert at the Universal Amphitheatre in Los Angeles on June 15, 1979, Frank introduced Harry James before an audience of sixty-two hundred people and said what a wonderful guy Harry was because when Sinatra was just starting out as a singer, James had let him out of his contract after only six months.

"And then there was Tommy Dorsey," said Frank. "And when I wanted to get out of my contract to him years later, it cost me seven million dollars." He stamped his foot on the stage, and stared down as if the bandleader were smoldering in hell for the wrongs he'd committed against his one-time singer. "You hear me, Tommy?" Frank yelled. "You hear me? I'm talking to you."

6

In 1942, driven by the tensions and deprivations of a country at war, people on the home front began spending lavishly for entertainment. They were so eager to be distracted that they flocked to theaters at all hours, forcing movie houses in Portland, Oregon, to stay open all night and feature a "swing-shift matinee" for workers from midnight to four o'clock in the morning. Live music was the best entertainment available, and the public handsomely rewarded its musicians, especially those singers whose way with a romantic lyric touched deep longings. Nelson Eddy was the highest paid musician in the country in 1942, commanding more than seven thousand dollars for a concert.

Managers of large theaters in New York City, Boston, and Chicago tried to book one of the big bands when they showed a new feature film. People wanted to hear Helen O'Connell sing "Embraceable You" with Jimmy Dorsey's orchestra or to listen to Eddy Duchin play "Stormy Weather." They loved swaying to Les Brown's orchestra and toe-tapping to Glenn Miller's "Don't Sit Under the Apple Tree."

Sinatra's last performance with Tommy Dorsey was in September 1942. From then on he was on his own.

Bob Weitman, manager of New York's Paramount Theater, booked Benny Goodman, the King of Swing and the country's number one bandleader, as the star attraction for the New Year's show that year. Featured with the famous clarinetist were singer Peggy Lee, Jess Stacy on the piano, and the Benny Goodman sextet. At the last minute, Weitman decided to add a scrawny singer who couldn't read a note of music but who had made the girls swoon when he performed the week before at the Mosque Theater in Newark, New Jersey.

"I still don't know exactly why I did it," said Weitman. "I had *Star Spangled Rhythm* as the picture for those weeks, and that certainly didn't need extra attractions. . . . Benny Goodman could pack the house himself. But there was something about this kid."

Sinatra had been a top band singer, but now he didn't have the Dorsey band behind him. And he knew that Benny Goodman, a serious musician, was conscious only of his clarinet and his orchestra, nothing else, certainly not of any new up-and-coming singers. The King of Swing had never heard of Sinatra. Billed as an "extra added attraction," the twenty-seven-year-old singer in the floppy bow tie was almost paralyzed by stage fright as he waited to walk to the microphone for that first show on December 30, 1942. It was a long wait. Benny Goodman dazzled the audience with his music for an hour before making his laconic introduction—"And now, Frank Sinatra."

Sinatra stuck his head and one foot out through the curtains—and froze. Immediately, the girls let out a scream. Sinatra still couldn't move a muscle. They sent up such a tremendous roar that the startled bandleader also froze, his arms raised on the upbeat. He looked over one shoulder and said to no one in particular, "What the fuck was that?"

Hearing him, Frank started laughing and ran to the microphone to sing "For Me and My Gal."

A few days later Nick Sevano brought a new press agent to the show.

"Up to this point," Sevano said, "the publicity had been handled by a guy named Milt Rubin, who was very close to Walter Winchell. Milt didn't fawn over Frank the way he was supposed to. In fact, he sometimes acted like Winchell was more important than our boy and that was his undoing. Then Manie Sacks suggested George Evans, who handled Glenn Miller and the Copa. He was the biggest thing to ever happen to Frank.

"I was bringing George Evans down the aisle to get closer to the stage," recalled Nick Sevano. "A girl stood up and threw a rose at Frank, and the girl next to her moaned a little. That's all George needed to see. A couple of days later, he created an absolute pandemonium for Frank."

The forty-year-old press agent engulfed everyone with his energy. Dynamic and hard-charging, he represented the best in the business: Duke Ellington, Lena Horne, Kitty Kallen, Dean Martin and Jerry Lewis, the Copacabana Club. He considered himself personally responsible for his clients' success and happiness, pushing himself tirelessly on their behalf. After seeing Frank sing at the Paramount, the astute press agent worked with dervishlike energy to turn the sparks of a tossed rose and a moaning teenager into a conflagration of screaming hysterical women. In the process, George Evans made his new client the most sensational singer in the country.

"I thought if I could fill the theater with a bunch of girls moaning, 'Oh, Frankie,' I've got something there," Evans said.

He hired twelve long-haired, round-faced little girls in bobby socks and paid them five dollars apiece to jump and scream and yell "Oh, Frankie. Oh, Frankie" when Frank started to sing one of his slow, soft ballads. He drilled them in the basement of the Paramount, directing them to holler when Frank bent and dipped certain notes. "They shouldn't only yell and squeal, they should fall apart," Evans said. He showed Frank how to caress the microphone, clutching it as if he were going to fall down. Then he suggested that when he sang "She's Funny That Way" and purred the words "I'm not much to look at, nothin' to see," one of the girls should interrupt and yell "Oh, Frankie, yes, you are!" On "Embraceable You," he suggested that Frank open his arms wide when he sang the words "Come to Papa, Come to Papa, do." Then Evans instructed the girls to scream "Oh, Daddy," telling Frank to murmur softly into the mike "Gee, that's a lot of kids for one fellow." Two of the girls were coached to fall in a dead faint in the aisle, while the others were told to moan in unison as loudly as they could.

To pack the theater to capacity, Evans distributed free tickets to hundreds of youngsters on school vacation. He hired an ambulance to sit outside and gave the ushers bottles of ammonia "in case a patron feels like swooning."

Evans knew it was one thing to be a popular band singer where the band and bandleader always dominate, and quite another for a singer to be a star on his own. Evans was going to give Sinatra everything he thought he needed to become that kind of star. He told a few select columnists that a new young singer was appearing at the Paramount. He said Frank was going to be bigger than Rudy Vallee and Bing Crosby because he made women fall on the floor. Photographers were alerted, and the next day's newspapers showed pictures of young girls being carried out "in a swoon" after seeing Frank Sinatra: Twelve were hired but thirty fainted.

By the end of the week, the ticket lines stretched around the block, and reporters were writing about the thrilling new crooner who cocked his head, hunched his shoulders, and caressed the microphone, all of which made young girls faint and old women scream.

The Paramount stayed packed for the four weeks of Benny Goodman's engagement, and Frank was named by *Metronome* as the top male vocalist in the country. Bob Weitman immediately signed him for another four weeks, saying it was the first time a performer had been held over since Rudy Vallee was the nation's singing idol in 1929. Then he hired extra guards for crowd control.

By this time, George Evans was in manic overdrive. He christened his client "Swoonatra" or "The Voice." He called his mooning fans "Sinatratics," and labeled the swooning phenomenon "Sinatraism," all of which was immediately adopted by the press. He encouraged bobby-soxers to form their own fan clubs, hold mass meetings, and write letters to the newspapers about their hero. Each fan club received a flossy embossed parchment charter signed by Frank.

Within weeks, Evans was calling reporters to tell them that more than one thousand Sinatra fan clubs had sprung up in the United States, among them the Moonlit Sinatra Club, The Slaves of Sinatra, and The Flatbush Girls Who Would Lay Down Their Lives for Frank Sinatra Fan Club, as well as the Frank Sinatra Fan and Mahjong Club, consisting of forty middle-aged Jewish women who met to play their favorite game while listening to Sinatra songs. Evans said more than two hundred fifty of the clubs published their own newspapers. Most reporters laughed, so Evans sent them copies of *Frank Fare*, the newspaper of a Newark, New Jersey, fan club called The Sighing Society of Sinatra Swooners, in which the editor wrote, "Cynical singers and orchestra leaders sneered at him at first, but we in the deepness of our hearts knew that our Frankie was straight and true and that someday he would be known and loved all over the world."

Evans circled this particular passage, and reporters dutifully wrote it up. He courted the press assiduously, knowing that published stories about Frank's fanatic fans and their bizarre behavior would set a pattern that even more youngsters would want to adopt. Consequently, he worked hard to arrange as many interviews as possible. He even devised a mass radio interview with two hundred high school editors quizzing Frank over WAAT in Jersey City, thereby ensuring stories in two hundred high school papers.

From the start, George Evans played Frank as a family man, the boy-next-door answer to girlish fantasies. Frank cooperated completely. He sat for every interview that George arranged and threw open his home to reporters and photographers. He posed patiently for any pictures they wanted to take of him and Big Nancy and Little Nancy in the kitchen, the bedroom, and the nursery. He put on a sailor cap and posed for pictures leaning on a lawn mower in the backyard. Soon, so much fan mail poured in that he hired two full-time secretaries to handle the letters and requests for photographs. This he did willingly. "I believe in publicity," he said. "It's the best thing to spend money on."

When Evans could not "sell" an interview, he invented a news event, like Frank Sinatra Day in Philadelphia, the "Why I Like Frank Sinatra" contest in Detroit, or New York's "I Swoon for Sinatra" contest. With Evans at the controls, the bobby-soxer brigade quickly grew into thousands of ecstatic, shrieking, rapturous fans.

"We hired girls to scream when he sexily rolled a note," said Jack Keller, who was George Evans's partner on the West Coast. "The dozen girls we hired to scream and swoon did exactly as we told them. But hundreds more we didn't hire screamed even louder. Others squealed, howled, kissed his pictures with their lipsticked lips, and kept him a prisoner in his dressing room between shows at the Paramount. It was wild, crazy, completely out of control."

So spectacular was the Sinatra publicity campaign that *Billboard* awarded Evans a scroll in 1943 for the "Most Effective Promotion of a Single Personality," which Evans proudly displayed on his office wall. "Frankie is a product of crowd psychology," he told the Chicago Tribune News Service. "And the girls loved it. Understand, it was the Sinatra influence that provided the initial impetus. But it was I, Evans, who saw the possibilities in organized and regimented moaning. . . . It's a big snowball now, and Frankie's riding to glory on it."

With the zeal of an empire builder, the devoted press agent began composing a biographical sketch of his client, which he distributed to the press. This was one of his most creative endeavors. After shrewdly assessing what the public wanted in its new boy singer, Evans lopped two years off Frank's age, asserting that the twenty-eight-year-old bobby-sox idol had been born in 1917 rather than 1915. That was intended to make him closer in age to his young fans. Ignoring Frank's expulsion from school, he elevated the high school dropout who had no interest in sports to a graduate of Demarest High who ran track, played football, leaped for basketballs, and sang in the glee club. Evans then promoted him from a lowly fly boy who bundled newspapers for *The Jersey Observer* to a full-fledged sports reporter. Both immigrant parents became native-born, and Evans made no mention, of course, of Uncle Babe's prison record or Uncle Gus's numbers operation. He raised Dolly from a Hoboken midwife with a thriving abortion business to a Red Cross nurse who had served her country in World War I. Marty was depicted as the head of the house. His place on the Hoboken fire department was left intact, with nothing said about how he got the job. Sensing that the public would not be endeared to a spoiled brat indulged by a mother as tough as a stevedore, Evans transformed Frankie into a poor, struggling little boy who barely survived the vicious gang wars in his slum neighborhood. He conjured up terrifying images of Hoboken brutes smashing one another with chains, knives, and brass knuckles. He depicted Frank as a Depression child who knew only poverty and deprivation. He was the American Dream personified.

But the most inventive part was Evans's description of his client as a loving family man. He insisted that Frank wear his wedding band, and frequently had him quoted saying such things as: "Nobody comes before my wife, Nancy. That goes for now and for all time." Giving "Mommy" full credit for his jaunty bow ties, Frank said, "We thought up that type of large bow tie as a trademark. Nancy shops around for bits of silk, keeps making new ones. I've got a hundred—I give lots away." At the end of his radio broadcasts he always said,

"Good night, Nancy." When Nancy became pregnant again in 1943, no one was happier than the avuncular Evans, who hoped that it would solidify Frank in the eyes of the public as a happily married man and keep him out of the gossip columns.

"God, how George tried to keep Frank and Nancy together!" said Ben Barton, who started a music company with Frank and Hank Sanicola in 1944 to publish all of Frank's songs. "He did everything he could to bust up Frank's outside romances."

"George was like a father to Frank, and he rode him hard about playing around with other women," said Nick Sevano. "He did everything he could to keep him with Nancy. He said his fans wouldn't tolerate him seeing other women when he was a married man with a three-year-old daughter at home and a baby on the way, and they'd drop him cold if he ever got a divorce."

Evans did more than lecture Frank on the subject of fidelity; he took it upon himself to befriend Nancy, and he slowly transformed her from a little Italian housewife into an extremely winning woman. Knowing that Frank was fatally attracted to glamour, he wanted Nancy to be able to hold her own. He sent her to a dentist to get her teeth capped and recommended cosmetic surgery for her nose, which seemed to overpower her small face and almost obliterate her deep brown eyes. He also made a series of appointments for her at Helena Rubinstein for makeup lessons and hair styling.

Then he took her shopping, insisting that she stop making her own clothes and spend money on something striking so that she would be beautifully dressed when Frank took her out, thereby making him proud of her. This was the hardest part for Nancy, who had been budgeting all her life. She believed in saving, and Frank in spending, so she handled the family finances. Always cutting corners, she asked her brother-in-law, Anthony Puzo, an accountant, to do their taxes, and took legal matters to Danny Figarelli, the brother-in-law who was a lawyer. She knew that the family wouldn't charge as much as outsiders. Ironically, the more money Frank made, the tighter Nancy held on to it.

When they bought their house in Hasbrouck Heights, New Jersey, in 1943, Nancy suggested that Frank call Don Milo, the Hoboken musician who had dressed him for the Major Bowes audition. Milo was now the purchasing agent for Republic Pictures and entitled to a forty percent discount on furniture. Nancy wanted a Stork Line bedroom set, plus new living room, dining room, and kitchen furniture, but she didn't want to pay full price. So Frank phoned Milo and Nancy bought everything wholesale.

She resented reimbursing Nick Sevano and Hank Sanicola for business expenses, especially when she suspected they were spending the money on entertaining other women for Frank, and she was almost niggardly about paying his other associates.

"He hired me to do some work for him at fifty dollars a week, but he got two months behind in paying me," said Milt Rubin, Frank's first press agent. "I asked somebody to find out why, and they told me that Nancy was handling the money and she felt that if she didn't pay people on time, they would work harder for Frank. I had to start suit to collect."

Money was the only weapon Nancy had to wield control over her husband's freewheeling style, and though he usually ignored her and continued spending, his associates couldn't be so cavalier. "Nancy really tried to hold us down," said Nick Sevano, "but money never ruled Frank. That was probably his best quality. When I was with him, he lived like King Farouk and spent all the time. He was always telling me to pick up six theater tickets for someone, to send flowers to someone else, to buy a gold lighter for this reporter and a gold watch for that one, to tip the maître d', tip the waiter, tip the hatcheck girl, tip the cabbie, tip, tip, tip. He never wanted anyone to think that he was not successful because he didn't have money, so he spent like crazy. And he never worried about going broke either. He said that he was the greatest singer in the world and that he'd always be able to make millions because he had such a fantastic talent. Hank and I thought he was nuts at times, but then, when you come from humble beginnings like we did, you tend to hang on to money for fear you'll never see it again. Nancy was like that, too, but not Frank. He always had money growing up because of his mom, and now he was always going to have it because of his talent."

Following his astounding success at the Paramount, the money rolled in as Frank signed contracts with *Your Hit Parade*, Columbia Records, and RKO. He made sure the press knew the astronomical sums he was making—$1,250 a week at the Paramount and $4,500 for a return visit, $2,800 a week on the *Hit Parade*, $1,000 for personal appearances on radio programs like *The Jack Benny Show, Amos 'n Andy,* and the George Burns and Gracie Allen show; $1,000 for a three-minute song in *Reveille with Beverly*, plus $25,000 for his first RKO movie, $50,000 for the second, and $100,000 for the third. "I'm in the $100,000 class now," he told the New York *Daily News*.

He had the swooners, but now he needed the sophisti-cates. So his agents accepted an April 1943 booking at the Riobamba, a sleek New York City nightclub that catered to socialites but was in financial trouble due to some recent cancellations. After much brokering, Frank was hired, but only as the "extra added attraction" for $800 a week. The two stars, monologist Walter O'Keefe and singer-comedienne Sheila Barrett, received $1,500 apiece.

Evans was worried. He knew how important it was for Frank to capture this sophisticated audience if he was to break into nightclubs and soar to the top. Hank Sanicola, also apprehensive, suggested more rehearsals, but Frank laughed. He had already seen the Riobamba. After looking the place over, he had turned to the owner and said, "You better push the walls of this joint out. I'm gonna pack 'em in."

Five days later, the nightclub was filled. By the end of the week, it was standing room only, and the club started making a profit. After two weeks, the two headliners were dropped, leaving only Frank and a line of chorus girls. His three-week engagement was extended, and his price upped to fifteen hundred a week. He was exultant and preening.

"I'm flying high, kid," he told a reporter. "I've planned my career. From the first minute I walked on a stage I determined to get exactly where I am; like a guy who starts out being an office boy but has a vision of occupying the president's office 'someday.' I hitched my wagon to a star and. . . ."

Composer Jule Styne sat in the opening night audience and partied with Frank until dawn. A few hours later, a messenger delivered to Styne a gold ID bracelet from Cartier inscribed: "To Jule Who Knew Me When. Frankie."

"Frank was a sensation, doing extra shows, and I went to the two-thirty A.M. show with a stop first in his dressing room," recalled Sammy Cahn. "The moment he saw me he put his arms around me and said, 'Did I tell ya? Did I tell ya?'

Of course, after that show, we all hugged and laughed and shouted. For us it was proof that the 'B' group now had an 'A' singer, which was the wire I promptly sent to the other members of the 'B' group back on the coast. The 'A' group of that era was Bing Crosby and Company.''

The next month, Frank returned to the Paramount, where he was besieged by thousands of screaming, swooning youngsters. They stormed the theater and broke down the doors to get inside, sweeping aside the police and security men as if they were cardboard cutouts.

"It was absolute pandemonium," said Nick Sevano. "This time, they threw more than roses. They threw their panties and their brassieres. They went nuts, absolutely nuts.''

The critics were flabbergasted. "The hysteria which accompanies his presence in public is in no way part of an artistic manifestation," said the *Herald-Tribune*. "It is a slightly disturbing spectacle to witness the almost synchronized screams that come from the audience as he closes his eyes or moves his body slightly sideways, because the spontaneous reaction corresponds to no common understanding relating to tradition or technique of performance, nor yet to the meaning of the sung text.''

"Hysteria to the point of swooning is definitely harmful," said a New York psychiatrist. "This is a nervous disease and a harmful thing. Apparently such singing upsets nerves that are already keen.''

"Mass frustrated love without direction," said a sociologist.

"His voice is an authentic cry of starvation," said a doctor.

"It's mammary hyperesthesia," said another.

"Purely mass psychology built up by his press agent," said a Brooklyn analyst. "They all work on one another. It's an emotional situation no different from the Holy Rollers.''

The head of the New York Police Department's missing persons bureau blamed Frank for the problem of runaway girls and recommended that he be exiled to New Guinea.

The education commissioner of New York City threatened to press charges against him for encouraging truancy, because thousands of girls were skipping school to hear him sing. "We can't tolerate young people making a public display of losing control of their emotions," he said.

One member of Congress excoriated him as "the prime instigator of juvenile delinquency in America."

Frank thrived on the controversy he was creating and

laughed when a magazine described his singing as "a kind of musical drug . . . an opium of emotionalism." He was not at all amused, though, when his voice was characterized as "worn velveteen," and he swore at the critic who wrote that "listening to The Voice is like being stroked by a hand covered with cold cream."

He snapped angrily at reviewers who said that he usually sang a half note or so off-key. "Nuts," he said. "If they knew music or at least knew enough to realize what I'm doing when I sing, they'd never say it. Those characters just don't know."

He scolded the critic who suggested that Tommy Dorsey and his band had made him a star. "Now when I sing, there is nothing to distract from me," he said. "Thirty-three musicians in the Dorsey band. It was like competing with a three-ring circus. Now I'm up there alone."

Frank was spending little time at home. Every bit of energy was directed toward his career, and he let *nothing* get in the way of that ambition.

Still, he also did nothing to protect his voice. On the contrary, he drank and smoked and sometimes did five shows a day. There wasn't much time for rehearsals, but he squeezed some in. He was constantly working, constantly in motion— whipping himself to glory.

He became so accustomed to the adulation of his young fans that he resented anything less from anyone else. If he read a negative review, he threw it on the floor of his dressing room and started ranting at whoever was standing there. "If it wasn't a bad review, then it was something else," said Nick Sevano. "Frank would always find a reason to start hollering about something. It was just frustration, but he scared most people to death because he acted like a madman. He'd just go crazy if things weren't done the minute he wanted them done.

"At the Paramount, we sent his shirts to the laundry every day because of all the makeup he wore, and we always wrote in indelible ink 'no starch.' One day they came back starched, and Frank hit the ceiling. He threw the shirts at me and started kicking them all over the floor, yelling and screaming and cursing. 'Fuck you,' he hollered. I threw the shirts right back at him and yelled, 'Fuck you, too, Frank. What the hell do you think you're doing? Are you crazy or something? It isn't my fault. I didn't starch the damn things.' He stormed out of the room and didn't speak for hours."

Behind Frank's back, his friends started referring to him as "the monster," and calling George Evans "Frankenstein." They knew better than ever to speak to Frank in the morning.

"It would take him two hours to wind up, and nobody talked until he was ready," said Nick. "Nobody would even go into the room until they knew what kind of mood he was in that day."

Axel Stordahl and songwriter Jimmy Van Heusen stood the best chance of eliciting good humor, but Frank screamed even at them occasionally. The two men were part of the entourage called The Varsity. It included his gofer/assistant Nick Sevano; his music company partner, Ben Barton; manager Hank Sanicola; bodyguard/boxers Tami Mauriello and Al Silvani; Jimmy Taratino, who wrote for the boxing magazine *Knockout;* along with lyricist Sammy Cahn and record company chief Manie Sacks.

The Varsity headed for cover the day that Frank read the review saying that he was nothing more than a love object of girls swept away by war hysteria. The reviewer dismissed his success as the result of "wartime degeneracy." Frank exploded. "The war has nothing to do with it. It just so happens that I am the greatest singing sensation of the last ten years."

The mere mention of the war galvanized Evans into action. He understood the resentment of those who felt that Frank had no right to be making thousands of dollars at home while so many brave American boys were dying for forty dollars a month, so he sent him to Philadelphia to sing for the boys in the naval hospital. Then he began volunteering him for as many war bond rallies as he could find. At a war bond auction at Bonwit Teller's in Manhattan, which Evans arranged and publicized, Frank sang songs for the highest bidders. The top bid of $10,000 was for "The Song Is You"; "Night and Day" brought $4,500. A Frank Sinatra kiss brought one hundred dollars.

Everyone seemed to be getting into uniform except Frank. Buddy Rich, Dorsey's drummer, joined the Marines. Ziggy Ellman, Dorsey's trumpeter, and Paul Weston, the arranger, joined the Army. Eddy Duchin was in the Navy and Glenn Miller was leading the Air Force band. Joe DiMaggio and Hank Greenberg, two of the biggest baseball stars of the day, also joined. And so did Frank's good friend, Tami Mauriello, the heavyweight boxer.

Evans kept telling reporters that Frank was a father before Pearl Harbor and his wife was expecting another baby soon, both legitimate reasons to disqualify him from the draft. In 1943 it seemed almost shameful for an able-bodied man to be seen at home. Already Frank had fought with a couple of soldiers who had seen him in a nightclub and yelled out, "Hey, Wop. Why aren't you in uniform?" A variation of that same question began popping up in the press. "I'll go any-time they say," said Frank publicly. "I'd like to join the Marines." Privately, he confided to columnist Earl Wilson that he would lose more than $300,000 worth of contracts if his career were interrupted with a stint in the service.

He was classified 1-A after his preliminary medical and said that he was "restless and ready to go." A month later, he was called back for a second examination and rejected for service as 4-F. "I've got a hole in my left eardrum," he said, referring to the puncture that had resulted from childbirth.

The bobby-soxers squealed with delight when they learned that their idol had been spared. The Varsity was relieved, and "the monster" noncommittal. The only statement came from Mama Sinatra, who was so taken with her fabricated image as a Red Cross nurse in World War I that she played it to the hilt. "Oh, dear," she said. "Frankie wanted to get in so badly because we wanted to have our pictures taken together in uniform."

7

For all the women in Frank Sinatra's life—the starlets and singers, waitresses and call girls—he much preferred the company of men, especially fighters and those who were attracted to boxing. Every Friday night in the early 1940s, he and The Varsity headed for the old Madison Square Garden on Fiftieth Street and Eighth Avenue to see the fights. No woman ever interrupted this weekly ritual. Going to the fights represented more than the spectacle of raw violence. There was also the camaraderie of like-minded men who enjoyed the sport and its elemental violence.

Some men took women—flashy women glamorous enough to instill envy and awe in other men—but, for the most part, this was a male arena where men watched other men in satin trunks pummel each other.

Before the action started, the air was visceral. The Garden was gamy and rife with gambling. Bets were made by small-time hustlers and high-stake gamblers, bookies and fight promoters. In one part of the Garden, several rows of men sat under a blue cloud of cigar haze. They wore fedoras and iridescent suits that shimmered under the glaring lights. Some of them sported tuxedos, as if they were dressed for the most important party of their lives. Others who sat ringside wore camel's-hair coats and diamond-encrusted gold pinkie rings that complemented their solid gold bridgework.

Frank liked to sit there with the subculture celebrities—

the restaurateurs and nightclub owners like Toots Shor, and crime syndicate bosses like Frank Costello. This is where Frank Sinatra paid his weekly respects to Willie Moretti (aka Willie Moore), the underworld boss of New Jersey, who was his neighbor in Hasbrouck Heights. Moretti was a short, garrulous man whose public recognition of Frank paved Sinatra's way with other mobsters.

"I never missed a Friday night," said Frank. "And the great fights I saw there and the great times I had I wouldn't trade for anything. Going to the Friday night fights was an event, a great event."

His passion for boxing had started in childhood with his admiration for his father, who fought thirty pro fights, and his three boxer uncles. Too small to carry on the family tradition, Frank, who weighed 127 pounds and whose hands swelled every time he landed a punch, became an avid fan. He enjoyed the heavyweight boxers' display of strength and toughness. He felt comfortable with these men and said he liked to associate with them because they were great company and had a sense of humor. "I remember teasing Marciano and Dempsey for that high-pitched voice each had," he said years later. "I'd say to them, 'You guys must have been hit in the crotch too many times,' and they'd laugh."

In 1943, Frank paid ten thousand dollars to buy an interest in heavyweight fighter Tami Mauriello. He attended all Mauriello's fights and accompanied him to the Gotham Health Club every chance he got. When Tami was drafted, he gave Frank his gold identification bracelet, which the singer wore as proudly as a high school girl wears her boyfriend's class ring.

With the induction of Tami and boxing writer Jimmy Tarantino, The Varsity was depleted by two, but there were always eager replacements and stand-ins more than willing to do Frank's bidding. Many of these men were uneducated Italians from the streets who shared an ethnic bond. The closest among them were the Sicilians, who accepted the ill-tempered yelling and tolerated the haranguing to be with a star who could introduce them to a glittering world of nightclubs and celebrities and potentially more money than they could ever make as blue-collar workers.

"We had some great times in those days," said Nick Sevano. "Frank was always going, going, going, and we were always with him, going to the theater, to the fights, to see

Zero Mostel or Billie Holiday, eating with George Raft and Betty Grable, going to the Stork Club, Lindy's and the Copa, flying to California, going to the Hollywood Palladium, meeting Spencer Tracy and Cary Grant. Those were the good times, the fun times, when Frank could make us forget what a pain in the ass he was."

The stage door at the Paramount was stacked six deep with petitioners begging for a coveted spot on The Varsity. It was there that Ben Barton had appeared one night and ended up starting the music company with Frank and Hank Sanicola.

Ben was more than a business partner. He became close with the Sinatras, stayed with them in Hasbrouck Heights, took care of Frank's parents, sent flowers to Dolly for Frank on Mother's Day, and, most of all, was Nancy's confidant, listening to her complaints about Frank's other women. He advised her to turn her eyes away and shut her ears. Long after their divorce he said: "If she'd done what I told her, she'd still be married to him. . . ."

Song pluggers pleaded with Frank for attention. Even Fred ("Tamby") Tamburro, Frank's bullying nemesis from the days of The Hoboken Four, came knocking.

"Frank, look," said Tamby. "You gotta do me a favor. A big favor. I just got married. Give me a job with you."

Sinatra knew he had forty-three sport jackets that he liked to have hanging a certain way, shirts that had to be carefully laundered—without starch—and exactly folded, and twenty-one pairs of shoes he insisted on lining up in a long, even row on the floor. He offered to take Tamby on as his valet.

"Me, shining your shoes and getting your shirts? Me?" Tamby refused to lower himself to the level of a manservant. Instead, he asked to use Sinatra's name for a year and bill himself as the man who originally sang with The Voice, but Frank refused.

"I can't understand why this man never helped me," said Tamby many years later. "I'm not the best singer in the world, but I'm not the worst either. I asked him to let me use his name for a year—to travel up and down the country and bill myself as Sinatra's original partner—but he said, 'No dice. No way.' "

Everyone in the entourage was covetous of his own position, and everyone was excited about going to Hollywood, where Frank was to star in *Higher and Higher* for RKO with Michèle Morgan and Jack Haley.

"This was Frank's first big film in which he was going to be the star, and all of us were pretty revved up about going with him," said Nick Sevano. "Except for Nancy. She was staying home because she was pregnant and had to take care of Little Nancy. She was fit to be tied about it and took it out on all of us. She was so upset because she was not included that she started raising hell with Frank. She was especially mad that I was going."

Friction between Big Nancy and Nick had been growing for months because Frank spent more time with his friend than with his wife. Nick lived with them in New Jersey. He was with Frank nightly, frequently staying with him in a suite at the Astor Hotel when it was too late to drive home.

"I was with him all the time in those days, and Nancy resented it," Nick said. "She was insecure and very jealous of anyone who was close to Frank. She hated Hank Sanicola, too, but Hank didn't come home at night with Frank and live with them in the house the way I did.

"Nancy would call Frank, and I'd hear him say, 'All right, Nancy, I'm coming home for dinner,' and then he'd never make it. Hours later, on the way home, he'd stew about it. He broke many, many promises in those days. Nancy would call Dolly, and Dolly would call Frank and say, 'You promised her, Frank. You promised Nancy that you would be there.' It was terrible, but Frank didn't have time to spend with a family. He was too distracted with getting ahead, with his responsibilities to his career, his work, his radio programs, his rehearsals, his appearances. He was running so hard in those days. Nancy didn't understand his ambitions.

"Then she'd blame me for carousing with Frank. She accused me of getting all the broads for him because I was a bachelor, but I can assure you that I never had to get any women for Frank in those days."

One day not long before Frank and his crew were to leave for the West Coast, Frank told Nick to run some errands, and make a few purchases. Nick was embarrassed to say that he'd run out of his expense money, and he could no longer bear going to Nancy because she questioned every purchase and every expense, wanting to know why it was bought, where, for how much, and for whom. So he crept into the master bedroom and took a ten-dollar bill from the top of the dresser. She saw him and later told Frank that Nick was stealing. She would not let up on the subject and finally forced her husband's hand.

A few nights later Frank and Nick left the Paramount and headed for Forty-ninth Street, where Frank kept his car parked for the ride back to New Jersey. On the way to the garage, Frank didn't say much, but when they reached the car, he didn't tell Nick to get in as he usually did. Instead, Frank lowered his head and said, "Why don't you stay at the hotel tonight, and I'll be in touch."

Nick realized there was severe conflict at home, so he agreed to stay in their suite at the Astor Hotel. "I sort of sensed that something was wrong, but I thought that he'd forget about it. I didn't take it too seriously until Hank called me the next day to say that Frank wanted me fired. I couldn't believe it. After more than four years of living and working together, he couldn't look me in the eye and tell me himself. If he'd just said he was under a lot of pressure at home, I would've understood, but he couldn't even do that. He couldn't communicate. I knew how much he hated confrontations but—I was dumbstruck by the whole thing, and in addition to being hurt, I was scared. I didn't know what I was going to do. I couldn't go back to Hoboken, not after everything I'd seen and done with Frank. I was desperate, just desperate."

People were shocked when they heard the news. Nick had been with Frank since 1939. He had designed Frank's clothes when Frank first went on his own, had handled all Frank's phone calls, letters, and public relations during the Dorsey days, always staying in the background. He ran all Frank's errands, shielded him from Nancy, and placated Dolly. He bought all the presents that Frank wanted to give and shouldered him in and out of cabs so that he would not be trampled by his young fans. He seemed to have dedicated himself to Frank.

He had even acted as his romantic emissary, flying to Saranac, New York, to visit Alora Gooding when she was hospitalized with tuberculosis. Frank had sent him because he couldn't go himself, and he didn't want Alora to be alone. Nick had gone and been snowed in.

One of Frank's entourage remembered the night Frank threw up all over Nick outside of Patsy D'Amore's Villa Capri in Los Angeles, and Nick carried him back to the Sunset Towers and put him to bed. He also recalled how much Nick hated hookers and how Frank used to send them around to his room as a joke. Nick had been Frank's Friar Tuck, his Sancho Panza.

Even Dolly Sinatra was stunned. She called Nick the minute she found out. "Don't worry," she said. "It's that bitch wife of his that's to blame. That bastard will call you. I'll get him on the phone to you. He'll know that you were the best friend he ever had. Don't worry." Two weeks later, she phoned Nick again: "Did that no good son of a bitch call you yet?"

"Frank never called, but those phone calls from Dolly gave me the confidence to keep going," said Nick. "Then Tommy Dorsey phoned and asked me to come with him."

Having sacrificed his best friend to his wife, Frank hired his Hoboken cousin, also named Frank Sinatra, but called Junior, to be his valet. Then he left for the coast with Axel Stordahl, Hank Sanicola, and George Evans to film *Higher and Higher*.

When he arrived in California, a screaming, clawing, hair-pulling crowd of five thousand teenagers mobbed the Pasadena station to meet his train on August 12, 1943. The minute the little girls spotted Frank and his red-and-white polka dot bow tie, they surged forward screaming and scratching and biting one another to get closer to him. Holding them back, police rushed Frank to safety in a nearby garage, where newsmen questioned him about his impending performance with the Los Angeles Philharmonic Orchestra, which was already a matter of controversy.

George Evans had convinced Stadium Concerts, Inc., the booking agency for most of the country's symphony orchestras, that they needed the crowd-drawing talents of his client to plump up their sagging box offices and pay off their deficits. Desperate to make money, they agreed, and booked Frank with the Cleveland Orchestra, the National Symphony in Washington, D.C., and the New York Philharmonic Orchestra at Lewisohn Stadium. Now he was scheduled to appear with the Los Angeles Symphony, and Hollywood's classical music lovers were outraged that a Tin Pan Alley crooner would be allowed in the Hollywood Bowl. They campaigned militantly against the Sinatra appearance.

"These classic longhairs really get me," Frank said. "It's no gag that I have a passion for classical music. I own albums and I attend concerts whenever I can. That's why I am willing to help out when philharmonic societies approach me.

It's pretty disheartening and disappointing to me that people like those opposing my appearance at the Hollywood Bowl think in those channels. I'm only doing it to help finance a field of music that I really love."

Years later, Frank Sinatra talked more of his love of classical music. He said that his own style, though originally in the Bing Crosby tradition, had developed into the *bel canto* Italian school of singing. And he said further that his first musical inspiration was from Jascha Heifetz's violin concerts. He said he liked the "fantastic things Heifetz did with the notes—holding them, gently sliding them, sustaining them. It was a whole new concept of phrasing to me, and terribly exciting."

More than eighteen thousand people turned out to sit under a harvest moon in the Hollywood Bowl, the largest crowd of the season. Most of them were under the age of sixteen, and could barely sit still as Vladimir Bakaleinikoff conducted the orchestra in a string of Russian classics. Finally, at ten P.M., Frank walked onstage with Morris Stoloff of RKO, who would conduct for him while Bakaleinikoff stepped aside. Aware of the ill feelings surrounding this part of the program, Stoloff turned to the orchestra and said, "You men know *your* kind of music and play it as though you loved it. Now, tonight I want you to play the kind of music Mr. Sinatra sings and loves with the same feeling."

Frank stepped up to the microphone as the girls began howling and screaming ecstatically. He smiled at their welcome but refused to sing until they were quiet. He began with "Dancing in the Dark," and several dozen photographers rushed the stage in a salvo of exploding flashbulbs. Next he sang "You'll Never Know," "Ol' Man River," and "The Song Is You." By the time he introduced "Night and Day," saying, "This is my favorite song of all time," the audience was wailing and gasping. "Girls, girls, please," he said, trying to quiet them. After nine sleepy ballads, he returned to the stage for encore after encore. Then he said to the audience, "I understand there has been a controversy out here over whether I should appear at the Bowl at all. Those few people who thought I shouldn't lost out in a very big way."

Rows and rows of girls screamed, "Oh, Frankie, we love you so," while a disgruntled army sergeant muttered, "After this, I hope they won't forget to flush the bowl."

Days later, the sergeant's comment appeared in *Time* magazine and roused George Evans to volunteer Frank for yet another war bond rally—to stave off the continued criticism about his draft-exempt status. With more than eleven million Americans in the service by this time, Evans was most sensitive about Frank's not being in uniform and made constant references to Frank's three-year-old daughter at home and the baby on the way.

In October 1943, Frank auctioned off his clothes over WABC radio in New York City, raising more than twelve thousand dollars in war bond purchases by shedding everything from his shirt to his shoelaces. Days after he disrobed, the U.S. Congress passed a resolution dropping draft deferments for pre–Pearl Harbor fathers.

Frank's success at home outraged soliders overseas. "I think Frank Sinatra was the most hated man of World War II, much more than Hitler," said writer William Manchester, who served in the Marines and was wounded on Okinawa. "Because we in the Pacific had seen no women at all for two years, and there were photographs of Sinatra being surrounded by all of these enthusiastic girls."

While Evans worried about his client's contribution to the war effort, Frank worried about his opening at the Wedgwood Room of the Waldorf-Astoria. In 1943, the Waldorf was one of the most famous hotels in the world. The lofty towers of the Art Deco palace on Fiftieth Street and Park Avenue admitted only high society, and the boy from Hoboken was apprehensive about the reception he might receive from the haughty sophisticates who were accustomed to liveried doormen, chauffeured limousines, and debutante balls. He was especially afraid of society chronicler Elsa Maxwell, the columnist, who had already charged him with "musical illiteracy" and derided his fans as "emotionally unstable females who paraded naked and unashamed for the drooling, crooning, goonish syllables of a man who looked like a second-string basketball player." She then recommended the girls be given "Sinatra-ceptives."

On opening night, Frank paced up and down in his dressing room, chain-smoking.

"Frank goes in to take a shower and falls," said Manie Sacks. "His ankle swells up. He says, 'I can't go on.' George Evans . . . and I knew it was fright—that he was looking for an out. We called a doctor, and he bandaged up the ankle.

"George and I decided to applaud like mad, so Frank

would at least hear a lot of noise from the first row. I was more frightened than Frank was. George didn't even sit down. He stood in the door and shivered.

"Frank sang for an hour and a half, until the captain came over and told Evans to ask Frank to stop so he could serve drinks."

After his last song, Frank thanked his audience profusely, saying, "I always dreamed of working at the Waldorf-Astoria— it's sort of the top."

Later that evening at a party given by Waldorf owner George Boomer, Frank, who had been coached by Evans, approached Elsa Maxwell. "You disapprove of me," he said, "and my mother agrees with you. She said, 'You tell that Miss Maxwell she is right!'"

"I disapprove of you, Frankie, only because I think it a pity for anyone with your naturally lovely voice to resort to such cheap tactics."

"My press agent, George Evans, thought up the squealing girls and the way I hold the mike," said Frank. "I do not like any part of it. But it all has made the headlines. And the headlines have made me, I guess."

Miss Maxwell mellowed. The next day she wrote up Frank's opening night, telling her readers, "He has found a setting to show off the sweetness of his voice."

A few weeks later, eager to please the society columnist, Frank agreed to sing at a benefit at the Hotel Pierre for a child-adoption center. The night of the benefit, he won the door prize.

"Driving home in my car, he held on his lap the little white fur jacket he had won and, again and again, picked it up to examine it, to admire it," said Elsa Maxwell, who had introduced Frank at the benefit. "'Nancy's never had a fur,' he said. 'Is this real ermine?'" Elsa Maxwell laughed and said that rabbit paws were a reasonable facsimile. (He gave the jacket to Nancy, and for Christmas he gave her a white mink coat, which he considered the height of sophistication. When she said that she wanted to dye it brown, he blew up.)

Now that Frank was a high-society success in New York, his mother's political stock soared in New Jersey. After his engagement at the Wedgwood Room, she asked him to sing at a rally for the Democratic mayor of Newark, Vincent J. Murphy, who was running for governor, and to say a few nice words about Jersey City Mayor Frank Hague, boss of Dolly's

Democratic machine. More than fifty thousand people turned out, and policemen and firemen worked overtime marshaling the crowds that poured into Lincoln High School to hear Hudson County's hometown boy.

No one enjoyed Frank's success more than Dolly Sinatra. As the mother of the most famous singer in the country, she now reigned supreme in Hoboken. Her husband was promoted to captain in the fire department, and she became the biggest celebrity in town. Every time a ribbon had to be cut to open a new music store, Dolly was there, swathed in the silver fox furs that Frank had given her. Hoboken Night at Yankee Stadium saw Dolly sitting in the best boxes drinking beer and eating hot dogs that somebody else always paid for.

"Everybody fussed over her once Frank made it big," said Minnie Cardinale, who had dipped chocolates with Mrs. Sinatra in Hoboken.

"It got so that she never paid her bills anymore," said Connie Cappadona, an interior designer Dolly hired to decorate her house.

Even the Catholics who had once shunned her because of her abortion business now came around and made her head of the Rosary Society at St. Ann's.

Dolly kept a supply of Frank's autographed photos on hand, and every time the delivery boy from the drugstore rang the doorbell, she poked her head out and said, "Do you want a lousy tip or a beautiful picture of my son?" The youngster always took the picture of Frank.

In addition to the silver fox furs and Miami Beach vacations that Frank paid for, Dolly and Marty Sinatra received money from their son on a regular basis. Firemen in Hoboken still remember the one-hundred-dollar check that arrived every Monday from Sinatra Enterprises.

In the tumultuous years since leaving Tommy Dorsey, Frank had become the most exciting entertainer in the country and swamped Bob Eberly, Dick Haymes, Perry Como, and Bing Crosby in *Downbeat*'s 1943 year-end poll of the most popular singers. No other singer had the battalions of devoted fans that Frank had. His teenage jumpers and screamers sent him hundreds of hand-knit sweaters, wrote hate letters to critical reviewers, and plastered lipstick kisses on his home in Hasbrouck Heights. They even wrote poetry to his three-year-old daughter, Nancy Sandra:

You'd probably laugh as little girls do,
And smile and act rather shy,
If you knew that the man whom you call Dad,
Is the one making us sigh.

Frank had touched the innocent sexual buddings of adolescent America as no one else before him. The shrewd
machinations of George Evans gave the young girls license to
express themselves by moaning and swooning and yelling.
He made it a fad to scream hysterically and to faint in the
aisles, and by doing so the bobby-soxers became part of the
show. He capitalized on the boy-crazy stage that all young
girls go through and gave them Frankie as their romantic idol,
their Prince Charming who would kiss them and caress them
with his songs.

All their girlish yearnings became centered on this fragile
young singer who talked to them as if they were equals,
sharing details of his family, and telling them about Big
Nancy and Little Nancy and the baby who was expected
soon. ("I want a boy so we can name him Frankie," he said,
"but if it's a girl, we'll name her Frances.") They listened
raptly to the words of his songs and responded when he
seemed vulnerable.

When he sang about nobody loving him, the little girls
shrieked with anguish, "Are you kiddin', Frankie?" "We love
you. We love you." When he closed his eyes and sang sadly,
"I'll Never Walk Alone," a youngster, nearly moved to tears,
shouted, "I'll walk wid ya, Frankie. Honest. I'll walk wid
ya." They wanted to hug and kiss this man who became the
personification of their fathers, uncles, brothers, and the kind
of man they dreamed of marrying. They fought for the chance
to touch him, but they also wanted to take care of him.

Frank returned their ardor in full. "I love all those girls
the same as they love me," he said. "I get thousands of
letters a week from girls who love me, but not in a *sex* way.
There is nothing degenerate about it. They wear Frankie
Sinatra bow ties just like I do and form Frankie Sinatra fan
clubs named after my songs. Every time I sing a song, I make
love to them. I'm a boudoir singer."

Most psychologists explained the Swoonatra craze as the
result of frustrated love induced by the pressures of war in
America in the 1940s—working mothers, absent fathers, and
the awful sense of impermanence. But there was something

deeper that made these youngsters identify with Frank Sinatra and idolize him.

"Most of his fans are plain, lonely girls from lower-middle class homes," said E. J. Kahn, Jr., in *The New Yorker*. "They are dazzled by the life Sinatra leads and wish they could share in it. They insist that they love him, but they do not use the verb in its ordinary sense. As they apply it to him, it is synonymous with 'worship' or 'idealize.'"

"Nearly all the bobby-soxers whom I saw at the Paramount gave every appearance of being children of the poor," wrote Bruce Bliven in *The New Republic*. "I would guess that these children found in him, for all his youthfulness, something of a father image. And beyond that, he represents a dream of what they themselves might conceivably do or become. He earns a million a year, and yet he talks their language; he is just a kid from Hoboken who got the breaks. In everything he says and does, he aligns himself with the youngsters and against the adult world. It is always 'we' and never 'you.'"

Years later, Sinatra talked about his bobby-soxer period and its effect on him: "I was—I was everything. Happy, I don't know. I wasn't unhappy, let's put it that way. I never had it so good. Sometimes I wonder whether anybody ever had it like I had it, before or since. It was the darndest thing, wasn't it? But I was too busy ever to know whether I was happy, or even to ask myself. I can't remember for a long time even taking time out to think."

Although Frank's appeal was primarily to women, there were a few male fans, but none so devoted as teenager Joey "GiGi" Lissa of Hoboken, who had idolized Frank ever since he saw him walking into the Cat's Meow poolroom in 1938 wearing a white trench coat.

Lissa's job was to clean Dolly Sinatra's house—a job it would seem every kid in Hoboken had at some time or other.

"When he was singing in New York, he always stopped at his mother's place before he went home to his wife, and one time I was cleaning Dolly's house when Frank walked in," Lissa said. "I was only fourteen years old, but he gave me his tie. It was maroon with yellow flowers. He used to let me walk with him up to the Crystal Ballroom and hold his glass. When I was in the service on Guam I robbed the USO of all its Frank Sinatra records and then when I had the midnight watch on my gunboat, I would be the mystery midnight disc jockey, and open all the phones to play Sinatra's music. All the ships in the fleet heard it and sometimes the officers came in and looked, but they always left me alone. Even Tokyo Rose mentioned it over the radio. 'We know who the mystery midnight disc jockey is playing all those Sinatra records,' she said."

Sinatra's female fans followed him like the Pied Piper to his performances and radio sessions for *Your Hit Parade*. They visited his white clapboard house on Lawrence Avenue in Hasbrouck Heights, sometimes standing for hours simply to stare at the windows. Other times, they rang the doorbell, knowing that Big Nancy would invite them in for Coke and cookies, and patiently answer all their questions about Frankie's favorite foods, favorite colors, favorite hobbies. They begged her for the clothespins that held his laundry on the line in the backyard, and they were thrilled when she allowed them to walk her to the store and to help decide what to feed Frankie for dinner. They seemed to know everything about him, including his fondness for giving friends nicknames. They had heard him call Bing Crosby "The King," Jimmy Van Heusen "Chester" (his real name), and Axel Stordahl "Sibelius." Now they wanted to know what he called his wife. "He calls me Mommy," Big Nancy said.

As far as they knew, the god they worshiped was a loving family man who cherished his wife and sang lullabies to his daughter. He seemed extremely boyish, wearing floppy bow ties and eating banana splits every day. He was friendly and so patient about signing autographs. He never got in a bad mood and never ever lost his temper. He seemed so vulnerable, so shy, so nice, so sincere. George Evans knew that the worshipful young fans needed to believe this myth to continue their adoration, and he nearly lost his mind trying to keep their shining image of Frankie intact.

8

Frank had not been present for the birth of his first child, Nancy Sandra, in 1940. Nor was he with his wife when their son was born on January 10, 1944, in the Margaret Hague Maternity Hospital in Jersey City, New Jersey. He was in Hollywood filming *Step Lively* and starring in a weekly radio show sponsored by Vimms Vitamins. But the ever-faithful George Evans was by Nancy's bedside to take care of everything.

Evans called Frank to give him the news and told reporters that the singer was very happy. "He wanted a boy very much," said the press agent. Then he headed for the florist and had three dozen red roses sent to Nancy from her husband with a card that read, "Congratulations to you, darling, and to the little guy for picking himself such a wonderful mom. All my love."

The next day, Evans arrived at the hospital early and helped get Nancy ready to meet the press in a pale blue quilted bed jacket that he had selected for the occasion. He propped a framed photograph of Frank next to her bed, fluffed the pillows, and told her to hold up the eight-pound-thirteen-ounce baby boy to admire the picture of his father, which would give photographers their best shot of the day. Then he called in the reporters and cameramen.

"I'm glad he's a boy because that's what Frank always

wanted—a junior," said Nancy. "When he was told by telephone last night, he was so excited he couldn't even talk."

Seeing the wirephoto of his wife and newborn son the next day, Frank said, "Fine-looking lad and no bobby socks, either." He told reporters that he didn't care what Frank, Jr., did when he grew up as long as he never became a singer. "No following in Dad's footsteps, that's for sure," he said.

The next day on his CBS radio show, Frank talked to his wife and baby over the air, saying, "I'd like to sing one of my favorite songs to my little son in New Jersey. So pull up a chair, Nancy, and bring the baby with you. I want him really to hear this."

Later Frank would admit that having the baby was an attempt to save a bad marriage. "I thought that another child would cement our marriage," he said, "and we had Frankie, Jr. But endless tours, nightclub work, and a hundred other business activities kept me away from home most of the time. Little by little, we [Nancy and I] drifted apart."

The radio show that starred Frank featured a line-up of beautiful female stars like Ginger Rogers, Judy Garland, Ann Sheridan, Joan Blondell, and Joan Bennett. It was one of the reasons he was in no hurry to return home. Despite his wife, his three-and-a-half-year-old daughter, and his newborn son, he stayed on the West Coast for two and a half months basking in the glow of being a movie star.

Higher and Higher had been advertised by RKO as Frank Sinatra's first film, which guaranteed record-breaking attendance by the nation's bobby-soxers. But not all the New York critics were enthusiastic. Dismissing *Higher and Higher* as *Lower and Lower*, Bosley Crowther in *The New York Times* wrote that "Frankie is no Gable or Barrymore," and the movie was nothing more than "a slapdash setting for the incredibly unctuous renderings of the Voice."

The New York Herald-Tribune was more respectful, saying that Frank "does his stint remarkably well for a comparative novice. His ugly, bony face photographs well; his voice registers agreeably enough on the microphone, and he handles himself easily, with occasional hints of comic authority."

The New Yorker faulted the movie as "not a particularly engaging film," but said Frank, as the star, "comes out fine. He has some acting to do, and he does it."

In Hollywood, however, the critics swooned. The *Los Angeles Examiner* said, "It's hard to dislike a guy who seems so friendly, simple, and natural . . . and Frankie seems that way on the screen because that's the way he is."

The Hollywood Reporter agreed: "The cinema captures an innate shyness in the singer who has uniquely become an idol of the airlanes and the bobby-sox trade. . . . People who have never understood his appeal to swooning fans, have even resented him, will have no trouble in buying the guy they meet on the screen here."

The *Los Angeles Times* said, "The crooner certainly doesn't fulfill the cinema's traditional idea of a romantic figure, which may be a break for him eventually. He plays himself in *Higher and Higher*, appears more at ease than we expected, and should find a place as a film personality with careful choice of subjects. Crosby did, didn't he?"

Frank stayed in Hollywood with his entourage and celebrated his new stardom. Most of them were without their wives and were gamboling like kids away from home for the first time—going to the fights, to the track, to Palm Springs, to Las Vegas, and to all of Frank's performances. On the weekend, they headed for Beverly Hills High School, where they had formed a softball team called The Swooners. Regulars included Frank, Sammy Cahn, Jule Styne, Hank Sanicola, actors Anthony Quinn and Barry Sullivan, and comedy writer Harry Crane. The cheerleaders were Virginia Mayo, Marilyn Maxwell, Lana Turner, and Ava Gardner, all wearing Swooner T-shirts.

Frank went home in March but stayed only a few weeks before returning to Hollywood to start work on *Anchors Aweigh* with Gene Kelly at MGM. He had told Nancy that he no longer wanted to live in Hasbrouck Heights; he loved the California sunshine, and after his good reviews he felt that his life was now in Hollywood. He wanted to be a movie star like Bing Crosby. He wanted to move to the West Coast and so did Nancy, but she was afraid to leave her family in New Jersey. Frank easily persuaded her with the promise of driving lessons and a new Cadillac. A few weeks later he bought Mary Astor's rambling estate in the Toluca Lake area of the San Fernando Valley, sight unseen.

Frank was a movie star now. But Nancy was still a little Italian housewife who was incredulous that her husband would be making more than one million dollars by the end of the year. "I couldn't believe it," she said. "Only millionaires made millions. All I could think of was the time six years ago when I had spaghetti without meat sauce because meat sauce was more expensive. And now Frank has made a million in a year!"

Nancy moved with the children to California and took her five married sisters with her. She even moved her sister, Tina, into the new house to act as her secretary and answer fan mail. Frank's mother was furious about all the Barbato girls going to California, but Nancy no longer cared what Dolly thought. The two women had long ceased to be allies. Nancy was delighted to be putting twenty-five hundred miles between herself and her mother-in-law.

"Nancy never liked Hoboken people," said Marion Brush Schreiber, "and when she came back from California for a visit, she acted real hoity-toity, saying, 'Oh, we're very close to Lana' and 'We see Lana all the time.' That kind of thing. It made Dolly want to kill her. You'd write a letter to Frank, and one of Nancy's sisters, Julie or Tina, would send you a reply. A nice letter, but it wasn't from Frank. That drove all of us crazy."

But Nancy was not to blame. Her life had changed so radically that she couldn't adjust to the glory and glamour of her husband. He regularly flew back and forth across the country for singing engagements on both coasts, leaving little time for his family in California. Frank was rarely home, but Nancy was there with the children. There were no governesses, only a weekly cleaning woman. Nancy remained a full-time housewife.

Spinning at the top of his fame now, Frank Sinatra's star was in the stratosphere, where there were no black storm clouds, only the limitless reaches of success. His name was known throughout the nation; his fans numbered in the hundreds of thousands; his voice echoed around the world on phonographs and radio; his friends were celebrated. His influence even reached to the White House.

On one of his trips to New York, Sinatra was sitting in Toots Shor's restaurant when Shor received a phone call from Democratic Committee Chairman Robert Hannegan inviting him and his wife to the White House for tea with President Roosevelt. There were to be only twenty people present, including Ed Pauley, treasurer of the Democratic National Committee, Senator Harley M. Kilgore of West Virginia, and former governors Keen Johnson of Kentucky and Frank Murphy of Michigan. Shor's wife was sick and could not attend, so he asked if he might bring Frank and, in addition, comedian Rags Ragland. Hannegan called the President's assistant, Marvin McIntyre, for permission. He got it. Stage and screen stars were always welcome in Franklin Roosevelt's White House, and Frank Sinatra was wanted especially because Bing Crosby had announced his support of Roosevelt's Republican opponent the week before. So the three men flew to Washington on September 28, 1944. Frank said that he wanted to talk to the President about the political campaign "because I'd like to do all I can."

Roosevelt had never endeared himself to Italian-Americans, especially after he said to the Attorney General: "I don't care so much about the Italians. They are a lot of opera singers, but the Germans are different. They may be dangerous." When Roosevelt ordered the internment of five thousand Italian-Americans, including opera singer Ezio Pinza, who was held at Ellis Island, Dolly Sinatra never forgave him. Berating Frank for not coming home to help her with a political campaign in Hoboken, she excoriated him with, "But you campaigned for that Roosevelt!"

Upon meeting the singer, President Roosevelt asked him to name the number one song on the hit parade. "Amapola," Frank said. The President looked puzzled. "He thought I was talking Italian," said Sinatra years later.

As Frank floated out of the White House, reporters asked him if he had sung for the President.

"No," he said. "I wish that I could have."

"What happened?"

"It was very nice," said Frank. "I told the President how well he looked. He kidded me about making the girls faint and asked me how I do it. I said I wished to hell I knew."

"Did he want any pointers?"

"No, he does very well himself."

"Naw, that's not what happened at all," interrupted Rags Ragland. "Frank was speechless when the President said how wonderful it was that he had brought back the art of fainting after it had been dead fifty years. Frank swooned himself. We had to pick him off the floor."

Frank told the reporters that he had voted for Roosevelt before and intended to do so again in November.

"Do you favor a fourth term?"

"Well," he said, "you might say I'm in favor of it."

The next day the President was criticized for inviting to the White House a 4-F singer who, unlike other stars, had yet to leave the country to make one USO tour.

"When our men are dying on foreign battlefields and fighting to maintain the foothold they have won in Germany, such a party is going from the tragic to the ridiculous," said the Republican senator from Indiana.

"That crooner!" said the Republican senator from Nebraska. "Mr. Roosevelt could spend his time better conferring with members of Congress who will have to pass upon his foreign policy. I have no objection to Sinatra, but the business of the American people comes first."

Frank's fan clubs were delighted with FDR for inviting their hero to the White House and one, Sinatra Slick Chicks of Chicago, offered the President a membership, which he accepted. This enraged Hearst columnists Westbrook Pegler, who denounced Sinatra as the "New Dealing Crooner," and Lee Mortimer, who said Frank didn't know anything about politics.

Frank didn't care. He donated five thousand dollars to the FDR election campaign, made a series of radio recordings for the Democratic National Committee, and spoke at Carnegie Hall.

"I'd just like to tell you what a great guy Roosevelt is," he said. "I was a little stunned when I stood alongside him. I thought, here's the greatest guy alive today and here's a little guy from Hoboken shaking his hand. He knows about everything—even my racket."

Many years later, Frank recalled his speech at a political rally at Madison Square Garden. "I said I was for Roosevelt because he was good for me. He was good for me and for my kids and my country, so he must be good for all the other ordinary guys and their kids. When I was through, I felt like a football player coming off the field—weak and dizzy and excited and everybody coming over to shake hands or pat me on the back. I'm not ashamed to say it—I felt proud."

He appealed to his fans, saying that they as the youth of America were entitled to the peace of tomorrow. "This peace will depend on your parents' votes on November seventh," he said, sending legions of screeching girls home to beg their parents to vote for Roosevelt.

On the morning of Columbus Day—October 12, 1944—thirty thousand frenzied bobby-soxers jammed Times Square, blocking traffic, stampeding bystanders, and crashing into store windows to get to the Paramount to see Frank, who was opening a three-week engagement of five shows a day. His last performance at the Paramount had been in May 1943, and his fans seemed to have proliferated like spores in those seventeen months.

"This is the worst mob scene in New York since nylons went on sale," said the police chief, surveying the human wall engulfing his patrolmen outside the theater.

The city went on emergency alert. Two hundred detectives, seventy patrolmen, fifty traffic cops, four hundred twenty-one police reserves, twelve mounted police, twenty radio cars, two emergency trucks, and twenty policewomen were dispatched to subdue the rioters.

The first thirty-six hundred girls admitted to the theater refused to give up their seats after the first show. Their pockets bulged with bananas and sandwiches as they settled in for the entire day. "Our folks would rather have us following Sinatra than chasing sailors and soldiers," said one seventeen-year-old fan. "And, besides, I always call mine twice a day to let them know I'm still here."

The minute Frank stuck his head through the stage curtain the girls stamped their feet and shouted and moaned in ecstasy. He blew them a kiss, and the uproar was so piercing and prolonged that he couldn't start singing. After five minutes of their nonstop screaming, he begged them to be quiet. "Please, please, please," he said. "Do you want me to leave the stage?"

"No, no, no!" they cried.

"Then let's see if we can't be quiet enough to hear a complete arrangement," Frank said.

Most of the teenage boys in the audience laughed at the swooners and enjoyed their hysterics, but one finally got fed up with all the adulation showered on the twenty-nine-year-old singer. Just as Frank reached the final bars of "I Don't Know Why I Love You Like I Do," Alexander J. Dorogokupetz took aim from the third row center and threw a raw egg that splattered in Frank's face. It slopped down the singer's chest onto his light gray jacket. Frank tried to keep singing, but Alexander fired again with another egg, which landed in his eye, and a third that grazed his bow tie. Before Dorogokupetz could fling his fourth missile, irate Sinatratics pounced on him, threatening to scratch his eyes out and pull his arms out of their sockets. One smashed him over the head with her umbrella. As the band played "The Star-Spangled Banner," Frank ran offstage.

A dozen uniformed police rushed to the battered culprit's rescue. They dragged him to the manager's office, where he was asked why he did it.

"I don't know why I did it," he said. "It just seemed like a good idea at the time."

Frank did not press charges, so four policemen escorted Dorogokupetz to the safety of the subway and sent him home to the Bronx.

The next day's papers carried headlines about the incident. "Sinatra Hit by Eggs; The Voice Scrambles Song," said one. "Hen Fruit Hits Heartthrob," said another. A group of sailors who read the stories of Dorogokupetz's egging began throwing ripe tomatoes at Frank's photographs on the theater marquee, leaving angry red splotches all over the boyish smile, the bow tie, and the curly forelock hanging down the forehead.

None of this diminished the bobby-soxers' idolatry. Their rush to touch Frank after every show necessitated posting security guards outside his dressing room.

"That dressing room was always jammed," recalled Mary Lou Watts, "especially when Frank's mother was there. She was a great big bossy lady and towered over her husband, who was about the size of a mushroom. He was as little as Frank, but that mother of his was huge and very domineering. Scare you to death."

On her regular pilgrimages to the Paramount, Dolly told reporters that Frankie was a fine boy. "He may be famous now, but he'll always be a baby to me," she said. "And I always told him to be nice to people as he goes up the ladder, because they're the same people he'll pass coming down. So far he has followed my instructions."

Most of Frank's friends from Hoboken waited in line to see him, including Tony Mac, who couldn't get backstage after the show. "When Frank came to the Union Club with Jimmy Durante I asked him why I wasn't allowed in to see him and he said, 'The signal was to say you was my cousin.' "

Marion Brush Schreiber was ushered in right away without knowing the password. She had kept her friendship with Frank from their days together on Garden Street, and he was very pleased to see her again. "He introduced me to the Ink

Spots," she said. "He was a great host; afterwards, he walked me to the elevator and kissed me good-bye."

Another backstage visitor was Fred "Tamby" Tamburro, who had moved back to Hoboken after turning down the job as Frank's valet the year before. Now he needed five thousand dollars to buy a tavern. His arrangements for financing had fallen through at the last minute, so he went to see Frank at the Paramount. Knowing that his former singing partner was making more than a million dollars a year, Tamby felt confident that Sinatra would lend him the money, but Frank turned him down cold.

Minutes later, while Tamby was still in Frank's dressing room, Buddy Rich, who was out of the service, stopped by and mentioned that he wanted to start his own band. Frank gave him forty thousand dollars on the spot. After Rich left, Tamby grabbed Sinatra and threw him up against the wall as he used to do when The Hoboken Four were touring for Major Bowes.

"He called the cops on me, but then changed his mind and told them to let me go," said Tamby. "He knew how it would look if his old partner was arrested for beating on him.

"A lot of people in Hoboken hate him 'cause he made it big. With me—I praise him to the sky as an entertainer. I told him to his face: 'Frank, as an entertainer, you're the tops. As a man—you stink.' "

Frank continually posed challenges to the ingenuity of his press agents. George Evans accompanied him on a train from New York City to Boston, where Frank was to address an interfaith tolerance rally of sixteen thousand teenagers in the Boston Garden. Evans, who was a committed liberal, was all for building on the image of Frank's wholehearted support for President Roosevelt.

But Frank had agreed to address the rally before he realized that it was the same night that Tami Mauriello was fighting in Madison Square Garden. By the time the train reached New Haven, Connecticut, he was getting restless. He told Evans he was going to the club car for a drink. An hour later, Evans went looking for him and discovered that Sinatra had got off the train at New Haven. When Evans told the thousands of youngsters in Boston Garden that Frank was unable to appear "because of a sudden illness," the distraught press agent knew it was best to leave town immediately. Had he remained in Boston overnight, Evans probably would have been lynched, for the morning papers carried pictures of Frank screaming his head off at Madison Square Garden for his favorite prizefighter.

Incensed, the rally's Boston promoters, who had been forced to refund a full house and to pay the musicians, threatened to sue Frank for breaking his contract. They also threatened to take the issue to the musicians union and demand that the union take action against Sinatra.

To deflect the growing controversy, Evans announced that Frank would make a series of addresses to high schools in several large cities early the next year. He urged the students, most of whom were devoted fans, to remain in school and to continue their education. "Mr. Sinatra will go to Washington this week to discuss the tour with education officials," he said. Although no one in Washington knew anything about Sinatra's pending visit, the announcement elevated him in the eyes of the public as someone who would use his influence and power to fight juvenile delinquency.

While George Evans handled things on the East Coast, his partner, Jack Keller, had his hands full in California, where the singer had stamped his feet in January and demanded that his part of the *Hit Parade* be moved from the CBS studio, with three hundred fifty seats, to the Vine Street Playhouse, with fourteen hundred seats. The move would amplify the volume of screams and sighs considerably.

Frank had hurled this demand at CBS less than an hour before broadcast time. In vain, officials had tried to explain to him that such a move would require several hours to reassemble all the special equipment. Frank said to move it anyway or he would not make the broadcast.

At this point, the American Federation of Radio Artists entered the dispute. "Either you go on tonight or you're through as far as AFRA's jurisdiction is concerned," he was told. Frank backed down.

To Jack Keller's dismay, the incident had made front-page news the next day. *Variety* quoted an AFRA spokesman as saying, "The kid's beginning to believe his own publicity, and that's fatal."

On his next trip to the West Coast, Frank alienated Hollywood with an ugly outburst during the filming of *Anchors Aweigh*. It was a characteristic explosion that would never have become a big story if a reporter had not been there to quote it.

"Pictures stink and most of the people in them do too," Sinatra said. "Hollywood won't believe I'm through, but they'll find out I mean it. It's a good thing not many of these jerks came up as rapidly as I did. If they had, you couldn't get near them without running interference through three secretaries."

Jack Keller exploded when he read that story. "Are you crazy? Are you nuts or something?"

At first, Frank denied saying anything, but Keller recognized the ring of truth in the quotes. He called everyone who had been on the set with Frank the preceding afternoon, and finally Frank admitted that he'd been hot and tired and might have said "something" to the United Press reporter who had been there interviewing Jose Iturbi. One of Frank's aides, Al Levy, said, "It was the hottest day of the year. Naturally he was tired, but that crack was never intended for that fat fellow with the glasses [the UP reporter]."

Keller called the reporter and apologized, asking if he'd be willing to carry a statement by Sinatra as a follow-up to his original story. The reporter agreed and Frank's statement, as written by Jack Keller, appeared as follows:

> It's easy for a guy to get hot under the collar, literally and figuratively, when he's dressed in a hot suit of Navy blues and the temperature is a hundred and four degrees and he's getting over a cold to boot.
> I think I might have spoken too broadly about quitting pictures and about my feeling toward Hollywood.
> I'm under a seven-year contract to RKO, which still has six years to run, and I have one more commitment at Metro following *Anchors Aweigh*, and believe me, I intend to live up to my contractual obligations.

Understandably, Jack Keller was delighted when Frank returned to the East Coast and the capable hands of George Evans. Unfortunately, Evans was not with his client the night Sinatra attacked one of the most powerful newspaper columnists in the country.

It happened late that election night of 1944. Frank was staying at the Waldorf-Astoria, where he was to begin his second singing engagement at the Wedgwood Room the next day. He had been told that Westbrook Pegler, the staunchly Republican columnist, was also staying at the hotel, and

Frank decided to taunt Pegler with President Roosevelt's stunning victory over New York Governor Thomas Dewey. As Sinatra told writer Dan Fowler: "We'd had a few drinks, and when it looked for sure like Roosevelt was in for his fourth term, somebody mentioned that Pegler was in the same hotel. We got to kidding about how he was probably taking Roosevelt's victory, and I said, 'Let's go down and see if he's as tough as he writes.' So we went down and knocked on his door. When nobody answered, we went away. Nobody broke in and busted up his furniture like it's been said."

A Pegler aide remembered the incident differently. "Peg was inside," he said, "and kept needling Sinatra through the door with things like, 'Are you that little Italian boy from Hoboken who sings on the radio?' Sinatra became so frustrated that he went back to his rooms and busted up his own furniture, throwing a chair out the window."

The columnist amplified his aide's version. "In the company of Orson Welles and others, Sinatra toured the circuit of expensive New York saloons known as the milk route and spent some time at the political headquarters of Sidney Hillman, which were the Communist headquarters too. He got shrieking drunk and kicked up such a row in the Waldorf that a house policeman was sent up to subdue him, and did."

The vendetta between the columnist and the crooner continued. A few nights later, Westbrook Pegler appeared in the Wedgwood Room for the late show. Frank saw him and told the management to get him out or he would not perform. Hank Sanicola pleaded with him to go easy. "Pegler is too powerful to mess around with," he said. Frank would not listen. Knowing he could not force the manager to evict him, Frank took advantage of the rule that once the show had started, no one could be seated. He sent one of his aides to fake a long distance phone call for the columnist, and two minutes before the show was to start, Pegler was paged. Seconds after he left the room to take the phone call, Frank stepped up to the microphone and started singing, apparently unmindful of the old Sicilian saying: "Keep your friends close to you; keep your enemies even closer."

Pegler retaliated by writing about Frank's arrest, six years before, on a morals charge. "It was in Bergen County that Sinatra was arrested in 1938 on a charge of seduction and causing the pregnancy of an unmarried young woman."

George Evans called him immediately, saying that the

complainant had seduced Frank and was arrested for annoy-
ing him. He added that the incident happened years ago,
when Frank was young and poor and unknown, pointed out
that the charges had been dropped, and he appealed to
Pegler to do the same.

The columnist responded by printing Evans's comment
and adding a few of his own. "No indictment was found, and
Sinatra was discharged. The incident would indicate a certain
precocity, however, for it will be observed that the facts of
the case never were tried and that this experience of the
youth so soon to become the idol of American girlhood was by
no means common to decent young American males, however
poor."

George Evans was nearly apoplectic. He made Frank
promise to do nothing further to antagonize Pegler, and Frank
grudgingly gave him his word of honor that he would not
incite the columnist to resume his attack. It was a promise he
kept for almost two years.

With a draft classification of 4-F, Frank did not have to worry about military service until 1945, when he was suddenly called up for a reexamination. "I'm awfully upset right now," he told reporters. "I'm going to visit my New Jersey draft board to find out my Selective Service status."

After three days of medical exams Frank was declared 2-AF, meaning that his punctured eardrum disqualified him from serving and that he was "necessary for the national health, safety, and interest," which would exempt him even from a war job. This new classification had been created when Congress passed a "work-or-fight" bill.

Then a newspaper headline asked, "Is Crooning Essential?" which stirred a national debate over Frank's draft status. An investigation was ordered by the New Jersey Selective Service Board, which announced that it was referring the matter to the appeals board in Washington "under a recent ruling governing the reexamination of outstanding athletes and stage and screen stars." This triggered bitter letters to the editor throughout the country.

"Can you tell me why athletes and stage and screen stars are so important that there must be some special dispensation concerning their war status?" the mother of an American soldier asked the *New York Sun*. "When the sons of ordinary citizens like myself go before a draft board, they go or not

Early Hoboken
days

(Courtesy of Richie Shirak)

Frank with his first
girlfriend, Marie
Roemer

*(Courtesy of Agnes
Carney Hannigan)*

The Hoboken Four
with Major Bowes

(Courtesy of Richie Shirak)

Frank and Nancy
on their wedding
day, February 4,
1939

*(Photo by Edward P.
Davis)*

The Voice

(Simon Nathan)

With Harry James
rehearsing for a
broadcast

(AP/Wide World Photos)

With Tommy
Dorsey and his
orchestra in
Ship Ahoy, 1942

(Courtesy of MGM/UA)

With George
Evans, his genius
of a press agent

(Courtesy of Phil Evans)

Photographers
recording Frank,
Jr.'s, birth, 1944

(New York Daily News
Photo)

Sinatra fans at the
Paramount, 1944

(New York Daily News
Photo)

Sailors pelting
Sinatra's picture
with tomatoes, 1944

(New York Daily News
Photo)

The "Crooner" meets the "Swooner" for the first time in Hollywood

(UPI/Bettmann Newsphotos)

Being welcomed
by his two Nancys,
1943

(New York Daily News
Photo)

With Gene Kelly
in *Anchors Aweigh*,
1945

(Courtesy MGM/UA)

Sinatra leaving Justice Court after Lee Mortimer's assault charge against him was dismissed at Mortimer's request, 1947. Frank had to pay the columnist $9,000.

(AP/Wide World Photos)

Sinatra arriving to testify before a grand jury about "Wrong door raid" on Marilyn Monroe, 1957

(AP/Wide World Photos)

Fire captain
Martin Sinatra
gives his son his hat
on "Frank Sinatra
Day" in Hoboken,
1947

*(UPI/Bettmann
Newsphotos)*

"Little Nancy" and "Little Frank," as they were known, at a radio broadcast in 1947

ABOVE Frank and Nancy at their New Year's Eve party, 1947

RIGHT Ava Gardner at the same party

In Reno with
manager Hank
Sanicola and
business partner
Ben Barton

(New York Daily News
Photo)

In Reno with
Ava Gardner

(New York Daily News
Photo)

With Aniello
Dellacroce,
underboss of
Gambino family

Leading a Los
Angeles orchestra

*(UPI/Bettmann
Newsphotos)*

Frank in rehearsal
in 1954

(AP/Wide World Photos)

depending on the word of the local examiners, and that's that."

One of the most damning letters came from the men of Ward 47-4, Hospital Plant 4118 in England, who had read that the girls back home were jumping into snowbanks and threatening to take their lives if Frankie were drafted.

"There are millions of GIs in the Army, so I don't see why there's so many tears for one man," wrote Pvt. Jerry M. Porcilli. "I am beginning to doubt if the girls back home are still civilized. My buddies agree with me that something should be done. Would you print this letter to show how the boys in the European Theater of Operations feel about the matter?"

On March 5, 1945, the New Jersey draft board declared there had been a "mix-up" and that Frank's 4-F classification was to be continued. Not everyone was satisfied. George E. Sokolsky wrote in the *New York Sun:* "The 4-F explanation is emotionally unsatisfactory. A few devils might be psychoneurotics, but surely that generalization does not explain all the exemptions, deferments, and 4-Fs that one notes on stage, screen, and radio. Nor do pierced eardrums. If it is policy to retain a number of actors at home to entertain the public on the theory that it is sound to spread good cheer, then that should be stated and explained. But how would that include Frank Sinatra, regarding whose induction there was so much publicity and then a silence? It gives the impression that his opportunity to continue his private business pursuits while other men of his age are forced to give up their careers and fight, even to death, for their country is a result of his political activities. Certainly, no man would want to be put in that position and no man would want to take advantage of it."

George Evans could not ignore this kind of public sentiment. He announced that Frank planned an immediate national tour of Army and Navy hospitals and that he would go overseas to entertain the troops in June.

"When Frank's manager asked me to put together a show to tour Europe with Frank for six weeks, I was torn apart," Phil Silvers recalled. "I was still on my honeymoon with Jo-Carroll. Yet Frank was a pal—if he needed me, I had to help. Jo-Carroll lost out to the tour. Frank left the details of the show in my hands because of my stage and USO experience."

Jo-Carroll Silvers, a former Miss America from Tyler,

Texas, was most understanding about that USO tour. "All
the stars had been going overseas except for Frank, who was
getting a lot of bad publicity because of it. He knew that he
finally had to go, but he was scared," she said. "He had
heard the rumors from the Victory Committee that the guys
were really going to let him have it. There were reports that
they were going to throw eggs at him and make fun of him for
not being in the service. For months, the servicemen had
been up in arms about Sinatra and all his swooners. They
resented their girlfriends' and wives' making fools out of
themselves over him. It was insulting to their manhood that
this skinny little 'shmo' was a sex symbol to women on the
home front. Now they were going to get even."

Silvers's unit included Saul Chaplin as accompanist, Betty
Yeaton, an acrobatic dancer, and Fay Mackenzie, an actress
with a fine singing voice. In May 1945, Frank met the group
in New York after making news by bumping an Iwo Jima
veteran to get a seat on the plane from Los Angeles. He was
further criticized for making his first USO tour a few days
after victory in Europe had been declared and the Germans
had unconditionally surrendered their entire military force to
General Dwight D. Eisenhower.

When the group landed in Rome, Frank refused to stay in
the three-floor walk-up hotel where they had been booked.
"We'll stay at the Excelsior," he announced. It was the best
hotel in town and booked to capacity, Silvers recalled, but
Sinatra somehow managed to get everyone in. Next, he decided that he wanted an audience with Pope Pius XII.

"Come on, Frank," said Phil Silvers. "What've you been
smoking?"

Frank called Myron Taylor, President Roosevelt's envoy
to the Vatican, and the appointment was made. Frank told
Silvers that he planned to tell the pope of a few things
happening in the United States that he might not be aware
of. "Like that bigot Father Coughlin in Detroit. This priest is
doing a lot of damage to the Church."

When the Sinatra group was ushered into a private room
of the Vatican, Frank knelt to kiss the ring of St. Peter. The
pope then asked him if he was a tenor.

"No, Your Holiness, I'm a baritone."

"Ah, and what operas do you sing?"

"I—ah—don't sing opera, Your Holiness."

"And where did you study?"

"I—ah—never studied."

Frank received his blessing from the pope without enlightening him about the fallibility of the Catholic Church in Detroit. His Holiness next turned to Phil, who was carrying rosary beads he had bought to have blessed for Bing Crosby. The pope seemed much more familiar with this singer than he had been with Frank and even gave Silvers an extra string of blessed beads for Mrs. Crosby.

Afterward, Frank punched Phil's arm hard and said, "You creepy bum! I take you in to see the pope—and you're plugging Crosby."

Phil Silvers had deliberated about how to introduce Sinatra to the troops.

"I knew Frank had to be presented in a very special way. I couldn't give him the usual build-up—'And here he is, the idol of America's youth!'—because those youths in uniform might have thrown C-ration cans.

"I suggested to Frank that he be presented as the underdog of the show. I would open with a few well-aimed Army jokes—food, the draft, civilian clothes. Then Frank wanders on, casually. Jokes about Frank: 'I know there's a food shortage, but this is ridiculous. He weighed twelve pounds when he was born, and he's been losing weight ever since.' Frank asks if he can sing. We go into my singing-lesson bit. I shape his tones, slap his cheeks, browbeat him, convince him he can't sing at all. Then my clarinet bit, for which Frank goes into the audience and heckles me. By this time I figured the men would be demanding, 'Let Sinatra sing!' The soldiers had been underdogs so long, I was sure they would love this underdog."

The routine worked. Frank made his first appearance before the troops and let Phil pull his ears, squeeze his cheeks, and slap him across the stage. The soldiers cheered loudly and then begged Frank to sing "Nancy with the Laughing Face," a song that Phil had written with Jimmy Van Heusen in honor of Little Nancy Sinatra's fourth birthday.

"He had those boys in the palm of his skinny hand," said Phil Silvers.

The New York Times agreed, saying, "The singer kidded himself throughout the program and had the audience on his side all the way."

After touring the Mediterranean theater, the group returned to the United States on July 6, 1945. Reporters were waiting at LaGuardia Airport in New York City, and Frank did not disappoint them. Minutes after alighting from the plane, he assailed the USO and the Army's Special Services for their handling of troop entertainment overseas.

"Shoemakers in uniform run the entertainment division," he said. "Most of them had no experience in show business. They didn't know what time it was. They might just as well be out selling vacuum cleaners."

With those words he demolished the good public image that he had established over the past few weeks. The backlash was immediate. The Army newspaper, *Stars and Stripes*, leaped to the defense of its men.

"Mice make women faint, too," said the newspaper. "He is doing an injustice to a group of people who are for the most part talented, hardworking, and sincere. There have been, of course, the usual prima donnas who have flown over, had their pictures taken with GIs, and got the hell home."

Defenders of the USO noted that Frank had made one of the shortest tours ever made by a big-name performer and asked why he had not been abroad before. Marlene Dietrich, who had spent months entertaining the troops, said, "You could hardly expect the European Theater to be like the Paramount."

Hearst columnist Lee Mortimer excoriated Frank and praised *Stars and Stripes* for answering "Sinatra's shrill solo by defending the brave, intelligent, and hardworking people who provided entertainment for troops under fire, while the crooner found safety and $30,000 a week behind a mike."

Mortimer disparaged "the 4-F from Hasbrouck Heights" for waiting until the hostilities were over in the Mediterranean "to take his seven weeks' joy ride, while fragile dolls like Carole Landis and aging, ailing men like Joe E. Brown and Al Jolson subjected themselves to enemy action, jungle disease, and the dangers of traveling through hostile skies from the beginning of the war."

Frank plaintively tried to defend himself. "I talked to thousands of guys over there. . . . They asked me to beef about the shows."

Once again, George Evans snapped into action, and soon the bad publicity was diluted by good reviews for Frank's campaign against racial injustice, the tolerance crusade that

Evans had promoted after the singer had skipped the interfaith rally in Boston. Since then, Frank had made a speaking tour of American youth centers. He had lectured high school editors and student council presidents in Philadelphia. He had talked in schools, auditoriums, and churches. He had written an article on juvenile delinquency and he had been applauded by the people he most admired, people who were educated and politically committed.

As an Italian-American, Frank had always resented being cast outside of the mainstream. He saw how his *paisans*, with their flailing gestures and exaggerated accents, were ridiculed as "eyetalians" and portrayed as illiterates and boors. He hated the discrimination.

"I'll never forget how it hurt when the kids called me a 'dago' when I was a boy," he said. "It's a scar that lasted a long time and which I have never quite forgotten. It isn't the kids' fault—it's their parents'. They would never learn to make racial and religious discriminations if they didn't hear that junk at home."

Evans encouraged in Frank a commitment to racial tolerance that was basic and emotional. "I'm not the kind of guy who does a lot of brain work about why or how I happened to get into something," said Frank. "I get an idea—maybe I get sore about something. And when I get sore enough, I do something about it."

As a liberal Democrat, Evans talked politics with Frank and introduced the singer to his politically active friends like the sculptor Jo Davidson. Soon Frank was quoting socialist philosophy to reporters. "Poverty. That's the biggest thorn," he said. "It comes down to what Henry Wallace said, to what he meant when he said every kid in the world should have his quart of milk a day."

He vowed to take his campaign for racial justice to the students of America, but with only an eighth-grade education he sometimes had trouble expressing himself. Growing up within the narrow confines of Hoboken, New Jersey, where there was no emphasis on learning, had limited him intellectually. Now, for the first time in his life, he began reading.

"I started with the most prolific [sic] books—I mean the kind that are easily understandable to a person like me, with a newly found job in my mind and in my heart," he said. He read *The History of Bigotry in the United States* by Gustavus Myers—"a great book," he said. He also read *The American*

Dilemma by Gunnar Myrdal, a study of blacks in the United States, and *Freedom Road* by Howard Fast, which describes the struggles of a group of blacks after the Civil War to take their place in a society promising equal opportunity. These books made a powerful impression on Frank, who embraced their teachings on the evils of racial prejudice and promised to dedicate himself to righting social wrongs. "I'm in it for life," he said. "After all, I'm only coming out for the basic American ideal, and who can object to that?"

Jack Keller said, "George Evans and I encouraged this newly developed social conscience, for we could see that along this road, except in the Deep South, it would certainly set Frank aside as 'a citizen of the community' as well as being a star. We convinced him to make a film entitled *The House I Live In*, which caused a lot of people to sit up and take notice. He even received a special Academy Award for it."

The ten-minute short, written by Albert Maltz, directed by Mervyn LeRoy, and produced by RKO, was made on a nonprofit basis, all proceeds going to organizations dealing with the problems of juvenile delinquency. In the movie, Frank teaches a lesson of religious and racial tolerance to a gang of kids.

The critics applauded. "*The House I Live In* is a short subject to make everyone concerned feel proud," said *Variety*.

"The picture's message is tolerance. Its medium is song. And its protagonist is Frank Sinatra—the bow-tied, fan-eared, scrawny-necked idol of the bobby-soxers, who has, amazingly, grown within a few short years from a lovelorn microphone-hugging crooner to become one of filmdom's leading and most vocal battlers for a democratic way of life," said *Cue*.

"This well-meaning project . . . part of a larger Sinatra crusade . . . was staged with free help from topflight Hollywood talent. They got the idea for the picture when they learned that Sinatra had been making spontaneous visits to high schools, where he preached little sermons on tolerance. The short's message should be clear enough to anyone," said *Time*.

The success of the film led Frank to Gary, Indiana, on November 1, 1945, to try to settle a strike by the white students of Froebel High School against the "pro-Negro" policies of their new principal, who had allowed the school's two hundred seventy black students to share classrooms with whites, to join the school orchestra, and to swim in the school pool one day a week. As a result, some one thousand white students had walked out, screaming and yelling and throwing bricks through the school windows. They refused to return as long as they had to share their facilities with the black students, and their parents supported them, fearing competition for their steel mill jobs from Gary's growing black population. After a four-day strike, the principal was as worried as the mayor. It was at this impasse that Frank was invited to address the students in hopes that he might be able to bring them together.

George Evans and Jack Keller briefed Sinatra on what to say and accompanied him to Indiana. They were met by the mayor and escorted to the school auditorium, where more than five thousand pupils and their parents had gathered at eight o'clock in the morning.

"George and I were standing in the wings, and although we had told Frank what to say, we were skeptical and pretty damned frightened as to what might happen," recalled Jack Keller. "Frank walked out onstage and stood dead center while all these rough, tough steel workers and their kids started catcalling and whistling and stamping their feet. Frank folded his arms, looked right down at them, and stared for a full two minutes, until there was a dead silence in the room. Evans and I were nervous wrecks wondering what in hell he was going to do.

"Without smiling, Frank kept staring at the audience. Finally he unfolded his arms and moved to the microphone. 'I can lick any son of a bitch in this joint,' he said. Pandemonium broke loose as the kids cheered him. They thought he was right down their street, and from then on, it was terrific."

Frank spoke earnestly. "I implore you to return to school. This is a bad deal, kids. It's not good for you and it's not good for the city of Gary, which has done so much to help with the war for freedom the world over.

"Believe me, I know something about the business of racial intolerance. At eleven I was called a 'dirty guinea' back home in New Jersey," he said.

"No, no, no," shrieked hundreds of girls in the audience. "No, Frankie, no."

"We've all done it," he said. "We've all used the words nigger or kike or mick or polack or dago. Cut it out, kids. Go back to school. You've got to go back because you don't want to be ashamed of your student body, your city, your country."

He pointed out that the Nazis used the method of divide and rule by pitting race against race. "Don't let it happen here," he pleaded. "I learned that a few people who have nothing to do with the Gary schools, who aren't even parents, have interfered and helped foment this trouble. Don't listen to them. Sit down and talk it over. If President Roosevelt could do it with Churchill and Stalin, then the kids of America can work out their problems too."

The priest onstage glanced at the mayor sitting next to him, and obvious embarrassment crossed the faces of the other civic and business leaders on the platform. Frank ignored their discomfort and proceeded to name one of the agitators, who was a local businessman. He called him "a cheap meddler" and "a two-bit politician who has had his name on the billboard two times but never was elected." "Surely you're not going to let a man like this influence you," he said. "You ought to run this bum out of town."

The priest stalked off the stage at this point and the mayor, red in the face, started to leave as well, but reconsidered and stayed in his seat. Frank finished by singing two songs and asking the kids to rise and repeat with him a pledge for tolerance. "We will strive to work together to prove that the American way is the only fair and democratic way of life." Then everyone sang the national anthem.

Sputtering with rage, the mayor accosted Frank as he was leaving. "Your remarks were most unfortunate. You were ill-advised in your statements, and what you said was a disservice to the cause and to the community."

Frank did not end the strike at Froebel High School, but for making the trip he received the first scroll presented by the Bureau of Intercultural Education in New York, where Eleanor Roosevelt was the keynote speaker. A month later, he received the annual unity award from the Golden Slipper Square Club of Philadelphia. The Newspaper Guild honored him with a Page One Award, and the National Conference of Christians and Jews cited him for "his outstanding efforts and contribution to the cause of religious tolerance and unity among Americans." He received the New Jersey Organization of Teachers award for "making the greatest contribution to racial progress and intercultural amity." His name was added to the 1945 Honor Roll of Race Relations by the curator of the Schomburg Collection of Negro Literature of the New York Public Library. Months later, the Catholic Youth Organization of Chicago presented him with their Club of Champions award, citing him as "an honest, fearless, and forthright fighter against intolerance, who has utilized his influence with a vast following to further those ideals which are the heartbeat of our democracy."

The liberal press applauded Frank for his tolerance crusade, but others criticized him for associating with groups such as American Youth for Democracy; Progressive Citizens of America; and the Independent Citizens Committee of the Arts, Sciences, and Professions, which was headed by his good friend, sculptor Jo Davidson. Gerald L. K. Smith, leader of the conservative America First party, testified before the House Un-American Activities Committee in January 1946 that Frank "acts as a front" for Communist organizations. Jack Tenney, chairman of the California State Senate Committee on Un-American Investigations, also accused him of being a Communist.

Casually dismissing the charges, Frank told *The Daily Worker:* "Somebody said I spoke like a Communist. You know, they call Shirley Temple [who was eighteen years old at the time] a Communist too. Well, I said, me and Shirley both, I guess."

Smith, who was hell-bent on destroying "Hollywood's left-wing cabal," called Frank a "Mrs. Roosevelt in pants," which delighted him.

"If that means agreeing with Jefferson and Tom Paine and Willkie and Franklin Roosevelt, then I'll gladly accept the title," Frank said.

Later, Gerval T. Murphy, a director of the supreme council of the Knights of Columbus, accused Frank of aligning himself with the Communist Party by speaking "at a Red rally of sixteen thousand left-wingers" in New York's Madison Square Garden.

"That was no Red rally," Frank said. "It was a rally sponsored by the Veterans Committee of the Independent Citizens Committee of the Arts, Sciences, and Professions. While Murphy was hunting witches, the committee was urging passage of legislation to provide housing for veterans. I was trying to help veterans get homes to live in. If that was subversive activity, I'm all for it. Murphy's statement was a complete distortion. The minute anyone tries to help the little guy, he's called a Communist. I'm getting so I expect crackpots to say things like that. The guy's a jerk."

When the congressional investigation into communism was focused on Hollywood, Sinatra said: "Once they get the movies throttled, how long will it be before the committee gets to work on freedom of the air? How long will it be before we're told what we can say and cannot say into a radio microphone? If you can make a pitch on a nationwide radio network for a square deal for the underdog, will they call you a commie?"

In the face of growing anti-Communist virulence, Frank later backed down and tempered his earlier statements. "I don't like Communists," he said, "and I have nothing to do with any organization except the Knights of Columbus."

"Frank was such an ardent liberal in those days," said Jo-Carroll Silvers. "So concerned about poor people that he was always quoting Henry Wallace. We both shared this political bond, more so than anyone else in our social group. In fact, both Frank and I were fairly close to the Communist Party line at that time. Neither of us was a card-carrying member, of course, but we were both very close to people like Albert Maltz who were, and we shared their beliefs for the most part.

"But Frank was unsettling, almost scary sometimes—a real contradiction. His temper was awful in those days. Phil and Sammy Cahn were frightened to death of him because he was so volatile. You never knew when he was going to explode. He was a sincere liberal and would take to the stump to criticize any racial prejudice, but then he was always mean to the little people around him. He seemed to enjoy making people look little in front of others. He thought it made him look big. Perhaps that's because Frank is physically small and slight, and needs to feel big and masculine. I don't know. He treated Hank Sanicola like a servant and made him wait on him all the time. He'd say, 'Match me,' and make Hank light his cigarette. He'd scream at Bobby Burns."

Formerly the band manager for Tommy Dorsey, Bobby Burns had gone to work for Frank after the war and had become his personal manager for a while. He traveled with Frank while Hank Sanicola stayed in L.A. to supervise Frank's business investments.

Next to President Roosevelt and Winston Churchill, another man Frank admired in 1947 was Benjamin "Bugsy"

Siegel, the West Coast Mafia chief for Murder, Inc. Siegel, who had been indicted for murder in 1940, described himself as a businessman. He did not mention his activities in book-making, gambling combines, a racetrack wire service, extortion, and narcotics traffic. He had moved at the top of Beverly Hills society ever since he had arrived from New York in 1934, where he'd been associated with Meyer Lansky, Frank Costello, and Charlie "Lucky" Luciano.

"Phil and Frank admired and adored Bugsy Siegel so much," said Jo-Carroll Silvers. "When we were in Chasen's [for dinner] and saw him, Frank and Phil would immediately stand up when he passed and, with real reverence in their voices, say, 'Hello, Mr. Siegel. How are you.' They were like two children seeing Santa Claus, or two little altar boys standing to pay homage to the pope. They were wide-eyed and so very impressed by this man, who was the chairman of the Mafia board then. Bugsy was handsome, charming, and very pleasant, but he also had an aura of danger about him that Frank would later cultivate. Phil and Frank were enthralled by him. They would brag about Bugsy and what he had done and how many people he had killed. Sometimes they'd argue about whether Bugsy preferred to shoot his victims or simply chop them up with axes, and although I forget which was his preference, I will always remember the awe Frank had in his voice when he talked about him. He wanted to emulate Bugsy."

Interestingly enough, the two men shared certain similarities. Both were notorious womanizers who took flamboyant lovers but always returned home to their long-suffering wives. Both traveled with entourages, possessed ferocious tempers, and had grandiose visions of empire-building. Bugsy dreamed of a gambling metropolis in the Las Vegas desert while Frank envisioned himself the kingpin of a million-dollar resort hotel two miles outside of Las Vegas. Bugsy's dream flourished, and the Flamingo Hotel launched Nevada as the gambling capital of the United States. Frank's luxury resort broke ground but was never completed. In May 1946, he would announce plans to build in Hollywood the largest sports arena on the West Coast, one to rival New York's Madison Square Garden, but construction was never started.

"Like Bugsy, Frank had a Mafia redneck mentality," said Jo-Carroll Silvers. "He always dressed well but in a vulgar, showy way. He was not funny like Phil and Harry Crane; he liked crude practical jokes but he was not a humorous man. Like gangsters, he gave great big crude showy presents. For our wedding he gave us a huge silver coffee service. That was part of his image of himself. He was quite Sicilian without any WASP overlay. His moods were such that there was a good Frank and a bad Frank, but he was openly good and openly bad. He didn't try to hide the dark side of himself in those days.

"He seemed to revere his mother but pay no attention whatsoever to his wife, Nancy. In the time that we were together from 1945 to 1950, I never once saw him talk to her or touch her or relate to her in any way. I knew he played around with other women because Phil had told me about the daisy-chain parties, but Nancy was still very much his wife, always quiet and in the background. I can still see her serving spaghetti to Frank and all his male cronies."

Jo-Carroll was outraged when her husband told her what went on at the Wilshire Towers apartment that Jimmy Van Heusen and Axel Stordahl shared. "This was where all the men were during the week for their bachelor orgies," she said. "They had a daisy chain going, and call girls were in and out of there all the time. One day Frank brought in Marlene Dietrich. Call girls were one thing, but Dietrich was something else. It was a joke to invite her, but she came because she had heard about Frank in those days."

Sammy Cahn was one of the men sitting around that apartment playing cards when Frank announced Miss Dietrich's arrival, and he described what happened: " 'Who do you think is going to walk into this room?' Frank said, and he named the lady who will be one of the great luminaries of the screen as long as movies are shown. Also one of the great all-around bedmates. I was somewhat skeptical. 'I'm not so sure the lady's going to walk in,' I said, 'but if she does and sees six or eight of us sitting around, she'll certainly leave.' Sinatra said, 'Screw her, let her leave.'

"I was wrong," said Sammy Cahn. "The lady walked in, smiled demurely, allowed Sinatra to take her hand and lead her into the bedroom."

This was not Frank's first public display of sexual prowess, nor would it be his last.

Every New Year's Eve, the men in Sinatra's group dressed in black tie and took their wives to Frank and Nancy's Toluca Lake home for a spectacular musical revue that was still remembered fondly decades later. "People begged to be invited," said Jo-Carroll Silvers. "These were phenomenal full-scale shows full of skits and songs that we rehearsed for months and months. In one, Sammy wrote me a song called 'I'm the Wife of the Life of the Party' and I brought the house down when I sang it." The song was a devastating satire with lyrics listing all of Phil Silvers's faults and irritating habits, including the comedy routines he did without ever being asked.

Comedy writer Harry Crane wrote many of the show's sketches, the best remembered being one in which Frank played a waiter in a restaurant where Sammy Cahn, Harry Crane, and Peter Lawford were eating dinner. When they finished, Lawford, renowned for being extremely tightfisted, summoned Frank. "Hey, waiter. I'll take the check now." Frank, who was carrying a tray piled high with dishes, was so stunned by Lawford's offer to pay that he fell over and dropped the tray, smashing all the dishes to the floor. In another, Frank appeared in blackface and sang his version of "Mammy."

As much work went into these New Year's Eve shows as into any Broadway production. Richard Whorf, director and designer, painted a huge drop curtain for the set. Jule Styne wrote all the music and Sammy Cahn all the lyrics. Frank spent weeks working as a carpenter and electrician, sawing lumber, hanging lights, and borrowing costumes and props from MGM, where he had recently signed a five-year contract. Theater chairs were set up in the living room, where everyone performed, including some of the wives, who were given minor roles.

People clamored for invitations, with some like Walter Annenberg flying in from as far away as Philadelphia. "Thanks a million for letting us come," he said. "If you have a party next year, please invite us and we'll fly out for it."

One New Year's Eve in 1945, Frank stood at the front door greeting his guests, while Nancy stayed in the kitchen fussing with the food. She still knew her place. Her husband was the center of everyone's attention; she was simply a satellite. He had received the greatest personal acclaim of any musical performer to date, and *Modern Screen* had named him the most popular screen star of 1945. In addition to his exploding fame, he was immensely rich. According to Walter Winchell, Frank Sinatra's earnings the previous year were "more than any other individual in the world." He was at the zenith of his success, whirling in a sphere of glamour and glitter where there was no longer any room for an Italian wife from Jersey City.

On the West Coast, away from the influence of his mother and George Evans, Frank took more extramarital liberties, to the acute embarrassment of his wife. It was becoming increasingly difficult for her to close her eyes to the little items that had been appearing in movie magazines about Frank and Lana Turner and Frank and Marilyn Maxwell. But she followed George Evans's advice, saying, "Everyone else may love Frank, but he loves me, and I'm the one he comes home to."

Nancy enjoyed having the New Year's Eve parties because they were in her home, where she felt most comfortable. Most of her guests were friends of long-standing with whom she felt secure. But this party did not bode well. As she was passing the hors d'oeuvres, she noticed a beautiful showgirl wearing a ring exactly like the one that Frank had given to her. And then she remembered. She had given the ring to Frank weeks before to take to the jeweler to be repaired. "I felt so humiliated," she said later. "I thought I would kill myself."

10

In 1946, Metro-Goldwyn-Mayer was the mecca of movie studios—the richest, the biggest, the best. Producing one full-length feature film every week, this fantasy factory boasted as its motto "More Stars Than There Are in the Heavens." By the time Frank Sinatra had his RKO contract renegotiated by MCA so that he could go to MGM, the Culver City studio had reached eighteen million dollars a year in profits—its largest ever. MCA agents Lew Wasserman and Harry Fried-man informed the studio that Sinatra wanted the "morals clause" changed, that he insisted on making at least one outside picture a year, plus sixteen radio guest appearances, and that he demanded the publishing rights to the music in alternate films. It took three months of negotiations, but MGM agreed to everything, including a twelve-week-a-year vacation. He was signed to a five-year contract at $260,000 a year.

Frank arrived on the MGM lot when the ten top movie stars in the world were Ingrid Bergman, Bing Crosby, Van Johnson, Gary Cooper, Bob Hope, Humphrey Bogart, Greer Garson, Margaret O'Brien, Betty Grable, and Roy Rogers. Frank was impressed but not intimidated. His records were selling at a rate of ten million a year, and for the third time he had won *Downbeat*'s award for the country's favorite male singer as well as *Metronome*'s award for best male vocalist. Unlike most contract players, he came to MGM as a star in his own right, with his own press agents, his own entourage, and a devoted army of fans.

Feeling as though he were in the most beautiful harem on earth, he tacked a sheet of paper to his dressing room door. On it were the names of the MGM actresses he most desired; over a period of time he systematically checked off each one.

One of the most dazzling was Marilyn Maxwell, an ex–band singer who was every man's fantasy of a movie star: tall and voluptuous, with white porcelain skin, long platinum hair, and a smile so inviting that only monks could resist. "She was gorgeous—simply gorgeous," recalled Nick Sevano, "and nice too. She spent hours showing me around Hollywood when I first came out because she knew that I had once been associated with Frank, and they were crazy about each other."

Marilyn, who was divorcing actor John Conte at the time, told friends that she was going to marry Frank, who had promised to divorce Nancy. In fact, Frank had asked his wife for a divorce, but Nancy refused even to consider it. In a rage, he stormed out of the house and left for New York to start filming *It Happened in Brooklyn* two weeks ahead of schedule. He asked Marilyn to meet him there on June 19 to go to the Billy Conn–Joe Louis heavyweight title fight with Toots Shor and his wife.

Toots was flabbergasted when Frank told him he was bringing Marilyn and strenuously argued against it. He said that a championship fight at Madison Square Garden was too public an occasion for him to be seen with anyone but his wife. Frank ignored him, so Toots called Manie Sacks and George Evans and pleaded with them to do something. Nothing worked until George Evans called Marilyn Maxwell personally and begged her not to go, effectively ending the relationship. Frank went to the fight by himself and sat with Joe DiMaggio and Marlene Dietrich.

Unaccustomed to taking orders, he resisted the studio regime throughout the shooting of *It Happened in Brooklyn* with Kathryn Grayson, Peter Lawford, and Jimmy Durante.

"I got a break when we were starting this new picture in New York," he said at the time. "We were shooting on the Brooklyn Bridge. We'd get out there in the morning and there'd be fog, so I wouldn't have to work all day."

MGM production memos show that even when the fog lifted, Frank did not work very much on either coast:

7/7:
Company had early call, stood by until 1:00 P.M., then called Sinatra to be ready at 3:15 P.M., sent car for him but could not locate him. Sinatra never came. Waited until 5:50 P.M. at doubletime on crew.

7/17:
Sinatra arrived from New York but reported he was ill and didn't work.

9/4:
Sinatra telephoned in to say he was ill but we were later informed that he had left for New York without permission.

9/10:
Bobby Burns phoned 9/10 and said Sinatra arrived from New York that morning, but was tired and would not report, that he would broadcast on Wednesday and report on Thursday.

9/12:
Called Sinatra for rehearsal but didn't report. He had an appointment to rehearse with Jack Donohue at 10:30 A.M. but didn't come in. Publicity Department also had made appointment with him to shoot magazine cover still. He finally arrived on lot at 2:20 P.M., shot the poster still, and then went to Stage 10 and ran through number once with Mr. Donohue. Sinatra said it was a "cinch," said he had an appointment and had to leave, which he did, without further rehearsing, at 2:45 P.M.

9/23:
Sinatra only worked part of day. He worked from 11:22 A.M. to 12:05, when dismissed for lunch. He was called back to rehearse at 1:05, but he did not report.

10/7:
He did not report. He was called to rehearse but because Durante was not available, Sinatra said he would not come in as he didn't see any point in rehearsing by himself. Mr. Donohue felt that he could have used Sinatra's services to good advantage, but Sinatra said he would not be in.

10/12:
Sinatra refused calls to come in and rehearse even though Mr. Durante was available.

11/7:
Left at 2:30 to appear on Burns & Allen broadcast.

In September, when Frank called in sick and left for New York without permission, he was flying to a friend in need. Phil Silvers was scheduled to open at the Copacabana on September 5 with Rags Ragland, who had died suddenly two weeks before. Besides being dearest friends, Phil and Rags were comedy partners from burlesque days, and Phil did not think he could do his act without him.

"He informed the Copa that because of Rags's death he could not carry out the contract," said Jo-Carroll Silvers, "but the Copa insisted he be there. He called Frank to help him out, but Frank said he was in the middle of a movie and couldn't leave MGM. Phil was heartsick and also scared to death. He'd never played the Copa before, and he felt that if he bombed there, his career would be over. He was panicked and so he called Frank again and begged him, but Frank said he just couldn't get away.

"On opening night, Phil was sitting in his dressing room after a bad dinner show when Frank stuck his head through the door and said, 'Here's your stooge.' "

With renewed confidence, Silvers strutted back onstage for the late show, with Frank sitting at a ringside table. "Turn on the lights," he said. "If there's anybody here who's famous, I'll introduce them." He looked directly at Sinatra. "Okay, turn down the lights," he said.

A few minutes later, he touched his tie, which was the prearranged signal for Frank to walk onstage and play the stooge. They repeated their highly successful USO routine in which Silvers slapped Frank, tweaked his nose, and pulled his ears while giving him singing lessons. The crowd gave Frank a standing ovation as he took his seat at ringside. Afterward, Phil called him back and they took their bows together. Then Phil stepped forward. "May I take a bow for Rags?" he asked.

The next day *Variety* headlined its story: "Sinatra's Stoogery for Phil Silvers NY Nitery Preem an Inspired Event."

It said: "That appreciative gesture by Sinatra understandably sets him in a niche all his own in the big, sentimental heart of show business."

With such positive publicity, MGM could hardly make an issue, but within weeks Frank had challenged them again by demanding that shooting be completed by a certain date so that he could do the Burns and Allen radio show. The director refused to accommodate him, and so Frank again left the lot without permission.

An MGM conference was called with studio head Louis B. Mayer presiding. Mr. Mayer ordered that Frank be officially notified by telegram of his improper conduct.

"Mr. Mayer stated that he wanted to go on record as to our attitude with respect to Sinatra's conduct," stated an MGM legal memo. "After some discussion it was decided that we would end the wire by notifying him that we do not condone or acquiesce in his course of conduct."

The next day, the telegram was sent, saying, in part: "No consent was given by us to such a radio appearance and your participation in such broadcast was in violation of your obligation and agreement under your contract with us. . . . These incidents are the culmination of a long series of violations of your contractual obligations to us."

Days later, an MGM executive gave Louella Parsons the story, which the Hollywood columnist printed in full, saying that Frank was being extremely difficult on the lot. She reprimanded him for his obstreperous behavior and predicted that if he did not improve, his days with MGM would be numbered.

Frank exploded when he saw her column. Without consulting Jack Keller, Frank sent a blistering wire in response:

> SUGGEST YOU READ THIS TELEGRAM WITH YOUR ARTICLE IN YOUR OTHER HAND. I'LL BEGIN BY SAYING THAT IF YOU CARE TO MAKE A BET I'LL BE GLAD TO TAKE YOUR MONEY THAT M-G-M AND FRANK SINATRA DO NOT PART COMPANY, PERMANENTLY OR OTHERWISE.
>
> SECONDLY, FRANKIE HAS NOT BEEN A VERY DIFFICULT BOY ON THE LOT. FRANKIE HAS ONLY BEEN HEARD FROM WHEN IT CONCERNS THE IMPROVEMENT OF THE PICTURE WHICH YOU WILL FIND HAPPENS IN MOST PICTURES WHERE YOU USE HUMAN BEINGS. . . . AS AN ADDED THOUGHT, I HAVE ALWAYS BEEN ONE OF THE MOST STALWART DEFENDERS OF THE PHRASE 'NOBODY IS INDISPENSABLE,' SO APPARENTLY YOUR LINE ABOUT MY BEING IRREPLACEABLE WAS ALL WET.
>
> LAST, BUT NOT LEAST, IN THE FUTURE I'LL APPRECIATE YOUR NOT WASTING YOUR BREATH ON ANY LEC-

TURES BECAUSE WHEN I FEEL I NEED ONE I'LL SEEK
ADVICE FROM SOMEONE WHO EITHER WRITES OR TELLS
THE TRUTH. YOU HAVE MY PERMISSION TO PRINT THIS
IF YOU SO DESIRE AND CLEAR UP A GREAT INJUSTICE!
FRANK SINATRA

Hollywood columnist Erskine Johnson criticized Frank for
the churlish display of temperament and the next day he, too,
received a Sinatra telegram:

JUST CONTINUE TO PRINT LIES ABOUT ME, AND MY
TEMPER—NOT MY TEMPERAMENT—WILL SEE THAT YOU
GET A BELT IN YOUR VICIOUS AND STUPID MOUTH.

Johnson offered to do battle either in a stadium or in his
office. "Don't bother to open the door, Frankie," he responded. "Just come through the crack."

Lee Mortimer gleefully saluted both writers. "May I welcome two distinguished members to the charmed 'Wise to the
Verce' Circle. They are Louella Parsons, movieland's greatest
columnist, who has been receiving nasty letters and wires
from Toots Shor's favorite crooner, and Erskine Johnson,
another Hollywood scribe, whom Frank promises to poke on
the nose when he sees him."

Frank complained bitterly about the unfairness of the
press. That year, 1946, the Hollywood Women's Press Club
voted him the undisputed winner of their "Least Cooperative
Actor" award.

On October 5, 1946, a sobbing Nancy Sinatra called George
Evans to say that Frank had walked out of their Toluca Lake
home and was looking for an apartment.

"He wants his freedom without a divorce," she cried,
telling Evans about the fight that had split them apart. Nancy
had expressed resentment over the $22,000 house that Frank
had bought for his parents in Hoboken and he had yelled at
her because her five married sisters and their children were
always underfoot. George listened sympathetically and decided to sit on the story for forty-eight hours while he tried to
persuade Frank to go back home. He warned him of the
repercussions, and explained that his fans would not tolerate
a separation, but Frank refused to budge.

That night he went to a party given by Sonja Henie,
where he danced all night with Lana Turner. The next day,

Evans was forced to announce the separation, which he had been trying for years to prevent. "It's just a family squabble," he said. "The case of a Hollywood career, plus a man-and-wife fight. There's no talk of divorce. I think they'll make up in a few days. Frankie has a few days off, so he's gone to a desert resort for a little privacy. This is the first public battle they've ever had, and I don't think it's serious. He will be back in three days to work on his current movie."

But Frankie spent those three days in Palm Springs, where he was seen dancing with Ava Gardner and dining with Lana Turner at the Chi Chi Club. The Hollywood press assumed that Lana, known as the Sweater Girl, was responsible for the break-up. "The items, even the innuendos, had some basis in fact," wrote Louella Parsons. "Frank was on a tear and he was tearing about publicly." Lana called Louella and tried to deny everything. "I am not in love with Frank and he is not in love with me. I have never broken up a home. I just can't take these accusations."

George dispatched Manie Sacks to California to see if he could bring about a reconciliation. Both men were concerned about the effect of the emotional tension on Frank. "It absolutely destroyed him," Evans said later. "You could always tell when he was troubled. He came down with a bad throat. Germs were never the cause unless there are guilt germs."

Two weeks later, Phil Silvers opened at Slapsie Maxie's in Hollywood, and had Frank join him onstage. As Frank was singing "Going Home," he saw Nancy sitting in the audience. Twice his voice quavered, and once he choked, but he made it to the end. Grim-faced and oblivious to the applause, he returned to his seat. Before he could sit down, Phil swooped over and steered him to Jule Styne's table, where Nancy was waiting with her eyes full of tears. Frank asked how the children were and put his arms around her as the audience cheered. They danced once, and left to spend the night at Frank's bachelor apartment before returning home the next day.

In expiation, Frank later bought Nancy a full-length ermine coat and an ermine muff. He promised her a house in Palm Springs that they would build together. He took her with him on his trip to New York in November, bought her a three-strand pearl necklace for Christmas, and held a press conference saying that they were definitely reconciled and looking forward to a long vacation together. That vacation was postponed for three months while Frank did retakes at MGM and badgered the studio for time off.

In January 1947, he received a call from Joe Fischetti, whom he had seen a few months earlier at the Chez Paree in Chicago. The two men, whose friendship dated back to 1938, reacted to each other like Sicilian brothers. Frank possessed glamour, and Joe, a cousin of Al "Scarface" Capone, came from the kind of family whose sense of honor Frank respected. The Fischettis were "made" men, *amici nostri*, who had taken the blood oath of Mafia brotherhood, and sworn to uphold *omertà*, the dark code of silence. They were *soldati* in the ancient and exclusive society of Cosa Nostra. Frank never used the word *Mafia*, a tenth-century Arabic term meaning "sanctuary." Instead, he simply referred to "the Boys" or "the syndicate."

Joe Fischetti had stayed with Frank at the Waldorf-Astoria in New York City in June 1946, under the assumed name of Joseph Fisher. The alias was necessary because the Fischetti name was known to the press and police. Charles "Trigger Happy" Fischetti was the mob's political fixer in Chicago, and his brother, Rocco, ran the syndicate's gambling concessions there. Joe was the youngest and best-looking of the Fischettis but, according to FBI files, "the least intelligent and least aggressive." He was not the underworld power that his brothers were, but he enjoyed the same associations.

The Fischetti brothers, along with Mafia bosses from across the country, were going to gather in Havana, Cuba, in February to pay respects to their exiled leader, Charlie "Lucky" Luciano. In his January phone call, Joe invited Frank to stay with them in Miami for a few days and then fly to Havana to meet "the man."

Luciano, a ruthless killer and master racketeer, had unified the Italian Mafia factions after Prohibition in the 1930s and had joined with the most powerful elements in Jewish and Irish crime circles to create the basis for the syndicate, with its division of families. He had been convicted in 1936 for running New York's largest prostitution ring, and sent to prison for ten years.

A few days before leaving Los Angeles, on January 31, 1947, Frank requested a gun permit and was fingerprinted. He said he wanted the right to be armed because he sometimes carried large sums of money. In exchange for a few days alone with "the boys" in Cuba, he promised to meet Nancy in Mexico City on Valentine's Day. After a stop in New York, he flew to Miami Beach, where he stayed with the Fischettis in Charlie's mansion on Allison Island. The night before leaving for Cuba, Frank and Joe visited the Colonial Inn in Hallendale, a luxurious gambling casino owned by New Jersey mobster Joe Adonis and Meyer Lansky, where Frank put on a free show for everyone. On February 11, they flew to Havana, where the Fischetti brothers and Frank were photographed walking down the steps of a Pan American clipper. Both Frank and Rocco were carrying attaché cases, which federal investigators suspected held two million dollars in cash for Luciano.

They checked into the Hotel Nacional, where thirty-six suites had been readied for the conclave, and within four days Frank met the major chieftains of America's underworld. He partied with Lucky Luciano, gambled in the casino with him, went to the races with him, and ate dinner with him. He even posed for a few photographs with him. He also enjoyed the company of Albert "The Executioner" Anastasia, Carlo Gambino, Willie Moretti, Vito Genovese, Frank Costello, Augie Pisano, Joe "The Fat Man" Magliocco, Joe Bonanno, Tommy "Three-Fingers Brown" Lucchese, Joe Profaci, Joe Adonis, Tony Accardo, Carlo Marcello, "Dandy Phil" Kastel, Santo Trafficante, and Meyer Lansky, all major mobsters.

Also present was Joseph "Doc" Stacher, who controlled the jukeboxes in Newark and operated slot machines for Lansky. Years later, in exile, Stacher recalled the underworld conference in Cuba in 1947: "The Italians among us were very proud of Frank. They always told me they had spent a lot of money helping him in his career, ever since he was with Tommy Dorsey's band. Lucky Luciano was very fond of Sinatra's singing. Frankie flew into Havana with the Fischettis, with whom he was very friendly, but, of course, our meeting had nothing to do with listening to him croon. The meeting took place in the Hotel Nacional and lasted all week. Everybody brought envelopes of cash for Lucky, and as an exile he was glad to take them. But more important, they came to pay allegiance to him."

A few days after Frank had flown to Mexico City to meet his wife, newspaper columnist Robert Ruark, who was in Havana, discovered the presence of Luciano and denounced

Frank for consorting with a deported drug peddler, procurer, and thug. Ruark wrote:

> If Mr. Sinatra wants to mob up with the likes of Lucky Luciano, the chastened panderer and permanent deportee from the United States, that seems to be a matter for Mr. Sinatra to thrash out with the millions of kids who live by his every bleat. . . . This curious desire to cavort among the scum is possibly permissible among citizens who are not peddling sermons to the nation's youth and may even be allowed to a mealy-mouthed celebrity if he is smart enough to confine his social tolerance to a hotel room. But Mr. Sinatra, the self-confessed savior of the country's small fry, by virtue of his lectures on clean living and love-thy-neighbor, his movie shorts on tolerance, and his frequent dabblings into the do-good department of politics, seems to be setting a most peculiar example for his hordes of pimply, shrieking slaves, who are alleged to regard him with the same awe as a practicing Mohammedan for the Prophet.

The effect of the column was astonishing. The United States immediately cut off all shipments of narcotic drugs to Cuba, and Harry J. Anslinger, Federal Narcotics Commissioner, said the ban would continue as long as the vice czar remained on the island. The next day, Cuban police arrested Luciano and threw him into a prison camp before sending him back to Italy. The episode became national news, and Frank was depicted as a friend of mobsters.

"Any report that I fraternized with goons and racketeers is a vicious lie," he said. "I was brought up to shake a man's hand when I am introduced to him without first investigating his past."

But Sinatra and Hank Sanicola later visited Luciano in Naples, where Frank gave the Mafia boss a solid gold cigarette case inscribed "To my dear pal, Charlie, from his friend Frank Sinatra."

Sinatra's response did not satisfy anyone, least of all Metro-Goldwyn-Mayer executives, who dispatched a representative to talk to Robert Ruark to "see if we can't straighten this whole thing out." In an effort to contain the damage, Frank's agents also sent a man to see the Scripps-Howard columnist to find out how many more columns he was going to do on Sinatra.

George Evans tried to salvage what he could of Frank's besmirched image by announcing that in his next film, *The Miracle of the Bells*, the singer was going to be cast as a Catholic priest and that he would donate his $100,000 wages to the church.

Ruark wrote another column, saying that he was not mollified.

> I was told a week earlier that some such effort would be made to remove the muck that Sinatra's association with hoodlums had left on his sinewy frame. As I say, it is elegant press relations—the best, because Sinatra, the mock clergyman, hurriedly wipes out the picture of Sinatra, the thug's chum.

Lee Mortimer, the entertainment editor of the *New York Daily Mirror*, berated Frank for befriending "cheap hoodlums," adding that his fans were morons to worship a man who wanted to socialize with gangsters.

A few weeks later, *It Happened in Brooklyn* was released to generally good reviews for Frank, except from Lee Mortimer.

"This excellent and well-produced picture . . . bogs down under the miscast Frank (Lucky) Sinatra, smirking and trying to play a leading man," wrote the columnist.

Frank had seethed over Mortimer's assaults in the past and more than once had threatened to get even. He told Joe Candullo, a friend who was a musician, to give the columnist a message: "If you don't quit knockin' me and my fans, I'm gonna knock your brains out."

"Every time Frank read one of Mortimer's columns, he went into a towering rage," said Jack Keller, "and threatened that the next time he saw this guy he was going to wallop him."

On April 8, 1947, Frank and Jack Keller were in Palm Springs relaxing with friends. Jack returned to Los Angeles in the afternoon and asked Frank to come with him, but Sinatra said he wanted to stay for the afternoon sun.

That night, Frank went to Ciro's, a Hollywood nightclub, and sat with several friends, including Sam Weiss, a two-hundred-pound music publisher, and his date, Luanne Hogan, a nightclub singer.

Around midnight, Frank saw Lee Mortimer leave with singer Kay Kino. With Sam Weiss behind him and three other men at his side, Frank jumped up and followed the couple to the front door. While Frank's men moved forward to hold Mortimer, who weighed barely one hundred twenty pounds, Frank lunged at the columnist. He called him a "fucking homosexual"—a "degenerate"—and slugged him behind the left ear. Mortimer fell, and Sinatra's friends pinned him to the ground while Frank continued slugging at him and screamed in his face, "I'll kill you the next time I see you. I'll kill you."

Nat Dallinger, a photographer for King Features Syndicate, who had been standing at the bar, saw the fight and ran to the columnist's rescue. "I rushed out and saw Mortimer go down and several men grab hold of him. I tried to pull them off, and somebody said, 'Are you going to get tough too?' I said, 'No, but four men against one are too many.' "

Frank and his friends finally backed off while Dallinger called the press and took the columnist to West Hollywood Emergency Hospital.

Before leaving, Frank told a reporter: "For two years he has been needling me. He has referred to my bobby-soxer fans as morons. I don't care if they do try to tear your clothes off. They are not morons. They are only kids, fourteen and fifteen years old. I think I have had more experience with their tactics than any other star in the country, but I have never beefed. Honestly, I intended to say hello to Mortimer. But when I glanced in his direction, he gave me a look. I can't describe it. It was one of those contemptuous who-do-you-amount-to looks. I followed him outside and I saw red. I hit him. I'm all mixed up. I'm sorry that it happened, but I was raised in a tough neighborhood, where you had to fight at the drop of a hat, and I couldn't help myself."

At two A.M., Jack Keller's phone rang. It was an Associated Press reporter asking where Frank was.

"He's in Palm Springs," replied Keller, who had left him there hours before.

"No, you're wrong," said the reporter. "He's in town, and he just hit a guy on Sunset Boulevard who's still rolling down the street."

"I just left him in Palm Springs," insisted Keller.

"Well, I know it was him," said the reporter. "He just hit a guy by the name of Lee Mortimer."

Before Keller died in 1975, he left tape-recorded reminiscences in which he told his version about what happened that night.

"After the AP guy called, the UP called and so did the downtown papers. Finally I just turned the phone off. Just about that time, a timid little knock comes on my door, and who's standing there but Frank.

" 'Jeez, I think we're in trouble,' he said.

" 'You bet your ass we're in trouble and we better get out of here before the reporters start showing up,' I said."

Both of them jumped into Frank's car and headed for Bobby Burns's house to decide what to do. At three A.M., Keller came up with the solution.

"There's only one thing to do," he said. "It's the only way to get out of this thing. Otherwise, you're going to have every newspaper in America against you, because regardless of what *they* think of this guy Mortimer, they resent anyone of their number being manhandled by an actor. So, Frank, you've got to pick up the phone and call all the papers and say, 'This is Frank Sinatra' and listen to their questions. Then you've got to tell each one of them that when you walked out of Ciro's, Mortimer and this Chinese dame were standing there and you heard him say to her, 'There's that little dago bastard now!'

"This is a slur on your nationality, and no one in their right mind would expect you to take this in good grace. Knowing your temper, the press will go along with you and be more or less on your side. It's the only thing you can do to come out of this looking good."

Frank seized on the suggestion and started making calls, the first of them to Hollywood columnist Hedda Hopper.

"Hedda, this is Frank Sinatra," he said. "I hate to wake you up. But I've been in a little fracas, and I wanted you to know the truth of what happened. Lee Mortimer has been poking at me in print for two and a half years. I saw him tonight at Ciro's, and he called me a name reflecting both on my race and my ancestry. I had no way of hitting back at him except with my fist. So this time I let him have it."

The next day the papers reported that Frank had floored Mortimer with one punch because he had called him a dago. Outraged by the reports, Mortimer denied the charge. "I was standing on the steps outside the restaurant when I was hit without warning," he said. He promptly swore out a warrant for Frank's arrest, charging him with assault and battery. Conviction carried a maximum fine of one thousand dollars or six months in jail, or both. He also sued Frank for twenty-five thousand dollars in damages.

Arrested the next day during a radio rehearsal, Frank sailed into the courtroom smiling and proclaiming his innocence. "I plead not guilty and wish a jury trial sometime late next month," he said. The sheriff revoked his gun permit, and the judge set bail at five hundred dollars.

The next day Mortimer reported that he had received two anonymous phone calls threatening him unless he dropped his charges.

"The first voice was guttural," he said. "After asking my name, the voice said, 'Get out of town. Get out of town immediately, and don't prosecute Sinatra.' The next call, the voice was lighter and smoother. I was told to get out of town right away and the person added, 'If you don't, we're going to take you over and take care of you.' "

The Hearst organization moved into action behind its columnist and gave the story headlines for five days in a row. *Time* magazine said that the space devoted to the episode was "almost fit for an attempted political assassination."

MGM attorneys investigated the case and found that there was no basis to Frank's assertions that Mortimer had called him "a dago," or "a dirty dago" or "a dago son of a bitch," as he had alleged on various occasions. Furthermore, MGM boss Louis B. Mayer was not about to tangle with the powerful Hearst organization, whose newspaper chain reached one out of every four readers in America. He demanded that the matter be settled at once. He told Frank to pay Lee Mortimer nine thousand dollars in damages, apologize publicly, and admit the truth. Jack Keller fought the decision.

"The MGM attorneys insisted that Hearst had gotten to the courts and that Frank was going to have to do thirty days in jail," he said. "I pleaded with him not to settle. I told him to do the time in jail because he'd get so much more publicity, but MGM prevailed on him and he paid the nine thousand."

Frank retained Pacht, Ross, Warner, and Bernhard, the law firm that represented Bugsy Siegel. Isaac Pacht and Siegel's lawyer, N. Joseph Ross, drafted a statement: "Frank stated that the whole episode arose when acquaintances stopped at his table and claimed to have overheard Mortimer make a remark which aroused Frank's anger and resentment. On further inquiry, Sinatra ascertained that Mortimer had made no remark and had not even known Sinatra was in the café and therefore that no provocation really existed for the subsequent occurrence."

A few nights later, Frank attended a party at Charles Feldman's house, where William Randolph Hearst, Jr., was a guest. "Young Bill," as the newspaper heir was known, looked askance as Frank walked into the room with his bodyguards. An argument ensued, and Frank left the party. Years later Hearst said, "I resented Sinatra surrounding himself with hood types rather than becoming a gentleman."

After the Mortimer fight, Frank received only negative press coverage from the Hearst papers. Since no star—not even Frank Sinatra—could survive a broadside from this behemoth chain and syndicate, George Evans flew to Hollywood to work on Louella Parsons, the Hearst columnist with forty million readers. He begged her to have lunch with Frank, but she refused. George kept calling. After five more invitations, she finally relented on condition that George pick her up at home and deliver her to the Beverly Hills Club, where Frank was to be sitting in a booth awaiting her arrival. Frank did as he was told and was there smiling as she walked in. He groveled.

"I know I did many things I shouldn't have, things I'm now sorry for," he said. He offered to escort the columnist to the Walter Winchell Tribute Dinner at the Mocambo a few weeks later.

Through the good offices of Marion Davies, Hearst's mistress for thirty years, Frank got an appointment with the press lord, who was eighty-four years old and in failing health. John Hearst, Jr., was visiting his grandfather in Marion Davies's pink stucco house at 1007 North Beverly Drive on the day that Frank arrived for his audience with William Randolph Hearst.

"He drove up by himself—no limousines, no bodyguards, no hangers-on. He was very contrite," recalled John Hearst.

Miss Davies smoothed the way for Frank. Like him, she had always admired Eleanor Roosevelt, hated Westbrook Pegler, and didn't have much use for Lee Mortimer. She had wanted to intercede for Frank, and so she had suggested that he come for tea with Hearst, knowing that he would be a charming visitor for the old man, who was too ill to see many people. Frank stayed at the Davies mansion for an hour; he got his pardon.

With the Hearst malediction lifted, Frank returned to work at MGM, where few people looked him in the eye. His studio bosses were chagrined by the reviews of his priestly role in *The Miracle of the Bells*. Although it was an RKO picture, MGM could not afford to see one of its highest paid properties devalued.

"Frank Sinatra, looking rather flea-bitten as the priest, acts properly humble or perhaps ashamed," said *Time*.

Frank took the bad reviews out on RKO and struck back when the studio required him to appear at the film's premiere in San Francisco.

"Frank did not want to go, but the producer, Jesse Lasky, pleaded with him to do it as a personal favor, so he agreed, but not with good grace," recalled Jack Keller. "Jimmy Van Heusen, Bobby Burns, and I went with him. We checked into the biggest suite in the Fairmont Hotel, with rooms covering half a floor. As we walked into Frank's suite, he went right to the phone and called room service. 'Send up eighty-eight Manhattans,' he said.

"Pretty soon all these carts came jangling up the hallway with waiters ready to serve the eighty-eight Manhattans. 'Where do you want them, sir?' Frank points to the entry hall. 'Just put them over there in the corner.'

"Well, Jesus, after three days the goddamn Manhattans were still sitting in the entry hall untouched."

At four A.M., Frank, who had insomnia, ordered a piano sent to his suite, which required waking the manager of the piano store and paying a truck driver triple wages to deliver it. The next night, Frank took a party of twenty people to four nightclubs and then back to his suite until seven A.M.

"Then Frank comes to me around nine A.M. and says, 'Let's go shopping.' I asked what we were going to buy and he said, 'What the hell's the difference? We'll think of something.' So we went to the best men's store in San Francisco. Frank asked me my size, walked over to the counter, and picked out eight cashmere sweaters in different colors. 'Just keep those,' he said. Then he went to the tie counter, where the best ties were selling for fifteen dollars a shot; he picked out two dozen for me. Then socks and shirts, totaling twelve hundred dollars' worth of clothes. He did the same for Van Heusen and Burns. He told the store to send them to the Fairmont and put them on his bill.

"The premiere went off beautifully, and Frank charmed everyone. The next morning, he wanted to fly directly to Palm Springs with Van Heusen while Bobby and I returned to Los Angeles, but the fog was so thick, you couldn't see out the windows. Frank was furious. How dare they do this to him! He had me call the airport but, of course, no planes were flying. He was irate. Then he turned to Van Heusen, who is a licensed pilot, and said, 'Charter a goddamn plane.'

"Van Heusen looked at him. 'Are you crazy? If the commercials aren't flying, who the hell is going to rent me a plane?'

" 'Don't argue with me,' yelled Frank. 'Get me a plane and let's get the hell out of here.'

"Van Heusen sat down and called every charter service. They all laughed at him. After an hour he said, 'Frank, there's no way out of here.'

" 'Don't tell me there's no way out of here,' roared Frank. 'We'll drive to Palm Springs.'

"We thought he was kidding, but he called Mario, the San Francisco chauffeur who drove him around whenever he was in town, and told him to get his ass over to the hotel. He then called the Blue Fox restaurant. 'Get your ass down to your goddamn kitchen,' he told the owner, 'and fix me up a great big picnic hamper with cold fried chicken, wine, cherry tomatoes—the works—and have it ready in an hour.'

"We tried to talk him out of it, but you could never talk Frank out of anything. He and Van Heusen left, and Burns and I waved them off as they headed for Palm Springs. We flew out in two hours, when the fog had lifted, and were in Los Angeles by three o'clock that afternoon. We didn't hear from Frank for almost a week. They had gotten hit by a blizzard and had to seek refuge in a farmhouse for three days. Every single thing on that trip was charged to RKO, and the limousine bill alone was something like eleven hundred and fifty dollars!"

Frank's next film for MGM was *The Kissing Bandit* with Kathryn Grayson, who strenuously objected to their love scenes. "I couldn't stand kissing him because he was so skinny, so scrawny," she said.

The critics also objected.

"Except for appearing gawky, which seems not very hard for him to do, and singing the Nacio Herb Brown songs rather nicely, he contributes little," said Bosley Crowther of *The New York Times*.

"While his songs aren't bad, his acting is," said Justin Gilbert in the *Los Angeles Mirror*.

To recoup their investment, MGM executives decided to put Frank back into sailor-suit musicals with Gene Kelly. This time, though, they gave top billing to Kelly, and kept their fingers crossed that they could repeat the success of *Anchors Aweigh* with *Take Me Out to the Ball Game* and *On the Town*.

"I made both of those films with Frank and Gene," said Betty Garrett, "and they were great to work with. We had weeks of grinding rehearsals before we ever started shooting, and we became very close. There was a lot of horsing around, especially with the dancers, patting each other on the behind, pinching, hugging, and all that. Frank worked hard on all the dances; he had a natural grace and moved easily. Gene never had him do anything terribly complicated, and in their numbers together, he geared them to what Frank could do. Frank was quick, but he hated to rehearse, particularly the book part, saying that if he did a scene more than once, he'd get stale.

"At other times, he could be perfectly awful, kidding around and wasting time. Frank did that a lot in *On the Town* when Gene and Stanley Donen were directing. In those days, any kind of disapproval from his coworkers or friends really upset him. He was very touchy about any sort of social ostracism. We knew this, so when he was late to one of our recording sessions and held up everybody for hours, including the orchestra, we decided as a joke to give him the silent treatment and not speak. I can't tell you how upset Frank got with us for doing that. He went crazy.

"Another time, he held Gene up and pushed his patience to the limit. Gene got mad at him and Frank suddenly got very remorseful and did a complete turnaround. While we went to lunch, he stayed there with Gene setting up for the next shot, which is normally the job of the stand-in. He adored Gene, and just didn't want to get on his bad side."

Frank, who was thirty-four years old when he made those two films, was sensitive about having the MGM makeup men fit him with hairpieces to cover his receding hairline and incipient baldness; he worried about covering the facial scars from his mastoid operations, and he fretted about having to have his large ears taped back. One day, he walked into Betty Garrett's dressing room, where she had a picture of her husband, Larry Parks, taped to the mirror. Frank looked at himself and then stared at the photograph.

"I hate your husband," he said. "He has what I call a noble head. I've got a head like a walnut."

"He just didn't seem comfortable with his looks," said Betty. "I remember the first day of shooting *On the Town*. I came up behind him and patted him on the fanny to wish him luck. We'd been doing that for six weeks in rehearsals, but this time he turned on me and snarled, 'Don't you ever do that again.' I couldn't figure out what was wrong with him until Gene told me that when they put the sailor pants on him, he didn't have any behind. In fact, he was actually concave. They had to call wardrobe and make symmetricals for him, which are like padded cheeks for the fanny. He was humiliated that he had to be built up like that, and didn't want any of us to find out.

"He was a sweet guy, though, and very good to me when we were doing *Take Me Out to the Ball Game*. I remember that we were doing a two-shot of a little scene together and they shot the master shot, then they shot over my shoulder to get a close-up of Frank and started to move the camera away. He yelled, 'Hey, wait a minute. How about a close-up of my girl here?' They gave me that close-up because of Frank.

"We used to talk a lot between scenes and he always talked about 'class.' It seemed to be his favorite word. He said that one of the classiest things he'd ever seen in his life was Gene Tierney walking into a Broadway theater one night wearing a white mink jacket. Frank went on and on about how she looked and how she carried herself. He was like a little kid talking about the queen. 'That's class,' he said. 'Real class.' It was sort of touching the way he described the scene as if it was almost unachievable for him. He also talked about Ava [Gardner] the same way, as if a woman like that was totally unobtainable for a man like him."

While Frank fantasized about Ava Gardner, Nancy clung fiercely to her reconciled marriage. She and Frank had tried for a new start by buying a $250,000 house—with a cobbled courtyard, swimming pool, and gardens—on Carolwood Avenue in Holmby Hills. They also designed a $150,000 air-conditioned house in Palm Springs with a swimming pool shaped like a grand piano. On June 20, 1948, they had their third child, Christina, who was a present for Father's Day.

Now that Nancy was firmly entrenched in Hollywood, she wanted nothing more to do with Frank's relatives from Hoboken, especially his Uncle Babe, who had been arrested several times for usury and loan-sharking. Now she was informed that Frank's cousin, Junior, was en route to California with his wife, Antoinette, and their four young children, including Frank's godchild, Salvatore.

"My husband worked for Frank until January of 1944," recalled Antoinette Sinatra, "when he returned home and got a job in the shipyards. Then he got a call from Hank Sanicola a few years later, and so we came to California and left everything behind in Hoboken. Hank put us up in a tiny, cramped trailer in a dirty pet cemetery in Tarzana. It was just awful, and I cried for days. Finally, I went to see Frank, who was doing *Your Hit Parade* for Lucky Strike. I started crying again, and he put his arm around me and said, 'What's wrong?' I told him, and he said he would take care of everything.

"He instructed Bobby Burns to get us out of the pet cemetery and take us up to the Sunset Plaza. Then he asked us to come to his house to see Nancy and the kids and have dinner. So Bobby drove us out to their house, but when Nancy saw us coming, she decided to be out. Little Nancy came to the door and said, 'My mother said to tell you she's not here.'

"I couldn't believe that an Italian girl could treat family this way, especially after everything I'd done for her. When she lived in Hasbrouck Heights, I used to run all her errands, go to the Italian market for her, pick up her groceries, and take her phone calls in the middle of the night when she'd be calling Junior to find out where Frank was and who he was with and when he'd be home. Now she'd gotten real fancy-pants and was acting like a louse to us just because we was from Hoboken. When I finally saw her a few days later, she offered us money to go back home. She said she didn't want us around and that she'd pay for us to go back where we belonged. We stayed, and my husband later went to Frank to borrow money for a down payment on a house, but Nancy found out about it and wouldn't let him loan us the money.

So he gave us five hundred dollars to buy a trailer in North Hollywood Park instead. I knew they were having marriage problems, but they always had those problems, so I didn't think much of it at the time."

Frank paid little attention to his wife. He showered her with gifts as if to salve his conscience and buy a little peace, but, ever restless, he continued seeking something else away from home, and not always with discretion.

One night late in the fall of 1948, he banged on Mel Tormé's door looking for Candy Toxton, a beautiful blond model he had known for some time. Toxton and Tormé had recently become engaged and were celebrating his birthday with a large group of friends.

"The party was in full swing when there was a knock on the door," recalled Tormé. "It was Frank with a magnum of champagne wrapped with a ribbon. I think there were two guys with him—Jimmy Van Heusen and someone else. I was astonished to see him. He had not been invited, and he was not too gracious. He handed me the champagne and said, 'Here ya go, Mel. Happy Birthday.' Then he charged in and started looking for my fiancée. He had been calling Candy and had not been able to get her on the phone because we were going together. Apparently, he had a big case on her. He even went upstairs looking for her. Finally, I went to him and said, 'Look, Frank, I don't know why you're here, but Candy and I are committed. We're spoken for, so to speak, and I'd be very grateful if you'd stop running all over the house looking for her.' We were young macho guys then, acting like two bulls locking horns over the heifer. It was pretty silly."

Frank and his male friends made these nocturnal rounds like a street-corner gang cruising the neighborhood looking for excitement and adventure. One night he found it alone with Ava Gardner in the desert and had to call Jack Keller at three o'clock in the morning to rescue him. The press agent was sound asleep when the phone rang. As he recalled the conversation, Frank said:

"Jack, we're in trouble."

"How can I be in trouble when all night I have just been lying here in bed?"

"This is no time for jokes, Jack. I'm in jail. Out here in the desert. Indio, California."

Frank told Jack that he and Ava had just "shot up the town."

"With what?" screamed Keller.

"Oh, you know them two thirty-eights I got the permits for? I keep them in the Cadillac now because I might get held up, traveling with all this jewelry on me and all. Well, tonight me and the kid here, we got a little loaded, see, and we drove down here from Palm Springs and we thought we'd have a little fun and we shot up a few streetlights and store windows with the thirty-eights, that's all."

"Oh, my God," said Jack. "Did you hit anybody?"

"Well, there was this one guy, we creased him a little bit across the stomach. But it's nothing. Just a scratch."

"Have you been booked at the police station? Do the newspapers know anything about it?"

"No, the chief here is a good guy. He knows who I am and all, and he ain't doing nothing until you get down here. You better make it fast, Jack."

Keller hung up and arranged to charter a plane in Burbank. He woke up a friend who was the resident manager of the Hollywood Knickerbocker Hotel and asked how much money he had in the safe. The man said he had thirty thousand dollars.

"I can't tell you why, but I need it all," said Keller. "I'll give it back to you first thing in the morning."

With thirty thousand dollars in cash, the press agent got on the chartered plane, arrived in Indio, and headed for the police station. While Frank and Ava slept in the squad room, Jack sat down with the chief, put his briefcase full of money on the desk, and said: "Okay, Chief, let's get down to business. How much to keep this whole thing quiet?"

According to Keller, the chief figured it was worth ten thousand dollars—two thousand for the officers who had made the arrest, two thousand to repair the damage to city property, one thousand to get rid of the hospital records on the man who had been hit, and five thousand for the chief himself. Keller counted out five one-thousand-dollar bills and fifty one-hundred-dollar bills. Then he asked for the names and home addresses of all the storekeepers whose places were shot up and of the man who was hit. The chief obliged.

Between seven and nine A.M. the press agent visited all the storekeepers at their homes and offered to pay them on the spot if they would give him an estimate of their damages.

All readily agreed. The man whose stomach had been creased with the bullet was more difficult. Although he did not know the name of his assailant, he felt that if he went to court, he might get a sizable judgment. He showed Jack where the bullet had gone through the front of his jacket, barely cutting the skin. He said he wasn't hurt very much, but it certainly scared him.

"I'll give you ten thousand dollars to help you get over your fright," said Keller. The man grabbed the money.

At ten A.M., reasonably sure that the shooting spree would never get into the newspapers, Jack put Ava and Frank into the chartered plane and took off with them for Los Angeles. He dropped Ava at her apartment and delivered Frank, cold sober, to his wife and children. Then he returned the thirty thousand dollars to his friend at the Hollywood Knickerbocker Hotel and called George Evans in New York.

The telephone calls went back and forth between coasts for days, with George screaming at Frank to stop seeing Ava Gardner, and Frank screaming back at him to mind his own business and slamming the phone down. But it was Keller, the original messenger of the bad news, who took the brunt of Frank's anger.

Of all George Evans's clients, Frank was still the biggest. Flexing his muscle, he demanded that George get rid of Keller and replace him on the West Coast. As much as George loved Frank, he refused to toss aside his friend and business partner.

"I can tell you that the soul-searching that went into that decision involved many hours of walking up and down Broadway late at night," said George Evans's oldest son, Phil. "My dad's decision not to fire Jack was based on the fact that no amount of success or reflected glory from Frank was worth selling your soul for. . . . My father kind of looked on Frank as a sort of son and a creation of his at the same time. He was a hero-builder and in a sense a worshipper as well. He didn't like to admit that anything would tarnish. He covered up a lot . . . but the drain on him during those years left some of us in the family with a sour taste . . . the price was very great in terms of stress, anxiety, and pressure. I'd say there were no more than two or three consecutive nights when there wasn't a phone call of some kind—Nancy crying, or Frank in a jam, or Lana, or Ava, or somebody. Dad would get home at one or two in the morning, and then at three or four the phone would ring from California. . . ."

The long distance yelling between George Evans and his client accelerated until Frank, in frenzied anger, fired his press agent of nine years—and all because of Ava Gardner, the woman whose green, yellow-flecked eyes seemed to radiate a light brighter than the sun itself.

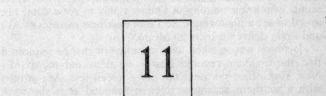

11

Ava Lavinia Gardner was born on Christmas Eve, 1922, in North Carolina, near Smithfield, in Grabtown, a squalid tobacco-farming community too tiny and unimportant to be marked on the map. Ava was the youngest of seven children of sharecropper Jonas Bailey Gardner, a lean, hard-drinking Catholic farmer, and his wife, Mary Elizabeth, a Scottish Baptist.

Even as a child, Ava was extraordinarily beautiful. Her almond-shaped eyes, high, full cheekbones, sensual mouth, long chestnut hair, and lissome body made her the prettiest girl in her high school class. Despite her beauty, she had few boyfriends because of the stern restrictions of her Bible-thumping mother.

At eighteen, Ava made her first trip out of North Carolina. She went to New York City to visit her oldest sister, Beatrice (Bappie), who was married to a photographer, Larry Tarr. Captivated by her beauty, Tarr took pictures of Ava and put one of them in his studio window, where it was seen by Barney Duhan, a young man who worked for Metro-Goldwyn-Mayer. Wanting a date with the model in the photograph, Duhan called Larry Tarr's studio, introduced himself as "Duhan from MGM," and asked if the model would contact his office as soon as possible. Bappie told him that Ava had returned to North Carolina. "But if you like, I can send for her," she said eagerly.

"No, no," said Duhan. "This is just routine. But send me the pictures of her anyway and I'll show them to Marvin Schenck, who's in charge of talent."

Tarr delivered twelve portraits of Ava to Metro's New York office that afternoon but heard nothing. On Ava's next visit to New York, Tarr called the studio to say that she was back in town. He spoke to Ben Jacobson, an MGM talent scout, who knew nothing of Duhan's ploy to get a date, but asked to see a photograph. So Larry took new pictures of Ava and again delivered them to Metro.

Jacobson was so taken with what he saw that he requested that the eighteen-year-old beauty be delivered to MGM's New York office the next day for a screen test. Ava arrived with a southern accent so thick it sounded as if she were speaking in a foreign language.

"Ahuhm Ahvuh Gahdnah," she said, drawing out her vowels until each one seemed to consist of several syllables.

The New York producer filming her turned off the audio and sent a silent print to California so they could at least see what she looked like before they heard her speak. Louis B. Mayer was bewitched and sent for her at once.

On August 23, 1941, Ava arrived in Hollywood. She was tested again, this time with sound.

"What do you do down there in Smithfield, North Carolina?" she was asked.

"Ahuh jes' wen' rown peekin' bogs oaf tabaccah plains," she said.

It took the producer several minutes to realize that she had said, "I just went around picking bugs off tobacco plants."

"She can't act, she can't talk, but she's a terrific piece of merchandise," said George Sidney, the MGM producer in charge of selecting new talent for the studio.

Metro signed Ava to a seven-year contract and turned her over to the studio voice coach, Lillian Burns, whose elocution lessons over the next few years purged the broad southern drawl. Still, Ava appeared only as an extra in walk-ons and supporting roles until 1945, when the studio began grooming her to be a movie queen.

By the time she came into Frank Sinatra's life, she was no longer a gawky innocent from the South. She had been seasoned by marriages to Mickey Rooney (1942) and bandleader Artie Shaw (1945), each of which lasted less than a year. She said the only tangible asset she received from either divorce was two years of analysis financed by Artie Shaw, which left her more confused than ever. "I don't want to read any more books on neurosis," she said. "Artie fed me that crap, and I'm so damned mixed up as a result, I don't know what I'm doing."

"Artie was a monster with great intellectual pretensions," said Jo-Carroll Silvers. "He just destroyed her, as he did many other beautiful women. As a result, I think Ava, who was Artie's fourth wife, spent the rest of her life trying to get back at men. She was sexually uninhibited, wild, all kinds of goodies and quick. You couldn't get ahold of her. She was gone and off with somebody else before you knew where you were. She was cruel that way, but so was Frank."

With her full lips and alluring eyes, Ava Gardner radiated accessibility, sending off signals of sweet and succulent sex, a rare commodity in a repressed era. She seemed to offer the promise of erotic nights and untrammeled sex. Hers was not the soft, round cornucopia of sex of Marilyn Monroe. This lithe beauty had no little-girl overtones, no extravagant padding. Although lean and spare, she was all woman—sensuous, ripe, seasoned. Ava was the mystery woman from out of town who would be loved for a night and whose name would never be learned. And Frank had been mesmerized from the first time he ever saw her.

"I still remember when she made the cover of some magazine," recalled Nick Sevano. "Frank looked at it and said, 'I'm going to marry that girl.' It was during the Dorsey days, and I wasn't about to remind him that he was already married."

Frank took an apartment in the Sunset Towers, where Axel Stordahl and Sammy Cahn also lived. "We'd yell back and forth to one another," said Sammy, "and guess who was living down below? If you looked down from Frank's terrace, you'd see, across the street, a series of little houses, one of them owned by Tom Kelly, a noted interior decorator; the occupant of that house was Ava Gardner. Just for mischief, Frank and I would stick our heads out the window and yell her name."

Ava never answered. She had met Frank at MGM and was not impressed. According to her friend, Ruth Rosenthal (Mrs. Milton Berle): "Ava disliked Frank intensely. She kept saying that she found him conceited, arrogant, and overpowering. They had instant hostility. I guess you could say this instant hostility was a precursor of a sudden romantic interest."

By the time the couple met again and spent a drunken evening together shooting up the streets of Indio, two combustibles had ignited, throwing off sparks that would singe everyone close to them. Frank was as much illusion and fantasy as the Great Gatsby, and Ava was as infantile and intoxicating as Daisy. Yet both belonged more to the aggressive world of Ernest Hemingway than to the sensitive realm of F. Scott Fitzgerald. Frank shared the Hemingway creed of *machismo* and the exaggerated sense of maleness, while Ava personified the sexual abandon of Lady Brett Ashley in *The Sun Also Rises*. Both espoused the Hemingway creed that *aficion* (passion) justified the expenditure of the self in public. Their tumultuous life together seemed to celebrate the "fiesta of life"—Hemingway's phrase for those "who give each day the quality of a festival and who when they have passed and taken the nourishment they need, leave everything dead."

Each must have seen a mirror image in the other, for the similarities between Ava and Frank were astounding. Both were sleek and catlike despite gargantuan appetites. Both were insecure about their lack of education; Frank had had only forty-seven days of high school before he was expelled, and Ava, although a high school graduate with one year of business school, still felt intellectually inadequate. Before marrying Artie Shaw, the only book she'd ever read was *Gone with the Wind*.

"You don't know what it's like to know you're uneducated," she said, "to be afraid to talk to people because you're afraid that even the questions you ask will be stupid."

Both Ava and Frank smoked cigarettes, drank hard liquor, cursed profanely, and worshiped F.D.R. Both loved blood sports; his was boxing, hers bullfighting.

Each rose to the top of show business. Frank did it with a voice of bedroom honey, Ava with alabaster beauty.

Both were nocturnal animals who thrived on partying well into the morning. Ava, who devoured movie magazines, told a reporter in 1948: "Deep down, I'm pretty superficial." In Frank, she found her temperamental double. Both of them seemed to crave action, excitement, and adventure—to be constantly in motion. Each seemed to have a savage dark side filled with a violent temper, mercurial moods, and raw jealousies.

"I'm possessive and jealous, and so is Frank," said Ava, trying to explain their cataclysmic fights. "He has a temper that bursts into flames, while my temper burns inside for hours. He never finished an argument. He'd just get up and walk away, leaving me frustrated and furious."

Their jealousies were intense and their retaliations were swift, sometimes cruel. One night at a club opening, Ava thought that Frank was singing to Marilyn Maxwell and stormed out. Then Frank discovered that Howard Hughes, one of Ava's previous lovers, was having him followed.

"We had one of our worst fights over that," recalled Ava many years later. "I had a rather valuable gold bracelet that Howard had given me. I got so mad during the argument that in order to prove to Frank that Howard meant nothing to me, I grabbed this bracelet and hurled it out of the window of the Hampshire House. I never got it back. I hope some lucky girl picked it up and sold it for what it was worth, which was quite a lot."

There was one striking difference between them: Ava was frighteningly insecure. Even after she became an international star, she remained full of misgivings. "You know I can't act worth a shit," she'd say when complimented on a performance. Frank, on the other hand, possessed confidence bordering on arrogance. Firmly believing that he was the best there was, he refused to be intimidated by competition. "I can sing that son of a bitch off the stage any day of the week," he'd say about his rivals.

Despite his own married status, Frank became so smitten with Ava that he didn't want her to see anyone else. But Ava, angry that he was taking so long to get a divorce, taunted him with other men, especially wiry Italian men. In desperation Frank turned to his good friend, Mickey Cohen, who had become the West Coast Mafia boss after the murder of Bugsy Siegel.

"He really had hot nuts for Ava Gardner," recalled Cohen years later. "There was a lot of heat, and my house in Brentwood was being watched around the clock. At the time, Sinatra calls and says, 'I got to see you on something important.' I says, 'Ya know ya don't want to come out here now, Frank. They got a twenty-four-hour detail on me.'

"But he insisted it was that important. So I said okay. Frank comes over to the house and says to me, 'Lookit, I want you to do me this favor. I want you to tell your guy, Johnny Stompanato, to stop seeing Ava Gardner.'

"So my answer was, 'Ya mean to tell me ya came all the way out here where they are recording everybody's name and number that comes near this house? This is what ya call important? I don't mix in with no guys and their broads, Frank. Why don't ya go on home to Nancy where you belong? You ought to go back to your wife and kids.' I talked to him like a friend. I mean, this is what a friend would say. Besides, I had troubles of my own."

Because of Frank's wife and three young children, his affair with Ava was conducted secretly at first. The public scandal this would have raised in 1948 could have caused MGM to drop Ava under the standard "morals clause" in her contract, which stipulated:

> The artist agrees to conduct herself with due regard to public conventions and morals and agrees that she will not do or commit any act or thing that will degrade her in society, or bring her into public hatred, contempt, scorn, or ridicule, that will tend to shock, insult, or offend the community or ridicule public morals or decency, or prejudice the producer (MGM) or the motion picture industry in general.

While "the Ava business," as Frank's friends referred to his furtive romance, was hidden from the public in the beginning, it was known to their friends who helped them meet on a regular basis during 1948 and 1949.

"Bobby and I had a house on the beach, and so Frank and Ava would be there all the time," recalled Betty Burns, the wife of Frank's manager. "We would be sitting in the living room and hear them upstairs in the bedroom quarreling and arguing. Ava would scream at Frank, and he would slam the door and storm downstairs. Minutes later, we'd smell a very sweet fragrance coming from the stairs. Ava had decided she wasn't mad anymore, and so she sprayed the stairwell with her perfume. Frank would smell it and race back up to the bedroom. Then it would be hours before he'd come back down."

With George Evans out as his publicist, there was no one to try to stop Frank's reckless romance. Nor was there anyone to contend with the press, which was now beginning to criticize his singing and question his appeal.

In 1949, there were no Sinatra discs among the best-selling records and most played on jukeboxes, prompting Lee Mortimer to gloat, "The Swoon is real gone (and not in jive talk)." He noted that the only Sinatra record in a list of the fifty most requested of disc jockeys was number forty-nine, suggesting that the bobby-soxers had "merely grown up and grown out of Sinatra" and that the swooning hysteria had just been "an unhealthy wartime phenomenon."

The *Downbeat* poll pushed Frank out of the top spots for the first time since 1943, elevating Billy Eckstine to first place and Frankie Laine to second while Bing Crosby and Mel Tormé tied for third. Frank could only manage fifth spot. This had not happened since he had become famous. He was not among the singers in a "Best Discs of the Year," 1949 compilation.

"To Frank Sinatra, I award a new crop of bobby-soxers," wrote Sheilah Graham. "The old screamers are now in their sedate twenties. And without hullabaloo, Frank's voice doesn't seem quite so potent. Am I right?"

Frank continued recording with Columbia Records, but the critics weren't enthusiastic. In March 1949, *Downbeat* said of a group of his sides recorded with Phil Moore: "They don't quite get the intimate between-you-and-me feel that was attempted, and Frankie hits a few off-pitch ones to boot."

That same month his movie *Take Me Out to the Ball Game* was released to a tepid review from Bosley Crowther in *The New York Times:* "Don't be surprised if you see people getting up for a seventh-inning stretch." *Time* magazine was similarly unimpressed: "It involves Frank Sinatra and Gene Kelly in a whirl of songs and dances that are easy to forget."

In May, Frank was dropped from *Your Hit Parade;* in August, *Downbeat* panned his new album, *Frankly Sentimental:* "Expertly done but Sinatra could never have become a name on this. . . . For all his talent, it very seldom comes to life." By December, the reviews were disheartening. " 'Lost in the Stars' seems pitched too low for Sinatra—he has trouble making the notes of 'dim' and 'him,' nor is he able to make the rather complex lyric hang together. On the simple 'Old Master Painter,' he fares better. A hit song . . . though Sinatra's is not the best record." By the time *On the Town* was released in December 1949, MGM had changed the billing, making Gene Kelly first and Frank second.

Having heard that his days at MGM were numbered, Frank had tried to get himself lent to Columbia Pictures for the part of Nick "Pretty Boy" Romano in *Knock on Any Door*. After reading the Willard Motley novel, Frank identified with Nick, the young slum kid on trial for murder. He approached Anita Colby, the former model who was working as an executive assistant to David Selznick.

"He asked me to call David to give him the role," she recalled. "He said that he was perfect for the part because he had grown up on the tough streets of New Jersey. I said that the part needed a younger man. Frank was thirty-four at the time, but he said, 'I look younger,' and he did, too. He said, 'That's my life. Everybody in my class either went to the electric chair or was hung. If I hadn't had a voice, I'd have been right along with the rest of them.' I talked to Selznick about Frank for the role, but David felt that he was just too old. The part went to John Derek instead."

As concerned as Frank was about his career, he was also passionately, wildly, and defiantly in love with Ava Gardner. In December 1949, he took her to New York with him while he did his NBC radio show, *Light Up Time*, with opera star Dorothy Kirsten. He wanted to introduce Ava to his parents.

Although Frank was still married, Dolly Sinatra no longer felt any loyalty toward her daughter-in-law. She accused Nancy of putting on Hollywood airs and thought Nancy was the reason Dolly did not see as much of Frank and her grandchildren as she wanted.

Frank and Ava stayed in Manie Sacks's suite at the Hampshire House, and they went to the premiere of *Gentlemen Prefer Blondes* accompanied by another couple to camouflage their being together in public. Four days later, Jack Entratter, the manager of the Copa, gave Frank a thirty-fourth birthday party, to which he brought Ava. The next month, when Nancy refused to give him a divorce, he walked out on her.

"Frank has left home, but he's done it before and I suppose he'll do it again," Nancy told the press. "I'm not calling it any kind of a marital breakup. He will come home. I'm not even calling it a separation. I've got something that is much too precious and fine to give up. It's unfortunate that Frank is who he is. If he wasn't a famous singer, known to all the world, we could have a quarrel just like any other normal married couple and no one would think anything of it."

Willie Moretti, Frank's *padrone* in Hasbrouck Heights, was shocked to read the news. While his Mafia sensibilities condoned murder, prostitution, and extortion, he prided himself on being a good family man, albeit one who suffered from syphillis. He revered his mother and respected his wife and children, holding the home as sanctified; he expected the same of Frank. He telegraphed him immediately, saying: "I am very much surprised what I have been reading in the newspapers between you and your darling wife. Remember you have a decent wife and children. You should be very happy. Regards to all. Willie Moore."

This was a separation that George Evans was not around to reconcile. He had to watch the personal and professional demise of his bobby-sox idol from afar. Discussing the matter with Earl Wilson one night at the Copacabana, he said: "I make a prediction. Frank is through. A year from now, you won't hear anything about him. He'll be dead professionally. I've been around the country, looking and listening. They're not going to see his pictures. They're not buying his records. They don't care for Frank Sinatra anymore. You know how much I talked to him about the girls. The public knows about the trouble with Nancy now, and the other dames, and it doesn't like him anymore."

"I can't believe that," said Earl Wilson.

"In a year, he'll be through," said the discarded press agent.

Temporarily free of Nancy, Frank publicly flaunted his love for Ava Gardner. Against everyone's advice, he insisted that she accompany him to Houston, where he had accepted a two-week engagement to open the new Shamrock Hotel. "This was a major mistake," he admitted later, "but I was so in love, I didn't care how bad it looked having her there while I was still married."

Following studio practice, Ava requested permission to leave Los Angeles. She had no film commitments pending, so MGM had no valid reason to deny it, but, fearing adverse publicity, the studio said no. She, too, refused to listen.

"Neither Metro nor the newspapers nor anyone else is going to run my life," she told her sister Bappie, who drove her to the airport.

That night, George Evans got into a loud argument with a

reporter while defending Frank and his illicit romance. The next morning, Thursday, January 26, 1950, the forty-eight-year-old press agent dropped dead of a heart attack. Frank was in El Paso with Jimmy Van Heusen, en route to Houston, when he got the news. He wired the Shamrock that he would be delayed because of the funeral and immediately returned to New York.

"For Frank, the sudden death of George Evans was an emotional shock that defies words," said Jimmy Van Heusen.

"George was the only one who would stand up and slug it out with Frank," said Budd Granoff, who had joined the Evans agency in 1948, and who became Frank's press agent after Evans died. "Everyone else would fall away. If Frank wanted something and George thought it was wrong, he would just stand up and tell him off. Everyone else more or less capitulated quickly. . . . The night before George died, he had been worked up about the Ava Gardner business. 'He's making a terrible, terrible mistake, and he doesn't know what he's doing,' he said. He cared so much for Frank, like he was a son or something."

Ever since Frank's first appearance at the Paramount in January 1943, George had been his mentor, guiding his career toward success. He had provided the strong father figure that Frank had never had, combining the unbridled drive of Dolly Sinatra with the gentleness of Marty.

"George and Jack Keller covered for Frank so many times," recalled one of Jack Keller's relatives. "Finally, it got to a point where they'd meet the press and say to reporters, 'Okay, we know what a son of a bitch he is and this is what he's done, but here is what you're going to print.' Then George or Jack would give them a story and that's what got printed. Both those guys spent their lives covering for Frank."

Emotionally committed to Frank's best interests, George had always been there to protect him from the consequences of his sexual indiscretions, his Mafia associations, his arrogance, and his temper tantrums. He had even managed to keep Frank's marriage intact by breaking up every extramarital affair before it took hold to threaten Nancy and the children. He had failed only once—when he underestimated Frank's passion for Ava Gardner—and that failure caused the first and final rupture between the two men.

After George Evans's funeral, Frank flew to Houston, where Ava was waiting. They went to dinner with Jimmy Van

Heusen at Vincent Sorrento's restaurant as guests of Mayor Oscar Holcombe. They were spotted by Edward Schisser, a photographer from the *Houston Post*, who approached them to get a picture. Schisser said that Frank threw down his napkin, reared back in his chair, and was ready to smash the man's camera. Ava screamed and hid her face in the folds of her mink coat. The owner, Tony Vallone, rushed over, and the photographer left without his picture. But the story appeared in the next day's paper and was picked up by the wire services, finally making public the secret romance of the last eighteen months.

Nancy was so humiliated by reading about her husband and Ava Gardner that when Frank admitted everything, she hired a lawyer and locked him out of the house. On Valentine's Day, 1950, she announced their separation. "Unfortunately, my married life with Frank has become most unhappy and almost unbearable," she said. "We have therefore separated. I have requested my attorney to attempt to work out a property settlement, but I do not contemplate divorce proceedings in the foreseeable future."

The press reaction was swift and harsh: Frank was depicted as a heel for treating his wife so shabbily, and Ava was labeled a "home wrecker." These pronouncements came easily in an era that revered tradition and repressed references to sex. This was a time of tightly held morals; when the Catholic Church forbade divorce and remarriage under pain of excommunication. The Hays Office, Hollywood's moral arbiter, demanded that movies show married couples wearing pajamas and sleeping in single beds. The word *virgin* was not mentioned on screen. The mores of the day condemned illicit romance, and Frank and Ava created such a public scandal with their love affair that they became front-page news. The Sisters of Mary and Joseph asked the students at St. Paul the Apostle School in Los Angeles to pray for Nancy, a poor woman whose husband wanted to divorce her.

Yet, when Frank returned to New York in March to open at the Copa, Ava went with him, ostensibly on her way to Europe to film *Pandora and the Flying Dutchman*. They both stayed at the Hampshire House again, prompting a sensational headline in the *Journal-American:* "Stars Staying at Same Hotel." Letters poured in vilifying Ava for her role in the break-up of Frank's marriage. Public sentiment was such that Frank felt compelled to deny the obvious.

"The fact that Ava and I have had a few dates means nothing," he said. "My marriage was already broken up long before Ava and I became interested enough in each other to have dates. I am separated from my wife and I don't intend to sit at home alone. I always stay at the Hampshire House, and Ava has always stayed there too."

Ava was so angry about the criticism that she threatened to skip Frank's Copa opening and leave early for Europe. "Since Frank is still officially married, it would be in the worst possible taste to discuss any future plans," she said. "One thing I'm sure of is that Frank's plans to leave Nancy came into his life long before I ever did."

Nervous about his first nightclub appearance in five years, Frank called Sammy Cahn and begged him to write some material for his three-week engagement. Although Frank had refused to speak to Sammy for over a year—"We had had a real falling out," recalled Cahn. "Someone told Sinatra that at a dinner party at my house his name was, as I believe they say, taken in vain. He thought I should have slapped the offending person's face."— Sammy obliged by providing him with a take-off on Frankie Laine's "Mule Train" and "The Cry of the Wild Goose," complete with coonskin cap, whip, and duck horn. Then Frank pleaded with Cahn to go to New York for his opening night. So Sammy took the Twentieth Century Limited and was there on March 28, 1950, along with Frank's parents, Phil Silvers, Manie Sacks, and two Mafiosi, Joe Fischetti and Willie Moretti.

Opening night, Frank was so distraught that he needed a doctor to give him a mild sedative. Before he walked onstage he was shaking, pale, and sweating. His voice had been wavering for weeks, his nerves were on edge, and he was frightened. The daily calls from Little Nancy asking when he was coming home reduced him to tears. Big Nancy sent him a good-luck telegram. Ava stayed in his dressing room until the last minute trying to soothe him, then took her place in the audience to cheer him wildly. He sang and danced and joked while launching an attack on the press that would become a standard part of his nightclub performances.

"My voice was so low the other night singing 'Ol' Man River' that I got down in the dirt, and who do you think I found throwing mud down there? Two Hollywood commentators! They got a great racket. All day long they lie in the sun, and when the sun goes down, they lie some more!"

The mobsters sitting ringside with Frank Costello, the Mafia owner of the Copa, roared their approval and clapped heartily, as did the rest of the nightclub audience. The reviews were mixed. "Today he may have less voice than ever before, but he has a compensating quality that considerably makes up for his vocal void," said *Variety*. "That would be salesmanship."

"Whether temporarily or otherwise, the music that used to hypnotize the bobby-soxers—whatever happened to them anyway, thank goodness?—is gone from the throat," said the *Herald-Tribune*. "Vocally, there isn't quite the same old black magic there used to be when Mr. Sinatra wrenched 'Night and Day' from his sapling frame and thousands swooned. . . . He relies on what vocal tones are operating effectively. . . . He uses carefully made musical arrangements during which the orchestra does the heavy work at crucial points."

At a late supper hosted by Manie Sacks, Ava, still fuming about the snickers she had heard during his singing of "Nancy with the Laughing Face," confronted Frank. "Did you have to sing that fucking song? It made me feel like a real fool."

"It's been a good-luck song for years," he said. "I sing it in almost every big show. It doesn't mean anything."

"Well, don't expect me to sit out there and get laughed at every night," she said. "Either the song goes or I go."

Frank dropped the song, and for the next ten nights Ava attended every show. On the eleventh night, she went to Artie Shaw's apartment for a party that she and Frank had fought bitterly about. She had gone to see Shaw perform at Bop City and then had talked to him at length about her problems with Frank, how jealous and possessive he was, how bored she was sitting around with Joe Fischetti, Frank Costello, and the rest of "the boys." So Artie had invited them both to dinner with some of his New York "intellectual" friends, but Frank had refused to go and threatened Ava if she went without him.

"That was a horrendous evening," recalled Artie Shaw many years later. "Frank hated me because I was with Ava. I don't know if hate was the word . . . he never sang for me; he wanted to but I told him that I didn't use boy singers. The only one I ever used was Tony Pastor, who kind of made fun of the lyrics. . . . There's a lot of vindictiveness in Frank, a lot of hatred there . . . but he can be shamed. He was shamed once by me. I saw it. He was shamed into becoming for about maybe five minutes a semi-human."

The shaming had occurred in New York when Frank had warned the bandleader to stop seeing Ava. Artie was not frightened.

"Are you as tough as you sound?" he asked.

"Yeah," snarled Frank.

"Then why do you need him?" said Artie, pointing to the massive bodyguard hovering over Frank.

Frank did not reply, but he now vented his rage on Ava.

An hour after she arrived at Shaw's apartment for the party, he called her. "Well, I just called to say good-bye," he said.

"Where are you going, Frank? Why can't I come too?"

"Not where I'm going, baby," he said.

Then came the sound of a pistol shot, a pause, and then another shot.

Ava dropped the phone and went screaming from the party in a panic, Artie and his friends accompanying her as she rushed to the Hampshire House and to Frank's suite on the eighth floor.

The producer, David O. Selznick, who was staying on the same floor, had heard the shots and called the front desk. "I think the son of a bitch shot himself," he said. The clerk telephoned the police.

Columbia Records chief Manie Sacks, who had a permanent suite down the hall, had also been startled by the shots. He ran into Frank's suite with Selznick and saw that Frank had simply shot his pistol into the mattress twice. Knowing that the police would be there quickly, he and Selznick grabbed the mattress with the two holes and carried it to Manie's suite, then rushed Manie's mattress back to Frank's bed. By the time the police arrived to search Frank's suite, there was no trace of bullets or bullet holes.

Breathlessly, Ava recounted her story to the police, but Frank, sitting up in bed in his pajamas, denied firing any shots.

"You're dreaming," he said. "You're crazy."

He said that he had called Ava to say good night and then gone directly to bed. The next thing he knew, the door had been battered down by firemen and his suite was full of people.

"I was staying there at the time," said actor Tom Drake.

"Everyone in the hotel was talking about Ava and Frank and their love affair, and now this! The corridor was full of police, firemen; you never saw anything like it."

"He shot the bullets through the mattress to scare her," said Artie Shaw. "Just did it to scare her. What a dumb, stupid thing to do."

MGM insisted that Ava leave at once for Spain to start work on *Pandora and the Flying Dutchman*. She had postponed the trip three times to remain in New York with Frank, but the studio could no longer afford the adverse publicity resulting from the volatile romance.

Months before, Metro had decided to terminate Frank's contract one year before its expiration, and studio lawyers, who had been negotiating terms with Sinatra's lawyers, agreed to pay him eighty-five thousand dollars in compensation. Before the check could be written, Nancy's lawyer, Greg Bautzer, hit the studio with a restraining order that forbade release of the money to Frank until Nancy's separate maintenance suit was settled.

On April 27, 1950, after prolonged discussions between MGM's publicity department and MCA, Frank's agency, a joint statement was released announcing Frank's departure. "As a free-lance artist, he is now free to accept unlimited, important personal appearance, radio, and television offers that have been made to him," said the deceptive release.

Unfortunately, there were few such offers because MCA agents were no longer knocking themselves out to get Frank bookings. His relationships with David "Sonny" Werblin in MCA's New York office and with Lew Wasserman in Hollywood had deteriorated because of his belligerent attitude.

"In those days, Sinatra had a temper, and when everybody didn't do what he wanted, he got upset," said the MCA agent who booked theaters. "As a result he'd say different things, 'screw you,' whatever. Sonny Werblin got blasted a lot and so did I. I was very close to Frank at one time, but he gave me a real bad time—real bad—and all I ever did was work for him and get him sensational deals. Frank wanted to be the top guy, and I mean the top. He wanted everybody to bow down to him, to kowtow, and not everybody would do it. So he vented his fury.

"Then Frank went to Jules Stein [chairman of the board of MCA] for a loan. Jules wouldn't give it to him, and that tore it for Frank. He didn't mince any words about it either. He was very unhappy and let everybody know about it. That started his big beef with Jules."

Frank needed money. With all that he had made, he had been financially reckless. When he had signed the contract on his Palm Springs home at the close of October 1948, he had demanded that it be ready for a New Year's Eve party. When the architect had explained that such speed would require triple shifts at exorbitant cost, he had answered, "Build it!" Now, with no movie contract and no bookings, he turned to his lawyer, Henry Jaffe, to make the deals that MCA had handled so expertly in the past. But it was hard for Jaffe to book an MCA client that MCA no longer supported. Justice Department documents show what happened when the lawyer went to NBC to discuss a weekly program for Frank for thirty-five hundred dollars a week to keep him in "eating money":

"Jaffe was sitting in the NBC executive's office and they were discussing the fifteen-minute show. While the executive was considering the possibility of using Sinatra on the show, he phoned Sonny Werblin of MCA and turned the intercom on so that Jaffe could hear the conversation between him and Werblin. Werblin, of course, did not know that Jaffe was sitting in the office hearing the entire conversation. When the executive suggested the possibility of using Sinatra on the show, Werblin attacked Sinatra vigorously, saying that he was no good, that he would not draw flies, and that the executive ought to drop the idea.

"After he hung up, the NBC executive turned to Jaffe and said, 'How can I hire Sinatra to do a show for me when his own agent thinks he is dead?' Jaffe was incensed. He went straight to George Heller of AFTRA (American Federation of Television and Radio Artists) and complained about MCA's double cross of Sinatra. Heller caught fire, and within a couple of days he had induced AFTRA to pass a resolution that MCA no longer be recognized as a talent agent for any of AFTRA's members. In effect, MCA was out of business for at least a day.

"Werblin and Wasserman were panic-stricken. Werblin called Jaffe and said, 'Kid, what are you doing to us? Why are you cutting our throat?' After Jaffe had made clear why he was taking the position, Werblin went to work and got MCA to cancel an indebtedness of some thirty thousand dollars that Sinatra owed to MCA for living expenses. . . ."

But there were no movie offers, and there were not many requests for personal appearances either. Frank still had his Lucky Strike radio show, *Light Up Time*, and through Joe Fischetti he was booked into the Chez Paree in Chicago. He also had another opening at the Copacabana, but the future looked bleak. He talked to Ava in Spain every day but could not promise her a wedding because Nancy, who had been "temporarily" awarded all property, a Cadillac, custody of the children, and most of Frank's available cash, remained convinced that he would come back home eventually and refused to give him a divorce.

"She has no plans for divorce," said her lawyer. "The separate maintenance suit is just her way of making Frank save his money. She'll put it all away as a nest egg. Then when nobody else wants him, she'll take him back, and they'll have something to live on."

Ava, impatient with the delays, retaliated with her co-star, Mario Cabre, a Spanish bullfighter, whose proclamations of love soon became international news, driving Frank into jealous frenzies.

"The understatement of the year would be to say that he was difficult," said Skitch Henderson, who was working as Frank's accompanist and conductor at the Copa. "Frank, you know, has always respected sidemen, so when the band played badly, he'd get hacked at me instead of them. He was bugged, too, because he couldn't get a hit record while a harmonica group had a million-copy seller in 'Peg o' My Heart.' One night, when the band was especially horrible, it all boiled over, and he turned to me and muttered very sarcastically, 'If I'd tried a little harder, maybe I could have gotten the Harmonicats to back me.' It cut me deeper than anything that has ever been said to me."

Frank's voice faltered, forcing him to cancel five days of his Copa booking. On the sixth day, he crawled out of bed only because he knew that Lee Mortimer had bet Jack Entratter one hundred dollars that he would never complete the engagement. That night, April 26, 1950, during the third show, he started to sing but no sound came forth. He had been struck by hysterical aphonia, an affliction that strangles the vocal cords.

"It was tragic and terrifying," said Skitch Henderson. "He opened his mouth to sing after the band introduction, and nothing came out. Not a sound. I thought for a fleeting moment that the unexpected pantomime was a joke. But then he caught my eye. I guess the color drained out of my face as I saw the panic in his. It became so quiet, so intensely quiet in the club—they were like watching a man walk off a cliff. His face chalk-white, Frank gasped something that sounded like 'good night' into the mike and raced off the floor, leaving the audience stunned."

The Copa announced the next day that Frank had suffered a submucosal hemorrhage of the throat and was ordered by his doctor to take a two-week vacation. He canceled the remaining two days of his engagement and headed straight for Ava in Tossa Del Mar on the Mediterranean coast with a ten-thousand-dollar emerald necklace. The press followed en masse.

"I have to keep my mouth shut," said Frank to reporters in New York. "Yes, I'll probably see Ava, but we'll be as well chaperoned as at a high school dance."

"Even if he has to hire sixteen duennas," said Jimmy Van Heusen, his traveling companion.

Upon his arrival in Spain, Frank was again besieged by reporters asking if he knew Mario Cabre. "I don't know him, but I have heard of him," said Frank, declining to elaborate.

That afternoon, the toreador declared his adoration of Ava to the Associated Press. "She is the woman I love with all the strength in my soul. I believe this love and sympathy are both reciprocal and mutual."

At a dinner Ava gave for Frank that night, he threatened her about the bullfighter. "If I hear that Spanish runt has been hanging around you again, I'll kill him *and* you!" he said.

"Be reasonable, Frank," she said. "We're in a fucking movie together, and he's supposed to be my lover—how can he avoid being near me? Besides, I haven't raised hell about Marilyn Maxwell, have I?"

"That's different. We're old friends and you know it."

"Well, Mario and I are new friends."

After five days of torrential rains, the bullfighter's public declarations of love, and continual queries from reporters who kept a twenty-four-hour vigil on the couple, Frank decided that the trip to Spain to see Ava had been a catastrophe.

"We know now that because of all this publicity it was a mistake for me to come here," he said. He left the next day for Paris, then flew to London, where British reporters were waiting at the airport. Stamping his foot on the runway, Frank lambasted the Spanish press for concocting a love triangle involving him and Ava and the bullfighter. "It's a lie, a vicious lie, and not a word of it is true. Why should Ava be the butt of this sort of vicious gossip? Ava was given a very bad shock by this business. She has come off very badly—it's a great shame. She's a wonderful person, and she's done nothing to deserve this kind of treatment."

Frank flew to New York, where he was again besieged by reporters hungry to know about Ava's bullfighter. "No, I didn't run away from him," he snapped, "and, no, he didn't cramp my style. They're working in a picture together, and that's all there is to it. Why should I be worried?"

By the time he arrived in Los Angeles to see Nancy and the children, the press was waiting for him at the airport. "When I got to Spain, I figured somebody would say something about romance," he said. "I'm not that naive. But I hadn't counted on that bullfighter. He was an added starter they ran in at the last minute. I never did meet him. I assume that what he said was just a publicity stunt."

Loathe to open new wounds, Frank and Nancy made an effort to be cordial and kind to each other, especially when dealing with the children, whom Frank was visiting as often as he could. Through their attorneys, though, they fought over money and wrangled about a property settlement of their community holdings, which totaled $750,000. That included their homes in Holmby Hills and Palm Springs, an office building Frank owned in Los Angeles, and the home he had bought for his parents in Hoboken, New Jersey. By June 1950, all they could agree to was conveying ownership of the Hoboken home to Dolly and Marty Sinatra. After rancorous negotiations, they both signed over their shares in the Hudson Street house, but beyond this they failed to agree on anything.

Nancy clung to every delaying tactic she could in hopes of outlasting Ava Gardner and bringing Frank back home. "What can she do for him in bed that I can't do?" she asked plaintively.

"She's miserable about all his gallivanting, but she's still very much in love with him," said her lawyer Gregson Bautzer, who was making Frank's life miserable.

"I'm the one responsible for that," said singer Kitty Kallen. "I'm the one who got Greg as Nancy's attorney. She was my best friend, and I was staying with her at the time while I was appearing at the Mocambo. Frank definitely wanted a divorce, and Nancy didn't know any attorneys. So I called Greg, and he got her such fantastic terms throughout the negotiations that when Frank found out I was the one who brought in Greg, that did it! I was on his list. He kept me from doing Jackie Gleason's television show and I didn't work Vegas for a long time. In fact, I didn't work for almost five years because of Frank's anger at me over that business. He didn't speak to me again for ten years, and then it was only because I was a friend of someone closely associated with the [Kennedy] White House."

Frank had agreed to pay Nancy $2,750 a month in temporary support. Later, he wanted so much to be free that he signed an agreement to pay her one-third of his gross income up to $150,000, and ten percent of the gross above that figure until her death or remarriage, with the payments never to fall below one thousand dollars a month. In addition, Nancy kept the Holmby Hills home, stock in the Sinatra Music Corporation, their 1950 gray Cadillac, and custody of the children. Frank kept the Palm Springs house, a 1949 Cadillac convertible, and all his musical compositions and records.

Without his salary from MGM, his financial resources plummeted. He had occasional club dates, but his record royalties were dwindling. He received six thousand dollars a month from Columbia Records, although the company was no longer selling ten million Sinatra records a year, as it had in 1946. His mentor, Manie Sacks, had gone to Capitol recently, leaving him under the direction of Mitch Miller, who nurtured such singers as Johnnie Ray, Frankie Laine, Jimmy Boyd, Jerry Vale, Patti Page, Tony Bennett, and Rosemary Clooney. With Manie Sacks gone, Frank was just another singer—a balladeer whose slow, sad songs were no longer selling.

"It was pathetic," recalled Harold Chapman, a Columbia Records engineer. "Sinatra would open his mouth and nothing would come out but a croak. Usually, when a singer is in bad shape, we can help him by extending his notes with an echo chamber. But Sinatra was one of the meanest men we ever worked for, so we engineers and musicians just sat on our hands and let him go down."

Frank was so financially strapped by the monthly payments to Nancy that he borrowed $200,000 from Columbia to pay his back taxes after MCA refused to lend him the money. From January 1 to June 30, 1951, he earned $328,050, of which Nancy claimed $67,805. When he paid her only a part of that amount, her lawyers quickly moved against his office building at 177 South Robertson Boulevard, where he was living, and forced him to sell.

Meanwhile, Columbia Records, which no longer could issue a new Sinatra record every month as it had in the past, instructed Mitch Miller to do everything possible to recoup their investment.

"I was flailing myself trying to get something that would work," said Miller. "I had made all these great records with him—'Nevertheless,' 'You're the One,' 'Love Me,' and 'I'm a Fool to Want You' —but they just weren't selling. We couldn't give them away. So I racked my brain trying to come up with something commercial. Frank's contract gave him full approval over all his songs, and he would not always record my suggestions. Once I met him at LaGuardia and brought him into the studio to hear two songs that I had arranged for him. I had his keys and had them arranged for him with chorus, orchestra, and French horns. It was the night before he was leaving for Spain to see Ava, and I wanted him to record both of them. Frank preferred recording at night because he said he was in better voice then, so I took him to the office with Hank Sanicola and Ben Barton, who were his music publishing partners. I played the songs for him. 'Frank, I think you could do great with these,' I told him. He listened and then looked at Sanicola and Barton, who gave him this sort of blank stare. 'I won't do any of this crap,' he said, and walked out. I scrambled around to salvage the date because the musicians and the chorus had to be paid. So I called Guy Mitchell, and he recorded both sides, which became instant hits: 'The Roving Kind' and 'My Heart Cries for You.' "

Another time, Mitch Miller suggested that Frank record a novelty song entitled "Mama Will Bark" with Dagmar, the one-name singer. This time, Frank agreed.

"He had been appearing at the Paramount with Dagmar getting great laughs from the audience with her dumb-blonde routine. Jackie Gleason was the opening act. Around that time, someone came to me with a song about a girl and a guy necking in the next room; the guy wanted something more but the girl resisted, saying, 'Mama will bark.' I thought it was a novelty that would either be an overnight smash or do nothing at all. I called Frank and said it might be worth a crack, so we got Dagmar and the two of them made the record. Frank wasn't embarrassed at the time, and if he had been, all he had to say was, 'I don't want this to come out,' and it would never have come out. But he never voiced any objections. Four years later, he came after me claiming I had ruined his career with that song."

For months, Henry Jaffe begged Bob Hope to feature Frank on his television show. Finally, Hope gave him a guest shot, for which Frank was very grateful. Then Jaffe got Frank a "network video package," which included a three-year contract with CBS for a one-hour weekly television variety show (*The Frank Sinatra Show*) and a radio show (*Meet Frank Sinatra*) that guaranteed Frank $250,000 a year. But the sponsors canceled after thirteen weeks.

"After Frank's first television show [October 7, 1950] bombed, I was called in to produce," said Irving Mansfield, "and I lived in hell for the next eight weeks. He was impossible to work with—absolutely impossible. A real spoiled brat. He was with Ava then, and the two of them were living in Manie Sacks's suite at the Hampshire House, and every day her life was a hell on earth because he was always accusing her of running out in the afternoon to sleep with Artie Shaw. Frank was insanely jealous of Shaw. Whenever he couldn't get her on the phone, he'd start screaming on the set that she was having an affair with Artie. 'I know she's with that goddamn Artie Shaw,' he'd yell. 'I know she's with that bastard. I'll kill her. I'll kill her. I'll kill her.' He was crazy on the subject.

"He was constantly surrounded by his entourage—Ben Barton, Hank Sanicola, some gorilla named Al Silvani, and a bunch of other hangers-on—and they shook and shivered every time he yelled. They talked in hushed tones and stood around him like goons protecting a gangster. I couldn't get near him. Dumb, isn't it, that the producer had to deal with the star through his flunkies and the three writers on the show, but that's the way it was. I went into the deal for a dollar a week so that I would have the right to quit on one week's notice. I knew it would be tough, but I never thought it was going to be as bad as it was . . . God!

"Frank was always late, sometimes two and three hours late; he hated to rehearse and refused to discuss the weekly format. Usually, he ignored the guest shots entirely. Once, he wanted to book Jackie Gleason, who was very hot at the time, but Frank would not rehearse. Even though he and Jackie were pals, Jackie refused to go on the air without a rehearsal, and we ended up having to pay him $7,500 plus expenses for being the guest star who did not do Frank's show. Another time I came to work and was told by the goons that Brian Aherne was the guest star for the following week. 'Frank wants to class up the show,' they said. What could I do? Aherne was a B actor with a mustache and no flair for television. He was a disaster, and Frank was furious afterwards. 'Why'd you put that bum on my show?' he screamed. 'It wasn't my idea,' I said. 'It was yours.' He refused to talk to me again for days.

"Frank was always washing his hands, constantly washing, washing, washing, as if he was trying to wash his life away or something. When he wasn't washing his hands, he was changing his shorts. He would drop his pants to the floor, take off his drawers, and kick them up in the air with his foot. Some flunkie would chase those dirty shorts around the room while Frank put on a clean pair. He must've changed his shorts every twenty minutes. I've never seen anything like it in my life."

Despite weekly shake-ups in the writing, planning, and production departments, Frank's show continued to receive poor reviews. In frustration, he blamed everyone around him. He lashed out at Mansfield and cursed the stagehands for being too slow. He castigated the critics who held up *The Dave Garroway Show* as the model he should emulate. He was especially bitter toward those who said guest stars like Perry Como stole the show from him. Mostly he blamed CBS for the technical mishaps and bad planning.

"Why can't the network smooth out the bugs on a show after it's been on the air five weeks?" he asked Jack O'Brian of the *New York Journal-American*. "I'm not a genius—I'm a performer. I can't think up the scripts. I certainly wish I could. I can't direct the camera work even if I wanted to. I'm onstage. They're not even pointing the thing at me!"

Frank banished Irving Mansfield from his sight but not before the producer invoked a clause in his contract and quit. The following Saturday, Frank showed up three hours late for rehearsal, but Mansfield no longer cared. This was his last Sinatra show, so he waited patiently for Frank to get started.

"During the rehearsal, I pressed the talk-back and said, 'Frank, I think we better go over that bit again. The dynabeams were off, the curtain was too slow, the—'

" 'I can't see in there. Who said that?' Frank asked.

"Irving Mansfield."

" 'Come on out here,' he yelled."

Mansfield walked out of the control booth, and Frank turned on him. "Listen, pal, I don't have time today to do it again, and I don't care what you like or don't like. You don't like me, either, do you?"

Mansfield felt the tension among the entourage standing in the wings. No one said a word. He looked the irate star squarely in the eye. "Frank, as an artist, you are incomparable. Nobody can touch you. But where you're a failure is as a human being."

"You're fired, pal," said Frank. "FIRED! Do you hear me?"

"Sorry, Frank. I already quit this morning," said Mansfield.

The show stumbled along for a few more months and could not hold its own against Sid Caesar and Imogene Coca's *Your Show of Shows*. Eventually, Frank lost his sponsors and his show.

Unable to find work in movies or television, he turned to his friends in the Mafia for nightclub bookings. Paul "Skinny" D'Amato booked him into his 500 Club in Atlantic City; Moe Dalitz let him sing at the Desert Inn in Las Vegas, Willie Moretti gave him several engagements at Ben Marden's Riviera in Fort Lee, New Jersey, and Joe Fischetti kept him working in Chicago.

Since their trip to Cuba together in 1947 to see Lucky Luciano, Frank and Joe Fischetti had become close friends. Frank introduced Al Capone's good-looking cousin to Ava's best friend and roommate, Peggy Maley, and the foursome spent many evenings together. Frank did many favors for the Fischetti brothers, who used his friendship to their best advantage. Government documents show that they once asked Frank to fly with them in a private plane from Las Vegas to Palm Springs to impress a starstruck automobile tycoon from Detroit whom they were romancing for an agency franchise. Frank made the trip, and soon after, the Fischettis opened crime syndicate car agencies in several large cities. The Fischettis also persuaded Frank to make a commercial "as a favor without charge," according to FBI files, for their friend, Peter Epsteen, who ran a Pontiac agency in Skokie, Illinois.

"Frank was begging for spots to sing at at the time," said Vincent "Vinnie" Teresa, a member of the Boston Mafia family. "The Palladinos [Joe Beans and Rocco] let him do his stuff at the Copa in Boston, and they paid him a good buck for it. He did all right, not sensational, but all right. Then he went to Joe Beans and asked if he could borrow some money. He told Joe that he could deduct what he borrowed the next time he came in to play the club. He said he'd be back to play the club. Joe was glad to help out. Sinatra paid Joe back what he owed him, but he never came back to play the club like he promised, because he and Joe had a falling out."

Another gangster who helped Frank during this time was Mickey Cohen, the West Coast Mafia boss with whom Frank and Hank Sanicola were financial partners in Jimmy Tarantino's gossip magazine, *Hollywood Night Life.* Tarantino, who later went to prison for extortion, used this entertainment weekly as a shakedown vehicle to terrorize Hollywood with its vicious "advertise or be exposed" techniques. Frank had invested fifteen thousand dollars in the magazine, which ensured him good publicity in it.

"I love Frank," said Cohen, "and I have a very great respect for him, and even when he was at his worst, I was his best friend. When Frank was going pretty bad, when he was getting kind of discouraged, I had this testimonial dinner for him at the Beverly Hills Hotel. I brought in his father and mother, and they put their arms around me and kissed me the same as they did Frank.

"His voice was even faltering a bit at the time. In fact, he sang a song that night, goddamn, that was really heartbreaking for me, because he really didn't sing like his old songs. It was a long song and he just wasn't himself—he wasn't the real Frank Sinatra.

"You know, I've been through much in my day. Many of my guys, people that I loved, were hit and buried and all that. It's very hard for me to cry, but really I felt sad that night for Frank. I was close to tears myself because his voice was really bad. And I think everybody in the audience could sense it.

"My guys had a private table alone for our own people. In fact, there was about fourteen of my own guys that fitted in with that type of doing—that could dress well enough and could carry themselves well. You know, there were some people that I had to keep out of certain places. They just were too crude, you know what I mean?

"A lot of people that were invited to that Sinatra testimonial, that should have attended but didn't, would bust their nuts in *this* day to attend a Sinatra testimonial. A lot of them would now kiss Frank's ass after he made the comeback, but they didn't show up when he really needed them. I don't know the names of a lot of them bastards in that ilk of life, but I remember the people that I had running the affair at the time telling me, 'Jesus, this and that dirty son of a bitch should have been here.' But I don't think anybody pulled any wool over Frank's eyes. . . .

"The testimonial instilled a little encouragement in him. At least it showed him that everybody wasn't down on him, I mean, everybody didn't think that he was all finished, and I really felt that he just had to find himself again. But his voice came back better than ever."

Americans focused on the Mafia and organized crime for the first time in December 1950 when Estes Kefauver, the Democratic senator from Tennessee, chaired hearings of the Special Committee to Investigate Crime in Interstate Commerce, popularly known as the Kefauver committee. For weeks, people sat riveted before television sets as the committee conducted its hearings on ninety-two days in various cities. Viewers saw gangsters like Meyer Lansky, Frank Costello, Mickey Cohen, and Willie Moretti dressed in shiny double-breasted suits take the Fifth Amendment—"I decline to answer the question on the grounds that it might tend to incriminate me."

To a man, they denied membership in the Mafia. Some claimed never to have heard of it, and others thought maybe they had read about it once or twice in the newspapers. Senator Kefauver tried to enlighten them and his thirty million viewers.

"The Mafia is a shadowy international organization that lurks behind much of America's organized criminal activity," he said. "It is an organization about which none of its members, on fear of death, will talk. In fact, some of the witnesses called before us, who we had good reason to believe could tell us about the Mafia, sought to dismiss it as a sort of fairy tale or legend that children hear in Sicily, where the Mafia originated. The Mafia, however, is no fairy tale. It is ominously real, and it has scarred the face of America with almost every conceivable type of criminal violence, including murder, traffic in narcotics, smuggling, extortion, white slavery, kidnapping, and labor racketeering."

During the committee's investigation, Senator Kefauver handed Joseph L. Nellis, one of the committee lawyers, a package containing eight eight-by-ten glossy photographs and told him to arrange a meeting with Frank Sinatra. "I almost fell off my chair," recalled the lawyer. "I opened the envelope and saw a picture of Sinatra with his arm around Lucky Luciano on the balcony of the Hotel Nacional in Havana; another picture showed Sinatra and Luciano sitting at a nightclub in the Nacional with lots of bottles, having a hell of a time with some good-looking girls. One picture showed Frank getting off a plane carrying a suitcase, and then there were a couple pictures of him with the Fischetti brothers, Lucky Luciano, and Nate Gross, a Chicago reporter who knew all the mobsters. Kefauver wanted to know more about Sinatra's relationship with Luciano, who was running an international narcotics cartel in exile. So I called Frank's attorney and arranged a meeting."

Sol Gelb, the New York lawyer Frank retained for this meeting, knew that a public appearance by Sinatra in the company of Albert "The Executioner" Anastasia and the henchmen of Murder, Inc., would finish him in show business. Even the news that the Kefauver committee was interested in Sinatra's Mafia relationships might be fatal to his faltering career, so Gelb agreed to produce his client only under the most clandestine circumstances. He insisted that Nellis conduct the interview at four A.M. on March 1, 1951, in a law office on one of the top floors of Rockefeller Center so that the press would never find out.

"It was an ungodly hour, but I was there with a court reporter when Frank arrived with his attorney," said Nellis. "He was very nervous. I remember, he kept shooting his cuffs, straightening his tie, and he smoked constantly. He knew that I was going to ask him about Willie Moretti and Lucky Luciano, but he didn't know about all the photographs that I had. He also didn't know that I had a report about a rape he had allegedly been involved in and the blackmail that had reportedly been paid to keep that story from ever being published."

Nellis began by asking Frank about his friendship with Joe Fischetti and his trip to Cuba in 1947 to see Lucky Luciano, whom the Kefauver committee had publicly pronounced as reprehensible. "There are some men who by their conduct in their life become a stench in the nostrils of decent American citizens, and in my judgment, Lucky Luciano stands at the head of the list," Senator Charles W. Tobey, a member of the committee, had said. Staff investigators had been informed by the U.S. Bureau of Narcotics that Frank Sinatra was suspected of delivering money to Luciano, so Nellis asked him about the luggage he carried on the plane and what it contained. Frank said that he was carrying an attaché case filled with his razor and crayons. Nellis tried again.

Q: There has been stated certain information to the effect that you took a sum of money well in excess of $100,000 into Cuba.
A: That is not true.
Q: Did you give any money to Lucky Luciano?
A: No, sir.
Q: Did you ever learn what business they were in?
A: No, actually not.

Nellis broached the subject of the rape by bringing up the name of Jimmy Tarantino: "We have information to the effect that you paid Tarantino quite a large sum of money to keep him from writing a quite uncomplimentary story about you."

A: Well, you know how it is in Hollywood. That dame, Florabel Muir, she runs a gossip column, had written some pretty bad stuff about me and some women in Las Vegas. Jimmy called up and said he had an eyewitness account of a party that was supposed to have been held down in Vegas in which some broads had been raped or something like that. I told Jimmy if he printed anything like that, he would be in for a lot of trouble.

Q: Did he ask you for money?
A: Well, I asked Hank Sanicola, my manager, to talk to him and that's the last I heard of it until Muir printed a story about it in the *Los Angeles Herald*.
Q: Did Hank tell you he paid Tarantino?
A: Well, I understand Tarantino was indicted and I don't

know the rest of the story, but the *Hollywood (Night Life)* quit publishing this crap afterwards.

Nellis then named a list of Frank's Mafia friends and acquaintances—Frank Costello, Joe Adonis, Abner "Longy" Zwillman, Meyer Lansky, Benjamin "Bugsy" Siegel—and asked how well he knew each of them.

A: No business. Just "hello" and "good-bye."

Q: Well, what about the Jersey guys you met when you first got started?

A: Let me tell you something, those guys were okay. They never bothered me or anyone else as far as I know. Now, you're not going to put me on television and ruin me just because I know a lot of people, are you?

Q: Nobody wants to ruin you, Mr. Sinatra. I assure you I would not be here at five in the morning at your lawyer's request so that no newsmen could find out we're talking to you if we intended to make some kind of public spectacle of any appearance before the committee.

A: Well, look, how in hell is it going to help your investigation to put me on television just because I know some of these guys?

Q: That will be up to Senator Kefauver and the committee. Right now, if you're not too tired, I want to continue so we can see whether there's any basis for calling you in public session.

Nellis continued with his roll call of Mafia names, asking Frank if he had ever been associated in business with Willie Moretti.

A: Well, Moore, I mean Moretti, made some band dates for me when I first got started, but I have never had any business dealings with any of those men.

Frank did not elaborate on his close personal relationship with Willie Moretti, who had helped him so much in the early days. Nor did he say that he, Frank, had shown his gratitude in 1947 by singing at the wedding of Willie's daughter in the Corpus Christi Church in Hasbrouck Heights. The garrulous Moretti had already testified before the committee, distinguishing himself as its most talkative witness. He had told the senators that he made a living by gambling ("Wherever there was a crap game, I was there") and amused them by saying that he had not done too well on the horses in 1948 but he had won $25,000 on President Truman's election.

By the end of his testimony, the wise-cracking gangster had talked himself to death. Ten months later, he was gunned down gangland-style in Joe's Elbow Room in Cliffside Park, New Jersey.

Joe Nellis did not know the extent of Frank's friendship with Willie Moretti, but he did have evidence of his many underworld associations. "What is your attraction to these people?" he asked Sinatra.

"Some of them were kind to me when I started out," said Frank, "and I have sort of casually seen them or spoken to them at different places, in nightclubs where I worked or out in Vegas or California."

Toward the end of the two-hour session, Nellis again asked Frank about his attraction to the underworld. "Well, hell, you go into show business, you meet a lot of people. And you don't know who they are or what they do," Frank said.

At this point, Nellis lost his patience. "I knew he was lying and being very cagey," he said many years later.

Q: Do you want me to believe that you don't know the people we have been talking about are hoodlums and gangsters who have committed many crimes and are probably members of a secret criminal club?

A: No, of course not. I heard about the Mafia.

Q: Well, what did you hear about it?

A: That it's some kind of shakedown operation; I don't know.

Q: Like the one you were involved with in the case of Tarantino?

A: I'm not sure that one was anybody's idea but Jimmy's.

The secret session broke up at 5:48 A.M. Nellis handed Sinatra a subpoena and said that he might want to question him at another time.

Later that morning, Nellis recommended to Kefauver that the singer not be called upon to testify publicly.

"Even though I recognized the inconsistencies in Sinatra's testimony and knew that he was lying at times, I also knew that he wasn't going to admit any complicity concerning Luciano or the Fischettis in terms of being a bagman or courier for them. Besides, we weren't out to destroy anyone or to sensationalize the hearings with Hollywood celebrities," he said.

Although Frank escaped congressional scrutiny in 1951, the case against him and his organized crime connections was far from closed. Five grand jury subpoenas would follow, along with two Internal Revenue Service investigations, a congressional summons, and a subpoena from the New Jersey State Crime Commission that he would fight all the way to the Supreme Court, and lose.

12

Encouraged by the public support she received from the Catholic Church as well as from the Hollywood press, Nancy Sinatra continued to refuse Frank a divorce, convinced that he would eventually come back home. She saw how physically drained he was by his tempestuous relationship with Ava Gardner, following her back and forth to New York, to Europe, to California. She knew of their ugly fights and Ava's resentment toward Frank's cronies, who were always hanging around. She also knew how much Frank missed the comforts of home, where she kept things as neat and clean as he liked, where there was always a jar of the homemade spaghetti sauce he loved in the refrigerator, and where she had always been uncomplaining about his male friends coming and going any hour of the day or night, and eating and drinking as much as they wanted. She saw how guilty he felt about leaving the children, especially Little Nancy, his favorite child. Besides, although Frank had walked out of the house in January 1950, he kept coming back, thereby prompting Nancy to drag out the legal proceedings as long as she could in hopes of outlasting Ava Gardner.

Ava, too, sensed Frank's ambivalence about a divorce, and after eighteen months she issued an ultimatum, stating that she would not see him again until he was a free man. Many of his friends hoped that this would bring him back to

Nancy, believing that his career would be revived if he returned home to his wife and children.

Frank had finally managed to snag the lead in *Meet Danny Wilson*, a Universal movie starring Shelley Winters, Alex Nicol, and Raymond Burr, for which he was being paid $25,000. Sinatra's friend Don McGuire had written the original screenplay about the rise of a brash but likeable young crooner who was backed by a gangster demanding fifty percent of all his future earnings. Frank played Danny Wilson, sang nine songs, and received lukewarm reviews.

"Frank Sinatra is obviously unfair to himself in *Meet Danny Wilson*. For Danny's rise to fame and fortune as crooner and bobby-sox idol is so much like Frankie's that the parallel is inescapable," said the *Los Angeles Times*.

Time magazine agreed. "The story cribs so freely from the career and personality of Frank Sinatra that fans may expect Ava Gardner to pop up in the last reel."

"This forgettable picture began shooting in chaos and ended in disaster," recalled Shelley Winters. "Frank was in the process of divorcing Nancy to marry Ava Gardner—I think he thought that's what he wanted. His children were quite young and there were always psychiatrists and priests and his kids visiting him on the set or in the commissary. . . . Sometimes the children would come to the commissary and I would join them. A priest from the Catholic Family Counseling Service would sometimes be with them. The priest was a very nice man, but the afternoons he visited Frank on the set we all might as well have gone home. Frank was truly impossible and so disturbed that he couldn't hear anything that anyone said to him, including the other actors, the crew, and the director, Joe Pevney.

"Everyone in Hollywood knew of his struggles 'to divorce or not to divorce,' and the columnists as well as the industry were giving him a very bad time."

The artistic chemistry between Frank and his headstrong leading lady soured immediately after rehearsals began, and their vicious arguments soon could be heard throughout the studio. He called her a "bowlegged bitch of a Brooklyn blonde" and she retaliated, denouncing him as "a skinny, no-talent, stupid, Hoboken bastard." One night they flew into such a rage at each other that Shelley slugged him, and Frank stormed off the set. "Contrary to other Italians I have known since, he didn't hit me back," said Shelley. "Maybe he went home and hit Ava Gardner."

The next morning, studio executives begged Shelley to make peace with her temperamental co-star. "Mr. Sinatra is going through a terrible and troubled period of his life and career," said Leo Spitz, the financial wizard of Universal. "He's going against all his religious training and has periods when he loses his voice, and it terrifies him. And he is not famous as an actor but a singer. . . . That's no excuse for him behaving so outrageously, but you're both liberals, and maybe with your ideals of brotherhood you can bring yourself to understand the reasons that are making him behave the way he did."

Shelley acquiesced and showed up the next day for shooting, but Frank was unrepentant. They rehearsed their scene, at the end of which he was supposed to look into the camera and say, "I'll have a cup of coffee and leave you two lovebirds alone." Instead, when the cameras started rolling, Frank changed the dialogue. "I'll go have a cup of Jack Daniel's or I'm going to pull that blond broad's hair out by its black roots," he said. Shelley slammed him over the head and stormed off the set, refusing to leave her home for two days. Finally, she received a tearful call from Nancy Sinatra begging her to go back to the studio to finish the picture. Nancy said: "Shelley, Frank doesn't get the twenty-five thousand dollars for the picture. The bank might foreclose the mortgage on the house. My children are going to be out in the street. Please finish the picture or they won't give me the twenty-five thousand dollars."

Again, Shelley relented and returned to the studio to finish the film, but she and Frank did not part friends.

Despite Frank's feelings of guilt about leaving his home, he finally decided to push Nancy hard for a divorce. After giving her a mink coat for her birthday, he pleaded for his freedom. She still remained unconvinced that he was sure of what he wanted, but this time he convinced her. "If I cannot get a divorce, where is there for me to go and what is there for me to do?" he asked. Nancy gave in. She notified her attorney of her decision and then called the press.

"Yes, we have come to a decision—the attorneys are working on it now," she said on May 29, 1951. "This is what Frank wants, and I've said yes. I refused him a divorce for a long time because I thought he would come back to his home. . . . I am now convinced that a divorce is the only way for my happiness as well as Frank's. I think it is better for the children too."

When reporters asked him if Nancy's decision now left him free to marry Ava, he snarled: "I'll flatten you if you ask me one more question about that. That's purely personal."

Three months later, Nancy still had not filed for divorce, so when Frank and Ava left for an Acapulco vacation in August, the press assumed that he was going to obtain a quick Mexican divorce and marry Ava, and they turned out in force to cover the story. When Frank saw all the reporters waiting for him at the Los Angeles airport, he refused to board the plane until they had been cleared from the runway. But the newsmen refused to move, and so Frank sprinted past them to the plane. The enterprising journalists had already found out that he had booked reservations in the names of A. L. Guest (Ava Lavinia, who was to be his guest) and Bob Burns (Frank's manager). At a layover in El Paso, the couple were again surrounded by the press. By the time Frank and Ava arrived in Mexico City, Frank was seething.

"Why can't you guys leave us alone?" he shouted. "This is silly. You can tell stateside for me that what we do is our own damn business. It's a fine thing when we can't go on vacation without being chased."

When a photographer took his picture in Acapulco, he exploded. His Mexican bodyguard, later identified by the United Press correspondent as a killer with a long record of murders, threatened to shoot the newsman if he didn't give up the camera.

A policeman took the camera and gave it to Frank, who destroyed the film and threw the camera back to the photographer.

"I told you guys to leave me alone," he screamed. "This is a private affair of my own. I don't have to talk to anyone. It wasn't the press who made me famous. It was my singing and the American public."

Frank turned on a reporter who was still taking notes.

"You son of a bitch," he yelled.

"Careful, Frankie," said the reporter. "We'll print this in the States."

"You miserable crumb . . . print that, you son of a bitch."

"We'll be glad to," said the reporter.

The story appeared in the United States the next day,

which further infuriated Sinatra, and, after three days, he and Ava cut short their stay and returned.

By the time their private plane landed at Los Angeles International Airport, the Hollywood press corps was waiting for them.

After clearing customs, he and Ava rushed for the black Cadillac convertible that Bobby Burns had left at the airport for them. "Kill that light," Frank screamed at the photographers. "Kill that light."

Jumping into the car, he started the engine, then headed straight for the reporters. The tires screeched. He almost hit several of them as he careened toward the runway, throwing airport officers into a panic. As he reached the airport gate, a photographer named William Eccles was standing with his camera cocked. Sinatra steered the car directly at him, grazing his leg with the bumper of the car.

"Next time I'll kill you," Frank screamed out the window. "I'll kill you."

"He turned the car into me and tried to scare me away," said Eccles. "I figured he'd swerve away from me, so I shot the picture and I didn't move. He slammed on the brakes, and at the last minute I jumped. I went up over the fender and rolled off on my stomach, dropping my camera. It was a hit-run case. I could have sued for money, but I wasn't after that. I was after respect for the press. I demanded a letter of apology. We got the letter a few days later."

Frank explained: "Maybe my car did brush a photographer's leg. I don't know. It was a madhouse. All we were trying to do was get away and they rushed the car. It was lucky someone didn't get killed."

Days later, Frank was in Reno establishing Nevada residency and singing at the Riverside Hotel. He'd also accepted a two-week engagement at the Desert Inn in Las Vegas. He was determined to force Nancy's hand by getting a Nevada divorce at the end of six weeks. On this trip, he made a concerted effort to get along with the press. In fact, he astounded Reno reporters by inviting all of them to his hotel suite, where he announced his plans. A few days later, Ava arrived to stay with him, and again he invited the press in to say that they would be married as soon as he got a divorce.

Over the Labor Day weekend, the couple went to Lake Tahoe with Hank Sanicola and his wife, Paula. Late in the evening of August 31, 1951, after a few hours of drinking and gambling at the Christmas Tree restaurant, Frank and Ava had another one of their terrible fights. It ended with Ava's hurrying back to Hollywood while Frank, despondent and depressed, returned to his chalet at the Cal-Neva Lodge and took an overdose of sleeping pills.

His valet, George Jacobs, found him in a stupor. Jacobs immediately called Sanicola, who summoned a doctor to pump Frank's stomach. The doctor, John Wesley Field, did not recognize Frank because he had recently grown a small mustache. Besides, as the doctor later told the sheriff, Frank identified himself as Henry Sanicola.

With George and Hank in the room, the doctor examined Frank's heart and pulse, which were normal but slow, and prescribed salts to induce vomiting and a stimulant to counteract the sleeping pills. Then, as required by law, he reported the incident to the sheriff, who sent a deputy sheriff to investigate. Three days later, the incident became national news, but by the time reporters showed up to ask questions, Frank and Ava were reunited and sitting together holding hands.

"I did not try and commit suicide," said Frank. "I just had a bellyache. Suicide is the farthest thought from my mind. What will you guys think of next to write about me?"

The reporters wrote what they were told: Frank didn't feel well, so he took "a couple" of sleeping pills, which produced an allergic reaction. "That's all there was to it—honest," he said.

Years later, George Jacobs confirmed that Frank had indeed tried to commit suicide that night over Ava Gardner. "Thank God, I was there to save him," he said. "Miss G. was the one great love of his life, and if he couldn't have her, he didn't want to live no more."

Frank was beset by a wife who wouldn't let go, children begging him to come home, and a lover angry about the bad publicity they were receiving and impatient to get married. In frustration, he lashed out at the press.

Ava, too, despised the press, but, understanding its power and influence, she always smiled for photographers and gave reporters some kind of a quotation. She insisted that Frank make an effort to get along with them, and he promised he would.

His reformation lasted only a few days. When his Nevada divorce became final a few weeks later, he became so enraged when he saw reporters waiting for him that he forgot his promise to Ava and called them all "newspaper bums."

"Why should I give the newspapers anything? I ought to give a cocktail party for the press and put a Mickey Finn in every glass," he said, prompting a headline that read: BELLIGERENT SINATRA GETS DIVORCE, SCORNS REPORTERS.

As soon as Frank was granted a Nevada divorce, Nancy filed legal papers objecting and refused to withdraw her objection until he agreed to pay her $40,000 in back alimony. Frank capitulated to every one of her financial demands, promising to pay her $65,000 immediately after she received a California divorce and $21,000 more by December 31, 1952, or she would have the right to take over the one asset he had left, the house in Palm Springs.

On October 31, 1951, Nancy was granted an interlocutory decree of divorce in Santa Monica after testifying to Frank's many acts of mental cruelty. Fifteen minutes later, the rejected wife left the court a rich woman.

Within a day, Frank and Ava obtained a marriage license in Philadelphia and vowed to be married privately—no press—at the home of Isaac "Ike" Levy, one of the founders of CBS. Manie Sacks, who was also from Philadelphia, helped Frank make arrangements for the secret Monday evening nuptials. Levy locked the marriage license in his office safe, and Mrs. Levy hired one of the city's best caterers and florists for the occasion. She told her decorator to get the Levys' Germantown mansion ready for twenty guests, and swore all the maids and butlers to secrecy.

On the Saturday night before the wedding, Frank and Ava invited Pamela and James Mason to a dinner celebration at The Colony in New York City. Later, they went to a Sugar Hill nightclub, where Ava soon decided that Frank was paying too much attention to a pretty woman sitting nearby. "It looks like I'm through with him," she said to Mrs. Mason. "I can't even trust him on the eve of our wedding."

Blinded by jealousy, she screamed at Frank and he at her. With a melodramatic flourish she yanked off her six-carat diamond engagement ring and threw it across the room. "Let's just call off this fucking wedding," she said, flouncing out of the club.

Frank ran after her, but Ava had already disappeared to the nightspots of Harlem. By the time he got back to the Hampshire House, where they were staying, she had moved out. Frank started drinking and called Manie Sacks. "The wedding's off," he said, "and what was to have been a celebration is a shambles." Sacks was now in the uncomfortable position of having to call Ike Levy. When talking to reporters later, Levy was exasperated.

"Make no mistake about it," he said. "There will positively be no marriage here today! They're like this war in Korea. They're always battling and getting nowhere."

It took the intercession of Axel Stordahl, James Mason, and Ava's sister, Bappie, but by Monday afternoon Frank and Ava had made up. That night, they went to Hoboken for one of Dolly Sinatra's famous Italian dinners.

"I don't even know the names of some of the things we had—chicken like you've never tasted in your life, some wonderful little meat things rolled in dough, and just about every Italian goody you can imagine," said Ava.

With the wedding on again, the secrecy was tightened, but reporters soon found out, by asking the city's top caterer, that it was to take place in Philadelphia on Wednesday evening, November seventh. This time it was Manie Sacks's brother, Lester, who volunteered his home for the event. That Wednesday, reporters in New York City waited outside the Hampshire House until Ava came out with Axel Stordahl, Frank's best man, and got into a waiting limousine. A few minutes later, Frank came out with Axel's wife, June Hutton, Ava's matron of honor.

"No questions, no questions," he said, brushing by the newsmen and putting his hand over the lens of a Movietone television camera just as the cameraman began filming the departure. The wedding party, which included Ben Barton, Frank's music publishing partner, and Dick Jones, an ex-Dorsey arranger, left for Philadelphia, where it was raining. When the limousine pulled up in front of Lester Sachs's fieldstone home, Frank saw the reporters standing in the drizzle.

"How did those creeps know where we were?" he yelled. "I don't want no circus here. I'll knock the first guy who attempts to get inside on his ass—and I mean it!"

Ava ran into the house, pulling Frank behind her. They were given a written request from photographers for pictures and a little cooperation. Frank ran back outside, shouting, "Okay, who sent the note? Which one?" He pointed from one photographer to the other. "Did you? Did you? You're not going to get any pictures. You'll get shots from the commercial photographer [Irving Haberman from CBS] when he gets around to it."

"I'll take my own pictures," said the note-sender.

"I'll betcha five hundred dollars you don't," yelled Frank. "If you do, I'll knock you flat on your ass."

An hour later, the twenty-nine-year-old bride walked down the steps on the arm of Manie Sacks. She wore a cocktail-length mauve and gray gown with a strapless top of pink taffeta.

"I was so nervous and excited," she said. "When Manie and I started down the stairs, he slipped, and we slid about three stairs before we regained our footing. But we did make it down the rest of the way, and as soon as I saw Frank standing there, I wasn't nervous anymore. He looked wonderful in his blue suit and gray tie and so composed. But he told me later he had the biggest lump in his throat. And all of a sudden I was in front of Judge Sloane."

They exchanged thin platinum rings, and seconds after the magistrate pronounced them man and wife, the thirty-six-year-old groom kissed his bride. Turning to the twenty assembled guests, he broke into a big smile. "Well," he said. "We finally made it. We finally made it."

Ava raced across the room and threw her arms around her new mother-in-law. Dolly promptly burst into tears and patted Ava's arm affectionately. She had favored the marriage from the very beginning. "I love that little girl," Dolly said. "She's brought my Frankie back to me."

Staunchly defending Frank and Ava, Dolly said, "I'd like to tell those hypocrites who send me letters without signing their names that say 'Aren't you ashamed, Mrs. Sinatra, aren't you ashamed that your boy divorced his wife and left three children just so he could marry that actress?' I'd like to tell them that Frank loves his three children as much as he loves anything else in the world—that I, his mother, am proud that he married a wonderful girl like his Ava."

Ava was the one and only woman in Frank's life Dolly truly loved, for Ava immediately became "famiglia" (family) —the beloved "figlia" (daughter-in-law). Dolly had tried to maintain cordial relations with Big Nancy because she wanted to see her grandchildren, but she gave her heart to Ava and quickly forgave her for not being Italian or Catholic. After all, Ava was an international beauty, of exotic plumage, not a drab little peahen like Nancy. Since the premiere of *Show Boat*, Ava had become one of the biggest movie stars in the world, and as such was the only woman good enough to marry Dolly's son, especially at this point in his life. With Ava beside him, he could scale the heights again. Dolly knew that Ava was already doing her part to help revive his movie career.

Besides, Frank was going to sing the following month for Prince Philip and Princess Elizabeth in London's Coliseum. To Dolly, Ava was the kind of woman a man could proudly introduce to royalty; Nancy was better left at home cooking and taking care of children. Years later, when Frank first performed before the British Queen, he said he was so excited that he called Dolly in Hoboken. "Guess who your son was with tonight?" he shouted. "The Queen of England!" His mother was unimpressed. "Lucky Queen," she said.

Ava enjoyed Frank's tough, profane, funny mother, and the two women spent many hours together shopping and drinking and laughing. The barefoot girl from Grabtown and the Hoboken midwife had a lot in common. Both were Christmas babies. Ava's birthday was December 24 and Dolly's December 25. Both were ardent Democrats and uninhibited. "They both cursed in Technicolor," said a friend of the family. Both adored Frankie and believed that he was the best singer in the world. Dolly was even known to smash a chair over the head of anyone who disagreed. Unlike the first Mrs. Frank Sinatra, Ava was not ashamed to visit Hoboken and walk down its blue-collar streets so her mother-in-law could show her off to all the star-struck neighbors and merchants.

"This marriage is blessed with good luck," said Dolly, an inveterate gambler. "You got married at the seventh hour on the seventh day of the eleventh month. Seven, seven, eleven. You can't miss."

Frank agreed with his mother. "We're over all our crises now," he said. "We have nothing to worry about anymore."

Ecstatic after the wedding ceremony, Ava went upstairs to change into her brown Christian Dior going-away outfit, her brown alligator shoes and purse, and the sapphire-blue mink stole that Frank had given her as a wedding present. He was already wearing the gold locket she had given him with a St. Christopher medal on one side, a St. Francis medal on the other, and her picture inside. They were going to honeymoon in Cuba for three days at the Hotel Nacional, which was owned in part by the crime syndicate.

When the bride came downstairs, Manie Sacks took her aside for a few seconds. "Look after him, Ava," he said. "He's had some hard knocks and he's very fragile. It isn't going to be easy living with a man whose career is in a slump."

"I'll do anything to make him happy," said Ava.

"Then," said Manie, "help him get back his self-confidence."

13

Both Frank and Ava came from families in which the mother was the dominant force and the father was sweet, passive, and ineffectual. What Ava did not know and Frank could not articulate was the importance of his not being emasculated the way his quiet little father had been. Marty Sinatra, racked by asthma all his life, rarely talked when Dolly was around. As much as Frank loved his father, he must have seen him as lacking a measure of masculinity for always yielding to his overpowering wife.

During his twelve years with Nancy, Frank had been in a traditional marriage: he was the breadwinner, she was the homemaker. There had never been any question about who was in charge. Now he was starting a totally different relationship: his career would be secondary to his wife's, and he would have to fight to assert his command. In a sense, he had married a surrogate Dolly, for Ava was almost as tough and independent as his mother. Although she suffered from deep insecurity ("Ava feared she could not really hold a man," said Hank Sanicola), she appeared so aggressive and combative at times that Jimmy Van Heusen soon called her "The Man." Having to pay Nancy $150,000 a year plus a percentage of his earnings made Frank financially dependent on Ava. It was her salary from MGM that paid most of their bills. She was the one with the flourishing career, and when the studio sent her to Africa to make *Mogambo*, Frank, who had nothing else to do, went along and carried her bags like a faithful courtier.

"Ava loved Frank, but not the way he loved her," said Hank Sanicola. "Twice he went chasing her to Africa, wasting his own career. . . . He needs a great deal of love. He wants it twenty-four hours a day. He must have people around—Frank is that kind of guy."

Ava never understood Frank's need to surround himself with an entourage, most of whom were Italian men like himself. Together, they comprised a modern version of the storefront club of the Italian neighborhoods they had grown up in. Their fathers and uncles went to those clubs to play cards and get away from their wives. Being with other men gave Frank an audience and helped to reinforce his sense of masculinity, but Ava hated to have Frank's men hanging around all the time, and this irritated him. He was accustomed to the good Italian wife who simply went into the kitchen and started cooking spaghetti for everyone when he brought the whole band home with him.

"The problems were never in the bedroom," said Ava. "We were always great in bed. The trouble usually started on the way to the bidet." A friend of Ava's explained: "There was a strong physical attraction on both sides, but they couldn't get together on the other things that are necessary in a relationship. Neither gave an inch, though I must say Frank worked harder on the marriage than she did. She's a very selfish girl."

"The trouble with Ava is that her whole concept of life comes from magazine illustrations," said another friend. "She used to come tripping down in the morning, put on a frilly apron, and prepare a five-course breakfast. Then she'd call Frank. He'd come down unshaven and hung over from the night before. He'd growl 'All I want is juice'—and more than likely she'd throw the juice at him."

By the time Frank married Ava, he had little work to do. Although he was still represented by MCA, the agency was no longer helping him. In fact, MCA agents were telling reporters that they had "to wait in line" to collect their commissions.

The dispute over commissions went back many years to the time Frank was singing on radio in a package show that he had put together himself. He was paid fifteen thousand dollars a week for the show, but when MCA demanded a ten percent commission on the gross, as was the practice, he balked. Frank felt that he had done all the work of getting the show, so he should not have to pay a full commission, and agreed to pay only a commission on his *net* earnings from the show. Because he was such an important client, MCA agreed. But now the agency was saying he still owed them forty thousand dollars in commissions from that show and implied that a client who was such a deadbeat should be dropped.

Frank laughed when he first heard the rumor. "How can you fire an entertainer who earned $693,000 last year?" he asked. The answer was extraordinary—a public notice in the trade papers declaring that Music Corporation of America no longer represented Frank Sinatra.

"Can you imagine being fired by an agency that never had to sell you?" said Frank. He despised MCA president Lew Wasserman so heartily for cutting him loose that he didn't speak to him for ten years. Wasserman remained unconcerned. MCA was the most powerful agency in the world, and a client like Sinatra, who was so hostile to the press, was a liability.

Without an agency, Frank turned to friends like Manie Sacks for help. And he appealed to Bob Weitman to book him into the Paramount for the opening of *Meet Danny Wilson* in March 1952. The Paramount had been the scene of his greatest box office triumphs, where thousands of bobby-soxers filled the theater and then ran up and down the aisles screaming his name and hurling themselves into the orchestra pit just to get closer to him. Five years later, he could not even fill the balcony.

The day after his opening the headline in the *New York World Telegram and Sun* said it all: GONE ON FRANKIE IN '42; GONE IN '52. The accompanying article was an open letter to the singer from Muriel Fischer. "I saw you last night. But I didn't get 'that old feeling' . . . I sat in the balcony. And I felt kind of lonely. It was so empty. The usher said there were 750 seats in the second balcony—and 749 were unfilled. . . . Later I stood outside the stage entrance. About a dozen people were waiting around. Three girls were saying 'Frankie' soft and swoonlike. I asked, 'How do you like Frankie?' They said, 'Frankie Laine, he's wonderful.' I heard a girl sighing, 'I'm mad about him,' so I asked her who. 'Johnnie Ray,' she cried. All of a sudden, Mr. Sinatra, I felt sort of old!'"

Frank played the Chez Paree in Chicago, a nightclub with seating capacity for 1,200, and brought in only 150 patrons. Columbia Records refused to renew his contract, and his fan clubs disbanded. His engagement at the Cocoanut Grove in Los Angeles was embarrassing, especially for some of his friends who didn't want to be seen attending. Sammy Cahn cringed when Frank gave him credit from the stage for some special material he'd written. "Believe me," said Cahn, "I could have done without it."

Although no one wanted to write stories about Frank anymore, he kept his publicity firm on a monthly retainer, but complained because he wasn't getting press coverage. Press agent Budd Granoff offered to reduce his fee, but pride kept Frank from paying a lesser rate than the other stars Granoff was handling.

"He was paying us four hundred dollars a week, and he felt it was too much money because he wasn't working and didn't have any money," said Granoff. "So I went to see him and said, 'Frank, you don't want to see anybody, you don't want to do any interviews, you're not doing anything, so why don't we cut the thing in half for the time being?' He got very angry. Referring to Dean Martin and Jerry Lewis, he said, 'How much is the skinny Jew-boy and the dumb Wop paying you?' I said four hundred dollars. He said, 'What is the fat boy paying you,' meaning Mario Lanza. I said four hundred dollars. He was very angry, very hurt. 'You don't change the fee,' he said. 'I change the fee, and I'll pay you four hundred dollars.' "

If Frank's career was sputtering, Ava's was soaring. She had been chosen to plant her hands and feet in wet cement in the forecourt of Grauman's Chinese Theater, a Hollywood honor accorded only the biggest stars, and one that Frank would not receive for another thirteen years. Later, MGM offered her a new ten-year contract for twelve pictures at $100,000 per picture. True to her word, she insisted that Metro hire Frank as her leading man for one of those movies. After the box office failure of *Meet Danny Wilson*, Universal had refused to renew his option for a second film despite his pleas, but he kept telling Ava that all he needed was one good role to put him over the top again. Dedicated to helping him in any way she could, Ava refused to sign her new contract until the studio lawyers added a clause entitled Services of Frank Sinatra, which stated:

(a) Should we buy the rights to and produce a photoplay based on "St. Louis Woman," we agree that she will be assigned to do this picture and we further agree that we will employ Frank Sinatra to appear in the photoplay.

(b) Should we not acquire the rights to "St. Louis Woman" or produce a photoplay based on this property, then we agree that at some time prior to the expiration of her contract, we will do a picture with her in which Frank Sinatra will also appear.

The next contractual battle was over inserting a pregnancy clause that would protect her from penalties should she be unable to work because of pregnancy. She had already announced that she and Frank wanted to have a baby. Actually, he wanted several. "I would like a dozen kids," he said.

Ava was convinced that most of Frank's misery was due to his rancorous press relations. She begged him to stop slugging reporters and cursing photographers, saying that he needed them to become a star again. But the last thing Frank wanted was to entrust his fate to the press.

"The newspapers—they broke up my home," he said. "They broke up my family. They ruined my life."

Shortly after his violent clash with reporters at the wedding, one of his publicists, Mack Miller, had conferred with him for three hours.

"Miller told Frank that if he didn't stop fighting with the press, he'd have to give him up," said a friend. "Miller said he wasn't worth what Frank was paying him if this kind of thing continued. Ava backed Miller up. She's no yes-woman."

Months later, Ava turned to Manie Sacks and together they convinced Frank that he no longer had any choice but to make amends with the press. The apologia was written by Irving Fein under Frank's name in a two-part series for the Hearst papers entitled "Frankly Speaking" in which Frank appeared to go down on his knees with his head bowed.

"The press generally has been wonderful to me, and I know that without their help I never could have become famous or earned more money than I ever believed existed when I was a slum kid in Hoboken," he wrote. "My only excuse for being abrupt and curt . . . is that I was nervous and distraught from the events of the past year."

He dragged out all the hoary tales of his so-called "slum"

childhood in Hoboken with its "race wars" and "vicious gang fights" and his "poor, poor" parents who "needed whatever money I could bring into the house," which drove him to "hooking candy from the corner store, then little things from the five-and-dime, then change from cash registers, and finally, we were up to stealing bicycles."

This, of course, shocked Dolly Sinatra, whose abortion earnings combined with her husband's wages had made her family one of the most comfortable on Garden Street. Having bought Frank's shiny new bicycles as a child, his new clothes, his car, his phonograph, and paid his charge account at Geismer's department store, and having given him an allowance which paid for presents for his friends, she was stunned by these recollections under her son's name. "I didn't know any of those things he said he did," she said. "I brought him up right."

Frank was equally imaginative about his Mafia friendships with Willie Moretti, Frank Costello, and Joe Fischetti. He asserted he barely knew Lucky Luciano, and despite the Italian police report of finding a solid gold cigarette case inscribed "To my dear pal, Charlie, from his friend, Frank Sinatra," he denied ever giving Luciano any gift. He cavalierly dismissed his twelve-year marriage to Nancy, saying that he had mistaken friendship for love. And he strained people's credulity when he said he had not dated Ava until after his separation from Nancy.

In a final grovel to the press he ended "his" series by saying, "Well, there it is. That's my side of the story, and I must say I feel better for having gotten it off my chest. I know that I never meaningly hurt anyone, and for any wrongs I may have done through emotional acts or spur-of-the-moment decisions, I humbly apologize."

"That should have told you right there that Frank didn't write that thing," said Nick Sevano. "He's never apologized to anyone in his life. It's just not in him."

The ghosted articles reflected how far Frank had fallen by 1952. With his career in tatters, he was willing to do anything to reclaim his stardom, and Ava vowed to stick with him through the climb back even if it jeopardized her own career. To prove it, she went on suspension at Metro to be able to accompany him to Honolulu for a booking. When they returned, the studio lent Ava to Twentieth Century Fox for *The Snows of Kilimanjaro*. It was based on Hemingway's short story about a mortally wounded big-game hunter who recalls the story of his life as he lies dying in a camp at the base of Mt. Kilimanjaro. Hemingway had asked that Ava be given the role of Cynthia, the Lost Twenties girl whom the big-game hunter had once loved and who dies during the Spanish Civil War. Ava was thrilled with the role, but Frank said she had to turn it down so she could be with him in New York.

"But it's the perfect part for me," she said.

"The perfect part for you is being my wife," said Frank.

Ava confided her problem to the scriptwriter, Casey Robinson. "She told me that Frank was so low, his career was so hopeless, that he needed her to go with him to New York, where he had a nightclub engagement," he said. "He insisted on it. It was quite a problem. So I sat down with Henry King [the director], went over the schedule, and changed things around. We had to promise to shoot Ava's part in ten days. On that promise, Sinatra gave a reluctant okay.

"Came the ninth day of shooting. We had only one more sequence to do. Frank kept calling her on the set and making her life pretty darn miserable. I like Frank now, but at the time I hated the little bastard because he was making my girl unhappy. Now I understand him, he was so beaten and insecure. Then came the last scene, the scene on the battlefield in Spain where Ava is dying. There was a problem: we had a great many extras, four or five hundred in all, and to satisfy the ten-day agreement we'd have to shoot into the night, which would have been horribly expensive. We decided to go over the ten days and break the agreement. When King and I told Ava, all hell broke loose. She became hysterical. She called New York, and Frank was furious with her. God knows how we got through that last day."

Ava signed autographs as "Ava Sinatra" and took every opportunity to defend her husband to the press. "Frankie's a great artist and terribly misunderstood, and even if I weren't married to him, I'd defend him," she told Hollywood columnist Sheilah Graham.

"Yes, I concede he has a quick temper, but if the press, and particularly the photographers, would stop baiting him for the sake of a story or picture, there wouldn't be so much tension in his relations with the press. It's mob psychology. One person or writer takes a crack at him, and others pick it up because it seems the thing to do. They know Frank can be needled, so they let him have it."

Years later, Ava reflected on what was happening to her husband when all he had was fading pride and a frayed voice. His moods swung from childish self-pity and the need to be reassured to a swaggering arrogance of barked orders and commands. She indicated that he resented her stardom and her possession of a much bigger name than his. But she also said they were happiest then because he was dependent on her.

"Yes, Frank was really up against it at that time," said Ava in 1982. "Unknown to the public, he was having serious problems with his voice, and his agents were having difficulty booking him into the top night spots. It seems hard to believe now, but he was having to play saloons and dates that were way beneath him."

She accompanied him on every one of these demeaning engagements, including one in Hoboken at the Union Club in September 1952. It was probably the final affront, illustrating how far he had fallen from his days as the bobby-soxers' idol when, in 1947, Hoboken had proclaimed a Frank Sinatra Day in his honor, presented him with the key to the city, and staged a grand parade led by his father's fire engine. This time there was no such acclaim.

"It was a Fireman's Ball in the fall of 1952 and Frank came because his dad asked him to be there," said his childhood friend, Tony Mac. "He came with Ava Gardner in a limousine and his mom made sure there were cops with billy clubs to help him get through the crowd. I remember the date well because Jimmy "Doo Doo" Shannon was dying of cancer, and this was about three weeks before he died. Doo Doo was one of the guys from the neighborhood, and Frank ate at his house all through grammar school. So we all went to see Frankie that night. I remember saying, 'How about coming to see Doo Doo Shannon. He's dying.' Frank said he just couldn't make it and leave Ava waiting in the limousine. He didn't have the time.

"He sang onstage that night and hit some clinkers, and so people booed him and threw fruit and stuff, kidding around. When he was singing on WAAT Radio, he hit clinkers then, too, and we laughed at him, but now, well, it was different. Oh, did he get mad."

Afterward Frank ran offstage and asked Tony Costello, one of the policemen, to show him out the back way. "I don't want to have to go out through there," he said, nodding peevishly to the crowd.

"I led him down the back steps to the street. There were no fans, nothing. As we shook hands and said good-bye, Frank said, 'Tony, I'll never come back and do another thing for the people of Hoboken as long as I live.' "

The next night Frank was singing at Bill Miller's Riviera in Fort Lee, New Jersey, and Ava, sitting ringside, saw Marilyn Maxwell walk in. As soon as Frank walked onstage and started singing, Ava was convinced that he was singing for no one else but his former lover. Hurling curses in the air, she stormed out of the club and boarded a plane for Hollywood. When she arrived, she sent her wedding ring to Frank with a bitter note. Sammy Davis, Jr., later saw Frank walking down a New York street all by himself, no fans, no friends, no entourage. "I've got problems, baby," Frank said. "That's what happens when you get hung up on a chick."

Frank also confided in Earl Wilson. "I never so much as looked at another gal since Ava. I'm nuts about her and I don't think it's dead, but it certainly is all up in the air now."

But he told other reporters that the disagreement was trivial. "We have a career problem," he said. "I'm going to see my wife in about ten days in Hollywood. I think everything will work out all right."

Frank followed Ava to the West Coast, but the volatile union erupted again days later in Palm Springs. Ava, who seemed to thrive on danger, laughed as she recalled the hair-pulling, glass-shattering event thirty years later.

"Frank and I were having one of our fights, as if that was anything new," she said. "Most of our fights were funny, but that one was the funniest of the lot.

"I was always deciding I couldn't go on living with him, and this was one of our spells apart when he was trying to talk me into going back. He told me that he had let Lana [Turner] have the house in Palm Springs for a week, and wanted me to go away with him someplace, but I had already arranged to be with my sister, Bappie. As usual, Frank didn't like any plan that didn't include him, so he started his usual line: 'Swell. You just go off with your sister, and I'll be in Palm Springs fucking Lana Turner.'

"I didn't really believe him, but I did start to think about it, and I decided I didn't like it too much. So I grabbed the car, collected Bappie, and off we drove to Palm Springs. As we got near the house, I suddenly saw Frank's car cruising around outside as if he was keeping watch on the place. As we got nearer, he drove away.

"When we got into the house, we found Lana there with Ben Cole, who was also a friend of mine, and they both seemed surprised and a little embarrassed to see me. They asked if I wanted them to go, and I said, 'Hell, no. There's plenty of room for all of us.'

"I hadn't been there more than ten minutes when the door bursts open and in storms Frank looking like Al Capone and the Boston Strangler rolled into one, and starts to abuse everyone present, mostly me. He seemed to be under the impression that we had been carving him up behind his back. He yelled at all of us and called Lana 'that two-bit whore,' and she burst into tears and got very small and said 'I'm not going to be talked about like that' in a very little-girl voice just like we were all in a Shirley Temple movie.

"Frank then said to Lana, Ben, Bappie, and me: 'Get the *hell* out of my house!' And I yelled, 'Fine! But since this is also *my* house, too, I'm gonna take out of it everything that belongs to me.'

"I started taking down pictures from the wall and Frank exploded. He grabbed everything I said was mine and hurled it outside onto the lawn. It was hysterical. Lana and Ben, who were both very frightened, fled from the house to look for somewhere else to stay, and when they came back for their things several hours later, we were still at it, and by that time the place was crawling with cops because the neighbors had called the police about all the noise. In the end, the local police chief, Gus Kettman, had to be called to keep the peace between us."

Lana Turner has her own vivid recollection of that Saturday, October 18, 1952. She said Ava had arrived unannounced as she and Benton Cole were sitting at the pool. "I was all the more startled to see her because she and Frank were separated at the time," said Lana, who apologized for the intrusion, saying that Frank had lent her the house. "'He didn't mention you'd be around.'

"'Oh, screw him,' said Ava. 'He doesn't know I'm here.'

"'Do you want us to leave?'

"'Oh, hell, no. There's room for all of us.'"

The three of them sat by the pool together and then went into the kitchen for fried chicken when a crazed Frank Sinatra burst through the back door with his eyes blazing and his face a Day-Glo red.

" 'I bet you two broads have really been cutting me up,' he said. We couldn't say a word, and I just kept shaking my head no because we hadn't even discussed him," said Lana. "With that he pointed to Ava and growled, 'You! Get in the bedroom. I want to talk to you!' With a shrug Ava headed for the bedroom I'd been using. Frank followed her, and before long, harsh words came from that bedroom, and a crash, as though a piece of furniture was being thrown."

Lana and Ben ran out of the house but, according to Lana, returned a few hours later concerned about what might have happened to Ava. "It was dark when we arrived at Frank's place, and a strange sight greeted us," she said. "Police cars were drawn up in front of the house, with red lights blinking, radios squawking. The glare of spotlights illuminated the house. The sounds of battle inside, I learned later, had grown so loud that neighbors had called the police."

Having already rented another house for the week, Lana and Ben asked Ava to join them, knowing that she could not stay with Frank. That evening, Frank moved into Jimmy Van Heusen's house, and Bappie took her battered sister to stay with Lana and Ben. "We did what we could to make Ava comfortable," said Lana. "Poor Ava. She was badly shaken, and after my own grim experience, I could sympathize with her humiliation. But alone in my room I was surprised that I also felt sorry for Frank. It was a bad time for him. His career had slipped badly, and he was losing Ava."

The fact that the police had been called to settle a dispute involving Frank Sinatra, Ava Gardner, and Lana Turner hit the newspapers with headlines that caused everyone in Hollywood to speculate about what had *really* happened to trigger such violence on Frank's part.

BOUDOIR FIGHT HEADS FRANKIE AND AVA TO COURTS screamed the *Los Angeles Daily Mirror*.

SINATRA-AVA BOUDOIR ROW BUZZES roared the *Los Angeles Times*.

Neither story stated exactly what had happened except that Frank had ordered Artie Shaw's second and fourth ex-wives (Ava and Lana) out of his Palm Springs house after a "dispute" and the police had been called "to restore peace." With so much left to the imagination and no comments from anyone involved, the only possible explanation for many people was that Frank had found Lana and Ava in bed together and had become so enraged by their lesbianism that he threw them both out and then started tearing the house apart. The whispered scandal was repeated with graphic detail for years and years until it became an accepted fact. "A lot of sick, vile rumors grew out of that incident," said Lana many years later.

Heartsick about what had happened, Frank called Ava frequently, but she refused to answer the phone and had the number changed the next day so he couldn't reach her. With all their plans in ruins—their trip to Ava's home in North Carolina, their trip to Africa, their baby—Frank was so distraught that, according to Jimmy Van Heusen, he often vomited. Frank called Earl Wilson and begged him to print his plea for a reconciliation. When Ava saw the column—"Frankie Ready to Surrender; Wants Ava Back, Any Terms"—she called Frank.

No one hoped more for a reconciliation than Adlai Stevenson, the Democratic nominee for President in 1952, who was running against Dwight Eisenhower and Richard M. Nixon. Nixon had charged that Stevenson would not end the war in Korea, which was America's most vexing foreign issue. He also said that a Democratic victory in November would mean "more Alger Hisses, more atomic spies, more crises." Hollywood's Democratic celebrities had rallied in support of Stevenson ("Madly for Adlai"), and Ava and Frank were among those touched by the magic of the man from Illinois. They had promised to make a joint appearance for him at the Hollywood-for-Stevenson rally on Monday, October 27, 1952, a few days before the presidential election. Ava was to introduce Frank, who had promised to sing "The Birth of the Blues" and "The House I Live In," but after the Palm Springs explosion, no one knew whether the battling Sinatras would show up, and if they did, who would introduce them to each other.

More than four thousand people jammed into the Palladium Ballroom that October night, and cheered when Ava walked onstage in a black satin strapless gown and a mink stole. Clutching the microphone, she said, "I can't do anything myself, but I can introduce a wonderful, wonderful man. I'm a great fan of his myself. Ladies and gentlemen, my husband, Frank Sinatra!"

Frank sang beautifully and said a few words for the candidate. He even posed for photographers with his arm around Ava. Stevenson lost the election, but he polled more votes than any previous losing presidential candidate in the nation's history. His greatest achievement, according to the Hollywood press, was reuniting Frankie and Ava.

Resuming their plans, they announced that they were leaving in a few days for Nairobi, where Ava would star with Clark Gable in *Mogambo*. Frank, who was without work, had agreed to accompany his wife, but he had instructed his agents to cable him when casting started on *From Here to Eternity*. Having read James Jones's novel about World War II—"It was an adventure-type story, which is the kind I like"—Frank saw himself as Maggio, the scrappy little private, and was convinced that the part would restore his career. He talked of nothing else.

Before they left, Ava phoned Joan Cohn, the wife of Harry Cohn, head of Columbia Pictures, to ask if she could see her. Mrs. Cohn said that she was sick in bed with the flu, but Ava insisted. "Please, Joan," she said. "It's very, very important."

"That was a very brave thing for Ava to call me like that and then insist on seeing me when I was ill," said Joan Cohn Harvey, "but she had a mission, and nothing was going to stop her. She came to the house alone in the evening and said that Frank must never know that she had been here. We both knew how much he needed and wanted to be the boss in that marriage.

"She took off her shoes and put her feet up on the coffee table. I was astounded because she had the tiniest little feet in the world for such a big girl. She was so very beautiful, but I wondered how those little feet ever held her up. I asked if she wanted something to drink, and was so surprised when she asked for vodka.

" 'God, Ava,' I said. 'You're going to ruin your skin.'

" 'What the hell,' she said."

After taking a few sips, Ava came straight to the point. "Joan, I've come to ask you a big favor. I want you to get Harry to give Frank the Maggio role in *From Here to Eternity*. He wants that part more than anything in the world, and he's got to have it, otherwise I'm afraid he'll kill himself. Please, promise me that you'll help. I'll do anything. Just get him a test. Please, Joan. Just a test."

Mrs. Cohn was stunned. It was absolutely unheard of for the wife of a star to come begging like this to the wife of a studio head, especially to the wife of Harry Cohn, who was renowned for being the nastiest man in Hollywood and who, until the war, had kept an autographed photo of Mussolini displayed in his office.

"Frank was at the bottom of the barrel then, and no one wanted him for anything, especially that role," said Joan. "I knew that he'd been pleading with Harry for the part of Maggio, but Harry had completely dismissed him. He thought Frank was nothing but a washed-up song-and-dance man. A has-been crooner. It was pathetic, really. But I was so moved by Ava that night and her devotion to Frank that I promised to help her in any way I could. As soon as I got out of that sick bed, I went to work on Harry."

14

Frank identified with Angelo Maggio, the tough little soldier in James Jones's novel, *From Here to Eternity*, who grinned and boozed and fought his way through the pre–Pearl Harbor army. Ruled by violent pride, the gritty Italian-American GI dies rather than allow the brutality of the stockade to break his spirit. From the moment Frank came across the character in the book, he wanted the role. He knew that this was a once-in-a-lifetime part that could reignite his waning star.

"I just felt it—I just knew it," he said, "and I just couldn't get it out of my head.

"I knew that if a picture was ever made, I was the only actor to play Private Maggio, the funny and sour Italo-American. I knew Maggio. I went to school with him in Hoboken. I was beaten up with him. I might have been Maggio. . . . When I heard that Columbia bought the story, I got Harry Cohn on the phone and asked him for a date for lunch. After we ate, I said to him, 'Harry, I've known you for a long time. You got something I want.'

"Harry said, 'You want to play God?' and I said, 'No, not that. But I want to play Maggio.' And then he looked at me funnylike and said, 'Look, Frank, that's an actor's part, a stage actor's part. You're nothing but a fucking hoofer.' "

Frank pleaded with him for more than an hour, saying he could play Maggio better than he could sing and dance. But for Harry Cohn, the subject was closed. He remembered

Frank's nonsinging performance in *The Miracle of the Bells*, which was a box office failure for MGM, and he wanted no part of it.

"Please, Harry," begged Frank. "I'll pay you if you'll let me play that role."

"Sure, Frank," said Cohn, who knew that Sinatra owed more than $109,000 in back taxes to the Internal Revenue Service. "Sure."

Frank's dreams outran his deficits. "I'm serious about the money, Harry," he said.

"Who mentioned money? But what about the money?"

"I get one hundred fifty thousand a film . . ."

"You *got* one hundred fifty thousand. Not anymore."

"Right," said Frank, "I used to get it, and I don't want anything near that much for Maggio."

"I'm not buying at any price," said Cohn, "but just for the record, what's yours?"

"I'll play Maggio for a thousand a week."

"Jesus, Frank, you want it that bad?" said Cohn. "Well, we'll see. I have some other actors to test first."

Frank called Abe Lastfogel and Sam Weisbrod, his new agents at the William Morris Agency, and told them about his talk with Cohn. He begged them to get him the role even if they had to sign him for fifty dollars a week.

"I'll do it for *nothing*," he said. "For *nothing*. You've just got to get it for me."

Since taking Frank on as a client, both agents had been doggedly trying to arouse interest in him, but everyone knew of his long string of flops and backed off. "Frank smelled like a loser in those days," said Abe Lastfogel, "but I promised him we'd start working on Fred Zinnemann [*High Noon* and *Member of the Wedding*], who was also our client, and had been named to direct *From Here to Eternity*. Fred didn't want to cast Frank in the role of Maggio because he said that everyone would think that he'd bastardized the book and made it into a musical instead of portraying a stark and tragic drama. He preferred the Broadway actor Eli Wallach for the part."

While Lastfogel and Weisbrod tried to persuade Fred Zinnemann, Frank called Buddy Adler, who was producing the picture for Columbia.

"It's an acting part, Frankie," said the producer.

"It's *me*," said Frank. "It's *me*."

Frank also called his friend Jack Entratter, who had left

the Copa and was now in Las Vegas running the Sands Hotel for Frank Costello and Joey Adonis, the two men Entratter had fronted for at the Copacabana in New York. Jack was a close friend of Harry Cohn and went fishing with him every other weekend. Aware of this, Frank begged Jack to talk to Harry about the role. Jack promised to do so, and later told Cohn that Frank wanted to play Maggio. But Harry Cohn had already made up his mind about the casting. He wanted Columbia stars in the movie, and suggested Robert Mitchum to play Sgt. Milton Warden, a role that finally went to Burt Lancaster; Aldo Ray to play Robert E. Lee Prewitt (Montgomery Clift won it); Joan Crawford to play the promiscuous wife of the captain (Deborah Kerr), and Eli Wallach to play Maggio.

Harry Cohn told his wife that he was being swamped with all sorts of appeals on Frank's behalf, even from Hollywood columnists who were writing about Frank's campaign to play the supporting character role with fifth billing in the credits.

Joan Cohn seized the moment to make good on her promise to Ava. "Why not consider Frank for the role?" she asked her husband. "He's Italian and scrawny, so he'd be perfect in the scene where skinny little Maggio has to go up against that great big Sgt. 'Fatso' Judson (Ernest Borgnine)."

"You, too, huh?" said Cohn to his wife. "I just don't think it would work. Besides, I'd have to test Frank, and you know he'd never lower himself for that."

"I bet he would," said Joan Cohn. "I'll bet you anything you want to bet that Frank Sinatra will do a test. Just try him, Harry. A test can't hurt, and then you'll know for sure."

Jonie Taps, a vice-president of Columbia Pictures and one of Cohn's closest associates, also pushed for giving Frank a test. "Harry still didn't like the idea," said Taps. "He said, 'Give me one good reason why I should put him in a picture?' I said, 'You may want Ava Gardner for a picture sometime. She loves Frank and she'll appreciate it.' Ava helped out, too, by giving Harry a call and asking him to cast Frank."

Finally, Harry Cohn called Frank and said that he shouldn't get his hopes up, but if he'd be willing to test for Maggio, he might be considered. Frank was ecstatic and agreed to the test. He waited weeks for Cohn to call him back, but he never heard a word. When Frank stopped by the studio to inquire, he was told that there was nothing definite to tell him yet. Then he read that Cohn and Fred Zinnemann were really interested in Eli Wallach for the role. In despair Frank left with Ava for Africa, telling his agents to cable him if there was any possible hope that he still might be tested. If so, he would fly back to Hollywood on a moment's notice and at his own expense.

The Sinatras flew to Nairobi on November 7, 1952, and celebrated their first wedding anniversary on a stratocruiser ten thousand miles from home. "We felt kinda sorry for ourselves," Frank later wrote in a letter, "but we exchanged our gifts and opened a not-too-chilled bottle of champagne to toast our first milestone." He gave Ava a huge globe-shaped ring studded with diamonds, which he charged to her, and she gave him a thin platinum watch.

"It was quite an occasion for me," she said later. "I had been married twice but never for a whole year." They arrived the next day and were met at the airport by Clark Gable, who whisked them through Kenya's crowded native districts to their bush site, where they lived in an opulent traveling tent complete with native servants and water carriers.

From the first day of shooting, *Mogambo*, a joint British and American production, was beset with unending difficulties. Temperatures soared to 130 degrees in the baked clay wastelands; alkali dust covered everyone; sleep was impossible because of bellowing hippos and howling hyenas. Pregnant, Ava suffered miserable morning sickness and quarreled constantly with Frank, who was bored and restless and unable to think of anything else but the role of Maggio.

To make matters even more unbearable, Ava did not get along with the director, John Ford (*The Grapes of Wrath*, *Tobacco Road*, *How Green Was My Valley*), who was gruff and harsh and refused to treat her like an MGM movie queen. She embarrassed him when he introduced her to the British governor and his wife.

"Ava, why don't you tell the governor what you see in this one-hundred-twenty-pound runt you're married to," Ford said.

"Well," said Ava, "there's only ten pounds of Frank but there's one hundred and ten pounds of cock!"

Ford wanted to kill her, but the governor and his wife roared with laughter. After a few such incidents the director developed a certain appreciation of his star and they soon became good friends. "She was a real trouper," he said later. "She was unhappy over Sinatra, but she worked her ass off just the same. I loved her."

Grace Kelly, too, was shocked at first by Ava's total lack of restraint, her uninhibited swearing, and the way she and Frank would take out their anger toward each other on whoever was standing around. "Ava is such a mess, it's unbelievable," Grace wrote in a letter to a friend. "Right now they are putting up a new tent for her—she just didn't like the other one because it was old—her tent is right next to mine—so I can hear all of the screaming and yelling."

Five days later Frank received a cable from the *From Here to Eternity* producer, Buddy Adler, to appear for a screen test. There was no offer to pay his expenses from Africa to California, but Frank did not hesitate. Charging the round-trip flight to Ava's MGM account, he left immediately for Hollywood.

"For the test, I played the saloon scene where Maggio shakes dice with the olives and the scene where he's found drunk outside the Royal Hawaiian Hotel," he said. "I was scared to death."

Adler was surprised to see Frank less than thirty-six hours after cabling him. "I was a little startled when I gave him the script of the drunk scene and he handed it back. 'I don't need this,' he said. 'I've read it many times.' I didn't think he had a chance anyway, so I said, 'Well, okay.' Since his was the last test of the day, I didn't intend going down on the stage. But I got a call from Fred Zinnemann, 'You'd better come down here. You'll see something unbelievable. I already have it in the camera. I'm not using film this time. But I want you to see it.'

"Frank thought he was making another take—and he was terrific. I thought to myself, if he's like that in the movie, it's a sure Academy Award. But we had to have Harry Cohn's okay on casting, and he was out of town. So Frank went back to Africa."

"I thought I'd collapse waiting for reaction to that test," said Sinatra later. "My agent sent word that Columbia was testing some other fellows, among them some fine stage actors. My chin hit my knees, and I gave up. Ava was wonderful at cheering me up, and said, 'I wish you wouldn't quit just because you got one telegram.' Clark Gable kept saying, 'Relax, skipper. Have a little drink and everything will be all right.' "

When Harry Cohn came back to town, he wanted to meet Eli Wallach and test him for the part. Columbia contacted Peter Witt, Wallach's film agent, and flew the actor in from

New York where he was starring on Broadway in *The Rose Tattoo*.

"That was quite an experience," said Eli Wallach. "I walked into Cohn's office and he said, 'He doesn't look like an Italian. He looks like a Hebe.' I screamed at him. 'Your name is Cohn. How dare you say that to me? I've been playing an Italian—Alvaro Mangiacavallo—for fifteen months now in New York, on the road, and in Los Angeles in Tennessee Williams's play, so don't talk to me about acting, and I've already spent five years in the army, so don't talk to me about the army!'

"I realized a second later that he had said it intentionally to aggravate me, to see if I would behave like the character. Then, of course, the actor part of me came to the fore, and I really let him have it. Then he said, 'You going to sign for seven years?' I said, 'No, I don't do that. I've never signed a seven-year contract.' I don't know if I floored him, but I can tell you that I never had much of a career in the movies."

Cohn told everyone that he wanted Eli Wallach for the role of Maggio, but he was having trouble negotiating with his agent. "By then we had three tests for Maggio—Eli Wallach, Harvey Lembeck, a well-known comedian of that time, and Frank Sinatra," said Daniel Taradash, the screenwriter. He had captured the essence of Jones's sprawling, 816-page novel and condensed it into a 161-page shooting script. "I remember when Frank came in from Africa to test. I saw him in the coffee shop, and he asked me, 'How do I play the scene and make Maggio laugh and cry at the same time?' He was so nervous. Eli Wallach made the best test of the three of them—no doubt about it. Everyone agreed. He was superb. Lembeck was not right; he tried too hard to be funny. Frank's test was good—better than expected—but it had none of the consummate acting ability of Eli Wallach.

"Buddy Adler said to Eli's agent [Peter Witt], 'We want your man,' and the agent gave a price two times as much as Columbia was going to pay. The agent said, 'Tennessee Williams's play, *El Camino Real*, is starting rehearsals and they want Eli. If I don't get that price, he's going to take the play.' This burned Cohn to the core. A guy coming into a prize part and demanding that much money was more than he would tolerate. 'Forget it,' he screamed. 'He's out. No way.' "

Wallach said that money had nothing to do with it. "I was offered the role of Maggio and was going to take it, but I had already committed myself to Elia Kazan to play in Tennessee Williams's play, *El Camino Real*, if they got the backing. When the money came through for the play, I grabbed it, because it was a remarkable piece of writing by the leading playwright in America and it was going to be directed by the country's best. There really wasn't much of a choice for me. As a stage actor I wanted to do the play, and so I turned down the movie and the role of Maggio. It just put my film debut off by a year or two, but I don't feel I lost out on some great thing."

When Frank heard that Eli Wallach had tested for the role, he became depressed, convinced that he no longer had a chance. He and Ava fought daily. She called Harry Cohn in Hollywood and pleaded with him to give Frank the role, saying that if Frank didn't get it, he would probably kill himself.

Shooting was scheduled to start in March and almost all the parts had been cast, except for Maggio. Fred Zinnemann, Buddy Adler, and Dan Taradash conferred with Harry Cohn in his basement projection room at home about the problem. After running the Wallach and Sinatra tests several times, Dan Taradash said, "Let's not be so dejected. Frank's not that bad. I know we were dazzled by Wallach, but let's try to take another look at Frank's test and see."

They ran the test again and again, trying to decide whether they should give the role to Sinatra or test someone else. Cohn went upstairs and got his wife. "I want you to go down there and look at the tests of Sinatra and Wallach," he said. "Then tell me which one you like the best. Tell me what you honestly think."

Joan Cohn watched the two tests and told her husband that she was captivated by Eli Wallach but thought he was too splendidly built to play Maggio. "He's a brilliant actor, no question about it," she said after watching the scene where Maggio strips down and gets into a fight with two military policemen, "but he looks too good. He's not skinny, and he's not pathetic, and he's not Italian. Frank is just Maggio to me."

"One crucial difference in Frank's favor was his size," said Dan Taradash many years later. "Eli was a pretty muscular guy with a great physique. He did not look like a schnook. He looked like he could take two MPs with no trouble at all. Frank, on the other hand, looked so thin and woeful and so pitifully small that the audience would cry when they saw this poor little guy get beaten up. Adler and Zinnemann and Cohn finally agreed, and that's how Frank got the role. It was by default and had nothing to do with a horse's head."

Taradash's allusion was to Mario Puzo's 1969 novel *The Godfather*, in which a famous Italian singer by the name of Johnny Fontane appeals to the Mafia don for help in getting a movie role that has been denied him. The godfather, who loves Johnny like a son, sends his *consigliori* to the West Coast to ask the studio head to reconsider. The movie magnate, who cares more for his thoroughbred horses than for humans, refuses; the Mafia lawyer asks him again, but the studio chief remains adamant. The *consigliori* returns to New York to give his boss the bad news, and a few days later the studio chief wakes up in bed next to the severed head of his most prized steed. He realizes that a man who would casually decapitate a $600,000 horse could just as easily kill him. So he reconsiders and gives Johnny the role, and with it Johnny Fontane regains his star status.

Puzo's novel, which sold millions of copies, reminded readers that there had once been another famous Italian singer whose career was brought back to life by a movie role that had at first been denied him.

By the time the book was published, Frank's organized-crime friendships were so well established that it was an easy leap for readers to assume that he, too, had received a godfather's help in obtaining the role of Maggio in *From Here to Eternity*.

"I heard the [BBC] interviewer say I got the Maggio role through the mob," Sinatra said. "Well—that's so far from the truth." In fact, he sued the British Broadcasting Corporation for saying that it was his crime syndicate ties that landed him the role; he won the lawsuit, and received a retraction.

For some, though, the suspicion always remained, understandably so, given Harry Cohn's organized-crime ties and Frank's various friendships within the Mafia. Later, one writer suggested that Frank Costello made an overture on Sinatra's behalf through Johnny "Don Giovanni" Roselli, the Las Vegas–Los Angeles capo Mafioso, to get Frank the role of Maggio. Harry Cohn wore a friendship ring from Roselli, the syndicate man identified in Justice Department files as the key "to keeping peace in the movie industry in Hollywood."

Years later, Frank proposed Roselli for membership in the Friar's Club.

Another writer, Leonard Katz, stated that when Sinatra asked for help in getting the role, Frank Costello simply contacted George Wood of the William Morris talent agency and some top movie executives on the West Coast. "It was a favor they couldn't refuse because of favors received in the past," he said. "Costello acknowledged to close friends that he was the one who got Sinatra the part, but he never talked about the circumstances in detail."

"Sinatra and Frank C. were great pals," said former columnist John J. Miller. "I know because I used to sit with Frank C. at the Copa, and Sinatra would join us all the time. He was always asking favors of the old man, and whenever Sinatra had a problem he went to Frank C. to solve it. Maggio would have been easy for Costello, who was tied in tight to George Wood, Sinatra's agent."

A vice-president of the William Morris Agency, George E. Wood was also a good friend of Vincent "Jimmy Blue Eyes" Alo, a member of the Vito Genovese Mafia family in New York.

"George [Wood] was perfect for Frank because he knew all the gangsters," said Abe Lastfogel many years later.

Some who said Frank had Mafia help getting the role of Maggio figured it came through George Wood to Jimmy Blue Eyes to Harry Cohn, but those who were involved with the movie deny it emphatically.

"There was absolutely nothing to that horse's head business," said Joan Cohn Harvey. "Nothing. Frank didn't get the part that way. Really."

"Preposterous," said Dan Taradash.

"Pure fiction, I assure you," said Abe Lastfogel.

"There were no horses' heads involved," said Fred Zinnemann. "Frank lobbied for the part by sending Harry Cohn and myself telegrams and singing them 'Maggio.' . . . His test was good and I saw no reason why he shouldn't do it. But there was no pressure. If I hadn't wanted him, he wouldn't have done it."

"As for the horse's head in Cohn's bed, Harry never owned a racehorse in his life," said Jonie Taps. "No one ever forced Harry Cohn to put Sinatra in *From Here to Eternity*. It just took a little needling . . . with a little help from Ava."

* * *

When Frank finally received the cable informing him that Maggio was his at eight thousand dollars, he was exuberant. Pacing up and down the tent like a panther, he kept saying, "I'll show those mothers. I'll show them."

This was the arrogant side of Frank that Ava detested, even more so now that she was undergoing her own personal crisis. She had decided to terminate her pregnancy and told her MGM publicist, Morgan Hudgins, that she wanted to fly to London for an abortion. Hudgins wrote to Ava's agent saying that she needed a little time off and that he would contact MGM in Culver City to make the necessary arrangements. He followed his letter with an urgent cable: PLEASE KEEP CONFIDENTIAL GARDNER INFORMATION MY LETTER TWO DAYS AGO STOP APPRECIATE DON'T DISCUSS WITH FRONT OFFICE YET STOP WRITING NEW LETTER TODAY.

An MGM executive cabled director John Ford, saying: CONFIDENTIAL: UNDERSTAND GARDNER CABLED AGENT SHE UNSETTLED AND NOT WELL AND PLANNING BRIEF TRIP TO LONDON FEEL THIS VERY UNWISE FOR MANY OBVIOUS REASONS UNLESS YOU DECIDE IT NECESSARY OTHERWISE SUGGEST YOU USE YOUR PERSUASIVENESS AND HAVE LADY STAY PUT.

After conferring with Ava and her publicist, Ford cabled MGM: GARDNER GIVING SUPERB PERFORMANCE VERY CHARMING COOPERATIVE STOP HOWEVER REALLY QUITE ILL SINCE ARRIVAL AFRICA DEEM IT IMPERATIVE LONDON CONSULTATION OTHERWISE TRAGIC RESULTS STOP SHOULD NOT AFFECT SCHEDULE WEATHER HERE MISERABLE BUT WE'RE TRYING NO MOZEL BUT HARD WORK REPEAT BELIEVE TRIP IMPERATIVE.

On November 23, 1952, a few days after Frank had flown back to the United States, Ava flew from Nairobi to London with her publicist and the wife of Robert Surtees, the cameraman. She stayed at the Savoy Hotel and then was taken to a private nursing home in the evening. Her publicist told the press that she had a tropical infection and was suffering from a severe case of anemia. Years later, Ava came closer to the truth when she told writer Joe Hyams that she had a "miscarriage."

"All of my life I had wanted a baby, and the news that I lost him (I'm sure that it was a boy) was the cruelest blow I had ever received," she said. "Even though my marriage to Frank was getting shakier every day, I didn't care. I wanted a baby by him."

The cameraman recalled it differently. "That isn't the

way it was at all," said Robert Surtees. "Ava hated Frank so intensely by this stage, she couldn't stand the idea of having his baby. She went to London to have an abortion. I know, because my wife went to London to be at her side at all times through the operation and afterward, and to bring her back on the plane. She told my wife, 'I hated Frankie so much. I wanted that baby to go unborn.' "

Frank flew back to Africa to spend Christmas with Ava. He had to borrow money to buy her his gifts, because she was still smarting over having to pay for her anniversary ring. She had been so angry about it, she complained to Robert Surtees. "You know what that son of a bitch did?" she said. "I got the bill for the ring!"

Frank and Ava flew to Paris for a few days of vacation in January, but their incessant fighting spun a poisonous web from which they could not extricate themselves. While in France, Frank received a cable from Cohn. MONTGOMERY CLIFT ALREADY PROFICIENT IN ARMY DRILL. SINCE YOU MUST DO SAME ROUTINE, SUGGEST YOU GET BACK FEW DAYS EARLY. Frank wired back: DEAR HARRY. WILL COMPLY WITH REQUEST. DRILLING WITH FRENCH ARMY OVER WEEKEND. EVERYTHING O.K. MAGGIO.

Frank returned to the States knowing that his marriage was in precarious shape, but he believed that everything would work out after he completed the forty-one days of shooting required for *From Here to Eternity*.

Frank was humbled to be working with such accomplished actors as Montgomery Clift, Burt Lancaster, Deborah Kerr, and Donna Reed. He was especially impressed with Monty Clift, who was playing Prewitt, his best friend in the film. Clift, a handsome but troubled man, possessed immense screen presence and tried for perfection in his role. For weeks before filming started he had been studying with Manny Klein, a well-known trumpeter, to learn how to play the bugle. Although he made no sounds on film, he was determined to make his throat and mouth movements on screen look exactly right. Monty also jogged every day to stay in shape for his fight scenes. He worked out regularly with a trainer and took boxing lessons from an ex-fighter, Mushy Calahan. He also boxed with the author of *From Here to Eternity*, James Jones, who had once been a Golden Gloves contender.

Frank hadn't seen this kind of driving perfectionism since

Gene Kelly's unsparing dance drills at MGM. Monty even had an acting coach who worked with Clift and Frank together on their scenes. "Monty was so intense about being Prewitt, he raised the level of the other actors," said Fred Zinnemann. "He cared so much, they started caring."

Clift also intimidated everyone in the cast. "The only time I was ever really afraid as an actor was that first scene with Clift," said Burt Lancaster. "It was *my* scene, understand: I was the sergeant, I gave the orders, he was just a private under me. Well, when we started, I couldn't stop my knees from shaking. I thought they might have to stop because my trembling would show. But I'd never worked with an actor with Clift's power before; I was afraid he was going to blow me right off the screen."

Shooting began in Hollywood on March 2, 1953, and moved to Hawaii for the exterior scenes at Schofield Army Barracks. The first day the cast was assembled, Zinnemann introduced Frank to the unit publicist, Walter Shenson.

"I went over to shake his hand and to say that I was going to be the publicity man on the film," said Shenson. "I asked him who his press agent was, and he said he didn't have one. I couldn't believe it. 'But who's putting all that stuff in the papers that I've been reading about you wanting the part and going after it and flying in for tests and flying back to Africa and all that stuff?'

" 'I did all that with Ava's help,' said Frank. 'She'd call Harry Cohn to lean on him, and then I'd call Louella Parsons, and later we'd both call Hedda Hopper.'

"I congratulated him on a splendid publicity campaign and told him that I could do a lot for him if he'd just behave himself with the press. He was a pussycat. 'Whatever you say, kid, whatever you say,' he said. So I started bringing around news people to interview him. A couple of times he said, 'I won't talk to that one. He was rude to Ava.' Then I'd remind him of his promise to cooperate, and he'd be a charmer.

"One day, I got a call from a press guy saying that the government had just released a statement that Frank owed $109,000 in back taxes. He wanted a comment from Sinatra, so I went to his trailer and told him. He looked at me very calmly and said, 'You don't think this is news, do you? If you owe $109,000, you know about it.' I explained that I was getting phone calls from the press wanting a statement. He said to tell them anything I wanted. 'If I do,' I said, 'it will have to be a quote from you.' 'Go ahead,' he said. 'Tell them whatever you want.'

" 'Surely your lawyers and accountants are working with the government, aren't they?' I asked. Frank said they were, so I went back and called all the reporters. 'Mr. Sinatra asked me to tell you the following: "My lawyers and my accountants are working with the government lawyers and accountants, and if it takes *From Here to Eternity*, I'm going to pay it all back." ' I later told Frank that I *had* to publicize the picture first and him second, but he thought that was brilliant."

Montgomery Clift coached Frank through every syllable of his part, spelling out every beat, every movement, every motion that Maggio made. He taught him not to rely on the words but to go beyond to the characterization. "Good dialogue simply isn't enough to explain all the infinite gradations of a character," Monty told Frank. "It's behavior—it's what's going on behind the lines."

Sinatra was grateful. "I learned more about acting from him than I ever knew before," he said. "But he's an exhausting man. After those army sergeants drilled us all day, we'd have dinner—usually at Monty's room or mine. Then Clift would jump up and say, 'Now show me how you do that about-face again.' I'd plead with him to lay off, but he'd start to practice all over again."

Most nights, Frank had dinner with Monty, Zinnemann, Deborah Kerr, and Burt Lancaster; afterward, he and Monty would grab their bottles and go to Frank's room, where he would try to call Ava in Nairobi. International calls took hours in those days, and Monty and Frank drank as they waited. By the time the Honolulu operator made a connection with Ava's African location, she was usually out for the evening, which gave Frank reason to drink the night away. Neither he nor Monty could stand being alone, so they spent endless hours together drinking, returning to their rooms so drunk that Burt Lancaster would have to put them both to bed.

Clift's drinking, exacerbated by his drug addiction, became uncontrollable during filming, and one night before the whole company was scheduled to leave for California, Monty and Frank showed up drunk for an important night scene. Within minutes Monty passed out, and the director was alarmed because the scene could not be postponed. Frank grabbed Monty, shook him, slapped him in the face, and then walked him to his trailer, where Frank spent the next hour sobering him up enough to go before the cameras.

"Frank was wonderful to work with about ninety percent of the time," said Zinnemann, who did not elaborate on the other ten percent.

On the last night of shooting, Frank turned on both Monty and Zinnemann as they began the scene in which Maggio is drunk and Prew is worried about his being caught by MPs. Frank and Monty had rehearsed the scene standing up, but, just before shooting, Frank decided that he wanted to do it sitting down. Zinnemann objected, but Frank insisted—loudly and profanely. Monty backed Zinnemann and remained standing to follow the script. This so angered Sinatra that he slapped Monty hard. The director tried to placate Sinatra by agreeing to film the scene with Frank sitting if he would also do one take standing. Frank refused and became extremely abusive. Alarmed by what was happening, Buddy Adler called Harry Cohn at the Royal Hawaiian Hotel, where he and his wife were dining with Air Force General and Mrs. O'Daniel.

"That call came in the middle of dinner," said Joan Cohn Harvey. "Buddy said if Harry didn't get over there fast—within the next five minutes—everything was going to blow up because Frank and Fred were really going at it. They were arguing about the way a scene was to be played. 'C'mon,' yelled Harry. 'We've got to go. That Buddy is so spineless.' "

Minutes later, an Air Force limousine arrived on the set and Harry Cohn jumped out in his white dinner jacket. "What the hell is going on here?" he yelled. He fired questions at everyone. How dare an actor tell the director what to do? Why wasn't the director following the script? Why can't the producer see that things are under control? He then threatened Zinnemann, saying that he would shut the picture down if things weren't done his way.

"I was on the sidelines watching but not hearing anything," said publicist Walter Shenson. "I could just see the pantomime of Harry Cohn running up in his white dinner jacket, striding into the middle of the set and making some pronouncement. Then he turned around and walked out and got back into the limousine. The next morning was Sunday, and I was on the beach with the rest of the crew. Cohn spotted me and asked if I had been there last night.

" 'Did you see that son of a bitch, Sinatra?' he asked.

" 'Yeah, I saw him but I don't know what was happening.'

" 'Well, that bastard guinea was trying to tell us what to do. You know where he is now? He's on an airplane going back to the studio.'

" 'How could you send him back without seeing the rushes?' I asked.

" 'I don't care,' said Cohn. 'The hell with him. That dirty little dago is not going to tell me how to make my movies.' "

The entire company returned to California a few days later to shoot interiors at Columbia Studios. By then Frank and Monty were inseparable friends and spent a great deal of time with James Jones.

"We talked about the injustice of life and love," said Jones, "and then Monty and I would listen to Frank talk about Ava Gardner."

One night during the course of the filming, Frank became so depressed by Ava's rejection that he threatened suicide. Monty talked him out of it.

"We would get very loaded," Jones said. "After dinner and a lot more drinks, we would weave outside into the night and all sit down on the curb next to a lamppost. It became our lamppost, and we'd mumble more nonsense to each other. We felt very close."

The rushes were so spectacular that Harry Cohn insisted the film be in the theaters by August. He was the first to recognize the film's quality. So proud was he of it, that for the first time in his career he allowed his name to appear in an advertisement before release, conveying to the public his pride in presenting *From Here to Eternity*. It became the biggest money-maker in Columbia's history. The final cost was $2,406,000; the first release grossed nineteen million. By fiscal 1954 gross income totaled eighty million. So great was the demand for seats that the Capitol Theater in New York City remained open almost around the clock; it closed only for an hour in the morning to let janitors sweep the floor.

Critics, as enthusiastic as the public, praised the film and everyone associated with it.

"*From Here to Eternity* . . . tells a truth about life, about the inviolability of the human spirit," said *Time* magazine. "[It says] something important about America. It says that many Americans, in a way that is often confused and sometimes forgotten, care to the quick about a man's right to 'go his own way,' though all the world and the times be contrary."

"[This is] a film almost as towering and persuasive as its source," wrote Bosley Crowther in *The New York Times*. "It captures the essential spirit of the James Jones study. . . . It stands as a shining example of truly professional moviemaking." The New York Film Critics named the picture the best of 1953 and gave awards to Burt Lancaster as best actor and Fred Zinnemann as best director. All five leading players were nominated for Academy Awards. So were the director, the screenwriter, the cinematographer, the film editor, and the sound man.

The most superlative reviews were for Frank, who surprised everyone by his performance and earned the respect of the industry, which immediately proclaimed his "comeback" as the most dramatic in show business. "He does Private Maggio like nothing he has ever done before," said *Time* magazine. "His face wears the calm of a man who is completely sure of what he is doing as he plays it straight from Little Italy."

"Instead of exploiting a personality, he proves he is an actor by playing the luckless Maggio with a kind of doomed gaiety that is both real and immensely touching," said the *New York Post*.

"Frank Sinatra is simply superb, comical, pitiful, childishly brave, pathetically defiant," said the *Los Angeles Examiner*. "Prew (Clift) is able to absorb 'the treatment' the army dishes out to him for his rebelliousness. Poor little Maggio succumbs to it, and Sinatra makes his death scene one of the best ever photographed."

The film seemed to elevate everyone connected with it.

"There was something magic about that picture," said Walter Shenson. "All of us went on to bigger and better things because of it. Frank's career took off, and so did Donna Reed's. Ernest Borgnine became a star; Dan Taradash became a producer at Columbia; our still photographer became a cinematographer, and I was made an executive. Harry Cohn felt that we were all a lucky bunch."

The camaraderie among the cast and crew of *From Here to Eternity* made the wrap party memorable. "We gave a party for the cast when it was over," said Joan Cohn Harvey, "and I still remember Frank sitting there telling everyone that in sixteen more hours he would be with Ava. 'She's the most

beautiful woman in the world. You know that, don't you?'
he'd say. 'Yes, Frank, we all know how beautiful Ava is,' I'd
say. 'She's not just one of the most beautiful women in the
world; she's *the* most beautiful,' he'd insist. He thought that
he was married to the most exquisite creature on the face of
the earth, and he was desperately in love with her. It was kind
of sad because all the rest of us knew that the marriage was
held together by mere threads at that point."

15

Frank acted as though once reunited with Ava they would live happily ever after. He phoned her in London, where she was to begin filming *Knights of the Round Table* for MGM, to say that he would be joining her in a few days. He wanted her to accompany him on singing engagements throughout Europe. He was in fine voice and looking forward to the trip. He promised her that it would be a second honeymoon for them and she accepted gleefully, once again defying the studio to take an unauthorized leave for three weeks to be with her husband.

Unfortunately, the second honeymoon turned out to be a disaster. They missed their London-to-Milan plane because their car broke down on the way to the London airport. Although they arrived with seven minutes to spare, and the British European Airways jet was still warming its engines, airport officials refused to let them board. Frank was enraged.

"I'll never fly BEA again," he yelled.

"I'd rather swim the channel," said Ava.

Frank checked other airlines to find one that would get them anywhere near Milan. The only service available was a BEA flight to Rome, which they took grudgingly. Waiting for them to deplane was an Italian photographer, and Frank berated him severely. Police were summoned to hold the photographer until Frank and Ava had left.

In Naples, Frank was greeted by a half-filled house, and

the audience booed him off the stage because Ava was not with him. During intermission, the theater manager refused to pay him, and Frank refused to resume singing. Impatient at being kept waiting, the audience booed and stamped and shouted. They were on the verge of rioting. The police were summoned, and the chief of Naples riot control visited Frank backstage accompanied by a platoon of fifteen policemen. They persuaded him to return to the stage.

"Ma vedere che passa," Frank told his audience. ("Take it easy.") *"Ma vedere che passa."*

When he ended the show after an hour and a half, the audience refused to leave the theater. They had paid $7.40 to hear Frank sing, double what they would pay to hear their operatic idol, Beniamino Gigli, and they expected a three-hour concert. They began screaming, *"Ruberia! Ruberia!"* ("Robbery!") Again police were summoned, this time to evacuate the theater.

In Copenhagen, Denmark, Frank couldn't fill half the house. In Malmö, Sweden, where he was performing in an outdoor park, it started to rain and became so cold that he said he would get sick if he continued, and therefore cut short his appearance by twenty minutes. He refused to stage a press conference and snubbed newsmen and photographers. The next day, a Scandinavian newspaper ran a cartoon showing a stage set with a mike, a slouch-hatted bodyguard with a tommy gun, a muffler, and a medicine stand, with the caption: "All is ready for Frank Sinatra's appearance." This was accompanied by an editorial stating, "Mr. Sinatra, Go Home!"

Frank canceled the rest of his tour and returned to London with Ava, where they fought so bitterly that they were almost evicted from their apartment.

Ava had three weeks' work to do on her film and asked Frank to stay with her so that they could return to New York together, but he refused, saying he had to leave immediately to rehearse for his engagement at Bill Miller's Riviera in Englewood, New Jersey. "I have a career, too, you know," he said.

Ava was so angry that she refused to notify him of her arrival in the U.S. a week later; he read of it in a newspaper. He was furious when he learned that she had gone to the Hampshire House, when she knew he was staying at the Waldorf Towers. Neither would telephone the other, but both talked freely to reporters.

"I saw a picture of Ava at the airport and that's the first inkling I had that she was in town," Frank said. "I don't understand it. We'd had no trouble. I can't make a statement because I don't know what she is planning. It's a crying shame, because everything was going so well with us. Something may work out, but I don't know."

Ava refused to be specific, but she indicated that perhaps marriage was too hard for her. "You start with love, or what you think is love, and then comes the work," she said. "I guess you have to be mature and grown up to know how to work at it. But I was the youngest of seven kids and was always treated like the baby, and I liked it, and played the baby. Now I'm having a helluva time growing up."

Dolly Sinatra was distressed by what was happening to her son. She called Ava at her hotel to find out what was wrong. "She said to please come right over," Dolly said. "She kissed me, and after a few minutes she began to cry. She had been tired, she said, when the plane came in, and when she didn't see Frank, she felt bad. Then she found out he was in Atlantic City with me and said, 'Mama, I don't know how to explain this, but I know how little you get to see him. I thought for once you're together, just the two of you, and I didn't want to spoil it.'"

Determined to bring them back together, Dolly invited Ava to dinner the next night. Then she called Frank. "I know he can be a little stubborn sometimes, and I decided to do this my way. I called him up and told him I was going to make a nice Italian meal the next night, Monday, and would he come over between shows.

"So he says to me, 'Who's gonna be there?' And I says, 'Never mind; you just come.' Ava got there first, at about six-thirty. Frank got there at seven. He walked in and I think he almost expected to see Ava there. He looked happy. They both did. But they were just standing there, not saying anything.

"This is where mothers come in. 'Hey,' I said to both of them. 'Come into the kitchen and see what I'm making for you tonight.' They both followed me in, and we walked to the stove, and I took the big spoon I use for stirring the gravy, and I made them both taste it. Then they both began to laugh and talk and before you knew it they were hugging each other, and then they grabbed me and the three of us stood there just hugging and laughing, and I think we all felt like crying a little bit too."

That night, Ava went back to the Hampshire House while Frank left to perform at the Riviera. "Stay up and wait for me, baby," he said. But after his last show, he went to Lindy's with the boys and did not show up until four A.M., which infuriated Ava.

"Isn't it kind of late to be coming home?" she asked.

Frank bristled. "Don't cut the corners too close on me, baby," he said. "This is the way my life is going to be from now on."

Ava related this incident to friends as evidence that the lovable Frankie she had married was now an overbearing, inconsiderate boor.

"When he was down and out, he was so sweet," she said, "but when he got back to the top again, it was hell. Now that he's got successful again, he's become his old arrogant self. We were happier when he was on the skids."

Frank argued that Ava had "a thing" amounting to aberrant jealousy. He said she constantly suspected he was involved in other romances, all of which he denied.

"If it took seventy-five years to get a divorce, there wouldn't be any other woman for me," he said. His friends had advised him to give her up, saying Ava was too complex and full of problems for him. "Sure, it's easy for somebody to say give her up—when they're not in love with her."

Dolly's "reconciliation" lasted only a few weeks, until Frank left for Las Vegas to appear at the Sands Hotel. Ava refused to fly to his opening because he hadn't called her. "Why should I go?" she said. "I've heard nothing from him since he left."

The night he left, she attended the premiere of *Mogambo* in Los Angeles wearing what the newspapers described as "a so-low-cut pastel satin gown, skin-tight from bustline to hemline and embroidered all over with beads, sequins, and paillettes. Skirt was slit to the knee in front. A long stole of white fox set off her short, short hair-do." The next day, Ava went to Palm Springs while Frank poured his heart out to Louella Parsons in Las Vegas.

"I can't eat. I can't sleep. I love her," he said.

"You should be telling that to Ava, not to me," said Louella. "Why in heaven's name don't you telephone her and tell her how you feel? I know she's carrying a torch for you a mile high."

"No, Ava doesn't love me anymore. If she did, she'd be here where she belongs—with me. Instead, she's in Palm Springs having a wonderful time."

"C'mon, Frankie. Why don't you telephone?"

"No, Ava's wrong this time. I've been wrong other times, but this time it's all her fault. She'll have to call me."

"Why 'wrong'?" asked Louella.

"She doesn't understand that I've got a career to worry about too," he said. "Why, Louella, she didn't even come to my opening here! Why would she do a thing like that to me? That's only part of it. Ever since our marriage, I've been at her beck and call. No matter where she's been, I've flown to her regardless of the fact that I also had some important engagements. But I was willing to neglect them for her. . . . She saw my mother. My mother said to her, 'All this fighting is no good. Why don't you telephone Frank?' "

Instead, Ava called her lawyer, Neil McCarthy, after seeing a photograph of Frank in the newspapers dressed as a clown at a Halloween party he threw at the Sands. Two gorgeous show girls flanked him. Ava told her lawyer that she wanted a divorce.

"Frank doesn't love me. He would rather go out with some other girl, almost any other girl," she said.

McCarthy advised her not to rush into the divorce court without first talking to her husband. He set up a meeting between them, and Frank flew to Los Angeles, but he canceled the meeting at the last minute. He resented being brought to heel by Ava and her lawyer for faults that he felt existed only in her imagination, so he flew back to Las Vegas.

On October 29, 1953, MGM announced that the marriage was over: "Ava Gardner and Frank Sinatra stated today that having reluctantly exhausted every effort to reconcile their differences, they could find no mutual basis on which to continue their marriage. Both expressed deep regret and great respect for each other. Their separation is final and Miss Gardner will seek a divorce." That night, a New York disc jockey played a Sinatra record, which he introduced as "Ava Gardner's newest release."

Ava announced that she was leaving for Rome to make *The Barefoot Contessa* with Humphrey Bogart. She said she was in no hurry to file for divorce but nonchalantly dismissed the possibility of a reconciliation. She invented and reinvented her marriage for reporters and ranged from sexually ridiculing Frank as "Mr. Sin-Nada" (nothing) to proclaiming him "the man I'll always love."

Frank was devastated and made no pretense about it. When reporters asked him about the break-up, he said, "I guess it's over if that's what she says. It's very sad . . . it's tragic. I feel very badly about it."

One friend suggested that he call Ava, and said she was as miserable as Frank was. "Then why is she going to Rome to make a picture?" Frank asked. "How are we going to make up if she's going to be so far away?" He never made the call.

A few nights later, the newspapers reported that Ava was seen dining quietly with Peter Lawford at Frascati's in Los Angeles. Knowing that Peter and Ava had dated years before, Frank flew into a rage and called Lawford, threatening him.

"Oh, God, he was furious with me for going out with Ava," said Peter Lawford many years later. "He screamed, 'Do you want your legs broken, you fucking asshole? Well, you're going to get them broken if I ever hear you're out with Ava again. So help me, I'll kill you. Do you hear me?' Then he slammed the phone down. I was panicked. I mean I was really scared. Frank's a violent guy and he's good friends with too many guys who'd rather kill you than say hello. I didn't want to die, so I called Jimmy Van Heusen and said, 'Please tell him nothing happened. Please.' Jimmy said not to worry. That Frank would get over it. He knew we'd been friends since 1945. Well, Frank got over it all right, but it took him six years!"

Out of his mind with grief over Ava, Frank flew to New York en route to a nightclub engagement at the Chase Hotel in St. Louis. He wandered around Manhattan like one of the damned, filled with remorse and self-pity, unable to focus on anything but his terrible personal loss. He began frightening friends by telephoning in a gloomy voice, "Please see that the children are taken care of," and hanging up.

On November 18, 1953, Jimmy Van Heusen, who had an apartment on Fifty-seventh Street, found Frank on the floor of the elevator with his wrists slashed. Van Heusen immediately called a doctor and rushed Frank to Mt. Sinai Hospital, but not before paying the man at the front desk of his building fifty dollars to keep quiet about the incident.

The people in charge of Frank's booking at the Chase

Hotel had no idea of what had happened, but they grew more concerned by the minute when he failed to show up for rehearsal.

"We were frantic," said the booking agent, "and we started calling all over. We called the Sands in Las Vegas; we called his home in Los Angeles; we called Palm Springs and New York, but no one could find him. Finally someone decided to call Morris Schenker, a lawyer in St. Louis who has ties to everyone, to see whether he could find out something. He called us back minutes later and said Frank would not be coming because he'd just slashed his wrists."

Frank's closest friend, songwriter Jimmy Van Heusen, had lived through the traumas of the Ava Gardner courtship and the tumultuous marriage. Affable and easygoing, he had never crossed Frank, no matter how deplorable Frank's behavior. He had harbored him in Palm Springs every time Frank stormed out of the house after a fight with Ava, and had spent those nights helping Frank drink his misery away.

When Van Heusen's apartment in New York had been the scene of one of the worst rows between Ava and Frank, with both of them cursing and screaming and breaking furniture, Jimmy had laughed it off. But having recently suffered what he thought was a heart attack, Van Heusen was now trying to protect his health. The sight of his bloodied friend was more than he could take. So he finally stood up to Sinatra and told him he would end their friendship forever unless Frank promised to seek psychiatric care.

Frank agreed, and upon his return to Los Angeles he began seeing Dr. Ralph H. "Romy" Greenson, who was Marilyn Monroe's psychiatrist and the brother-in-law of Milton "Mickey" Rudin, who had become Frank's attorney when he signed with William Morris.

Frank remained in Mt. Sinai while his representatives fielded questions from the press. His agent said that Frank was "not seriously ill"; his doctor said he was suffering from "complete physical exhaustion, severe loss of weight, and a tremendous amount of emotional strain." The slashed wrists were dismissed as "an accident with a broken glass," and Frank signed himself out two days later, saying he felt "just fine." However, the William Morris agency was concerned about his state of mind and assigned George E. Wood to stay with him constantly, to do his bidding, to soothe and calm him and keep him from harming himself.

"George was supposed to keep Frank from slashing his wrists again," said Abe Lastfogel, the agency president. "He was perfect for Frank because he knew all the gangsters—Meyer Lansky, Vincent 'Jimmy Blue Eyes' Alo, Frank Costello—all of them!"

Wood was an agency vice-president making twenty-five thousand dollars a year, plus bonuses and an unlimited expense account. Despite his importance, George became a virtual baby-sitter for Frank, and never left his side. "When Frank ate, I ate," he said. "When he slept, I slept. When he felt like walking, I walked with him. When he took a haircut, I took a haircut. I loved the guy."

The heartbreak Frank suffered over Ava seeped into his music, giving new poignancy to lyrics of loss and loneliness. The songs he sang in the clubs expressed the brooding melancholy he was feeling at the time. Charged with more power and emotion than ever before, his voice resonated with deep pain and turbulent longing as he sang "I'm a Fool to Want You," making each word seem like a cry of anguish for being so ensnared by Ava.

Like the blues singers of old, Frank poured out his feelings, making his soulful ballads sound like anthems of remorse. He laid himself bare during this period, and his plaintive voice touched the hearts of listeners, who could almost feel the pain of this heartbroken man. "Don't Worry 'Bout Me," "My One and Only Love," "It's a Blue World," and "There Will Never Be Another You" sprang from his agony and grief. His intonation imparted a deeper, more personal meaning to Harold Arlen's and Ira Gershwin's:

The night is bitter,
The stars have lost their glitter.
The winds get colder.
And suddenly you're older.
And all because of a gal that got away.

Generations of men sitting in bars drinking and brooding about their own broken romances and sexual betrayals identified with this macho man who was brought to his knees by lost love. They heard him introduce songs about men who have been done wrong by women, saying, "Shake hands with the vice-president of the club," and they understood and commiserated. In a few years, he would give these same men musical aphrodisiacs with which they could seduce their women, but right now his was a soul in abject misery, and his music reflected it.

"It was Ava who did that, who taught him how to sing a torch song," said Nelson Riddle. "That's how he learned. She was the greatest love of his life, and he lost her."

Critic George Simon wrote that Frank "produced some of his most emotional recordings during this period," but the country was more interested in the belting renditions of Frankie Laine and Eddie Fisher than the searing torch songs of Frank Sinatra.

After leaving Columbia Records in 1952, Frank had not been able to get a contract with any recording company, including RCA Victor, where his good friend, Manie Sacks, was vice-president. Finally, the William Morris agency managed to obtain a one-year contract for him with Capitol Records, a fledgling Hollywood company, provided that Frank forfeit an advance and pay all his own studio costs.

June Hutton and Axel Stordahl persuaded Dave Dexter of Capitol to take a chance on Frank. The producer went to his boss, artists and repertoire chief Alan W. Livingston, and urged him to call Sam Weisbord and draw up a Sinatra contract. "I don't know if he can come back on records," Dexter told Livingston, "but I promise his output will be musically good—you won't hear any barking dogs." After the contract was signed, Livingston called Frank to discuss his choice of arrangers and the type of orchestra that should accompany him.

"By the way, your producer will be Dave Dexter," he said. "He's raring to help you kick off a whole new career."

"That bastard?" screamed Frank. "I won't work with him. He's the jerk who rapped my records in *Downbeat*. Screw him, who needs him?"

Embarrassed, Livingston went into Dexter's office to tell him what had happened. Dexter was furious. "Here's a guy who is dead on his ass," he said. "He's been deserted by all but a few of his friends, he's without a job, and he's brushed off every day by the record companies, the picture studios, and the radio and television networks. But I believe in his basic talent just as the Stordahls do, and I'm the only guy in the world who's willing to risk my job in spending $100,000 or more of my company's money trying to bring the son of a bitch back—and he fluffs me. Next time you talk to him, Alan, tell him to shove it. The feeling is mutual."

Livingston reassigned Frank to a more placid Voyle Gilmore, who chose Nelson Riddle to be his arranger. Axel Stordahl and June Hutton were dropped by Capitol a few months later.

"Handling Sinatra is like defusing a ticking bomb," said Dave Dexter in 1976. "I look back now and I'm grateful that the job went to someone else."

It was Voyle Gilmore's patience combined with Nelson Riddle's swinging arrangements that would carry Frank to the top of the music world again, restoring him as the country's number one pop singer.

The collaboration with the quiet, aloof arranger who had once worked with Tommy Dorsey provided a fine showcase for Frank's rich voice and emerging new style. The driving basses and swinging reeds of Nelson Riddle supplanted the fluffy lush strings and slow tempi of Axel Stordahl, creating some of the best popular music of the era. Riddle bestowed on Frank a swinging ballad style coupled with a jazz-influenced, finger-snapping spontaneity that characterized his music and came to be known to Sinatra fans as the Capitol Years (1953–1961).

"Working with Frank was always a challenge," said Riddle. "And there were times when the going got rough. Never a relaxed man, as Nat Cole was, for example, he was a perfectionist who drove himself and everybody around him relentlessly. You always approached him with a feeling of uneasiness, not only because he was demanding and unpredictable, but because his reactions were so violent. But all of these tensions disappeared if you came through for him.

"I suppose, over our eight years of partnership, he threw out an average of about one arrangement a year—not bad going. But there'd never be any anger—after the first time through he'd just say, 'Let's skip that one,' and go straight on to the next. He'd never give out any compliments either. If he said *nothing*, I'd know he was pleased. He just isn't *built* to give out compliments, and I never expected them. He expects your best—just that.

"Frank is an instinctive musician. After a steady partnership, I worked for him off and on until 1978 for a total of twenty-five years. Then there wasn't much for me to do anymore. I never really had an argument with him, but then I don't argue. I hold my temper too long, but that's why I could work with Frank, I guess. He's very tough on people. For example, if I wasn't conducting the orchestra to his liking, he'd shove me out of the way and take over. If he asked for diminuendo from the orchestra and didn't get it immediately, he'd take things into his own hands, and you can believe that they damn well played softer for him than they did for me. When he'd take over conducting like that, I'd feel awful, but I didn't do it fast enough for him, and I guess I'd have to say I'm in total accordance with that kind of behavior. He showed me how to insist on certain things from an orchestra, so I guess you could say I learned from Frank like he learned from me. But we always did things his way. He knows what's good for him and for the music."

The emergence of the long-playing record (LP) in the 1950s was important to a singer like Sinatra, who preferred to build a mood with his music and sustain it with songs that followed one general theme, as he did in albums like *Come Fly with Me*, *Songs for Swingin' Lovers*, and *Only the Lonely*. The single recording he made with Nelson Riddle of "Young at Heart" became one of the most popular songs in the country in 1954, but Frank's musical longevity remained in the LP albums he produced. His first Capitol album, *Songs for Young Lovers*, hit the album charts in 1954, two weeks after "Young at Heart" made its *Billboard* debut.

Brooding over Ava, Frank barely weighed a hundred and twenty pounds. He did everything he could to endear himself to her, hoping to change her mind about the divorce; he called her repeatedly and sent her all his records. He even had a large coconut cake delivered by Lauren Bacall, who was going to Rome to join her husband, Humphrey Bogart, Ava's co-star in *The Barefoot Contessa*.

The touching gesture was not appreciated. "She couldn't have cared less," said Lauren Bacall. "She wanted me to put it down on some table she indicated—not a thank-you, nothing. . . . Her reaction had only to do with Frank—she was clearly through with him, but it wasn't that way on his side."

"Betty [Bacall was born Betty Persky] got a little miffed about that cake," recalled Verita Thompson, Bogart's hairdresser. "She had felt responsible for her charge and had hand-carried it by taxi and limousine and several thousand miles across the Atlantic by plane to ensure its arrival in one piece. And when she finally presented it to Ava, Ava thanked her but pushed it aside and didn't even open the box. The action was so uncharacteristic of Ava that we figured it signaled the end of her relationship with Frank."

It was no secret that Ava had started a love affair with a Spanish bullfighter, Luis Miguel Dominguin, who, after Manolete's death, was considered the greatest bullfighter in the world and revered in Spain as no movie star had ever been.

But Bogart kidded her about the affair. "I'll never figure you broads out. Half the world's female population would throw themselves at Frank's feet, and here you are flouncing around with guys who wear capes and little ballerina slippers." Ava arched her eyebrow and told Bogie that he was being nosy.

She had already rented a house in Madrid and was planning to go there for Christmas to be near Dominguin, but at the last minute Frank called, saying he could not get through the holidays without seeing her. Unable to stay away any longer, he flew to Spain to celebrate her birthday. After the Christmas holidays, he accompanied her back to Rome and stayed with her in her apartment.

Ava had been posing in Rome for sculptor Assen Peikow for a classic Greek statue to be used in a cemetery scene, and Frank was bewitched by the white alabaster model of her face and body. At the end of the filming, the movie company gave him the statue, which he later installed in his backyard like a shrine.

Frank returned to Hollywood, admitting that his plans for reconciliation had failed. "We are trying to work out our problems," he said, "but there are still problems."

Sinatra remained so tortured by Ava's affair with the great matador that years later, when he was approached to play Manolete, he turned the part down, claiming that the American public didn't like bullfighting. Sammy Davis, Jr., tried to persuade him otherwise, but couldn't. "Maybe the subject brought back memories he wanted to forget," Davis said.

Suffering bouts of insomnia and depression, Frank no longer wanted to live alone, so he moved his friend, Jule Styne, into his five-room apartment on Wilshire Boulevard. "He *literally* moved me in," said the composer, who had been staying at the Beverly Hills Hotel. When Styne asked for his room key, the desk clerk informed him that Frank Sinatra had come to the hotel, packed all of his belongings, and moved him out. "I stood there wondering what this was all about," said Styne. "I couldn't understand Frank's motives. I knew he was going through hell with Ava and perhaps he just wanted company. I was flattered, of course."

The nights were the hardest for Frank, and he tried to fill them with dates and nightclubs and card games with the boys. "One time he called us over to play cards, and when we got there he was on the phone to his first wife, Nancy," said one friend. "Sometimes he needs advice or wants somebody to talk to or maybe he's just lonely, so he calls Nancy. Well, this time she was mad at him. She wouldn't talk to him.

"By the time we got the game started, he didn't even want to play anymore. He went into the den, opened a bottle, and started drinking alone. Okay. So we keep the game going awhile, and then Sammy Cahn gets up and he goes in to try to get Frank to join us. So what does he see?

"There's Frank drinking a toast to a picture of Ava with a tear running down his face. So Sammy comes back and we start playing again. All of a sudden, we hear a crash. We all get up and run into the den, and there's Frank. He had taken the picture of Ava, frame and all, and smashed it. Then he had picked up the picture, ripped it into little pieces, and thrown it on the floor. So we tell him, 'Come on, Frank, you've got to forget about all that. Come on and play some cards with us.' He says, 'I'm through with her. I never want to see her again. I'm all right. I've just been drinking too much.'

"So we go back to the game, and a little while later Sammy goes back to Frank, and there he is on his hands and knees picking up the torn pieces of the picture and trying to put it back together again. Well, he gets all the pieces together except the one for the nose. He becomes frantic looking for it, and we all get down on our hands and knees and try to help him.

"All of a sudden, the doorbell rings. It's a delivery boy with more liquor. So Frank goes to the back door to let him in, but when he opens it, the missing piece flutters out. Well, Frank is so happy, he takes off his gold wrist watch and gives it to the delivery boy."

Despite his regular trips to the psychiatrist, Frank's depression over Ava seemed to deepen. Some friends felt that he enjoyed wallowing in his misery.

"I come home at night and the apartment is all dark," said Jule Styne. "I yell 'Frank!' and he doesn't answer. I walk into the living room, and it's like a funeral parlor. There are three pictures of Ava in the room, and the only lights are three dim ones on the pictures. Sitting in front of them is Frank with a bottle of brandy. I say to him, 'Frank, pull yourself together.' And he says, 'Go away. Leave me alone.' Then all night he paces up and down and says, 'I can't sleep, I can't sleep.' At four o'clock in the morning, I hear him calling someone on the telephone. It's his first wife, Nancy. His voice is soft and quiet, and I hear him say, 'You're the only one who understands me.' Then he paces up and down some more and maybe he reads, and he doesn't fall asleep until the sun's up. Big deal. You can have it."

Everywhere Jule went, people asked what it was like living with Frank Sinatra; Jule told them in excruciating detail. Soon Jule's stories of Frank's drunken crying jags over Ava, his insomnia, his truculent depressions, and his late-night calls to Nancy got back to Frank. Eight months after Jule had been moved in, he came home to find a note from his host: "I'd appreciate it if you'd move." He received no further explanation, no apology, no good-bye. So he packed his bags and returned to the Beverly Hills Hotel, wondering what he had done.

"I was told to leave in no uncertain terms," he said, figuring the reason was Frank's anger that Styne's best-selling song, "Three Coins in the Fountain," which he wrote with Sammy Cahn, had been given to another firm for publication and not to Sinatra's firm, the Barton Music Corporation. Ironically, the song that Frank sang in the movie became a hit for the Four Aces and not for Frank.

"Why didn't he get angry with Sammy Cahn too? It was Sammy's song as much as it was mine," said Jule.

Frank did not speak to Jule again for five years, and it took Jule that long to figure out that he had been kicked out because of the personal stories he told about Frank's anguish and grief over Ava. Years later, he admitted that Frank's request for him to leave was justified.

Ava did not apply for her divorce until 1954, when she established residency in Nevada, and even then she did not proceed, because she insisted that Frank pay the legal costs and he refused. Nothing was made final until 1957. And even after the divorce, Frank still kept talking about his beautiful ex-wife. While making movies he kept her picture taped to his dressing room mirror and told anyone who asked, "I know we could have worked it out. . . ."

"He never got her out of his system," said Nick Sevano. "She had a hold over him no other woman ever had."

His friends and associates agreed. Even the women he dated, most of whom were tall, thin, and brunette, knew that they had been chosen to be surrogates. Most did not mind.

"It was nightmare time after Ava," said Norma Ebberhart, a beautiful actress with one blue eye and one green eye. "We spent a lot of nights together in Palm Springs trying to chase those nightmares away."

Frank fell into many arms trying to recover from Ava, and reached out to every woman around him for comfort. He proposed to some but forgot most, running away as soon as they wanted more than he wanted to give.

"He was wonderful and I liked him very much," said Vanessa Brown, "but I just didn't want to marry him. He asked me several times, but I think he was looking for someone to take care of him—a basic, old-fashioned girl who would cook and clean and keep house. He needed that. It bothered him very much that I never had any food in the house. He said, 'Can't you make some pasta or something?' "

He swore to Mona Freeman that he didn't care if he ever saw Ava again, and he said the same to Judy Garland, whom he dropped abruptly when she wanted to become the next Mrs. Sinatra. Elizabeth Taylor got the same treatment toward the end of her unhappy marriage to Michael Wilding when she found herself pregnant by Frank and wanted to marry him. He arranged an abortion for her instead.

No one woman seemed to be able to wipe away the scars of Ava Gardner.

"He always told me one of the things that fascinated him about Ava was that there was no conquest," said comedian Shecky Greene. "He couldn't conquer her. That is where the respect comes. He never got her. He couldn't control her or dominate her. He'd get drinking and tell me how she always called him a goddamned hoodlum and a gangster. He'd never take that from anyone else but Ava. She was always a challenge to him, and he needs that. It's a definite part of his personality."

16

The night of March 25, 1954, Frank Sinatra walked into the Pantages Theater on Hollywood Boulevard with his thirteen-year-old daughter, Nancy, who was wearing a white ermine cape, and Frankie, Jr., ten, sporting a bow tie just like his father's early trademark. Young Frank's mimicry of his father had started when he was a year old, and by the time the boy was ten, Sinatra was to comment about his son, "He's so like me it's frightening."

Big Nancy had remained at home with the youngest child, Christina, six. She had cooked a spaghetti dinner during which the children gave their father their own Academy Award, a St. Genesius medal bearing the inscription: "To Daddy— All our love from here to eternity."

After Columbia Pictures removed Frank from the star line-up of Montgomery Clift, Burt Lancaster, Deborah Kerr, and Donna Reed, and reduced him to the rank of a supporting player, he became the odds-on favorite to win the Oscar for Best Supporting Actor. Also nominated were Eddie Albert (*Roman Holiday*); Brandon de Wilde (*Shane*); Jack Palance (*Shane*); and Robert Strauss (*Sialag 17*). Despite such formidable competition, reporters wrote about the awards as if Frank had already won.

"I ran into person after person who said, 'He's a so-and-so but I hope he gets it. He was great,' " said Louella Parsons.

"So if Frank doesn't step up to get his Oscar, he and the rest of the audience will be surprised numb."

A week before the awards ceremony, Frank was eating dinner at La Scala in New York with Jimmy Van Heusen, Hank Sanicola, and music publisher Jackie Gale. As Frank left for the airport to fly to Los Angeles, the men raised their glasses. "Bring back that Oscar," they said. "I'm gettin' it," said Frank.

Despite his optimism, Frank made his son and daughter promise not to be disappointed if he didn't win. "Don't you be either," they said in unison.

The film itself won eight Academy Awards, tying the all-time record of *Gone with the Wind*.

That night Frank sat nervously as Mercedes McCambridge walked on stage to make the presentation for best performance by an actor in a supporting role. When she announced him as the winner, the audience cheered wildly and Little Nancy burst into tears. Frank leaned over to kiss her and grabbed young Frankie's hand. Then he dashed toward the stage. Hugging the gold statue close to him, he thanked Harry Cohn, Fred Zinnemann, and Buddy Adler. Later, he said he regretted not thanking Montgomery Clift as well, but he never mentioned Ava, who had done as much as anyone to get him the role.

He took the children home and gave their mother the small Oscar medallion he had received for her charm bracelet. Then, clutching his trophy, he drove to his apartment, where a few friends had gathered to congratulate him.

"Frank walked up the path holding that Oscar and looking so alone that it almost broke my heart," recalled actress Charlotte Austin. "Here it was the biggest night in his life, and the only woman he cared about was five thousand miles away in Spain with another man. Frank was very quiet and happy, though, and acted as if he didn't quite believe it had really happened to him. We had a great time. Gene Kelly was there. Adolph Green and Betty Comden, Jule Styne, Sammy Cahn, and Bert Friedlob, the producer. The first thing Frank did was call his mom in Hoboken. She must have done most of the talking because all we could hear him say was, 'Yes Mama, no Mama, yes Mama.' "

Variety proclaimed Frank's victory "the greatest comeback in theater history." The Associated Press concurred. "Frank Sinatra, a wartime crooning idol of the nation's bobby-soxers,

Frank Sinatra and Lauren Bacall holding hands in 1958 and neither confirming nor denying marriage plans

UPI/Bettmann Newsphotos)

With Mrs. Eleanor Roosevelt during rehearsal for Frank's television show, 1960

(UPI/Bettmann Newsphotos)

Some of the "Rat Pack"—Frank, Dean Martin, Sammy Davis, Jr., Peter Lawford, Joey Bishop—in *Ocean's Eleven*, 1960

(AP/Wide World Photos)

STAIR-4

Frank escorting
Mrs. John F.
Kennedy to her
box for the pre-
inauguration gala
he staged

*(UPI/Bettmann
Newsphotos)*

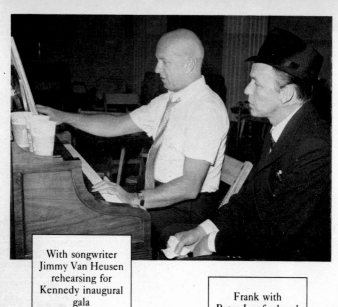

With songwriter
Jimmy Van Heusen
rehearsing for
Kennedy inaugural
gala

*(UPI/Bettmann
Newsphotos)*

Frank with
Peter Lawford and
Attorney General
Robert Kennedy,
1961

*(UPI/Bettmann
Newsphotos)*

Frank with his
parents at the 50th
anniversary party
he gave them, 1963

(Irv Wagen)

Nancy Jr. dancing
with her grandfather
at the party

(Irv Wagen)

Chicago Mafia boss,
Sam Giancana

(AP/Wide World Photos)

George Jacobs,
Sinatra's valet,
reaching for a trash
can to throw at a
news photographer
after his estranged
wife testified he
often received
generous tips from
"Mr. Sam"
Giancana

*(Los Angeles
Herald-Examiner)*

Frank and daughter Nancy celebrating safe release of Frank, Jr., after his kidnapping, 1963

(AP/Wide World Photos)

Frank and his 19-year-old girlfriend, Mia Farrow, sailing from Hyannis Port, Massachusetts, after visiting members of the Kennedy family, 1965

(AP/Wide World Photos)

Mia Farrow
Sinatra in Miami
with her husband,
1967

(AP/Wide World Photos)

Frank with
producer Brad
Dexter (left) and
director Sidney J.
Furie, during
filming of *The
Naked Runner*, 1967

(Courtesy of Brad Dexter)

Frank as Maggio in
*From Here to
Eternity* with
Montgomery Clift
and Burt Lancaster

(AP/Wide World Photos)

Frank at Caesars Palace in Las Vegas, sporting a mustache and the beginnings of a goatee, 1969

(AP/Wide World Photos)

Rehearsing a dance routine for a 1973 TV special with Gene Kelly, 25 years after they starred together in musicals

(AP/Wide World Photos)

Frank Sinatra's
attorney, Milton
(Mickey) Rudin, at
a 1974 news
conference after
Frank's Melbourne
concert was
cancelled

*(UPI/Bettmann
Newsphotos)*

Frank escorting
Jacqueline Kennedy
Onassis to '21' after
she attended his
concert. To his
immediate left is
his close friend,
Jilly Rizzo

(AP/Wide World Photos)

ABOVE So tight is security around Sinatra that he has had it written into his contracts that not a single soul, no matter how famous, is to be allowed backstage, or even to approach him. Yet members of the nation's most powerful Mafia family managed to get his attention in 1976 at the Westchester Premier Theatre. Top row: Paul Castellano, Gregory De Palma, Thomas Marson, Carlo Gambino, Jimmy Fratianno, Salvatore Spatola; bottom row: Joe Gambino, Richard Fusco

BELOW Frank with his bride Barbara Marx and Nancy and Ronald Reagan, 1976

(New York Daily News *Photo)*

Frank Sinatra, Jr.

*(Copyright ©
Stanley Tretick)*

Rat Pack reunion:
Burt Reynolds,
Dean Martin,
Shirley MacLaine,
Sammy Davis, Jr.,
and Frank during
filming of
Cannonball Run II,
1984

(AP/Wide World Photos)

Addressing the President and First Lady at their second inaugural gala

(Terry Arthur)

With daughter Tina and the Reagans in the Blue Room after Frank received the nation's highest civilian award, the Presidential Medal of Freedom

(Copyright © Stanley Tretick)

Doonesbury

BY GARRY TRUDEAU

"HIS LOVE OF COUNTRY, HIS GENEROSITY FOR THOSE LESS FORTUNATE, HIS DISTINCTIVE ART...

6-10

...AND HIS WINNING AND COMPASSIONATE PERSONA MAKE HIM ONE OF OUR MOST REMARKABLE AND DISTINGUISHED AMERICANS...

...AND ONE WHO TRULY DID IT HIS WAY."
— Ronald Reagan
May 23, 1985

MEDAL OF FREEDOM RECIPIENT FRANK SINATRA DOING IT HIS WAY WITH TOMMY "FATSO" MARSON, DON CARLO GAMBINO, RICHARD "NERVES" FUSCO, JIMMY "THE WEASEL" FRATIANNO, JOSEPH GAMBINO AND GREG DEPALMA.

Doonesbury

BY GARRY TRUDEAU

"HE HAS CARRIED ON HIS CRAFT WITH DISTINCTION AND HIGH PROFESSIONALISM...

6-11

HE HAS APPLIED HIS TALENTS TO THE BENEFIT OF MANKIND...

...AND TO THE UPLIFTING OF THE HUMAN SPIRIT."
— Citation for honorary degree, Stevens Institute, May 23, 1985

DR. FRANCIS SINATRA UPLIFTING THE SPIRITS OF ALLEGED HUMAN ANIELLO DELLACROCE, LATER CHARGED WITH THE MURDER OF GAMBINO FAMILY MEMBER CHARLEY CALISE.

Doonesbury

BY GARRY TRUDEAU

♪ *"THESE LITTLE TOWN BLUES..."* ♪

OUCH!

6-12

WELL, MAYBE THAT'S ENOUGH DANCING FOR TONIGHT, MOMMY.

OH, RONNIE, IT'S STILL SO EXCITING TO LISTEN TO FRANCIS' RECORDS...

I'M SO GLAD HE'S FINALLY GOTTEN THE RESPECT HE DESERVES. FIRST THE MEDAL, THEN THE DOCTORATE. AND HE LOOKED AS HUMBLED BY IT ALL AS A FIVE-YEAR-OLD BOY!

THAT'S **DR.** SINATRA, YOU LITTLE BIMBO!

YES, SIR, **DR.** SINATRA. WOULD YOU LIKE ANOTHER CARD?

Doonesbury

BY GARRY TRUDEAU

WHADDA YA MEAN, YA *GOTTA SHUFFLE! DEAL*, SISTER!

I'M SORRY, DR. SINATRA, THOSE ARE THE HOUSE RULES.

READ MY LIPS, HONEY! I SAID, *DEAL THE CARDS!*

I COULD LOSE MY JOB, DR. SINATRA.

YOU'RE *DAMN RIGHT* YOU COULD LOSE YOUR JOB! GET ME YOUR (EXPLETIVE) BOSS!

BUT...

GET ME YOUR (OBSCENE GERUND) *BOSS*, YOU LITTLE (ANATOMICALLY EXPLICIT EPITHET)!

OBSCENE GERUND?

Doonesbury

BY GARRY TRUDEAU

FRANKIE! HELLUVA SHOW! LOVED IT! YOU STILL GOT THE GOLDEN PIPES, AMICO NOSTRA!

THANK YOU, DON. I APPRECIATE THAT.

FRANKIE, I WANT YOU TO MEET SOME FRIENDS OF MINE.

I CAN'T, DON. I'VE GOT TO GO SEE ABOUT GETTING THIS BROAD FIRED FROM THE CASINO.

FRANKIE. SIT DOWN. SHOW SOME RESPECT. I'M SITTIN' WITH MADE GUYS HERE.

MADE GUYS? YOU'RE ALL MURDERERS! WOW! NO KIDDING?

HEE, HEE! WHAT I TELL YOU? SAME SKINNY KID WITH STARS IN HIS EYES!

LET ME GO GET A PHOTOGRAPHER!

Doonesbury

BY GARRY TRUDEAU

CHERYL, WHAT'S THIS NONSENSE ABOUT HAVING TO SHUFFLE BEFORE DEALING TO DR. SINATRA?

I WAS JUST FOLLOWING HOUSE RULES, SIR.

HOUSE RULES? CHERYL, THERE WOULDN'T *BE* A HOUSE IF NOT FOR THE BUSINESS DR. SINATRA PULLS IN!

YOU TOLD US NO EXCEPTIONS, SIR.

WHAT'S THE *MATTER* WITH YOU, GIRL? FRANK SINATRA IS *ABOVE* THE RULES! HE'S *ABOVE* SIMPLE COURTESY! HE DOES IT *HIS* WAY!

BUT...

SLAP HER AROUND, STEVE!

PLEASE, FRANK, I CAN HANDLE THIS!

SORRY ABOUT THE DISTURBANCE, FOLKS.

climaxed a thrilling career comeback in winning an Oscar for the best supporting role. A year ago the spindly crooner was considered washed up in Hollywood."

Psychiatrist Ralph Greenson, who had now been treating Frank for three months, watched the awards on television. As Frank ran up to the stage to get his Oscar, the psychiatrist said to his wife, "That's it. We'll never see him again." Dr. Greenson knew his patient well. The next week Frank called and canceled his appointment, saying he no longer needed to probe his past with a psychiatrist.

"I found out all I wanted to know," he said. Later, he completely dismissed psychoanalysis. "I've never gone in for that analysis bit, and I don't intend to start now. All I know is that I'm feeling great, and I'm not askin' myself why. The time you start talkin' to yourself is when you're unhappy, and I'm happy with what I am. So long as I keep busy I feel great."

Keeping busy meant constant movement and incessant action. Even Frank couldn't explain his restlessness. "This is something I can't help," he told film director Vincente Minnelli. "I have to go. No one seems able to help me with it—doctors, no one. I have to move."

Frank's success in *From Here to Eternity* brought him the kind of work that had eluded him for years. "The greatest change in my life began the night they gave me the Oscar," he said. "It's funny about that statue—I don't think any actor can experience something like that and not change."

Financially, Frank had been revitalized a few months before, when he was approved for a Nevada state gambling license, and bought two percent of the Sands Hotel for $54,000. During the hearing before the State Tax Commission, one commissioner had objected to his application, saying that he should use the purchase money to pay his back taxes. Frank explained that he was paying the I.R.S. $1,000 a week for every week he worked and had already reduced his $109,000 debt to $90,000.

"In the past ten years I've paid the government over a million dollars in income tax, and I don't think they're too concerned about my not paying them $90,000," he said. Worried about Frank's ties to organized crime, the commissioners questioned him about his friends and associates. "My interest is purely as a business investment," he said, "and my participation would be limited to helping co-produce the dinner shows."

Robbins E. Cahill, one of the commissioners, later expressed the board's concern about Frank's Mafia associations. "Entertainment people are always closely connected to the element that we always feared in those days because both of them had money. I think, like a lot of great entertainers, Frank knew many, many hoodlums."

After deliberating on and off for fourteen months, the commission finally approved the application that would eventually make Frank a multimillionaire.

"I can't tell you how happy this makes me," he said at the time. "I've been trying for more than a year to get a foothold in Las Vegas because I believe it has a great future. I want to be a part of that future. . . . You know, an entertainer's life is somewhat uncertain. It all depends on the whims of the public. When I am finished as an entertainer, I want to have an investment that will insure the education of my children and a sufficient income for me. I think this Sands investment will keep me very comfortably."

In addition to mobster Bugsy Siegel's Flamingo, there were only four hotels on the Las Vegas strip, but Frank knew the city would eventually be a boomtown for gamblers. It couldn't miss; it was the only place in the country that had legalized casino gambling. Frank's two percent interest in the Sands, which grew to nine percent, was a testament to his good relations with the underworld, for the new luxury hotel was at that time controlled by more Mafia groups than any other casino in Nevada.

Justice Department files indicate that one stockholder was persuaded to sell two of his five shares of stock in the Sands to Sinatra for $70,000, giving Frank his initial two percent. Informants told the FBI that Vincente "Jimmy Blue Eyes" Alo then gave Frank "a gift of seven percent of this hotel," bringing his share to nine percent.

The number one man at the Sands was Joseph "Doc" Stacher, a New Jersey gangster who was second only to Meyer Lansky in the syndicate and looked on Frank as his son. Stacher's police record listed atrocious assault and battery, robbery, larceny, bootlegging, hijacking, and murder investigations. The casino's official greeter was Charles "Babe" Baron, once suspected of murder. Some of the less visible gangsters involved with the Sands included Joe Fusco of the old Capone mob, Meyer Lansky, Abner "Longy" Zwillman, Anthony "Joe Batters" Accardo, Gerardo Catena, acting boss of the Genovese family in New York, and Abraham Teitelbaum, a former attorney for the Capone mob who frequently stated: "Alphonse Capone was one of the most honorable men I ever met."

Years after he fled the U.S. and went into exile in Israel, Doc Stacher admitted that the mob had offered Frank a share in the Sands so that he would draw the high rollers.

"I was the man who built the Sands," Stacher said in 1979. "To make sure we'd get enough top-level investors, we brought George Raft into the deal and sold Frank Sinatra a nine percent stake in the hotel. Frank was flattered to be invited, but the object was to get him to perform there, because there's no bigger draw in Las Vegas. When Frankie was performing, the hotel really filled up."

For the next thirteen years, Frank would reign supreme at the Sands, eventually becoming vice-president of the corporation and earning over $100,000 a week when he performed. His drawing power was such that he could do no wrong in the eyes of the Mafia owners. When they gave him three thousand dollars a night to gamble with, he often went through the money in twenty minutes, but they extended credit, frequently allowing him to play no-limit games, and sometimes even ignoring his markers. They built a three-bedroom suite on the ground floor for him because they knew he was afraid of heights—he always booked hotel suites on low floors— and they installed a private swimming pool for him protected by a stone wall. Later, he insisted they put in a health club with a sauna and steam bath as well. They ordered the Italian breads, prosciutto, and provolone that he loved flown in from New York.

Frank performed in the Copa Room and opened his show by saying, "Welcome to my room." Because he filled the house, the casino was his kingdom. If a room service waiter brought him a hamburger that was too well done, there was a good chance that it would be thrown against the wall, and the chef fired. If he didn't like the color of a telephone, he tore it out of the wall. Bellboys were kept on duty just to take care of his early morning requests for pizza or blueberry pie. He "comped" all of his friends with free food and free drinks for days at a time, and expected each of them to perform at the Sands exclusively. If they didn't, they were no longer his friends, as Judy Garland found out when she accepted a Las Vegas engagement at another hotel.

"My playing the New Frontier was strictly a business deal," she said, "but Frank took it as a personal rebuff. His attitude since then, to be polite, has been pretty repulsive."

Frank made movies at the Sands, recorded albums, sponsored boxing matches, threw glamorous opening night parties, and made it the place to go to on the Las Vegas strip. He frequently flew in Hollywood celebrities, and crowds jammed the casino just in hope of seeing a star having a drink or placing a few bets. Hank Greenspun, publisher of the *Las Vegas Sun*, wrote a front page editorial saying that when Frank Sinatra was in town, it was the economic equivalent of three conventions.

"I'm very grateful to Frank because he made my husband a great deal of money," said Corinne Entratter, wife of the president of the Sands. "Of course, my husband made Frank even more, and for a while, everyone benefited from having Sinatra at the Sands. It was after they started making so much money they didn't know what to do with it that they had problems. In the beginning, everyone pulled together; afterwards, they wanted to kill each other.

"Everyone made more money when Frank played the strip, especially cab drivers and hookers," she said. "Frank loved hookers, and used them a great deal. He preferred them because he didn't have to deal with them emotionally. And he always paid them well."

Over the years, prostitutes became a staple in Sinatra's life, and not just in Las Vegas. "I remember when Frank and the Rat Pack were doing *4 For Texas* . . . and a whole gang of prostitutes—well, they were call girls, they weren't actually prostitutes—were shipped up there to the boondocks . . . they were also going to act as girls sitting at a bar in the movie, and the man in charge, an older gentleman, very moral and proper, who had to handle arrangements was so upset," said Lor-Ann Land, a secretary on the film. "He had to pay them more than scale and he didn't know how to figure it all out. How to designate what they were *really* being paid for. . . ."

Frank was one of the pioneer entertainers in Las Vegas, along with Jimmy Durante, Joe E. Lewis, Sophie Tucker, Ted Lewis, Tommy Dorsey, Danny Thomas, Tony Martin, Nat King Cole, "Fat Jack" Leonard, and the Will Mastin

Trio featuring Sammy Davis, Jr. Of them all, Frank became the star most identified with Las Vegas over the years.

Las Vegas was an open city in the 1950s—open to mobsters, to gamblers, to hookers. No legal apparatus had been established to prevent owners from "skimming" the take: understating the gross receipts from gambling, then reporting as revenue only what was left. There was no law limiting the amount or size of cash transactions, and no requirement that they be reported to the Internal Revenue Service. This made casinos perfect places for criminals to hide or launder illegal money. There were no cameras in the counting rooms in those days. Casino directors regularly took money off the top of the nightly take, and after pocketing their own share, dispatched Mafia couriers, who delivered illegal millions in skimmed money to the real owners—the participating syndicate bosses, who expected a share of the skim in return for their initial investment. Owning a piece of a casino meant that you owned part of a money forest where you simply shook the trees and watched thousand-dollar bills fall like leaves. As Meyer Lansky said, "The only man who wins in the casino is the guy who owns the place."

Conceived and built by the Mafia, Las Vegas remains a town where the mob feels comfortable and where hoodlums are welcomed with open arms.

"You'll find the mob people get the finest suite of rooms—rooms that might cost three hundred bucks a day—and invitations to the best shows in town, and we never pick up a tab because it's all on the house," said Vinnie Teresa of the New England Mafia. "I don't know how many times I got telegrams inviting me to the biggest hotel in Las Vegas because Frank Sinatra or Sammy Davis was in town that week. All the mob would show up for their shows. 'Come on down and be our guest . . . we have a suite of rooms reserved for you,' one of the hotel's bosses would say. Why? They want you because you're a gambler and because suckers love to see tough guys just like they like to see big-name entertainers. They love to walk into a casino or a card room, spot you, and whisper in someone's ear: 'Hey, Joe, do you know who that guy is? That's Vinnie Teresa from the New England mob.' If a place gets the name that mob people come in regularly, suckers will flock there just to gape at mob people like they were movie stars and to get next to a table to watch how you gamble. . . . Before you know it, they're into the game themselves, and they're dropping a bundle.''

Frank had begun going to Las Vegas with his gangster friends shortly after he moved to the West Coast, sometimes dropping thousands of dollars at the tables. Gambling was second nature to him. He had grown up with a mother who had her own bookie and frequently woke up the neighbors by playing boccie (an Italian bowling game) outside their windows with truck drivers, challenging them to five-dollar throws. Accustomed to his father's regular poker games, Frank became familiar with betting on all sports, especially boxing and horse racing. His Uncle Gus ran numbers in Hoboken and was arrested several times for possession of lottery slips; his Uncle Babe was arrested more than twenty times for crimes like usury and loan-sharking, often lending money to gamblers at illegal interest rates.

Frank had an affinity with the men who ran Las Vegas; he felt at home in their nocturnal environment, and gambled with abandon. One evening, he lost over fifty thousand dollars at baccarat. He first played this fast, big-money card game in the south of France and was so enthralled by the action that he insisted the Sands start its own baccarat game in 1959.

"I've seen Frank go up to the baccarat table with ten thousand dollars, sit down, put the bundle on the table, ride it up to thirty thousand, lose it, and walk away from the table with a shrug,'' said vibraphonist Red Norvo.

Away from Las Vegas, Frank continued to gamble by telephone, calling in his roulette bets. He chose roulette, he said, "because you can't shoot craps by phone."

"Frank destroys money," said Joe DiMaggio.

"He'll bet on anything," said Al Algiro.

Frank's good fortune held throughout 1954. He was named the most popular male vocalist in the year-end *Downbeat* poll, an honor he had not received since 1947. The magazine also selected him as the Top Pop Records Personality of the year, and *Metronome* christened him Singer of the Year for his best-selling single, "Young at Heart," and his album, *Swing Easy*.

Feeling the need to chronicle his comeback, Frank placed a full-page ad in *Billboard* at the end of the year enumerating the various awards he had received, the films he had in release (*Suddenly* and *Young at Heart*), the film he was shooting (*Not as a Stranger*), and the film he was scheduled to start (*Guys and Dolls*). He signed the ad, "Busy, busy, busy—Frank."

But his string of good luck was broken at two A.M. the morning of December 9, 1954, as he was leaving the Crescendo on Sunset Boulevard with Texas oilman Bob Neal, model Cindy Hayes, and Judy Garland. After hearing Mel Tormé sing, the foursome sneaked out of the nightclub hiding drinks under their coats. As they walked into the foyer, Jim Byron yelled to Bob Neal. Byron, who was Mel Tormé's publicist, was in a telephone booth calling his answering service for messages. Not recognizing Judy Garland, who was six months pregnant, he asked Neal who the woman was because he wanted to tell the Hollywood columnists that Frank Sinatra and his friends had stopped by to hear his client. Neal told him and returned to the group, telling Frank what Byron wanted.

In a rage, Frank lunged at the telephone booth, shouting, "Get out of there, you bastard. Get out of there. What business is it of yours who we're with? You fucking parasite. You're nothing but a leech. You're a newspaperman. I hate cops and I hate reporters. Get out of there right now and take off your fucking glasses."

Shaken by the outburst, Byron stumbled out of the telephone booth. Frank continued to berate him as he made his way to the parking lot.

"Why don't you go out and make a decent living and not suck off other people?" Frank screamed. "You leech."

"And who are you, Frank? You're dependent on other people. You're dependent on the press and the public."

"I am not," yelled Frank. "I have talent and I am dependent only on myself."

Frank slammed his left fist into the side of Byron's face, and the publicist retaliated with a few kicks and one flailing blow to the nose that caused Frank to yell, "He hit me, he hit me!" Parking lot attendants separated them.

The next day, despite eyewitness accounts, Frank gave another version of the events: "He was trying to make it seem an illicit date or something, and anybody who thinks that has got to be a pretty sick guy. Especially when Judy was six months pregnant. I told him I resented his calling Judy a 'broad' and I added if he didn't know who Judy Garland was, he must have been living under a rock. I went back to Byron and told him to take his glasses off. Then suddenly two guys held my arms and Byron tried to knee me. He succeeded in denting my shin bone and clawing my hand. I couldn't do anything because I was held by two men. I broke loose. It ended when I gave him a left hook and dumped him on his fanny. Then I got scared. It was obvious he didn't know how to defend himself, and I didn't want any trouble. It ended there."

"I didn't get really mad at him until an hour or so later, when I emerged from the daze to contemplate his 'I've got talent, I've got talent,'" said Jim Byron. "If show business talent allows you to do this, then I suppose the talent of an atomic scientist who had perfected a new bomb would permit him to blow up the world.

"I never sued him even though the public and press were in sympathy with me. The police were sufficiently mad at Frank for his 'I hate cops' to call me and offer me protection if necessary. It wasn't necessary. I wasn't going ahead with anything."

Frank's behavior appalled journalists, many of whom recounted his fistfights with Lee Mortimer in 1947 and photographer Eddie Schisser in Houston in 1950, his threats to kill reporters in Mexico City, and the automobile incident with Bill Eccles at the Los Angeles airport. Some remembered that in 1949 at parking meter executive Donald Duncan's Palm Springs home, Frank slugged the bartender, Jack Wintermeyer, for not giving him the extra dry martini he had requested. Wintermeyer was taken to a hospital and treated for a gash on his forehead but he, too, refused to press charges after holding a "peace meeting" with Frank.

Yet there was also the Frank Sinatra who rushed to the hospital bed of Lee J. Cobb after he nearly died from a heart attack in June 1955. He was felled by a massive coronary shortly after divorcing his wife. Having named people as Communists before the House Un-American Activities Committee, Cobb had few friends left in Hollywood. There was no work for him and he was trying to support himself and his two children while on the edge of bankruptcy.

"I was in a low mental state then," he said. "I was sure my career had come to an end. Then Frank called and in his typical, unsentimental fashion, moved into my life. He flooded me with books, flowers, delicacies. He kept telling me what fine acting I still had ahead of me, discussing plans for me to direct one of his future films. He built an insulated wall around me that shielded me from tension, worry, and strain."

Frank paid all the hospital bills not covered by Cobb's insurance and then moved him to a rest home in the hills above Los Angeles for six weeks, again paying all expenses. He called him every day and visited regularly.

"That's where I first met Lee," said Cobb's future wife, "and he was so grateful to Frank, so surprised, and so very touched. It was the kind of instant generosity you rarely see. The amazing thing is that Frank and Lee were not close friends at the time. They knew each other, but that was it."

The two men had met as co-stars in *The Miracle of the Bells* in 1949. Both were gamblers and shared the same kind of liberal politics. Frank admired Cobb's acting talent and said that he should have won the 1954 Academy Award for his performance as Johnny Friendly in *On the Waterfront*.

"After the rest home, Frank moved Lee into his own home in Palm Springs, and then he moved him into a beautiful apartment in Los Angeles," said Mrs. Cobb. "It was one of those places that very rich people live in—clean and beautiful, with walls that are all quilted and comfortable. I don't know if Frank picked it out, or someone on his staff, but he paid for everything. He was wonderful during those critical months, and yet very elusive. He was never there to be thanked or hugged or shown any kind of gratitude. He didn't seem to like that or want that.

"He and Lee had long talks about life and death because Lee was so close to dying at one point. Frank seemed to understand how hard it was sometimes to keep on going, how elusive the will to live can be. He said that you really had to scrape bottom before you could appreciate life and start living again. Frank had been through bad times, too, and I think he sensed a soulmate in Lee. Maybe he was so grateful for having made a comeback that he extended himself to someone in need—the kind of need he himself had once known. I don't know, but it was a felicitous life-saving moment for Lee, and maybe in its way it was for Sinatra, too."

Frank's comeback seemed to produce generosity in him that was not unlike his mother's garnering votes by distributing food baskets to the needy while making her political rounds in Hoboken.

When Sammy Davis, Jr., lost his eye in an automobile

accident in 1954, Frank drove seventy miles from Los Angeles to San Bernadino Community Hospital to see him, and insisted that Sammy use his house in Palm Springs to recuperate.

When Charlie Morrison, owner of the Mocambo in Los Angeles, died in 1957, leaving his widow with a stack of debts and no insurance, his creditors threatened to close the club, forcing his wife into bankruptcy.

"Charlie had thousands of friends, but we had about four dollars," she said. "Then Frank called me up. He said, 'Mary, I don't have anything to do for two weeks. How about me coming into the Mocambo with Nelson Riddle's orchestra?' He had never sung at any club in Hollywood, and it was like New Year's Eve every night. We took in over $100,000 in those two weeks, and I gave old Charlie a millionaire's funeral. It kept me going for a year besides. Celebrities were shoving against celebrities, and the waiters were able to pay off the mortgages on their homes."

When Bela Lugosi committed himself to a hospital because he was an addict, Frank wrote him a sympathetic note, accompanied by a huge package of delicacies. "It gave me such a boost," said Lugosi in 1955. "It was a wonderful surprise. I've never met Sinatra, but I hope to soon. He was the only star I heard from."

Even close friends had trouble understanding the extremes in Frank that could drive him to physical brutality one minute and sweet generosity the next.

"To this day Frank doesn't know how to express affection," said Phil Silvers. "He does it with expensive gifts."

Frank's psychiatrist analyzed his generosity as the need to dominate people as his mother did. "His generosity means that he himself is the ever-bountiful, giving person," said Dr. Ralph Greenson.

"He was real good to his girls," said his makeup man, Beans Ponedel. "He gave them all parts in his movies. He did it for Gloria Vanderbilt in *Johnny Concho*, but she walked out; he did it for Shirley MacLaine (*Some Came Running*); he did it for Joi Lansing (*A Hole in the Head*); he did it for Natalie Wood (*Kings Go Forth*)."

Some people saw Frank's generosity as a means of making amends for past wrongs. "I remember Frank reaming out his manager, Bobby Burns, in front of everyone one night—screaming and yelling and cursing him up one side and down the other," said Mitch Miller. "He never apologized because Frank cannot say 'I'm sorry,' but the next day Burns found a brand new Cadillac in the driveway from Frank. Is that generosity, or simply extravagant reparation? I don't know."

At one movie location, Frank used generosity to make amends for an outburst. "That prop boy I yelled at a few minutes ago—I understand his wife is sick," he said to Beans Ponedel. "Send her flowers and make sure that we pay all the medical bills."

Some thought Frank's generosity stemmed from his need to be respected by people he respects, like an old Italian padrone, but one old friend dismissed it as nothing more than showing off.

"He's just like Lucky Luciano—always having to play bigshot," said the friend. "When Lucky was in prison, he had all the money in the world to buy favors, and no inmate ever had to want for a few dollars as long as word of his need reached Luciano. You can imagine all the fawning and kowtowing that went on over those donations. It's the same thing with Frank."

"There are times when Frank behaves despicably," said former reporter Kendis Rochlen. 'He'll be nasty, rude, inconsiderate, uncooperative, and ungrateful. Then he'll turn right around and quietly do something generous and considerate for someone without even expecting thanks. . . . In fact, he seldom makes known some of the nice, generous things he does for people he happens to admire. I guess he's too busy alienating reporters, hating cops, and sneering his way onto the cover of *Time* magazine."

Frank's spontaneous acts of kindness laid the foundation for his reputation as a generous, giving man and provided his press agents with what they needed at other times to cover his atrocious behavior.

17

Frank wanted the role of Terry Malloy in *On the Waterfront* so that he could return to Hoboken as a conquering hero. The producer, Sam Spiegel, wanted Marlon Brando to play the part. "I wanted Frank to play the priest, but he wanted to play the Marlon Brando role," said Spiegel.

Smarting over losing the lead to Brando, an actor he despised—Sinatra called Brando "Mumbles" and "the most overrated actor in the world"—Frank sued Sam Spiegel for $500,000, claiming breach of contract. He and Spiegel later settled the lawsuit amicably, without any exchange of money.

In 1954 and 1955 Frank made more movies than any other star in Hollywood. He played a psychopathic assassin in *Suddenly;* a saloon pianist in *Young at Heart;* a physician in *Not as a Stranger;* a theatrical agent in *The Tender Trap;* the proprietor of "the oldest established permanent floating crap game in New York" in *Guys and Dolls;* and a drug-addicted card dealer, Frankie Machine, in *The Man with the Golden Arm,* which was his favorite movie and the one that earned him an Oscar nomination for best actor.

"I'm in demand—fortunately, yes," he said in 1955. "All these wonderful roles came together—*Guys and Dolls, The Tender Trap, Golden Arm*—and I have got five (*Johnny Concho, High Society, The Pride and the Passion, The Joker Is Wild,* and *Pal Joey*) planned ahead, including two for my own company—a pretty even split between straight parts and musicals, but I don't call it a comeback. I wasn't away anywhere."

Frank resented the press for writing up his current success as a "comeback," thereby implying that he had returned after a long period of failure. At the *Guys and Dolls* premiere in Hollywood, he opened the program prepared by the studio advertising department and found his show business career described "with ups and downs matching the steepness of a Himalayan mountain peak. After soaring to what was almost national adulation a dozen years ago, a combination of poor roles, a bad press, and other things sent his career zooming downward. He was reputedly washed up. Today his 'second career' is in high gear." Frank was furious.

The next day, he screamed about the program's summary of his career. "Where do they get that stuff—'He was reputedly washed up.' 'My career zoomed downward.' 'My second career.' Maybe I didn't make movies for a couple of years, but I bet I made more money on TV, in nightclubs, and making records than half the stars in Hollywood."

Still, Frank couldn't ignore his meager record sales in the bad years, and he was embarrassed by some of the recordings he had made at Columbia Records. "Nowadays I hear records I made three or four years ago and I wish I could destroy the master records," he said. "It was all because of emotion. No doubt about it."

When Columbia reissued those records to cash in on his new success, Frank retaliated by denouncing the company, saying that he had been forced to record music licensed by Broadcast Music Inc. (BMI), in which Columbia's parent company, CBS, had an interest. He gave scathing interviews to the press and sent telegrams to senators and congressmen, demanding antitrust action against Columbia to bar broadcasters from owning music publishing and recording firms.

The focus of his anger was Mitch Miller, director of artists and repertoire, whom he accused of ruining his career by selecting inferior songs with cheap musical gimmicks such as barking dogs and washboards for accompaniment.

"Before Mr. Miller's advent on the scene, I had a successful recording career which quickly went into decline," said Frank. "It is now a matter of record that since I have associated myself with Capitol Records, a company free of broadcasting affiliations, my career is again financially, creatively, and artistically healthy."

Mitch Miller was outraged by Frank's attack. "His career went down the drain because of his emotional turmoil over Ava Gardner," he said. "I had nothing to do with him losing his movie contract, losing his television show, losing his radio show. I had nothing to do with him losing his voice. He should look to himself as the cause of his own failure and stop trying to blame others. Besides, his contract gave him total control over all his material. He didn't have to do anything he didn't want to do. And as far as gimmicks go, let me tell you that the microphone is the greatest gimmick of all. Take away the microphone and Sinatra and most other pop singers would be slicing salami in a delicatessen."

Despite the angry telegrams, no congressional action was taken against Columbia Records or Mitch Miller, but Frank became obsessed with hating Miller and refused all entreaties by friends to make up. When Erroll Garner recorded "On the Street Where You Live," he called Frank in Las Vegas and played the recording for him.

"Wonderful, wonderful," said Frank. "Whose orchestra is that with you?"

"Mitch Miller," said Garner.

Frank hung up the phone.

Years later, Miller was in Las Vegas staying at the Sands, and Jack Entratter dragged him over to Frank to shake hands. "It's time you two became friends again." he said. Miller very agreeably extended his hand and said, "Hi, Frank, how are you." Frank, who was sitting with a large table of friends, looked up and said, "Fuck off."

"It was very embarrassing," recalled Miller, "and it's kind of crazy because I never really did anything to him except record some great records."

Columnist Dorothy Kilgallen experienced the same kind of rage after her 1956 newspaper series entitled "The Real Frank Sinatra Story" appeared in the *New York Journal-American*, detailing, among other things, Frank's romances with Anita Ekberg, Gloria Vanderbilt, Kim Novak, Jill Corey, Jo Ann Tolley, Melissa Weston, and Lisa Ferraday.

"A few of the women, like Ava and Lana, were public idols themselves and priceless examples of feminine beauty," she wrote. "Many more, of course, have been the fluffy little struggling dolls of show business, pretty and small-waisted and similar under the standard layer of peach-colored Pan-Cake makeup—starlets who never got past first base in Hollywood, assorted models and vocalists, and chorus girls now lost in the ghosts of floor shows past. Others belonged to the classification most gently described as tawdry."

Frank sent Miss Kilgallen a tombstone carved with her name. Then he incorporated her into his nightclub act, ridiculing her as "the chinless wonder." At the Copa he said, "Dorothy Kilgallen isn't here tonight. I guess she's out shopping for a new chin." At the Sands, he held up one of his car keys and said, "Doesn't that look like Dorothy Kilgallen's profile?" He continued his unstinting vitriole for the next nine years, refusing to relent until the day she died. Informed of her death in November 1965, he said, "Well, guess I got to change my whole act now."

After directing *Not as a Stranger*, during which Frank went on a drunken bender with Robert Mitchum and Broderick Crawford, tore down the walls of his dressing room and ripped out phones, Stanley Kramer swore he would never use him again, even if Kramer had to go begging with a tin cup. Yet, months later and against his better judgment, he signed Frank to play Miguel, the Spanish peasant boy in *The Pride and the Passion* which began with sixteen weeks of filming in Spain in April 1956. Spain was tantalizing to Frank because Ava was there, living a few miles outside of Madrid, but he later regretted signing the contract as much as Kramer did.

His contract specified that "no other artist is to receive better living accommodations than those provided for Sinatra; that he is to be paid ten thousand dollars per week and supplied with twenty-five dollars per day for tips and incidentals, plus reasonable baggage allowance."

Sinatra refused to stay on location "in the sticks" with Cary Grant, Sophia Loren, and the rest of the cast, insisting on his own suite at the Hotel Castellana Hilton in Madrid. He also insisted on having a car at his disposal and demanded that Kramer pay five thousand dollars to transport his Thunderbird from Los Angeles to Madrid. Kramer offered him a fifteen-thousand-dollar Mercedes with a chauffeur instead. Frank wanted a convertible, and refused to work until he got one; the transatlantic negotiations between his agents and the director's lawyers over the car went on for weeks.

"His entrance to Spain was preceded by this controversy," said novelist Richard Condon, who was a publicist at the time. "Kramer prevailed on the transportation, but Francis would not forgive him. They argued through intermediaries also over a stereophonic record player for Frank's hotel suite, and on the first night of shooting in a village south of Madrid, Frank summoned Kramer to him before the assemblage of the extras, crew, and players, and said that if Kramer didn't get him out of there and back to the hotel by eleven-thirty that night that Frank would piss on him. That got things off to a lame start."

The director became alarmed about Frank's heavy expenses after the first week and cabled company lawyers in Los Angeles about his $644 bill for long distance calls and cables, one of which went to his Chicago bookie.

"The ten thousand pesetas cash were spent entertaining Sinatra's various friends and hangers-on," wrote the director's assistant. "I hope to be able to resolve this problem in some reasonable manner with Sinatra, but will be careful not to take a stand so equivocal that it is difficult to back out of."

Yet, the next week, Frank flew Peggy Connolly in to stay with him and gave the twenty-four-year-old singer the right to charge anything to his account, including her beauty salon bills, jewelry from Loewe's, gloves, a key ring, dolls, flowers, caviar, and an $850 handbag. Peggy was a beautiful brunette who had been dating Frank for a few months. When reporters asked her about the possibility of becoming the next Mrs. Sinatra, she said, "Nothing is impossible. You never know when you're going to get married."

A few days after her arrival, Frank was sitting in his hotel suite with Richard Condon and others when Ava called. Frank sauntered to the phone to talk to her.

"You goddamned jerk," she yelled so loudly that everyone in the room could hear. "You've been here how many days and you don't even call me."

"I've been busy," said Frank.

"What's happening?"

Peggy Connolly walked into the room and listened to Frank's end of the conversation. A few minutes later, he hung up.

"Was that Ava?"

"Yes, it was."

"Are you going to see her?"

"Maybe."

"Well, I won't like it at all. I didn't come here so you could see Ava."

Frank looked at her for a few seconds and then very

calmly told her to go back into the bedroom, pack her bags, and leave. Weeks later, he sent her a twenty-thousand-dollar grand piano and begged her to return. She did, but not even Peggy Connolly could make Spain tolerable for Frank. He complained to everyone. "Who found this creepy place, a drunken helicopter pilot?" he asked Kramer, fuming about the primitive state of telephone service in Franco's Spain. He had mailed 143 letters to the United States and on the back of each envelope he had written "Franco is a fink" in English.

"Sixteen weeks," he said. "I can't stay in one place sixteen weeks, I'll kill myself." He harangued the director about his taking so long to shoot, complained about the script, and refused to rehearse. "Let's get this circus on the road. Forget rehearsals. Just keep the cameras turning," he said, refusing to do more than one take.

He threatened to walk off the movie, and the director knew better than to invoke the legalities of his contract. The year before, Frank had walked out on the 125-member company filming *Carousel* in Boothbay Harbor, Maine, when he was told that the movie was being shot both in standard thirty-five-millimeter CinemaScope and a new fifty-five-millimeter wide-screen process, requiring at least two takes for every shot.

"I will not make two pictures for the price of one," Frank had said as he stormed off the set. Twentieth Century Fox sued him for one million dollars for breach of contract, but Sinatra could not have cared less.

"They just didn't know how to handle Frank," said Beans Ponedel. "You can't ever tell him to do something. You've got to suggest. He was always yelling at Kramer, 'Don't tell me. Suggest. Don't tell me. Suggest.' "

"When Sinatra walks into a room, tension walks in beside him," said Stanley Kramer. "You don't always know why, but if he's tense, he spreads it. When we were shooting in Spain, he was impatient. . . . He didn't want to wait or rehearse. He didn't want to wait around while crowd scenes were being set up. He wanted his work all done together. He was very unhappy. He couldn't stand it, he wanted to break loose. Eventually, for the sake of harmony, we shot all his scenes together and he left early. The rest of the cast acquiesced because of the tension, which was horrific."

To distract Frank, the unit photographer, Sam Shaw, took

him on cultural excursions to the Prado art museum and engaged him in discussions about art.

Frank had first discovered art back in the '40's, when he was appearing at the Paramount. He went to the Museum of Modern Art one day, and, as he said later, "I just couldn't believe it, all those paintings." He began experimenting on his own, drawing a lot of clowns first and then branching out into street scenes and backyards.

"I had the sense that Frank was sort of looking to Sam [Shaw] for whatever might have been culturally missing in his life," said Jeannie Sakol, a former free-lance journalist on location in Spain. "When Sam started talking about art, Frank became really fascinated. Sam was a mentor and opened a door to things that Frank had never seen before. He was in a fretful mood, though, and not terribly happy at the time. I remember one night Sam and I and Frank went out to dinner, and I nearly died of embarrassment. The waitress served us chicken and came back to the table to see if there was anything else we wanted. Frank picked up a chicken leg and moved it up and back in his mouth, back and forth, back and forth. . . . Sam cajoled him out of it finally, and he put it down, but he was aching for some action. Clearly, I wasn't it and the waitress wasn't it, and what was going on wasn't doing it for him either. He was kind of a bad boy."

Yet this man who could be so appallingly vulgar in public was also a man of taste with an extraordinary collection of Fabergé boxes, Steuben glass, and Indian crafts, as well as other American art and Impressionist paintings—including Pissarro, Dufy, Boudin, and Corot.

In Spain, Frank became agitated over an item in the *New York Journal-American* that cast an aspersion on Ava and her relationship with Sinatra. He was so determined to find out where the item had come from that he hired a private detective in New York.

"He called me in and said, 'I have to find out who gave that item. That's all there is to it,' " said Richard Condon. "Well, he did find out, and to have a rapprochement we arranged a dinner for Frank and Ava and two beards—myself and Otto Preminger. Throughout dinner, Frank and Ava never spoke to us—not one word. They were holding hands all night long and gazing sappily at each other, and when the last course was over, they stood up and left the room, leaving Otto and me with each other."

The reconciliation with Ava lasted only one evening. Since there was no hope for a renewed marriage, Frank wanted to leave Spain as soon as possible. On July first, he refused to work unless Stanley Kramer would promise him that he would be finished on or before July 25, 1956. Kramer explained that he had done his best to revise the schedule but still needed him until August first. Frank stamped his foot and demanded that he be let go on July 28; Kramer said he would try. Frank said that wasn't good enough; he was leaving July 28 whether Kramer was done shooting or not. The director reminded him of his contract, and Frank told him to sit on the contract; he was leaving on the twenty-eighth. This prompted a flurry of cables back and forth from the director to the production lawyers to Frank's lawyers and to his William Morris agent, Burt Allenberg. Disregarding the threat of suspension, Frank left on July 28, and the picture was completed without him.

Despite the dissension making the film, Frank received good reviews for his performance. "As the virtual star, the cannon [the Spanish peasants transport the cannon to outside the walls of Avila to destroy a French-occupied fort] does nobly—if it doesn't exactly out-act Sinatra, Grant, and Miss Loren, it is usually there, like Everest," wrote Hollis Alpert in the *Saturday Review*. "While the gun deserves a special Academy Award, Mr. Sinatra must be commended for his restrained and appealing *guerillero* leader, Mr. Grant for his stalwart, understated British captain, and Miss Loren for her good looks."

Time magazine applauded Frank "despite spit-curl bangs and a put-on accent."

The accent was something he had worked on with a Spanish-speaking friend, who was a musician. "He had prepared for the part of the simple shoemaker's son who leads the revolution against the French by having the script recorded by a heavily accented Spanish voice, which Frank memorized to get the speech exactly right," said Richard Condon. "This was, unfortunately, recorded by an Argentinian who, among other things, pronounced *yes* as "jess," making Frank sound, in the role, as if his dad had somehow scraped together enough money to send his boy to a preparatory school in Buenos Aires circa 1801."

Upon leaving Spain, Frank leaned out his hotel window and yelled, "Franco is a fink!" On the trip home with his publicist Warren Cowan, and his wife, Ronnie, Frank never stopped denigrating the Spanish dictator.

"He just hated Spain," said Ronnie Cowan, who started what she called a "little sexual number" with Frank on that trip to the United States that would be "an on and off thing" for almost twenty years. "He liked to make love lying on the floor listening to his own records. It was great!" she said.

Most women, married or single, made themselves readily available to Frank wherever he went, but he seemed to prefer the few who were indifferent to him. He spent weeks pursuing an actress whose dramatic dark beauty rivaled that of Ava Gardner's.

"I wasn't the least bit attracted to Frank and I hadn't liked his singing either," said this woman. "I thought he was a bum from the wrong side of the tracks, and I was quite a snob in those days. I was accustomed to monumental men with great style. Frank was not someone I wanted to be seen with, but after he works his charm on you for a while, he gets better.

"Swifty Lazar kept calling and calling me to go out with Frank, and I kept saying no. Swifty lived near Frank and was always getting him girls. He took the scraps that Frank did not want; he always said he liked the fallout. Swifty took me to Romanoff's one night, and Frank was there. I'd seen him at the Bogarts' party the week before, when he kept following me around the house. Literally following me. I had ignored him then, or at least tried to, but he kept following me, and Lauren Bacall kept following him. Finally, he turned to her and said, 'She's ignoring me.' Bacall put her hands on her hips and said, 'Yeah, she's ignoring you right into the sack.' She thought I was playing hard to get, and she knew that Frank was interested. She felt very threatened. At Romanoff's, she was sitting in Frank's lap, and her husband, Humphrey Bogart, was next to them. Frank kept asking me to dance, saying, 'Why won't you let me take you out? I think you are so beautiful. I want to be with you. Please.' "

Frank showered the beautiful actress with flowers and kept begging her to go out with him. After several pleading phone calls from Swifty Lazar, she finally agreed to accompany Frank to San Francisco, where he was making an appearance for the United Nations.

"He picked me up and drove to the airport," she said. "I remember when I got in the car, the radio was playing one of his records, and he said, 'That's your boy.' I forget which hotel we stayed in, but Frank had arranged for a room for me and one for him, which I found very considerate. I spent the night in his room, of course, but still thought it was very nice of him to arrange for two rooms. After checking into the hotel, we went to his suite and the phone was ringing as we walked in the door. Frank answered it and said, 'Yes, Captain. Okay, General. Yes, boss. Uh-huh. Okay, boss. Bye-bye.' It was Lauren Bacall. He shook his head, saying she was too pushy for words. I was quite surprised that she'd called him, knowing we were together, but I hadn't realized the extent of their relationship at the time."

When they returned to Los Angeles, Frank insisted that the actress come back to his apartment, where his houseboy was cooking a special pasta dinner with his favorite lemon meringue pie with criss-crosses on top.

"I just wanted to go home, take a shower, and relax, but Frank insisted that I have dinner with him. I finally agreed but said I would have to leave right after the lemon meringue pie. When we got to his apartment, his houseboy came out to get his bags. A few minutes later, I saw my bags coming in too. Frank said, 'Take them to my room.'

" 'Oh, no,' I said.

" 'Please. You must stay with me.'

" 'No, Frank. I can't. I've had a wonderful time, but I do want to get home. I really insist. I must.'

"Suddenly, his face twisted and contorted like a prune and he dropped to the floor, put his face in my lap, and started crying. He sobbed like a baby. 'Please don't believe what you hear about me,' he said. 'Please stay with me. I won't hurt you. Don't be afraid. Please, please stay with me.' It was quite unsettling, but I finally left.

"A few days later I agreed to go to Palm Springs with him. He said he wanted to cook pasta for me. In his house, there was an icon to Ava—a little painting of her on the wall going up the stairs with a candle underneath that he lit every day. It was a shrine to her. He talked about her all the time and how she had walked out on him and how he had lost his voice. He said he was so depressed that he wouldn't go out of the house during the day because he didn't want anyone to see him. He kept talking about the pain he felt at being rejected, and the terrible humiliation. I'll never forget it."

*   *   *

As if to get even, Frank seemed to need to humiliate others, women especially.

"He's a little twisted sexually," said Jacqueline Park, an actress who later became the mistress of Jack Warner. "There are a lot of odds and ends in his sex life. He loved call girls for orgies and he liked to see women in bed for kicks, but not all the time. . . . I didn't see him again because he wanted me to go to bed with another woman. . . . There were a lot of women who fell in love with Frank but he'd reject them and throw them over. There's a monster in him who wants to screw the world before it screws him—hurt people before they hurt him. Then he feels guilty about being so ugly, and that guilt makes him a Mr. Nice Guy and so he does favors for some of the girls he's used or rejected. When Joi Lansing, who was a regular bedmate of Frank's for years, was dying of leukemia, he paid for all of her hospital bills."

Judy Garland experienced the same type of treatment. After her marriage to director Vincente Minnelli broke up, she fell in love with Frank and confided to Joan Blondell that he would be her next husband. One night, she invited him to her house for an intimate dinner, and he accepted. She set the table beautifully with silver for two, but Frank never showed up and never called to explain why. Humiliated, she called Blondell in tears and begged her to come over to keep her company. "Oh, please, come," she said. "I'm alone in this big place I've taken. . . ." Joan went over and, after a few drinks, Judy told her that Frank had stood her up. A few months later, when Judy entered the Peter Bent Brigham Hospital for "exhaustion," Frank bombarded her with telephone calls and sent daily gifts of flowers, perfume, lingerie, and records. One night, he flew a planeload of mutual friends to Boston, and with the hospital's permission, took Judy out for the evening.

Although Frank dated other women, his secret relationship with Lauren Bacall was already being whispered about among their close friends. Noel Coward, who attended Frank's New Year's party in Palm Springs, commented on her possessiveness in his diary January 1, 1956, saying, "Frankie is enchanting as usual and, as usual, he has a 'broad' installed with whom he, as well as everyone else, is bored stiff. She is blond, cute, and determined, but I fear her determination will avail her very little, with Betty Bacall on the warpath."

As the party ended, Frank asked the Bogarts to stay on.

Lauren Bacall wanted to, but her husband insisted they leave. In the car going home she said, "We should have stayed."

Her husband disagreed. "No, we shouldn't," he said. "You must always remember we have a life of our own that has nothing to do with Frank. He chose to live the way he's living—alone. It's too bad if he's lonely, but that's his choice. We have our own road to travel, never forget that—we can't live his life."

There was no one in Hollywood whom Frank admired more than Humphrey Bogart. He worshiped the cynical, outspoken fifty-six-year-old actor as an artist, and looked up to him as a kind of mentor, continually asking him what books to read, knowing that Bogart had a thorough grounding in the classics. Bogart had attended Trinity and Andover in preparation for Yale, but had joined the navy instead of going to college. He was everything Frank wanted to be—educated, sophisticated, respected. On screen, Bogie was the ultimate tough guy and in person he had an intractable sense of self.

Bogart, in turn, was amused by Frank's mercurial temperament. "He's kind of a Don Quixote, tilting at windmills, fighting people who don't want to fight," he said. "He's a cop-hater. If he doesn't know who you are and you ask him a question, he thinks you're a cop. Sinatra is terribly funny. He's just amusing because he's a skinny little bastard and his bones kind of rattle together."

Much as he enjoyed Sinatra's company, Bogart said, "I don't think Frank's an adult emotionally. He can't settle down." Later, he told reporters that Frank's idea of paradise is a place where there are plenty of women and no newspapermen. "He doesn't realize it, but he'd be better off if it were the other way around."

Bogie and his wife formed a group known as the Holmby Hills Rat Pack, which was dedicated to drinking, laughing, staying up late, and not caring about public opinion. Frank was named pack master, Judy Garland, first vice-president, and her husband Sid Luft, the cage master. Agent Irving "Swifty" Lazar was recording secretary; Nathaniel Benchley, historian; and Lauren Bacall, den mother. Bogie was in charge of Rat Pack public relations because he was always good for an uninhibited quotation, and the press had real affection for him. The more he abused them, the more they liked him. David Niven, Mike Romanoff, and Jimmy Van Heusen were also members of this group, which Bogart said existed "for the relief of boredom and the perpetuation of independence. We admire ourselves and don't care for anyone else."

Some Hollywood Republicans like William Holden resented Bogie's Rat Pack, which adored Franklin Roosevelt, Harry Truman, and Adlai Stevenson. "Their conduct reflects on the way a nation is represented in the eyes of the world," said Holden. "It might sound stuffy and dull, but it is quite possible for people to have social intercourse without resorting to a rat pack and even to drink or do anything without resorting to a rat pack. People have worked for years to lend some dignity to our profession, and the rat pack reflects on the community and on my children and on their children and everybody's children."

On February 29, 1956, Humphrey Bogart was diagnosed as having throat cancer. He required surgery and radiation treatments to contain the malignancy. Unfortunately, the doctors operated too late, and Bogie had less than a year to live. As one of his closest friends, Frank visited him regularly when he was in town.

"It wasn't easy for him," said Lauren Bacall. "I don't think he could bear to see Bogie that way or bear to face the possibility of his death. Yet he cheered Bogie up when he was with him—made him laugh—kept the ring-a-ding act in high gear for him. He did it all the only way he knew how, and he did it well."

Bogie loved to hear about the practical jokes Frank played on their friend, Swifty Lazar, and applauded the lengths to which he would go to torment the tiny, bald-headed agent whose obsession with cleanliness was a familiar joke within the Rat Pack. Bogie used to take off Swifty's shoes and socks and rub his bare feet in the carpet just because Lazar couldn't bear naked contact with any floor. Bogie was delighted when Frank called him about hiring a plasterer to go into Lazar's apartment and brick in his clothes closet with drywall so that when Swifty walked in he thought he was in the wrong apartment. Finally realizing it *was* his apartment, he went crazy when he couldn't get to his little suits and velvet slippers. He started screaming at Frank and banging on his door, refusing to speak to him for weeks afterward. Another time, Frank took Lazar's favorite hat and served it to him under poached eggs, which amused Bogart no end.

In October, when Frank was playing the Sands, he sent a

chartered plane to Los Angeles to fly Cole Porter, Martha Hyer, Harry Kurnitz, Nancy Berg, Mike and Gloria Romanoff, the Burt Allenbergs, and Lazar to Las Vegas to celebrate Lauren Bacall's thirty-second birthday. Bogie did not attend. Instead, he spent the day on his boat with his son.

"He was somewhat jealous of Frank," said Lauren Bacall many years later. "Partly because he knew I loved being with him, partly because he thought Frank was in love with me, and partly because our physical life together, which had always ranked high, had less than flourished with his illness."

This was the closest Bacall ever came to admitting her passion for Frank during the time that her husband was dying. "It was no secret to any of us," said playwright Ketti Frings, who visited Bogart at home during his last days. "Everybody knew about Betty and Frank. We just hoped Bogie wouldn't find out. That would have been more killing than the cancer."

On Monday, January 14, 1957, Humphrey Bogart died, three weeks after his fifty-seventh birthday. Frank was performing in New York at the Copa when he got the news. He canceled his next two appearances, telling his agents, "I can't go on. I wouldn't be coherent." He called Lauren Bacall in California and offered her his house in Palm Springs for two weeks, then canceled three more shows. But he still couldn't bring himself to fly to the West Coast for the funeral.

The rest of the Bogart Rat Pack was there in full force, with David Niven, Swifty Lazar, and Mike Romanoff serving as pallbearers. Adolph Green and Betty Comden flew in from New York. Nunnally Johnson flew in from Georgia. Frank remained in Manhattan. He pleaded laryngitis, but close friends suspected that he had developed a crippling case of what George Evans once called "the guilt germs."

18

Frank made front-page headlines in February 1957 with a Hollywood scandal that lasted for months.

WITNESS SAYS SINATRA LIED blared the *Los Angeles Mirror-News*.

SINATRA AND "PRIVATE EYE" TO FACE PERJURY QUIZ roared the *Los Angeles Examiner*.

At issue was Frank's honesty in relating what had happened the evening of November 5, 1954, when he and Joe DiMaggio were suspected of staging a raid on an apartment in which Marilyn Monroe was supposedly having a lesbian relationship. Sinatra and DiMaggio were attempting to get evidence to use in the divorce she was seeking from DiMaggio, but they never caught Marilyn because the wrong apartment door was broken down.

After *Confidential* published a story entitled "The Real Reason for Marilyn Monroe's Divorce from Joe DiMaggio," which detailed the break-in, the California State Senate Investigating Committee began probing how stories about movie stars were leaked to exposé magazines. Frank was subpoenaed to testify about his part in the midnight raid. At first he refused, saying he didn't have any information relevant to the case. Then he threatened to sue the chief of police of Los Angeles, the police captain in charge of intelligence, and the two police detectives who served the subpoena on him in bed at four A.M., claiming that the service was improper.

"It was a good thing I was asleep," said Frank, "or I might have gotten a gun."

"It seems to me that somebody is attempting to take the spotlight away from the real issue in this matter," said the police chief, dismissing Frank's threat.

Finally forced to testify, Frank swore under oath that he had simply driven DiMaggio to the scene of the raid, where they were met by Philip Irwin and Barney Ruditsky, the two private detectives they had hired to gather evidence on Marilyn. Frank claimed that while he stood by his car smoking, DiMaggio; Billy Karen, the maître d' of the Villa Capri; Hank Sanicola; and the two detectives crashed into the apartment of Florence Kotz.

DiMaggio later claimed that he hadn't broken into the apartment either; Billy Karen said he didn't remember what happened; Hank Sanicola said that he and Frank stayed at the Villa Capri restaurant all night; and Barney Ruditsky was excused from testifying because of a heart ailment.

Philip Irwin testified that "almost all of Mr. Sinatra's statements were false." The twenty-four-year-old detective said that he was afraid to say much more because of his fear of Sinatra and the possibility of physical violence.

"Do you still fear him?" asked the committee counsel.

"Still very much so," said Irwin.

"What do you fear?"

"I'm afraid of being beaten up again."

"Aside from being beaten up, have you no other fears?"

"Yes," said Irwin. "I have other fears."

When asked why he was so frightened, the young man said that he had been beaten up after he sought out Frank to tell him that he had nothing to do with leaking the story to *Confidential*.

"And why did you seek out Mr. Sinatra?"

"Because I feared him—from rumors I had heard; I didn't want what happened [later] to happen."

The detective told of being badly beaten by men he had never seen before, and his story was corroborated by State Investigator James J. Callahan, who said: "Irwin had a black eye. I don't think his nose was broken, but it was very badly bruised. He had severe welts from his shoulder to the belt line. His arms and legs had been kicked. He was pretty thoroughly worked over."

The detective testified that Frank had accompanied the

men into Mrs. Kotz's apartment after Ruditsky had broken down the door. He said that Frank had turned on the light, causing the woman to scream. When Frank saw they were in the wrong apartment, he ran out with his friends and drove to the Villa Capri restaurant.

The landlady of the building also testified that she had seen Frank enter the building and run out of Mrs. Kotz's apartment a few minutes later.

With so many conflicting testimonies, the county grand jury decided to investigate the "wrong door raid," and hearings were set for March. Although Frank was represented by Martin Gang and Mickey Rudin of Gang, Kopp & Tyre, he called the Mafia's lawyer, Sidney Korshak, in Chicago for help. Korshak was renowned among gangsters as a man who could get just about anything accomplished with a couple of phone calls. Frank later hired Fred Otash, a private detective, to try to prove that he did not perjure himself before the State Senate Committee. By the time the grand jury convened, Frank and his friends had their previously divergent stories straight. Frank testified for fifty minutes, sticking to the story he had given the State Senate Committee. When asked how jurors could possibly reconcile his testimony with that of the detective Philip Irwin, he said, "Who are you going to believe, me or a guy who makes his living kicking down bedroom doors?"

Frank escaped indictment, and perjury was ruled out by the district attorney, who said: "There is definitely a bald conflict in the testimony. But the transcript falls short in its present form of showing the complete elements of a perjury."

DiMaggio and Monroe divorced several months later, but the friendship between Joe and Frank ended when Sinatra started dating Marilyn and passing her around to his friends. Joe never forgave Sinatra or Peter Lawford for allowing Marilyn's affair with Robert Kennedy to take place. He was bitter about them after her suicide and barred both men from attending her funeral in 1962.

In 1957, Frank was just beginning to test the effectiveness of litigation as a means of punishment. His first target was investigative reporter Bill Davidson, who had published a three-part biography of Frank in *Look* magazine, which earned Davidson the University of Illinois's Benjamin Franklin Award for the best article depicting a person living or dead in an American magazine for general circulation.

"I think the turning point of Frank's antipathy to the press—and that's the mild word—began with Bill's article," said Richard Condon. "Because we were in Spain shortly after that, and Frank was just rabid about the press at that time, just wild, and he mentioned Bill."

The first article, "Talent, Tantrums and Torment," appeared May 14, 1957. Infuriated, Frank sued Davidson and *Look* magazine for $2,300,000, claiming that he had been libeled as a "neurotic, depressed, and tormented person with suicidal tendencies and a libertine." His sixteen-page complaint charged that the article was "lewd, lascivious, and scurrilous, containing innuendos and references of the same nature and type as are contained in articles published in what are popularly known as scandal magazines."

He specifically denied the story of his appearance at the Democratic Convention in Chicago the summer before, when he sang the national anthem, and then rebuffed the Speaker of the House, Sam Rayburn, who put his hands on his arms, and said, "Aren't you going to sing 'The Yellow Rose of Texas' for us, Frank?"

Sinatra supposedly looked at Rayburn coldly and said, "Take your hands off the suit, creep." Speaker Rayburn sent a telegram denying the incident, but Davidson had an eyewitness source to the contrary.

The second article in *Look* appeared a week later, concentrating on Frank's vendetta with newsmen and why he was so afraid of personal publicity. It dispelled the legend of him as a poor little kid from the slums who ran with street toughs in Hoboken. Instead, he was depicted as a spoiled Mama's boy, who was dressed in Little Lord Fauntleroy suits as a baby, and fussed over by his grandmother, who raised him while his mother took care of political business. The article quoted neighbors who remembered him as the richest kid on the block and far too frail to have ever been in the many fights he later bragged about.

There was one major omission from the article. Davidson wrote that there had been an abortion mill in the Sinatra neighborhood and alluded to Dolly's role as a midwife, but made no connection between her and the abortion business that Frank wanted to keep hidden from everyone, especially his children.

The third installment, "Blondes, Brunettes and the Blues," detailed the women in his life, from Nancy Barbato and Ava Gardner to unknown secretaries and starlets like Joan Blackman who, when asked her identity, was introduced by Frank as "Ezzard Charles." The next day the *Los Angeles Mirror-News* reported: "Ezzard was an eyeful in shocking-pink gown, shoes, coat, and lipstick."

Seven months later Frank dropped the lawsuit and replaced it with a new one that charged Davidson and *Look* with invasion of privacy. He said that he wanted to directly challenge the right of the press to report the personal lives of celebrities.

"I have always maintained that any writer or publication has a right to discuss or criticize my professional activities as a singer and an actor. But I feel that an entertainer has a right to his privacy, and that his right should be just as inviolate as any other person's right of privacy."

Admitting that it was a test case to change existing law, Frank asked only for "damages proved in excess of three thousand dollars."

Look magazine welcomed the challenge.

"The press has not only the right, but a duty, to publish facts pertaining to public figures and, in so doing, to examine them to see what makes them tick, how they stack up on analysis, and what they are, not simply as professional performers but also as persons," said the magazine's counsel.

The suit never went to trial because Frank dropped it, but not before sending a message to publishers, editors, and writers that anyone who dared to write about him in depth and without his permission could be subject to costly litigation.

"Mickey Rudin told me later that he had not wanted to file that lawsuit," said Bill Davidson. "He said: 'We all advised Frank to forget it, but he wouldn't let go.' Sammy Davis, Jr., said that Frank hated me because he thought I had called his mother an abortionist. Sammy tried to tell him that I'd simply reported an abortion mill in the neighborhood, but he wasn't able to pacify Frank at all.

"Three or four years later, my wife and I were having dinner at Romanoff's on the Rocks in Palm Springs, and Frank was in the back room at a private party. He must have been tipped off that I was there because he charged out of the back room and came barrelling towards our table, absolutely purple with rage. I thought he was going to kill me.

Dean Martin ran out and bodily dragged him back, saying, 'Get back in here, Frank. Don't start anything.' "

Unable to accept the fact that his life was not off base to the press, Frank tried to control what was written about him by refusing interviews to reporters who asked personal questions.

"He was making *Pal Joey* at the time Bill's articles were published, and he hit us with a long list of press people who were not allowed on the set," said a publicist for Columbia Studios.

One writer was threatened. Movie actress Gloria Rhoads wrote a book involving Frank that she submitted to him for approval before publishing.

"The book wasn't intended to embarrass Mr. Sinatra," she said, "but evidently they thought it was. When I brought it to them to get Mr. Sinatra's approval, one of his closest advisors told me: 'If you pursue this, you will never work another day in Hollywood. We are very powerful, and we don't hesitate to use this power. We can call up any top studio and tell them not to use you, and they will not.' And I haven't worked a day since then."

Zealously guarding his privacy, Sinatra built a wall of secrecy around the women in his life. He was humiliated when his affair with Shirley Van Dyke became public in 1957 after the thirty-two-year-old film actress took an overdose of sleeping pills. Recovering in General Hospital after being revived by police, she said that she had known Frank for fourteen years. "I've dated him on and off since I met him," she said.

Frank admitted that he had obtained bit movie parts for her since she came to Hollywood, but he refused to comment on the contents of her suicide note, which said, "The one I've really loved, Frank Sinatra, you've done me wrong. You're so big and I'm so small."

During 1957, Frank was being seen with Lauren Bacall, escorting her to premieres, dinner parties, and weekends in Palm Springs.

"Frank and I had become a steady pair," she said. "We flew to Las Vegas for *The Joker Is Wild* opening—he took me to the *Pal Joey* opening in town—at all his small dinner parties, I was the hostess. People were watching with interest. It seemed to everyone—to his friends, to mine—that we were crazy about each other, that we were a great pair; that it wouldn't last; that Frank would never be able to remain constantly devoted, monogamous—yet that maybe with me, he would."

Bacall galloped toward marriage while Frank tried to rein her in, calling friends and asking them to get him out of the relationship. One night, Jule Styne invited them for a quiet dinner.

"Well . . . you know . . . going with Betty . . . I'd like to make it more than a quiet dinner," said Frank. "I'd like to have someone else talking, or else it gets too serious between her and me."

To please Frank, Jule invited Mike Todd and Elizabeth Taylor. And to please Mike, he invited Eddie Fisher and Debbie Reynolds because they were having marital troubles.

"So there we were at the Beachcomber's," said Jule Styne. "First there was a great confrontation between Sinatra and Bacall. In the middle of it, my girl turns to Frank and says, 'You'd be lucky to marry her.' Well, that's the last thing Frank wants to hear, and I give my girl a nudge, but immediately Frank hates me and my date. Next thing, there's a big hassle between Eddie and Debbie, and they're carrying on across the table from each other. And Mike, trying to settle it down, says, 'Come on, Debbie, Eddie's a nice kid.' In the meantime, Liz is irritated because she's being ignored and sitting in the middle of this battlefield, and she tells Mike to mix out. Mike turns to me in a stage whisper and says, 'Thanks, Jule, this is a wonderful idea. We ought to make it a regular weekly event.' "

It was months of what Bacall described as an "erratic" courtship. Frank would be "wildly attentive" one minute, and sullen the next. "He'd had so many scars from so many past lives—was so embittered by his failure with Ava—he was not about to take anything from a woman," she said. " 'Don't tell me—suggest.' God knows how many times I heard that. But I didn't know how to suggest."

Deeply in love, she wanted nothing more than a wedding ring from Frank, but he vacillated until the evening of March 11, 1958, fourteen months after Bogart's death, when he finally proposed.

"I must have hesitated for at least thirty seconds," she said later.

That evening, they went to the Imperial Gardens on

Sunset Boulevard to celebrate with Swifty Lazar. A young girl came to their table asking for autographs. Frank said, "Put down your new name." After "Lauren Bacall," Mrs. Bogart wrote "Betty Sinatra."

"I was so happy, I wanted everyone to know that we were getting married, but I kept my mouth shut," she said.

Frank left the next day for Miami, and Lazar took Bacall to the theater. During intermission, a columnist asked her if she and Frank were going to get married. "Why don't you telephone Frank in Florida?" she said before admitting the truth, which Swifty confirmed minutes later. That night, she saw the headlines on the early edition of the morning paper: SINATRA TO MARRY BACALL.

Not knowing how he would react, Bacall phoned Frank in Miami to tell him what had happened. He didn't call her back for days. When he did, he said, "Why did you do it? I haven't been able to leave my room for days—the press are everywhere. We'll have to lay low for a while, not see each other for a while."

That was the last Lauren Bacall ever heard from Frank Sinatra. He didn't speak to her again for six years, and then only in rage. When reporters asked him about the marriage report, he said, "Marriage? What for? Just so I'd have to go home earlier every night? Nuts!"

That night, Ava called Frank from Spain. "I hear you called off the marriage," she said.

"What marriage?"

"The marriage to Betty Bacall."

"Jesus. I was never going to marry that pushy female."

Ava gleefully related the story every time the Sinatra-Bacall affair was mentioned to her. Not so gleeful was Lauren Bacall, who wrote in her autobiography years later how devastated she was by Frank's rejection. "To be rejected is hell, a hard thing to get over, but to be rejected publicly takes everything away from you," she said. "But the truth also is that he behaved like a complete shit. He was too cowardly to tell the truth—that it was just too much for him, that he'd found he couldn't handle it."

Frank resented her book. "I think it was unfair, because there is another side to it," he said, "but I'm not going to give it. Some things should rest."

19

Frank's three-year contract with the American Broadcasting Company for three million dollars in upfront cash, plus a share of the profits, was one of the most phenomenal television deals ever signed. Known in 1957 as "the third network," ABC-TV sweetened the deal by buying stock in Frank's motion picture production unit, Kent Productions, which gave him handsome capital gains tax advantages. The company also agreed to let him film his thirty-six half-hour shows and keep sixty percent of the residuals. With the shows on film, Frank figured they would be shown again and again, with his corporation, Hobart Productions, collecting most of the money.

"This guarantees me seven million dollars, and most of that will go into a trust fund for the children. For years, I've been looking to get into a position to set aside money for them, and this is the one way I can do it."

The network gave Frank complete artistic control, allowing him to develop each show in his own way, a degree of freedom that was unheard of in television. "If I flop this time, it'll be my own fault—and that's the way I want it," Frank said.

In 1952, he had signed with CBS, the biggest television contract to date, but his ratings had been so low that the show lasted barely a year. Afterward, he had blasted the industry.

"Television stinks," he had said then. "Except, of course, if you can do a filmed show. That way, you avoid a lot of the panic and no-talent executives who get in it from merely writing an essay on fire prevention in the first place. The only time any of these bums have even been in the theater was when they bought a ticket. . . . My blood boils when I see the mediocrities sitting on top of the TV networks."

Now, five years later, with his records selling in the millions and his movies (*Johnny Concho*, *Meet Me in Las Vegas*, *High Society*, *Around the World in 80 Days*) box office successes, he was the number-one star in Hollywood. His weekly series was being hailed by ABC-TV as the smash entry for the new fall season.

Yet, loath to rehearse, Frank dashed off eleven shows in fifteen days, sailing through with little attention to detail. At CBS, one show would have taken seven days to film, and the star would have been required to rehearse. At ABC, Frank made his stand-in, Dave White, do the rehearsing while he simply jumped in at the last minute to do the filming.

"It was a brutalizing experience for actors who take their work seriously, let me tell you," said actor Maurice Manson. "I only lasted one day with that man, and one day was too much for me.

"We were doing a four-person skit—a light comedy bit with me as the producer, Frank as the talent scout, and Kim Novak as the girl who is discovered and taken to a drama teacher, played by Celia Lovsky. As the movie producer, I was sitting at my desk going through scripts. Frank was supposed to knock on the door and then walk into my office. When I heard him knock, I said, 'Come in.' Frank opened the door and then fell to his knees, and started barking like a dog. I thought he'd had an epileptic fit or something, but when all his stooges on the set laughed uproariously, I realized that it was his idea of a joke. I didn't think it was a bit funny myself and was quite unnerved. We started again, and this time he got through the door. As the camera came in for closeups, I said the lines from the script: 'Well, what do you think of the girl?' The film was rolling as Frank said, 'Don't know. I haven't had a chance to feel her up yet.' Again his stooges screamed and hollered as though that was the funniest thing in the world, so Frank kept it up all day. We finally got something in the can after a few hours of nonsense, but it was awful, and Celia and I looked horrible, probably because we were both so done in by Frank's antics.

"I'm sure that he wasn't being malicious and trying to

make us look bad. It's just that he didn't care about the acting or the ensemble. He wouldn't take the time to rehearse. He wouldn't even learn his lines. He just read them off the TelePrompTer. He was forty-two years old at the time, but he acted like a stupid teenager. It was a case of arrested adolescence."

The series made its debut on October 18, 1957, with the *New York Herald-Tribune* hailing it as "a triumph in almost all departments," while *The New Yorker* criticized it as "underorganized and a little desperate; and that for a show described as 'the most expensive half-hour program in history.' "

By November, *Variety* had dismissed the series as "a flop, rating and otherwise." *The New Republic* said it was suffering from that "terrible disease that afflicts television variety shows. It has no name, but the symptoms are superficial smoothness, lack of emotion, cheerful banality, and something that can only be called intentional dullness."

Dean Martin was Frank's guest star the next month, which the *Chicago Sun-Times* found regrettable. "They performed like a pair of adult delinquents, sharing the same cigarette, leering at girls, breaking up on chatter directed to the Las Vegas fraternity, plugging records, movies, and the places where they eat for free, and swigging drinks at a prop bar." Some critics objected to Frank's use of such words as "broads" and "mother grabbers," and others found Dean so nonchalant as to be indifferent. The chemistry between the two men, who were close friends, did not ignite ratings.

Even Frank's Christmas show with Bing Crosby was condemned by *Variety* as "static, studied, pretentious, and awkward. . . . Even discounting the often sloppy production . . . the absence of central theme or point of view, the fact is that Sinatra never seemed at his best or at his easiest, and the attitude infects his guests."

Network executives were panicked by Sinatra's low ratings, which placed the show a sorry third to *M Squad* and *Mr. Adams and Eve*, which starred Ida Lupino and Howard Duff. But Frank remained calm and confident. "Those guys in the gray flannel suits—I just don't dig 'em," he said. "You'd think they'd give a show a chance to build. But no. The show wasn't on two weeks before the complaints started coming in."

In February 1958, *TV Guide* described the show as "one of

the biggest and most expensive disappointments of the current season," and by March Frank was starting to say that he was too busy with movie commitments to continue the series. It was dropped after twenty-six weeks, and the post mortems blamed his arrogance.

"Mr. Sinatra, the artist whose best we have tasted and enjoyed, was simply making a fast buck," wrote Harriet Van Horne in the *New York World Telegram*. "He didn't just walk through his show, he shambled, shrugged, and could [not] have cared less."

"It would be charitable to suggest that the shows were unrehearsed," wrote Paul Molloy in the *Chicago Sun-Times*. "It would also be an indictment of sloppy performance. For I couldn't escape the feeling that Sinatra's thinking was something like: 'Let's give the peasants out there a few songs and jokes and get this nuisance over with.' There is effrontery about this attitude that has no place in show business."

Jack Donohue, Frank's director, said he was temperamentally unsuited to a medium that demanded careful rehearsals. "There are quite a few performers who have no business on television each week, and Sinatra is one of them," he said. "I just feel that nobody—Frank included—can race through three shows a week. He hates to rehearse, and he was always late for rehearsal. He'd show up late and say, 'What do I do, Jack?' and I'd tell him we had a run-through, then a dress rehearsal, and he'd say, 'Oh, no! Do we have to do this twice?' So I'd say: 'No, Frank, you don't have to, but the rest of the cast does. Maybe you know your lines, but the rest of the cast doesn't, so we're going to do this my way.' I have actually played his part in the run-through and dress rehearsal, and the first time Frankie had a whack at it was when we were on the air."

Although the series was canceled, ABC recouped some of its investment the following year when Frank hosted four one-hour specials, but he was never again able to make his mark in television. "I hate the fric-frac of it all," he said. "I'll do a special now and then but no more of this series crap. Lucy [Lucille Ball in *I Love Lucy*] can have it."

He threw himself into a killing pace of movie-making (*Some Came Running, Kings Go Forth, A Hole in the Head*, and *Never So Few*) and nightclub appearances (the Fontainebleau in Miami, the Copa in New York, the Chez Paree in Chicago, and the Sands in Las Vegas). All of Frank's work catapulted him to number one among the ten biggest money-making movie stars in 1958, who included Glenn Ford, Elizabeth Taylor, Brigitte Bardot, Jerry Lewis, Rock Hudson, William Holden, James Stewart, Yul Brynner, and Marlon Brando.

Yet his attitude toward work—especially his unwillingness to rehearse—irritated people. Director Billy Wilder, a good friend of Frank's, refused to work with him, saying: "I'm afraid he would run after the first take—'Bye-bye, kid, that's it. I'm going, I've got to see a chick.' That would drive me crazy." Asked if Sinatra was unprofessional, Wilder said, "I think this: if, instead of involving himself in all those enterprises, nineteen television shows and records by the ton and four movies all at once and producing things and political things and all those broads—his talent on film would be stupendous. That would be the only word. Stupendous. He could make us all, all the actors that is, look like faggots."

Shirley MacLaine, who had been given her part by Sinatra in *Some Came Running*, agreed. "His potential is fantastic. The only thing . . . The thing is, I wish he would work harder at what he's doing. I don't think that when you polish something you can help but improve it. He won't polish. He feels polishing might make him stagnant. He doesn't even like to rehearse. . . . Some people say he behaves the way he does because he isn't sure of himself, or because he hates himself. With this man, it's nothing as simple as that. Maybe it's something like this: he won't extend himself all the way because he's such a perfectionist. . . . What I mean by that is that if he shows anybody he's working hard and it doesn't come off, he's got no excuse. If he's not working hard, they can't point at him and say it's not right, because he can then say, to himself at least, 'Well, I wasn't working up to my peak.' I do think he works at singing. But at acting, the way he goes, he always knows that people will say, 'My goodness, think of what that man could do if he *really* worked. . . .' Now that I think of it, maybe he is afraid. Maybe he's afraid to see what might happen if he worked up to his whole potential. It might destroy everything he's done by playing it casual."

Still, Frank was the hottest property in show business, and, as such, he fully expected to win the first annual Grammy of 1958 for best male vocal and for his new album, *Only the Lonely*, which he and Nelson Riddle believed to be their finest work to date. But the new award, voted on by members of the National Association of Recording Arts and Sciences, went instead to Domenico Modugno for best male vocal ("Nel Blu Dipinto di Blu—Volare"), and to Henry Mancini for best album (*The Music from Peter Gunn*). All Frank got was an award for the best album cover.

"He was so upset about not winning a music award that he refused to let any of the photographers take our picture that night," said Sandra Giles, the actress who accompanied him to the Grammys. "He wasn't nasty to me, but he was very moody and drank a lot afterwards. I was very young then, and didn't know how to handle him. Looking back, I guess I should've been grateful that Elvis didn't win anything!"

The musical arrival of the former truck driver from Tupelo, Mississippi, had appalled Frank. Elvis Aaron Presley, the gyrating crooner who wiggled and shimmied as he sang his rockabilly songs, was driving young females into screaming paroxysms of delight with his jumping guitar and long sideburns. Elvis's clamorous shouts and sexual moans unleashed a frenzy in teenage girls unmatched since The Voice himself had hordes of bobby-soxers shrieking at the Paramount. Yet Frank viewed the twenty-four-year-old singer as a degenerate redneck and musical abomination.

"His kind of music is deplorable, a rancid-smelling aphrodisiac," he said.

So incensed was he by Elvis the Pelvis that he wrote a magazine article in *Western World* denouncing rock 'n' roll and all its practitioners: "My only deep sorrow is the unrelenting insistence of recording and motion picture companies upon purveying the most brutal, ugly, degenerate, vicious form of expression it has been my displeasure to hear, and naturally I'm referring to the bulk of rock 'n' roll.

"It fosters almost totally negative and destructive reactions in young people," he said. "It smells phony and false. It is sung, played, and written for the most part by cretinous goons and by means of its almost imbecilic reiterations and sly, lewd—in plain fact—dirty lyrics, it manages to be the martial music of every sideburned delinquent on the face of the earth."

Frank excoriated Elvis for appealing to music's lowest common denominator. He hated his glittery suits and blue suede shoes. While Frank clung to slow, yearning ballads, he condemned the hillbilly interloper for taking these same traditional rhythms and changing them into something blatantly

sexual. Perhaps most of all, he resented Elvis for carving a
new place and direction in music that had the potential to
challenge his own. And that is exactly what Elvis did. By
1956 he had been acclaimed as the king of rock 'n' roll, and
although Frank felt that rock music had no place on the Top
40 charts, Elvis dominated the number-one position for three
decades.

Even after his death, Elvis remained on top of the all-
time sales list, with The Beatles and Stevie Wonder as
runners-up. Perry Como captured the twenty-second spot,
while Frank ranked near the bottom at thirty-fourth.

Despite his personal feelings about Elvis, Frank was pragmatic enough to recognize Elvis's phenomenal appeal. As a
way of cashing in on it, he decided to welcome Elvis home
from a two-year stint in the army in 1960 by paying him
$100,000 for a ten-minute appearance on his last ABC-TV
special.

"You should make in a year what Frank is losing on this
show," said Sammy Cahn of the "Welcome Elvis" telecast.
"But he wants to prove he can go big on TV."

After years of trying, Frank finally proved it. Thanks to
Elvis, Trendex gave his ABC special a whopping 41.5 rating,
the highest of any show in five years.

Presley, who wore black leather jackets and white socks
that went unchanged for days, was not a man Frank could
ever feel comfortable with. He was not "cool" in the sense of
the members of Sinatra's Rat Pack, who wore snap-brim hats
and sharkskin suits from Sy Devore's Hollywood men's store.
The group Sinatra formed after Bogie's death consisted of
Dean Martin, Peter Lawford, Sammy Davis, Jr., Joey Bishop,
and Shirley MacLaine as mascot. It was as dedicated to
drinking as Bogie's—Bogie's principle was that the whole
world was three drinks behind and it was time to catch up.
But in Frank's Rat Pack, personal homage to their "leader"
was all important: Frank was addressed as "the pope," "the
general," and "el dago."

The new Rat Pack developed its own vocabulary, in which
all women, except Mother, were "broads." God was "the big
G" and death "the big casino," as in, "Did you hear that
so-and-so just bought the big casino," meaning that so-and-so
had just died. "Dullsville, Ohio" was anywhere but Vegas
and "a little hey-hey" was a good time. "Bird" was the male

organ, and the term was constantly used as a jovial greeting, as in, "How's your bird?" At a party, when Frank was bored, he'd say, "I think it's going to rain," which meant that he wanted to go someplace else, and everyone had to leave. "Clyde" was an all-purpose word that could mean anything, but when applied to Elvis Presley and his guitar, it meant "loser, a shmendrick."

They called themselves the Clan for a while, until that became politically embarrassing, and they hastened to make it known that they had nothing to do with the Ku Klux Klan.

The Rat Pack satisfied Frank's lifelong absorption with male company and met his craving for attention. The group's slavish devotion to "the leader" seemed humorous until the day Sammy Davis, Jr., gave an interview to Jack Eigen in Chicago, acknowledging Frank's need to belittle others.

"I love Frank and he was the kindest man in the world to me when I lost my eye in an auto accident and wanted to kill myself. But there are many things he does that there are no excuses for," said Sammy. "Talent is not an excuse for bad manners. . . . I don't care if you are the most talented person in the world. It does not give you the right to step on people and treat them rotten. This is what he does occasionally."

"That was it for Sammy," said Peter Lawford. "Frank called him 'a dirty nigger bastard' and wrote him out of *Never So Few*, the movie we were starting at the time. He had originally had the part created so that Sam could be in the movie, but now he had it rewritten again for Steve McQueen. For the next two months Sammy was on his knees begging for Frank's forgiveness, but Frank wouldn't speak to him. Even when they were in Florida together and Frank was appearing at the Fontainebleau and Sammy was next door at the Eden Roc, Frank still refused to speak to him. He wouldn't even go over to see his show, which was something we always did when one or the other of us was appearing someplace. He left word with the doorman that Sammy was not to come in. If he did, Frank said he'd walk out."

Sammy had not only criticized Frank, but he had done so in Chicago, where it was broadcast over the radio and later picked up by all the media, and where Frank's Mafia friends would hear it. Chicago was home to his close friend, Joe Fischetti, whom he'd made his talent agent at the Fontainebleau; to Sam Giancana, the chief of the Chicago Mafia, who wore Frank's sapphire friendship ring; to Tony "Joe Batters"

Accardo, the former Chicago syndicate boss for whom Frank had given a personal home recital the year before.

"That was the unforgivable part—to embarrass Frank in front of the Big Boys," said Lawford. "Those Mafia guys meant more to him than anything. So Sammy was quite lucky that Frank let him grovel for a while and then allowed him to apologize in public a couple of months later. It could have been a lot worse, given Frank's temper. You have no idea of that temper. He can get so mad that he's driven to real violence, especially if he's been drinking, and I'm not kidding. I know. I've seen it. One time at a party in Palm Springs, he got so mad at some poor girl that he slammed her through a plate glass window. There was shattered glass and blood all over the place and the girl's arm was nearly severed from her body. Jimmy Van Heusen rushed her to the hospital. Frank paid her off later and the whole thing was hushed up, of course, but I remember Judy Garland and I looking at each other and shivering with fright at the time. I did everything I could to avoid setting off that temper, but sometimes it was impossible. Look what happened when he heard I'd gone out with Ava. He threatened to kill me and then didn't speak to me for five years. He got over it one night at Gary and Rocky Cooper's dinner party. I had married Patricia [Kennedy] by then, and she was his dinner partner. I think we were very attractive to Frank because of Jack [Kennedy], who had been elected senator from Massachusetts and was getting ready to run for president. Anyway, that night at the Coopers got us back together again, and we started seeing Frank all the time. We went around the world together, we named our daughter after him [Victoria Frances], we set up corporations to produce each other's movies, and we went into the restaurant business together, but even Pat, who adored Frank, was still scared of his temper.

"On New Year's Eve in 1958, we met him for dinner at Romanoff's with Natalie Wood and R. J. Wagner. He wanted us to go to Palm Springs afterwards, but when he went to the gent's room, the girls said that it was too chilly to go that night. They preferred driving in the morning, but then we said, 'Who's going to tell him?' Knowing his temper, Pat out and out refused to say anything, and Natalie didn't even want to be in the same room when he was told. Finally, R. J. insisted that I be the one to do it, so when Frank got back to the table, I explained as gracefully as I could that we'd prefer joining him in the morning. Well, he went absolutely nuts. 'If that's the way you want it, fine,' he said, slamming his drink on the floor and storming out of the restaurant. I rang him the next morning and his valet, George Jacobs, answered and whispered hello. He said that Frank was still asleep because he hadn't gotten to bed until five A.M. Then he said, 'Oh, Mr. Lawford. What happened last night? I better tell you that he's pissed. Really pissed off. He went to your closet and took out all the clothes that you and your wife keep here and ripped them into shreds and then threw them into the swimming pool.' That gives you an idea of Frank's temper and why I say that Sammy was very lucky to have gotten off so lightly."

Dean Martin maintains that he holds his friendship with Frank because they always keep it light. "I don't discuss his girl with Frank or who he's going to marry. All I discuss are movies."

Frank had first seen Dean Martin at the Copa back in 1948 when Martin was paired with Jerry Lewis, and Frank's comment then had been, "The dago's lousy, but the little Jew is great." But after Martin and Lewis split, Frank gave Dean one of his first acting roles in *Some Came Running* in 1958, and the two men became fast friends. They had a lot in common: both were Italians from blue-collar towns, neither had a high school education, both were singers who couldn't read a note of music, both enjoyed gangsters (federal wiretaps show that Dean was close to Sam Giancana and Paul "Skinny" D'Amato), both adored their mothers and took good care of their parents, both preferred spending nights drinking with the boys. They even shared similar phobias: Frank's was a fear of heights and Dean's a fear of elevators. As they became close, their parents became friends and their children grew up with an "Uncle Frank" and an "Uncle Dean."

Frank was not simply the leader of the Rat Pack. He had also assumed the position of *il padrone* in Hollywood, where he was approached by Twentieth Century Fox executives to be master of ceremonies at the luncheon on September 19, 1959, honoring Soviet Premier Nikita Sergeivich Khrushchev and his wife, Nina. This unprecedented visit to America by the Soviet head of state brought out more than four hundred of Hollywood's most glamorous stars, including Marilyn Monroe, Elizabeth Taylor and Eddie Fisher, Cary Grant, Bob

Hope, Richard Burton, Rita Hayworth, Gregory Peck, June Allyson, and David Niven. Militant anti-Communists like Adolph Menjou and Ronald Reagan refused to participate, but the most important movie executives in the industry were on hand to pay their respects, to eat squab, drink California wine, and listen to Khrushchev and Spyros P. Skouros, president of Twentieth Century Fox, debate the respective merits of communism and capitalism. To the chagrin of everyone but the visiting Russians, Khrushchev appeared to win the argument, leading one man to observe, "A twentieth-century fox visits Twentieth Century Fox!"

Shortly after he arrived in California, Khrushchev was informed that he could not visit Disneyland because the Los Angeles Police Force could not ensure his safety. He was furious, and his famous temper that had driven him to bang on the table with his shoe at the United Nations now erupted at the luncheon. "What is it?" he asked his assembled guests. "Why am I not allowed to go? Do you have rocket-launching pads there? I do not know. Is there an epidemic of cholera there or something? Or have gangsters taken hold of the place that can destroy me? That is the situation I am in—your guest. For me the situation is inconceivable. I cannot find words to explain this to my people."

Immediately, Frank turned to Mrs. Khrushchev and said that he would take her to Disneyland himself, giving her a personally guided tour. The sweet-faced, gray-haired woman broke into a big smile and sent a note to her husband sitting at another table, but a security officer returned to tell her that such a tour would be impossible. "I tried, honey," said Frank, patting her hand.

After lunch, the Khrushchevs were shown a lively sequence from *Can-Can*, the movie being filmed at Twentieth that starred Frank with Shirley MacLaine, Maurice Chevalier, Louis Jourdan, and Juliet Prowse. With the help of an interpreter, Frank explained the proceedings. Grinning, he said that the first number would be a song by Louis Jourdan and Maurice Chevalier. "It's called 'Live and Let Live,' and I think it's a marvelous idea," he said. "The movie is about a bunch of pretty girls and the fellows who like pretty girls."

Khrushchev smiled and applauded loudly after Frank's remarks.

"Later in the picture, we go into a saloon. A saloon is a place where you go to drink," said Frank with a straight face.

At this, Khrushchev laughed loudly. For the next few minutes, the Twentieth Century Fox sound stage was like the Copa Room of The Sands in Las Vegas as Frank sang "C'est Magnifique." After his song, he turned the show over to the dancing girls, saying they were all his nieces. Khrushchev smiled as Shirley MacLaine and Juliet Prowse pranced onto the stage with shrill cries, kicking their legs and whirling their skirts. But when they flounced their backsides to the audience in a traditional can-can number, the Soviet premier was frowning. He pronounced the dance and the dancers "immoral," saying: "A person's face is more beautiful than his backside."

Frank was on his best behavior for the Soviet visit, and as Mrs. Khrushchev's luncheon partner, he demonstrated great charm and gallantry, looking intently at the pictures she showed him of her grandchildren and telling her about his own children.

On the subject of his children, Frank dropped his ring-a-ding-ding act to become a soft and doting father who was far too indulgent at times. He gave his eldest child, Nancy, a mink coat for her sixteenth birthday and the first pink Thunderbird in the United States when she was seventeen, as if these presents would make up for his leaving the house when she was only ten years old. Nancy, who adored her father, never blamed him for the divorce. "My father may have left home, but he never left his family," she said.

"Nancy was clearly the favorite. No doubt about it," said Doug Prestine, a close friend and neighbor of the Sinatra children. "Tina was too young to be affected by the favoritism, but it sure was tough on Frankie. Big Frank spoiled Nancy to the neglect of Frankie, and it hurt him a lot. He never got the equivalent of anything that she got, none of the trips with Big Frank or any of the super gifts, and certainly none of the attention and affection. It was Nancy who got to be on Frank's television show with Elvis Presley, not Frankie. Nancy had a huge bedroom in their Bel-Air house on Nims Road and Frankie had a real tiny one. Nancy had loads of clothes but Frankie barely had any. Big Frank gave Nancy her own television set, and poor Frankie didn't even have a radio of his own. One day, the rivalry really got to him, and the two of us pulled one of the parts out of Nancy's television set so that it wouldn't work anymore. That sabotage was more than just prankishness on Frankie's part. He was hurting from being so ignored by his dad and struck back at Nancy. There was always a distance between them because of his dad's overindulgence towards her.

"I still remember when we were walking home from school one day and, completely out of context, Frankie turned to me and said, 'You don't know how lucky you are to have a real father.' Even though we were only about thirteen years old at the time, I knew that that statement was significant; I just didn't know what to say to him. Big Frank would come around when he was in town, or for a special occasion like Thanksgiving, but then he'd be gone for months at a time. He called a lot, but that wasn't enough for the kids. At least, it wasn't enough for Frankie.

"One night, the two of us were watching television in the library of the Sinatra house when Big Frank crashed through the gate in his Eldorado Cadillac with the hand-brushed stainless steel top. He was real drunk and wearing a white dinner jacket that was torn and dirty, as if he'd been in a fight or rolling around the gutter someplace. He wasn't the least belligerent. In fact, he was kind of friendly. He slurred his words and said, 'What are you two doing?' I was stunned to see him in that condition because I'd never seen a grown-up drunk before, but Frankie wasn't surprised at all. He very matter-of-factly went outside, got his dad out of the car, and carried him into the house, where we tried to wash him up and poured some coffee down him. Then Big Frank passed out on the couch, and we went back to watching TV. Frankie acted like it happened all the time."

Early on, young Frank saw how much his sister and his mother adored his father. Hungry for some of that same affection, he began fashioning himself in his father's likeness, imitating his mannerisms, his singing, his speech.

"If I stand in front of the fireplace with my hands behind my back, he does the same thing," Frank said of his ten-year-old boy. "He kills me. When I do a television show, he'll quote everything I said the next time I see him."

Frank's way of demonstrating love was through lavish gifts, and his former wife and children always looked forward to opening "Daddy's presents."

"I was one of Nancy, Jr.'s closest friends and I remember the first Christmas that I spent with the Sinatras," said Rona Barrett, the Hollywood commentator. "It was incredible. There was a stack of Frank's presents higher than the tree for Nancy and Tina, and a brand-new car with a red satin ribbon on it for Nancy, Sr., but scarcely anything for Frankie. It was so pathetic. The girls got furs and diamond bracelets and cashmere sweaters and silk blouses and loads of one-hundred-dollar shoes. I'd say each one of their piles was worth at least fifteen thousand dollars, but poor Frankie didn't get more than five hundred dollars' worth of gifts. I really felt sorry for him."

Much of Frank's fathering fell to his valet, George Jacobs, and to his secretary, Gloria Lovell, who remembered all the children's birthdays, shopped for all their presents, and called them on a regular basis.

"I feel like I raised those kids," said George Jacobs. "For a while when Frank and Nancy weren't speaking to each other I was the go-between. Young Frankie and I got to be real good pals. He's a sad little guy, but sweet. A nice kid. I'd drive around with him, and when I'd bring him back home, Nancy, Sr., would be there, asking, 'Well, what did Frankie say? What did he talk about? I don't want you teaching my son no jive.' I never did tell her what Frankie talked about, and I never told Frank either, because I didn't want to break the kid's confidence. With all those damn women around, he needed some man to talk to, and his dad just wasn't around that much."

"Poor Frankie. He's had it tough being Frank's son," said Nelson Riddle, the father of six children, and someone Frank, Jr., had confided in over the years. "Frankie's not an athlete like Dean Martin's kid; he's not a great student; he's not a comedian or a back-slapper. He's an introspective little guy. Broods a lot. Frank has never taken the time to know his son, and what he does know, he doesn't like.

"[Frankie] never had a father who took responsibility for him. I don't mean financial responsibility because Frank's always been generous to his family with money, but a son needs more than that. He needs a man he can look up to. I've talked to Frankie a lot, and I know he doesn't like his dad, but deep down he wants to be loved by him. He can't get that love, though. He knows it. He doesn't fawn like the girls do. He's been left out ever since he was a little kid."

Always self-conscious about his own lack of education, Frank wanted his children to finish high school and pleaded with them to go to college, hoping that at least one Sinatra might earn a degree. Trying to please him, Nancy, Jr., enrolled at the University of Southern California but lasted only a semester before dropping out; Frankie also attended USC, but after a year he, too, quit; and Tina never even applied. There was no motivation toward higher education at home and certainly no need to learn a profession. The children knew they would never have to rely on a job. Frank had established trust funds for all of them that would be worth millions.

Frank's children were proud of him. They looked up to their father as the most important man in Hollywood. They saw movie stars approach him with reverence and fear, and even felt themselves treated with deference just because they were his children. To them, he seemed like the most influential man in the country. He knew important people all over the world—the Pope, the Queen of England, Eleanor Roosevelt, and the Shah of Iran. He had recently become a close friend of John F. Kennedy, the most electrifying young politician in the United States, and he was close to the chieftains of the underworld—all of which convinced Little Nancy that her father possessed magic.

"Daddy is the most charismatic figure of the twentieth century," she said.

20

Sam Giancana smoked Cuban cigars, drove a pink Cadillac, and talked out of the side of his mouth. He had fourteen aliases, but was known mostly as Sam Flood, Momo Salvatore Giancana, Moe or Mooney Giancana. He frequently introduced himself as Dr. Goldberg or Mr. Morris, but to Frank he was simply Sam.

A short, dour little man, he sat in the Armory Lounge in Forest Park, Illinois, and ordered killings as easily as he ordered his linguine. Some of the victims were simply shot, while others were hung on meat hooks and tortured with electric cattle prods, ice picks, baseball bats, and blowtorches. By 1960, Giancana had eliminated more than two hundred men.

This short, balding man with a sixth-grade education was known as Chicago's Mafia boss. He was the successor to Al Capone, and as such he was a top member of La Cosa Nostra, the national crime syndicate. He controlled all the protection rackets, pinball machines, prostitution, numbers games, narcotics, loan sharks, extortionists, counterfeiters, and bookmakers in the Chicago area.

In Las Vegas, he owned points in the Riviera, the Desert Inn, and the Stardust, which brought him hundreds of thousands of dollars in skimmed money. He also had Mafia business interests in Miami Beach, St. Louis, Arizona, California, Mexico, and Central and South America. The estimated annual take from these enterprises was two billion dollars, of which forty to fifty million went directly to him. Outside of the Armory Lounge, he conducted business on the golf course or in a hearse, to avoid federal eavesdropping.

Sam had served time in prison and been arrested more than seventy times for assault with intent to kill, contributing to the delinquency of a minor, burglary, assault and battery, larceny, possession of burglar tools and concealed weapons, bombing, and gambling. He was arrested three times for murder.

A dapper little man, Giancana wore sharkskin suits, alligator shoes, silk shirts, a gold monogrammed leather belt buckle, and a star sapphire pinky ring that was a gift from Frank Sinatra. When he knew he was under FBI surveillance, he added a black fedora and a pair of black wraparound sunglasses.

"Frank never called him or any of his killers Mafia—they were always 'the Boys' or 'the Outfit,' " said Peter Lawford. "But they were Mafia all right. . . . Because of Giancana, he kowtowed to the Chicago mob. Why do you think Frank ended every one of his nightclub acts by singing 'My Kind of Town Chicago Is'? That was his tribute to Sam, who was really an awful guy with a gargoyle face and weasel nose. I couldn't stand him, but Frank idolized him because he was the Mafia's top gun. Frank loved to talk about 'hits' and guys getting 'rubbed out.' And you better believe that when the word got out around town [Hollywood] that Frank was a pal of Sam Giancana, nobody but nobody ever messed with Frank Sinatra. They were too scared. Concrete boots were no joke with this guy. He was a killer.

"Giancana was always summoning Frank and Dean to perform for him, and they always went. They both flew to Chicago on four different occasions that I know of, and sang free of charge. One time, Giancana made Frank and Dean and Sammy sing for engagements at the Villa Venice, and they did that gig free of charge, too. Frank once went to Chicago by himself to do a command performance for Sam at Giannotti's Restaurant and Cocktail Lounge in 1962. I spent a lot of time with Frank when Giancana was around. They were very close friends. I was with Frank and Giancana in Miami at the Fontainebleau, where Sam kept a permanent suite and Frank performed every winter. Down there, Sinatra liked to get together with Joe Fischetti, or Joe Fish as he called himself in those days. Frank and Fischetti and Giancana would run around throwing cherry bombs at everyone. Sam threw one under my chair once, and I wanted to go for his neck, but, of course, I could hardly do that, could I?"

Both Giancana and Sinatra possessed mercurial temperaments characterized by wild mood swings and frightening unpredictability. Both wore toupees, gambled, owned points in Las Vegas casinos, drove shiny cars, traveled with an entourage, and relished beautiful women. Both were lavishly generous, bestowing new cars like bread crumbs. More important, each had something the other wanted. For Frank, it was the power derived from associating with an underworld capo; for Giancana, it was the opportunity to enrich Mafia coffers by using the biggest entertainer in Hollywood as a draw.

"Frank wanted to be a hood," said Eddie Fisher. "He once said, 'I'd rather be a don of the Mafia than president of the United States.' I don't think he was fooling."

Frank knew that Giancana was in the Las Vegas Black Book, which listed—with their pictures, aliases, and FBI numbers—the eleven men not allowed on the premises of any casino in the state. So he took care to hide Giancana in his dressing room when Sam visited the Sands. The gangster don rarely visited the casino because of the federal agents on the premises. FBI records state that Frank telephoned Giancana in Chicago, asking for him by the code name of James Perno (Sam's relative), not knowing that their conversations were being recorded. In conversations with his girlfriend Phyllis McGuire of the three singing McGuire Sisters, Sam referred to Sinatra as "the bird" or "the canary." And the FBI reports show that when the two men traveled together in Hawaii, Frank made hotel reservations for Sam, and that Sam used the code name of J. J. Bracket.

Frank did not try to hide his association with Giancana from anyone except the federal agents who followed Sam everywhere. He was proud of his friendship with the Capone capo, and introduced him to his friends, among them Yul Brynner, Greg Bautzer, and Dana Wynter. Frank fixed him up with women in Las Vegas, Miami, and Hollywood, and included him in the dinner parties he gave at Las Brisas, an exclusive resort in Acapulco. Once, he sat Sam next to a New York socialite, and introduced him as "Sam Flood."

Frank played golf with Giancana in Nevada, and opened his house to him in Palm Springs, occasions that were wit-

nessed by FBI agents. One Easter, his former wife, Nancy,
helped him entertain Giancana and Phyllis McGuire in the
desert. Later, when he was with Ava Gardner, Frank took
Sam and Phyllis to meet his parents in New Jersey, where
Dolly cooked them one of her big Italian dinners. As a favor
to Sam, Frank gave Phyllis a role in his movie *Come Blow Your
Horn*. Giancana visited her on the set regularly and became a
source of fascination to the cast and crew.

"He was there every day on the film, sort of hovering
around," said William Reed Woodfield, the unit photographer. "He was rather dour. He didn't sit around and say, 'We
bumped off so-and-so today,' or any of that stuff. I asked
Frank once what the Mafia was and he said, 'Oh, it's, you
know, just a bunch of guys.' "

Frank treated the crime overlord with deference. "If Sam
said something, Sinatra was on his feet, saying, 'I'll get it for
you, I'll get it for you,' " recalled Victor LaCroix Collins,
road manager for the McGuire Sisters. "He was like a bum
boy. He just kissed Sam's butt left and right. He didn't dare
do anything else."

Phyllis McGuire saw the same thing. "Frank was in awe
of Sam," she said. "He adored him. They were the best of
friends."

The star sapphire ring that Frank had given to Giancana
was part of an Italian friendship ritual that symbolized lifelong bonding.

"Those love rings are some kind of Mafia deal, something
among the Italians," said Joseph Shimon, a former Washington, D.C., police inspector who later became a close friend of
Sam Giancana and a partner in Operation Mongoose, the
CIA-Mafia plot to kill Fidel Castro. "I was with Sam at the
Fontainebleau when Sinatra was appearing, and Frank must
have called our suite twenty times trying to get together with
Sam. He wouldn't leave Sam alone. Finally, Sam said, 'We're
going to have to see him sometime. Might as well get it over
with now, but watch what you say because the guy's got a big
mouth.' Sam was referring to the way that Frank bragged
about his Mafia friends all over the place. Sam maintained
that Frank's mouth was the reason Charlie 'Lucky' Lueiano
got in so much trouble in 1947, because Frank was in a bar
running his mouth about going to Cuba to see him and some
guy tipped off the feds. Anyway, we went down and met

Frank at the bar. I was sitting next to Sam when Sinatra walked over.

" 'I can't even keep up with you,' Sinatra said. 'Where you been keeping yourself.'

"Sam said, 'Look, I'm busy. You know I got to keep moving around.'

"Frank looked down at Sam's hand. 'I see you're wearing the ring.' Sam said that he always wore it.

" 'Oh, no, you don't,' said Sinatra. 'I heard you hadn't been wearing the ring. I heard you never wore it.'

"God, it seemed so ridiculous to me. He was talking like some frustrated little girl with a broken heart. Finally, I couldn't help it. I said, 'What is this? Are you two bastards queer for each other or what?' Sam fell off his chair laughing, but Sinatra was very embarrassed and turned his back on me. He didn't know who I was. He knew I was with Sam and Johnny Roselli and Bob Maheu but he didn't know why."

From the beginning, Giancana knew of Frank's commitment to the presidential campaign of John F. Kennedy, beginning with a series of meetings held at the Lawfords' during 1959 to try to build a broad base of support for Kennedy throughout California.

"I was at some of those meetings," said former congressman Tom Rees. "Frank was there and quite a few other show business people. There was internecine warfare going on in the state in terms of what were we going to do: Would we come up with a favorite son? What about people such as Adlai Stevenson and the others? Should we file a separate Kennedy slate?"

Always a strong Democrat, Frank had idolized Franklin Delano Roosevelt in 1944 and contributed five thousand dollars to his campaign. He had supported Harry Truman in 1948 and had sung for Adlai Stevenson in 1952 and 1956, but this time he was personally committed to the candidate in a way he had never been before. Jack Kennedy—young, brilliant, rich, and handsome—was an extraordinary man from an Irish-American dynasty, and his impact on Frank was remarkable. In turn, Jack Kennedy enjoyed his glamorous Hollywood romps with Sinatra, who personified the sleek, swinging, emancipated male who can do anything he wants and never pay the consequences.

"Let's just say that the Kennedys are interested in the

lively arts and that Sinatra is the liveliest art of all," said Peter Lawford at the time.

"His [Kennedy's] fondness for Frank was simply based on the fact that Sinatra told him a lot of inside gossip about celebrities and their romances in Hollywood," said Dave Powers, Kennedy's closest aide. "We stayed with Frank in Palm Springs one night in November 1959 after a big fundraiser in Los Angeles. You could tell when Sinatra got up in the morning because suddenly music filled the house, even the bathrooms. Frank was a terrific host, and we had a great time. When we left, he gave me, not Jack, a box of jewelry to give my wife to make amends for keeping us the two extra days."

George Jacobs, Frank's valet, a black man, served Kennedy what he called the house special. "With Frank, it's spaghetti for breakfast, lunch, and dinner," he said. "I was serving him by the pool, and Frank told JFK to ask me about my stand on civil rights. I didn't like niggers and I told him so. They make too much noise, I said. The Mexicans smell, and I can't stand them either. Kennedy fell in the pool, he laughed so hard."

On the eve of the New Hampshire primary, Kennedy flew to Las Vegas to watch the summit meeting staged at the Sands by the Rat Pack during the filming of *Ocean's Eleven*, which was a lighthearted tale of the mob and their casinos. Frank introduced Jack to the audience as Dean lurched from the wings. "What did you say his name was?" asked Martin. Kennedy laughed along with everyone else as Martin and Sinatra, whom Joey Bishop introduced as "the Italian bookends," wheeled their bottle-bedecked "breakfast" bar onstage to choose a suitable juice while Joey whispered to the audience, "Well, here they are folks—Haig and Vague. . . . In a few minutes they'll start telling you about some of the *good* work the Mafia is doing."

Minutes later Sammy Davis, Jr., flew out to smash a cake in Bishop's face, and then Dean staggered out, picked up Sammy, and handed him to Frank, saying, "This is an award that just arrived for you from the NAACP." Later, while Dean was singing, Lawford and Bishop strolled across the stage in their shorts and tuxedo jackets. Jack Kennedy enjoyed the impromptu japes and boys-only bonhomie.

Fascinated by the spellbinding power of great screen personalities, Kennedy gravitated to the Rat Pack, which Frank renamed the "Jack Pack" in his honor. His interest in Hollywood came in part from his father, Joseph P. Kennedy, who predicted in the 1920s that film would equal the telephone as a new industry. Recognizing the power of movies to create illusion and fantasy, the elder Kennedy had bought a production company called Film Booking Office, and for two years he made movies. Then, through a series of complicated transactions and mergers, he had become part of RKO, one of the biggest Hollywood studios. During this time, he began an affair with Gloria Swanson, the glamorous actress. He took her on family vacations with his wife, and introduced her to his children.

Beginning as far back as 1945, Jack Kennedy spent as much free time as possible in Hollywood, romancing movie stars like Gene Tierney. Once his sister, Patricia, married Peter Lawford in 1954 and bought Louis B. Mayer's house in Santa Monica, Jack had a real base of operations in southern California. He used it frequently and in time began to socialize with the Rat Pack at Puccini's, the Beverly Hills restaurant that Frank and Peter owned with Hank Sanicola and Mickey Rudin.

Through Peter, whom Frank now called "brother-in-Lawford," Kennedy became a close friend of Sinatra, who introduced the young senator to many women. FBI files contain information regarding some of the women that the two men enjoyed in Palm Springs, Las Vegas, and New York City. The files also mention that Kennedy and Sinatra were "said" to be the subjects of "affidavits from two mulatto prostitutes in New York" in possession of *Confidential* magazine, which ceased publication in 1958. The Justice Department files also state: "It is a known fact that the Sands Hotel is owned by hoodlums, and that while the Senator, Sinatra and Lawford were there, show girls from all over the town were running in and out of the Senator's suite."

"I'm not going to talk about Jack and his broads . . . because I just can't," said Peter Lawford in 1983, "and . . . well . . . I'm not proud of this . . . but . . . all I will say is that I was Frank's pimp and Frank was Jack's. It sounds terrible now, but then it was really a lot of fun."

Among the women Frank introduced to Jack Kennedy was a striking twenty-five-year-old brunette named Judith Campbell (later Judith Campbell Exner), with whom Sinatra had had a brief affair, which ended when she refused to participate in his sexual parties, telling him that his tastes were "too kinky" for her. "You're so square," Frank had said after he brought a black girl to bed with him and Judith. "Get with it. Swing a little."

Frank introduced her to Jack Kennedy in Las Vegas and provided his own suite for the room service lunch the two shared on February 8, 1960, a lunch that launched a two-year affair that would include twice-a-day phone calls, a four-day stay at the Plaza Hotel in New York City, and romantic interludes in Palm Beach, Chicago, Los Angeles, and Jack Kennedy's home in Georgetown while Jackie was away. They met twenty times for intimate lunches in the White House in 1961, and telephone records show that Judith called him seventy times.

Knowing that Judith Campbell had started an intimate relationship with Kennedy, Frank introduced her to his other good friend, Sam Giancana. He told her: "Wake up and realize what you've got in the palm of your hand." Both men enjoyed a simultaneous intimacy with the young woman, who unintentionally but inexorably brought the underworld into a relationship with the White House.

"Jack knew all about Sam and me, and we used to discuss him," said Judith Campbell Exner in 1983. "He was angry about my seeing him. He had all the normal reactions that would take place between two people that cared for each other. Yes, he was jealous."

Extolling "that old Jack magic," Frank worked closely with Ambassador Kennedy throughout Jack Kennedy's presidential campaign, especially in New Jersey, which was a key state, and where Sinatra's mother's connection with Mayor John V. Kenny of Jersey City proved beneficial.

Not everyone in the Kennedy camp was pleased with Frank's involvement. "We wouldn't let him campaign openly in the primaries," said Paul Corbin, a Kennedy aide. "We couldn't even let Peter Lawford in because of the Rat Pack image. Frank made his contribution to the Wisconsin and West Virginia primaries over the jukeboxes—that's it."

Throughout both primaries, voters heard the smooth, insouciant Sinatra voice singing "High Hopes" with the lyric reworked by Sammy Cahn:

K-E-double-N-E-D-Y,
Jack's the nation's favorite guy.
Everyone wants to back Jack,

Jack is on the right track.
And he's got HIGH HOPES,
High apple-pie-in-the-sky hopes.

"I went into every tavernkeeper in the state and paid them twenty dollars to press that button and play Frank's song for Jack, but that's all he did in West Virginia," said Corbin.

But unbeknownst to Corbin and the rest of Kennedy's political operatives, Frank made a much more substantial contribution to the West Virginia primary. FBI wiretaps showed large Mafia donations to the state campaign that were apparently disbursed by Sinatra. This under-the-table money was used to make payoffs to key election officials. And Sinatra's friend Sam Giancana dispatched Paul "Skinny" D'Amato to the state to use his influence with the sheriffs, who gambled in the illegal gaming rooms of Greenbriar County. These men controlled the state's political machine, and many of them were gamblers who had been customers at Skinny's 500 Club in Atlantic City; some still owed Skinny money, and others were more than happy to do him a favor, which was rewarded from a cash supply of more than fifty thousand dollars. Their job was to get the vote out for Kennedy—any way they could.

Owning a few politicians in Illinois, Giancana knew the advantages of being close to political power, and decided to help Frank help the Kennedy campaign, figuring that if JFK won, Frank would be able to put an end to the federal surveillance Giancana was now experiencing every time he turned around. It wasn't that John F. Kennedy was his favorite candidate; he was simply the least undesirable at the time.

Kennedy had not wanted to enter the West Virginia primary, but after an indecisive win over Hubert Humphrey in Wisconsin, where his victory was discounted because it came from strongly Catholic districts, it was felt he had to go into West Virginia to prove that he could draw Protestant votes. Frank was concerned about West Virginia because he knew that it was virulent anti-Catholic territory. Furthermore, the United Mine Workers there had already endorsed Hubert Humphrey in retaliation for Bobby Kennedy's role as chief counsel of the McClellan rackets committee. This made Giancana's money and men all the more important.

With Skinny D'Amato quietly working the hollows of West Virginia, Ambassador Kennedy recruited Franklin D. Roosevelt, Jr., to stump the state with his son, knowing that the Roosevelt name was revered throughout West Virginia. The ambassador also had FDR, Jr., send letters postmarked Hyde Park, New York—President Roosevelt's home—to every voter, praising Senator Kennedy. The ambassador knew it would be almost impossible for any miner to vote against a man endorsed by the son of the president who gave coal miners the right to organize and to make a living wage for the first time in their lives. Throughout the state, Franklin Roosevelt, Jr., held up two fingers pressed tightly together, saying, "My daddy and Jack Kennedy's daddy were just like this."

"Frank Sinatra would've done anything to get Jack elected, so it's kind of ironic that he almost capsized the campaign early on when he tried to break the blacklist by hiring Albert Maltz," said Peter Lawford. "God, was that a mess. The ambassador took care of it in the end, but it was almost the end of old Frankie-boy as far as the family was concerned."

On March 21, 1960, Murray Schumach wrote a story in *The New York Times* disclosing that Frank had hired Maltz, one of the Hollywood Ten, to write a screenplay of *The Execution of Private Slovik*, a book by William Bradford Huie about the only American soldier executed by the U.S. Army for desertion since the Civil War. Frank planned to direct and produce the story himself.

Frank's friendship with Albert Maltz had started in 1945 when Maltz wrote the Academy Award–winning short against racism, *The House I Live In*. But then Maltz had been imprisoned, fined, and blacklisted for refusing to answer the questions of the House Un-American Activities Committee, and he had moved to Mexico in 1951. It was there that Frank called him with the screenplay offer that would break the blacklist.

Sinatra's decision to hire Maltz unleashed the most rabid partisans from both sides of the "Red or dead" issue. Only months earlier, Otto Preminger had announced that Dalton Trumbo, another blacklisted screenwriter, had written the script for *Exodus*, which would soon be released. Preminger's bold act was the first chink in the seemingly impregnable blacklist. The director's stand encouraged Kirk Douglas to use Trumbo for the script of *Spartacus*, the story of a Roman gladiator based on a book by Howard Fast, then an avowed Communist.

By announcing the signing of Maltz before the movie was

shot, Sinatra joined a select group of men determined to bring an end to the invidious blacklist.

"I had not worked on a film in Hollywood since 1948," said Maltz, "and I, like others who were blacklisted, kept hoping that the blacklist would be broken, so to receive Frank's call in 1960 was enormously exciting to me. I went up to see him, and we discussed the story, which we both agreed would say that the enemy in the war was not the United States Army, but the war itself. I point this out because of the irony of being blacklisted as a subversive who was trying to overthrow the government of the United States, and here I was setting out to say that the enemy in the war was not the United States, but war itself. Frank said that he had been thinking of hiring me for a long time and that it was very important to him to do so and to make this film. He said that if anyone tried to interfere with his hiring me, they were going to run into a buzz saw. He anticipated all the problems and the outcry from the American Legion types, but he said he didn't care. He wanted to break the blacklist. So he decided to make the announcement in advance of my doing the screenplay. . . . Frank said he would announce my being hired, but we set no date, so I left for New York. While there, I got a call from Frank's lawyer, Martin Gang, who asked if I would mind if the announcement was put off until after the New Hampshire primary, in which Kennedy was running."

Concerned that delaying the announcement might dilute its effectiveness in breaking the blacklist, Maltz called Frank at the Fontainebleau in Miami, where he was appearing. "I asked him openly if he wanted to delay because he was raising money for Kennedy and was worried that being publicly involved with a blacklisted writer might dry up finances, but he said, 'No, I support Kennedy because I think he's the best man for the job, but I'm not doing anything special for him.' So I suggested we make the announcement right away, and he said fine."

Hours after the announcement, the Hearst press bludgeoned Frank in editorials across the country, demanding that he fire Maltz immediately. "What kind of thinking motivates Frank Sinatra in hiring an unrepentant enemy of his country—not a liberal, not an underdog, not a free thinker, but a hard revolutionist who has never done anything to remove himself from the Communist camp or to disassociate himself from the Communist record?" asked the *New York Mirror*.

In contrast, the *New York Post* proffered "An Oscar!" to Frank, writing, "He has joined the select company of Hollywood valiants who declared their independence from the Un-American Activities Committee and the American Legion. . . . In defying the secret blacklist that has terrorized the movie industry for more than a decade, Sinatra—like Stanley Kramer and Otto Preminger before him—has rendered a service to the cause of artistic freedom. . . ."

In Washington, a Senate investigating subcommittee announced that it would be sending men to Hollywood "within a week" to look into attempts by Communists to infiltrate the motion picture industry. Actor John Wayne said, "I wonder how Sinatra's crony, Senator John Kennedy, feels about him hiring such a man? I'd like to know his attitude because he's the one who is making plans to run the administrative government of our country."

Outraged by Wayne's attack, Frank bought full-page ads in the Hollywood trade papers: "This type of partisan politics is hitting below the belt. I make movies. I do not ask the advice of Senator Kennedy on whom I should hire. Senator Kennedy does not ask me how he should vote in the Senate. . . . I spoke to many screenwriters, but it was not until I talked to Albert Maltz that I found a writer who saw the screenplay in exactly the terms I wanted. . . . Under our Bill of Rights I was taught that no one may prescribe what shall be orthodox in politics, religion, or other matters of opinion."

Frank stated that as director and producer of the film: "I and I alone will be responsible for it. I am concerned that the screenplay reflects the true pro-American values of the story. I am prepared to stand on my principles and to await the verdict of the American people when they see *The Execution of Private Slovik*. I repeat: In my role as a picture-maker, I have—in my opinion—hired the best man to do the job."

That statement aroused widespread enmity and attacks by veterans' groups throughout the country. The *Los Angeles Examiner* stated: "You are not giving employment to a poor little sheep who lost his way. . . . You are making available a story wide open for the Communist line."

Despite the outcry, Frank stood firm, insisting upon his inalienable right to hire whomever he wanted.

Then prospective television sponsors threatened to withdraw if he did not disassociate himself from Maltz at once.

"General Motors called me up—we had three Pontiac specials set—and they said that if he doesn't rescind that association with Maltz, we're pulling out," said Nick Sevano. "If he doesn't fire him in the next twenty-four hours, we're canceling all our business dealings. I had recently gone back into business with Frank, and I had $250,000 at stake in those GM specials, so Hank [Sanicola], Mickey Rudin, and I flew to Palm Springs to try to talk Frank into firing Maltz, but he wouldn't budge. 'Fuck 'em,' he said. 'There will be other specials.' When I pleaded with him to change his mind, he got so mad he fired me, and we had to break up our management company."

When priests stood up in their pulpits to sermonize against Frank, Ambassador Kennedy became alarmed and called Cardinal Spellman in New York and Cardinal Cushing in Boston, only to be told that Sinatra's consorting with Communists could damage his son's campaign among Roman Catholics. A few days later, Governor Wesley Powell of New Hampshire accused Senator Kennedy of "softness toward communism."

"That's when old Joe called Frank and said, 'It's either Maltz or us. Make up your mind,' " said Peter Lawford. "He felt that Jack was getting rapped for being a Catholic and that was going to be tough enough to put to rest. He didn't want him to get rapped for being pro-Communist as well, so Frank caved in, and dumped Maltz that day."

Bowing to Ambassador Kennedy, Frank issued a public statement: "In view of the reaction of my family, my friends, and the American public, I have instructed my attorneys to make a settlement with Albert Maltz and to inform him that he will not write the screenplay for *The Execution of Private Slovik*.

"I had thought the major consideration was whether or not the resulting script would be in the best interests of the United States. Since my conversations with Mr. Maltz had indicated that he has an affirmative, pro-American approach to the story, and since I felt fully capable as producer of enforcing such standards, I have defended my hiring of Mr. Maltz.

"But the American public has indicated it feels the morality of hiring Albert Maltz is the more crucial matter, and I will accept this majority opinion."

Frank had finally succumbed, after being subjected to public and private pressures few people ever experience in a lifetime. Family, friends, business associates, religious leaders, politicians, a galaxy of editorial writers and columnists had all advised—some demanded—that he throw Maltz to the wolves, or face the pack himself. Even after his statement, the controversy raged on like a fire in an oil well, stopping only when it ran dry.

An eight-column streamer in Hearst's Los Angeles flagship paper ran in red above its own masthead: SINATRA OUSTS MALTZ AS WRITER. In an editorial headed "Sinatra Sees the Light," the *Examiner* commended Frank for his "maturity" in firing the blacklisted writer. In New York City, the *Post* condemned him for capitulating "to the know-nothings of cinema and journalism." *Publishers Weekly* agreed: "Chalk up another victory for lynch-law mentality."

Frank paid Maltz's agent $75,000, the full price he had agreed to pay for the screenplay, but he was too embarrassed to call the writer to explain what had happened or to apologize for going back on his word. He also abandoned the idea of directing and producing the Private Slovik story.

A few nights later, Frank saw John Wayne at a celebrity-packed benefit dinner in the Moulin Rouge nightclub. Frank, who had been drinking, approached the six-foot-four-inch actor on the way to the parking lot.

"You seem to disagree with me," he said.

"Now, now, Frank, we can discuss this somewhere else," said Wayne.

Frank snarled at the actor, but friends stepped in to hold him back. Wayne walked away and Sinatra stalked to his car after turning on the one newsman present: "I guess you'll write all this down."

Angered, Sinatra stepped in front of a moving car, forcing the parking lot attendant behind the wheel to jam on the brakes, bringing the car to a screeching halt.

"Hey, Charley! You almost hit me! You know what I'm insured for?" Frank yelled. Confused and shaken, the parking lot attendant shook his head. Frank raced around to the driver's side of the car, shoved the attendant, and tore the shirt off another. "Can you fight?" he yelled. "You'd better be able to."

"Aw, Frank, he wasn't trying to hit you with the car,"

said another parking attendant, Edward Moran. "He's only trying to make a living."

"Who the fuck are you?" Frank roared, pushing Moran, who started to strike back trying to defend himself. Before the twenty-one-year-old could land a blow on Frank, the large fists of Big John Hopkins were punching Moran's head and face. Hopkins, who had been standing a few feet away, was six feet tall, weighed 220 pounds, and worked for Sammy Davis, Jr. Moran claimed to the police that as Hopkins beat him up, Frank yelled, "Tell that guy not to sue me if he knows what's good for him! I'll break both his legs."

Hopkins and Frank jumped into Sammy's Rolls-Royce and drove off, while the parking lot attendant was taken to Hollywood Receiving Hospital and treated for facial cuts and bruises. He later filed suit against Frank for violent assault, asking $100,000 in damages.

At that point, Big John Hopkins stepped forward to say that Frank wasn't to blame. "There's a little mixup and I'm standing right in the middle," he said. "I separate them. Someone gets hurt in the separation and it isn't me. And it isn't Frank." Before the case went to trial, Frank agreed to settle—no sum was disclosed.

Following the Maltz episode, Frank avoided publicity until the Democratic National Convention in Los Angeles in July. By that time, the Dodgers were on a winning streak and the city was strewn with baseball pennants and political bunting. The Democrats arrived early to stage a $100-a-plate fund-raising dinner at the Beverly Hilton to be attended by 2,800 people, including all the Hollywood stars Frank could turn out—Judy Garland, Janet Leigh, Tony Curtis, Sammy Davis, Jr., Shirley MacLaine, Peter Lawford, Angie Dickinson, Milton Berle, George Jessel, Joe E. Lewis, and Mort Sahl.

Jack Kennedy sat at the head table next to Garland. Frank sat at the end with the rest of the Democratic candidates—Adlai Stevenson, Stuart Symington, and Lyndon Johnson. After winning seven primaries and campaigning in fifty states, Jack Kennedy had arrived in Los Angeles with over 700 of the 1,520 delegates pledged to him. He was confident that by Wednesday, July 13, he would have the 761 votes necessary for a first ballot nomination.

Frank and the rest of the Rat Pack opened the convention

ceremonies in the sports arena on Monday, July 11, singing "The Star-Spangled Banner," which was marred only by the delegates from Mississippi, who booed Sammy Davis, Jr. The jibes were so loud and ugly that Sammy lost his composure. As Davis tried to blink back his tears, Frank whispered to him: "Those dirty sons of bitches! Don't let 'em get you, Charley. Hang on. Don't let it get you!" But unable to hide his humiliation, Sammy left after the national anthem while Frank, Dean Martin, Peter Lawford, Janet Leigh, and Tony Curtis took their places on the floor in front row seats reserved for the press. They prowled the aisles restlessly, wanting to be part of the Kennedy power-brokering that was being handled by Kenny O'Donnell and Larry O'Brien. Although reporters, delegates, and even the Speaker of the House of Representatives were barred from the floor unless they could produce a highly coveted pass, Frank and the Rat Pack wandered at will from one delegation to the next, impervious to barriers and restrictions. Conscious of television, Frank had painted the back of his head black so that the cameras would not pick up his shiny bald pate.

Ambassador and Mrs. Kennedy stayed at Marion Davies's mansion in Beverly Hills, and while Rose attended the convention every day, her husband entertained labor leaders and big city bosses at home. On Wednesday, July 13, the day of the nominations, Frank was sitting with Jack Kennedy and his father when David McDonald, president of the steelworkers union, arrived.

"Bobby was there . . . and quite a number of the members of the Kennedy family were there," recalled McDonald. "I walked in and said hello to everybody. Jack said, 'Would you like a drink, Dave?' I said, 'Yes, I'd love a beer.' He said, 'Right out there.' So I went out there and Frankie Sinatra, of all people, was the bartender. So Frank said, 'What would you like, Dave?' I said, 'Got an ice cold beer here?' He said, 'Sure.' I said, 'Frank, would you do me a favor? How about calling [my wife] Rosemary. She couldn't be here because she has this terrible headache from the demonstration.' So he called Rosemary. Her headache stopped immediately because she was such a great admirer of Sinatra, of his singing ability, anyway."

Jack Kennedy stayed at the house with his father to watch the nominating speeches while Frank returned to the convention hall, where the Stevenson demonstrators were threatening to tear down the hall in their fervor. As Senator Eugene J. McCarthy (D-Minn.) stepped to the podium to make his eloquent nominating speech for Stevenson ("Do not reject this man who has made us all proud to be Democrats. Do not leave this prophet without honor in his own party."), the convention turned into a screaming, screeching mass of waving straw hats and blowing horns beseeching the heavens to thunder in praise of their man. Frank sat backstage, glumly watching the wild Stevenson demonstration. After five minutes of pandemonium, he signaled the orchestra leader, Johnny Green, giving him the "cut" sign with his hand to his throat, and effectively put a stop to the outpouring of adulation.

Minutes later, Minnesota Governor Orville Freeman made the nominating speech for Kennedy, which didn't match McCarthy's rousing speech for Stevenson, but that made no difference, because by 10:07 P.M., when the roll of states was called and Wyoming gave its fifteen votes to Kennedy, the Democratic nomination was his. The convention hall erupted with excited Kennedy delegates screaming "All the way with JFK." The Rat Pack jumped up and down, pounding one another on the back. "We're on our way to the White House, buddy boy," Frank said to Peter Lawford. "We're on our way to the White House."

Frank had arranged for political satirist Mort Sahl to address the convention before Kennedy's acceptance speech the next night. Months before, Sinatra had solicited material from the thirty-three-year-old comedian for a Kennedy joke bank to compete with one Bob Hope was doing for the Republicans. Sahl had amused the Kennedys with his caustic political humor, referring to White House Press Secretary Jim Hagerty as "Ike's right foot," and deriding Eisenhower as the president who rode to the White House like a hero on a white horse. "Four years later we've still got the horse, but there's nobody riding him," he had said.

Given these Republican jibes, Frank had figured that Sahl would provide good entertainment for 100,000 cheering Kennedy partisans. He certainly didn't expect the comedian to make fun of the candidate, and he cringed when Sahl opened by announcing that Nixon had sent a wire to Joseph P. Kennedy, saying, "You haven't lost a son. You've gained a country. Congratulations." It was no better when Sahl ended by saying, "We've finally got a choice, the choice between the lesser of two evils. Nixon wants to sell the country, and Kennedy wants to buy it."

After that evening, Frank's relationship with Sahl was never the same.

The convention over, Frank campaigned hard for the Kennedy-Johnson ticket. He appeared before two thousand women at Janet Leigh's Key Women for Kennedy tea and sang three songs. He sent a $2,500 check to the campaign headquarters. He brought Hollywood friends to the Democratic Governors' Ball in Newark, New Jersey, and sang before forty thousand people. He staged luau benefits in Hawaii during the filming of *The Devil at 4 O'Clock*, and campaigned with Peter Lawford throughout the islands.

"Frank and I won Honolulu for Jack by one hundred twenty-eight votes," said Lawford. "We hit all the islands, just the two of us. I'd smile and Frank would sing, picking up local bands along the way."

Frank also arranged a behind-the-scenes meeting for Ambassador Kennedy with his good friend, Harold J. Gibbons, national vice-president of the Teamsters Union, so that the ambassador could try to heal the wounds caused by Bobby's investigation of labor racketeering and get labor's endorsement for his son's presidential ticket. The teamsters never endorsed Kennedy, but Frank's friend Sam Giancana steered teamster dollars out of their $200 million pension fund into the Kennedy campaign. Giancana did it partly to get Kennedy elected— and thereby end his own surveillance—but he also must have wanted to please Frank, with whom he now had a common business interest. A few months before, Giancana had quietly made preparations to become a secret owner of the Cal-Neva Lodge in Lake Tahoe. The owners of record were to be Frank Sinatra, Dean Martin, and Hank Sanicola.

Curiously, former Ambassador Joseph P. Kennedy was staying at Cal-Neva at the time as Sinatra's guest, and, according to Justice Department files, "had been visited by many gangsters with gambling interests." The Justice Department refused in 1985 to release any further information to explain the "deal" made between Joseph Kennedy and the "gangsters with gambling interests."

Seeing an opportunity to embarrass the Republican nominee, Frank gave Bobby Kennedy, JFK's campaign manager, a copy of a private investigator's report disclosing that Richard

Nixon had made periodic visits to a New York psychiatrist, Dr. Arnold Hutschnecker, news that would have been highly damaging if published in 1960. Bobby Kennedy's aide recalled that Sinatra, who personally employed the private investigator, was surprised when Bobby refused to use the information and locked it in his office safe instead. "Frank then sent a reporter around to try to surface it, but Bobby was out of town at the time," said the aide. "He never said anything to Frank, but he sat on the report and refused to make it public."

On September 12, 1960, Frank set aside politics for the wedding of his beloved daughter, Nancy, to Tommy Sands at the Sands Hotel in Las Vegas in front of thirty-five friends and family. Little Nancy had intended to marry Sands in the winter of 1960 after Tommy's Air Force tour of duty was completed, but she pushed the marriage ahead because "my father goes to Honolulu to make a picture. . . . I couldn't get married without my father."

Her mother watched with mixed emotions as Nancy, Jr., rushed into marriage with the young singer who, as a teenage idol, had sold a million copies of "Teen-age Crush" for Capitol Records. "It's my own life happening twenty years later," said Big Nancy.

The twenty-three-year-old groom wore his airman third class Air Force uniform and the bride wore a white streetlength dress designed by her father's designer, Don Loper. Frank refused to pose for photographers. "This is Nancy's day, and I don't want to horn in," he said.

Frank cried when he saw his twenty-year-old daughter ready to walk down the aisle. "He looked at me in my white gown and veil," she said. "He saw the bouquet and the little diamond star earrings he'd given me for a wedding gift. He just stood there with tears streaming down his face.

" 'I love you, chicken,' he said.

"I said, 'I love you, too, Daddy.' And off we went down the aisle, both in tears."

Later Nancy said, "You know what most mothers give their daughters for a wedding present? Silver or china or money for a romantic trip. My mother gave me a sewing machine."

The marriage was to be tough for Tommy because Nancy was constantly calling her father for advice, and begging him to put Tommy in his movies. Tommy insisted that they move to New York to be away from the Sinatra influence. "Frank let me know that he felt it was a foolish idea, that I'd be hurting myself professionally by pulling up stakes and moving away from Hollywood," said Sands. "I didn't care though. I had to do what I thought was best . . . Nancy was unhappy about leaving her family, all her childhood ties, and it was only natural for her father to give me his advice because she was involved."

"I remember when we went to the Sinatras one Christmas when Nancy was married to Tommy," said Mickey Rudin's former wife, Elizabeth Greenschpoon. "Nancy opened her present from her father, which was a ten-thousand-dollar leopard coat. That was something Tommy could never have afforded to give her, and when she opened the present she started screaming. Everyone oohed and aahed over Frank, and poor Tommy left the room."

Five years later, Tommy Sands would walk out on Nancy, saying he no longer wanted to be married to her. Once again, she would see her father cry as she collapsed in her mother's Bel-Air home, where she stayed in bed for weeks.

On Election Day, November 8, 1960, Frank stayed in his office at Essex Productions in Los Angeles. His secretary, Gloria Lovell, kept an open telephone line to Jake Arvey in Chicago, where Giancana controlled the first ward and several river wards. Arvey, Democratic National Committeeman from Illinois and a close friend of Giancana's, reported the state's returns to Frank every half hour. By midnight, NBC's John Chancellor was predicting a Republican sweep, with Richard Nixon the winner. At three o'clock in the morning, Chicago Mayor Richard Daley called Dave Powers in Hyannisport. "We're trying to hold back our returns," he said. "Every time we announce two hundred more votes for Kennedy in Chicago, they come up out of nowhere downstate with another three hundred votes for Nixon."

At 3:10 A.M., Nixon made a television appearance in the Ambassador Hotel in Los Angeles with his wife, Pat, who was on the verge of tears, but he refused to concede the election. This so angered Frank that he picked up the phone and called the hotel, demanding to be put through to Nixon's suite. The operator refused to connect him. "Do you know who this is?" he screamed. "This is Frank Sinatra, and I want to talk to Richard Nixon." He was determined to tell the Republican candidate to give up and get it over with, but he couldn't reach him.

A few hours later, Jake Arvey called Frank to say that the black wards in Chicago were coming in strong for Kennedy, but in the end he carried the state by only 8,858 votes. The national election was so close that Kennedy won by only 118,550 votes out of 68,832,818 cast.

Although Chicago's Mayor Daley later took the credit for Kennedy's election, gangsters around the country pointed with pride to the syndicate control of the West Side Bloc, which produced that victory.

"The presidency was really stolen in Chicago," said Mickey Cohen, the Los Angeles mobster.

Sam Giancana later bragged about his contribution to John F. Kennedy's victory. As he frequently told Judith Campbell: "Listen, honey, if it wasn't for me, your boyfriend wouldn't even be in the White House."

Skinny D'Amato credited Sinatra's mobilization of mob support for the victory. "Frank won Kennedy the election," he said many years later. "All the guys knew it."

A month after the election, a contractor and construction crew began breaking ground around Sinatra's Palm Springs compound to add a heliport and a large new guest house with a dining room capable of seating forty for the future president and his Secret Service agents. Frank spared no expense on this project and paid hundreds of thousands of dollars in overtime to get the job done in a hurry. Frank worked with the carpenters day and night and even flew in lumber by helicopter, for he was convinced that his house on Wonder Palms Road would become the Western White House, a vacation retreat for the president of the United States.

$$
\boxed{21}
$$

The *Caroline*, the Kennedys' private plane, landed in Washington, D.C., on January 6, 1961. Frank jumped out with Peter Lawford and a little dog wearing a black sweater. A maroon Lincoln Continental limousine whisked them off to the National Guard Armory, where they would be spending the next thirteen days planning an inaugural gala to honor the president-elect the night before his swearing-in. This invitation-only show for ten thousand people paying one hundred dollars apiece for seats and ten thousand dollars for boxes would raise over one million dollars to cover the Democrats' campaign deficit.

"It will be the biggest one-night gross in the history of show business," said Frank.

He had thought of little else since the election, when he began making calls all over the world to assemble an impressive array of stars to pay a show business tribute to the president who so loved Hollywood. He persuaded Ella Fitzgerald to fly in from Australia to sing for five minutes, Shirley MacLaine was coming from Japan, Gene Kelly from Switzerland, Sidney Poitier from France, and Keely Smith and Louis Prima from Las Vegas. Frank negotiated with Leland Hayward to release Ethel Merman from *Gypsy* for one night and managed to close another Broadway show, *Becket*, for the evening to free Anthony Quinn and Sir Laurence Olivier. Sinatra wanted Fredric March to do a dramatic reading of

Abraham Lincoln's farewell speech, the one he delivered from the back of the train that took him from Springfield to Washington. Frank called Eleanor Roosevelt, who, despite her support for Adlai Stevenson, was thrilled to participate. He engaged Sammy Cahn and Jimmy Van Heusen to write special songs, and Goodman Ace, Norman Corwin, Jack Rose, Leonard Gersche, and Mel Shavelson to write dialogue. Joey Bishop was to be master of ceremonies, and Leonard Bernstein promised to conduct "Stars and Stripes Forever." The rest of the cast consisted of Harry Belafonte, Milton Berle, Nat King Cole, Helen Traubel, Juliet Prowse, Mahalia Jackson, Alan King, Jimmy Durante, Pat Suzuki, Kay Thompson, Bette Davis, Janet Leigh, and Tony Curtis, plus Nelson Riddle and his orchestra. Only Dean Martin, locked into a movie, and Sammy Davis, Jr., who had recently married Swedish actress Mai Britt, would be conspicuously absent.

Sammy Davis did not want his interracial marriage to mar the gala in any way. He had postponed his wedding until after the election, because Frank was to be best man and Sammy didn't want that fact to hurt Kennedy's chances for election. "Right or wrong, fair or not, my wedding was giving the Nixon people the opportunity to ridicule Kennedy and possibly hurt him at the polls," he said. "And every survey showed that [Kennedy] couldn't afford to lose a single vote. I could imagine the pressure Frank must be under. He must have eighty guys telling him, 'Don't be a fool. You've worked hard for Kennedy, now do you want to louse him up?' "

"This is the most exciting assignment of my life," said Frank, who had planned every gala detail accordingly. Before leaving California, he spent ninety thousand dollars at Rusar's jewelry store in Beverly Hills creating silver cigarette boxes with the inaugural invitation inlaid on top to be given to the participating stars. He had spent thousands more ordering a custom-designed wardrobe, including an Inverness cape with a red satin lining, black patent leather pumps, a silk top hat, swallowtail coat, striped trousers, a double-breasted gray suede weskit, black calfskin oxfords, and white kid gloves. And, in case he spilled anything, he ordered everything in duplicate.

The day of the gala, snow started falling softly on Washington and continued until the city was blanketed under huge white drifts that covered cars and buried shrubs and fences. By evening all traffic was stalled on snow-choked streets, and the National Guard had to be called in to plow the city's main arteries. By nine P.M. the armory was only half full, and Frank and Peter Lawford were pacing back and forth, waiting for those performers still stuck in the storm. By ten P.M. the president-elect and Mrs. Kennedy had yet to arrive, and the show was an hour and a half late. Finally, their police car pulled up to the entrance, and Frank went into the swirling snow to escort Jacqueline Kennedy up the stairs, trying to stay clear of her white organza skirt.

At eleven P.M., with many seats empty, the lights went down and Frank walked onstage.

"We know it's a great party," he said, "because who else could run up a debt of two million dollars in three months without a credit card?"

For the next three hours, a priceless collection of show business talent led by the son of Italian immigrants saluted the first Irish-American ever elected to the presidency.

Seconds after the finale, John F. Kennedy went up onstage to thank the stars. "I'm proud to be a Democrat, because since the time of Thomas Jefferson, the Democratic Party has been identified with the pursuit of excellence, and we saw excellence tonight," he said. "The happy relationship between the arts and politics which has characterized our long history I think reached culmination tonight.

"I know we're all indebted to a great friend—Frank Sinatra. Long before he could sing, he used to poll a Democratic precinct back in New Jersey. That precinct has grown to cover a country. But long after he has ceased to sing, he is going to be standing up and speaking for the Democratic Party, and I thank him on behalf of all of you tonight. You cannot imagine the work he has done to make this show a success. Tonight there are two shows on Broadway that are closed down because the members of the cast are here. And I want him and my sister Pat's husband, Peter Lawford, to know that we're all indebted to them, and we're proud to have them with us."

After the gala all the stars were bused downtown to Paul Young's restaurant, where Ambassador Kennedy held a glittering dinner for everyone. When Frank complimented him on the splendor of the evening, the seventy-two-year-old host said, "Wait until you see the party we throw four years from now!"

Hours later, Frank was wearing his Inverness cape with the red satin lining and waiting to be driven to the Capitol in time for the noon swearing-in. And that evening, January 20, 1961, while the President and First Lady made their rounds of the five inaugural balls, Frank gave a party at the Statler Hilton for the stars who had participated in the previous evening's gala.

By the time the President made it to the second ball at the Statler, he was so curious about Frank's party that he excused himself, leaving his wife and Vice-President and Mrs. Johnson sitting in the presidential box while he bounded upstairs to see the stars. He apologized for interrupting. "I'm sorry," he said, walking over to Frank's table, "I didn't know you were eating."

"That's class," said Frank later. "That's real class."

Everything about Jack Kennedy impressed Frank, who was still reeling from the thanks he had received from him the night before. He paid to have the President's remarks reprinted in *Variety* and played the recording of that evening over and over for his friends, saying, "I only wish my kids could have seen it. I can't find the words. I'll never be able to find the words."

"After the inauguration we all had to sit around Frank's hotel suite at the Sands in Las Vegas and listen to that record of Kennedy thanking him," said the woman who was living with Jimmy Van Heusen. "Frank would stand by the mantel and play it over and over, and we had to sit there for hours on end listening to every word."

Frank framed the President's note of thanks and put a gold plaque on the door of the bedroom where Kennedy had slept when he visited Sinatra in 1959, although he confused the date, saying "John F. Kennedy slept here November 6 and 7, 1960."

Visitors were always shown the "Kennedy Room," where Frank exhibited his presidential mementos, including photographs of himself with Jack Kennedy and the half-dozen notes that JFK had dashed off to him during the campaign, each framed as beautifully as a precious painting. Aware that Nevada was one of the two western states that went for Kennedy in the election, Frank was pleased to point out the note that said: "Frank—How much can I count on the boys from Vegas for? JFK."

Upon returning to the West Coast, Frank sent the President every one of his albums, plus tapes of Rat Pack hijinks in Las Vegas. In return, President Kennedy sent him a thank-you note on White House stationery; that, too, was framed and hung in the Kennedy Room.

Returning home was a letdown for Frank, and he seemed out of sorts. He performed at the Sands in Las Vegas and flew to Miami for his opening at the Fontainebleau. There he spent time with Sam Giancana, who was working on a CIA plan to assassinate Fidel Castro. Back in California, Sinatra was still in a foul mood. He stayed at his Palm Springs house and entertained a regular crowd of friends, including Marilyn Monroe, Pat and Peter Lawford, Sammy Davis, Jr., and Mai Britt, and Jimmy Van Heusen. Long days were spent at the pool lying in the sun, and in the evening everyone ate one of Frank's Italian dinners served by George Jacobs.

"Frank was awful during this time," said one of the guests. "He yelled at Marilyn, saying 'Shut up, Norma Jean. You're so stupid you don't know what you're talking about.' She was drinking out of a flask by that point and rather pathetic. He barked at George constantly: 'George, get this; George, fill the drinks; George, clean my ashtrays; George, clear the table.' He never said 'please' or 'thank you' and was always yelling at that poor guy, but George never said a word. He just took it all with silent dignity."

Frank's agitation was due, in part, to Desi Arnaz, who rented space to Frank's production company at Desilu Studios. As president of Desilu, Arnaz was responsible for developing *The Untouchables*, a popular weekly television show about Eliot Ness battling the Chicago mob in the days of Al Capone, when Sam Giancana was Capone's driver. The Chicago names being mentioned on the series were making Giancana and Tony Accardo extremely uncomfortable. They didn't want to see their notorious predecessors depicted as murderers, so they secretly backed the Federation of Italian-American Democratic Organizations in starting a boycott against the show's sponsor, Chesterfield cigarettes. In March 1961, Chesterfield bowed to the pressure and withdrew its sponsorship. But that wasn't enough for Sam Giancana. He wanted Desi Arnaz killed.

In April, after an evening of drinking in Palm Springs, Frank announced that he was going to take care of Desi.

"I'm going to kill that Cuban prick," he said.

With actress Dorothy Provine beside him, Frank drove to the Indian Wells Country Club, followed by Jimmy Van

Heusen and his date, to wait for Desi's usual arrival at the restaurant there.

The two women sat in silent terror as Frank said he was going to stop the show and put Desi out of business. Van Heusen tried to cajole Frank into leaving. Every five minutes he said, "Well, looks like Desi isn't going to show. Let's shove off," but Frank refused to move. Minutes later, Desi walked in flanked by two huge Italian bodyguards, each one standing well over six feet and weighing at least three hundred pounds.

Seeing Frank sitting at one of the tables, Desi yelled across the restaurant at the top of his drunken voice, "Hi ya, dago." Thinking Frank was there to have a good time, Desi walked over with the two bodyguards. With a tight jaw, Frank introduced him to his group, which was holding its breath in anticipation of mayhem. Frank turned to Desi and told him what he and some of his influential Italian friends thought about the show making the Italians gangsters. "What do you want me to do—make them all Jews?" said Desi. He said that he wasn't afraid of Frank's friends, and the argument went on from there. Frank admitted he'd never seen *The Untouchables* but said he knew what he was talking about because "I *always* know what I'm talking about. That's how I got where I am."

Desi laughed. "Oh, yeah," he said in his thick Cuban accent. "Well, I remember when you couldn't get a yob. Couldn't get a yob. So why don't you forget all this bullshit and just have your drinks and enjoy yourself. Stop getting your nose in where it doesn't belong, you and your so-called friends."

Unruffled, Desi meandered back to the bar with the two bodyguards, leaving Frank full of unspent bluster. Obviously embarrassed, he looked around the table and said, "I just couldn't hit him. We've been pals for too long."

"Yeah, what's the point," said Van Heusen soothingly.

As they were leaving, Frank spotted two women sitting at a nearby table and invited them to join the group at Van Heusen's house for a party.

At four A.M., the group headed for Van Heusen's house in Palm Desert, relieved that the crisis over Desi Arnaz had been averted. They didn't know that Frank was so upset that he would soon move his production company out of the Desilu Studios. But they saw how humiliated Frank felt to have backed down on his threats when he walked into Jimmy's den, where a large Norman Rockwell portrait hung on the wall. One of the composer's most treasured possessions, it portrayed Van Heusen sitting at the piano in his pajama top, and it was a special gift from the artist. Grabbing a carving knife from the kitchen, Frank lunged at the painting and slashed the canvas to shreds.

"If you try to fix that or put it back, I will come and blow the fucking wall off," he said.

Van Heusen did not say a word; the women exchanged frightened glances. Finally, one of the two women picked up at the country club said solicitously, "I love your records, Frank."

Looking at her contemptuously, Sinatra said, "Why don't you go slash your wrists."

After Frank had left the house, Van Heusen's date asked, "How could you stand there and let him do that?"

"Tomorrow he'll be so sorry that he'll send me some print worth five thousand dollars or something."

"What difference does that make?" she asked. "That can't replace a Norman Rockwell."

She was unable to comprehend why this very strong man acquiesced to Sinatra, whom he addressed as "your eminence" to his face and referred to behind his back as "the monster."

"Why do you put up with his craziness?" she asked. "Pick up hookers for him? Go over there all the time and stay up with him until all hours of the morning and sit back and watch him treat people like dirt?"

"Because he sings my songs, that's why. I'm a whore for my music."

Jimmy Van Heusen had learned long before to tolerate the strange twists in Frank's psyche that drove him to savage behavior. Other close friends made the same allowances.

"Yes, there is a cruel streak in Frank, no question about it," said Anthony Quinn, "but I still love the guy. He's what all men are and not one man in a million ever is. Thomas Wolfe said that. I guess what I love is the Frank that sings. That's when he's really himself. I love what he says in his songs. I don't love everything that Frank does or the way he treats people at times, but anyone who sings like he does cannot be a really bad man."

Frank frequently tried to make amends for his bizarre behavior with an act of generosity. A few days after he ruined the Norman Rockwell painting, he sent his friend an expensive Japanese print as Van Heusen had predicted, and it was accepted without any recrimination.

Still, the violence within Frank kept people at bay, leaving some of the women in his life to receive the roughest treatment, possibly because they came to know him so intimately. During the time Natalie Wood dated Frank, he insulted her so terribly at a party in his home that she went screaming from the table in tears. Even so, he threw her a surprise party on her twenty-first birthday, and on her twenty-second he sent her twenty-two bouquets, and had them delivered one by one hourly. He also ordered twenty-two musicians to serenade her.

"He was Dr. Jekyll and Mr. Hyde, and sometimes you didn't know which one you were going to get," said Judith Campbell. "Frank's Dr. Jekyll was a charmer, but his Mr. Hyde was frightening, truly frightening."

"It was really something to see," said the woman who lived with Jimmy Van Heusen. "Frank would bring someone to the desert for the weekend, and, of course, we'd have to be there, so I saw a lot of what I call Frank's 'before-and-after' treatment. Before bed, he would be so charming. The girl was 'mademoiselle this,' 'darling that,' and 'my sweet baby.' He was [a] cavalier, a perfect gentleman. You never saw anything like this man in your life. He'd jump across the room to light a cigarette. He'd fill her glass with champagne every time she took a sip. With a hand on her neck he'd say, 'You're beautiful tonight,' or he'd whisper loudly enough for all of us to hear, 'No one prettier has ever been in my house. You look radiant, gorgeous.' Then the next day we'd go over for his interminable pool party, where everyone drank for hours, followed by his spaghetti dinner, which was followed by more drinking. It was the next day that we'd always find the other Frank, the one who wouldn't speak to the girl, who had been the most beautiful woman in the world the night before. Sometimes he wouldn't even go near her, nor would he tolerate any affectionate overtures from her. Humped and dumped. The minute the conquest was achieved, kaput. The girl could pack her bags. I saw so many of them leave his house in tears."

Paul Chandler, who worked as a houseman for Frank for

many years, said one of his jobs was to drive the women home the next morning. "Frank was just like a child. He wanted every new toy there was, and then after he played with it, he'd just toss the toy away. Those girls were no more than toys to him. Some mornings, I'd get to the house and find four or five of them in the bed at the same time, and all colors of girls, too, let me tell you," he said.

It was this "swinging" image of Frank that so fascinated President Kennedy, who delighted in hearing reports of what Frank was doing, and especially with whom. During her visits to the White House, Judith Campbell was quizzed by JFK endlessly. "Almost immediately, Jack started pumping me for gossip, most of it directed at Frank," she said. " 'What was Frank doing? Was it true that he was seeing Janet Leigh?' We always went through the same old routine."

"It's true that Jack loved hearing about Frank's Hollywood broads," said Peter Lawford. He added that the President enjoyed movie and show business gossip so much that he subscribed to *Variety* to keep up with what was going on.

"During one of our private dinners, he brought up Sinatra and said, 'I really should do something for Frank.' Jack was always so grateful to him for all the work he'd done in the campaign raising money. He said, 'Maybe I'll ask him to the White House for dinner or lunch.' I said that Frank would love that, but then Jack said, 'There's only one problem. Jackie hates him and won't have him in the house. So I really don't know what to do.' Here was the President of the United States in a quandary just like the rest of us who are afraid to upset our spouses. We joked for a few minutes about stuffing Frank into a body bag and dragging him around to the side door so the gardeners could bring him in like a bag of refuse and Jackie wouldn't see him. We also talked about sneaking him in in one of John-John's big diaper bundles. The President brightened up a few minutes later and said, 'I'll wait until Jackie goes to Middleburg, and I'll have Eunice be the hostess.' So that's what he did. When Jackie left, Evelyn Lincoln called Frank and invited him to the White House. He flew to Washington for the day and a car drove him up to the southwest gate. Even without Jackie there, the President still wouldn't let him come in the front door. I don't think he wanted reporters to see Frank Sinatra going into the White House. That's why he never flew on *Air Force One* and was never invited to any of the Kennedy state dinners or taken to Camp David for any of the parties there. He got to Hyannis once, but that was only because Pat and I invited him."

Still, Frank stayed in close contact because President Kennedy frequently called him in Los Angeles. Frank's secretary, Gloria Lovell, would interrupt business meetings to tell him that he had a White House call and Frank would pick up the phone, saying, "Hi ya, Prez." If he took the call privately, he always told the men what the President said when he returned to the meeting.

"After each one of those calls, Frank pranced around so proud of the fact that the President was ringing him up," recalled one associate.

Since the gala, Frank had seen the President in person only once and that was briefly when he visited the White House with Judy Garland and Danny Kaye. The minute they were ushered into the Oval Office, Kaye started jumping up and down, climbing behind the desk, peeking around the flag and playing the clown. The President quickly signaled his military aide to shut the door and make sure that no photographers were let in, including Cecil Stoughton, who was acting as the official White House photographer. Kennedy did not want "unpresidential" photographs published of entertainers cavorting in the Oval Office. When the meeting was over and the three stars were escorted out, Frank tried to hang back to have a one-on-one talk with Kennedy, but to no avail.

Frank got the chance in September 1961, when the President invited him to Washington to thank him for all his work on the gala. Before going to the Oval Office, Frank stopped by the press office to see press secretary Pierre Salinger, who had become a good friend. He was noticed by reporters, which fueled speculation about his close friendship with the President.

At a press conference, Salinger was asked about the relationship:

Q: Pierre, one other thing, was Frankie Sinatra a guest at Hyannisport last week?

A: No.

Q: Or any other weekend?

A: No.

Q: In *Show Business Illustrated* [it was said] that the President on Inauguration Day went to see Sinatra to thank him for his participation in the gala.

A: No, that's not true.

Q: Has Sinatra ever been a guest of the President and his wife anywhere?

A: No.

Technically, Salinger was correct. Frank didn't go to Hyannisport until the day after the news conference, on September 23, 1961.

The day of his White House visit, Frank was given a grand tour of the family quarters and taken out to the Truman Balcony for drinks.

"I still remember how he showed the White House maître d' how to make Bloody Marys with his own fantastic special recipe," said Dave Powers, a presidential aide. "He sat on the balcony sipping his drink and looking out at the sun streaming in and the wonderful view of Washington we got from there. He turned to me and said, 'Dave, all the work I did for Jack. Sitting here like this makes it all worthwhile.' Then I went out and got some of the big mounted color photographs of the President and we had one signed for him. ["For Frank—With the warm regards and best wishes of his friend. John F. Kennedy."] He also signed one for his daughters and for his son. It was a new photograph of the President, and Jack wanted him to have it. He liked Frank a lot."

The next day, September 24, 1961, Frank flew to Hyannisport with Pat Lawford, Ted Kennedy, and Porfirio Rubirosa and his wife, Odile, on the Kennedys' plane. When fog closed the Hyannis airport, the group flew to New Bedford, Massachusetts, where they decided to take a taxi the rest of the way. Frank strolled off the *Caroline* holding a glass of champagne and followed by his twelve pieces of luggage, a case of wine, a dozen bottles of carefully wrapped champagne, and two loaves of Italian bread for Ambassador Kennedy. He whistled for two cabs to drive the group and the parcels, including three cartons of ice cream in dry ice, to the Kennedy compound, fifty-three miles away.

When they arrived at the Kennedy compound, the presidential flag was flying to indicate that John F. Kennedy was in residence. Driving past the White House communications trailer, the group was dropped off at the ambassador's house, where Peter Lawford was waiting and the dinner table was set for twenty-six. The next day, everyone went cruising with the President on the *Honey Fitz* and listened to Frank talk about his trip to Italy and his audience with Pope John

XXIII. Peter Lawford laughed out loud. "All your friends in Chicago are Italian too," he said.

On the subject of Frank's Mafia connections, Lawford later grew serious and formally approached his brother-in-law by making an appointment to see the attorney general in his office at the Justice Department. There Lawford begged Bobby to listen to Sinatra's pleas for Giancana. Robert Kennedy intended to make Frank's mobster friend the Justice Department's top priority in Chicago and curtly told Lawford to mind his own business.

That three-and-a-half-hour cruise off Cape Cod later brought President Kennedy stinging criticism from people who objected to his socializing with Frank Sinatra and being seen with the much-divorced Porfirio Rubirosa, former Dominican ambassador and onetime son-in-law of Rafael Trujillo, dictator of the Dominican Republic. Plucky Pierre, as Kennedy called his rotund press secretary, tried to quash the criticism by telling reporters that the Rubirosas were guests of Ted Kennedy and that Frank was a guest of the Lawfords. He emphasized that Frank had not been the guest of President and Mrs. Kennedy anywhere: "Mr. Sinatra went up there to confer with Ambassador Kennedy about a souvenir recording of the inauguration gala. The record will be a money-raiser for the Democratic Party."

During that visit, the President mentioned the $100-a-plate fund-raiser he had to attend in November at the Hollywood Palladium and expressed hope that Frank could attend; Frank said he wouldn't miss it.

He then told the President about his interest in making *The Manchurian Candidate*, a psychological thriller based on a novel by Richard Condon about two American soldiers who are captured by the Communists during the Korean War and brainwashed. One of the soldiers (Laurence Harvey) is programmed to assassinate a presidential candidate so that the Communist-backed candidate will become president. The other soldier, to be played by Frank, is deprogrammed by a psychiatrist and then works with the FBI to investigate Harvey. Frank had been approached with the property by George Axelrod and John Frankenheimer and wanted to make the film. It would be distributed by United Artists as part of the fifteen-million-dollar contract Frank had with the company. The problem was that Arthur Krim, president of United Artists, refused to distribute the movie. He was national finance chairman of the Democratic Party at the time and, as such, very protective of the Kennedys. He felt that the film was too politically explosive. Frank disagreed and took the matter directly to President Kennedy, who said that he had no objection whatsoever to seeing the film made. In fact, he enjoyed Condon's novel and thought it would make a great movie. So Frank asked him to call Krim, and he agreed to do so.

"That's the only way that film ever got made," said Richard Condon. "It took Frank going directly to Jack Kennedy."

On matters involving his Mafia friends, Frank was not so successful. Shortly after his September visit to the White House and his stay in Hyannisport, Sam Giancana was talking to his West Coast operative, Johnny Roselli, who had been Frank's house guest in Palm Springs. On federal wire taps of December 6, 1961, the two gangsters talked about Frank's promise to intercede with Attorney General Robert F. Kennedy, whose Justice Department had stepped up its investigation of Giancana.

ROSELLI: . . . He [Frank Sinatra] was real nice to me. . . . He says: "Johnny, I took Sam's name, and wrote it down, and told Bobby Kennedy, 'This is my buddy, this is what I want you to know, Bob.' " Between you and I, Frank saw Joe Kennedy three different times—Joe Kennedy, the father. He called him three times. . . . He [Frank] says he's got an idea that you're mad at him. I says: "That, I wouldn't know."

GIANCANA: He must have a guilty conscience. I never said nothing. . . . Well, I don't know who the fuck he's [Frank's] talking to, but if I'm gonna talk to . . . after all, if I'm taking somebody's money, I'm gonna make sure that this money is gonna do something, like, do you want it or don't you want it. If the money is accepted, maybe one of these days the guy will do me a favor.

ROSELLI: That's right. He [Frank] says he wrote your name down. . . .

GIANCANA: Well, one minute he [Frank] tells me this and then he tells me that and then the last time I talked to him was at the hotel in Florida a month before he left, and he said, "Don't worry about it. If I can't talk to the old man [Joseph Kennedy], I'm gonna talk to the man [President Kennedy]." One minute he says he's talked to Robert, and the next minute he says he hasn't talked to him. So, he never did talk to him. It's a lot of shit. . . . Why lie to me? I haven't got that coming.

ROSELLI: I can imagine. . . . Tsk, tsk, tsk . . . if he can't deliver, I want him to tell me: "John, the load's too heavy."

GIANCANA: That's all right. At least then you know how to work. You won't let your guard down then, know what I mean. . . . Ask him [Frank] if I'm going to be invited to his New Year's party.

ROSELLI: I told him that's where I usually go for New Year's with Sam. But he says, "I have to be in Rome the twenty-seventh."

GIANCANA: Too fucking bad. Tell him the Kennedys will keep him company.

ROSELLI: Why don't you talk to him [Frank]?

GIANCANA: When he says he's gonna do a guy a little favor, I don't give a shit how long it takes. He's got to give you a little favor.

Frank had been steadily losing clout with the Boys over his dwindling influence with the Kennedys. FBI records indicate that when in 1961 Carlos Marcello, the *capo di tutti capi* (boss of all bosses) of Louisiana, who headed one of the oldest and most deeply entrenched Mafia families in the United States, had become one of Bobby Kennedy's targets for deportation, the New Orleans don contacted Santo Trafficante, head of the Florida Mafia family, who in turn called Frank to use his influence with "the President's father" on Marcello's behalf. But Trafficante's efforts failed and may have only intensified federal efforts against Marcello, who was eventually deported to Guatemala.

Mafia leaders by this time realized they had vastly overrated Frank's influence with the Kennedys. They could no longer count on him to run interference for them. Despite the syndicate's "donation" to the Kennedy campaign, on telephones tapped by federal agents, Johnny Roselli discussed the problem with Sam Giancana, remarking that Frank was powerless to help them at all. Roselli suggested that Sam not rely on Sinatra anymore and try something else to get rid of the FBI agents who were shadowing him constantly.

ROSELLI: He's got big ideas, Frank does, about being ambassador, or something. You know Pierre Salinger and them guys. They don't want him. They treat him like they treat a whore. You fuck them, you pay them, and they're through. You got the right idea, Moe [one of Giancana's nicknames], go the other way. Fuck everybody. We'll use them every fucking way we can. They [the Kennedys] only know one way. Now let them see the other side of you.

Giancana's increasing disIlusionment with Frank was obvious on December 4, 1961, when he spoke to Chuckie English, one of his lieutenants, about money that Sinatra's record company, Reprise, owed someone.

ENGLISH: They owe that guy $14,000 and wouldn't pay.

GIANCANA: Why?

ENGLISH: I don't know. What do we do?

GIANCANA: Tell him to sue the [obscenity deleted]. Do it fast, too.

FBI wiretaps picked up another of Giancana's conversations blaspheming Frank as a liar. "If he [Kennedy] had lost this state here he would have lost the election but I figured with this guy [Sinatra] maybe we will be all right. I might have known this guy [obscenity deleted]. . . . Well, when a [obscenity deleted] lies to you."

Later, when Sam and Johnny Formosa, another gangster, discussed their feelings of betrayal over Frank's failure to "deliver" his friend, President Kennedy, and get rid of the federal agents who had marked Giancana as a target for early prosecution, they mentioned the Rat Pack.

FORMOSA: Let's show 'em. Let's show those asshole Hollywood fruitcakes that they can't get away with it as if nothing's happened. Let's hit Sinatra. Or I could whack out a couple of those other guys. [Peter] Lawford and that [Dean] Martin, and I could take the nigger [Sammy Davis, Jr.] and put his other eye out.

GIANCANA: No . . . I've got other plans for them.

Those "other plans" became clear the following year as Sam spent thousands of dollars renovating the Villa Venice in a Chicago suburb, and transformed the syndicate-owned restaurant into a red-tasseled nightclub with seating capacity for more than eight hundred people. Sam kept the Venetian gondolas outside on the river near the entrance and added Italian music as well as shuttle-bus service to a Mafia casino known as the Quonset Hut two blocks away. There he installed two dice tables, roulette wheels, and blackjack tables, all rigged to favor the house. His scheme called for bringing into the Villa Venice top entertainers who would attract high-rolling patrons, who in turn would be charged one hundred dollars and later steered to the illegal gambling down the road.

Through wiretaps installed in the Armory Lounge in another Chicago suburb, the FBI learned that Giancana had spoken with Sinatra in New York and met with him in Los Angeles to arrange for the entertainment. Sam planned to open on October 31, 1962, with Eddie Fisher, who would be followed by Sammy Davis, Jr., Dean Martin, and Frank himself.

Everyone agreed to perform without fee, although Frank was permitted to cut an album of his performances with Dean and Sammy for his new company, Reprise Records. He hoped to sell one million copies of the album for $4.95 each, which would net him fifty cents an album, a total of $500,000. Frank sent Mo Ostin from Reprise to Chicago a week ahead of time to work out the musical arrangements, and then he insisted on a private train to transport himself and Dean Martin from Hollywood. His demands irritated Giancana, who complained bitterly to a friend in a conversation recorded by FBI wiretaps.

"That Frank, he wants more money, he wants this, he wants that, he wants more girls, he wants . . . I don't need that or him. I broke my ass when I was talking to him in New York."

FBI agents interviewed each one of the headliners at the Villa Venice, and each one admitted he was performing there as a favor. Eddie Fisher referred to his good friend, Frank Sinatra, saying, "I'm here because a friend asked me to do him a favor." Frank, who was making $100,000 a week in Las Vegas, said he was performing free as a favor to Leo Olsen, who was the nightclub's owner of record, a front for Sam Giancana. Sammy Davis, Jr., was a little more forthright when agents questioned him about cutting short his lucrative Las Vegas engagement to work at the Villa Venice for nothing.

"Baby, that's a very good question," he said. "But I have to say it's for my man Francis."

"Or friends of his?"

"By all means."

"Like Sam Giancana?"

"By all means."

When asked to elaborate, Davis gulped his drink and exhaled. "Baby, let me say this. I got one eye, and that one eye sees a lot of things that my brain tells me I shouldn't talk about. Because my brain says that, if I do, my one eye might not be seeing anything after a while."

Jammed for three shows a night, the Villa Venice did record business during the Rat Pack's run, attracting mobsters from across the country. Dean Martin joked openly about suspicion of Frank's hidden ownership. When Sinatra yelled for someone to hand him a stool to sit on, a stagehand tossed one out of the wings onto the floor.

"I thought you owned some of this," said Dean to Frank. "And that's how they treat you."

A few minutes later, Martin brought down the house when he pointed in the direction of the club's penthouse apartment and cautioned Sinatra and Davis: "Hold the noise down. There's a gangster sleeping up there."

For Frank's opening night, Joe Fischetti flew in from Florida with a contingent of gangsters, as did Jim DeGeorge from Wisconsin. Sitting ringside with Sam were several of Chicago's Mafia lieutenants: Marshall Califano, Jimmy "The Monk" Allegretti, Felix "Milwaukee Phil" Alderisio, and Willie "Potatoes" Daddano, one of Sam's personal assassins. Sam showed up every night with a phalanx of gangsters dressed in sharkskin suits and black fedoras, escorting wives in mink coats with teased bouffants.

Sam, a widower, took Judith Campbell to Eddie Fisher's opening, and during the run of the Rat Pack he entertained lavishly in his upstairs suite in the restaurant while down the road in the Quonset Hut the fixed wheels hummed and the loaded dice rolled. By the end of the month, his "other plans" for Frank and the Rat Pack had enriched him by over three million dollars in unreported, tax-free cash. The next day, the Quonset Hut closed, and the Villa Venice suspended its entertainment policy.

"It was a sucker trap set by Sam, plain and simple," said Peter Lawford, who had not been invited to participate, "and Frank lent himself and Dean and Sammy and Eddie Fisher as bait to bring in the high rollers while Sam and the Boys fleeced them." Lawford added, "I guess it was either that or die."

Sam was so grateful to the entertainers who performed at the Villa Venice that he sent each an expensive present. Sinatra's gift was seven thousand dollars' worth of Steuben crystal.

"It was gorgeous, absolutely gorgeous," said Phyllis

McGuire, who selected the teardrop pattern. "I got Frank full service for thirty—the martini glasses, white wine glasses, red wine glasses, champagne goblets, and water tumblers. I even called his secretary, Gloria, to see if he'd like it monogrammed. She said Frank had trouble with monogrammed things because people liked to keep them."

Phyllis had suggested crystal after seeing the one piece of plain stemware Sinatra had in Palm Springs. "It was a gift from Ruth Berle, and Frank tried to tell me it was Steuben, but I knew better," she said. "I told him it's not Steuben unless it says Steuben on the bottom. I turned his silly glass over and showed him that it was not Steuben. He still didn't believe me. So Sam told me to get him the real thing and then maybe he'd know the difference. I guess that's why he never said thank you for the crystal. He was too embarrassed. You see, Frank will never admit a mistake."

22

"I know that certain people in the Chicago organization knew that they had to get John Kennedy in [the White House]," said mobster Mickey Cohen. "There was no thought that they were going to get the best of it with John Kennedy. See, there may be different guys running for an office, and none of them may be . . . what's best for a combination. The choice becomes the best of what you've got going. John Kennedy was the best of the selection. But nobody in my line of work had an idea that he was going to name Bobby Kennedy attorney general. That was the last thing anyone thought."

By appointing his thirty-five-year-old brother to the nation's top law enforcement position, Kennedy sounded a clarion call to attack organized crime on a national scale. As chief counsel to the McClellan committee, Bobby had exposed corruption in fifteen unions and fifty corporations, helping convict labor leaders like Dave Beck, Jr., president of the Teamsters Union. Now, as attorney general, he rallied Justice Department lawyers to "the conspiracy of evil" that he said was organized crime, and he declared that it would be his major concern. He quadrupled the staff and funding of the organized crime section and appointed Edwyn Silberling to compile a list of top racketeers to be targets of prosecution. Included were some of Frank Sinatra's closest Mafia friends: Sam Giancana, Mickey Cohen, Johnny Roselli, Anthony "Big Tuna" Accardo, Santo Trafficante, Jr., and Carlos Marcello.

So driven was Bobby Kennedy in his pursuit of gangsters that he prosecuted Joey Aiuppa of the Chicago mob for violating provisions of the Migratory Bird Act. "Bobby's instructions were: 'Don't let anything get in your way,' said Henry Petersen, a senior aide in Kennedy's Justice Department. "'If you have problems, come see me. Get the job done, and if you can't get the job done, get out.'"

During one of many meetings the attorney general held with his bright young staff, one lawyer stepped forward to complain about the President's friendship with Frank.

"We are out front fighting organized crime on every level and here the President is associating with Sinatra, who is in bed with all those guys," he said.

The attorney general said, "Give me a memorandum and give me the facts."

A series of three reports were prepared on Frank in 1962. They showed that he had repeated and personal associations with ten of the leading figures of organized crime, detailing the times and dates these gangsters telephoned Frank at home, using his unlisted number. The report also enumerated special favors that Frank had performed for these men over the years.

"Sinatra has had a long and wide association with hoodlums and racketeers which seems to be continuing," stated the Justice Department report. "The nature of Sinatra's work may, on occasion, bring him into contact with underworld figures, but this cannot account for his friendship and/or financial involvement with people such as Joe and Rocco Fischetti, cousins of Al Capone; Paul Emilio D'Amato, John Formosa, and Sam Giancana, all of whom are on our list of racketeers. No other entertainer appears to be mentioned nearly so frequently with racketeers.

"Available information indicates not only that Sinatra is associated with each of the above-named racketeers, but that they apparently maintain contact with one another. This indicates a possible community of interest involving Sinatra and racketeers in Illinois, Indiana, New Jersey, Florida, and Nevada."

The part that disturbed Bobby Kennedy the most detailed Sam Giancana's repeated visits to Sinatra's home in Palm Springs.

Bobby had become even more alarmed on February 27, 1962, when he received a memo from FBI Director J. Edgar

Hoover: While investigating Johnny Roselli, agents had found many calls to Judith Campbell. A check of her telephone records disclosed several phone calls to Evelyn Lincoln, President Kennedy's personal secretary in the White House, as well as to Sam Giancana. Bobby did not know then that Frank Sinatra was the link between Judy Campbell and the President, and Judy Campbell and Sam Giancana, but he did have enough information about Sinatra's connections to organized crime to dissuade his brother from accepting Frank's hospitality as planned in March 1962. Bobby immediately stepped up surveillance on Giancana as well as on Judith Campbell, and dispatched J. Edgar Hoover to give the FBI reports to the President while he called Peter Lawford to cancel the President's weekend stay at Sinatra's house.

Peter pleaded with Bobby to reconsider, but the attorney general was adamant, saying that under no circumstances could the President of the United States stay at the home of a man who also played host to Sam Giancana and other hoodlums. Peter then appealed directly to the President, who agreed with his brother.

"I can't stay there . . . while Bobby's handling [the Giancana] investigation," said the President. "See if you can't find me someplace else."

"It fell to me to break the news to Frank, and I was frankly scared," said Lawford, who winced when he recalled the situation twenty years later. "When I rang the President, I said that Frank expected him to stay at the Sinatra compound, and anything less than his presence there was going to be tough for Charley here to explain. It had been kind of a running joke with all of us in the family that Frank was building up his Palm Springs house for just such a trip by the President, adding cottages for Jack and the Secret Service, putting in twenty-five extra phone lines, installing enough cable to accommodate teletype facilities, plus a switchboard, and building a heliport. He even erected a flagpole for the Presidential flag after he saw the one flying over the Kennedy compound in Hyannisport. Now, no one asked Frank to do any of this, but he really expected his place to be the President's Western White House. When Jack called me, he said that as President he just couldn't stay at Frank's and sleep in the same bed that Giancana or any other hood slept in. 'You can handle it, Petah,' he said to me. 'We'll take care of the Frank situation when we get to it.' I made a few calls, but in

the end it was Chris ...
who arranged everything ...
Secret Service stayed next ...
Frank didn't speak to him fo ...
the one who really took the bru ...
responsible for setting Jack up to sta ...
... ll people—the other singer and ...
like that k never forgave me. He cut m ...

... is the real reason wh ...
... dinner ... You ...
everything ...

Frank could ... lieve what Lawford told ... the President was coming to ... Springs and would s... t Bing Crosby's because Bobby didn't wan... ... stay with Frank. Unable to appeal to Ambassador Kennedy, who had been struck mute with a stroke a few months before, Frank called the attorney general in Washington. Bobby explained that it was impossible for the President to stay at his house because of the disreputable people who had been his houseguests.

"Frank was livid," said Peter. "He called Bobby every name in the book, and then rang me up and reamed me out again. He was quite unreasonable, irrational, really. George Jacobs told me later that when he got off the phone, he went outside with a sledgehammer and started chopping up the concrete landing pad of his heliport. He was in a frenzy.

"When Jack got out here for that weekend [March 24–26, 1962], he asked me how Frank had taken it. I said, 'Not very well,' which was a mild understatement. The President said, 'I'll call him and smooth it over.' So he did. After the conversation, Jack said, 'He's pretty upset, but I told him not to blame you because you didn't have anything to do with it. It was simply a matter of security. The Secret Service thought Crosby's place afforded better security.' That's the excuse we used—security—and we blamed it all on the Secret Service. We'd worked it out beforehand, but Frank didn't buy that for a minute, and, with a couple of exceptions, he never spoke to me again. He cut me out of all the movies we were set to make together—*Robin and the 7 Hoods*; *4 for Texas*—and turned Dean and Sammy and Joey against me as well."

Lawford was so distraught about Frank's reaction that he sent his personal manager, Milt Ebbins, to talk to him.

"Frank was terribly hurt, and Peter was the culprit. Frank blamed him for getting Crosby's house," said Ebbins. "I made a special trip to his office, I'll never forget it, on Sunset Boulevard. I spent three hours with him. I said, 'Frank, this

y he didn't. . . .' I told him everything,
know what he said? 'Well, maybe we'll have
xt week,' but they never did. . . . Afterwards, Frank
d not help Peter at all. None of Frank's friends would ever
hire him."

Close identification with the dynamic young Presid
had given Frank a special aura in Hollywood, whe how's
asked him, "What do you hear from Washin To be cut off
Jack?" "Have you been to Hyannisport, heaven slammed in
from this power was to have the geed by Kennedy's decision
his face. He was so deeply
to stay at Bing Crosby's estate instead of his own that he left
town for the weekend. To close friends, he damned Peter
Lawford and denigrated Bobby Kennedy, talking about the
hypocrisy of accepting hoodlum money to get elected and
then refusing to accept hoodlum friendship, but Frank never
said a negative word about the President.

No one understood the importance of a good public image
better than the Kennedys, who lived by the creed of their
father: "You must remember—it's not what you are that
counts, but what people think you are."

As President, Jack Kennedy cared intensely about the
image he projected. So much so that when Warner Bros.
started to cast the movie, *PT 109*, based on his World War II
exploits, he insisted on seeing the tests of the stars being
considered to portray him.

"When he learned that they were making the movie, we
asked that the President be allowed to approve the man
chosen to portray him," said Pierre Salinger. "Especially
since the picture would be shown overseas and could dissemi-
nate an image that might be very bad for the U.S. if not
handled with dignity."

This attention to image was not lost on Frank, who admitted that his own was lacking. He called a meeting with his
lawyer, Mickey Rudin, and his two publicists, Henry Rogers
and Warren Cowan of Rogers and Cowan, to deal with the
problem.

"What the hell is wrong?" he asked them. "I have the
worst image in the world. The press keeps rapping me. My
reputation is going downhill more and more every day. I have
the best public relations men in show business working for
me, and my image stinks. What the hell is wrong?"

"The only thing wrong with your image is you," said Henry Rogers. "You have been doing outrageous things, you have been making outrageous statements, you have been offending the press outrageously."

Rogers and Cowan had been handling Frank's public relations for seven years, trying to mollify the reporters and photographers he periodically abused, but Frank had frequently disregarded their advice and called his own shots.

When Samuel Goldwyn arranged for some of the stars of *Guys and Dolls* to be on the *Ed Sullivan Show* in 1955, Frank discovered that he was to appear without pay while Marlon Brando and Jean Simmons were receiving fees. He took the matter to the Screen Actors Guild, and Sullivan bought a full-page ad in *The Hollywood Reporter* to protest. He commented on Sinatra's low TV rating and added: "P.S. Aside to Frankie boy: Never mind that tremulous 1947 offer: 'Ed, you can have my last drop of blood.' "

Rogers and Cowan cringed when Frank insisted on responding with full-page ads in the Hollywood trade papers: "Dear Ed: You're sick. Frankie. P.S. Sick, sick, sick!" And they were no happier when he walked into the Stork Club one night and saw columnist Dorothy Kilgallen, who was wearing sunglasses. Getting up from his table, Frank walked past her and dropped a dollar bill into her coffee cup, saying, "I always figured she was blind."

Rogers and Cowan tried to stop Frank from sending angry telegrams, but he persisted. When *Time* magazine reported that he was about to buy a Palm Beach estate and nightclub to get even with a nightclub owner who had refused to offer him five thousand dollars for one appearance, Frank wired *Time*: I AM GLAD TO SEE THAT YOU ARE STILL BATTING A THOUSAND REGARDING ANY INFORMATION CONCERNING ME. AS USUAL YOUR INFORMATION STINKS. I NEED A HOUSE AND A NIGHTCLUB IN PALM BEACH LIKE YOU NEED A TUMOR!

When Frank refused to be fingerprinted by the New York police for a cabaret license, his publicists backed him all the way, saying it was the principle of the thing. Rogers and Cowan, not knowing of Frank's old New Jersey arrests, told the press that he did not have a police record.

Henry Rogers became so frustrated with Sinatra's behavior that when Frank asked him why he did not have a good public image, he impulsively said that Frank was his own worst enemy.

Silence followed Rogers's rebuke, but Frank did not flinch. He asked Rudin's opinion, and Cowan's, and listened to both men discuss his poor public persona and what could be done to rehabilitate it. They decided that Frank should undertake a "people-to-people" type of personal appearance tour and do benefits around the world that would raise money for handicapped children.

Having decided on a European tour, Frank then fired Rogers and Cowan and hired another publicist, Chuck Moses, a serious, conscientious public relations man.

"Frank wanted to be not just an entertainer and an important factor in show business," said Moses, "but he also wanted to play a role in the community other than that which is always imagined of him. He was very serious about this. . . . He wanted to do good. He wanted to change his image."

It was no longer enough for Frank to be the most famous Italian-American singer in the world or an international movie star; he had to be esteemed and venerated. In Sicily, such men are revered as *uomini rispettati*—men of repsect; men who are honored by village folk, whose hands are kissed, whose advice is heeded, whose greeting is cherished.

"Frank is totally committed to public respectability," said Richard Condon, "but on his terms, and being a friend of the President . . . was in his eyes the ultimate respectability."

"The breach with JFK was brutal for him," said Chuck Moses, who had the task of reshaping Frank's public persona, and who began by trying to get rid of the Rat Pack image. "It gives the public a wrong impression," he said. "People think Frank and Dean and Sammy and a few others are inseparable. Sure, they're good friends, but Frank has many other friends, interests, and activities."

The first step in remaking the Sinatra image was the European concert tour arranged by Mickey Rudin in 1962 to benefit underprivileged children and to introduce his client as a philanthropist with a social conscience.

"I was married to Mickey at the time, and together the two of us had to go out and get Frank concerts," said Elizabeth Greenschpoon. "We went all over the world—to Rome and Tokyo and London, and I watched Mickey create an atmosphere of demand for Frank, that he was desirable. Never mind the henchmen and goons. Mickey made them book Frank. Because of my husband's strong ties to Israel, he also managed to get a youth house named for Frank because supposedly this was a tour to benefit children and youth. I say 'supposedly' because the real purpose was to benefit Frank. He needed a good press at the time, and Mickey saw to it that he got one."

In Tokyo, they gave Frank the key to the city and named an orphanage for him.

In Hong Kong, hundreds of children lined the streets waving garlands of flowers in his honor.

In Nazareth, they presented him with a silver-embossed Bible in a ground-breaking ceremony for the Frank Sinatra International Friendship Youth House. But this antagonized the Arab League, which promptly banned his movies and records.

In London, Princess Margaret shook his hand and Lord Snowden bowed in admiration.

In Paris, General de Gaulle made him an officer of the "Order of Public Health."

Throughout the ten-week tour, the press coverage was outstanding because Moses had hired a still photographer, a three-man television team, and two publicity people to accompany Frank. Photographs of him holding blind children in Greece and talking with crippled children in Italy appeared around the world, inspiring newspapers to commend "the new Frank Sinatra." In Japan, they hailed him as "a nice, gentle guest," in Israel as "a tough dandy."

His return to the United States was heralded as "Do-Gooder Frank Flies Back Home." He was honored by the Variety Club of Southern California for "services in behalf of children everywhere" and was presented with a silver plate by the Columbian Foundation. He told reporters that as an overprivileged adult he wanted to help underprivileged children.

"I think we raised something like a million dollars for children's institutions. I wish it was five million," he said, noting that his most moving experience had occurred while visiting with a six-year-old blind child. "It was windy, and I brushed the hair out of her eyes and told her that the wind had been blowing up her hair. She stopped me cold when she said, 'What color is the wind?' "

Chuck Moses designed new press kits with a biography of Frank that began: "Frank Sinatra's life has moved into a new phase. . . ." Moses also arranged as many interviews as he could, believing that Frank would gain more by talking to reporters than by beating on them.

"Frank cared very much about the press and what they wrote about him," said Moses. "He insisted that I take a nice big suite in every hotel we checked into so that I could have reporters up. I had to be very careful when I announced his engagement to Juliet Prowse because Frank was concerned about Nancy, Sr. He knew that she [still] expected him to come back to her, and he really didn't want to hurt her. Six weeks later, I had to announce that the engagement was broken because of 'a conflict of career interest.' Juliet just refused to give up her dancing and be the kind of stay-at-home wife that Frank wanted, but I couldn't go into that kind of detail with reporters. Because of the personal nature of those two announcements, they were probably the toughest I had to make."

Frank's image campaign suffered a slight setback a few months later when he fought with a photographer in a San Francisco nightclub because he had not asked for permission to take Sinatra's picture. The photographer's camera was smashed and the film ruined.

"It is true that Frank was unhappy with the way the picture was taken," said Moses. "He likes photographers to ask his permission to take pictures and to address him as 'Mr. Sinatra.'"

Joe Hyams of the *Herald-Tribune* approached Moses about doing a *Playboy* interview with Sinatra, which Moses instantly recognized as an ideal showcase for "the new Frank" to talk about his good works and philanthropy. But Frank refused to sit still for the in-depth tape-recorded interview that *Playboy* required for its question-and-answer format. Billy Woodfield, the photographer, who was working with Frank at the time, urged him to reconsider and take advantage of the forum, pointing out that the magazine reached millions of people each month, but Frank still declined. Woodfield persisted until Frank finally said, "Well, why don't you put something together for me—something controversial—shake 'em up a little, and I'll take a look at it."

When Woodfield tried and was unable to develop anything, he called Mike Shore, who was in charge of advertising for Reprise Records. Frank admired Shore and frequently referred to him as a genius. Fascinated by the idea of creating such an interview, Shore sat down at a typewriter and wrote out the questions he imagined that *Playboy* would ask and then answered them as he thought Sinatra might, given a worldly and compassionate philosophy. Shore centered the interview on the fundamentals that move and shape men's lives—God, religion, and the progress of civilization toward disarmament and against nuclear war. He showed Frank as a man with a great understanding of the human condition, making him sound as literate as Adlai Stevenson and as humane as Albert Schweitzer. Shore pitted him firmly against bigotry and nuclear testing, in favor of admitting mainland China into the United Nations, and resentful of organized religion. Throwing in a few Las Vegas idioms to make it sound like Frank, Mike Shore "asked him" if he believed in God, and answered eloquently for him.

"I believe in you and me. I'm like Albert Schweitzer and Bertrand Russell and Albert Einstein in that I have a respect for life—in any form. I believe in nature, in the birds, the sea, the sky, in everything I can see or that there is *real* evidence for. If these things are what you mean by God, then I believe in God, but I don't believe in a personal God to whom I look for comfort or for a natural on the next roll of the dice. I'm not unmindful of man's seeming need for faith; I'm for *anything* that gets you through the night, be it prayer, tranquilizers, or a bottle of Jack Daniels. But to me religion is a deeply personal thing in which man and God go it alone together, without the witch doctor in the middle."

A few days later, Woodfield presented the synthetic interview to Frank, who was immensely impressed with what Mike Shore had written and was eager to have it appear as his own in the magazine.

Mickey Rudin objected, arguing that the content was much too controversial, especially the atheism.

"Rudin said, 'Frank, you can't say this. You can't sign this piece,' " Woodfield recalled. "We all sat there and Frank looked at me, and Frank, Jr., was in the room, and Hyams was sitting there. . . . I looked at Frank, Jr., and I looked at Frank and said, 'Frank, it's your decision. If you believe what this interview says, that these things are your beliefs, and you are afraid to say them in America, what are you saying to your son about America?' Frank looked at me and said, 'You're absolutely right.' He picked up a pen and signed [the release form]."

Mike Shore also signed a release, giving the copyright to

Frank, and the interview appeared in the February 1963 issue of *Playboy* billed as "a candid conversation with the acknowledged king of showbiz." The magazine received many letters commending Frank's pacifist views about total global disarmament. Yet close friends knew him to carry a gun and be militant about a strong national defense. So much so that during the Cuban missile crisis he had put his pilot, Don Lieto, on twenty-four-hour emergency notice and equipped his private plane with enough water and canned food to survive for a month in case the crisis evolved into war and they had to fly to a safer place.

Among the impressed *Playboy* readers who read the intelligent discourse under Frank's name was Kris Kristofferson, who was on the Gulf of Mexico agonizing over the end of a song he was writing.

"I was struggling with the last line," he said, "but when I read Frank's interview, I flashed on that part where he talks about being for anything that helps you get through the night. That's where I got the last line and finished my song—'Help Me Make It Through the Night.' "

While Frank worked at improving his public image, he continued to try to improve his relationship with Jack Kennedy. For JFK's birthday in May 1962 he had sent him a huge rocking chair made out of flowers. A White House aide described the gift as "so gaudy and outlandish that we sent it out the same day and the President didn't even look at the thing." Still, Kennedy acknowledged the gift in a letter to Sinatra: "I was delighted with this lovely remembrance and thought you might like to know that the youngsters over at Childrens' Hospital also had the opportunity of sharing, with me, your more than generous gift."

A few months later, Frank wired the White House that he had arranged with United Artists to provide President Kennedy with a print of *The Manchurian Candidate*.

Although now removed from the Kennedys' sphere, Frank remained politically committed to the Democratic Party and had campaigned hard in 1962 for Edmund "Pat" Brown, who won the governorship of California when he beat Richard Nixon.

"Frank traveled all over the state campaigning for me and raising money. Then he staged an inaugural gala in Sacramento like the one he did for Jack Kennedy in Washington," said Pat Brown.

Of primary importance to Frank at the beginning of 1963 was the fiftieth wedding anniversary party he was planning for his parents in February. To celebrate their golden anniversary, he had already purchased a sixty-thousand-dollar home for them in an exclusive residential section of Fort Lee. His mother had promptly filled it with brand new furniture, another gift from Frank. The principal adornment in her living room was an artificial Japanese cherry tree surrounded by plaster statues of the saints, small founts of holy water, photographs of Pope John XXIII, Ava Gardner, Pope Paul, and Dean Martin, plus an autographed chair from Sammy Davis, Jr. That house on Abbott Boulevard, which was firmly situated in Bergen County, the most prosperous part of New Jersey, was the culmination of all Dolly Sinatra's dreams of upward mobility. Thanks to her son, she was now wearing the fur stoles, mink coats, and pearl brooches that other, respectable women of Bergen County wore. Her reputation as "Hat Pin Dolly" was far behind her.

In honor of their fiftieth anniversary, Frank bought Dolly a $25,000 diamond bracelet from Tiffany, which was delivered to her home in an armored truck. He also obtained a Papal Blessing, which he sent to his parents in a letter, saying, "The sands of time have turned to gold, yet love continues to unfold like the petals of a rose, in God's garden of life. . . . May God love you, through all eternity. I thank Him, I thank you for the being of one. Your loving son, Francis."

For the evening of February ninth, he reserved the large dining room of the Casino in the Park in Jersey City, New Jersey, for a champagne dinner for three hundred people. It was to follow a special high mass at St. Augustine's Roman Catholic Church, where Dolly and Marty were to renew their marriage vows.

Frank had sworn his mother to secrecy on the party and threatened to leave if there was press coverage or any photographers allowed inside. He had left the invitation list up to her, so Dolly invited most of Hoboken. The notable exception was her sister, Josephine Monaco, Frank's favorite aunt, to whom Dolly had not spoken since 1957, when *Look* magazine quoted her as saying that Dolly turned over the rearing of young Frankie to her mother, Rosa Garavante. In that article, Josie also punctured the cherished myth of Frank's nearly dying the day he was born and being saved by his grandmother, who held him under the cold water faucet until he came to life.

"I never could understand that story about Frank's grandmother saving his life," Josie said. "She wasn't even there during the delivery."

Also missing from the invitation list was Frank's Irish godfather, Frank Garrick. Even after thirty years Dolly and Frank still nursed a grudge against the former newspaperman for firing Frank.

"My son is like me," Dolly was fond of saying. "You cross him, he never forgets."

Frank dreaded returning home and facing relatives and the friends of his youth. His relatives said that he was so nervous about going back to Hudson County that his stomach started turning flips and he had to take a tranquilizer.

"He's a coward when it comes to Hoboken," said his cousin. "He just can't cope with it. When he sees somebody from his childhood, it seems to bring back everything and he tries to ignore it."

The night of the party the jovial Dolly, wrapped in mink, arrived leading her husband, Marty, by the hand. They were quickly surrounded by news photographers and television cameramen.

"Get all your pictures now, boys," yelled Mrs. Sinatra, posing cheerfully, smiling and waving to the press. "There won't be any later because Frankie will be here and you know how he feels about you fellas. So snap away now."

While his parents were being escorted through the front entrance of the restaurant, Frank arrived at the side door with Paul "Skinny" D'Amato and Henri Gine, a former adagio dancer who had worked with Sinatra for years, attending to his parents, running all kinds of errands. They were escorted by mounted policemen and sixty security guards. Two men from the sheriff's office dressed in tuxedos were to accompany him all night so that no one could approach him.

Staring straight ahead, Frank strode into the room and did not stop to greet anyone. He joined his daughter, Nancy, and her husband, Tommy Sands, at the head table, where he greeted his parents and then sat down next to a few priests and his quiet aunt, Mary. He fidgeted and squirmed as the master of ceremonies read a personal message of congratulations from President and Mrs. Kennedy. He did not sing or make a speech of any kind. Nor would he talk to any of the old Hoboken friends he hadn't seen for twenty years. He watched his parents dance to "The Anniversary Waltz" and smiled as Nancy danced with her grandfather, but he declined to lead his mother around the floor or to dance with his daughter. Two or three persons snapped pictures of him at the family table, which irritated him no end. "Mom, what did I tell you about pictures?" he said. Dolly shrugged. "What can I do, son? They're guests."

There was no way in the world that Dolly was going to allow this event to go unrecorded. Despite Frank's orders to the contrary, she was determined to get pictures taken that evening. So she bought film and flashbulbs for three of her friends, paid them each five dollars, and instructed them to photograph the family table throughout the evening. To see to it that Frankie wouldn't object too strenuously, she made sure that one of the friends was a Catholic Sister in a black habit draped with rosary beads.

WELCOME TO FRANK SINATRA'S CAL-NEVA LODGE, said the road signs leading to the casino hotel overlooking Lake Tahoe's Crystal Bay. The border dividing California and Nevada ran right through the middle of the property, intersecting the swimming pool and pushing drinkers to the California side while gamblers stayed on the Nevada side.

"This is the only place in America where you can walk across the lobby and get locked up for violating the Mann Act," Frank said, greeting nightclub guests in his Celebrity Room.

Surrounded by small bungalows or chalets on the North Shore of Lake Tahoe in the High Sierra, the Cal-Neva Lodge had undergone renovation since Frank bought into it.

"We have obtained a loan of . . . $1,500,000 . . . for expansion of the lodge," said Paul "Skinny" D'Amato, explaining the enlarged casino, additional hotel accommodations, and the acoustically perfect showroom that Frank had insisted be built for performers. Skinny had discussed the Cal-Neva with another mobster over a telephone that was tapped by federal agents. The FBI knew that Skinny was Sam Giancana's man at Cal-Neva, the person placed there to keep track of the count from the drop boxes at the gambling tables, and to look out for hidden interests. And they knew also from wiretapped conversations between Sam and Johnny Roselli that Giancana was a hidden owner of the Cal-Neva.

ROSELLI: Aren't you going to be tied up with the Cal-Neva?

GIANCANA: I am going to get my money out of there and I'm going to wind up with half of the joint with no money. Not going to make any difference. . . . That joint ain't going to be no good because it's a very short season.

The Cal-Neva was open only from June through the Labor Day weekend in September, but the owners wanted to make it a year-round operation. FBI reports suggested that Giancana had tried to borrow three million dollars from the Teamsters Central States pension fund for the purpose, but Jimmy Hoffa had turned him down.

This enraged the Mafia don, who complained bitterly to a friend. "Once I got $1,750,000 from him in two days. Now all this heat comes on and I can't even get a favor out of him now. I can't do nothing for myself. Ten years ago I can get all the fucking money I want from the guy, and now they won't settle for anything."

Frank packed the Celebrity Room with performers like Eddie Fisher, Vic Damone, Red Skelton, Victor Borge, Lena Horne, Dean Martin, Joe E. Lewis, and Juliet Prowse to draw high-rolling summer crowds, while Trini Lopez and Buddy Greco played the Cabaret Lounge.

Nevada records show that as of August 15, 1961, Frank owned thirty-six and six tenths percent of the Cal-Neva; as of May 15, 1962, his interest rose to fifty percent. The other two owners of record were Hank Sanicola, who owned thirty-three and one third percent, and Sanford Waterman, who owned sixteen and two thirds percent.

"Frank loved owning that place," said Chuck Moses. "He was always arranging parties, chartering planes, and flying up groups like Lucille Ball, Richard Crenna, and Marilyn Monroe. There were two crap tables there, and all those celebrities would get lucky and win, so he really took a loss."

"Frank was a most convivial host," said San Francisco columnist Herb Caen. "He was great fun and sort of nice to people—except every now and then when he'd flip out. Some guy would come over with his girl and say, 'Frank, I want you to meet my girl.' He'd do one of his mood turns and snarl at the guy: 'You want me to meet your girl? What does your girl want? Does she want to meet me? Can't she speak for herself? Who are you to do her talking? Is she deaf and dumb, this girl of yours? Can't she speak up? Speak up, girl, speak up. Hey, girl, ya want to meet me? Ya want to meet me?' By that time the couple were in complete shock, and the rest of us were so embarrassed we didn't speak. Later, we'd say, 'For Christ sake, Frank, what's the big deal?' He'd say, 'I don't know. I can't help it. They're just so goddamn dumb.'

"Most of the time, though, he was great fun. I saw him a lot at Cal-Neva when Sam Giancana was there. In fact, I met Giancana through Frank. He was a typical hood—didn't say much. He wore a hat at the lake and sat in his little bungalow receiving people. He and Frank were obviously good friends."

The mere presence of Sam Giancana at Cal-Neva was illegal in Nevada, because he topped the Gaming Control Board Black Book list of men not permitted on the premises of any casino in the state.

"In order to avoid the possibility of license revocation for unsuitable manner of operation, your immediate cooperation is requested in preventing the presence in *any licensed establishment* of all persons of notorious or unsavory reputation," the board's orders declared.

"This was always of great concern to Hank," said one of Sanicola's business associates. "He agreed to go into Cal-Neva with Frank only on the condition that Giancana stay away. Hank put in $300,000 of his own money and didn't want to lose his investment. He knew if Sam was around, the place would be turned into a garage. But Sam was as big a ham as Frank and he started coming around a lot, which made Hank real nervous because there were always a lot of federal agents swarming around Giancana. One night he had to take Sam out the back way because of the agents. Hank kept telling Frank that there was going to be trouble because Giancana was always hanging around, but Frank told him that he was a worrier. 'Not to worry,' he'd say. 'Not to worry.'"

During the summer of 1962 Sanicola had had his hands full with federal agents investigating a prostitution ring at Cal-Neva that used women flown in from San Francisco. The operation was conducted openly from the main registration desk of the lodge.

Then there was the attempted murder of an employee, shot on the front steps of the lodge. A few weeks after that, Marilyn Monroe tried to commit suicide there, but she managed to contact the Cal-Neva operator in time to be rushed to the hospital to have her stomach pumped. (A few days later, in Los Angeles, she died of another overdose.)

The most worrisome event had taken place the night after the lodge opened, on June 30, 1962, when Deputy Sheriff Richard E. Anderson had come to pick up his wife, Toni, a cocktail waitress working the late shift. Anderson was aware that his wife, a brunette beauty, had been known to the staff as one of Sinatra's girlfriends before her marriage. Although she and Anderson had been married for three months, he still resented the proprietary way Frank acted toward Toni and warned him to keep away from her. As Anderson stood talking to the dishwashers late that night in the Cal-Neva kitchen, Frank entered and asked him what he was doing there. Anderson said that he was waiting for his wife. Frank tried to throw him out, and a few minutes later the two men started fighting. Anderson punched Frank so hard he was unable to perform for the rest of the week.

"The next day everyone was talking about the fight and the way Frank threatened Anderson. Everyone knew about Frank's temper, but no one paid any attention until a couple of weeks later . . ." said Bethel Van Tassel, a former newspaper columnist.

At 10:26 P.M. on the night of July 17, 1962, Dick Anderson and his wife were driving on Highway 28 not far from the Cal-Neva. They were on the way to the Crystal Bay Club for dinner after a day spent working on the house they were building. Coming toward them at high speed was a late-model maroon convertible with California license plates. The Andersons' car went off the road and smashed into a tree. Dick Anderson was killed instantly. His wife was thrown from the car and suffered multiple fractures. The occupants of the maroon convertible never stopped, and the deputy sheriff investigating the crash could not determine the cause of the accident.

"We have not found any reason why Anderson should have lost control of his car or driven off the road as he did," he said, adding that Anderson might have been blinded by the bright lights of the oncoming car or deliberately forced off the road.

"It's still a mystery," said Dick Anderson's mother, Louise, twenty-four years later. "An FBI man and some people in the community thought that Frank Sinatra had something to do with the accident. That's something they didn't prove or didn't try to prove.

"After the dispute, my son told me that Sinatra went to

the sheriff in Reno and told him to just can my son, to suspend him—to get rid of him. When Dick was killed, he was under suspension. The sheriff's office still gave him a military funeral, but he was under suspension on account of Sinatra. My husband and I still think that Frank Sinatra had something to do with Dick's death, either directly or indirectly . . . I just never went into it . . . because I thought, well, Sinatra is very powerful . . . Richard had four children and I didn't want anything to happen to them or to us, so we just dropped it. Now I'm seventy-nine years old and I don't care what happens to [my husband] or to me. I don't think they would ever come after us."

"There were a number of circumstances that led to suspicions that actually the automobile accident wasn't an accident," said Ed Olsen, Chairman of the Nevada Gaming Commission, in 1972 in his oral history at the University of Nevada. "But on the other hand, there was never anything concrete or provable; the matter was ultimately dismissed . . . even though there were reports from both law enforcements that [Toni Anderson] had told conflicting stories about her relationship with some of the Sinatra people and indicated there might have been something else to the accident than an accident. But as I say, there was never anything proven."

Toni Anderson told her friends she was frightened, and she did not return to her job.

By 1963, FBI agents had Sam Giancana under constant surveillance, which is why Frank's name was mentioned so frequently in FBI reports. The two men were frequently together by this time, spending Easter in Palm Springs, vacationing in Hawaii in May, traveling to New York in June, playing golf at Lake Tahoe in July. Sam came to know the FBI agents following him by name—Bill Roemer, Marshall Rutland, Ralph Hill—and railed at them at every turn.

"Why don't you fucks investigate the Communists," he would scream. "I'm not going to take this sitting down. I'm going to light a fire under you guys, and don't forget that."

In July 1963, Giancana became so exasperated, he sent one of his Mafia lieutenants, Charles "Chuckie" English, with a message for Bill Roemer, who was standing outside the Armory Lounge in a Chicago suburb. "If Bobby Kennedy wants to talk to Sam, he knows who to go through," English told the agent.

"Who?" said Roemer. "Frank Sinatra?"

"You said it, I didn't," said English.

Giancana had given up on Frank's influence with the Kennedys to rid him of the FBI's surveillance. Over federally tapped phones, he discussed Sinatra's political impotence with associate John D'Arco:

GIANCANA: He [Sinatra] can't get change for a quarter.

D'ARCO: Sinatra can't?

GIANCANA: That's right. Well, they [the Kennedys] got the whip in their office, and that's it, and they got the money behind them, so they are going to knock us guys out of the book and make us defenseless. They figure if you've got the money, you got the power. If you don't have the money, you don't have the power.

Giancana sued in U.S. District Court in Chicago to enjoin the Bureau from harassment, claiming the FBI was depriving him of his constitutional rights to privacy. The court ruled in favor of the gangster, fined the FBI five hundred dollars, and ordered the agents to reduce their surveillance by parking at least one block from Giancana's home and remaining one hole behind him on the golf course. But this did not stop the agents from following him to New York City in June 1963, when he, Phyllis McGuire, Frank, and Ava Gardner went to New Jersey for dinner with Frank's parents. Although Frank and Ava had been divorced for eight years, Frank still saw her frequently.

"We had a great time," said Phyllis McGuire. "We took Dolly and Marty a bottle of Crown Royal in a purple felt bag. Ava was so fascinated with it that she couldn't wait until we got there to have a shot, which she chased with beer. She was adorable, and Dolly loved her. There was nothing Mama Sinatra wanted more than to get Frank and Ava back together again."

But Frank and Ava couldn't reach a reconciliation. Frank's Mafia friendships still irritated her. "Ava didn't like those types of people at all," said Phyllis. "She hated the image. It wasn't just Sam, either. Frank had others around him all the time, and when Ava found out that Johnny Formosa had stayed with him in Palm Springs, she really gave him hell."

The next night, the McGuire Sisters appeared on *The Ed*

Sullivan Show. After the telecast, Giancana took everyone out to celebrate.

"We went to Trader Vic's, which was closed because it was Sunday," said Victor LaCroix Collins, the McGuire Sisters' road manager. "But Sam knocked on the door and another dago opened it and said, 'We're closed.' Sam said, 'Yeah, well you just opened,' and, by God, they opened. We had a real drunken brawl in there. It was the McGuire Sisters; Sam; the musical conductor, Tony Riposo; Frank; and Ava Gardner, who is the most foul-mouthed woman I ever met. The two of them [Frank and Ava] got into the worst fight you ever saw . . . the names they called each other! She called him a bastard and said he was nothing but a stupid frigging Wop. Even though we were all feeling real good and half drunk by then, everyone looked at one another when she said this and then looked at her, but she just kept on like none of us were there. . . . Frank kept telling her to shut up. . . . Then they stormed out and the rest of us went to Phyllis's apartment on Park Avenue. A little while later Sinatra showed up with Sammy Cahn. It was raining to beat the devil, and so Sinatra started bending everyone's umbrella, thinking that was real funny. Or else he was still mad at Ava."

Ava had been staying with Frank at his apartment in New York City, and he was doing all he could to please her. Jilly Rizzo, Frank's close friend and bodyguard and the owner of Jilly's, Frank's favorite New York bar, was doing all he could to help Sinatra please her. He enlisted Mike Hellerman to run down to Mulberry Street with him to get the littleneck clams that Frank wanted to serve her. When Frank asked where he could take Ava to dinner without drawing a crowd of reporters and photographers, Jilly recommended the Hawaii-Kai, saying no one would expect to see him there.

"The following day, Jilly and I went up to Sinatra's apartment," said Mike Hellerman. "He was as happy a guy as I've ever seen. We were all sitting there on the couch, talking, when the doorbell rang. Suddenly, Ava walked out of another room all dressed, carrying a suitcase, and headed straight for the door. She opened it, turned, and gave a little wave, saying good-bye to Frank. Then she walked out. None of us knew what to do. We were so embarrassed for Frank. We were flabbergasted. Frank was stunned. Jilly told me later that the guy at the door [waiting for her] was a Spanish airline pilot."

Ava had had enough of Sam Giancana and, according to Victor LaCroix Collins, Sam had had enough of her. "Sam didn't like her at all," said Collins. "He always said that she was a crazy bitch. I only met her that one time, but I'd met Frank before, when Sam and the girls and I spent Easter with Sinatra and his former wife, Nancy, in Palm Springs. That was in April of 1963, and it was another drunk. Sam sent him Easter lilies, which I remember because I had to sign the card for him as Dr. Goldberg—he'd never sign his name to anything—and we had a big fight about how to spell Sinatra's name. We spent the day sitting in Frank's den watching him listening to his own music. I helped Nancy make cold meatball sandwiches in the kitchen."

"It wasn't that memorable a weekend," said Phyllis McGuire. "Frank is one of the most insecure people I've ever met in my life. He's so damn boring. His stories haven't varied in the last twenty years. He talks about when his father brought him the horse in this little bar in Jersey . . . and after the horse is in the bar, his father couldn't get the horse back out. And how much he loved his father when really all the time it was his mother that he feared. His mother dressed him like Little Lord Fauntleroy. Martin Sinatra was a fabulous man, but he was quiet and sweet. Frank's mother was the ballsy one. The boss of that whole family."

During that weekend, Nancy Sinatra took Phyllis into Frank's bedroom and pointed to the photograph of Ava Gardner next to the bed. Then she pointed to the pictures of Nancy, Jr., Tina, and Frank, Jr., sitting on the bureau. "Ava couldn't do that for him," she said, looking at her children's photographs. "Despite all the women he's had, I'm the only one who gave him children."

Walking to the bureau, Nancy opened her jewelry box to show Phyllis all the pearls that Frank had given her through the years. Holding up strands of chokers and long ropes and delicate necklaces, she cited the occasion for each gift. "He got these for me when we were in New York and these I got because . . ."

Phyllis listened with sympathy as Nancy displayed her pearls. "It was so pathetic," she said, "but Nancy is a very sweet lady and has handled herself very well, considering.

It's no secret that the dream that keeps her alive is of Frank returning to her someday. It's so sad, so very sad."

The McGuire Sisters were scheduled to perform at Cal-Neva the week of July 27, 1963. Sam accompanied Phyllis to Lake Tahoe and stayed with her in Chalet Fifty. During the day, FBI agents photographed Giancana and Frank playing golf on the South Shore. In the evening, the two men met in Chalet Fifty for drinks and had dinner together in the Cal-Neva dining room. Victor LaCroix Collins joined the girls and Sam for drinks in the chalet, but soon became irritated with Phyllis, who playfully punched him in the arm every time she passed his chair.

"The dame's got quite a blow on her, and my arm was getting sore," he said. "So I told her, 'You do that again and I'm going to knock you right on your butt.' A half hour later, she punches me again, and so I grabbed her by both arms and meant to sit her in the chair I got out of, but I swung her around and she missed the chair and hit the floor. She didn't hurt herself . . . but Sam came charging over from across the room and threw a punch at me wearing a huge big diamond ring that gouged me in the left eyebrow. I just saw red then and grabbed him, lifted him clean off the floor, and was going to throw him through the plate glass door, but thought, 'Why wreck the place?' So I decided to take him outside and break his back on the hard metal railing on the patio. I got as far as the door and then got hit on the back of the head. I don't know who hit me from behind, but the back of my head was split open. It didn't knock me out, but I went down and Sam was underneath me. He had on a pearl-gray silk suit, and the blood from my eyebrow was running all over his suit. I had a hold of him by the testicles and the collar and he couldn't move. That's when Sinatra came in with his valet, George, the colored boy. They were coming down to join the party.

"The girls were screaming and running around like a bunch of chickens in every direction because nobody knew what was going to happen. . . . George just stood there with the whites of his eyes rolling around and around in his black face, because he knew who Sam was, and nobody ever fought with Sam, least of all me, a short little guy. . . . Sinatra and George pulled me off Sam, who ran out the door. Then Sinatra called me a troublemaker, and said the gangsters were going to put a hit out on me because of this fight. I told him the only way they'd get me is from a long distance with a high-powered rifle because none of them had the guts to hit me face to face. 'I'm not afraid of nothing, Wop,' I said, and he started yelling that I was going to lose the place for him because of this fight. Because of the notoriety he was going to lose all his money. I said, 'What do you mean, your money? You don't have a dime in the place. It's all Mafia money and you know it.' He and George ran out then, and I left the next day for Nebraska. . . . Later I wrote in my diary for July 27: 'One son of a bitch of a day and night.' "

The FBI agents reported Giancana's presence to the Nevada Gaming Control Board, which began an investigation. On August 8, 1963, Ed Olsen, chairman of the Nevada Gaming Commission, called Frank at the Sands in Las Vegas, saying he wanted to meet with him at five o'clock.

"We interviewed him at length, and he acknowledged that he had indeed seen Giancana," said Olsen. "He said he'd seen him rather briefly coming out of Phyllis's cabin and that they just exchanged greetings, and that was all . . . he had no further knowledge of it or anything else."

Having been informed of the fight by the FBI agents, Olsen's investigators flew to Nebraska to interview Victor LaCroix Collins, who confirmed the FBI's report, but Frank denied knowing anything about the fight. "If there was a rumble there while I was there, they must be keeping it awfully quiet," he told Olsen. Chairman Olsen asked him to repeat that assertion under oath, but Frank refused, saying that he never talked under oath without consulting with his attorney.

"[Sinatra] explained his philosophy to us in a very reasonable manner," Olsen said later. "He wasn't cantankerous or anything of that nature. . . . He said that he was acquainted with people in all walks of life and that Giancana was one of those that fit into that category. I asked him if he didn't feel that his association with Giancana and people of that notoriety, whether it be in Palm Springs or Chicago or New York . . . didn't reflect to his own discredit and also to the discredit of gambling in Nevada. Sinatra nodded at that, and volunteered only a commitment that he would not see Giancana or people of that type in Nevada and he would continue to associate as he wished when he wasn't in Nevada. As he said, 'This is a way of life, and a man has to lead his own life.' "

By Labor Day weekend, the press was looking into the story that the Nevada Gaming Control Board was investigating the presence of Sam Giancana at the Cal-Neva Lodge. Frank's attorney denied any wrongdoing to the *Los Angeles Herald Examiner*.

"There's no truth to the fact any underworld figure was at the lodge or got in a fight there," the attorney said. "Your information was wrong."

Olsen told the paper that the investigation could not be concluded until "certain discrepancies in the information provided by various people at Cal-Neva could be resolved."

When Frank read the story, he was incensed. He told his accountant, Newell Hancock, to phone Olsen to come to the lodge for dinner "to talk about this thing."

Olsen did not think such a visit appropriate because the board was investigating Cal-Neva. "But [Frank] kept insisting and I kept refusing," said Olsen. "The more I refused, the madder he got, until he seemed almost hysterical. He used the foulest language I ever heard in my life." Finally, Olsen agreed to meet with Frank in the gaming commission office, and the meeting was set for three-thirty P.M. on September 1.

But Frank did not show up. At four P.M. he called Olsen in a rage. "You're acting like a fucking cop," he said. "I just want to talk to you off the record."

Olsen explained that he wanted the meeting on the record in his office in the presence of others, including his secretary, who would make a record of the conversation.

"Listen, Ed, I haven't had to take this kind of shit from anybody in the country, and I'm not going to take it from you people," said Frank. "I want you to come up here and have dinner with me . . . and bring that shit-heel friend, La France. [Charles La France was the board's chief investigator.] It's you and your goddamn subpoenas which have caused all this trouble."

Olsen said that the publicity was not caused by his subpoenas because no one knew about them except those subpoenaed for interviews.

"You are a goddamn liar," said Frank. "It's all over the papers."

"No, they are not," said Olsen.

"I'll bet you fifty thousand dollars."

"I haven't got fifty thousand dollars to bet."

"You're not in the same class with me," said Frank.

"I certainly hope not," said Olsen.

"All right, I'm never coming to see you again. I came to

see you in Las Vegas and if you had conducted this investigation like a gentleman and come up here to see my people instead of sending those goddamn subpoenas, you would have gotten all the information you wanted."

Pointing out that Skinny D'Amato refused to be interviewed and that the maître d'hôtel had obviously lied, Olsen said that he wasn't satisfied that Frank had told the truth either.

"I'm never coming to see you again," Frank repeated.

"If I want to see you, I will send a subpoena," said Olsen.

"You just try and find me, and if you do, you can look for a big, fat surprise . . . a big, fat, fucking surprise. You remember that. Now listen to me, Ed . . . don't fuck with me. Don't fuck with me. Just don't fuck with me."

"Are you threatening me?" asked Olsen.

"No . . . just don't fuck with me and you can tell that to your fucking board and that fucking commission too."

At six P.M., two audit agents from the board arrived at Cal-Neva to observe the count of gambling table drop boxes. When Skinny D'Amato informed Frank of the agents' presence, Frank told him, "Throw the dirty sons of bitches out of the house."

Because the employees had already started the count, the agents left, but they returned two days later. At that time, Skinny tried to bribe them with one hundred dollars each. The agents turned down the bribes and reported the attempt to Olsen, who decided to issue a complaint seeking the revocation of Frank's license at Cal-Neva and the Sands. He cited several grounds: violating Nevada's gambling laws and regulations by permitting Giancana's presence at Cal-Neva, trying to intimidate and coerce the chairman, Olsen, and members of the Gaming Control Board, hiring people who proffered bribes, instructing employees to resist subpoenas, and associating with people who were harmful to the gaming industry.

Frank was given fifteen days to answer the charges. Hank Greenspun, publisher of the *Las Vegas Sun*, hurried to his defense, writing daily front-page columns in his paper extolling Frank's generosity and philanthropy.

"I cannot think of any individual who has possibly been more instrumental in spreading the name and fame of Nevada to the outside world than Frank Sinatra," he wrote. "I think [revoking his license] is a rotten, horrible, mean, and cheap way to repay this man for all the good he has brought this state."

The governor, Grant Sawyer, disagreed. "Threats, bribery, coercion, and pressure will not be tolerated, and the full weight of the state's gaming control machinery will be brought to bear on any person who wishes to test us," he said. "Nevada's gaming authorities hold a sacred trust from the people, and no man, regardless of his wealth, social status, or business and political connection, is bigger than this trust."

The governor said that he had received several phone calls from wealthy men who talked about resolving the "Sinatra problem" and about making large contributions to his coming election campaign. "I told them that the rules were made for everybody, including Mr. Sinatra."

The governor's position was supported by the lieutenant governor, Paul Laxalt, who felt it was about time that the state did something about Sinatra.

But while the case was pending, President Kennedy came to Nevada and was given a caravan tour through Las Vegas. Riding in the first car with Sawyer, Kennedy said to the governor, "Aren't you people being a little hard on Frank out here?" Sawyer said that the matter was out of his hands and that the issue would be settled legally. He later told Ed Olsen what the President had said, and Olsen was flabbergasted by Kennedy's intervention in Frank's behalf.

"That's about the highest degree of political pressure that you could ever put into the thing," Olsen said many years later. "There was this very definite suggestion from the President of the United States that, frankly, we were being a little tough."

On the other hand, Sam Giancana was disgusted with Frank for losing his temper. "He [Sinatra] called Ed Olsen a cripple," said Phyllis McGuire. "Sam couldn't get over the fact that Frank had done that. Sam said, 'If he'd only shut his damned mouth.' But Sam never could figure out why Frank would deliberately pick fights . . . he would always say to him: 'Piano, piano, piano' (Softly, softly, softly). 'Take it easy, take it easy.' Sam could never get over the hotheaded way Frank acted."

Cal-Neva became a running issue in the nation's newspapers, because it coincided with the public testimony of Cosa Nostra gangster Joseph Valachi. Appearing before Senator McClellan's rackets committee, Valachi named Sam

Giancana as the chief of the Mafia's Chicago family, adding that the Chicago hoodlums are "the smart guys" of the syndicate.

When reporters asked Frank if he had harbored the top "smart guy" at Cal-Neva, he said he had no idea Sam was on the premises. "I'll fight the charges," he said in New York, where he was performing at a United Nations benefit.

As Frank mounted the dais of the General Assembly hall, he said, "Anybody want to buy a used casino? I didn't want it anyway."

Mickey Rudin retained Harry Claiborne, a Las Vegas criminal attorney, to represent Frank in the action brought by the board. On September 27, 1963, Claiborne, who later became the first federal judge to be convicted of tax evasion, subpoenaed Olsen for a deposition. He and Rudin cross-examined the board chairman for four hours. Once they realized that Olsen had a statement from Victor LaCroix Collins about the fight with Giancana in Chalet Fifty as well as a memorandum of Olsen's telephone conversation with Frank, and memoranda prepared by those who were listening in on an extension, they decided not to fight the action.

Rudin called Frank and then called Jack Warner to discuss leasing Sinatra's casino holdings, totaling $3,500,000, in exchange for a business arrangement that would align Frank with the studio.

"I was with Jack at that time and remember very well how he bailed Frank out of the Cal-Neva mess," said Jacqueline Park, Warner's mistress for seven years. "Jack agreed to buy something like two-thirds of Reprise Records and sell Frank one-third of Warner Bros. Records. He also made a movie deal with him, which enabled Frank to move his Sinatra Enterprises to the Warner Bros. lot, but Frank wouldn't agree to anything until Jack promised to make him assistant to the president. That was the biggest thing Jack did for him because that title helped Frank save face and tell the press that he was going to concentrate on the movie business from now on."

The day after the joint announcement by Sinatra and Warner of their new merger, Frank walked around flashing a certified check from Warner Bros. for one million dollars.

"This is what I call real pocket money," he bragged.

Jackie Park remembered that Sinatra's actions caused press

speculation about whether he would eventually try to buy Warner Bros. Pictures, Inc.

"Jack went crazy when he read the newspapers," said Jackie Park. "We were in New York at the Sherry Netherland having breakfast in Jack's suite. He was screaming mad and showed me a newspaper article. 'You see, this is what I get for trying to be a nice guy to that son of a bitch,' he yelled. He called Frank and said, 'You better understand something, Frank, and understand it now. I'm the president of Warner Bros. Pictures, and my brothers and I own the studio. . . . I'll blow the whistle on you if you try anything funny. You tell your friends that I'm not afraid of them. I didn't get this far to have a gang of ruffians for partners.'

"Jack was jumping to conclusions, assuming that Frank had had something to do with the speculation, and he was hysterical, absolutely hopping mad. I only heard his end of the conversation, but Frank must have been trying to placate him because Jack said, 'I'm not getting excited, Frank . . . just as long as we understand each other. I have friends too.' When Jack hung up, he was red-faced and angry and patting the sweat from his forehead. He said he needed a drink, and swished down a Jack Daniels like it was water. 'Whether or not you're afraid, you must never show it,' he said, 'and the worst people you can show fear to are gangsters. Then they try to take over, you understand?' I said I understood."

The next day, Jack Warner issued a statement clarifying the position of Frank Sinatra in the corporation:

Since there has been considerable uninformed comment about this relationship, it is appropriate that these inquiries be answered [he stated]. Warner Bros. Records is owned two-thirds by Warner Bros. Pictures and one-third by Mr. Sinatra. That company is in the business of producing phonograph records which are distributed on the Warner Bros. and Reprise labels.

As to motion pictures, there is an agreement between Warner Bros. Pictures and Artanis Productions, Inc. [Frank's corporation name, Sinatra spelled backward], an independent producer, as the result of which Artanis produces features at Warner Bros. Studios, which are released by Warner Bros. Pictures. Mr. Sinatra owns substantially all of the stock of Artanis Productions and is the president of that company. Mr. Sinatra does not own any stock of Warner Bros. Pictures, Inc.

This association, plus the warm friendship that exists between Mr. Sinatra and myself, has led to a certain amount of speculation that I am considering Mr. Sinatra as my successor as president of Warner Bros. Pictures—or that Mr. Sinatra desires to be my successor. There is no evidence or reason for such speculation.

The day before Frank was supposed to answer the charges of the Nevada Gaming Board, Harry Claiborne issued a statement to the press saying that Frank had decided to disassociate himself completely from the gaming industry and would give up his half interest in Cal-Neva as well as his nine percent interest in the Sands.

"I have recently become associated with a major company in the entertainment industry, and in forming that association I have promised not only to devote my talent as an entertainer to certain of our joint investments, but I have agreed to devote my full time and efforts to that company's activities in the entertainment industry."

The board immediately revoked and terminated Frank's gaming license, stating that "all the allegations of the complaint as to Park Lake Enterprises and Frank Sinatra are deemed admitted by reason of their failure to file any notice of defense as required by law. . . ."

Castigating him as a discredit to the industry, they ordered him to get out of gambling by January 5, 1964, which meant he had to dispose of property worth $3,500,000.

A few weeks before the board's order, Hank Sanicola and Frank had broken up their partnership. Hank had been so enraged about the trouble with Giancana that he had refused to take Frank's call. This had so incensed Frank that he refused to show up for his scheduled performances at Cal-Neva, leaving Hank to search frantically for a last-minute replacement.

"He [Hank] called me, and I arranged for Jack Jones to take over the billing," said Chuck Moses. "I went out and got the best, most expensive gold watch in existence and had it inscribed, 'For Jack—Thanks so much. Frank.' But there was nothing I could do to get Frank and Hank back together again."

Speaking to each other only through intermediaries, Hank

told Frank that he wanted out of Cal-Neva, precipitating the worst fight the two men had had since they had first started working together in 1936.

"Out of Cal-Neva, out of everything," said Frank, instructing Mickey Rudin to buy out Hank's interest in all the financial ventures they had put together in twenty-seven years. Frank was so strapped for cash at the time that in lieu of money, he gave Sanicola all the Sinatra music companies— Barton, Marivale, Sands, Saga, Tamarisk, and Ding Dong Music—containing catalogues of more than six hundred songs, an inventory worth close to one million dollars.

"In the beginning, Hank was indispensable to Frank," said Ben Barton. "He rehearsed him, ran his errands, fought his fights, and kept him protected. He did everything for Frank. Everyone tried to get the two of them back together, but once Frank cut him off, that was it."

"It's true that Frank barely spoke to Hank again," said Nick Sevano, "and the day of Sanicola's funeral, sixteen years later, Frank drove around the church with Jimmy Van Heusen so everybody could see him in the car. I don't know if he wanted people to think that he'd come to the funeral or just wanted to show everyone that he carried a grudge to the end and wouldn't come inside to pay his last respects. I don't know. I gave up trying to figure out Frank a long time ago."

Cal-Neva also ended Frank's friendship with Sam Giancana because the gangster never forgave him for losing his temper with Ed Olsen.

"I talked to Sam the next day, and he told me that Frank cost him over $465,000 on Cal-Neva," said Joe Shimon, a former D.C. police inspector who was a good friend of Giancana. "He said, 'That bastard and his big mouth. All he had to do was keep quiet, let the attorneys handle it, apologize, and get a thirty- to sixty-day suspension . . . but, no, Frank has to get on the phone with that damn big mouth of his, and now we've lost the whole damn place.' He read him off for using all that filthy language with Ed Olsen and said he was a stupid fool. He never forgave him. He washed Frank right out of his books."

Even one of Frank's closest friends took Olsen's side. Seeing Olsen at the Sands a few months after Sinatra's license had been revoked, Sammy Davis, Jr., approached the Gaming Board chairman and said he'd like to speak with him privately.

"Oh, God, I thought, here comes a brawl for sure," recalled Olsen. "Davis gets me off in a corner, and I don't know whether he had a few drinks or what. He had just come off the stage not ten minutes before, so I'm sure he couldn't have had. And he undertakes to tell me in many of the same four-letter words that Sinatra used what a great thing I had done. He says, 'That little son of a bitch, he's needed this for years. I've been working with him for sixteen years, and nobody's ever had the guts to stand up to him!' Coming from Sammy Davis, Jr., that just threw me. And he went on for, oh, five or ten minutes of . . . the same thing."

24

Frank was on Stage 22 of the Warner Bros. lot making *Robin and the 7 Hoods* when he got the news of John F. Kennedy's assassination. For the first time in a long time, he went to church to pray. Years later, when he learned that Lee Harvey Oswald had watched *Suddenly* a few days before shooting the President, he withdrew the 1954 movie in which he played a deranged assassin paid to kill the president. He also forbade the re-release of *The Manchurian Candidate*, his 1962 movie dealing with a killer who is brainwashed to gun down a politician.

That November evening, Frank called the White House. He expressed his sympathy to Patricia Lawford, but did not talk with her husband, Peter.

"Frank was pretty broken up when he talked to Pat and would have given anything to come back to Washington for Jack's funeral, but it just wasn't possible to invite him," said Lawford. "He'd already been too much of an embarrassment to the family."

When Frank returned to work a few days later, he was dismayed by the comments he heard among the cast and crew. Over the loudspeaker system he said, "I have heard some unfortunate remarks on this set about Texas. This indicates that we are still not unified, despite the terrible happenings of the past week. I beg of you not to generalize about people, or make jokes about anyone from Texas. Or say anything that will keep us divided by malice or hatred. Now is the time for all of us to work together with understanding and temperance—and not do or say anything that will prevent that. . . ."

A few weeks later, Frank turned to Peter Lawford for help when Frank's nineteen-year-old son was kidnapped at gunpoint on December 8, 1963.

"Frank woke me up with his phone call a few hours after they grabbed young Frankie," said Lawford. "There was no hello, no apology, nothing like that. He just said for me to call Bobby and get the FBI in on the case and get back to him in Reno. I called the attorney general right away and he told me to tell Frank that they were doing everything they possibly could. Bobby had put men on the detail, and FBI agents in Nevada and California were working around the clock. He'd also ordered roadblocks set up at all state borders and police were checking all the cars. Bobby said, 'I know how Frank feels about me, but please tell him that everything is being done, and we'll get his boy back as soon as possible.'

"Bobby called Frank himself the next day, but I gave him Bobby's message that night, and he listened. I think he said thank you before hanging up, but that was the last time we ever spoke to each other. We hadn't been in much communication since the President had stayed at Bing Crosby's house in Palm Springs—and to make things just terrific for me with Sinatra, Jack had stayed at Bing's on two different trips. I did see Frank briefly when we took Marilyn [Monroe] up to Cal-Neva, but he got so mad at her after she overdosed and had to have her stomach pumped that he just snarled at everyone. Young Frankie's kidnapping was the only time I'd ever really heard him kind of scared. He sounded quite frightened."

Frank, Jr., had quit school to start a singing career of his own. He had worked a while with the Dorsey orchestra and now was playing a lounge act in Tahoe. He tried to imitate his father's style, singing in a tuxedo like his dad, telling some of his father's stale saloon jokes, and performing some of his father's most famous songs, but he was a pale imitation.

The kidnapping began on Sunday night at nine-thirty P.M., when Barry Worthington Keenan, twenty-three, and Joseph Clyde Amsler, his best friend from high school, also twenty-three, knocked on Frank, Jr.'s, door at Harrah's Lodge in Lake Tahoe. Frank, Jr., was eating dinner with Joe Foss, a musician in the Tommy Dorsey Orchestra, before their first show in the lounge. Pretending to be from room service, the two amateur kidnappers barged into the room, bound and gagged Foss, and carried Frank off at gunpoint to their car, a 1963 white Chevrolet Impala with a broken muffler, which carried them through a mountain blizzard to a rented house in Los Angeles, where they held young Frank for ransom.

In a few minutes Foss freed himself and called the hotel's press agent, who called the police. Frank's manager, Tino Barzie, called Frank, Sr., who was at his home in Palm Springs. He chartered a plane and flew to Reno, where he was met by Bill Raggio, the district attorney of Washoe County. The two men were joined by four FBI agents from Nevada; Frank's lawyer, Mickey Rudin; and Jim Mahoney, the new Sinatra publicist who had replaced Chuck Moses by promising Frank a golf tournament in his honor.

Blocked by the blizzard and unable to drive or fly to Lake Tahoe, Frank set up headquarters at the Mapes Hotel in Reno. He was soon joined by Jack Entratter and Jilly Rizzo. After calling his former wife, Nancy, who was in Bel-Air, and his mother and father in Fort Lee, New Jersey, he waited for sixteen sleepless hours for the kidnappers to contact him.

On Monday, December 9, at 4:45 P.M., he finally received the first of seven calls. Following the script that kidnapper Keenan had written, a confederate, John Irwin, forty-two, called Sinatra to say that his son was safe. He said the kidnappers would call him later.

"They haven't asked for money yet," Frank told reporters that evening. "They know I would give the world for my son. And it's true."

When the ransom call finally came, Frank said, "You can have anything—a million dollars—anything." But inexplicably, the kidnappers' script asked for much less, $240,000, in used currency.

"Fine, fine, anything, okay," said Sinatra.

"We'll make another phone contact about the exchange," said Irwin. "Discretion will be the demeanor."

Frank called a friend, Al Hart, president of the City National Bank of Beverly Hills, to make arrangements for the ransom money, and flew to Los Angeles to await further instructions. He went to his former wife's home in Bel-Air. Reporters were waiting outside to cover the biggest name kidnapping in America since the Lindbergh baby was abducted in 1932.

Hart assembled the money at the bank, and Frank, accompanied by an FBI agent, delivered it in a brown paper bag according to the kidnappers' complex instructions. After fifty-four hours, young Frank was released two miles from his mother's home in Bel-Air and taken to the home by a Bel-Air patrolman who recognized the young man. He hid in the car's trunk to avoid newsmen, and his father was so grateful to the driver for bringing Frankie home that he gave him one thousand dollars.

"Father, I'm sorry," said Frankie as he crawled out of the car trunk.

"Sorry? Sorry for what?" said Frank as he threw his arms around his son. "You're alive, and that's all that matters."

"Don't cry, Mother," said Frankie. "I'm well. I'm in good shape."

Frank went to the phone to take a call from Attorney General Robert F. Kennedy. He then called Frankie's grandmother in Fort Lee. "Mom, we have him back. He is alive. He is well and will call you this afternoon. He is with the doctor right now."

Dolly Sinatra burst into tears. "I was saying the Rosary when the call came," she told reporters keeping vigil outside her home in New Jersey. "I dropped my rosary beads and dropped down in a near faint. This is the happiest moment of my life. We are leaving for California on the twentieth. We will spend Christmas together—the whole family."

The three kidnappers were captured the next day, and most of the ransom money was recovered. Frank hired a Pinkerton guard for Nancy's Bel-Air home and dispatched one of his personal bodyguards, Ed Pucci, to travel with Frankie to make sure nothing happened to him. He then called Chasen's to deliver enough food and liquor for a three-day party to celebrate his son's return as well as his own forty-eighth birthday. He invited all the FBI agents who had worked on the case as well as Dean Martin, Jimmy Van Heusen, Jack Entratter, Gloria and Mike Romanoff, and a Palm Springs neighbor, Abe Lipsey. "Getting Frankie back is the best birthday present I could ever have," Frank told his friends.

The next night, he flew to Las Vegas with Jill St. John to celebrate the Sands's eleventh anniversary party. Red Skelton joked about the kidnapping. "Frank called me and asked me to come over and I told him, 'How can I? You marked all the money.' "

Don Rickles cracked, "Do you know why the kidnappers let Junior go? Because they heard him humming in the trunk."

"It's a week I never want to live through again," said Frank. "I'm so happy that it turned out the way it did. I am happy that the FBI did such a magnificent job in capturing the three men, because I know it will act as a deterrent to other punks who want to try something like this."

To show his gratitude to the federal agents who worked on the case, Frank sent each one a gold watch from France worth two thousand dollars. They were made out of twenty-dollar gold pieces and had black velvet bands. But the FBI returned the watches to Sinatra with a letter from Dean Elson, special agent in charge of the Las Vegas office, telling him that they were not allowed to accept gifts. A few weeks later, Frank bought another two-thousand-dollar watch and sent it off to FBI director J. Edgar Hoover in Washington with thanks for all that the FBI had done to end his son's kidnapping. Frank also enclosed the other watches for the agents who worked on the case. This time, they were not returned. Amused, Sinatra assumed then that he'd made a mistake the first time around by not sending a gift to the director.

During the kidnappers' trial a few months later, Barry Keenan tried a bizarre defense. He said that the kidnapping was a hoax in which Frank Sinatra, Jr., participated to get publicity for himself and his budding new singing career. The jury did not believe the story and sentenced all three men to life in prison, but the idea of a hoax took root and dogged young Frank for many years.

"When the Independent Television News in London broadcast that it was just a publicity stunt on my part, Dad sued them for libel and collected a lot of money," said Frank, Jr. "I forget how much we won, but I know that we donated the judgment to charity. Dad just wanted to keep the record clean and prove to the world that there was no hoax involved."

Years later, Barry Keenan admitted that he had indeed made up the hoax story that had caused young Sinatra so much embarrassment.

"That kidnapping scarred young Frank for life," said Nelson Riddle. "It brought him the wrong kind of publicity and alienated him even further from his father . . . but I think he's turned out remarkably well given all that. He's had the best mother in the world."

Big Nancy devoted her life to her children, but made no secret of her desire to reconcile with their father, preferring to retain the status of a divorced woman and be Mrs. Barbato Sinatra for life than to remarry and lose the Sinatra name. She told friends, "Once you've had the best. . . ." Crushed by Frank's engagement to Juliet Prowse in 1962, she said sadly, "Frank and I are a closed chapter. He wants a new life." When the engagement was called off forty-three days later, she knew better than to hope for too much, for Frank had already told the press, "I love Nancy, but I'm not in love with her."

Still, she raised her children to lionize their father, and she encouraged their dependence on him.

"I saw how close the family was when I did a play—*Remains to Be Seen*—with Tommy Sands in Chicago," said Patricia Bosworth. "The whole Sinatra clan was there. I think even Frank, Jr., came down at one point. Every night they would go back to the hotel and call Daddy whether he was in Vegas or Beverly Hills, or wherever he was, and they would all talk to him except for Nancy, Sr., who sat on the couch watching television movies and eating big bags of hard candy. She kept saying, 'Oh, what a life we had . . . I can't help loving him still. . . . He's a wonderful father, a wonderful father.' One night she was watching Barbara Stanwyck on television and she said, 'Barbara Stanwyck is just like me,' meaning, I guess, that they both had lost their husbands to other women."

Frank left the child rearing to Nancy, a strong, pragmatic woman who allowed him to be the soft, indulgent father. When Nancy, Jr., was nineteen years old, she became pregnant. Her mother took her to have an abortion.

"In those days, you didn't sleep with anyone before marriage and you never had an abortion," said Nancy, Jr. "I explained my reasons, and my mother understood. She never once made me feel guilty. Neither did my father. They simply didn't want me hurt."

"Little Nancy was a real daddy's girl and she probably wouldn't have married Tommy [Sands] if Frank hadn't approved," said Corinne Entratter. When Nancy pressured her father to give her husband movie work, Frank agreed to cast him in *Come Blow Your Horn*, but knowing that the director and producer did not want him, Tommy said he wasn't right for the role and refused the part.

"Nancy put terrible pressure on her father to get Tommy in the movies," said Chuck Moses. "Frank finally cast him in *None but the Brave*, which was the movie he directed in Hawaii, the first one he did under his new agreement with Warner Bros."

That movie, a co-production of Japanese and American companies, nearly cost Frank his life on location in Hawaii. On Sunday, May 10, 1964, he invited several people to spend the day with him on the beach in front of the house he was renting in Kauai. His executive producer, Howard Koch, and his wife, Ruth, were there with Brad Dexter, a rugged, strapping actor who played the rough sergeant in the film. Dick Bakalyan, another actor, and Jilly Rizzo and his blue-haired wife, Honey, whom Frank had nicknamed the "Blue Jew," were also there. Murray Wolf, a song plugger, was up in the house, fifty yards away. Sensing Sinatra's restlessness, Koch had excused himself to go back to work.

"Frank was getting itchy," he said. "I was going back to the desk to do some rescheduling to see if we couldn't finish [shooting] sooner."

"It was a sun-drenched afternoon and we were all on the beach enjoying the ocean and that great tropical sun," recalled Brad Dexter. "The waves were billowing higher and higher, though, and I noticed a treacherous riptide developing with a very strong undertow. I warned everyone to be careful in the water. Frank asked me to go to the house to bring him some wine and soda, so I went on up. While I was collecting everything in the kitchen, I heard Murray screaming hysterically from the living room that Frank was drowning. I ran in and found Murray framed in front of the huge bay window in an emotional frenzy, pleading with me to save Frank's life."

Dropping the wine and soda, Dexter tore out of the house, running at full tilt down the long, winding path that led to the water's edge. When he got there, he could barely see the bobbing heads of Frank and Ruth Koch in between the crashing waves. Everyone on the beach was paralyzed by fear and drawing away from the shoreline as Brad raced past and, in a running dive, plunged into the ocean.

Fighting his way through the waves, he reached Ruth Koch first. "Save Frank," she said, gasping for air. "I can't go on." Holding her head out of the water, Dexter tried to shake the submissiveness out of her.

"Nobody's going to die," he said. "We're all going to come out of this alive. C'mon, fight. C'mon. You're going to be okay."

He held Ruth under one arm while he swam to Frank, who was even farther out. He was already suffering from hypoxia, a lack of oxygen, and his oxygen-starved brain was impairing his vision.

"I can hear you, but I can't see you," he cried, his face a pale shade of blue.

"Frank was pathetic, helpless like a baby, and he kept sputtering to me, 'I'm going to die. I'm finished. It's all over, over. Please take care of my kids. I'm going to die. My kids. I'm going to die,' " said Dexter. "I tried desperately to instill in him the will to fight for his life. I kept slapping him repeatedly on the face and back with stinging blows. I pulled him up and out of the water, over and over again, but he was as limp and lifeless as a rag doll. It was like grabbing a handful of jelly. He was so soft—there was no muscle tone, no firmness to hold on to, only squishy flesh. I yelled at him to help save himself, but he kept saying, 'I'm going to die, I'm going to die.' I tried to get him angry enough to start fighting back by calling him a fucking lily-livered coward. A spineless, gutless shit. But he didn't react. He seemed like he wanted to die, like he had no will to live. He just caved in.

"With one hand, I grabbed him by his ass and pulled him up and out of the water, but his body was a dead weight. Then I realized that he was unconscious, and so was Ruth. I had to fight continuously to hold them up and out of the crashing waves, praying that someone on the beach would summon help soon. I kept slapping them, pulling them out of the water, hoisting them up for air, but they were two dead weights. I cradled one in each of my arms and treaded water, trying to keep us all afloat, knowing that time was running out.

"I caught a glimpse of the beach far in the distance and saw four heads in the ocean coming towards us. I don't remember how long it took for them to reach us, but the time seemed endless. Someone later said that it was forty-five minutes. It seemed like forever until those lifeguards reached us with their surfboards and lashed Frank and Ruth on top with ropes to hold them in position. Then they slowly reversed their course and paddled them back to land, leaving me to fend for myself. I rolled over to float, and to try to regain the strength I needed to swim back, but I was nearly done for. All I wanted to do was sleep, but I fought that deep fatigue, knowing that if I gave in to it, I'd be finished forever, and for what? For two people who wanted to die? Who had given up trying to save their own lives and could[n't] have cared less about mine? That thought inflamed me, and I swam like a crazy man with an extravagant passion to live, defying the waves to take me under. By some miracle that I don't understand to this day, I reached the beach before the life-saving party. I hit the shore and ran down to the point where Frank and Ruth were still in the ocean. I went in to help carry them out. Both were unconscious.

"I stretched Frank out on the sand and gave him artificial respiration. Once he started vomiting the water out of his lungs, I turned him over to the lifeguards. Jilly Rizzo ran up to me and shouted, 'You're a hero, Brad. You're a hero. Without you, Frank would be dead.' "

Dexter walked back to his hotel room and passed out for a few hours. When he returned to Sinatra's house, it was overrun with people—newspaper reporters, photographers, island officials, friends, members of the cast and crew, and representatives of the Red Cross. The first news bulletins that flashed worldwide reported that Frank had drowned. When Dexter walked into the room, Sinatra was sitting in an easy chair, talking to his daughter, Nancy, who was on Oahu, the main island, with Tommy for the weekend. Frank, in his bathrobe and slippers, was trying to comfort her and assure her that he was alive and well.

"He looked up at me when I entered the room and I observed that he was still in a state of shock," Dexter said. "His eyes were bloodshot, and he had the expression of a felled ox. When our eyes locked, it seemed that he didn't know what to say. He was embarrassed. He hung up the telephone and said, 'My family thanks you.' It was such a strange remark, almost as if I had put him in the uncomfortable position of having to thank me for saving his life. He never thanked me then or later, and I realize now that my rescue efforts probably severed the friendship right then and there by depriving him of the big-benefactor role which is the one he liked to play with his friends. The Chinese say when you save a life it belongs to you forever. Frank would have much preferred performing the grand dramatic gesture himself and saved my life so that I would be the one who owed him and would be indebted to him for life, not vice versa. I didn't see the love-hate relationship all that clearly at the time, but it certainly became obvious later on."

Although Frank never thanked Brad Dexter, he drew him closer, bringing him into his immediate circle of friends, and giving him a place of honor alongside the writer, Harry Kurnitz, whom he idolized. Frank seemed to turn to the rugged actor for protection, much as a small boy relies on his strong brother; he confided in him and for a while the two men seemed inseparable. Frank affectionately nicknamed him "Serb" because the actor was Yugoslav and spoke Serbo-Croatian. Frank told him that he was haunted by terrible nightmares of the drowning, and admitted his fear of going to sleep because he'd wake up in the middle of the night, shaking and sweating, unable to free himself from the crushing waves that were pounding him. He talked about his fear of dying but never wanted to know the details of the extraordinary rescue effort that kept him alive and for which the Red Cross awarded Dexter a citation of honor. Frightened by his own vulnerability, Frank refused to discuss his brush with death publicly, and dismissed it nonchalantly, saying, "Oh, I just got a little water on my bird. That's all."

The night after the near tragedy, Jilly Rizzo called Brad to say that "the boss" wanted him to come to the house for dinner because George Jacobs was preparing spaghetti pomodoro, Frank's favorite, and Patsy D'Amore, who owned the Villa Capri in Hollywood, had flown over some fresh Italian bread and prosciutto.

"Frank appeared uptight and depressed when I arrived," said Dexter. "I didn't realize how angry he was until we sat down to dinner and George started serving the spaghetti. Frank took one forkful and then started yelling that it was not prepared properly. George stood there quaking in his boots, not saying a word as Frank seized the platter and threw the spaghetti in his face, screaming, 'You eat it. You eat this crap. I won't.' George didn't flinch. He just peeled the spaghetti off his face and went back to the kitchen. I was so stunned by what Frank had done that I could barely speak. Finally, I

said, 'That was unkind, Frank. A very unkind thing to do.'
He yelled 'Goddamn it. That bastard doesn't know how to
cook al dente, and that's the only way I'll eat it!'

"George Jacobs was a terrific guy with a great sense of
humor who took care of all Sinatra's needs. He was his valet,
chauffeur, cook, bartender, social secretary; he did everything for Frank, everything. He was totally devoted to him,
traveled around the world with him, and was always at his
beck and call. To see him so humiliated by Frank was quite
disturbing. I thought maybe Frank was suffering from the
aftershock of almost drowning and just wasn't quite himself.
We were scheduled to shoot early the next morning, so I
excused myself at that point and returned to the hotel, but I
couldn't help thinking what bizarre behavior that was for a
man who was at death's door twenty-four hours before. How
important could a plate of spaghetti be? After what Frank
went through, why wasn't he grateful just to be alive? I asked
myself that question over and over until I realized that he was
unconsciously lashing out at me for putting him in the awful
position of having to be grateful for his own life. He couldn't
deal with his feelings toward me, so he took it out on poor
George, a black man who would never fight back and whom
Frank treated like chattel or a piece of property that he
owned and could discard at will."

In the next three years, Dexter would often see that
sudden searing anger overtake Frank like a violent squall,
plunging him from gracious charm into malevolent cruelty.
"After a while, I got so I could see it coming," he said. "I
could tell in Frank's eyes when that horrible mood change
was about to happen. There is some emotional conflict deep
inside him that is triggered off by God knows what, and when
it comes rushing to the surface, he explodes and hurts someone either physically or psychologically. Frank is a true manic-
depressive and careens from great waves of elation to bouts of
morose despair. It's always in the depressed state that he gets
ugly and vents his rage, like the time he urinated on Lee
Mortimer's grave. Afterwards, he screamed, 'I'll bury the
bastards. I'll bury them all.' "

In his manic phase, Frank seemed like the greatest Italian
host since Lorenzo de Medici. He spent money lavishly,
wining and dining his friends with unstinting generosity,
flying them around the world in his private plane, and swamp-
ing them with expensive gifts. He tipped waitresses and

hatcheck girls with handfuls of hundred-dollar bills, an act of largess that worried his lawyer, Mickey Rudin, who often counseled him to be more careful about spreading around so much cash.

Frank's casualness about money jolted Dexter one night in 1964 when the two men met to have dinner at LaRue's. Later, they climbed into Frank's Dual Ghia and headed for the Sunset Strip to have a nightcap in the old Scandia restaurant. Then they drove back to Frank's apartment on Doheny, where they went inside to discuss their next movie project.

"That's when he remembered the briefcase which was on the backseat of the car," said Dexter. "I hadn't even noticed it, but I went out to the garage and brought it into the apartment. 'Open it up,' he said, and when I did, I nearly had a cardiac arrest. That damn briefcase was filled with cash—stacks and stacks of hundred-dollar bills. I don't know how much money a briefcase holds, but this one was filled to the top. I couldn't believe he'd been driving around all night with that valise lying so visible on the backseat, where parking lot attendants, or anybody else for the matter, could've easily taken it.

"'God in heaven,' I said. 'Someone could've swung with this.'

"'Don't worry about that,' said Frank. 'There's more where that came from.'" Dexter dropped the subject.

During the filming of *Von Ryan's Express* in Rome, Dexter was dismayed to see his friend spend money so recklessly. One weekend when he was bored and wanted company, Frank summoned the city's best haberdashers to bring their most luxurious items to his villa. They spread out a dazzling array of men's accessories—silk shirts, ties, beautiful cashmere sweaters, eighteen-carat-gold cuff links, scarves, alligator belts, handkerchiefs, and slacks. Throwing open the door, he invited everyone in—Jack Entratter, Jim Mahoney, Jilly Rizzo, Dick Bakalyan, and Dexter.

"Help yourselves, fellas. I'm gifting today," he said.

Swarming into the room, the men grabbed the opulent items like little boys diving for baseball cards. Everyone loaded up, except for Brad Dexter. "What are you being so generous for?" he asked. "You don't need to lay it on like this."

"It means nothing to me, Brad. Take something. Help yourself."

Dexter shook his head and walked out of the room.

At the age of forty-nine, Frank was still buying friendship the way he had growing up in Hoboken when he took the neighborhood boys to Geismer's and let them use his charge account.

"I saw so much of that in Frank," said Dexter. "It made me sad. His father, Marty, was also bothered by all the hangers-on who exploited him. I met his parents in Palm Springs and Marty and Dolly thanked me profusely for saving Frank's life. 'I trust you because of that,' Marty told me the next morning when we had breakfast together. 'I don't trust these other bums. Why is my son always surrounded by freeloaders? Please take care of him, Brad. I feel better when you're around him. Promise me. Like you did in the water.' The old man really got to me, and I promised him that I'd do my best. For that reason, I always felt protective towards Frank and did my damnedest to keep him out of trouble."

Having accepted a role in *Von Ryan's Express*, Dexter had traveled to Europe with Frank for location filming in 1965. Sinatra had picked him for the part of the heroic captain, while he played the lead, Colonel Ryan, a man so feared and hated that his soldiers called him Von Ryan. Frank was making the film because Harry Kurnitz had told him the war story was more worthy of his talents than the "home movies" he'd been making with the Rat Pack.

The studio had leased an eighteen-room villa for Frank in Italy, complete with helipad. It was situated outside of Rome because he refused to come into the city.

"He was mad at the city then," said Howard Koch. "They gave him a hell of a bad time a few years ago—1953, was it? Don't know exactly when, but I guess he was kind of on his ass and doing a concert tour. Anyway, something went wrong, and they booed him—*booed* him. I guess he's been sore ever since."

Refusing a limousine, Frank made Twentieth Century Fox charter a helicopter each day for his personal pilot, Don Lieto, to fly him from the Villa Apia to Cortina D'Ampezzo, high in the Dolomite Alps, so he could avoid the Italian paparazzi. The rest of the cast and crew traveled by car, an hour each way. He insisted that the director, Mark Robson, revise the shooting schedule to film all Sinatra's scenes consecutively so that he wouldn't have to wait for setups and angle shots. On the set, the tension between Frank and

Robson was excruciating as the director tried to explain the folly of shooting according to Frank's whims.

"I know all that," said Sinatra. "I didn't tell you how to schedule the picture. I just told you what I wanted, and you told me, in front of witnesses, that you could do it. That was the deal. So now *do* it! You hear?"

The cast held its breath waiting for Robson to explode, while Frank's friends egged him on with contemptuous asides.

"For them, Sinatra seemed a kind of loaded gun which they would point at the director's head," said Saul David, the producer.

"Sinatra never seemed to be alone," said his co-star, Trevor Howard. "There were always four men with him. Fellows who never took their hats off, even in nightclubs. It's all a bit like a gangster film. A few days before Sinatra arrived on location in Cortina, the bodyguards flew in. They found there wasn't a single Sinatra record on the jukebox, so they took it apart and stocked it with nothing but Frank's songs. All part of the service, I suppose."

Given the director's methodical style and the star's extreme impatience, an eruption was inevitable. It occurred a few weeks into shooting, when Frank stomped off the set and refused to return. The studio tried to appease him by putting a yacht at his disposal for a ten-day cruise.

"We went to Portofino and Santa Margherita and Rapallo and then came back," said Dexter. "The most memorable moment was pulling up alongside Aristotle Onassis's yacht, the *Christina*, and seeing Jackie Kennedy, the president's widow, on board. I pointed her out to Frank, saying that she was an attractive woman with a good background—the kind of woman he should be interested in. He looked over at her and shook his head. 'It would never work,' he said. 'Never.' I sensed that he felt Mrs. Kennedy was unobtainable to someone like him.

"He'd already been paid a visit by Ava Gardner, who was the greatest love of his life. She was in Sicily making *The Bible* with George C. Scott and flew up to see him after a big fight with Scott. She stayed at the villa for a couple of days. I came over one night to have dinner with them and she was lovely. Frank was still trying to revive the relationship, but she started to hit the bottle and . . . It was painful for Frank to see the woman he adored destroying herself with booze. He never got over her. Ever."

After a few weeks in Italy, *Von Ryan's Express* moved on to Spain. The night before filming was completed there, Brad and Frank attended a dinner party at the Belgian consul's home in Malaga. They returned to the Pez Espada hotel in Torremolinos and stopped in the bar after midnight for a drink. Minutes later, an aspiring young actress sat down and tapped Frank on the shoulder. As he turned around, the young woman threw her arms around him and the flashbulbs popped as Frank pushed her away.

Furious with what he saw as a ruse, he screamed that no one was allowed to take his picture without permission. A stuntman who was with them grabbed the photographer, lunged for the camera, removed the film, exposed it, and smashed the camera on the floor. The hotel manager threw the couple out, and Sinatra and his party finished their drinks and left. As Brad and Frank passed a big painting of Francisco Franco, Spain's Fascist dictator, they spat on the floor.

Hours later, the police arrived looking for the assailants the girl had described after filing charges against Frank and Brad, alleging they had tried to kill her. Under the Spanish system of *denuncio*, any person could accuse another of a crime and it became the burden of the accused to prove himself innocent. Furthermore, police could detain anyone for questioning, without official charges, for a seventy-four-hour period. So the Guardia Civil (Spanish police) arrived at the hotel, armed and unsmiling, to arrest Sinatra and Dexter. They took them to Malaga, booked them, and threw them into separate cells.

Dexter insisted on phoning the U.S. ambassador in Madrid, and Frank vented his rage on the police.

"What the hell is this?" he yelled. "You cops are just like the gestapo. I'll be damned if I'll be treated like a criminal because some broad throws a glass in my face. Get the goddamned ambassador on the phone."

They were released after being questioned over and over again about the incident at the bar. When the police prefect demanded 25,000 pesetas ($416), Dexter objected strenuously, but Frank said he'd pay any amount of money to get out of that jail. When producer Saul David paid the fine, they were released.

Forbidden to return to the hotel to pack their belongings, they were escorted by the police directly to the airport, put on a jet, and flown to Paris, where they checked into the George V Hotel.

"I'll never go back to that fucking country again," Frank said. "I hate those dirty Fascist bastards."

The next day, they flew to New York and stayed in Frank's apartment on the East Side. To celebrate his return home, Frank invited a few friends, including Brad and Jimmy Van Heusen, to dinner at the Colony restaurant, where Gene, the captain, always gave him the best table in the house. After a few drinks, Frank started glowering at the Portuguese waiter, who he thought was Spanish. A few more drinks and he was convinced that the waiter was from the Malaga police force. He turned to Dexter.

"Look at that son of a bitch," he said. "He looks just like the prefect of police. Look at him."

Dexter agreed that the waiter possessed the same saturnine features that came out of the Spanish Inquisition, but he wasn't convinced he was part of Spain's secret police force.

"What are you talking about?" Frank yelled. "This guy is from Malaga and he's spying on us. Look at the way the son of a bitch is looking at me. Look at him watching our every move!"

In full fury, Frank flagged the captain and said, "I don't want this bastard around here. I don't want him serving this table. I want him out of here. This guy is no good. He's a spy. Get him out."

To emphasize his point, Frank stood up and tipped the table over, splashing drinks and crashing plates and glasses to the floor, which sent shards of china and crystal flying. Food splattered in all directions. A squad of waiters hustled to hunt down the rolls scattered around the room, while the captain solicitously assured Frank that he would replace the waiter immediately.

"Poor Gene shunted everyone out of the room and sent in a whole new crew to take care of our table," said Dexter, laughing as he recalled the incident. "Sometime later, when we were back in California, I read in the paper that Spain was celebrating the twenty-fifth anniversary of the benevolent reign of Francisco Franco. I showed the article to Frank, and we both laughed about it. Then he called his secretary, and said, 'I want to send a telegram. Send it to Francisco Franco in Spain with a copy to the Secretary of State in Washington, D.C., and the American ambassador to Spain, Robert Forbes

Woodward: 'Congratulations on the twenty-fifth year of your benevolent regime in leading the people of Spain. Now drop dead. Frank Sinatra.' "

The cast and crew of *Von Ryan's Express* returned to Hollywood in October 1964 for thirty days of interior shooting at Twentieth Century Fox. A bewitching nineteen-year-old girl with long golden hair appeared every day at the door of the sound stage in a gauzy nightgown that fell to her ankles. The sun streamed through the sheer gossamer of her gown, outlining her slender form. Half waif, half siren, she brightened considerably as Frank walked on the set, but she remained standing at the door, backlighted by the sun.

"He arrived, and I thought, 'What a super looking man,' and that's how it began for me," said Mia Farrow, the innocent-looking waif who ushered in the most violent period of Frank Sinatra's life.

25

Of the seven children born to director John Farrow and actress Maureen O'Sullivan, their first daughter—Maria de Lourdes Villiers Farrow—was a true child of Hollywood. Born in Beverly Hills on February 9, 1945, her godfather was the famous director George Cukor; her godmother was Louella Parsons, movieland's most powerful columnist; and her best friend was Liza Minnelli, daughter of Judy Garland and Vincente Minnelli. Her decision to become an actress surprised no one.

"I discovered that only in drama class could I manipulate people, amuse them, even make them notice me through this marvelous game of pretending, where I didn't have to be me," she said.

After graduating from Marymount High School, Mia went to New York and landed an ingenue role in the off-Broadway revival of *The Importance of Being Earnest*. Excellent reviews led to her discovery by television talent scouts, who chose her to play Alison Mackenzie, the brooding, bewildered heroine of *Peyton Place*, which was to become one of 1965's top three television shows.

Back in Hollywood before the televising began, she boldly announced her ambitions. "I want a big career, a big man, and a big life. You have to think big—that's the only way to get it. . . . I just couldn't stand being anonymous. I don't want to be just 'one of the Farrows,' third from the top and fifth from the bottom."

No man in Hollywood at the time was bigger than Frank Sinatra, and from the minute she saw him, she was mesmerized. "I liked him instantly," she said. "He rings true. He is what he is." She had already declared her preference for older men after flirtations with Yul Brynner and Kirk Douglas: "I love older men. I feel much more comfortable with them. They're exciting, they've lived. They have marvelous experiences to share. I don't have boyfriends or girlfriends my age. They frighten me."

So she visited the set of *Von Ryan's Express* every day in the transparent gown she had borrowed from the wardrobe department.

"We were doing some pickup shots at Twentieth Century Fox and Mia would invite herself on the set every day to look at Frank and admire him," recalled Brad Dexter. "At the end of the first week, Frank and I and Billy Daniels, the cinematographer, were leaving for Palm Springs in Frank's little French jet. Mia was standing there looking up at him as we were walking out, so he said, 'See ya later. We're going to grab the jet and hit the desert for the weekend.' She nearly knocked him over when she said she wanted to go with us. 'How come you never invite me to come along?' she asked. Frank did a double take. 'Huh? Are you kidding? Would you like to come?' Mia beamed and said, 'Sure.' He explained that there was only room for the three of us, but that if she was serious, he'd send the plane back. He did, and that's how she came to spend her first weekend with Frank in Palm Springs, which started the romance."

Frank took her to a screening of *None but the Brave*, and she told him he was a better director than her father, who had died a few years before. He took her to Thanksgiving dinner at the home of Bill and Edie Goetz and told her to clean her plate. For Christmas, he gave her a solid gold cigarette case in which he'd inscribed, "Mia, Mia, With Love, from Francis." She filled it with joints of marijuana that she rolled herself. He called her on the set of *Peyton Place* every day, and she told reporters, "I'm so happy. Someone I love just called me."

Standing five-five and weighing only ninety-eight pounds, she mocked her spindly little figure: "My measurements are 20-20-20."

She looked as delicate as a porcelain doll, with moon eyes, snow-white skin, and coltish legs. Her voice trembled with breathlessness as she talked about mysticism, Zen, yoga, and extrasensory perception. She frequently made statements about her soul: "Sometimes I think I'd like to put my soul somewhere where nobody could get it. I'd have a castle with a moat and drawbridge and people could never stomp on me and take chunks out of my soul until there's nothing left. Or maybe I'll have a house with a garden that runs wild, and when I go outside I'll wear long black boots so that the snakes can't bite me. The world is full of them, you know."

With her long blond hair streaming down her back and her wide innocent blue eyes, she seemed pure and fresh and ingenuous. In her little smocks and tights, she was a universe away from the sequined décolletage of Jill St. John and Angie Dickinson and the hardened slickness of the rest of the women in Frank's life. Although Mia was shrewd, ambitious, and extremely manipulative for such a young woman, she appeared naive and helpless to Frank, and he wanted to protect her, to provide for her, to pet her.

"Men had an instinctive desire to protect Mia," said her mother. "That's the secret."

When Mia told Frank the story of going to the prom and not being asked to dance by any of the boys, he gulped. He told her she was beautiful, but she didn't believe him, she said, because all her life she'd been called "Mouse . . . I was a skinny, runty thing," who had suffered a bout with polio. He was moved by the bare little apartment duplex she lived in with her deaf Angora cat, Malcolm, and he wanted to shower her with luxuries, but Mia didn't seem interested in material things. She later accepted a nine-carat diamond ring, a mink coat, and a diamond bracelet as big as a manacle, but she said she never cared about money.

She called him "Charlie Brown" for the sweet, round-faced character in the *Peanuts* comic strip, and he called her "doll face." She entered his life at a time when middle-aged America was trying to be young again, to disprove the buttons and banners of the flower children proclaiming: "Don't trust anyone over thirty!" He was almost fifty years old; she was nineteen.

In the beginning of their relationship, Frank and Mia spent many quiet weekends together at his house in Palm

Springs. His men friends dismissed her as just another one of Frank's "broads," but the women knew better.

"Mia was a very clever young lady, and she knew exactly what she was about and what she wanted," said Edie Goetz. "She was crazy about Frank, and she intended to marry him."

"Jack and I spent a weekend with them in Palm Springs," said Corinne Entratter, "and when I saw her standing by the mantel petting her great big white long-haired cat and being completely aloof and indifferent to everyone around her like she was on the third ring of Saturn or something, I thought, 'Yep, Frank's going to marry this one.' She was just kookie enough."

Jack Warner and his mistress, Jackie Park, also spent a weekend in Frank's house in Palm Springs, which was still filled with photographs of Ava Gardner.

"There was one of Ava in the bathroom, in the bedroom over his bed, in the living room, and even one in the kitchen, but Mia never said a word about them," said Jackie Park. "I told her that I had known her father and was amused when she said, 'Oh, Daddy was so pure and holy, he should have been the pope.' I was kind of taken aback by that one because I'd had a rollicking sexual relationship with John Farrow and I certainly didn't remember him as pure and holy! I asked her if she was happy with Frank, and she said, 'Yes, we're going to get married. I just know we are. This is my destiny, and there is nothing I can do about it.' I thought at the time that she was seeking a replacement for her dad, whom she adored."

During these weekends in Palm Springs, Frank entertained friends like the Goetzes, Rosalind Russell and her husband, Freddie Brisson, Claudette Colbert and her husband, Dr. Joel Pressman—"that stuffy, older crowd that he cultivated to be more respectable," said Dexter. "I called them 'the late show.' " Mia tried her best to act as Frank's hostess on these occasions, but she had not mastered all the niceties. Once, he asked her to do the seating for a dinner party, but she stumbled, trying to seat men next to women without putting them next to their wives. Embarrassed, Frank told her to sit down and did it himself. The next day, she sent him a letter apologizing for her lack of finesse, and saying that she was simply not sophisticated enough for him.

She also said that she would understand if he never called her again. He called the next day.

Frank's involvement with a nineteen-year-old was a source of great amusement to many of his friends. "I've got Scotch older than Mia Farrow," said Dean Martin.

"If Frank marries that girl, his kids are going to call her Mamma Mia," said "Fat" Jack Leonard.

"Frank didn't have to buy Mia a diamond ring," said Eddie Fisher. "He gave her a teething ring."

Although younger than two of Frank's children, Mia dismissed the thirty years between them. "I know there's a big age difference, but it doesn't really matter to me," she said. "Frank is exciting and fascinating. He's the most captivating man I've ever known. I've never encountered anyone sweeter or more considerate. He is everything a girl could want."

For his part, Frank said, "I really like this one. . . . I'm pushing fifty, but what the hell? Let's say I've got five good years left. Why don't I enjoy them?"

Some friends observing the romance between the hipster and the hippie remembered how outraged Frank had been by the 1957 film *Love in the Afternoon*, starring Gary Cooper and Audrey Hepburn, and how he had scolded the director's wife about what he thought was a degenerate story.

"He was quite vehement about it," said director Billy Wilder. "So vehement that he made my wife cry. He said he didn't like the picture because he thought it was immoral for an elderly man to make love in the afternoon to a young girl."

In August 1965, Frank chartered the *Southern Breeze*, a one-hundred-sixty-eight-foot glistening white yacht with a crew of twenty-three, to cruise the waters off New England. At $2,000 a day, he paid $60,000 in advance for the month, and invited nine guests: Bill and Edie Goetz, the Freddie Brissons (Roz Russell), the Joel Pressmans (Claudette Colbert), Sears, Roebuck heir Armand Deutsch and his wife, Harriet, and Mia Farrow.

When the television starlet took leave of *Peyton Place* to make the trip, the screenwriters did not know whether she was going to get married, so they wrote her character into a four-week coma, figuring if she returned, the character could recover; if she married, the character would die. All this gave rise to speculation that the cruise would be a honeymoon for Frank and Mia, and reporters pursued them everywhere the yacht dropped anchor. Photographers snapped pictures of them shopping ashore hand in hand, eating clams together, laughing, whispering, and hugging as though oblivious to the headlines they were creating across the country.

Mia's mother as well as Frank's mother seemed incredulous, and when reporters asked whether marriage was in the offing, the mothers denied it.

"Marry Mia?" laughed Maureen O'Sullivan. "If Mr. Sinatra is going to marry anyone, he ought to marry me!"

"My son is just helping this girl become a star," said Dolly Sinatra. "How many times has Frank helped somebody to the top? This is what he is doing now. He has done it before. He is doing it now. And he will do it again. This Mia, she's a nice little girl, but that's all. Remember, Frank's children are older than this girl. I'm going to spend the next two days in New York City with my son in his apartment. I'm sure I have some influence left with him. If there is any truth to these rumors—which I personally know there is not—I will use my influence to discourage any marriage."

In 1962, Frank had broken his engagement to Juliet Prowse because she would not give up her career to be his wife. She had changed her mind later and telephoned Frank with the happy news, but, according to Nancy, Jr., "when Juliet called my father, he said, 'Forget it, baby,' and hung up." He had sworn that he would never again share a wife with her acting career as he had done with Ava Gardner. He had recently told Mia the same thing, and repeated it in an interview with *Life* magazine in April 1965: "I don't say marriage is impossible, but if I would marry, it would have to be somebody out of show business, or somebody who will get out of show business. I feel I'm a fairly good provider. All I ask is that my wife looks after me, and I'll see that she is looked after."

Mia was not ready to give up her career. "I want to go on to do good things, make good movies, do good things on the stage. *Peyton Place* is making it all possible. And the wonderful thing about all this is the feeling it gives you of being wanted. When you go to a party or walk into a room, everywhere, everyone looks at you differently and they treat you differently. It's a lovely feeling.

"I want to marry Frank," she said. "I love him, but I know if I do, my career is over and it really hasn't even begun. I like being what I am. Wanting the career is as much a part of me as my mind and heart. If I marry, something of me will be lost and I just won't be the same person. That wouldn't be fair to either of us. I think I'll wait, but. . . ."

In Newport, Rhode Island, as Roz Russell left the yacht, reporters swarmed around her to ask whether Frank and Mia were married yet.

"I can assure you they are not getting married here," she said. "Not on this voyage. There is no suggestion of it."

The yacht stopped at Hyannisport so Frank could go to the Kennedy compound and visit with Ambassador Joseph Kennedy, who was still unable to talk because of his stroke. Frank took Mia with him anyway, knowing that the sight of a pretty nineteen-year-old blonde would cheer the aged patriarch immensely. In Edgartown, Massachusetts, Mia and Frank refused to answer reporters' questions about any plans for marriage. Claudette Colbert was shocked by the queries. "Good gracious, no. As far as I can determine, Mia and Frank are simply good friends," she said. "Mia is a charming girl and Frank does like her an awful lot, but it doesn't seem like Frank would marry such a young girl. . . ."

Next day's paper carried the headline: MIA NOT MRS. YET.

At Martha's Vineyard, tragedy befell the cruise as the yacht's third mate drowned after heroically saving another crew member.

"Sinatra was shocked and appalled by this event, which put an end to the vacation," said the yacht's captain.

"It had been the most closely observed cruise since Cleopatra floated down the Nile to meet Mark Anthony," said *Time* magazine.

Mia had ingratiated herself with all of Frank's friends, from the patrician Edith Mayer Goetz to the publican Jilly Rizzo. But his family was less than enchanted, especially Nancy, Jr., who cringed every time she saw pictures of her father with the actress who was five years her junior.

Nancy and her mother were planning a celebration for Frank's fiftieth birthday in December and had invited hundreds of people, including the President and Vice-President of the United States, who had both declined, but the two Nancys were in a quandary wondering what to do about Mia. They didn't want to invite her, but they were afraid not to. For months, this birthday, which also commemorated Frank's twenty-five years in show business, had been assuming the dimensions of a royal celebration, with CBS-TV News filming a special on Frank's life to be shown in November, NBC-TV televising a Sinatra spectacular for the same month, and *Billboard* publishing a one-hundred-page issue entitled "The Sinatra Report." *Life* magazine published a double cover with a twenty-two-page spread on Frank. It was the biggest layout accorded an entertainment figure in the magazine's history, and Reprise Records released one of his best albums, the hauntingly beautiful *September of My Years*, which won a Grammy.

"It was the CBS special that started causing a few problems," recalled Laurence Eisenberg, one of Frank's publicists with Jim Mahoney and Associates. "Frank had insisted that Walter Cronkite not ask any personal questions and Don Hewitt, the producer, agreed that the program would show only the 'professional' side of Sinatra—that meant no personal questions about Mia or the Mafia. Well, there was at least one question about whether or not he planned to marry Mia and maybe a couple about some of those 'alleged relationships.' "

Two weeks before the show was to be aired, Mickey Rudin sent CBS a letter demanding to review the program before it was broadcast. When CBS declined to make the show available, Rudin fired off another letter charging the network with a "breach of understanding." Rudin said Frank expected treatment similar to that accorded cellist Pablo Casals, violinist Isaac Stern, and contralto Marian Anderson in previous CBS-TV portraits, and withdrew his permission to use material that he had already furnished for the news special. The network also received five identical telegrams from Dean Martin, Alan King, Sammy Davis, Jr., Soupy Sales, and Trini Lopez demanding that CBS delete them from the program, as well as wires from Nancy, Sr., and Nancy, Jr., saying the same thing. But CBS refused to alter the show, and the resulting publicity about "Sinatra: a CBS News Documentary" made it sound as though the public could look forward to the biggest exposé in television history at ten P.M. on November 16, 1965.

Despite the furor, the program, which won the Arbitron ratings for that time slot, was a highly flattering hour showing Frank cavorting with Dean Martin and Sammy Davis, Jr., telling jokes and singing during a recording session and at a benefit for prison inmates. The critics were disappointed.

"We expected a tiger last night and we got a pussycat," said the Associated Press.

". . . Journalistically it was a placebo of rewrite," said Jack Gould in *The New York Times*, adding, "[It] wasn't authorized but it could have been."

The *Chicago Daily News* wrote: "Frank Sinatra owes CBS one more telegram. This one should say, 'Disregard all previous telegrams from me and my friends and thanks for the fair, honest treatment.' "

The *Los Angeles Times* said: "Sinatra and his loyal clan could not have put together a more flattering look at their leader."

Jack O'Brian in the *New York Journal-American* wrote: "Sinatra had the chance to deny most of his established affinity for underworld characters, and not a cock crowed during that denial, which was virtually the comedy high point of the show."

The *Herald-Tribune* said: "CBS and the public have been had. . . . Frank Sinatra not only perpetuated his public image. He gilded the self-made lily. . . . Once more, but this time under the CBS News aegis, he offered only the public image—the dedicated singer, the generous benefactor, the deep thinker, the happy comrade, the firm executive, the devoted parent—he wants the public to accept as the whole man."

The Sinatra camp was delighted with the documentary. Jilly Rizzo sent a telegram to Frank, boasting: WE RULE THE WORLD!

Jim Mahoney suggested a public relations gesture toward CBS-TV. "Shall I drop a line to Hewitt?" he asked Frank, but Sinatra was still angry at Walter Cronkite for asking him if he was going to marry Mia—even though that segment had not been aired. "Can you send a fist through the mail?" he asked.

The crowning event of his fiftieth birthday celebration was the dinner party given for him on December 12 at the Beverly Wilshire Hotel by his former wife, Nancy, and his daughter, Nancy, Jr., who had relented and said that he was welcome to bring Mia if he wished. He declined, knowing how uncomfortable everyone would feel. Milton Berle was the master of ceremonies for the evening, which featured a filmed parody of the CBS-TV interview prepared by Jack Haley, Jr., and Sammy Cahn showing scenes from various

Sinatra movies. George Burns and Jack Benny did comedy sketches, Tony Bennett sang, and Sammy Davis, Jr., jumped out of a cake to amuse the one hundred fifty guests. Tina Sinatra helped with the party and did a little skit with her sister, but their brother, Frank, Jr., did not attend.

After midnight, when everyone had gone, Frank was seen sitting alone in the ballroom with Brad Dexter sobbing because his son had not been there to share the evening with him.

"Everybody was here and it was a glorious party, but the one person in the world I would have wanted more than anybody else was my boy and he didn't even send me a telegram, or a card, or anything," said Frank.

Dexter tried to comfort his friend, saying that Frank, Jr., probably had tried to call.

"My son never calls me," said Frank. "He puts as much distance between us as he possibly can."

Frank drove to Mia's apartment that night as he had promised to do. When he walked in, he was surprised to see that she had cut off her long golden hair.

"I chopped my silly hair off because I was bored with me," she said.

Once he recovered from the shock Frank said, "It's terrific. Now you can go out for Little League like the rest of the boys!"

Mia told Corinne Entratter that she'd done it because she'd become too prideful about her long hair. "Mia was always so vain about her hair, always twisting it and pushing it, so I was quite shocked when she clumped it all off. I asked her why she'd done it and she said, 'I just thought I should not have anything I should be vain about.' It was almost like something a nun would say."

The next day, when Mia joined Frank and Brad Dexter for lunch at the Beverly Wilshire, Sinatra greeted her by saying, "Hiya, Butch!"

For weeks, Frank and Dexter had been discussing plans for launching a new phase in Frank's career that would concentrate on his acting. Having been made vice-president of Sinatra Enterprises in charge of production, Dexter was looking for the kinds of properties that would showcase Frank as an actor and do away with the japing antics of his last few movies, which Bosley Crowther of *The New York Times* said were characterized "by many globs of sheer bad taste that manifest a calculated pandering to those who are easily and crudely amused." The critic dismissed *Von Ryan's Express* as "outrageous and totally disgusting," and said that *Marriage on the Rocks* was nothing more than "a tawdry and witless trifle about a bored married man."

"It is provoking to see this acute and awesome figure turning up time and again in strangely tricky and trashy motion pictures that add nothing to the social edification and encouragement of man," he said. "One after another of his pictures in the past several years has been a second- or third-rate achievement in dramatic content and cinema artistry, and the only thing to be said for a few of them is that they have galvanized and gratified some elements that prefer lurid action and bravado to solid commentary and sense. . . . What grieves a long-time moviegoer is to remember how bright and promising he used to be, beginning with his charming performance with Gene Kelly in the musical *Anchors Aweigh*."

Frank was aware of the shortcomings of his recent movies and said, "I guess the trouble has been that at the time I did these pictures, nothing better seemed to be available. It all boils down to material."

Brad Dexter hoped to resurrect Sinatra's film career with quality work.

"I wanted Frank to develop the professional pride in his movies that he had in his recordings," he said. "We talked about it a lot and he said that he wanted to inherit Bogart's mantle and be an actor's actor, so I started looking for the best stuff I could find for him. I brought him *Harper*, and he loved the story, but Mickey Rudin blocked the deal because he didn't want Elliott Kastner and Jerry Gershwin, who owned the property and developed the script, to get paid $400,000 to produce a picture which might only make it on Sinatra's name. The movie went to Paul Newman instead, and everyone made a fortune. I wanted Sinatra Enterprises to acquire Anthony Burgess's *Clockwork Orange*, so I sent the book to Frank and told him to read it. He called me back saying he couldn't understand a word and didn't see it as a movie, so I had to turn it down. The movie was later made by Stanley Kubrick and made millions.

"Finally, I got Frank to agree to do *The Naked Runner*, a suspense drama in which he was to play an unwitting assassin, a role that would capitalize on his explosive, combustible personality. Frank was all for it, and so I started production work in London in 1966, but there were problems, real problems, because Frank was going through his Mia period and was beset trying to decide whether to marry her or not. It was a bad period for him and . . . everything ended in disaster."

On June 8, 1966, Frank took nine persons, including three women and Dean Martin, Jilly Rizzo, and Richard Conte to the Polo Lounge of the Beverly Hills Hotel to celebrate Dean's forty-ninth birthday. Shortly after midnight, Frederick R. Weisman, fifty-four, president of Hunt's Foods and brother-in-law of multimillionaire philanthropist Norton Simon, walked in with Franklin H. Fox, a businessman from Boston. The two men had come from a rehearsal dinner at Chasen's for the wedding of their two children and wanted to toast the future as prospective fathers-in-law. Walking past Sinatra's table, they sat in a booth nearby and ordered drinks.

Conversation was difficult for them because of the noise from the Sinatra table, so after a few minutes, Weisman leaned over and asked Frank and his party to keep it down, adding that their remarks were offensive to the women in the room. Frank looked at the man with contempt. "You're out of line, buddy," he said, turning back to his raucous table.

Franklin Fox watched Sinatra look closely at the man who had dared to criticize him, and heard him make an anti-Semitic remark, adding, "I don't think you ought to be sitting there with your glasses on talking to me like that."

Weisman rose to object to Sinatra's slur, holding up his hand to ward off any possible blows, but Frank was on his way out. It seemed as though he had dismissed the incident, but a few minutes later he stormed back to the Weisman table.

"He came back to vent his anger, and Fred stood up," said Franklin Fox. "My efforts were simply to keep Sinatra away from him, and I did that by sidearming him. I was standing in front of Fred when Sinatra threw the telephone. . . . Dean Martin was trying to get him out of there, and the next thing I knew Fred was lying on the ground, and Sinatra and his party had walked out. I was trying to help Fred on the floor. . . . When we weren't able to revive him, we called an ambulance and he was carried out of the room on a stretcher."

Still unconscious twenty-four hours later, Weisman was taken to the intensive care unit of Mt. Sinai Hospital, where he was in critical condition for forty-eight hours and not expected to live. On Saturday, June 11, he underwent cranial surgery to correct the effects of a skull fracture. By the next day, he started showing signs of regaining consciousness, but there was damage from the blow, which caused what his doctors called "retrograde amnesia."

Awaiting Weisman's recovery, the police investigating the brawl were having trouble locating the rest of the principals.

"Sinatra has been in hiding," said Police Chief Clinton H. Anderson, "but we'll get him. We want to find out the cause of the fight and the physical condition of Weisman at the time."

Frank telephoned the Beverly Hills police from his home in Palm Springs and said that the fight was all Weisman's fault. "This man said, 'You talk too fucking loud, and you have a bunch of loud-mouthed friends,' " said Frank. "I thought he was kidding; then I realized he wasn't. . . . He hit me, and at once another man jumped between us. The top of the cocktail table at which I was sitting was broken from its base as Weisman fell across the table and then to the floor. I at no time saw anyone hit him and I certainly did not. I looked behind me, and as I left, I saw a man on the floor."

Dean Martin, who had gone to Lake Tahoe, verified Frank's story by phone.

"Martin had nothing to say, as you might expect," said the chief. "He said he didn't see anything."

A year later, Dean admitted to Italian journalist Oriana Fallaci, "The cops came. We said we didn't know who did it and walked out. But we did, yeah."

In Palm Springs, Frank was worried as he waited to see if Weisman would live or die. Mia had flown to be with him, as had Jack Entratter and his wife, and together the four of them kept a death watch.

"That's the only time I think I ever saw that man scared," said Corinne Entratter. "For two weeks, we all sat there staring at each other. Mia and I tried to learn how to play backgammon. Nobody went anywhere. We were like prisoners. We just didn't go anywhere. We just waited it out. Nobody knew how it would come out."

Although Weisman was showing steady improvement, the bulletins from the hospital were not encouraging at first. "His condition from the operation is satisfactory, but he remains in serious condition and still is unconscious," said a hospital spokesman. Three days later he regained consciousness but the hospital reported his condition as "still serious." Weisman recognized family members but could not remember anything and kept introducing his wife to his doctor. By June 27, he had recovered enough to talk to the police about what had happened that night in the Polo Lounge, but he said he could only remember what happened leading up to the fracas. From the moment he was struck, his memory was gone. His family was so outraged by what had happened to him that they wanted to press criminal charges against Sinatra. But, as they later confided to friends, they had received anonymous phone calls threatening to harm their children, so they were afraid to act.

Frank's long history of violence so intimidated the Weismans that they decided to forget the whole affair.

"He wants the case closed," said Weisman's attorney, Grant B. Cooper. "A further investigation as to whether he was hit, pushed, or fell is not necessary."

"We don't want to talk about it. There is just nothing to say," said Weisman's wife.

"There's nothing to settle. We just want to forget it ever happened," said his brother.

On June 30, the Los Angeles district attorney announced that he was closing his investigation. "In the absence of any other evidence, we have concluded no prosecution is indicated, and that this case is closed," he said.

A few days later, Frank gave Mia a nine-carat diamond engagement ring he had bought at Ruser's jewelry store in Beverly Hills for $85,000. He presented it to her on July 4 during the weekend they spent in Mt. Kisco, New York, with Random House publisher Bennett Cerf and his wife, Phyllis. Cerf, whom Sinatra called The Bookmaker, had been an adoring fan of Frank's since he had first heard him sing in the early forties. Their friendship had become close in the early sixties when Frank was a bachelor and would use the Cerfs' Mt. Kisco home for a month-long summer retreat.

On July 5, Sinatra left for London to start filming *The Naked Runner*. A few days later, Mia walked into P. J. Clarke's in Manhattan flashing the stupendous diamond. "It's a friendship ring from Frank," she said.

Remembering what had happened to Lauren Bacall when she talked to the press about Sinatra's marriage proposal, Mia's mother quickly called Frank in London and asked what she should say about the ring. She received his permission to announce the engagement with no definite date for the wedding.

"I couldn't be more delighted," Maureen O'Sullivan told the press. "Frank is a wonderful person, and I know they'll be happy together."

That night Sinatra had dinner with Brad Dexter at The Colony in London, a gambling club managed by George Raft. They played a little blackjack and returned to their suites in Grosvenor Square, where Frank announced his plans to marry Mia. He asked Brad what he thought about it, and Dexter didn't lie to his friend. "It's too big an age difference, Frank. You're talking about thirty years in age. It doesn't make sense. When she's forty you'll be seventy, but if that's what you want, go ahead and marry the girl."

"Well, don't you think it's a good idea?"

"No, I really don't."

"Why don't you approve? The age business doesn't mean a thing. Besides, she's a good kid and I'm lonely. I need somebody."

"I know you're lonely, but I think you're confusing the love you have for your son with what you feel about Mia. Junior won't respond to you, but Mia does."

Erupting in fury, Frank swept the table lamps to the floor with a loud crash and threw an ashtray at the window, shattering the glass into glistening shards. Without a word, he grabbed the telephone and placed a call to Jack Entratter at the Sands in Las Vegas. Glaring at Dexter, he barked orders at Entratter to get a marriage certificate, line up a judge, order cake and champagne, and prepare everything necessary for a wedding.

"Make all the arrangements," he said, "because I'm leaving London tomorrow, and Mia and I are getting married."

Then he called Mickey Rudin and told him to find his pilot, Don Lieto, to pick him up and fly him to New York. He called Bill and Edie Goetz in Los Angeles and told them they were to be best man and matron of honor in forty-eight hours. Then he called Mia and told her to fly from New York to California and from there to Las Vegas without saying a word to anyone, including her mother.

"I sat there as he made all these calls, wondering if he'd gone crazy," said Dexter. "Since he just seemed to get madder and madder, I finally left and went to bed around five A.M. Frank flew out of London the next day, and Mia's doom was sealed."

Arriving in New York on July 18, Frank had dinner with his former girlfriend, Peggy Connolly, and hardly acted like a man about to be married. The next day, he flew to Las Vegas and arrived at the Sands accompanied by Mia, Bill and Edie Goetz, and his valet, George Jacobs. Judge William P. Compton was waiting with a marriage license that had been witnessed by Harry Claiborne and Jack Entratter. Minutes before the ceremony, Frank took George Jacobs aside and said, "Call Miss G," their code name for Ava Gardner. Jack Entratter tried to dissuade George from making the call, but George insisted.

"It'll be my ass if I don't get hold of that lady before someone else does, and I'll find her if it's the last thing I do," he said, heading for the phone. "She's the love of his life, and you know it!"

Ava's comment on the nuptials was succinct and bitter. "Ha!" she said. "I always knew Frank would end up in bed with a little boy." Later, she dismissed her former husband as "a scared monster. He was convinced there was no one in the world except him," she said.

At five-thirty P.M. on July 19, 1966, Frank took Mia into Jack Entratter's living room, where the strains of Frank's new record, "Strangers in the Night," were faintly audible over the hotel's speaker system. The judge read a four-minute civil ceremony. Frank slipped a gold wedding band on Mia's finger, kissed her three times, and the judge pronounced them husband and wife.

"Let's break out the wine and caviar," Frank said.

"I've never seen such anxiety before," recalled Edie Goetz. "They were both so nervous you couldn't believe it. Frank's face was flushed and he twitched nervously as they repeated their vows."

The twenty-one-year-old bride turned and hugged her sixty-six-year-old matron of honor, saying, "This is the happiest day of my life."

Grinning, Frank led her from the air-conditioned room into the 107-degree heat to pose for wedding pictures on the patio of Entratter's Oriental garden. Saluting reporters with his hand raised upward, he said, "My bride."

"This is a big day, fellas. I can't think of what to say. We just decided to get married last week. We were both out west, it seemed right, and we're in love, and it was logical."

"Will Mia accompany you to London?" asked a reporter.

"Oh, yes, by all means, yes," said Frank.

After a quick glass of champagne, the couple was in a limousine en route to the airport to fly to Los Angeles.

"I gave a wedding dinner for eighteen [no members of Frank's family among them] and they spent the night here with us so that no one would know where they were," said Edie Goetz, who took credit for finally persuading Frank to get married. "Billy and I both said, 'Oh, go ahead and do it. She's crazy about you.' "

The news of the marriage stunned Frank, Jr., who was in Cocoa Beach, Florida, performing at the Koko Motel. "I think you got the wrong party, pal," he said when asked how he felt to be one year older than his stepmother. "I don't believe it. I just don't believe it." That night, before singing what he called his Sinatra Songs, he told his audience: "I'm going to devote exactly five minutes to my father because, as he once confided in a moment of weakness, that's exactly how much time he devoted to me."

Frank and Mia began their honeymoon a few days later in New York City, where Frank socked a photographer who was trying to take a picture of them entering the "21" club for a party hosted by the Bennett Cerfs. The next night, Frank and Mia went to Fort Lee, where Dolly Sinatra had been cooking for two days, preparing ravioli, scallopine, scungilli, stuffed green lasagne noodles, fettucine, corkscrew pasta, macaroni, spaghetti, and sausage gnocchi. She loaded her tables with cheese, cold cuts, and sweet sugary desserts. She'd done the same thing when Frank had brought Ava Gardner to Hoboken fifteen years before, but that had been an occasion to celebrate. Ava was a big movie star and one of the most beautiful women in the world. Mia Farrow was just a girl, younger than Frank's two older children, and she'd never even been in a movie.

"Dolly, who always praised Ava Gardner, wasn't impressed with Mia at all, but she was putting on a good show for Frank," said Al Algiro, a close friend of Dolly and Marty who had helped with the dinner. "It was a great party. Toots Shor was there and that comedian Joe E. Lewis and Jilly Rizzo, of course. Nancy, Jr., [who was in New York at the time] came and so did Rosalind Russell and Freddie Brisson and Liza

Minnelli, who smoked little cigars all night. Mia dressed kind of funny, with long white stockings like a nurse and a short little dress that almost came up to her hips, it was so short. She didn't say much the whole evening. After everyone left, Dolly said, 'Well, what do you think?' I shrugged and said Frank was over twenty-one and could marry whomever he wanted. 'Yeah, I suppose,' she said. 'But this one don't talk. She don't eat. What's she do?' Then she shook her head and said, 'It won't last long, so I guess it's a good thing they weren't married in the Church. . . .' "

26

The Sinatras continued their honeymoon in London in a penthouse apartment in Grosvenor Square while Frank worked on *The Naked Runner*. On weekends, he and Mia flew to the south of France and stayed in Jack Warner's villa in Cap d'Antibes, but within three weeks he grew restless. Bored with the movie, he wanted to go home.

"We had a location shoot up the Thames River about eighteen to twenty minutes by helicopter from London," said Brad Dexter. "I had made the run a couple of times with the chopper pilot to make sure he knew the route because Frank insisted on flying rather than driving to save time. He also expected everything to be run with military precision. The morning of the shoot, the British government summoned my pilot and gave me a substitute who had never flown the route before. We picked up Frank and took off just as the fog came in. Minutes later, the pilot lost his direction. Frank, who had barely spoken to me since returning to London, asked how long the flight was. I told him eighteen to twenty minutes, so he sat back, tight and taut, without saying a word. After eighteen minutes in the air, he said, 'Well? Where's the location?' I couldn't see a damn thing, so I asked the pilot and he admitted that he was lost.

"Frank went nuts. 'I don't stand for excuses, goddammit,' he said. 'I don't work with incompetents. We should've been there by now. I don't know why the hell I ever came to

England. I hate this goddamn country. I don't know why I'm making this lousy picture.' He went on and on, building a huge resentment toward the movie.

"After forty-five minutes the pilot finally drops us down on the location spot, where the director, Sidney Furie, is waiting, ready to talk to Frank about his scene, but Frank jumped out of the chopper and said, 'I don't want to work. I don't want to act. I'm sick and tired of this "mother" movie. I think we ought to dump the whole thing, change the location, and get the hell out of here. Let's go back to Palm Springs and shoot it in the desert.' With that, he walked off and stood under a tree, pouting. The director, a sensitive, creative guy, who had been working his arse off for nine months, couldn't believe his ears. 'This is terrible, Brad,' he said. 'Just terrible. I can't make a picture under these conditions with a man who is totally and completely uncooperative.' He started crying hysterically. 'I'm quitting the picture,' he sobbed. 'I'm not going to work with such a cretin. I'm walking off the picture now.' With that, he jumped in his jeep and drove off, leaving me in the middle of England without a director, with a petulant star who's being paid one million dollars but refuses to work, and a crew of fifty guys who're getting paid to stand around and watch this craziness."

Hailing another jeep and driver, Dexter sped off to find the director, who was roaring down the highway nursing his bruised feelings. Catching up to him, Dexter pulled him over to the side of the road and begged him to return to the picture, swearing that he would bring Sinatra around. After an hour of persuasion, the two men returned to the location and the director set up for his shot with Frank, who was still standing by himself under the tree.

Dexter approached him. "Look, Frank, the director is ready to shoot now. The scene is all set up. I know you're uptight and you've got some problems, which are none of my business, but this could be a wonderful picture for you if you would only participate. The important thing is that the clock is running and all this time is costing money—your money and Warner Bros. money. So why don't you come back with me now and do the scene. Be a professional and let's make this picture work."

Sinatra looked at his friend with venom, turned on his heel, and walked to the set. Approaching the director, he said, "Okay, what do you want me to do?"

For the next three days, shooting in England went according to schedule, and the cast and crew looked forward to moving to Copenhagen for the next location site.

"All of us were due to film in Denmark," said Derren Nesbitt, Frank's British co-star. "Then my schedule was changed, and I didn't have to go. Sinatra knew I was disappointed, so he arranged for me and my family to join them. He had a car pick us up at our home in the country and take us to the airport, then his private plane to Copenhagen. When we arrived, he'd left a manila envelope for us with money. I remember remarking how difficult it would be to spend this amount in ten days, and then the same amount arrived again in a plain manila envelope every morning at the hotel. We had a wonderful time. He was very generous."

In Denmark, Frank told Dexter that he wanted the weekend off to fly back to Los Angeles to star in a benefit for Governor Edmund "Pat" Brown, who was running for his third term. Brown's Republican challenger was Ronald Reagan, a former actor and president of the Screen Actors Guild, who was making his first run for public office.

"I told him to take the time off and I'd shoot around him for a few days," said Dexter. "I was a big Pat Brown supporter myself and thought it was a worthy cause, especially against Reagan, whom Frank and I both couldn't stand."

Sinatra's antipathy toward Reagan in 1966 was intense. "He hated the guy, just hated him," said a woman who lived with Jimmy Van Heusen. "We'd be at some party, and if the Reagans arrived, Frank would snap his fingers and say, 'C'mon, Chester. We're leaving. I can't stand that fucking Ronnie. He's such a bore. Every time you get near the bastard, he makes a speech and he never knows what he's talking about. The trouble with Reagan is that no one would give him a job.' This happened time and time again because Frank could not abide being in the same room with the Reagans. Every time they'd walk in, we'd have to walk out, and each time we'd have to listen to Frank's diatribe against Reagan all over again."

"It's true that Sinatra despised Ronnie almost as much as Richard Nixon," said Peter Lawford. "He said he thought he was a real right-wing John Birch Society nut—'dumb and dangerous,' he'd say, and so simple-minded. He swore he'd move out of California if Reagan ever got elected to public office. 'I couldn't stand listening to his gee whiz, golly shucks crap,' he said. Frank couldn't stand Nancy Reagan, either; he said she was a dope with fat ankles who could never make it as an actress. He took every opportunity he could in Las Vegas to change the words to 'The Lady Is a Tramp'; instead of singing 'She hates California, where it's cold and it's damp,' Frank would sing, 'She hates California, it's *Reagan* and damp . . . that's why the lady is a tramp.' "

Shecky Greene said that Frank was vehement on the subject of Reagan. "We were all at a house in Miami watching Joey Bishop's show on television one night when Reagan came on to welcome Joey," said the comedian. "Frank immediately got crazy and started screaming things and calling Reagan every name in the book. He hated the guy and cursed him out all night long."

After the "Night of Stars" fund-raiser for Governor Brown at the Los Angeles Sports Arena, Frank produced another benefit for him in San Francisco. It featured Dean Martin, Ella Fitzgerald, Joey Bishop, Connie Francis, Trini Lopez, Dan Rowan and Dick Martin, the Four Step Brothers, and Nelson Riddle's orchestra, and raised $175,000. Reagan tried to counter Sinatra's swinging appeal with folksy Republicans like Irene Dunne, Roy Rogers, John Wayne, and Pat Boone, whom Frank ridiculed, saying, "If I had a son, I'd like him to be like Pat Boone—till he was three hours old."

"Frank campaigned hard for me throughout the state," said Governor Brown. "He raised a lot of money and staged both my inaugural galas." He did not have the chance to stage a third gala because in 1966 Reagan defeated Brown by almost one million votes.

Before the election, Frank had instructed Mickey Rudin to call Brad Dexter in London to say that he was not returning and for Dexter to put all the footage together from *The Naked Runner*, bring it back to California, and finish the film there. Dexter refused, saying he had production commitments in England. Rudin insisted, but the producer ignored him. Determined to complete the picture, Dexter met with the director and started reshaping the script so they could finish without Frank.

"We'd steal takes from scenes that he'd already done before," he said. "That's how we got all our close-ups."

Days later, as Dexter recalled, Rudin arrived in London to deliver Frank's ultimatum in person.

"As Sinatra's lawyer, I want to inform you that my client

gave me instructions to give to you," he said. "You are to wrap all the film and return to California to finish the picture. In other words, stop shooting now or get out."

Dexter refused to do either, saying that he was going to deliver the picture to Jack Warner at Warner Bros. upon completion. "I'm not going to contribute to Frank's delinquency, and if he won't come back here and lend himself as an actor to this film, then we'll do it without him. Now you go back and tell him that, Mickey, and stop bothering me."

The lawyer returned to California while Dexter remained in London for two months finishing *The Naked Runner*.

"Upon completion, I returned to Los Angeles and drove to the Sinatra offices at Warner Bros., where Milt Krasney [Vice-President of Sinatra Enterprises] said, 'Welcome back, Brad. I was instructed to inform you by Mr. Rudin that you are fired off the picture and that you are to pack your things and clear them out of the office and vacate the premises immediately.' I told him that he couldn't fire me and neither could Mickey Rudin. There's only one man who owns this company, and if he wants to fire me, that's fine, but he's going to have to do it, I said. It was nine o'clock in the morning and I picked up the phone and asked for the tie line to Frank's house in Palm Springs.

"George Jacobs answered and said Frank was asleep. I insisted that he be awakened. Minutes later, Frank came on the line and in a sleepy voice said, 'How are you? How was the flight? You sure took your time in getting back here.' I told him that the picture was finished for him to look at, but that I'd just been informed by Milt Krasney via Mickey Rudin that I was fired and was to leave the lot immediately. 'I'm not taking orders from any of your lackeys,' I said. 'If you want to fire me, fire me, but I want to get it straight from you—no one else. Do you understand, Frank?' There was a long pause on the phone and then a click. He'd hung up.

"Since he didn't have the guts to fire me, I went ahead and finished the picture in California. I had already been paid $35,000, but was still owed a balance of $15,000, so when the film was completed, I sent a telegram of resignation to Sinatra with a copy to Rudin and asked for the remainder of my producer's fee. I waited a few months, but never heard a word. Nor did I ever receive my final payment. By that time, though, I was producing over at Paramount and it was worth $15,000 to me just to be rid of Frank Sinatra and never have to have anything more to do with him. That meant not having to sit up with him every night until he could go to sleep; not having to be around continual brawls and cherry bombs and drinking until the last bottle was empty and the last song sung. Frank's a sick guy in many ways, and that sickness becomes a heavy burden for those close to him after a while."

Some people in Hollywood were shocked that the friendship between the two men did not survive making the movie together, and Sinatra's publicist was called upon to explain.

"When the picture was finished, Frank asked to see a rough cut," said Jim Mahoney. "Dexter told him this was impossible; the film was not yet suitable for viewing. He was the producer, of course, but he seemed to have forgotten it was Frank who gave him the job. Anyway, that was the end of it."

Years later, when asked about his near drowning and the man who had rescued him, Sinatra said, "Brad didn't really save my life. It was an old guy on a surfboard." After that he often referred to Dexter as "Brad who?"

In November 1966, Frank began his first engagement in Las Vegas since marrying Mia. She attended his opening night at the Sands, where the standing-room-only crowd stretched to catch a glimpse of her as she walked to her ringside seat on the arm of her husband's close friend, Joe E. Lewis. She gazed at Frank adoringly as he sang his songs and the crowd exploded with applause. Midway through his performance, he paused to introduce the celebrities in the audience and then used the racial tensions growing in east Los Angeles for a repartee which made people extremely uncomfortable.

"Smokey the Bear was supposed to be here tonight . . . you all know Smokey. That's Sammy Davis. But he couldn't make it. He has an opening of his own . . . down in Watts. It's a gas station. He calls it Whitey's. He sells three kinds of gas . . . regular, ethyl, and burn, baby, burn. But Sammy's okay. He had a wedding anniversary recently, and I sent him a gift—yeah, I sent him and Mai a love seat covered in zebra skin, so when they sit together they won't be so conspicuous. . . . Well, let's see. What else is new? Oh, yeah. I got married. . . . She's here," he said, pointing to Mia, who stood up to receive thunderous applause from the audience.

"Yeah, I sure got married. . . . Well, you see I had to. . . . I finally found a broad I can cheat on. . . ."

A gasp rose from the crowd and heads swiveled to spot Mia's reaction, but she had lowered her head in shame. Sensing the audience's disapproval, Frank tried to continue as if nothing had happened.

"Ain't she pretty?" he said, pointing to his young wife, but by then he had lost the rapport with his audience. "I guess I'd better sing. I'm in a lot of trouble."

That evening, Frank and Mia and the Sinatra entourage stopped at the Aladdin to watch Joe E. Lewis's midnight show. Frank jumped up onstage to help the comedian with his material.

"I really came in to see Jackie Mason," he said. "Nah, I'm just kidding. . . . If that bum came out here on the stage now, I'd bite him on the neck. He's a creep. . . ."

Mason's lacerating jokes about Frank's marriage to Mia inflamed Sinatra, who did not find references to his hair transplants and elevator shoes funny. Nor was he amused when the comic talked about the couple's nightly ritual: "Frank soaks his dentures and Mia brushes her braces . . . then she takes off her roller skates and puts them next to his cane . . . he peels off his toupee and she unbraids her hair. . . ."

The next day, the comedian said he received an anonymous call threatening his life if he continued making such jokes, but he did not alter his act or change his material. Six days later, an armed assailant climbed onto the patio of his hotel room in Las Vegas and fired three bullets, which shattered a glass door and lodged in the mattress of his bed.

"I told the police that Sinatra's people had been calling me and telling me to lay off," said Mason, who was convinced that someone was trying to kill him. "Maybe it was some kook who wanted to impress Frank."

The Clark County sheriff's office in Las Vegas investigated, but closed the case two days later, saying that despite the evidence of the three pistol shots, there was no motivation for the shooting.

"I knew that Sinatra owned Las Vegas when the detectives there made me the prime suspect and asked that I take a lie detector test," Mason said.

Three months later, Mason appeared in Miami at the Saxony at the same time Frank was appearing at the Fontainebleau. Mason continued telling his Sinatra jokes and related what had happened to him in Las Vegas. "I have no idea who it was who tried to shoot me. . . . After the shots were fired, all I heard was someone singing: 'Doobie, doobie, doo.'

"I was threatened four times that week by friends of Sinatra who came to my dressing room and said I'd better stop talking about Frank and making cracks about him in my show, but I didn't think much about it. Since Las Vegas, I was no longer mentioning Mia Farrow, and the jokes about Frank were harmless. Like I'd say: 'I see Sinatra has another girl. Boy, the way he goes from one girl to another . . . well, any psychiatrist will tell you that this denotes a basic insecurity—I should be so insecure!' "

At five A.M. on Monday, February 13, 1967, Jackie Mason was sitting in a car in front of his apartment in Miami with Myrna Falk, a receptionist, when an unidentified man yanked open the door on the driver's side and with a fist wrapped in metal smashed into Mason's face, breaking his nose and crushing his cheekbones.

"We warned you to stop using the Sinatra material in your act," Falk heard the attacker tell Mason.

Although he could never prove any involvement and tried to make excuses for Frank at the time, Mason remains convinced that Frank was responsible.

"I know it was his doing," he said many years later. "He's a vicious bastard, and yet people act like fawning idiots around him. Look at Alan King. Frank pushes him around and Alan takes it. He never made it big, so he wants to be with the biggest and will do anything to be in Frank's company. Ordinarily, he struts around like a putz, but then Sinatra walks in, and Alan goes duh, duh, duh. Cowering to Sinatra makes him feel important, I guess. It just makes me sick."

Everywhere Frank went during his faltering marriage to Mia Farrow, especially when he was in Miami and Las Vegas, violence seemed to erupt. Shortly after they were married he had agreed to let her pursue a movie career, saying, "I love her and I must be fair. She has talent." Later he resented her being away from him, and the longer she was gone, the more violent he became, throwing furniture out of his penthouse window or lobbing cherry bombs.

Compounding his marital problems was a subpoena from the federal grand jury in Las Vegas seeking evidence that casino owners had skimmed profits from their receipts before taxes and then diverted those funds to underworld figures with hidden interests in the casinos. The grand jury wanted to question Frank about his relationship with Sam Giancana and his ownership interest in the Sands and Cal-Neva. Sinatra fought the subpoena and tried to get out of testifying, but was finally forced to appear on January 26, 1967. "We wouldn't let him out of it," said William G. Hundley, former chief of the Justice Department's organized crime section. "He was very unhappy."

At the same time, Frank was being subpoenaed for a deposition by the *Miami Herald* in a ten-million-dollar libel suit brought by the Fontainebleau Hotel for a two-part series in which the hotel was reported to be deeply involved with Mafia figures. The newspaper asked Frank about his underworld friendships with Sam Giancana ("I've met him") and Vincent "Jimmy Blue Eyes" Alo ("I just ran into him") and Meyer Lansky ("I met him many years ago"). Frank claimed he saw Joe Fischetti only "occasionally" and knew of no connection between Fischetti and the Fontainebleau, although Justice Department files show that Fischetti was paid $1,080 a month for helping arrange Sinatra's appearances at the hotel. "Through Sinatra [he] brought other big name entertainers to the hotel. As a result, Fischetti achieved a position of prominence at the Fontainebleau and gained considerably along financial lines," stated one FBI document.

Under oath, Frank denied knowing Charles and Rocco Fischetti. He also said he had never stayed at the Fontainebleau when Giancana was there, although many people, including former D.C. police inspector Joseph Shimon, knew differently.

Although Frank was forced to give one deposition, he refused to cooperate when the newspaper's attorneys called him back for further questioning. Circuit Court Judge Grady Crawford ordered him to appear for a second deposition, but Sinatra left town. He also refused to testify at the trial and threatened to boycott his own performance at the Fontainebleau to avoid being subpoenaed. Under no circumstances was he going to talk about the incidents of violence that had taken place at the hotel during 1967 when his beefy bodyguards had left bruised and bloodied bodies in his wake.

"I remember the first time I saw that side of him I was shocked," said Mrs. Tony Bennett. "We had come to Miami to have dinner with him. Afterwards, a group of us went into the Fontainebleau coffee shop, where this little old guy grabbed Frank's hand and started shaking it. 'Oh, Frank Sinatra,' he said. 'You are my idol. You are the greatest.' He was a janitor or somebody who worked there and he was in awe to see Frank Sinatra walk in, but Frank must have been in pain from arthritis or something because he grabbed his hand back and said, 'Get away from me, you creep. Get away.' The poor man was so bewildered, he didn't know what to do. Suddenly, two of Frank's goons went over to the guy; one held up his jacket as a shield so the rest of us couldn't see the other one bashing in the guy's face. When the jacket came down, the little man was on the floor and his face was bleeding and torn. I heard a woman crying, 'He loves you. Why did you do that? He loves you.'

"I was so insulted that this kind of barbarity would happen while we're sitting there, and no one would say a thing. Here we are, respectable people, and this is happening right in front of us, and we don't do anything about it. 'I want to get of here,' I said, and we left, but none of us said anything to Frank. That's what upset me so. I thought Tony was a coward for not saying something, and I was furious at him, but he's always been indebted to Sinatra for turning his career around, so he wasn't going to say a word against him. Frank had told *Life* magazine in 1965 that Tony was the best singer in the business, which renewed national interest in him, so he just looked the other way when Frank's goons started beating up on that guy. He [Tony] was such a coward. Then I read in the paper the next day that some sailor had been robbed and beaten up in New Orleans and that when Frank had read about the incident, he'd arranged to pay the sailor's hospital bill and given him a few hundred dollars to make up for what he'd had stolen. That doesn't square with what his goons had done the night before, but then Frank is a very complex guy."

The bodyguards protecting Frank were huge, hulking men like Ed Pucci, Andy Celentano, and Jilly Rizzo. They bulled passage through crowds and intimidated with their bulk and menacing demeanor. Referring to them as "my dago secret service," Frank equipped each with a walkie-talkie radio and a custom-made enamel lapel pin similar to those worn by the Secret Service agents protecting the president.

"I know all about his goons," said Shecky Greene. "I was appearing with Frank at the Fontainebleau at that time when he put me in *Tony Rome*, the movie he was making in 1967. Both of us were drinking too much in those days and neither one of us was the world's nicest drunk. I had to get dressed standing in the grease with the busboys. I told him I couldn't work where I had to dress in the basement. He told me to take his dressing room, which was right off the stage, of course, so I took it and was getting ready to open. Frank came down and finished dressing with me. A minute before I was to go onstage, he said, 'Shecky, stick with me and I'll make you the biggest star in the business.' I looked at him and said, 'If being a big star means being like you, then I don't want it.' Frank Sinatra is not my idea of show business. George Burns, yes. Cary Grant, yes. Bob Hope, by all means, but not Frank Sinatra. I walked onstage that night and did my performance. Later, things got a little bloody.

"At four in the morning, my head was split open by Andy 'Banjo' Celentano, Frank's bodyguard. Joe Fischetti came at me with a blackjack three feet long, and I broke his nose. Then he begged me on his hands and knees not to call the boys in Chicago, which is where I'm from. I've still got scars all over my head from that fight, and if you put a nickel in them, they will all play Sinatra's songs. Now, I didn't hear Frank order that beating, so I can't swear that he did, but I can tell you what was happening during that time and you tell me. The air was volatile and violent around him all the time. We played the same audience every night, and when I was onstage, there was nothing but laughter. Yet when Frank came out, that same audience erupted and people started fighting, drawing guns, and swearing to kill one another.

"Frank had so many people sucking around him then, it was sickening. And those bodyguards would attack on command, so naturally people were frightened. Even if he doesn't order the beatings, he allows the violence to happen by having those guys around. He wanted me to go on tour with him, but I couldn't kiss his ass, so that was the last time we worked together."

Even Mia grew exasperated with the rude humor of his entourage. "All they know how to do is tell dirty stories, break furniture, pinch waitresses' asses, and bet on the horses," she said.

One night at the Sands, Frank threw a box of cupcakes at one of his friends, splattering frosting on the expensive gown of a woman at an adjoining table. Mia was embarrassed. "Oh,

Frank, you're so childish," she said. Momentarily stung by the rebuke, Frank scooped up two handfuls of ice cubes from the ice bucket in the middle of the table and pelted the guests around him. Again, Mia scolded him. "That's not only childish, it's dangerous," she said. "You could knock someone's eyes out." Without a word, Frank stalked out of the room.

Normally, Mia was proud to sit at the Sands or the Fontainebleau listening to the audience rustle with excitement when her husband walked onstage.

"He rocks a room," she said. "Nothing I could ever do in films would make me as proud as I am of him then. He gets away with the squarest lines, and he worries about his lyrics, but he's an artist. He's groovy, he's kinky and—above all—he's gentle. Nancy is writing a book about her father, and she's calling it *A Very Gentle Man*. That's him."

Mia was ambitiously pursuing her own career soon after their wedding and she had flown to London to be in *A Dandy in Aspic* with Laurence Harvey, telling reporters that it was all right for Sinatra to be married to a professional actress.

"There would be no point in having a wife who stayed home and cooked his spaghetti for him," she said. "Any number of women could have done that." She said she would not make movies with her husband because she did not want to live off his famous name. "I've got to do things on my own. If I were his leading lady, too many people would think he just handed me the role," she said. Frank agreed. "I don't think a man and his wife should act together," he said. "At least, that goes for us."

In 1967, Mia signed with Paramount to make *Rosemary's Baby* and begged her agent to call David Susskind in New York for the role of the mute in *Johnny Belinda*, which was being made as a television movie for ABC. Susskind said absolutely no. The agent asked why, and the producer gave him four reasons: "She can't act, she's too thin, she's Frank Sinatra's wife, and she has the sex appeal of Spam."

"Be reasonable, David," said the agent. "She doesn't need sex appeal to play a deaf mute, does she?"

Susskind conceded that point, but said his mind was made up. "I don't want any trouble on this production, and with the wife of Frank Sinatra, you've automatically got trouble," he said.

The next day, Mia called him herself to plead for the

part. "Please, please, please reconsider me," she said. "I'd give anything in the world to play that part. Please reconsider me for it."

"I can't chance it, Mia," said Susskind. "I know your husband doesn't want you to work, and he's not all that keen on me anyway. It just won't work."

"Mr. Susskind, my career is very important to me," said Mia. "I need a role like this. Please listen to me. I'm an actress first and a wife second. Please."

After several days of negotiating, the producer relented and cast Mia in the role that had won an Academy Award for Jane Wyman in 1948.

Rehearsals started in California, but midway through, Mia was hospitalized.

"I started to worry because we only had a week or so to go before airing and I needed to make a decision about replacing her," Susskind said. "So I flew out to the Coast, and she showed up for work with black welts all over her body. She was bruised from head to foot, with mean red gashes and marks all over her arms and shoulders and throat as if she'd been badly beaten. She looked like she'd been roughed up pretty bad. I sat down with her and said, 'Mia dear, I don't think someone wants you to do this role.' She lowered her eyes and said that she still wanted to do it. She begged and pleaded with me and said she would be fine. She pointed out that most of the damage was done below her face, so we could cover her up with makeup, which we did, but in certain lights you could still see those awful welts. I felt so sorry for that poor kid."

Months later, Susskind and his wife were sitting in one of their favorite New York restaurants, where they had come to know the mistress of Vincent "Jimmy Blue Eyes" Alo, a member of the Vito Genovese Mafia family, and through her, the mobster himself.

"Mary, the Mafia mistress, called me one night and insisted on seeing me on urgent business," said Susskind. "She was so uncomfortable about what she was trying to tell me that she couldn't get it out for at least an hour. Finally, she said, 'David, someone doesn't like you . . . someone wants to hurt you and hurt you bad. Nothing fatal. He doesn't want to kill you. Just break an arm and a leg. . . . It's Sinatra. He's put the word out to get you. You used his wife in a movie when he didn't want his wife to work. He's mad, and he's going to get other gangsters to do it for him. My guy says that no one touches anyone in the East without his okay, and that if anyone touches you, he won't be alive the next day. But he says that you're not to go to Las Vegas or Miami. He can't control what goes on there.'

"I said I would never think of going to either place, but I sure as hell didn't want to be told I couldn't go," said Susskind. "But I saw how serious she was, so I said that I would stay out of those places for the next year or so. Naturally, my opinion of Frank Sinatra is biased as a result. I think he's an ill-bred swine who operates on the level of an animal, with no sensibilities whatsoever."

Frayed at the edges, Frank's marriage began unraveling because he thought that Mia enjoyed being a movie star more than being his wife. He now resented her ambitions and retaliated with a couple of brief sexual escapades during the making of *Tony Rome* in Miami while she was in London. Mia called him every day from England and made two transatlantic flights to spend weekends with him, but she refused to exchange her career for the full-time role of Mrs. Frank Sinatra. She did agree to work with him in his next movie (*The Detective*), which was to be filmed in New York in the fall, and she arranged her schedule to accompany him to Las Vegas for his two weeks at the Sands over the Labor Day weekend.

Howard Hughes had bought the hotel in July 1967, adding the Sands to his long list of casinos, including the Desert Inn, the Castaways, the Frontier, and the Silver Slipper, prompting Johnny Carson to greet his audiences: "Welcome to Las Vegas, Howard Hughes's Monopoly set. You ever get the feeling he's going to buy the whole damned place and shut it down?" Frank, too, poked fun at the eccentric billionaire's 1967 buying orgy of casinos, hotels, airports, and television stations. "You're wondering why I don't have a drink in my hand," he said to his audience one night. "Well, Howard Hughes bought it!"

Frank's animus toward Hughes stretched back to 1945, when the billionaire first courted Ava Gardner with extravagant presents, putting limousines and chartered jets at her disposal whenever she wanted to go shopping in Mexico or see bullfights in Spain. Frank remembered bitterly how Hughes had hired detectives to follow him and Ava in 1950, but he seemed to have forgotten that when MGM had dropped him,

Ava had gone to Hughes to get him movie work at RKO, Hughes's studio.

Expecting to make a killing, Frank made it part of his contract renewal with the Sands that Hughes buy the Cal-Neva Lodge from him, which he had leased to Warner and others for the last four years because he was prohibited from running it himself. But Hughes was not interested in the Lake Tahoe property and refused Frank's calls to discuss the matter. Unaccustomed to such a rebuff from the Sands, where his every whim had been indulged for the past fifteen years, Frank began negotiating with Caesars Palace, the newest, most luxurious casino in Las Vegas. Still, he considered the Sands his domain, and no one—not even the richest man in America—could dismiss him so casually.

Frank exacted retribution over Labor Day, the casino's largest-grossing weekend, by pleading "desert throat" at the last minute, claiming that he was unable to perform. He flew to Palm Springs with Mia, and Sammy Davis, Jr., substituted for him. He returned a few days later, but by the weekend he was in a frenzy, lashing out at pit bosses, cursing at cocktail waitresses, and frightening other employees, including the security guards.

"I built this hotel from a sandpile, and I can tear the fucking place down, and before I'm through that is what it will be again," he said.

Hughes's top aide, Robert Maheu, wrote a memo to his boss about Frank's behavior: "Last night, he drove a golf cart through a plate glass window and was disgustingly drunk. In an effort to protect him from himself, Carl Cohen [the Sands's executive vice-president, in charge of the casino,] stopped his credit after he had obtained thirty-thousand-plus in cash and had lost approximately fifty thousand dollars. Sinatra blew his top, and late this afternoon called me to tell me that he was walking away from the Sands and would not finish his engagement. One of the reasons Cohen cut off his credit is that this SOB was running around the casino stating in a loud voice that you had plenty of money and that there was no reason why you should not share it with him since he had made the Sands the profitable institution it is."

Frank signed a three-million-dollar contract with Caesars Palace on September 11, 1967, that guaranteed him $100,000 a week—the highest salary then paid a performer in Las Vegas. He returned to the Sands and went on a drunken rampage at five A.M., slamming his fist on the bell clerk's desk and demanding to know Carl Cohen's room number. The clerk refused to divulge it. This further incited Frank, who grabbed a house phone and demanded to be connected with Cohen's room. The terrified operator connected him with her supervisor, Frances Scher, who decided to put the call through. Cohen was asleep and did not answer. Ten minutes later, Frank called the operator again, asking for Jack Entratter, who had left a Do Not Disturb notice on his phone. The operator told Frank, who yelled: "You had better get him and tell him I will tear up this goddamn fucking place and I'll jerk out every wire in the phone room, too."

Accosting a security guard, Frank demanded to be taken to the switchboard room, but the guard refused. Frank screamed at him, but the guard said that he did not take orders from him. Thrusting his finger at the guard, Frank said, "You're pretty tough with a gun, aren't you. Well, I'll take that gun away and shove it up your ass."

Finding the phone room on his own, Frank pounded on the doors and threatened to kick them in. "Open up this fucking door," he screamed. The three telephone operators inside became so fearful that they called the security office and pleaded for someone to come to their aid.

Accompanied by Jilly Rizzo and a man named Stanley Parker, Frank returned to the hotel lobby and called Carl Cohen, demanding to see him at once. Cohen agreed, and at five forty-five A.M. he appeared in the Garden Room and sat down at a table with Frank and Parker. He asked Parker to leave, saying the conversation was private. "You son of a bitch, he can hear anything I have to say to you," said Frank.

"What did you call me?"

"You heard me, you son of a bitch. What are you so nervous about?"

"You just got me out of bed."

Frank kept repeating his question. "What are you so nervous about?"

Cohen rose from the table and said, "I'm tired of this one-sided conversation. Fuck you. I'm not going to listen to this bullshit."

Getting ready to leave, Cohen backed his chair away from the table, but when Frank saw that he was actually going to walk out, he threw a handful of betting chips in his face.

Then he lifted the table and spilled the contents in Cohen's lap.

"I'll get a guy to bury you, you son of a bitch mother-fucker. You kike," Sinatra screamed.

The ethnic slur galvanized Cohen. He smashed his right fist into Frank's face, splitting his upper lip and knocking the caps off two front teeth.

"You broke my teeth," Frank screamed. "I will kill you, you motherfucker son of a bitch."

Frank lunged toward Cohen, who calmly stepped aside as a security guard intervened.

"Get him, Jilly. Get him," Frank yelled to his friend, but Rizzo remained immobile.

Thrashing about in rage, Frank grabbed a chair, but instead of hitting Cohen, he missed and hit the security guard, opening a gash in his scalp that required two stitches. Apologizing to the man, he continued screaming at Cohen, who was leaving the room. "I'll get a guy to bury you, mother-fucker."

Nevada Governor Paul Laxalt ordered an investigation, and the district attorney, after reading the sheriff's report, considered filing charges against Frank.

"I don't feel he should have the right to tear apart a hotel or run wild," District Attorney George Franklin said. "If he gets out of control, he should be handled like anyone else."

At the Sands, Cohen was being treated like a conquering hero, especially by employees who had suffered Frank's wrath over the years. Some even considered giving him a testimonial dinner, and one wrote a letter to the editor of the *Las Vegas Sun* citing incidents of the dehumanizing treatment employees had been subjected to by Frank. According to the letter, Frank once threw a hamburger against a dressing room wall because it was not prepared to his liking and then had the employee who brought it to him fired.

"Now, after a few days and a few drinks," the letter said, "this sheer genius of a man staggers into the office and as he blurringly gazes about decides the phone on his desk doesn't match the new orange sweater he's wearing. He calls you and demands an orange phone immediately. But you don't respond quickly enough. He calls you some choice words, and the filth of them pleases him so much, he directs them to the female help as well. His reasoning is, no orange phone, no phone at all, and he proceeds to tear all the phones out before he sets fire to the office and breaks the windows."

The employee, who asked that his letter be published without his name, stated that there were many more Sinatra tantrums that were even more brutish than those recounted.

Frank had his defenders. Among them was Hank Greenspun, publisher of the *Las Vegas Sun*, who had chastised the Nevada Gaming Board for revoking Frank's license in 1963. This time, Greenspun defended Frank's actions on the front page of his newspaper: "Not everybody in the world of theatricals can be Ronald Reagan or Shirley Temple . . . [Sinatra's] value to Las Vegas is legendary, for every night he performs here is New Year's Eve. So should he be condemned for celebrating a Happy New Year even if the calendar doesn't justify the occasion?"

Frank's former wife, Nancy, chimed in, saying that he was justified in wreaking mayhem on the Sands and its employees.

"I don't blame him," she said. "What else could he do when they shut off his credit in the hotel that he practically built up from the ground."

Pointing out that Frank could have been prosecuted for disorderly conduct, assault and battery, and malicious destruction of property, D.A. George Franklin said that Frank's conduct was reprehensible.

"You don't go running around a hotel screaming four-letter words and breaking windows," he said. "He did nothing but a disservice to this community by that kind of behavior."

But the district attorney could not prosecute because no one would press charges.

Frank blamed his friend of thirty years—"Where was Jack Entratter when Carl Cohen tried to kill me?"—and walked out on the rest of his engagement.

Carl Cohen became famous in Las Vegas when posters of Frank with his teeth knocked out sprang up around town with the captions: "Hooray for Carl Cohen," and "Elect Carl Cohen Mayor."

27

Shortly after Governor Pat Brown's defeat by Ronald Reagan in 1966, Frank made an overture to the Vice-President of the United States, Hubert H. Humphrey.

"It was in the Waldorf [Astoria] Towers, where the Vice-President and his wife were staying at the time," said Norman Sherman, Humphrey's press secretary. "The phone rang, and someone said that Frank Sinatra would like to make a courtesy visit as an admirer of Mr. Humphrey. The Vice-President agreed to see him, so Frank stopped by on a Sunday afternoon with Mia, who was quite kittenish and curled up on the couch beside him, but didn't say a word. She just listened as Sinatra and Humphrey reminisced about the big bands in the 1930s in South Dakota. Hubert was a nut on boxing and knew all sorts of trivia about who weighed what and which contender won what crown, so they shared that as well. There was an instantaneous bonding between them, an immediate good feeling that led to a nice friendship. Humphrey thought highly of Frank, but then he thought highly of everyone. And let's face it, friends were not that easy to come by then, especially in the entertainment industry, which was so violently opposed to President Johnson's Vietnam policies."

The cheery politician from Minnesota enthusiastically supported the United States involvement in Vietnam. Frank, in turn, supported Humphrey and became a hawk on the war as well, while his flower-child wife stood with the doves, who deplored the bombing and bloodshed. Mia could not understand her husband's zest for napalm and defoliation, and neither could his liberal friends, who were appalled by his support of the Johnson-Humphrey ticket. Opposing Vietnam, they supported Senator Eugene J. McCarthy, an eloquent antiwar candidate.

The war in Vietnam would continue to haunt Frank for many years, causing dissension at the Academy Awards in 1975, when he was sharing the honors as master of ceremonies. When producer Bert Schneider won an Oscar for the best documentary for his searing antiwar film, *Hearts and Minds*, he read a telegram from Dinh Da Thi, chief of the Viet Cong delegation to the Paris peace talks, thanking "all our friends in America for all they have done on behalf of peace" and expressing "greetings of friendship."

Backstage, Bob Hope and Frank sputtered with indignation. Together they hastily scribbled a statement, which Frank later revised and read, disavowing all responsibility for the reference and apologizing that it had taken place.

Hearing Frank's disclaimer, Shirley MacLaine, also one of the evening's hosts, exploded. Accosting him backstage, she demanded to know who sanctioned such a statement on behalf of the Academy of Motion Picture Arts and Sciences. Jolted by this attack from a former lover and member of his Rat Pack, Frank disavowed any responsibility.

"Bob and Howard (Koch) made me do it," he said. "They handed me this piece of paper, and I read it."

After the ceremony, Bert Schneider said, "As a member of the Academy's Board of Governors, I resent Frank Sinatra taking this as an Academy point of view. He's a gutsy guy. Why didn't he come out and say he helped write it and it was his own point of view?"

But at the height of the controversy over the Vietnam War, Frank did not have a point of view that he could articulate sensibly. He took his directions from the politicians he supported. In 1968 he called Vice-President Humphrey's office in Washington and spoke to his administrative assistant, William Connell.

"There is a great deal of misunderstanding and confusion about the Vietnam situation," he said. "People are asking me questions that I cannot answer. I don't think the questions they ask are being answered in a way that they can accept."

He went on to say that he didn't know how to respond to the administration's critics. Connell suggested sending the critical questions to Humphrey in a letter so that the Vice-President could provide him with some useful answers.

Instead, Frank sent a letter to several hundred people, saying that he was writing "at the special request of Vice-President Hubert Humphrey." He asked for a brief outline of "those points of our country's present policy in Vietnam you find most puzzling and confusing and about which you have not as yet found satisfactory or clear-cut answers." He assured everyone that he would transmit their questions to the Vice-President and that "he, in turn, will forward the compilation to President Johnson."

Days later, Mr. Johnson was horrified to read in the *New York Post* that Frank Sinatra, "at White House request," was canvasing intellectuals on what measures to take in Vietnam. He summoned his national security advisor, Walt Rostow, and then called the Vice-President, who called Connell, who then wrote an apologetic memo to Bill Moyers: "Sinatra *was* trying to be helpful. He wants to help the President and the Vice-President, and he can be especially helpful in raising money for the party. He just got carried away by a casual conversation."

The debate over Vietnam seemed to exacerbate the differences between Frank and Mia: He drank Jack Daniels; she smoked marijuana. He got drunk; she got stoned. He gave her diamonds; she wore wooden love beads. He enjoyed nights out at Jilly's; she liked disco dancing at the Daisy. He relished boxing; she studied transcendental meditation. He liked eating Italian; she picked at yogurt and bean sprouts. He gambled; she did needlepoint. He thrived in Las Vegas; she flourished in India with the Maharishi Mahesh Yogi.

The final rupture in the marriage came in the fall of 1967 when Frank, who was in New York, called Mia in California to say that she was to start work with him in *The Detective*. She said she couldn't because she was still working on *Rosemary's Baby*. Frank ordered her to walk off the set and report to work with him. She refused. He then called Bob Evans at Paramount and demanded her release, but Evans said the director, Roman Polanski, needed her for another month. Frank insisted that his wife be released at once, but Evans said, "While she's working for us, she's Mia Farrow, not Mrs. Sinatra."

Frank again called Mia and repeated his order that she walk off her movie, but she remained intractable. She went to the Factory discotheque that evening in a group that included Senator Robert F. Kennedy, with whom she danced most of the night. Reading about his wife dancing with his enemy enraged Frank as much as Mia's refusal to obey him. Without a word to her, he called his lawyer, Mickey Rudin, and instructed him to draw up divorce papers. Then he sent Rudin to Mia's trailer on the Paramount lot the day before Thanksgiving to serve notice on her that he was filing for divorce. Minutes later, his publicist, Jim Mahoney, announced the couple's "trial separation."

"We were just ready to roll when Sinatra's lawyer, Mickey Rudin, turned up," recalled Roman Polanski. "He said he had some important papers for Mia, so I called a break. . . . After a few minutes, Rudin emerged [from her dressing room] and left without a word. When it was time to resume shooting, no Mia. I knocked on the door. No response. When there was no answer to my second knock, I just went in.

"There she was, sobbing her heart out. She managed, haltingly, to tell me that Rudin had come to inform her that Sinatra was starting divorce proceedings. What hurt her most was that Sinatra hadn't deigned to tell her himself, simply sending one of his flunkies. Sending Rudin was like firing a servant. She simply couldn't understand her husband's contemptuous, calculated act of cruelty, and it shattered her."

Leaving the studio in tears, Mia fled to the $300,000 English Tudor house that Frank had bought for her in Bel-Air. He had filled it with new furniture and forty-eight place settings of Gorham's "Chantilly" silver in hopes that she might want to be a hostess instead of an actress.

"I had nothing I wanted to live for," Mia said later. "That kind of lostness, that kind of unhappiness can be so destructive, and so bewildering. . . . When my marrige was over, I believed it just wasn't possible. . . . You see, that marriage was terribly important to me. That promise. I believed and trusted in that commitment as I've never believed or trusted in a commitment before."

Reflecting on why the "gentle, quiet man" she had married had walked out on her, she said, "Maybe it bothered him not being young. He felt things getting away from him.

My friends from India would come into the house barefoot and hand him a flower. That made him feel square for the first time in his life."

A few weeks later, Frank invited Mia to spend Christmas with him and twenty of his closest friends in Palm Springs.

"He called and asked how everything was," she said. "Without even realizing that I was saying it, I blurted out: 'Frank, may I come back?' He told me that he had invited a lot of people to spend the holidays with him in Palm Springs and that if I didn't mind a crowd, he would be happy to have me there too. I would have taken him up on the offer if the crowd had been big enough to fill the Colosseum.

"All our friends were there [the Deutsches, the Goetzes, the Brissons, the Cerfs, Harry Kurnitz, Bubbles and Arthur Hornblow, Pamela and Leland Hayward, Ruth Gordon and Garson Kanin]. It was a fun crowd. Every night at eleven P.M., Frank had two movies just flown in from Hollywood for the guests to watch if they didn't want to drink or play cards or talk. . . . I never had such a marvelous time. Frank was surrounded by the people he likes best, me included. And he was so relaxed and happy. I have never seen him so happy."

Mia said this to a reporter shortly after her holiday with Frank in Palm Springs, but she soon realized how transitory that Christmas interlude had been when Frank never called. So she flew to the Himalayas to meditate with her guru.

"I had nothing, just the remnants of a marriage," she said. "So I latched on to what seemed to be the nearest hope. It wasn't just a whim; my life was crumbling, it really was. My marriage was gone."

The trauma of divorcing his young wife hit Frank hard early in 1968 when he was filming *Lady in Cement* in Florida during the day and performing at the Fontainebleau at night.

"He was real upset," recalled Al Algiro, who worked as an extra. "I remember Pat Henry messed up his lines real bad, and after three takes Frank got so mad he went over and slapped Pat in the face a few times and told him to shape up. Also, when Lainie Kazan played her scenes too close to his lips, he got pissed off and said, 'Are we supposed to kiss in this scene?' That was a real putdown for Frank to say in front of everyone. This was Lainie's big chance at a movie career, and she was trying so hard."

Refusing to do more than one take and ripping out handfuls of the script to save time, Frank treated the director,

Gordon Douglas, like a lackey who was on the film simply to accommodate him. At Frank's insistence, Douglas scheduled his scenes so that he never had to come to work before noon; the sets were pre-lit, and his double plotted every move so that by the time Frank arrived, he could complete action on one set and proceed to the next without delay. The film was finished within six weeks and the post-production details fell to Michael Viner, the twenty-one-year-old assistant to the producer.

"At the end of the film, there were a couple of problems involving Sinatra," he said." One night, he was so mad at the scriptwriter, he ripped a fire ax out of its casing and chopped down the door to his room, which cost us a few hundred dollars. Then there was a prostitute who complained that Frank and his pals had not treated her quite right. She said that after an all-night party, Frank had invited her to stay for breakfast and called for an order of ham and eggs, which he then ate off her chest with a knife and fork. She threatened to sue Twentieth Century Fox because of that incident, but we settled before it got to court."

Bolstered by hormone shots of testosterone regularly administered by a nurse, Frank indulged himself sexually with a variety of women and most were thrilled to be in his company.

"I was just a little twenty-six-year-old secretary from Chicago when I met him at the Fontainebleau," said Nancy Seidman. "He invited me to spend the weekend with him, which was incredible, even though he came down with pneumonia, and was very, very sick. He ran a temperature of 104 degrees, and I stayed up and took care of him, changing his pajamas, which would get soaked every few hours from his fever. . . . Mia Farrow kept calling the suite, but Frank wouldn't take her calls. Then Eddie Fisher came in to ask if he should marry Connie Stevens. . . . Jilly was there all the time. . . . People were so reverential . . . I was very taken with the whole scene. It was quite exciting. . . ."

Hearing that Frank was ill, Mia flew to Florida to be by his side, but she left a few days later, looking wan and pathetic. Frank then summoned Ava Gardner, who arrived with a maid, a secretary, and twenty-nine pieces of luggage. She stayed only briefly. "During the night there was one of those wild parties, and a piano got pushed out of an upstairs window," she said. "That was too much for me. Next day, I left." Dolly and Marty Sinatra arrived a few days later.

"All I need is for Nancy, Sr., to arrive, and all the people close to me will have checked in," Frank said.

"The Mia thing was hard," said Nancy, Jr. "I don't care who you are, or what age you are, you suffer through something like that just like everybody else."

"If we could make it through Mia, I guess we can endure anything," said Frank, Jr.

Gathering his family around him, Frank tried to ease his anguish, but the impending divorce disturbed him. He offered Mia generous alimony, but she refused any kind of financial settlement, saying all she wanted was his friendship. She kept the jewelry he had given her and the forty-eight place settings of silver, but she moved out of the home in Bel-Air, taking only her clothes and her stuffed animals from the bedroom.

"When I got married, all that sudden money I never used at all, you know? It wasn't my money, after all," she said. "That was his money. We kept separate bank accounts, although I didn't really have any money to speak of . . . there was no fear about being broke."

Agreeing to a quick divorce in Juarez, Mexico, Mia refused to charge Frank with mental cruelty, saying the only acceptable ground would be incompatibility. "I didn't seem to be able to please him anymore," she said. She asked the court to restore her maiden name.

The night before the decree was granted, Mia was in Hollywood at the Daisy when George Jacobs walked in with his date, and Mia grabbed him for a dance. Since it was the eve of her divorce, that dance with her husband's handsome black valet became a gossip item on Rona Barrett's television show. When George returned to Sinatra's house in Palm Springs, where he was living, Frank refused to speak to him.

"The maid came to me and said, 'Mr. Sinatra wants you to get out of the house,' " said Jacobs. "This was the day of the Mia divorce. Frank had locked himself in his room and wouldn't come out. I banged on the door and said, 'What's wrong? What's going on?' He wouldn't open the door. 'Mickey will tell you. Mickey will tell you,' he said. 'Call Mickey.' So I called Rudin and waited an hour for him to get back to me.

"He told me that the stuff Rona Barrett reported really stirred Frank up, that I'd better take a few days off and, in the meantime, move all my belongings out of the house. I tried to explain that I didn't do anything. All I did was walk into the Daisy with my date and see Mia, who was sitting there getting stoned. She wanted to dance, so we danced a couple of times. That was it, but everyone around the old man—Jilly and all of them—poisoned his mind until he actually believed that his valet was sleeping with his wife. I couldn't believe that he'd ever think I'd do something like that to him. After fourteen years together, he dropped the net on me just like that, and he couldn't even look me in the face to do it. He couldn't fire me in person. He had to have his prick lawyer do it for him.

"I was so mad afterwards that I threw away everything he'd ever given me—two-thousand-dollar watches, suits, sweaters, shirts, shoes, coats, cameras, radios—everything. I didn't want anything from the bastard around. I got twelve thousand dollars in severance pay and blew it, and then I sold all my shares in Reprise Records.

"I had been so close to that man. I even signed his name better than he did. In fact, I did all the autographs. 'Just give it to George,' Frank would say whenever someone wanted a signed Sinatra picture. I went everywhere with him. I nursed him through his suicide attempt in Lake Tahoe. I helped him get through Ava, who was the only woman he ever loved. I was even the nurse after his hair transplants from Dr. Sammy Ayres, who had done Joey Bishop first and then Frank. I drove all the girls to Red Krohn [Dr. Leon Krohn] for their abortions, and I treated each one of those dames like a queen because that's what he wanted me to do. The women that man had over the years! I still remember Lee Radziwill sneaking into his bedroom. How do I know? I heard her. I always had a room next to Frank so he could slap the wall for me if he needed anything.

"Yeah, I was at Cal-Neva with Giancana, and I was with him a lot when he visited Frank in Palm Springs. The guy was great with tips. I knew them all—Sam and Joe Fischetti. I even knew Moe Dalitz when he was calling himself the entertainment director of the Desert Inn. Don't that beat everything? The entertainment director!"

Devastated by the firing, Jacobs reminisced about the years he worked for Sinatra, saying that what he missed most was the riotous merriment.

"We had some funny, funny times together because Frank was always doing numbers on people. He loved practical jokes. Like the time he walked in when Milt Ebbins [Peter

Lawford's personal manager] was shaving and said, 'Let me see that, Milt.' Wham! He threw the razor out of the window. 'What time is it, Milt?' He'd take Ebbins's watch off his wrist and throw that out the window, too. He was always doing crazy stuff like that. Years later [after the break with Frank], I thought I'd write a book about those funny times and I sat down with Joe Hyams. We got about thirty-two pages written before the word got out and oh, God! Rudin hit me with a letter you wouldn't believe. I told him I'd never hurt Frank. I loved the guy. I just wanted to write about the good things. Not the bad stuff; nothing about the Mafia, none of that stuff. I even said they could have the galleys and if there was anything they wanted to take out of the book, it would be cut out, but Rudin wouldn't hear of it. Man, when that word got around, I couldn't get anybody to hang out with me. They all thought they'd be shot in the knees because Frank was mad."

The night the divorce was granted, Johnny Carson announced the news to his *Tonight Show* audience by saying: "Hear about the trouble at Frank Sinatra's house? Mia Farrow dropped her Silly Putty in Frank's Poligrip."

During this time, Sinatra was seriously involved in Hubert Humphrey's 1968 presidential campaign. Lyndon Johnson had announced that he would not seek a second term as President. Senator Robert F. Kennedy declared his candidacy, which only caused Frank to intensify his efforts for Humphrey.

"Bobby is just not qualified to be president of the United States," Frank said.

Kennedy's candidacy rekindled Sinatra's hatred for the man who had put Sam Giancana in prison and sent Jimmy Hoffa, another good friend, to the penitentiary for mail fraud and jury tampering.

"I remember Frank saying if Bobby Kennedy got elected, he will point his finger at all of us and say: 'You are under arrest,' " said Mrs. Ted Allen, wife of one of Frank's favorite photographers.

In May 1968, Frank flew to Washington with his Chicago Mafia friend, Allen Dorfman, to attend a party for Humphrey in columnist Drew Pearson's Georgetown garden. Seeing Dorfman, a mob-connected associate of Jimmy Hoffa, socializing with Sinatra and the Vice-President made a *Washington*

Post reporter curious about the relationship among these three men. Approaching Dorfman, the reporter asked if he was there to make a deal: Humphrey's pardon of Jimmy Hoffa in exchange for helping get Humphrey elected. Dorfman replied bluntly. "Yeah . . . we're here to buy everybody in town who's for sale." After the party, Frank met Mrs. Jimmy Hoffa and Teamster Vice-President Harold Gibbons for dinner.

The next night, following a Big Brothers benefit, Drew Pearson and Humphrey took Sinatra to the White House for a late night visit with Lyndon Baines Johnson. Frank's animosity toward Bobby Kennedy was the only thing that made him partially acceptable to the President, who had never forgotten Sinatra's rebuke to his fellow Texan, House Speaker Sam Rayburn, at the 1956 Democratic National Convention, nor his idolatry of John F. Kennedy in 1960. Johnson showed his disdain when Sinatra was ushered into the Lincoln bedroom well past midnight.

Lady Bird was already in her nightgown and the President was lying on a table getting a massage. Humphrey stopped by the canopied bed to talk to Mrs. Johnson while Frank walked over to the famous mantelpiece on which Jacqueline Kennedy had placed an inscribed plaque before leaving the White House. He looked closely at the inscription: "In this room lived John Fitzgerald Kennedy with his wife Jacqueline—during the two years, ten months and two days he was President of the United States—January 20, 1961–November 22, 1963."

President Johnson watched him examining the plaque. He then jumped off the massage table, grabbed an old souvenir booklet about the White House dating back to the Kennedy administration, and thrust it in Frank's face.

"I don't suppose you read, but this has lots of pictures. Here's something else," he added, handing Frank one of the presidential souvenirs he gave to his women visitors. "It's a conversation piece," he said of the lipstick with the White House seal on it. "It'll make a big man of you with your women."

Reeling from the insults, Frank turned and walked out of the room in a quiet rage, not realizing that he had seen his mirror image in the coarse Texan. Both men needed to be the focus of other men's eyes, and they dominated their own worlds by the sheer force of their personalities. Both were unscrupulous, admirable, treacherous, devoted, and mean. Both were adored by their mothers, supporting Sigmund Freud's thesis that "a man who has been the indisputable favorite of his mother keeps for life the feeling of a conqueror, that confidence of success that often induces real successes." The thirty-sixth President of the United States and the country's most popular singer were so alike that they circled each other warily. Both were naturally attracted to the ebullient Humphrey, who flattered each of them unashamedly.

"I will appear in ten major cities stumping for the Vice-President," Frank told the press. "We'll start in Oakland, California, and then hit Minneapolis, Cleveland, Detroit, New York, and Chicago, among others."

But Frank was unable to attract any of his celebrity friends to the Humphrey cause. Shirley MacLaine and Sammy Davis, Jr., were campaigning for Bobby Kennedy. Sammy Cahn wrote the Kennedy campaign song to the tune of "My Kind of Town." Bill Cosby, Nancy Wilson, Andy Williams, Gene Kelly, Jack Lemmon, Gregory Peck, and Rod Steiger also campaigned for Kennedy. Paul Newman, Robert Vaughn, Dick Van Dyke, and Carl Reiner supported Eugene McCarthy. Frank was the only major Hollywood star to support Hubert Humphrey, and he was of inestimable worth to the Vice-President because his concerts attracted thousands of devoted fans who would pay hundreds of dollars to watch him enwrap his soul in song. He enlisted the support of his daughter, Nancy, who had started singing after her divorce from Tommy Sands in 1965 and had become a pop sensation with her hit song, "These Boots Were Made for Walking." That song, plus the recording of "Somethin' Stupid," which she made with her father, had been number-one songs in America and England in 1967.

"I'm trying to help draw crowds who will contribute to the campaign," said Frank. "I won't make any speeches. I'll leave that to the politicians. I'll just sing. And I hope that the Vice-President will be with me on all ten of those appearances. I think all Americans should get out and contribute to the candidate of their choice. It's getting so expensive, it is almost impossible for candidates to campaign properly."

Frank worked harder for Humphrey than he had for any other political candidate. Records in the Vice-President's Minnesota archives show frequent phone calls and regular correspondence between the two men and their staffs. In addition to his concerts, which raised thousands of dollars, Frank advised the candidate on the best makeup to wear for television. He recommended special lighting for Humphrey's political commercials and even suggested dying his hair to look a little younger. He called Bennett Cerf at Random House, who agreed to lead an effort to place an advertisement for Humphrey in *The New York Times* signed by leading editors and publishers. At his own expense, Frank made a sixty-second videotape soliciting funds for the campaign, and he spent his own money on voter registration drives.

The rioting that followed the death of Martin Luther King, Jr., in April 1968 convinced Frank that the black vote would be decisive in the election. He opened his home to Black Panther groups from Watts and other parts of the country, trying to persuade them to vote for Humphrey.

Ironically, his concern for civil rights did not extend to his nightclub performances, which were filled with crude racial jokes and bigotry. Appearing with Count Basie and Ella Fitzgerald one night, Frank tried to amuse his audience:

"The Polacks are deboning the colored people and using them for wet suits," he said.

Looking at Basie's all-black band, he said, "I'd publicly like to thank the NAACP for this chess set they gave me."

He called Johnny Mathis the "African Queen," and used Sammy Davis, Jr., as a foil, complaining about the watermelon rinds in his dressing room and commenting that in a top hat Sammy "looked like a headwaiter in a rib joint." Sammy Davis would sometimes cringe, but he would never say a word to Frank.

Although grateful for Frank's public support and his immense fund-raising ability, some people close to Humphrey worried about his friendship with the singer. Washington attorney Joseph L. Nellis, the former Kefauver committee counsel who had interrogated Frank in 1951 about carrying money to Lucky Luciano in Cuba, wrote the Vice-President a private memo warning him about Sinatra's Mafia connections. He mentioned Frank's Washington meeting in 1968 with Allen Dorfman, a Chicago mobster who was trying to get teamster boss Jimmy Hoffa out of prison. He also cited Frank's 1967 chairmanship of the Italian-American Anti-Defamation League on whose letterhead was at least one man connected to organized crime. The group, which sought to improve the image of Italians in the United States, drew heated criticism from *The New York Times* for selecting Frank as their national leader.

"I concluded my memo by saying: 'It's true you need support from every segment of the population, but surely you would agree that you don't need support from the underworld, and Frank Sinatra is unquestionably connected with the underworld,'" said Nellis. "Hubert later told me that he would be careful about the friendship, but he couldn't set Sinatra aside because Frank was too powerful a supporter in Hollywood and the money he raised was just too great to discard him. 'You just don't turn your back on that,' he said."

Another Humphrey stalwart, Martin McNamara, former assistant U.S. attorney in Washington, D.C., was concerned enough about Frank's involvement in the campaign to contact Henry Peterson, head of the organized crime section in the Justice Department. He sent a memo about this meeting to Bill Connell: "[Peterson] said that there is presently under way an investigation which has arisen out of IRS investigations into the relationship between the entertainment industry and the Cosa Nostra. That as far as Sinatra personally is concerned, there is a three months' old investigation in their division which will probably extend for another two to three years. In other words, there is no likelihood of any criminal charge situation arising in the immediate future.

"For our own guidance," McNamara continued, "we should be aware of the fact that Joe Fischetti and Ben Novak of the Fontainebleau are regarded as being fronts for substantial investments of hood money. The same is true of Paul D'Amato, who runs the 500 Club in Atlantic City. Another name mentioned was that of Sam Giancana, the head of the Chicago syndicate, now in Mexico City, who is one of the ten most important racketeers in the world. All these names are individuals with very close personal relationships with Sinatra and, in essence, Sinatra is their pawn and in their debt for having picked him out of the entertainment doldrums a few years back."

In August 1968, a week before the Democratic National Convention, *The Wall Street Journal* ran a long front-page story entitled "Sinatra's Pals—Gangster Friendships Cause Singer Trouble/But He Isn't Fazed." It said that for nearly thirty years some of Frank's best friends had been mobsters. "Not just two-bit hoods, either; Mr. Sinatra hobnobs with the Mafia's elite," wrote Nicholas Gage, detailing Frank's relationships with Willie Moretti, Lucky Luciano, Joe Fischetti, and Sam Giancana. Gage cited Frank's ownership of an interest in the Berkshire Downs racetrack in Massachusetts, saying that Frank and Dean Martin were directors of the track in 1963 and that it was secretly owned by Raymond Patriarca, the New England Mafia boss, and Gaetano "Three-Finger Brown" Lucchese, the late head of one of New York's five Mafia families.

"In recent months, gangsters have not appeared conspicuously in Mr. Sinatra's entourage, but he is known to have seen them privately," said Gage. "Last October, Mr. Sinatra came to New York to make a speech. According to police reports, he also drove up to Trumbull, Conn., to visit the home of Dave Iacovetti, a member of the Mafia's Carlo Gambino family in New York."

These stories of his Cosa Nostra connections so infuriated Frank that he canceled his scheduled appearance at the convention luncheon for Mrs. Humphrey, where he was to be the master of ceremonies and sing for two thousand women delegates. He also canceled his appearance at a gala honoring Mayor Richard Daley.

Hypersensitive to press criticism, Frank worried about reflecting negatively on the Vice-President. "He'd say to me: 'Should I do this? I don't want to embarrass him,' " recalled Nick Kostopolous, one of Humphrey's advance men.

After the convention, Frank continued to campaign hard for the Democratic ticket, saying, "I'll do anything to defeat that bum Nixon."

Frank did not have the same inside sources that he'd had in 1960, when Sam Giancana and Skinny D'Amato made such vital contributions to the election of John F. Kennedy. This time, too many disillusioned Democrats stayed away from the polls to protest the war in Vietnam. In one of the closest elections in American history, Humphrey lost the White House by fewer than 300,000 votes to Richard Nixon.

As a consolation prize, Frank sent Humphrey an expensive set of golf clubs, plus a set of Mark Cross luggage, and encouraged him to take advantage of his new-found leisure.

28

The poor health of Frank's father had worsened. On Sunday, January 19, 1969, Frank flew his parents to Houston's Methodist Hospital so that Dr. Michael Ellis DeBakey could examine Marty for an enlarged aorta. DeBakey, a pioneer in artificial heart pump research, was celebrated as one of the finest heart surgeons in the world. Frank had been recommending him to friends for years—and paying their expenses at the Fondren-Brown Cardiovascular Center, where DeBakey operated. Now he was bringing his seventy-four-year-old critically ill father.

Frank and his mother spent most of the day and night by Marty's bedside as DeBakey's team of doctors ran tests to determine whether surgery was necessary. Two days later, Marty seemed to be resting comfortably. Assured by the hospital that he was "progressing nicely," Frank left Houston for New York while Dolly stayed with her husband. The next day, January 24, Marty's heart gave out and the former fire captain from Hoboken died of cardiac arrest at seven fifty-five P.M. Frank flew to Texas to take his father back to New Jersey for the last time.

Frank buried him with a requiem mass at Fort Lee's Madonna Church, which was jammed with five hundred people, most of whom hadn't even known the quiet little man but who had come only to see Frank Sinatra and his show business friends. The funeral procession included twenty-five limousines, ten carrying the two hundred fifty floral arrangements sent from Hollywood and Las Vegas.

"Dolly called me right after Marty died and said I had to be with her for the funeral," said Sister Mary Consilia. "She insisted I walk down the aisle with her in my nun's habit and stand in the line of mourners. The first pew in the church was Little Frank, Big Frank, Dolly, and me. She knew that they [the two Franks] wouldn't be taking Holy Communion, so I took her to the rail and lifted up the black veil she was wearing so she could receive. Behind us were Big Nancy and Little Nancy, who had recently become engaged to Jack Haley, Jr., who had given her a big beautiful diamond ring made in the shape of a butterfly. He was there at the funeral, too, and so was Tina. . . ."

After the solemn high mass celebrated by three priests, the cortege proceeded to the Holy Name Cemetery in Jersey City, followed by a horde of curiosity-seekers who yelled and waved and stamped their feet trying to get Frank's attention. The two Franks guided Dolly to the gravesite, where she said good-bye to her husband of fifty-five years. Wailing with grief, she seemed on the verge of collapse; Frank summoned a police escort to take them back to Fort Lee.

"[Dolly] wanted me to do some errands for her," Sister Consilia said, "but I didn't have the convent car, so Frank said he'd give me one and, sure enough, two nights later I got a nice green paneled Pontiac station wagon. It came with a plaque that said Sinatra Enterprises and a tape deck with all of Frank's tapes. I drove Dolly all over in that car. I went with her to the Fontainebleau—Frank made all the arrangements and saw to it that we had our own suite—and then when he got on her a little bit for being so heavy, she went to Duke University to go on the rice diet. I went with her then, too, because she didn't want to be alone. We had a lot of fun together, me and Dolly. She considered me her property. She had me do things for her all the time."

As the paterfamilias, Frank reached out to take care of those who took care of his mother.

"I got into all of his concerts free," said Sister Consilia. "His secretary would hold tickets for me, and I'd just walk backstage to say hello to Frank before the show. You know that no one gets backstage to see Frank. He has his bodyguards standing there, and you can't pass through them unless you have permission, but I always got through because

I'd go to Jilly, and he'd let me back to see Frank. Of course, it wasn't the same after Dolly died, but while she was alive I saw all his concerts."

"Frank was good to his folks, real good," said Al Algiro. "He bought them their place in Fort Lee and was always sending Dolly diamonds and furs and stuff like that. Marty got a lot of real nice golf sweaters. One time, Frank came to visit with Rosalind Russell and Charlotte Ford, and he wanted to watch Frankie Junior's television special, but all Marty and Dolly had was a little black and white TV set. Frank nearly went nuts. 'You mean this is all you got?' he said. He couldn't believe it. The next morning, he sent over three huge twenty-five-inch color sets, and Dolly called me to come and install them."

After his father's death, Frank raised $805,000 to endow the Martin Anthony Sinatra Medical Education Center adjoining the Desert Hospital in Palm Springs. He also wanted to build a house for his mother next to his own in the desert. He was determined to move her out of the grimy industrial East, with its insufferable weather. But when he broached the subject of her moving to the West Coast, Dolly wouldn't hear of it. She was adamant about never leaving New Jersey.

"She told me she didn't want to go to Palm Springs because she didn't like Frank's friends," said Nancy Siracusa, the food editor of the *Hudson Dispatch*. "Dolly said, 'I don't want to move out there with all those bigshots.'

"One reason Frank wanted to get her out with him is because he didn't want her involved in the community here. He said he didn't like people using her and the Sinatra name, but Dolly loved throwing benefits like the one she did at the Stanley Theater in Jersey City for the St. Joseph's School for the Blind. She raised thirty thousand dollars that night and had everyone there, including the governor, and John V. Kenney, the big political boss of New Jersey. That's when she wanted Jimmy Roselli to sing, but he refused to do it; Frank got so mad at him for turning down his mother that he never spoke to him again."

Frank continued to beg Dolly to move to Palm Springs so that he could take care of her, but she said she would never leave her husband's grave untended in Jersey City. Who would visit it and take flowers? Who would have the commemorative masses said at the Madonna Church? Frank promised to move his father's remains to a crypt in the Desert Park

Memorial Cemetery, a few minutes drive from his house in Palm Springs, if she would change her mind.

Dolly had stayed at her son's compound many times and knew of its splendor—the pools and tennis court and guest houses, the railroad box car that had been converted into a health spa, the helipad and all the servants. She still didn't want to make the move. Frank pleaded, saying he wanted her to be able to spend more time with her grandchildren. He even dangled the prospect of great-grandchildren in front of her, saying how terrible it would be if she were not there to share those joys with her family.

He flew to Fort Lee with architectural blueprints for the house he wanted to build for her next door to his own on the grounds of the Tamarisk Country Club.

"Dolly just didn't know what to do," said Al Algiro. "She worried about moving away from her friends, but Frank promised that she would never be homesick because he'd fly any of us out there anytime she wanted. She told him she didn't want to live in the desert during the summer when the temperature soars to 120 degrees before noon, so he promised her a condominium in La Jolla or Del Mar near the racetrack, which she loved. After a while, she just couldn't keep saying no."

When Dolly finally gave in, Frank built her a five-bedroom house, bought her every piece of Italian Provincial furniture she wanted, plus every kitchen appliance available. For her staff, he hired a cook, a gardener, three maids, and a team of security guards.

The most persuasive reason for Dolly's move to Palm Springs was simply to see her son, because come October 1969 Frank could no longer visit her in New Jersey without being arrested. He had refused to appear before the State Commission on Investigation to answer questions about organized crime and was being threatened with possible contempt for declining to answer a subpoena. In return, he had sued in federal court, contending that the commission's subpoena was illegal and that the State Commission was unconstitutionally created. ". . . Notwithstanding the fact that I am of Italian descent," he stated, "I do not have any knowledge of the extent or the manner in which 'organized crime' functions in the State of New Jersey or whether there is such a thing as 'organized crime.' "

By this time, Frank had assumed a permanent defensive stance about his Cosa Nostra relationships. In large part, he blamed Mario Puzo for his uncomfortable position in society, because of Puzo's Mafia novel, *The Godfather*, which had been published in 1969. There were so many similarities between the fictional Johnny Fontane and Sinatra that little was left to the imagination, especially Frank's.

"How close do you want to get to a singer who knew a president who was assassinated?" he asked angrily. "I read off Puzo one night in Chasen's. What phony stuff! Somebody going to the mob to get a role in a movie. Puzo turned out to be a bum. He prostituted his own business making up such a phony story. I screentested for Cohn, and he hired me for the role [in *From Here to Eternity*]. Period."

Jilly Rizzo, who was present at the Chasen's confrontation, said he thought Frank was so angry he wanted to kill the author, but was restrained. Instead, he berated Puzo, who was so humiliated by Frank's shouting that he walked out of the restaurant. Frank yelled after him, "Choke. Go ahead and choke, you pimp."

Days later, Frank's suit against the New Jersey State Commission on Investigation was dismissed by Federal Judge Coolahan, who ruled that the investigative body was indeed legal and valid.

Frank appealed the verdict to the U.S. Supreme Court, but by a 4-3 vote, the court rejected Frank's arguments and refused to prevent his arrest for declining to answer the commission's subpoena. His lawyer's argument that Frank would be caused irreparable harm by appearing before the commission was not persuasive. Senator Clifford Case (R-N.J.) introduced a bill in the United States Senate, called "The Frank Sinatra Amendment," which would make it a criminal offense to flee across a state line to avoid testifying before a state crime investigative commission.

Frank still refused to bow to the subpoena. The commission announced that it was prepared to seek his indictment on a criminal contempt charge, an extraditable offense that could return him to the state in handcuffs. At that point, he gave in.

"Can you imagine what the headline would have been?" asked his lawyer. "Frank simply couldn't afford that kind of publicity, even though we felt that the commission moves against him were unconstitutional."

His lawyer agreed to produce Frank for questioning only if the commission would hold a secret session in Trenton at midnight on February 17, 1970, to avoid reporters and photographers. The commission agreed, and Frank testified for one hour and fifteen minutes, telling them absolutely nothing about his Mafia relationships.

Q: Do you know Willie Moretti?
A: No.
Q: Ever meet him?
A: I'm not sure whether I ever have, because it seems so long ago that I had a house in Hasbrouck Heights, New Jersey, my wife and I. We bought a house, and the man from whom we bought the house, I think, brought him to the house one day to meet me.
Q: Do you know Meyer Lansky?
A: I've met him.
Q: Who is he?
A: I just read in the papers that he was an undesirable.
Q: You have never heard that "Skinny" D'Amato is a member of Cosa Nostra?
A: Never.
Q: Are you familiar with Sam Giancana's reputation as a member of Cosa Nostra?
A: No.
Q: Are you familiar with Joseph Fischetti's reputation as a member of Cosa Nostra?
A: No.
Q: Are you familiar with Lucky Luciano's reputation as a member of Cosa Nostra?
A: No, sir.
Q: Are you familiar with Willie Moretti's reputation as a member of Cosa Nostra?
A: No, sir.
Q: Are you familiar with Joe Adonis's reputation as a member of Cosa Nostra?
A: No, sir.

The commission member asking the questions seemed incredulous. "I have been using the word *Cosa Nostra*. If I were using the word *Mafia* with respect to any of those people named above, would your answers be different?"

Frank said that his answers would remain the same.

Q: Do you know anybody who's a member of Cosa Nostra?
A: No, sir.

Q: Do you know anybody who's a member of the mob?

A: No, sir.

Q: Do you know anybody who's a member of any organization that would come under that category of organized crime?

A: No, sir.

When one of the commissioners asked Frank if he knew Harold "Kayo" Konigsberg, a New Jersey extortionist and loan shark, Frank said he did not know the man and had never met him. Perhaps, but Frank's name had surfaced during a 1961 FBI wiretapped telephone conversation between Konigsberg and Angelo "Gyp" DeCarlo, a lieutenant in the Mafia family formerly headed by Vito Genovese, in which the two mobsters talked about how they would raise the money to take over a hotel in Jamaica.

"Do you know where I'll get it from?" Konigsberg said. "Frank Sinatra."

"I'm going down there to Florida next week," said DeCarlo. "I'll see Sinatra and have a talk with him."

"Is he going to be in Florida next week?"

"He'll be there until the twelfth or thirteenth [March]," said DeCarlo. "I'm going down there Friday, so I'll see him before he leaves."

Frank was asked whether he knew Generoso Del Duca, a member of the New York Mafia, and he said no.

"Ever meet him?" asked one of the commissioners.

Again Frank said no, although he had been in a Miami nightclub with Joe Fischetti and Del Duca a few years before, when Del Duca had a heart attack and died in Frank's arms. Del Duca's body was sent to New York the next day for burial. Frank and Tony Bennett canceled their midnight shows in Miami to fly to the funeral home in New York. At two-thirty A.M., they were admitted to pay their last respects. They checked into a hotel and the next morning visited Mrs. Del Duca before flying back to Miami. Unaware of this incident, the commission could not ask Frank why he went to such great lengths to pay tribute to a man he said he didn't know.

The commission dropped its contempt charges against him the next day, saying "he has fully and completely answered all our questions."

Having been forced to testify once, Frank knew that he was now vulnerable to a subpoena from any investigative body in the country looking into organized crime. Without political protection of any sort, he was defenseless.

"For many years, every time some Italian names are involved in any inquiry—I get a subpoena," he said. "I appear. I am asked questions about scores of persons unknown to me. I am asked questions based on rumors and events which have never happened. I am subjected to the type of publicity I do not desire and do not seek."

Courting respectability, he instructed his press agents to push his trip to London in May 1970 to perform in Royal Festival Hall for the National Society for the Prevention of Cruelty to Children, headed by the queen's sister, Princess Margaret. His second performance benefited the Alexandra Rose Day Charity, sponsored by Princess Alexandra, the daughter of the late Duke of Kent. His publicists made a point of telling the press that Frank was not accepting a fee for either concert and was even paying for Count Basie's orchestra so all the proceeds could go to charity. Pictures of him being feted by royalty flashed across the wire services.

The U.S. ambassador to the Court of St. James, Walter H. Annenberg, and his wife, Lenore, sent formal invitations to an embassy party in his honor, where he was cheered by socialites and diplomats. Saluting the assembled lords and counts and dukes, Frank said, "Bless your distinguished little hearts."

He returned to California in time to take part in the gubernatorial race between Governor Ronald Reagan and Jesse Unruh, former speaker of the California Assembly and once described as the century's most important state legislator. Unruh, a disciple of Bobby Kennedy, had done nothing to help Hubert Humphrey in his race for the presidency in 1968, and now Frank was going to retaliate by announcing his support for Reagan.

"He [Unruh] hurt my man badly in Chicago," said Frank. "In fact, he hurt the whole Democratic Party. Humphrey didn't lose. His people lost for him. . . . If Reagan ran for president against Humphrey, I'd come out for Humphrey."

Ronald Reagan did not seem quite so "boring and stupid" to Frank as he once had. On July 9, 1970, Frank announced his support for the Republican incumbent, proving the wisdom of the old Sicilian adage: "The enemy of my enemy is my friend."

On the same day, Governor Reagan, railing against "welfare cheats," withdrew ten million dollars in aid for California's aged, blind, and disabled, which shocked Frank.

"Did he do that? Did he really do that?" he asked, stunned by the news. "Well, I suppose you don't withdraw your support for a candidate over one issue, but I'll look into it. And you can bet I'll speak to him about it."

Upon reading of Sinatra's defection, Democrats cringed. "I can't believe it," said former Governor Edmund "Pat" Brown. "Frank has always been a good Democrat and one of my strongest supporters. He knows the tragedy of the Reagan administration, and maybe we can get him to change his mind."

The Democratic National Committeeman dismissed the endorsement as "one of the most insignificant occurrences in the annals of California politics."

Joey Bishop said, "It's a shock."

"It figures," Peter Lawford said.

Steve Allen wrote an open letter to Frank, saying he could not understand how a lifelong liberal could suddenly begin supporting a conservative like Ronald Reagan, who in 1962 had said of America's blacks, "In their own country, they're eating each other for lunch." Allen listed the governor's reactionary positions on prison reform, medical care for the aged, farm labor, hunger, the generation gap, taxes, campus unrest, political integrity, antiwar demonstrators, education, consumer interests, capital punishment, and mental health, begging Frank to set aside his "Sicilian vengeance" and return to the Democratic fold.

"They say your hatred of Senator Bob Kennedy was so great—because he kept you away from the confidence of his brother, the president—that you have waited a long time to get revenge and would not even be denied by the senator's assassination. The word is, Frank, that all you can do now that Bobby is gone is 'get even' with his man, Jesse Unruh, and the Kennedy-McCarthy types who work for him," wrote Allen. "Only a few thousand people may read this letter, Frank. I offer you access to a few million if you'd like to visit my TV show and explain your position."

Frank did not respond, but he hastened to reassure the world of his political affiliation, saying, "I'm an Italian Democrat all the way. On that score, I could never change."

To prove his point, he said that he was supporting Edmund "Jerry" Brown, Jr., for secretary of state in California,

John Tunney, another California Democrat, for the senate against George Murphy, the MGM song-and-dance man, and Susan Marx, widow of Harpo Marx, who was running for the state assembly. He then urged all Democrats to campaign against Nixon.

"He's running the country into the ground," said Frank. "He scares me. I wouldn't be surprised if they dump him in 1972. Whatever the situation, the Democrats have got to get together and beat Nixon in 1972."

But he confounded party loyalists by endorsing Republican John Lindsay for mayor of New York City and contributing ten thousand dollars in New York to Republican Governor Nelson Rockefeller's reelection campaign. Yet he also gave $1,500 to New York Democratic Congressman Seymour Halpern, $500 to Kenny O'Donnell, JFK's appointments secretary who was running for governor of Massachusetts, and $500 to George Wallace, the segregationist governor of Alabama.

Unbeknownst to Frank, an IRS investigation was under way at Caesars Palace into the relationship between the entertainment industry and the Mafia. Frank was among the targets of IRS surveillance.

On Sunday, September 6, 1970, during the graveyard shift, the IRS undercover agent working in the cashier's cage in Caesars watched as one of Sinatra's entourage came to the window with a pile of black chips and walked away with some $7,500 in cash. The undercover agent had been watching Frank carefully for weeks, because Frank had vast sums of money in markers (IOUs to the hotel) that were not being deducted from his salary or paid back by winnings.

"About an hour later, the same guy comes back to the window with some more black chips and cashes them in," said the agent. "That's when we knew that Sinatra was using us for petty cash. Whatever he was winning off the marker, he was putting into his pocket, and whenever he ran out of money to bet, he just signed another marker for ten grand. . . . It was a way for him to get some easy money. . . . We were concerned about his paying his back markers . . . Sinatra told people that he didn't have to pay his markers. He said that when he performed at Caesars and then sat down to gamble, he attracted enough big money around him so that the casino made out and profited enough so that they didn't need to collect from him."

When the undercover agent got a call at around five A.M. from the blackjack pit saying that Frank had signed another marker, he called Sanford Waterman, the casino manager, who got dressed and came downstairs. After being told what was happening, the manager, who had been part owner of the Cal-Neva with Sinatra in 1963, stood quietly in a corner and waited for the man to approach the cage again. When he did, Waterman nodded, giving his approval to cash in Sinatra's chips, and then went to the blackjack pit to confront Frank.

"Sandy walked up to him and said, 'I want ten thousand dollars, in markers,' " recalled the agent.

" 'What's the matter? My money isn't good here?' said Frank.

" 'Yeah, your money is good as long as you've got money. You don't get chips until I see your cash.'

"That's when the trouble started and Frank called Waterman a kike and Sandy called him a son of a bitch guinea. They went back and forth like that in front of a big crowd of people, including three security guards, until Sandy whipped out his pistol and popped it between Sinatra's eyeballs. . . . Sinatra laughed and called him a crazy Hebe. . . . He said he'd never work at Caesars again and walked out. . . . Frank had carte blanche at Caesars—complete run of the casino— but it's getting heavy when you have built up so much in markers and maybe fifty percent of it is petty cash in your pocket. This must have been going on for a long period of time, because Waterman got pretty excited about it."

The next day District Attorney George Franklin said he was going to call Frank for "a little talk" to ask him about his ties to the Mafia.

"One remark he supposedly made to Waterman as he was going out the door was, 'The mob will take care of you,' " said Franklin. "I want to ask him about who owned the nightclubs where he sang in the early days, who started him on his way, and his friendships with the underworld."

Sheriff Ralph Lamb was outraged. "Waterman was booked [for pulling a gun]. If Sinatra comes back to town Tuesday, he's coming downtown to get a work card, and if he gives me any trouble, he's going to jail. I'm tired of him intimidating waiters, waitresses, and starting fires and throwing pies. He gets away with too much. He's through picking on little people in this town. Why the owners of the hotels put up with this is what I plan to find out."

The next day, the charge against Waterman was dropped.

"My reports indicated Waterman still had fingermarks on his throat where Sinatra grabbed him," said the district attorney. "There seems to be reasonable grounds for making the assumption that Sinatra was the aggressor all the way."

Immediately, Jim Mahoney, Frank's press agent, started phoning reporters.

"I think it ironic that a gun was pulled on Sinatra and when all is said and done, he appears to be the heavy," Mahoney said. "A man was accused of a crime, whether true or not. Frank kept quiet like a gentleman. So everybody's taking potshots at him. Frank isn't running for office. The guys in Las Vegas are."

The continuing international press coverage of the incident finally forced Frank two weeks later to defend himself.

"There was no such argument about credit or for how much I was going to play," he said. "As matter of fact, I just sat down at the blackjack table and hadn't even placed a bet, since the dealer was shuffling the cards. At that point Waterman came over and said to the dealer: 'Don't deal to this man.' I got up and said, 'Put your name on the marquee and I'll come to see what kind of business you do' and I walked away. . . . As for his injuries, I never touched him . . . and as for the remarks attributed to me relative to the mob, they're strictly out of a comic strip.

"If the public officials who seek newspaper exposure by harassing me and other entertainers don't get off my back, it is of little moment to me if I ever play Las Vegas again," he said.

He said he was through with the gambling capital. "I'll never set foot in the whole state of Nevada again," he said. "I have no intentions of going back—now or ever. I've suffered enough indignities."

When reporters asked him about the incident, Governor Ronald Reagan rallied to Frank's defense.

"Why don't you fellows ask me about the good things he's done, like Richmond, Indiana," he said, referring to the benefit Frank and Jerry Lewis had staged to educate the nine children of former police chief Don A. Mitrione, who had been kidnapped and slain in Uruguay by Tupamaro leftist guerrillas.

The next month, Frank began campaigning in earnest for Reagan, performing at fund-raisers in Los Angeles and San

Francisco, mesmerizing $125-a-plate audiences with the silky ballads and love songs he used to sing in Las Vegas. Reagan, obviously grateful for such support, jumped onstage to express his thanks.

"Most people believe that politics is a game of quid pro quo," he said. "But I want to assure you that following Frank's endorsement of me, it is only sheerest coincidence that there is going to be a freeway run right though the lobby of Caesars Palace."

29

Vice-President Spiro T. Agnew, who called a Nisei reporter a "fat Jap," and referred to Poles as "Polacks," was frequently greeted by placards that said: APOLOGIZE NOW, SPIRO. IT WILL SAVE TIME LATER.

Despite Agnew's racial slurs, Frank was his biggest supporter, especially when he took on *The New York Times* and *The Washington Post*, referring to them as "the eastern liberal establishment press."

He concurred with Agnew's opinion that "some newspapers dispose of their garbage by printing it."

He relished Agnew's sesquipedalian labeling of Democrats as "nattering nabobs of negativism," "pusillanimous pussyfooters," "vicars of vacillation," and "hopeless, hysterical hypochondriacs of history." Frank cheered him as he denounced "radical liberals" as "solons of sellout" and "pampered prodigies." Frank applauded his "politics of polarization" and hailed him for assailing the administration's critics as "an effete corps of impudent snobs who characterize themselves as intellectuals."

Frank agreed with Agnew about "the disease of our times" being an artificial and masochistic sophistication, and said that was what concerned him most about American life.

"It's the amorality," said Frank. "And so much restlessness. I guess we just got used to a way of life in my age bracket. Things are confusing a lot of Americans. Take the protestations, called for or uncalled for. I'm not against protestations, if they're for a cause. But I don't like rebellion without a cause. It's frightening."

He felt secure and comfortable with Agnew, who decried student protestors, antiwar demonstrators, flag burners, rioters, draft dodgers, narcotics, and the Students for a Democratic Society (SDS).

Vic Gold, Agnew's press secretary, commented on the shared politics of the two men. "After Frank and the Vice-President became friends, Shirley MacLaine, who was one of the radical liberals the Vice-President was talking about, was quoted as saying, 'I wonder what Frank Sinatra and Spiro Agnew talk about,' " he said. "Frank heard that and said, 'Tell her: We talk about you, dear. We talk about you.' "

"There was instant chemistry—personally and politically— between Sinatra and Agnew," said Peter Malatesta, special assistant to the Vice-President and a nephew of Bob Hope, "and because of that we started spending a lot of time with Frank in Palm Springs. He treated the Vice-President like royalty, even named the guest house he had built for JFK after him and filled 'Agnew House' with specially monogrammed matches and stationery.

"Life on the Sinatra compound was full of excitement and luxury. Every night was a party, with regulars that included the Ronald Reagans, Roz Russell and Freddie Brisson, Jimmy Van Heusen, the Milton Berles, the Bennett Cerfs, Dr. Michael DeBakey, Jilly Rizzo, and Barbara and Zeppo Marx. Of course, after Frank and Barbara started dating, we didn't see much of Zeppo, which kind of upset Mrs. Agnew, who saw Barbara slipping out one morning and realized that she had been sleeping over. Judy Agnew thought Zeppo was a great friend of Frank's and that was quite unsettling to her. I mentioned to him that the Veep's wife was a little undone by the Barbara business, but Frank just shrugged and said he couldn't let her go home at night because a coyote might get her!

"His setup in Palm Springs was perfect. There was enough security to satisfy the Secret Service and enough luxury to satisfy everybody else. Every bedroom had two bathrooms so that husbands didn't have to share with wives, and each had medicine cabinets perfectly stocked at all times. There were also 'his' and 'her' closets in the bedroom, each with a new pair of slippers and a bathrobe. The guest suites all had a hotline to the full-service kitchen on the compound, which provided twenty-four-hour service, and yet if you wanted privacy, you could use the Pullman kitchen in the bedroom that was fully stocked with food and liquor.

"Life with Frank was sweet, which is why the Vice-President made eighteen trips to Palm Springs in a year and a half. The Agnews spent Easter, Thanksgiving, and New Year's there, and after Frank's retirement, things really started to swing!"

Frank's March 1971 announcement of his retirement came after a year of dwindling record sales and miserable movie reviews. On his album of Rod McKuen songs *A Man Alone*, Frank had sung splendidly, but his recitation of McKuen's mawkish poetry might have contributed to the meager 63,500 copies sold, which compared poorly with his previous average of 150,000. When he listened to his voice on his next album, *Watertown*, even he was chagrined. Some critics felt it was too progressive for his traditional audience, but not enough so to attract the children of Woodstock. The album sold only 35,000 copies. *Sinatra & Company*, released in 1971, showed Frank trying to stay contemporary, attempting to adapt his very personal style to the shifting mores of music by singing some of the hits of John Denver and Peter, Paul and Mary. For the man widely described as the greatest popular singer of the twentieth century, the album sold poorly.

The box office returns on *Dirty Dingus Magee* were even more disappointing. Playing a frontier rascal in his fifty-fifth movie, Frank was crucified by the critics, who charged him with crude double entendres and witless burlesquing, suggesting that perhaps his time as a leading man had passed.

"What we're supposed to find so funny is merely disgusting," said the *Los Angeles Times*.

"Sinatra, who proved his acting abilities in such pictures as *From Here to Eternity* and *Man with the Golden Arm*, merely lends his presence here and not too much of that," said Arthur Knight in *Saturday Review*.

Describing the movie as a shabby piece of goods masquerading as a Western, Roger Ebert in the *Chicago Sun-Times* said Frank had not made a good movie since *The Manchurian Candidate* in 1962. He held him responsible for the failure of *Dirty Dingus Magee*, saying, "I lean toward blaming Sinatra, who's notorious for not really caring about his movies. If a shot doesn't work, he doesn't like to try it again; he might be late getting back to Vegas. What's more, the ideal Sinatra role requires him to be in no more than a fourth of the scenes, getting him lots of loot and top billing while his supporting cast does the work."

After the clash with Sanford Waterman at Caesars Palace, there was no Vegas to return to, for Frank had vowed never to set foot in Nevada again. At fifty-five, he enjoyed good health, except for persistent pain following surgery on his right hand for a condition known as Dupuytren's contracture, a shortening or distortion of muscular tissue in the palm, which made two of his fingers bend inward like claws.

"He isn't really sick or doddering or dying from an incurable ailment," said Nancy, Jr. "He's very much alive and well and kicking . . . but he says it's the end of an era, and he's right. His kind of show business era has ended. So he's going to take it easy and enjoy himself."

After publicly announcing his retirement in a letter printed by syndicated columnist Suzy (Aileen Mehle), his favorite reporter and occasional date, Frank carefully orchestrated his farewell performance for June 13, 1971, at the Motion Picture and Television Relief Fund benefit at the Los Angeles Music Center. He chose songs to represent periods in his life, and mirrored the moods of a generation that remembered the big band sounds of Tommy Dorsey and the swooning at the Paramount.

"Here's the way it started," he said, slipping into "All or Nothing at All," his first hit record after leaving Tommy Dorsey and going on his own.

"That was the beginning," he told the audience, which included Vice-President and Mrs. Agnew, Governor and Mrs. Reagan, and Presidential Advisor Henry Kissinger. He sang "I've Got You Under My Skin," and "I'll Never Smile Again," and "Nancy," and "Fly Me to the Moon," and "The Lady Is a Tramp," and "Ol' Man River." He sang with power, giving each lyric exquisite phrasing, each word melodic shading, and the audience came roaring to its feet four times to give him a standing ovation. Then he sang his signature song, "My Way," belting out the words so closely associated with his life. Then, with dramatic flourish, he announced that having built his career on saloon songs, he would end it the same way. The stagelights went dark, with only a pin spot picking out his profile in silhouette as he started singing "Angel Eyes." He lit a cigarette and let the smoke envelop him. As he sang the last line, he strolled offstage into the darkness, refusing to do an encore.

He had made fifty-five films, more than one hundred albums, and some two thousand recordings.

But Frank's announced retirement was not convincing to everyone.

"He'll be back with a whole series of comebacks," said Sammy Davis, Jr.

"No, no, he's serious," said Nancy Sinatra, Jr.

"I think he'll be back," said Bing Crosby.

"No way," said Frank. "After thirty-five years in show business, I think I've had it . . . I'm tired. I'm through and I'm not kidding. It's over."

His family shared the farewell performance with him: his mother, his first wife, Nancy, Nancy, Jr., with husband, Hugh Lambert, and Frank's youngest and most beautiful child, Tina, now twenty-three, with her fiancé, Robert Wagner (a relationship that Wagner ended in 1972).

Following the performance, Frank attended a party in his honor at the home of Rosalind Russell, then flew with the Agnews to Palm Springs.

"What a touching night that was," recalled Peter Malatesta. "The Vice-President and his wife went to bed while I sat up with Frank all night drinking Stolichnaya and listening to him talk about the old days and his tough childhood. He talked about politics and told me how crude Lyndon Johnson was, lying nude around the White House getting massages in the middle of the night. That was the night Frank told me he had worked for the CIA under Johnson. I was stunned when he said that, but I didn't ask any questions and he didn't offer any explanations."

Frank accompanied Agnew on *Air Force Two* on many of his official trips and became so enamored of political life in Washington, D.C., that he and Mickey Rudin leased a house on Embassy Row with Peter Malatesta, where they entertained frequently when they were in town. But the growing friendship between Agnew and Sinatra soon became a matter of controversy within the White House.

"We kept hearing that the Vice-President's association with Frank was politically damaging, but Agnew did not agree," said Agnew's press secretary, Vic Gold. "Paul Harvey

tore into him on the radio for befriending Frank, and William
Loeb, publisher of the Manchester *Union Leader* in New
Hampshire, wrote him a stinging letter about the relationship. Agnew responded, saying: 'Dear Bill, I appreciate your
comments, but I want to say that Frank Sinatra is a friend of
mine. He's been a good friend and never asked me for
anything. I found this strange criticism coming from someone
who has taken financial support from a convicted felon like
Jimmy Hoffa. Sincerely, Ted Agnew.' "

"Frank demonstrated the same kind of loyalty to Agnew
when President Nixon wanted to replace Agnew on the ticket
with former Texas governor John Connolly.

"Frank said he wanted to make Spiro president in 1976
and the only way to do it was to keep him on the ticket in
1972," said Malatesta, "so we started a huge write-in campaign about how great Agnew was, to make Nixon look
foolish if he dropped him. We denied knowing anything
about the write-in, of course, but we had it financed with
private contributions," Malatesta continued. "Then we staged
a big fund-raiser in Baltimore at the Lyric Theater. Bob Hope
[Malatesta's uncle] was the master of ceremonies. Frank got
everyone to perform, turned out a bunch of stars to attend,
and then came out of retirement to sing a tribute to Agnew to
the tune of 'The Lady Is a Tramp.' Frank's rendition was
'The Gentleman Is a Champ.' He had Pat Henry there and
Nelson Riddle's orchestra. It was quite an evening and it
kept Agnew on the ticket."

Standing outside the theater that night was a U.S. marshal
waiting to deliver a subpoena to Frank from the House Select
Committee on Crime, which was investigating the influence
of organized crime on sports and horse racing and wanted to
question Frank about his investment in Berkshire Downs in
Hancock, Massachusetts. A last-minute telephone call from
Senator John Tunney (D-Calif.) stopped the summons from
being served.

Having raised $160,000 for John Tunney's election cam-
paign the previous year, Frank was a valued constituent, and
when Mickey Rudin asked the senator to call the committee
chairman, he gladly did so, saying Frank would be perfectly
willing to come and tell everything he knew if the committee
would only "invite" him instead of issuing a formal subpoena.

The year before, on the occasion of Frank's retirement,

John Tunney had stood on the floor of the United States Senate to proclaim his constituent "the greatest entertainer the country has ever had." He was joined by other senators from both parties representing states where Sinatra's appearances had raised a lot of money: Alan Cranston of California, Howard Cannon of Nevada, Jacob Javits of New York, Charles Percy of Illinois, Hubert Humphrey of Minnesota.

"Senator Tunney didn't want us to embarrass Mr. Sinatra when he was here to sing for the Vice-President," said Claude Pepper (D-Fla), chairman of the House Select Committee on Crime. "He wanted us to accommodate him as much as possible and let Mr. Sinatra testify in closed executive session. I told him we wouldn't treat a celebrity any differently from any other witness."

Mickey Rudin flew to Washington to talk to the committee about keeping Frank from an open congressional hearing that would be covered by the press.

"He is psychotic about testifying before committees under oath," said the lawyer, who seemed unconcerned about his client's Mafia friendships. "Frank knows twenty of these guys."

"What do you mean 'these guys'?" asked Chris Nolde, a committee staffer. "Do you mean organized crime figures?"

"Yeah," said Rudin, who talked openly about Frank's friendship with Gaetano Lucchese, Sam Giancana, and Joe Fischetti.

Nevertheless, the committee agreed to extend an "invitation" to Frank rather than a subpoena, and scheduled his appearance for June 4, 1972. But Sinatra flew to England that day and refused to return to testify. Incensed by the rebuff, the committee issued a second subpoena and ordered federal marshals to stand at every port of entry in the country awaiting Frank's return. This brought calls from the Vice-President's staff, several congressional friends, and Harold Gibbons of the Teamsters Union. As a result, Congressman Pepper withdrew the second subpoena and issued Frank another "invitation" to appear on July 18 while promising to limit the questions to his holdings in the mob-infiltrated racetrack.

"The day before he was to testify," said Peter Malatesta, "Frank scheduled a meeting with Mickey Rudin, Vic Gold, and myself at the Madison Hotel in Washington to discuss the approach he should take before the committee. We talked for three hours and counseled him to be firm but docile and very, very low-keyed. He even made notes. Later, when he had dinner with Agnew, he was steaming over the press and kept saying, 'Why can't they ever tell the good side? They're just after me because my name ends in a vowel.' The next day, he went up to the hill and gave the committee hell, promptly forgetting everything we had told him to do."

As soon as he was sworn in, Frank started berating the congressmen for not immediately refuting the testimony of Joseph "The Baron" Barboza, a self-described syndicate enforcer who had said that Frank was a business front for Raymond S. Patriarca, head of the New England Mafia family. Waving a newspaper clipping at the committee, he read the headline: WITNESS LINKS SINATRA WITH REPUTED MAFIA FIGURE.

"That's charming, isn't it? That's charming," he said sarcastically. "That's all hearsay evidence, isn't it?"

The committee counsel, Joseph Phillips, acknowledged that it was.

"This bum went running off at the mouth, and I resent it," said Frank. "I won't have it. I am not a second-class citizen. Let's get that straightened out."

Asked to rebut the allegation that he had knowingly bought into a Mafia-controlled venture when he invested $55,000 in Berkshire Downs, Frank snapped at the counsel. "I don't have to refute it because there's no truth to it."

"Tell us about the first contact you had with anyone in relation to Berkshire Downs?"

"The first and only contact I had was with a man named Sal Rizzo."

"How did you know Mr. Rizzo?"

"I met him."

"How?"

"I can't remember where or how, but I met him and we got to talking about it and I liked his idea about the investment."

"What did he tell you about the investment that you liked?"

"I just liked the idea for five percent of the racetrack I might do well with it," said Frank.

"Well, could you tell us whether you were introduced to Mr. Rizzo by Mr. Lucchese?"

"I was not."

"Did you know Mr. Lucchese?"

"I met him."

"Could you tell me how well or how often you met Mr. Lucchese?"

"Once or twice, a long time ago."

"Could you tell us under what circumstances you met Mr. Lucchese?"

"I can't remember that."

Exasperated by the evasive answers, the counsel said, "Well, I am trying to learn, Mr. Sinatra, how it is that Mr. Rizzo could make such a favorable impression on you in such a short period of time." Frank didn't say.

Later, Charles Carson, the racetrack's comptroller, testified that Frank and Rizzo were childhood friends. He said that Rizzo told him: "I have known Sinatra since New Jersey. I was a neighbor of his and knew the whole family. Now that he is in the money, I can talk with him just like I talked with him before."

The committee tried to resolve the conflicting testimonies the next day when Salvatore Rizzo appeared, but Rizzo invoked the Fifth Amendment on thirty-four of the forty-six questions asked. He refused to say whether he knew Frank, for how long, whether he sold him Berkshire Downs stock, or had lived in Frank's old New Jersey neighborhood.

But Rizzo had testified in 1968 to the Florida State Beverage Commission about Frank's investment in Berkshire Downs, and that testimony was read into the House Crime Committee record:

Q: Did Frank Sinatra receive money in your track up there?

A: Yes.

Q: How long have you known Mr. Sinatra?

A: Fifteen or twenty years.

Commenting on the earlier testimony, the House committee counsel said, "It appears, Mr. Chairman, that either Mr. Sinatra's testimony before this committee was false, or the testimony of Mr. Rizzo before the Florida State Beverage Commission was false. In either case, one of the gentlemen has committed perjury."

New England Mafia boss Raymond Patriarca was brought before the committee from the Atlanta Federal Penitentiary, where he was serving ten years for murder conspiracy. Asked if he had ever met Frank, the mobster said, "I never met

Frank Sinatra personally. I seen him on television and at the moving pictures."

"Did you ever have any business dealings with him?"

"No, sir."

"Did you ever purchase any stock from him?"

"No, sir."

"Anybody on your behalf do it?"

"I claim my Fifth Amendment privilege."

"Do you have any knowledge that anyone associated with you had any business dealings with Sinatra?"

"I claim my Fifth Amendment privilege."

While Patriarca said he did no business with Frank directly, he would not deny that a front man did it for him, which left real questions about Sinatra's testimony. But the committee members seemed so chastened by Frank's outrage that they all but apologized for calling him to testify.

"You're still the chairman of the board," said Representative Charles Rangel (D-NY).

After ninety-five minutes, Frank swaggered out of the room, clearly the victor. He sent the committee an $18,750 bill for his expenses, which he said included chartering a jet at $1,200 an hour to fly back from Europe to testify. He was not reimbursed.

Still steaming about the indignity he had been subjected to, he commissioned New York journalist Pete Hamill to write an essay in his name for *The New York Times;* it was printed on the op-ed page on July 24, 1972. Frank upbraided the committee for invading his privacy, trying to besmirch his good name, and he accused members of seeking publicity at his expense during an election year.

The committee backed off and no further action was ever taken, prompting one congressional investigator to say with a sneer, "I call it the committee that *was* a crime!"

One of the first people to congratulate Frank on his performance before the House Select Committee on Crime was President Nixon, who exulted in the committee's public embarrassment. Frank was touched by the phone call, and despite his animus toward Nixon over the years, decided to support the President for reelection in 1972. He even contributed $53,000 to the cause.

His action stirred outrage among those close to him, especially his outspoken daughter, Tina, who said she was horrified by her father's support of the Republican Party. Mrs. Milton Rudin, the wife of Sinatra's lawyer, wrote him a letter expressing herself on the "monstrosity" of his actions.

"When Frank came out for Richard Nixon, I wrote him a letter and told him to take me off his Christmas list—no more big, fancy, showy presents—because with Nixon in office we were going to be in for hard times," she said. "I said we'd probably never even see Christmas, let alone have money to spend what with all Nixon was spending to bomb Vietnam and Cambodia. . . . I was disgusted with Frank and told him so. I told him what I thought of him for endorsing such a man. I signed the letter and sent it.

"His office called me three different times to make sure there wasn't some mistake. I said the only mistake was Frank's endorsement of Richard Nixon. Well, my husband must've gotten a call from Sinatra, because he came roaring home, screaming, 'How dare you? How dare you?' He wanted to throw something at me, and I knew then that my marriage was over. . . . Frank never spoke to me again, and no matter how many years go by, he will never forgive me. If I had a career to ruin, I'm sure he'd try to do it. He's a vengeful man that way. . . . I've known Frank a long time. He was a patient of my brother, who was a psychiatrist—Dr. Ralph Greenson. And that was in the early 1950s. That's how long I've known Frank Sinatra.

"Rudin's reaction was almost funny . . . but sad, too, because Frank is not a good friend to Mickey . . . even though Mickey has protected Sinatra, his family, and his children with his understanding and compassion.

"Sure, Frank sent him a very expensive Oriental desk when he was traveling in the Far East and thousands of dollars' worth of Dunhill fishing tackle for his new boat, but so what? He still treats him like dirt. . . . I remember when he called Rudin a foul name and they hung up on each other. . . . Mickey is Jewish and I am Jewish, and when people get mad they say things, and no matter how they try to retract them later, I still feel wounded. And Sinatra knows how to wound people. . . . When we were sitting down as a family to our Passover Seder, Frank called constantly and would not leave Mickey alone. Mickey said, 'Enough is enough. I'm getting out.' He wanted to get rid of him then, but he never did.

"I don't know if Frank is Mafia or not, but I do know that

he has been involved with some very unethical people. Mickey always left the house to find a pay phone to talk to Frank about certain things. When we got divorced, I found out that Mickey had put everything in my name, including Jilly's restaurant and Frank's house in Palm Springs. I had to sign about forty quit claims and that's when I decided to take back my maiden name so Mickey couldn't borrow against any of my property or use my name for whatever reason."

Despite Mrs. Rudin's objection, Frank stood staunchly behind the Nixon-Agnew ticket and even campaigned with the Vice-President, oblivious to the Watergate scandal swirling around the White House. He helped Agnew court the Jewish vote by making him part of the program when he received the Medallion of Valor of the State of Israel. On election night, Frank flew to Washington to be with the Agnews and help them celebrate when the Republican ticket carried forty-nine states.

Now Frank could look forward to four years of uninterrupted power and prestige as the best friend of the Vice-President of the United States. Despite his work for Kennedy in 1960 and for Humphrey in 1968, he had never flown on *Air Force One*, nor had he been invited to a White House state dinner or a weekend at Camp David. Now all that a grateful President and Vice-President could bestow would be his. They began by offering him the opportunity to stage another inaugural gala, but he declined, preferring to be viewed as a statesman. "He simply doesn't want to be treated as a performer anymore," said his publicist, Jim Mahoney. "He will be at the inaugural, but not to perform."

Frank flew to Washington in January 1973 with Barbara Marx, newly divorced, to throw a series of pre-inaugural parties with Peter Malatesta in the mansion they had leased on Embassy Row.

"Everyone came to those parties," said Peter Malatesta. "The Agnews, Henry Kissinger, Eva Gabor, Senator Barry Goldwater, Attorney General John Mitchell and his wife, Martha; astronauts including Alan Shepard, and all the ambassadors of Italy, Saudi Arabia, Tunisia, and Morocco," said Peter Malatesta. "The night before the inaugural, Louise Gore [Republican National Committeewoman from Maryland] was giving a bash for the Republican Finance Committee at the Jockey Club, so I told Frank he should really go. He wasn't sure he wanted to, but I told him it was the most important party of the weekend and that if he wanted to meet the cream of the Republican crop, he'd be there. So he went and, oh, God, what a disaster that was!"

Earlier in the evening, Frank had gone to the Kennedy Center to be master of ceremonies for the inaugural's American Music Concert. He wanted his comic, Pat Henry, to be part of the program as well, but the comedian had not been cleared beforehand and the Secret Service refused to let him participate. Frank protested, but the Secret Service remained firm, saying that without security clearance no one was allowed onstage to perform for the President. Refusing to emcee the evening without his comic, Frank stormed out, leaving Hugh O'Brian to fill in for him.

When he reached the Fairfax Hotel for Mrs. Gore's party, he had to cross a long line of photographers and reporters in the lobby. Among them was Maxine Cheshire, society columnist for *The Washington Post*. Frank had encountered her several months before, when he was getting out of Ronald Reagan's limousine at the dinner Agnew was giving for all the governors at the State Department. Frank had never forgotten her because she had approached him with the most embarrassing question he had ever been asked in the company of dignitaries.

"Mr. Sinatra, do you think that your alleged association with the Mafia will prove to be the same kind of embarrassment to Vice-President Agnew as it was to the Kennedy administration?"

"Nah, I don't worry about things like that," Frank had said with great aplomb. "I look at people as friends and that's all I worry about." He moved quickly to join Governor Reagan without a word of rebuke to Mrs. Cheshire, but her question rankled him for months.

Now as he saw her approaching Barbara Marx at the Fairfax Hotel, he exploded. "Get away from me, you scum," he shouted. "Go home and take a bath. Print that, Miss Cheshire. Get away from me. I don't want to talk to you. I'm getting out of here to get rid of your stench."

Turning to the people around him, he said, "You know Miss Cheshire, don't you? That stench you smell is coming from her." In full fury, he turned on her and screamed: "You're nothing but a two-dollar cunt. C-u-n-t. You know what that means, don't you? You've been laying down for two dollars all your life."

He reached into his pocket, pulled out two one-dollar bills, and stuffed them into the plastic glass Mrs. Cheshire was holding. "Here, baby, that's what you're used to." Grabbing Barbara he said, "Let's get the hell out of here."

"I couldn't believe it," said Malatesta, who was standing by Frank's side. "Here I was, all set to introduce him to the Republican hierarchy, and he's got to play Johnny Macho! I nearly died. As Frank and Barbara left, I ran to the bar for a few quick pops to get the nerve to go back home. When I walked in, Frank and Barbara were sitting in the living room in the two wing chairs, staring at the wall. No words. Nothing. Finally Frank said, 'I told you we shouldn't have gone.'

"He was so upset that he did not leave the house for two days, and he canceled his appearance at several inaugural events. The President was enraged when he heard what happened, and then the White House started getting on my back because Nixon had already asked Frank to appear at the state dinner for the president of Italy, and Haldeman [White House Chief of Staff] was now trying to get him to cancel because they didn't want to be tarred with the Maxine incident. He blamed Agnew for bringing Sinatra into GOP court circles to begin with, and wanted us to tell Frank he couldn't sing for Prime Minister and Mrs. Guilio Andreotti. There's no question that everyone in Washington was shocked by Sinatra's behavior, and every newspaper in the country was writing about it. I was a mess trying to figure out how to keep everything intact. Then Frank nearly blew everything sky high.

"He sent his driver out to every pharmacy in town to buy up hundreds of bottles of vaginal sprays and douches and wrote a note to Maxine saying she would know how to use those products and why. He asked me to have them delivered to her at *The Washington Post*, and I thought, Oh, God, not this on top of everything else. So I called Rudin and told him what had happened. Mickey told me to just say I did it, but not to do it. He said he had too many problems with him as it was and that he didn't need that one. So I didn't send them, although Frank thought I did."

The attack on Mrs. Cheshire seemed indefensible, even to Frank's closest friends, and Edward Bennett Williams, the attorney for *The Washington Post*, asked Mickey Rudin for "an acceptable apology," which was not forthcoming. Mrs. Cheshire threatened to sue for slander, if for no other reason than to force that apology.

"If he had attacked me as a reporter, I would have taken it, but he attacked me as a woman," she said. "I feel I owe it to my children to sue. I'm square enough that virtue means something to me. I take my reputation and the sanctity of my home very seriously."

In the end, she decided against a lawsuit, but Frank never apologized for his vulgar tirade against her. In fact, he laced into the press months later.

"I call them garbage collectors: the columnists without a conscience, the reporters who take long shots based on the idea that where there's smoke there's fire, all for the sake of a story," he said. "I'm blunt and honest. I could easily call them pimps and 'hos' [whores]. They'd sell their mother out. How dare they say what they do about me?"

As always, Frank's seventy-nine-year-old mother back in Palm Springs supported him. Dolly Sinatra listened to the graphic details of his performance in Washington without raising an eyebrow. Nor did she blanch when told that her son had called Mrs. Cheshire one of the vilest words in the English language. In fact, she bristled only when she heard about the two one-dollar bills he had stuffed into the reporter's glass.

"Hmmmpf," she snorted. "Frank overpaid."

Frank had won the Jean Hersholt Humanitarian Award in 1971, and had received the annual Screen Actors Guild Award in 1972 for his generosity "to persons whom he has never even met." A visiting Englishwoman who was forced by a New York cab driver to pay $237.70 for a thirty-dollar ride had received a check from Frank for $250 with a letter from his press agents: "Our client, who has always been royally treated by the English, was very upset about your experience with the taxi driver. He has asked us to send you this check to make up for the money you lost and he sincerely hopes the rest of your trip will be a pleasant one."

When Mr. and Mrs. Sam Labeiko, an elderly immigrant couple, were to be evicted from their $46.80-a-month apartment on Manhattan's Lower East Side because they couldn't pay a ten-dollar rent increase, Frank provided them with a lawyer to fight their cause.

When Sharon Ehlers, a seventeen-year-old cerebral palsy victim, and her parents were stranded in New York City after a car thief stole their specially converted minibus, Frank dispatched his Gulfstream jet to fly them back to California. The girl, paralyzed since birth, could say only "mommy," "daddy," "yes," and "no," but her father expressed the family's gratitude. "Whoever would think that a fellow like Frank Sinatra would think of a fellow like me," he said.

When Judy Wyatt was a sophomore at a San Antonio school for the orthopedically handicapped and was to undergo a fourth operation on her paralyzed leg, Frank offered to pay her hospital bills. Told that the costs were covered by the crippled children's division of the Texas health department, he offered a one-thousand-dollar contribution to her doctor's charity of choice, and then gave her family a sizable check.

"We lived in a housing project at the time, but he made it possible for us to move to this house," said Mrs. Wyatt. "He has given us a completely different life."

When Emogene Slayden of West Frankfort, Illinois, who was born with no arms and only one leg, lost her welfare payments because of a technicality in the law, Frank sent her one thousand dollars so she could hire a housekeeper to cook and clean and help her get dressed. "I just wanted to run out and buy the biggest color television I could find and then I could say Frankie bought me a television, but I didn't dare," she said. "I needed the money to live."

When Bernice Mitchell of Desert Hot Springs, California, lost most of her welfare grant due to a cut by the California health department and could not afford to buy Christmas presents for her son, Frank personally delivered a red bicycle to her eleven-year-old boy, saying it was a gift from Santa Claus sent by way of Governor Reagan.

When Mario Victoria, an eight-year-old boy from El Monte, California, who was suffering from two malignant brain tumors, had to celebrate Christmas early because he would die before December, Frank sent him a check for five hundred dollars.

When Morgan Rowe, a ten-year-old boy from Gainesville, Florida, fell from a tractor into a spinning thrasher that mangled his arms and upper torso, Frank sent him a check for fifteen thousand dollars.

All of these spontaneous acts of generosity, accounts of which were published in newspapers around the world, contributed to Sinatra's international reputation as a humanitarian and helped to bring him innumerable honors. He won the March of Dimes Foundation's Man of the Year Award in 1973, followed by the Thomas A. Dooley Foundation's "Splendid American Award." He shared the latter tribute with his good friend Vice-President Agnew a few months after the inaugural, when both of them appeared at the organization's annual fund-raising dinner at the Plaza Hotel in New York.

"We chose Sinatra and Agnew because they reflect the true spirit of the 'ugly American,' " said Dr. Verne Chaney, president of the foundation that sponsors medical aid and health education in Southeast Asia. "They are people who reflect well the image of what this country stands for, the qualities that make people great—strength, integrity, courage, and forthrightness. No matter what Americans may think of them, these two men have a good image abroad. Besides, if we had chosen two Peace Corps volunteers, nobody would have paid to come."

The favorable press coverage of this event persuaded President Nixon to reinstate Frank as the featured performer at the White House state dinner on April 17 for the Italian prime minister and his wife. Frank gratefully came out of retirement for this occasion and was so excited by the invitation that he took all three of his children to Washington so they could hear the President of the United States praise him to the hilt: "Frank Sinatra is to American music what the Washington Monument is to Washington—he's the top.

"This house is honored to have a man whose parents were born in Italy but yet from humble beginnings went to the very top in entertainment," Nixon said.

The two hundred twenty guests in the East Room sat enraptured as Frank sang a medley of his classics, including "Moonlight in Vermont," "Fly Me to the Moon," "Ol' Man River," "I've Got the World on a String," "One for My Baby," "I've Got You Under My Skin," and "Try a Little Tenderness."

"When I was a small boy in New Jersey, I thought it was a great boot if I could get a glimpse of the mayor in a parade," Sinatra said. "Tonight, here with my President, the Italian prime minister, and their guests, it's quite a boot to me. I'm honored and I'm privileged to be here. Today, after the rehearsal, I looked at the paintings of President and Mrs. Washington and thought about the modest dignity of the presidency up through the years to now and our President. It makes me very proud of my country. I love my country. We all do. That's just it. I thank you, Mr. President, for inviting me here. It was wonderful to perform for the prime minister of my father's country." As a patriotic encore, Frank sang "The House I Live In," which brought Nixon jumping to his feet to lead the applause.

"Those of us who have had the privilege of being in this

room and who have heard many great performances know that once in a while there is a moment when there is magic in this room, when a singer is able to move us and capture us all, and Frank Sinatra has done that tonight, and we thank him," said the President.

"Lovely words, sir," said Frank, his eyes filling with tears. "See you very soon."

"July," said Nixon. "I've got to practice. I haven't played golf for a year."

Before Frank left that evening, the President took him aside and told him to seriously consider coming out of retirement. "After tonight, I'll have to think about it," said Frank.

The rapport between Sinatra and the White House gave rise to FBI allegations, later dismissed, that his endorsement of the Nixon-Agnew ticket and his fifty-thousand-dollar campaign contribution, plus an "unrecorded contribution" of $100,000 in cash, had paved the way for the prison release of his distant relative, Angelo "Gyp" DeCarlo, the underboss of New York's Mafia family. Having served only nineteen months of a twelve-year sentence for extortion, DeCarlo, who was described by prosecutors as "violent . . . homicidal . . . and a man who orders executions," had received a commutation from President Nixon on December 20, 1972. The official reason given had been that DeCarlo was suffering from terminal cancer, but weeks later the FBI had learned that "certain associates" of DeCarlo credited the release to Frank's intervention with the White House. Furthermore, *Newsweek* magazine reported that DeCarlo, though ailing, was "back at his rackets, boasting that his connections with Sinatra freed him."

After a two-month investigation, the Justice Department announced that although Frank's name had been mentioned frequently on wire-tapped conversations of DeCarlo from 1961 to 1965, there was no evidence that he used his influence with the President to get his Mafia relative released.

Senator Henry M. "Scoop" Jackson (D-Wash.) was not convinced. He charged that the pardon "bypassed normal procedures and safeguards." He said his Senate Permanent Investigations Subcommittee had turned up information that raised "serious and disturbing questions as to the reasons and manner in which Angelo DeCarlo was released from federal custody," but the mobster died in 1973 before the senator's investigation was completed, and none of the information was released.

* * *

At the time, Frank was working to keep his good friend Spiro Agnew out of prison. Involved in a criminal Maryland kickback scheme, the Vice-President was being investigated for bribery, extortion, and tax fraud. Records of his election campaigns had been subpoenaed to determine possible violation of criminal laws covering conspiracy.

"We were at Sinatra's house in Palm Springs when the news broke that Agnew had been taking cash payoffs since 1967 of at least $100,000," said Peter Malatesta. "We flew back to Washington right away with Mickey Rudin, whom Frank sent off to Baltimore to find out what was really going on. Rudin came back three days later saying that the Vice-President was dead-ass guilty. 'So is Marvin Mandel,' he said, 'but he has his ducks in a row better than Agnew.'

"I asked Mickey who he had talked to and he said, 'Some guys.' I asked what guys, and he put his fingers to his nose and squashed it, whatever that means. I was stunned.

"Vic Gold had joined us, and Rudin was outlining a plan of action, saying that he could put together a cartel of the five best criminal lawyers in the country to defend Agnew and no jury in America would convict him unanimously. He reasoned that if Agnew would fight a long court battle, some of the Watergate pressure would be taken off Nixon. 'After all,' Rudin said, 'a court case like this could drag on for years, and the man *is* innocent until proven guilty.' He said that no one would dare attempt to force Nixon out of office because then Agnew would automatically become president, even if he were still on trial. He felt that Agnew would never be impeached by Congress, so he said that the best thing for him to do is stay and fight."

"Mickey analyzed the Agnew situation brilliantly," said Vic Gold, "and he was not in the least surprised by the cash payoffs. He said, 'Let me tell you something about your man: He's very close with a dollar. Every time he opened his wallet and handed Peter money to get something, it was always a fresh bill. That told me something . . . that he did everything by cash. That went out in Al Capone's time. I tell all my clients not to do anything except by check or with a piece of paper.' Despite that, though, Rudin and Frank both wanted Agnew to fight back, and so did I."

The Vice-President tried to follow the advice by branding as "damned lies" the reports that he took cash kickbacks from Maryland contractors, but federal prosecutors had sworn statements from some of the men who made the payoffs.

"I am innocent of the charges," Agnew maintained. "I will not resign if indicted."

But by October 10, 1973, he had no other choice. He had to give up the vice-presidency if he wanted to avoid criminal prosecution. He resigned and then pleaded nolo contendere to one count of income tax evasion.

Frank felt heartsick. "As a citizen who loves America, and as a good friend of Mr. Agnew, this indeed is a sad day," he said. "Certainly, I offer whatever sympathy and support my friend may need. It takes great courage to pursue the route he has chosen. And I have every hope that in the months and years to come, his action will result in a greater public understanding of his feelings and position as the man in the arena."

Frank sprang into action for his beleaguered friend, whose net worth of $198,000 was disappearing rapidly. Without his yearly salary of $62,500 as vice-president, Agnew was forced to sell his house in Bethesda and liquidate his stocks to pay his legal fees. He also lost his substantial government pension. Facing a $147,500 bill from the state of Maryland, plus disbarment proceedings, the former vice-president was nearly destitute.

Frank sent Agnew $30,000 the day after he resigned to pay his $10,000 tax evasion fine and his family living expenses while he tried to find a job. He also lent him $200,000 to pay his back taxes, interest, and penalties, and then sent letters to his close friends, asking them to donate at least $3,000 each to help defray Agnew's legal bills. The figure was kept at $3,000 so the donor would not have to pay federal gift taxes, but the response was unenthusiastic. Most recipients pretended the letter got lost in the mail, but William J. Green, chairman of the Clevepak Corporation, and one of Frank's closest friends, openly refused to contribute, and said that Frank was putting too much pressure on their friendship by soliciting money for a man like Spiro Agnew.

Frank contacted W. Clement Stone, the Chicago insurance tycoon who thought up PMA (Positive Mental Attitude), and set up a meeting to discuss a possible defense fund that would pay the legal bills. The multimillionaire philanthropist agreed to help, but the fund raised only $40,000, barely covering the lawyers' retainer fee.

Frank contacted publishers to see how much they'd offer for Agnew's memoirs. He wanted at least $500,000 but was politely rebuffed.

"Mr. Sinatra called me as a friend, hypothetically, to ask me if we would be interested if Agnew were to write a book," said Thomas Guinzburg, then of Viking Press. "I told him it would depend entirely on what kind of book it was. If he [Agnew] came clean and said what happened and why it happened, it would be a valuable book. But I don't think the American public is ready to buy a defense that says 'I was just a good, honest, Greek boy minding my own business when a millionaire came along and said to me, "Here's $5,000 for grocery money, Ted." ' "

Frank received a lot of hate mail because of his unstinting support for Agnew.

"I was criticized because Agnew was a friend of mine, and I stayed a friend after he had his troubles," he said. "I don't know about walking away from people when they've got troubles. I never knew that side of life. His problems were up to the law, not me. I'm just a friend."

As Agnew was forced off the national stage, Frank bounded back on, announcing the end of his two years of retirement in the most expensive television special of 1973.

"I didn't realize how much I'd miss this business—the records, the movies, the saloons," he said. "So here I am for all the young people who wanted to know what I used to work like. . . ."

Backed by a fifty-four-piece orchestra with twenty violins that softened a ravished voice, Frank looked older and considerably heavier as he sang of how grateful he was to be back. His song told the audience that he couldn't say goodbye.

Despite the carefully orchestrated special, the ratings were poor and the reviews disappointing.

"Not much of the voice remains, but the showmanship of Frank Sinatra is still enough to carry an hour special," said *Variety*. Still, Frank was jubilant to be performing again and he followed his television special with the album, *Ol' Blue Eyes Is Back,* ignoring critics like the one from the *Toronto Globe and Mail,* who called him "a vocal has-been, ripping off those who care about his music rather than his personality."

Proud of the album, Frank played the master tape one night for a few friends, including Ed McMahon, Tom Malatesta, Peter's brother, and Vic Gold, who recalled McMahon's unsettling observation of his friend.

"When Sinatra walked into another room, Ed, who was sitting on the floor, said, 'Whenever I see Frank, I think of that poem, "Richard Cory," by Edwin Arlington Robinson. "So on we worked, and waited for the light, And went without the meat, and cursed the bread; And Richard Cory, one calm summer night, went home and put a bullet through his head." ' "

Weeks later, Frank stunned everyone by announcing his return to Caesars Palace. His mother, who had threatened to return to New Jersey if he ever went back to Las Vegas, was angry, until she learned that Sanford Waterman, who had pulled a gun on Frank in 1970, had been arrested for racketeering and was no longer at Caesars. George Franklin, the district attorney who had wanted to prosecute her son, had been defeated for reelection, and the sheriff, Ralph Lamb, now was ready to welcome him back to town.

With Caesars Palace under new management and willing to pay Frank $400,000 a week in addition to providing free bodyguards "to avoid any unpleasant incidents," Dolly Sinatra agreed to go back to Las Vegas for Frank's opening night, an event that sold out every hotel in town and packed 1,300 people into the casino's Circus Maximus showroom.

To mark the occasion, Caesars Palace presented each guest with a medallion that was inscribed: "Hail Sinatra, The Noblest Roman Has Returned," making January 25, 1974, an opening night unmatched in Las Vegas history, with an unprecedented number of stars in attendance, rounded up by the hotel's publicity staff. Everyone from Eddie Albert to Leslie Uggams showed up. The Sinatra family, including Nancy, Jr., and Hugh Lambert, and Tina with her husband, Wes Farrell (a marriage that was to last only eleven months), sat ringside with Dolly and Big Nancy. The only one missing was Frank, Jr., who pleaded a previous engagement.

Frank insisted the press coverage be limited to a select group of reporters and refused entry to *The Washington Post.*

Jim Mahoney explained: "It's nothing personal, but *The Washington Post* is not welcome wherever Frank Sinatra performs."

His obvious enthusiasm about being back before a live audience heightened the excitement of the evening and infused his performance with an electricity that brought the audience to its feet several times.

"I hope you're as pleased to see me as I am to see you out there," he said in his opening remarks. "When you get out of show business, it's a little dangerous because all of a sudden you're out of touch. . . . Also, it was a little tough to wake up and find out that Rodney Allen Rippey [the black child actor who became famous for a hamburger commercial on television] had replaced me. . . . I only saw him once. He was in an alley giving Sammy Davis some of his old clothes. . . . Sammy gave me this jacket—a present for the opening and I said, 'Gee, it's so soft. What's it made of?' He said, 'My Uncle Webb.' "

Frank gave his usual performance of exceptional vulgarity and exquisite taste, a swine one minute as he lashed out at female columnists, and particularly graceful the next as he sang his soft, sad ballads, playing the audience like a sweet harp. Applauding the old insouciance, Charles Champlin in the *Los Angeles Times* praised his astonishing gifts of phrasing, control, and feeling, which he said proved beyond doubt the still youthful tenderness of his voice. "The night was not an unmitigated triumph, though," Champlin wrote. "Midway along, Sinatra paused to sip a glass of wine . . . and revive his animosities towards the ladies of the press. . . . Whatever the distant provocations, the savagery of the attacks invited sympathy for his victims and put gall in a winy evening."

To trumpet his comeback, Frank launched an extensive ten-city concert tour, his first in six years, to benefit Variety Clubs International. Every performance sold out weeks in advance as he made his triumphant march across the country, leaving spellbound audiences in his wake. The only criticism arose when he stopped singing and started talking. Skewering the press, he criticized Edwin Newman of NBC-TV, sneered at Eric Sevareid of CBS-TV, and ridiculed Barbara Walters, calling her "the ugliest broad on television."

His most searing remarks were directed at Rona Barrett, who had recently published her autobiography. In it she wrote that she felt Frank, Jr., had staged his own kidnapping to get his father's attention. She also observed that anyone seeing Frank with his daughter, Nancy, "would quietly walk away with a funny, gnawing feeling: If they weren't father and daughter, they could certainly pass for lovers. . . ."

Frank's rage could not be contained: "Congress should give Rona Barrett's husband a medal just for waking up beside her and having to look at her. . . . She's so ugly that her mother had to tie a pork chop around her neck just to get the dog to play with her. . . . What can you say about her that hasn't already been said about—(pause)—leprosy. . . . I promise not to say anything about Rona Barrett tonight. I really mean that. A lot of my friends were upset about the fact that I was even bothering about her, so I'm not going to mention her name. I'm also not going to mention Benedict Arnold, Aaron Burr, Adolf Hitler, Bruno Hauptmann, or Ilse Koch—she's the other two-dollar broad—the one who made the lampshades."

The success of his U.S. tour led to a five-country tour through Europe, his first since 1962. But Frank canceled his appearance in West Germany because of what he called "scurrilous attacks" by its press, and then flew to London, where he lambasted the Germans from the British stage.

"What gives with these Germans anyway? I've done nothing to them," he said. "I could have answered and told reporters to 'look to the sins of your fathers.' I could have mentioned Dachau, the concentration camp. . . . I don't understand the German press. They call me a super-gangster. What's that? Al Capone? He wasn't one. It's ridiculous, who the hell needs it anyway?"

The British audiences gave him standing ovations, while the British press wrote rave reviews, but Prince Charles, the future king of England who had met Frank twice, said he was distressed by the "creeps" and "Mafia types" Sinatra surrounded himself with.

"He's a pretty strange person," said the prince. "He could be terribly nice one minute and . . . well, not so nice the next."

In France, they referred to Frank's bodyguards as "gorilles."

The tour ended with an international incident in Australia when Frank insulted the country's press corps. Darting past reporters in Melbourne, he spat at the reporters waiting to interview him before his rehearsal at Festival Hall. One newsman had managed to reach him by phone earlier in the morning to ask what he had eaten for breakfast and Frank slammed the phone down without responding.

"The idiot," Frank said. "What the hell does he care what I had for breakfast? I was about to tell him what I did after breakfast."

He refused to be interviewed after his rehearsal, and when he returned to his hotel and found more television cameramen waiting for him, he exploded, a signal for his bodyguards to fly into action.

According to one of the cameramen, one of Frank's bodyguards wrapped an electric cord around his throat and warned, "Things are going to get physical."

Reporter Hilary Sexton emerged from the fray with cuts on her face.

"Sinatra's goon squads blocked the way and then attacked the newsmen," said Jim Oram of the Sydney *Daily Mirror*.

That evening, Frank appeared at Melbourne's Festival Hall before a sold-out house of eight thousand people, who clapped, cheered, and stamped their feet with approval.

"Too much booze, too many smokes, too many long, long nights have taken the glow from his voice, but no one gave a damn," wrote the Sydney *Daily Mirror*. "For Sinatra still has the phrasing which cannot be surpassed, the timing, the splendid arrogance of remarkable talent."

During his "tea break," Frank sat on a stool to talk to the audience and castigated Australia's reporters.

"They are bums and parasites who have never done an honest day's work," he said of the men. "Most of them are a bunch of fags, anyway." He called the women "broads and buck-and-a-half hookers."

"Ladies and gentlemen, I'm a little tired tonight. I had to run all day because of the parasites who chased us. . . . They won't quit. They wonder why I won't talk to them. I wouldn't drink water with them, let alone talk to them. It's the scandal men that bug you and drive you crazy, and the hookers—the broads of the press are the hookers. I hope I don't have to explain to you the word *hooker*," he said, "but I'm not particular, I'd give them a dollar fifty. . . . We who have God-given talent say to hell with them. . . ."

The next day, the country was in an uproar. "Who the hell does this man Sinatra think he is?" demanded Neville Wran, leader of the Labor party in New South Wales.

A member of the National Parliament reproved Frank's "goon squads masquerading as security guards."

Jim North of the Australian Journalists Association said, "I will call on 114 affiliated unions and ask them to blackball Sinatra unless he apologizes for calling our women journalists whores."

The Stagehands Union refused to work, so Frank's $650,000 Australian concert tour was canceled.

The Waiters Union refused to serve him, so room service at his hotel was cut off.

The Transport Union workers refused to refuel his Gulfstream jet, blocking his departure until he said he was sorry.

Refusing to apologize to members of the press, Frank demanded that they apologize to him "for fifteen years of abuse I have taken from the world press." Then he retreated to his hotel while Mickey Rudin called the president of the Australian Labor Party, Robert Hawk, to ask whether the singer would be allowed to leave the country.

"If he can walk on water," said the labor leader. "There will be no boat and no plane leaving until your man apologizes."

With Jim Mahoney playing golf in Scotland—an absence that would cost the publicist his job a few weeks later—Rudin was forced to handle the press himself. He called a press conference to say that his client was regretful but unrepentant, and wanted him to investigate the possibility of taking legal action against the unions.

"I'd like to believe this is not Fascist Spain or Germany in Hitler's time," said Rudin. "We are astounded that the decisions of a few union leaders can apparently deprive a man of his living, can stop him leaving a country, or possibly even stop him being fed."

Rudin spent the next three hours negotiating with the Labor leader Hawk over a public statement that would satisfy the Australians while preserving Frank's pride. He said that the singer "accepts that working members of the Australian media would be doing less than their professional duty if they did not make every effort to keep the public informed about the visit of an international celebrity." The union leader recognized "the unique international stature of . . . Sinatra and his understandable desire to be protected therefore from an uninhibited exposure to the media."

The final result was a joint statement that without an

explicit apology said Frank "did not intend any general reflection upon the moral character of working members of the Australian media. . . ."

U.S. editorials cheered the Australians for forcing Frank to his knees.

"Americans by now are pretty well inured to the antics of their elderly, ill-mannered and foul-mouthed matinee idol, Frank Sinatra," said the *Washington Star*. "Australians, to their credit, are not. . . . [They] . . . have a refreshingly direct and forthright manner of handling such things, and we heartily applaud their actions in this case. If American unions—and audiences—showed the same resolution, we might spare ourselves a great deal of unnecessary unpleasantness."

"The Aussies, being the nice people they are, passed up their golden chance, which was to find a nice, slow freighter and send [Frank Sinatra] to sea with ample time to reflect on the ingratitude of people who refuse to accept wealth and fame as reason to excuse pigpen manners," said the New York *Daily News*. "They let him continue his tour and so he will come back to his homeland under his own momentum, where nearly everybody understands what an honor it is to be kicked in the groin by so famous and talented a man, and where bulky henchmen can help Frank impart the wisdom to any who may need persuading."

Bob Hope regaled audiences with his account of the episode: "They finally let Frank out of the country right after the head of the union down there woke up one morning and saw a kangaroo's head on the next pillow."

Back in the United States, at a nightclub engagement at Lake Tahoe, his first since the Cal-Neva days with Sam Giancana, Frank offered a mock apology to the prostitutes of the world for putting them in the same category with female journalists:

"I want to apologize to all the hookers, who are the Madonnas of the Evening, for comparing them to newswomen," he said. "Newswomen sell their souls. Who'd want their bodies?"

Proceeding to New York, where he performed on live television before a capacity audience at Madison Square Garden, he again spewed hateful venom at the press, but held himself in check until the commercial breaks.

"A funny thing happened in Australia," he said. "I made

a mistake and got off the plane. You think we've got trouble with one Rona Barrett, but they've got twenty in Australia and each one's uglier than the other. . . . Those nickel-and-dime garbage dealers make Rona Barrett look like a nun."

The audience screamed its approval, but the ratings were abominable. Frank's show, ballyhooed as "a once in a life-time event 'live' at Madison Square Garden," fell to number forty in the week's ratings, an indication that most of the country preferred watching *Kojak* and reruns of *Father Knows Best*. Even the critics were disparaging, especially Rex Reed, who said that Frank was sloppier than Porky Pig, with manners more appalling than a subway sandhog.

"All of which might be tolerable if he could still sing," wrote Reed. "But the saddest part, the hardest part to face about this once-great idol now living on former glory, is that Frank Sinatra has had it. His voice has been manhandled beyond recognition, bringing with its parched cloak only a painful memory of burned-out yesterdays. Frank Sinatra has become a bore."

Berating him for "spitting libelous insults at the female members of the press when he should be arrested," and telling offensive racial jokes "so old they were hairy," Reed scolded Sinatra for "making apathy and arrogance a lifestyle."

With that syndicated review, Rex Reed earned Frank's undying enmity, and his animosity scraped new depths. He had never forgiven the critic for once saying that Nancy, Jr., dressed like a pizza waitress, and Sinatra now unleashed his fury in attacks that were usually too crude to be printed.

Since his comeback, it seemed that Frank's strained relationship with the press had suffered even greater stress, as if he were blaming reporters and critics for the shortcomings of his aging voice.

He seemed to think that if he flung enough acid, journalists and critics would see the error of their ways and pay him homage the way they had done in earlier years. Nothing less than adulation would suffice. Criticism of any kind produced attacks that were unsparing in acrimony and, at their worst, alarmingly irrational.

He barred *Women's Wear Daily* from covering him after its critic savaged one of his performances: "The Voice is now the Void . . . a performance of self-destructive vulgarity. The ego-infested arrogance of a man who has made the sentiment of 'My Way' stand as his musical epitaph has totally surrendered any musical relevance by catering to the coarse and useless windbag within."

When an entertainment writer in Reno, Guy Richardson, expressed a lukewarm attitude toward Sinatra, he was flabbergasted to receive a telegram from Frank calling him a "bigot," and saying that he was "yellow from top to bottom." He was even more stunned when Frank warned Harrah's Club that he would walk off the stage if anyone from the Reno newspapers dared to attend one of his shows. When the publisher and editor of the *Reno Evening Gazette* and the *Nevada State Journal* appeared for one of his performances, they were barred.

In Toronto, Frank made the critics pay for their tickets to review him, an extremely rare thing for a performer to do. When one of his bodyguards punched a free-lance photographer from the *Toronto Star,* the newspaper wrote about it, causing Frank to roar onstage that evening, waving a copy of the paper, which described his "squad of menacing bodyguards."

"I have only two uses for newspapers—to cover the bottom of my parrot's cage and to train my dog on," he told his audience.

He was incensed at Mike Royko of the *Chicago Daily News* for writing about his "army of flunkies" and "full-time police guard" while in the Windy City. He called the Pulitzer Prize–winning columnist "a pimp because you are using people to make money just as [pimps do]."

So he used his concert series in Chicago to berate the columnist. "At least, we didn't invite Jerko or whatever his name is," he told one audience of six thousand. "Do you know he was our lookout at Pearl Harbor? I'd like to hire Chicago Stadium and box him for charity. We'll pay him a thousand dollars for every round he lasts. He won't make two dollars."

Violence had accompanied Frank for years, but most people were reluctant to fight back. One who did was Frank J. Weinstock. An insurance agent from Salt Lake City, he sued Sinatra for assault and battery, claiming that Frank had ordered him beaten up by Jilly Rizzo and Jerry "The Crusher" Arvenitas in a Palm Springs restaurant. In his complaint, he said he had been in the men's room of the Trinidad Hotel on May 5, 1973, when Frank entered with his bodyguards and said, "There's the wise ass and smart son of a bitch who's going to intercept my woman." Frank had been having dinner with Barbara Marx and others. Weinstock was in the restaurant with his wife and some relatives. His complaint described what happened next.

"You're kidding," said Weinstock. "You can't believe what you're saying. I don't know your woman. I've never seen her before in my life. I don't know what you're talking about. Look, Sinatra, aren't you the Sinatra I read about in books who can have all the girls he wants, a great well-known, notorious lover? Do you really mean you're afraid of me, a hick from Salt Lake City, Utah, bothering a man of your obvious prowess?"

"Have some respect for the boss," said one of Frank's henchmen. "Keep your hands down if you want to live, you know, you do what we tell you to do, you know. You put your hands up again and I'm going to bust every bone in your body. If you want to live, if you want to stay from getting killed, you'll keep your hands down."

"Look, you son of a bitch, the name is Frank or *Mister* Sinatra," said Frank, who then snapped his fingers to his entourage. "Okay, boys."

Weinstock said that minutes later, back in the cocktail lounge, he was rushed by several men and left with rib injuries, facial cuts, and bruises all over his body. Terrified, his sister ran up to Frank.

"Mr. Sinatra," she said. "You must have made a mistake. That's my brother. Please help him."

"Don't talk to me, baby," said Frank.

With that, he and his party left by the kitchen door. Weinstock summoned police and was taken to the station, where he was told by an officer that this kind of skirmish wasn't at all unusual for Frank on his home ground of Palm Springs. Weinstock later was told that one policeman wanted to arrest Sinatra that night but was stopped by his superior officers and later fired.

Unable to get the Palm Springs police to file charges, Weinstock decided to sue for $2,500,000 in damages.

Immediately after filing suit, Weinstock said he began getting anonymous phone calls threatening him, his wife, and his child. "I had a lot of those calls. Always from men saying I better back off and drop the charges or I'd be sorry," he said. "I hung up on them, but it was very frightening."

"My client only sustained minor injuries," said Marvin E. Lewis, Sr., the San Francisco attorney handling the case, "but it's time someone put a stop to Sinatra's bullying behavior."

To that end, Lewis planned to parade through the courtroom former victims of Frank's bodyguards, including Frederick Weisman, who had been badly clubbed in the Beverly Hills Polo Lounge in 1966, as well as Eddie Moran, the parking lot attendant who was beaten up in 1960. He planned to subpoena files from newspaper morgues to prove what he claimed was Frank's penchant for bullying. But the court ruled that such evidence was inadmissible. Lewis also planned to investigate Sinatra's finances so he could prove that his client deserved a multimillion-dollar judgment. Knowing Frank's influence in Palm Springs, Lewis filed suit in federal court in Los Angeles.

"I don't trust trying a case against Sinatra in Riverside County," Lewis said.

The trial started shortly after Frank returned from Australia, but he did not appear in the courtroom. Nevertheless, Marvin Lewis addressed the jury as if he were present.

"We're trying this case because a man has taken the law into his own hands," he said. "We're not going after him just because he has money, but the only way to punish a man of his wealth is through his pocketbook. What should we be suing him for? Bananas?"

Frank's attorney maintained that Weinstock was drunk and had approached Barbara Marx, offering to show her the way to the ladies' room, on the night in question. Jilly Rizzo admitted that he had hit Weinstock, but only after the businessman had supposedly called him "a guinea bastard." He denied that he was Frank's bodyguard.

"Sinatra don't need no protection," said Rizzo. "He's man enough to stand up and defend himself in his own way like any man should."

The trial lasted two weeks and the jury came back in favor of Frank and his sidekick, Jerry "The Crusher" Arvenitas, but awarded Weinstock $101,000 in damages in a judgment against Jilly. The judge overturned the jury's verdict and granted Rizzo a new trial. But both sides agreed to settle out of court.

"I felt that justice had not been done," said Marvin Lewis, "but I was glad that we at least had gotten a [jury] verdict against Jilly. That way they couldn't walk off and say that they had no responsibility. But I know it would have been a different story if I'd had the opportunity to cross-examine Frank Sinatra and have the jury see him under cross-examination. . . . I thought they would be so angry at him for not coming into court and not going on the stand to give his view of what had happened that it would work against him. I really believed that. Evidently, it didn't."

31

"If I had as many love affairs as you've given me credit for, I'd now be speaking to you from a jar in the Harvard Medical School," said Frank in a speech to Hollywood press agents. Yet this man, described by *Playboy* as "a bona fide sex idol with the stamp of his epoch on him," sang pleadingly for "one last caress" before "it's time to dress for fall," and women responded generously. Some, including Pamela Churchill Hayward, he would have married, but the British beauty had declined the offer shortly after the death of her husband, producer Leland Hayward, in March 1971. Six months later, she married Averell Harriman.

"Frank is very good to widows," said Joan Cohn Harvey. "I know, because after Harry died, he made a pass at me, but I wasn't interested. I didn't need the rush, and I told him so. Somehow I managed to say no nicely enough because I got roses the next day, and we remained friends."

Edie Goetz was not so fortunate. After her husband's death in 1969, Frank had courted her romantically, although she was several years his senior.

"Frank took such good care of me, and was so good for me after Billy died," she said. "We traveled everywhere together. He took me to Palm Springs and to New York for Arthur and Bubbles Hornblow's twenty-fifth anniversary party. . . . And, oh, the presents. . . . He bought me stereo speakers for the house, and one Christmas he gave me an embroidered bag—you couldn't see the embroidery under a magnifying glass it was so fine, and inside there was a solid gold box which was engraved: 'To Edie, With Much Love—Noel. Francis.' When he married Mia, he gave me a double Fabergé frame with his picture and hers. Later, he told me to take Mia's picture out and put two of him in, so that's what I did. . . . We had such a friendly love affair. . . . He called me 'sexy.' . . . It was gay and fun. . . ."

Then one night while they were sitting in the library of Edie's Holmby Hills mansion, Frank suggested turning their relationship into something more permanent. Edie, the daughter of Louis B. Mayer and one of Hollywood's most important hostesses, was horrified at the prospect.

"Why, Frank, I couldn't marry you," she said bluntly. "Why . . . why . . . you're nothing but a hoodlum. . . ."

Without saying a word, Frank left the house and never spoke to Edie Goetz again.

Other women, like Hope Lange, Lois Nettleton, and Victoria Principal, might have longed to become the next Mrs. Frank Sinatra, but they were simply pretty interludes along the way for Frank, who had sworn off marriage. "I've been married three times and that's enough," he said. "I'm *not* getting married again!"

"It was a happy time, his mellow period, after he'd retired and before he went back into show business," said Victoria Principal. "We were very discreet. Few people even knew about our relationship. But I will always treasure the memory of those happy months we had together."

It was during that retirement period that Frank had begun seeing Barbara Marx, who was still married to her second husband, Zeppo, the youngest of the Marx Brothers. She and Zeppo lived near Sinatra on the Tamarisk golf course in Palm Springs. An excellent tennis player, Barbara had been frequently invited to Frank's house as a doubles partner for Spiro Agnew.

"That's how the relationship started," recalled Peter Malatesta. "At first she just came over for tennis, but after a while she was there all the time."

Shortly before Barbara accompanied Frank to the Nixon-Agnew inaugural in 1973, she sued Zeppo for divorce. She was awarded $1,500 a month alimony for ten years, plus a

1969 Jaguar. Frank immediately replaced it with a brand new one.

Born October 16, 1930, in Glendale, California, Barbara Jane Blakeley had aspired to be a beauty queen and after high school had entered several local contests. She was crowned Belmont Shore Fiesta Queen in Long Beach in 1946. The next year, she was named Miss Scarlet Queen with the sole duty of christening a tuna boat of the same name. After her marriage to Robert Harrison Oliver, an executive with the Miss Universe pageant, she opened a modeling school. She served as a hostess for the Junior Chamber of Commerce and coached the beauty contestants, saying that a girl had to learn how to tuck in her fanny if she wanted to get anyplace. She warned contestants that the majorette strut would cause "posterior proliferation."

After divorcing her husband, she took her young son, Bobby, and moved to Las Vegas, where she became a showgirl at the Riviera Hotel. She also modeled for the California designer, Mr. Blackwell, who became famous for his annual list of the World's Ten Worst Dressed Women.

"Barbara is not a woman of humor, nor is she very intelligent, but she's beautiful, she's sweet, and she's incredibly patient," Blackwell said. "I started designing in 1956, and she was my number one model. She was always prepared when she walked down the runway, and in New York she spent her last buck to find the best pair of high heels to make my clothes look better. She knew I liked high heels, and so she wore them. She's very accommodating that way.

"We were very poor then and had to share a hotel room to save money. We used to spend hours together talking about our dreams for the future, and Barbara said she needed to marry a man of position. She was very ambitious. Not for a career, because she really didn't want to work, but she said she needed to marry a man of means. She loved jewelry.

"So we both set out to save her from the bar stools of Vegas. You see, during the shows, the dancing girls would sit on the stools and attract customers. They had to get acquainted with the big rollers, so to speak. That's how she met Zeppo, who was about twenty years older than she was and part of the Marx Brothers comedy team. He was an inveterate card player, but he was the most famous and important man she had met up to that point, and so she set her sights for him. I helped by borrowing jewels and mink coats for her to wear when she went out with him so that she would look good—like she didn't have to marry for money, you know what I mean? She desperately wanted to marry Zeppo because of the good life he could give her and her young son.

"After three years, Zeppo finally proposed and they were married in 1959. That got her into the Palm Springs Racquet Club and the Tamarisk Country Club, which was very important to her. She became good friends with Dinah Shore. Zeppo brought her into a new world of money and social prominence that she had never known before. He wasn't the classiest man in the world, I'll grant you that, but he was the best that Barbara could do for herself at the time . . . and he was a good launching pad to get Frank later on. . . . When Zeppo finally asked her to get married, she told me that there wouldn't be much cash available to her because he lived off a trust fund, but he promised that she could charge everything she wanted and live very comfortably."

"Barbara's life hasn't been a bed of roses," said Dinah Shore. "Her son, Bobby, has always been the most important thing in her life. It wasn't easy raising him alone in Vegas. She was determined that life run smoothly for Bobby, and it has. He's a wonderful young man."

The Marx marriage lasted thirteen years—until Barbara fell in love with Frank.

"Zeppo told me, 'She left me with a deck of cards and an old Sinatra album,' " said his nephew, Arthur Marx. "My dad [Groucho] was giving Zep one thousand dollars a month to live on before he died in 1979."

Everyone seemed to like the pretty, blue-eyed blonde who was uninhibited in her devotion to Frank, helping him with his parties, accompanying him on the golf course, traveling with him around the world. She got along as well with Rosalind Russell as she did with Jilly Rizzo.

"She's just perfect for him," said Phyllis Cerf Wagner. "If Frank feels like cooking an Italian dinner, that's what she feels like doing. If Frank feels like going out and going to a nightclub, that's what she feels like doing. If Frank feels like picking up and coming to New York or going to Europe or having her go with him to every performance and bring friends, that's what she feels like doing."

As bright and shiny as the California sun, Barbara looked like a blond Ava Gardner without the layers of sensuousness—

and without Ava's fiery temperament. Calm and reassuring, she was willing to let Frank shine alone in the spotlight while she stood by his side contentedly. She was more interested in setting up tennis games, playing gin rummy, and shopping with her girlfriends than in pursuing a career. Friendly and uncomplicated, she posed no threat to Frank, nor was she someone who would make him feel intellectually inferior. Like a California sunflower, she was pretty, cheerful, and hearty enough to survive his tempers and moods.

The only drawback to the relationship was Frank's mother, Dolly, who could not stand Barbara, and took every opportunity to tell her so. Mrs. Sinatra's maid, Celia Pickell, who worked for her for ten years, cringed every time the two women were in the same room together.

"Dolly would say just horrid things to Barbara, and there was nothing none of us could do to stop her," she said. "Dolly would say real loud, 'I don't want no whore coming into this family.' If she had to eat at the same table with Barbara, it was awful. She'd say horrible things, and Barbara would go running from the table in tears, but there was nothing Frank could do about it. He'd say something like, 'Aw, Mom,' but that was it. The first wife, Nancy, was very good to Mrs. Sinatra, but Dolly never liked her either. I remember when Dolly went to the hospital in Houston, Texas, and I went down there with her. Nancy, Sr., came to see her, and Dolly said, 'What did you come out here for? We don't need you.' Poor Nancy said, 'Why do you say those things? Your son sent me to help you.' But Dolly wouldn't be nice. 'Well, we don't need your help. So go.' Dolly spoke her mind about everything."

Despite his mother's objections, Frank continued seeing Barbara, though he sometimes subjected her to insults and abuse.

"In the south of France, he slapped her across the face for laughing at him, and she could not come out of her hotel room for two days," said Gratsiella Maiellano, girlfriend of Pat DiCicco, a good friend of Frank's. "It was in the lobby of the Hotel de Paris, and Frank told her to go to her room and shut up or else he would kill her. . . . We had been sitting at the pool looking at a Spanish magazine picture story of Frank, and I was translating it for everyone. He had been taken in by a girl reporter at the Marbella Club. She had fooled him and never said she was a newspaper girl. Frank took her to dinner and put his arm around her, and she sold those pictures to a magazine and wrote a story about him, how coarse he was, how sullen. She wrote that Frank was so ill-bred that he ordered a bottle of Château Lafite to be sent to the kitchen, not knowing that only the nouveau riche would do something that boorish. He was really pissed off when we started laughing. That's when he hit Barbara and made her go to the room."

Still, Barbara wanted to marry Frank and began pressing him to make their relationship permanent. He refused, and at the end of 1974 he ended the relationship.

"Frank had all sorts of problems deciding whether he really wanted to be married again—whether he *should* be married again," said Dinah Shore.

Barbara sought refuge with her best friend, Bea Korshak, wife of the Mafia's labor lawyer, and admitted the frustration of living with a man who refused to marry her. The Korshaks took her to dinner that evening at Gatsby's with Cyd Charisse and Tony Martin. Barbara confided that her on-again, off-again relationship with Frank was finally off—for good.

"This time, I'm through with that bastard," she said. "I've had it."

A few days later, a watered-down version of that conversation was reported in Joyce Haber's column in the *Los Angeles Times*, accompanied by a photograph of Barbara, who was incensed to see the story in print. That night, she carried on about the press in general and Miss Haber in particular until agent Swifty Lazar said, "If you don't want to be written about, you should have stayed married to Zeppo."

Frank had flown to New York City, where he was seen having dinner with a former girlfriend, Nancy Gunderson. When he returned to the West Coast, he saw the *Los Angeles Times* item and called Barbara for dinner, resuming their relationship. But she did not accompany him on his next trip to New York City, where Frank was to sing with Ella Fitzgerald and Count Basie at the Uris Theater, so he escorted Jacqueline Kennedy Onassis, who showed up for his opening night with Jilly Rizzo. Backstage later with the Peter Duchins, Jackie was starry-eyed. "I wish it were all starting again," she said breathlessly.

Jackie's feelings toward Frank had changed dramatically since the days when she was married to John F. Kennedy and wouldn't let Sinatra into the White House. The thaw had occurred during her marriage to Aristotle Onassis, when Frank invited the couple to attend his concert in Providence, Rhode Island. Jackie flew up with the Sinatra party and met Ari later at Jilly's for Chinese food. Shortly after Onassis's death, Jackie was lunching with attorney Edward Bennett Williams at the "21" club. Frank was there as well and wanted to extend his condolences, but hesitated to approach the table without their permission. He sent a waiter over with a note, asking if he might stop by when they finished eating.

No sooner had the pictures of Jackie and Frank taken at the Uris Theater hit the press than Barbara decided to fly to New York to join him, vowing never to leave his side. She accompanied him on his European concert tour in January 1976, and in Israel she wrote a wish on a piece of paper and although she's not Jewish, stuck it between the ancient stones of the Wailing Wall, begging God for a marriage proposal. By May 18, her prayers were answered with a seventeen-carat diamond engagement ring that cost Frank $360,000.

"Barbara is wearing a diamond engagement ring as big as Hoboken, New Jersey," wrote syndicated columnist Suzy, who broke the news.

"Yes, it's true," snapped Frank, "but it's nobody's goddamned business."

Unable to face his mother with her future daughter-in-law, Frank sent Mickey Rudin to break the news. Dolly reviled him, calling the lawyer a son of a bitch who was robbing her son blind.

"Oh, don't say those things, you hurt my feelings," said Rudin, trying to placate Dolly.

A few hours later, Frank went over to his mother's home, but before he could say hello, according to Celia Pickell, she started yelling at him.

"You fucking no good bastard, you were going to get married and not even tell me, weren't you?" she hollered.

"You know I can't tell you because you always give me hell, Mama," said Frank, looking like a frightened little boy.

"Then Barbara tried to be nice again, and she and Frank went out and bought some dresses for Dolly so she could pick one to wear to the wedding," recalled Celia Pickell. "Barbara brought them over, but Dolly wouldn't speak to her. She said she was going to keep all the dresses because that would mean less money to be spent on Barbara. She kept saying, 'I don't want no whore coming into this family,' but we'd tell her how nice Barbara was, and she finally gave in and resigned herself to the marriage, but she didn't like it one bit."

Everyone else wished Frank and Barbara well, including some of their former spouses.

"She'll make him a wonderful wife and hostess," said Zeppo Marx. "She plays golf well and tennis well. She's an all-around good girl. He'll never find anyone better, that's for sure."

Ava Gardner, who had relied on Frank for years, said, "I'm glad he has found happiness with Barbara. Even though we were divorced long ago, I've always counted on Frank to advise me in business affairs. He's always been so generous with his time and interest. I'm sure his new wife won't object if I continue to call on him in the future."

To throw off the press, Frank announced that he and Barbara would marry on October 10, 1976, at the Beverly Hills home of Kirk Douglas, all the while planning a secret July 11 ceremony at Sunnylands, the Walter Annenbergs' thousand-acre estate in Rancho Mirage, California. Not even the 120 guests knew for sure that they were invited to a wedding, but they suspected because their invitations for "an engagement party" were imprinted with "Pray Silence," one of Frank's favorite expressions, and called for neckties, which seemed extremely formal for the 115-degree weather.

A few close friends like Dinah Shore and Johnny Carson did not receive invitations because Frank was still fuming about their treatment of Spiro Agnew. Carson had refused to have the former vice-president on *The Tonight Show* to plug his book, and while Dinah had Agnew on her television show, she asked him a question that Frank found too probing. Because of that question, Frank barred her from the wedding, although Dinah was one of Barbara's closest friends.

The only invited guest who declined was Frank, Jr., who pleaded a singing engagement on the East Coast. As a wedding present, he sent his father a carton full of paperback sex manuals.

"What the hell is this supposed to mean?" Frank asked him.

"Well, fourth time. There must be something wrong," said Junior. "I figured maybe you needed some help."

Sworn to absolute secrecy about the wedding plans, Barbara was put to the test when Zeppo called her on July 10 to ask whether she and Frank were getting married the following day.

"Oh, no, dear," she said. "Frank and I aren't getting married until October tenth."

After Zeppo made another call and found out that the wedding was indeed set for the next day, he shook his head sadly.

"It really hurts me that she felt she had to lie to me," he told a reporter. "It must have been orders from Sinatra.

"Frank doesn't seem embarrassed that he stole my wife. We remain very friendly. And I've never said anything bad about him. I think Barbara and Frank will be very happy, and I believe she will fit into the Sinatra family. Now she is with someone younger—someone she really wants to be with. But I wouldn't dream of attending their wedding . . . not that I've been invited."

The next day at three P.M. armed guards stood outside the gates of the Annenbergs' estate to ensure that no reporters or photographers were admitted. Pacing up and down in front of the black marble fireplace in the Annenbergs' drawing room, the sixty-year-old bridegroom waited with Judge James H. Walsworth, while his forty-six-year-old bride changed into her wedding dress, a drifting beige chiffon by Halston. After a few minutes Frank became impatient. "Hurry up, Barbara," he said. "Everyone thought I would be the one who wouldn't show up."

Minutes later the beautiful blonde appeared on the arm of her father, Charles Blakeley, and stood alongside Frank, who was flanked by his best man, Freeman Gosden (Amos of *Amos 'n' Andy*), and Bea Korshak, the matron of honor, who was wearing the antique sapphire and diamond necklace that Barbara and Frank had given her the night before. Reading the civil wedding vows, Judge Walsworth asked Barbara: "Do you take this man for richer and for poorer?"

"Richer, richer," said Frank, causing everyone to burst into laughter.

"All she wants to do is make Frank happy. That's her goal," asserted Barbara's mother, Irene Blakeley. "And he wants her to have the best of everything."

After the ceremony, a champagne reception was held in the Annenbergs' marbled atrium decorated with bouquets of bouvardia, garlands of gardenias, and huge sprays of lilies of the valley. The bride cut a four-tiered wedding cake with a knife festooned with stephanotis. As she and Frank paused to make a wish, presidential contender Ronald Reagan piped up: "If you can't think of anything you want to ask for, I can make a suggestion." Everyone laughed.

Waiting outside for the guests, who included Spiro Agnew, Jimmy Van Heusen, Gregory Peck, Dr. Michael DeBakey, Leo Durocher, and Sidney Korshak, were air-conditioned buses to transport everyone a few blocks to the Sinatra compound for an elaborate seafood dinner and a view of the couple's wedding gifts to each other: hers was a $100,000 peacock blue Rolls-Royce with license plates reading BAS-I for Barbara and Sinatra; his from her was a $100,000 gray twelve-cylinder Jaguar.

The couple planned to honeymoon with three couples from New York—the Morton Downeys, the Bill Greens, the Paul Mannos—and set off the next day for Frank's mountain chalet in Idylwild, about fifty miles from his Palm Springs compound. Frank stayed up late drinking with Bill Green that night and didn't go to bed until four A.M., hours after Barbara was asleep. As he stood up to retire, he walked over to his friend, and cupped Green's face in his hands.

"Bill, sometimes I wish someone would really hurt you so I could kill them," he said. This was his way of telling his friend how much he cared for him.

Although she had been living with Frank for years, marriage opened up a whole new world to Barbara, who suddenly found new respect and attention as Mrs. Frank Sinatra. *Town and Country* wanted to photograph her; Charlotte Curtis, society editor of *The New York Times*, interviewed her; designers threw open their doors to her, knowing that Frank would shower her with clothes, jewelry, and furs.

"He's turned every single day into Christmas," said Barbara, who exulted in her new possessions. "It knocks me out. Maybe I appreciate it more because I didn't always have all this."

Frank gave his bride free rein to redecorate his Palm Springs compound. "Do what you want," he told her. "Do it exactly the way you want it, and then I want to see it."

With no financial restraints, Barbara started refurbishing. She commissioned a new master bedroom, new dressing rooms, new closets, and a new bathroom. She also ordered new furniture in soft shades of orange, Frank's favorite color, and jolted the salespeople at Kreiss in Los Angeles when she made a down payment on some dust ruffles and a few pieces of wicker.

"Mrs. Sinatra opened her purse and took out ten thousand dollars in cash that still had the Caesars Palace wrapper on it," said Bahman Rooin, a Kreiss salesman. "That was the way she made the down payment on her order."

Embracing her husband's life, Barbara followed Frank everywhere.

"I travel with him, that's really our life," she said. "We're really on the road most of the time, and a plane is almost our home or a hotel, or whatever. . . . So in order to try to make some kind of normalcy out of it, out of that crazy kind of life, I travel with him and try to make it as comfortable as possible."

Frank's opening nights in Las Vegas were always an exciting spectacle that brought the entire Sinatra family together, with Barbara sitting ringside for every performance. Dolly especially loved the neon lights and all-night glitter of these occasions, when movie stars like Kirk Douglas and Cary Grant flew from Hollywood to be in the audience to pay homage to her son. She also enjoyed the bawdy comedians of Las Vegas, especially Don Rickles. She laughed uproariously at his insulting humor, which was not unlike her own, but if she were traveling with Sister Consilia, she refused to let the nun attend the show with her.

"He's too off-color for you, Sister," she said.

The smiling, gray-haired Dolly would spend hours in the cavernous casino of Caesars Palace playing the slot machines. Whenever she ran out of money, she dispatched a courier to her son, who peeled off several hundred-dollar bills so she could continue feeding the one-armed bandits. She even had a slot machine at home that she had rigged. The eighty-two-year-old matriarch was catered to at the casino, where she knew all the pit bosses and dealers and bookmakers. She relished the attention they showered on her as Mama Sinatra. She accepted it as her due.

For her son's opening on Thursday, January 6, 1977, Dolly and her New Jersey houseguest, Anna Carbone, a doctor's widow from Cliffside, made plans to take a chartered Learjet from Palm Springs to Las Vegas. Dolly much preferred going on her own to being part of her daughter-in-law's entourage on an earlier flight.

At four P.M., the two women were picked up by one of

Frank's employees and driven to the airport, where they boarded the small, luxurious jet, which was stocked with a fruit basket, liquor, cookies, cheese, and crackers for the twenty-minute flight to Las Vegas. The pilot and co-pilot greeted them and radioed the control tower for permission to take off.

The tower radioed back that the pilot would have to wait twenty minutes because there was another plane in the vicinity flying at a higher altitude. At four fifty-five P.M., the twin-engine Learjet taxied down the runway and disappeared into low clouds. Instead of making a scheduled right turn toward Las Vegas, the plane inexplicably turned left and headed for the San Gorgonio Mountains, forty miles off course.

The pilot, who had flown this route many times before, knew that the mountain range was in his path, but he couldn't see it. At the altitude they were flying the precipitation that hit the ground as rain was a white swirl of blinding snow in the sky. He radioed the tower asking for permission to increase his altitude from nine thousand feet to seventeen thousand feet to escape the snow-capped monster looming ahead—the highest peak in southern California. The tower granted permission but retracted it. Flying at 375 miles an hour, the pilot begged the air traffic controller to change his mind—and fast—but it was too late. The response was garbled, and the blip representing the Learjet vanished from the radar screen as the plane slammed into the icy, unyielding 11,502-foot mountain. The impact was so powerful that the wings and tail were sheared from the fuselage. The sudden, violent deceleration hurled the crew, the passengers, and their luggage across the snowswept folds of the mountain, scattering limbs and shredded pieces of clothing in the trees.

The operators of the Learjet service, Jet Avia, Ltd., immediately contacted Sinatra's attorney, Milton Rudin, who flew from Los Angeles to Las Vegas to tell his most important client that his mother's plane had disappeared in a turbulent snowstorm. Shaken but bolstered by hope that she would survive, Frank decided to go on with his opening night show as if nothing had happened. Without alluding to the missing plane, the sixty-one-year-old entertainer sang so smoothly and joked so easily that his audience gave him a standing ovation.

When there was no word by midnight, Frank began to lose hope, and when the rescue efforts had to be called off because of snow and driving winds, he canceled the rest of his engagement and returned with his wife to Palm Springs to wait. Frank, Jr., joined him a few hours later, as did Jilly Rizzo and Mickey Rudin.

Early the next day, the weather had improved enough for Civil Air Patrol helicopters to circle the mountain ridge to search for some trace of wreckage, but there was nothing. Hope that Dolly might be alive all but faded, and the vigil in the Sinatra compound became a deathwatch.

The next morning, Frank was so tormented by the image of his mother buried alive under a freezing blanket of snow that he insisted on going up with one of the Air Patrol helicopter pilots, Don Landells, to search for her. Twisted with grief, he boarded the plane and sat in silence, straining to catch a glimpse of anything moving below. The pilot circled for hours, but there was no trace of the jet or of any of its passengers. All that could be seen was the rescue team in bright orange parkas slogging their way through the towering snowdrifts. The longer the helicopter hovered over the mountain, the more hopeless the situation looked. Finally, Frank signaled the pilot to return home. He called the San Bernadino sheriff from his compound to say that he did not want the rescue team to take any unnecessary risks while searching for the crash site.

The next morning, Sunday, January 10, Landells went up again and flew over the estimated site of the crash. This time, he noticed a bit of disturbed snow in a sparsely wooded area. Circling lower, he spotted Dolly's large muumuu dress hanging from a tree. He also saw the fuselage resting against a sharp cliff and bits and pieces of bodies strewn along the mountain ridge. After notifying authorities, he called the Sinatra house and told Mickey Rudin that there was no longer any hope.

Although Frank had expected to hear the worst, he could not quite accept the fact that his mother had not somehow managed to survive. She had been the most important person in his life, the one most responsible for his incredible success. It was her temperament that had shaped Frank and her ambitions that had fueled him.

He closeted himself with his grief. No one, not even his wife or children, could reach him. Months later, he said, "Her death was a shame, a blow. Especially because of the manner in which she died. She was a woman who flew maybe five times a year. I could understand if it happened to me."

Frank buried his mother with a requiem mass at St. Louis Roman Catholic Church in nearby Cathedral City, where she had prayed every Sunday; he laid her to rest alongside his father in Desert Memorial Park. Carrying the coffin were Jimmy Van Heusen, Dean Martin, Leo Durocher, Pat Henry, and Jilly Rizzo.

"My father was devastated by his mother's death," said Frank, Jr. "The days after were the worst I had known. He said nothing for hours at a time, and all of us who were nearby felt helpless to find any way to ease his agony. . . . Back at home after the terrible hour at graveside, I felt it best not to leave him alone. Sitting with him and watching the tears roll one by one down his face made me feel even more desolate than I had on the night the kidnappers dragged me out into the snow half-dressed."

"The death of Frank's mother was a trying and difficult time for Frank," said Barbara. "It's the only time I have seen him that sad."

"This was the first time Frank broke down in public," said his mother-in-law, Irene Blakeley.

Abashed by his public tears, Frank later was asked if he cried alone, and said, "Well, I don't do that. I haven't done that in a long time, except for recent grief, but pretty much alone. I would think so. It's a kind of a—it's a personal and an embarrassing moment, I think, particularly in a man, you know."

Frank turned to his long-neglected religion for reassurance, clinging to the Catholic priests who had been so much a part of his mother's life. Her death seemed to bring him painfully in touch with his own mortality, and, as if in atonement, he began inching his way back to the church. Soon he decided that he wanted to return to the sacraments and to remarry his Protestant wife of six months in front of a Catholic priest. To do that, though, she would have to take instruction, and he would have to obtain an annulment of his first marriage, which had taken place in Our Lady of Sorrows Church in Jersey City. There was no need to annul the marriages to Ava Gardner and Mia Farrow because those had not been performed in the Catholic church and therefore were not recognized as valid. Only the 1939 marriage to Nancy Barbato—the marriage that had produced his three children—counted in the eyes of the church. Consummation of a marriage no longer precluded an annulment. The revised Code of Canon Law would make it easy for him to dissolve that first marriage, and Barbara readily agreed to do whatever was necessary to qualify as a Catholic.

"Let me tell you that after his mother died, Frank became a totally committed Catholic, and Barbara then took instruction to convert," said Richard Condon. "I remember one evening we were having dinner at '21' in New York at a big round table, and I was with Barbara. Somehow we got to talking about her difficulty in understanding what the priest was teaching her about being in a state of grace. Now, I resigned from the Catholics when I was thirteen, but I still remembered the theory well, and we spent forty minutes at the table talking about a state of grace. I have no reason to believe in the month I spent in Spain with Frank [during the making of *The Pride and the Passion* in 1956] he was even a service Catholic—I mean the type who goes to mass every day or even on Sunday—but after his mother died, he became devotedly Catholic. Devotedly. Perhaps it was the apparition of death. . . ."

Frank's rush to Catholicism startled people who remembered him as virulently anti-Catholic, especially those who had attended the party given by Billy and Audrey Wilder in Malibu when Frank was married to Mia Farrow. He had spent most of the evening in a corner with model Anita Colby disparaging the church while she, a devout Catholic, smiled tolerantly. "Don't worry, Frank. We'll get you in the end. We'll get you in the end." He laughed at her. "He thought I meant we'd poke him in the bottom," she said many years later, "but what I really meant was that Catholicism is the toughest religion to live by but the greatest one to die by and that's when Frank would come back."

Frank had experienced what he regarded as the hypocrisy of the Catholic church in Hoboken, where the Italians had to go to St. Ann's in Little Italy and were not allowed to go to Our Lady of Grace with the uptown Irish and Germans. And that uptown church had barred him from hiring the orchestra for its Friday night dances because his mother had been convicted of performing abortions.

"He wasn't a churchgoer, and neither was I," said Nick Sevano, his childhood friend. "We observed the religion as descendants from Italian immigrants that were Catholic, but it was something that we just observed. There were other Italians more observing than us."

"His parents were devout Catholics and they worried about the consequences of his divorces, which in those days were considered anathema for a Catholic and synonymous with eternal damnation," said Thomas F. X. Smith, former mayor of Jersey City. "In the 1960s, St. Peter's College gave a dinner honoring the pope's encyclical 'Rerum Novarum,' and Richard Cardinal Cushing of Boston was the featured speaker. At a reception beforehand, Dolly and Marty, both in their sixties at the time, were dying to meet the cardinal, especially Dolly, who was overwhelmed by the prospect. I made the introduction, and Cardinal Cushing gave them a warm reception, but poor Dolly burst into tears because of the divorce business. The cardinal immediately put his arm around her and said, 'Now, where is that skinny son of yours? He came up to Boston a while back, raised a ton of money for a children's home, and then left before I could thank him for how well he's doing the Lord's work.' That was the best thing he could've possibly said to Dolly at the time, because she was so worried about the state of her son's soul."

Eager to please his mother, especially after his marriage to Barbara, Frank had listened to a mobster who had come up with the scam of promising him membership in the exalted Knights of Malta in exchange for ten thousand dollars and a few songs. Jimmy "The Weasel" Fratianno knew that Frank had been trying to be accepted by the oldest and most exclusive social order of chivalry in the world. The Maltese Cross, which is awarded for outstanding accomplishment and service to humanity, had been given to only seven hundred people in a thousand years, and Frank longed to be among the American knights approved by the Vatican, who included Lee Iacocca, president of Chrysler Corporation; Barron Hilton, president of the Hilton Hotel Corporation; Robert Abplanalp, the aerosol magnate; former New York mayor Robert Wagner; and J. Peter Grace, chairman and chief executive officer of W. R. Grace & Company. Thus, when the Mafia murderer proposed to induct Frank into what Fratianno called the Red Knights and said it was a division of the Catholic organization that did not require Vatican approval for induction, Sinatra leaped.

"I've been trying to get into the Knights of Malta for

fifteen years," he said. "My mother's a devout Catholic, and I know this would mean so much to her."

Fratianno then introduced him to a Hungarian "Knight of Malta" named Ivan Markovics. Mickey Rudin judged Markovics to be a con man preparing to rip Frank off with a fraudulent scheme, but Sinatra didn't listen to his lawyer. Blinded by the respectability he thought such an award would bring, he insisted on writing a check for ten thousand dollars, and promised to do a benefit for the Knights at the Westchester Premier Theater, an affair that would later prove to produce money for the mobsters behind the scenes. Days later, Fratianno called Rudin to say that Frank had been approved as a "Knight," and Frank ecstatically made arrangements to receive his scroll, medals, diplomatic passport, and flag at the house of his neighbor and friend, Tommy Marson, in Rancho Mirage. Fratianno had promised him that a prince of Italy and cardinals in scarlet silk robes would induct him into the sacred knighthood.

A few days later, Frank was summoned to Tommy Marson's house, where Ivan Markovics was decked out in a red silk robe with a white Maltese cross and gold medals hanging from silk ribbons around his neck. With great flourish, he presented Frank with a scroll embroidered with Latin words, a red silk box with gold medals, a red flag with the white Maltese cross, and a red passport with a Maltese cross. Afterward, he began telling Frank about the great investiture they planned for him. "As you know, I personally went to Rome and spoke with Prince Petrucci, accompanied by two cardinals from the Vatican. They will bring a special papal blessing for you and your mother."

Continuing the charade, Markovics said: "It looks quite promising that Prince Bernhard of Holland will also attend if we can arrange for his transportation. And there are many prominent members in the United States who would like to personally welcome you into the order on the day of your investiture if transportation can be arranged for them."

"That's no problem," said Sinatra. "I'll have a plane for them at LaGuardia and arrangements will be made for their stay at the Canyon here in Palm Springs. Can we do it in December?"

"We better think in terms of January or February . . . I've got to organize all these people, send out invitations. It all takes time, but believe me it will be worth it. It's going to be the most fantastic affair imaginable, something deserving of a man of your exalted station in life."

Sinatra smiled. "Well, well," he said. "Recognition at last."

Dolly's plane crashed before the investiture took place, so she never knew of her son's pseudo-knighthood or how the Mafia had duped him. Having paid ten thousand dollars for membership, Frank proudly flew his Knights of Malta flag from his Palm Springs home and gave Barbara the Maltese cross to wear when they entertained at benefits with Barron Hilton, who is a *real* Knight of Malta.

Determined to honor his mother's memory in the best way he could, Frank applied for an annulment of his marriage to Nancy Barbato. His decision so rocked the family that his daughter Nancy called a UPI reporter in Los Angeles in a rage, hoping the wire service would write a story about it. The children believed that the church dissolution would mark them as illegitimate in the eyes of society, though in fact an annulment does nothing to affect legitimacy or the laws of inheritance. Frank had to send a priest to convince his children that the dissolution of his marriage to their mother would not harm them in the least.

In 1977, when the Catholic bishops of the United States removed the penalty of excommunication from Catholics who divorce and remarry, it became far easier to have a marriage annulled. No longer is it necessary to apply to Rome, to hire a canon lawyer, to pay thousands of dollars to the Vatican. Nor is it required to have the consent of the marriage partner. Annulments can now be granted by the diocesan marriage tribunal after application by one spouse, and the process takes from six months to two years. Few are denied.

Frank received his annulment in 1978, but he did not announce it then or when Reverend Raymond Bluett married him and Barbara in Palm Springs. It was when he was photographed taking Holy Communion in St. Patrick's Cathedral in New York the following year that a rash of press stories appeared around the world.

"Did Frank Make the Vatican an Offer It Couldn't Refuse?" asked the *Los Angeles Herald Examiner*.

"Sinatra Stars in Storm over Catholic Divorces," said the London *Observer*.

The letters-to-the-editor columns reverberated for weeks

with outrage from readers who were unaware of the dramatic
new changes within the Catholic church and resented what
they thought was Frank's new standing. Reverend Edgar
Holden, O.F.M., wrote to the *Daily News*: "If Frank Sinatra
received Holy Communion . . . I'm happy for him. I'd also
presume he felt he had a right in conscience to do so. As for
his first marriage being annulled, that's none of my business,
or, for that matter, anyone else's."

Most readers disagreed. "The fact that Sinatra obtained
this annulment three marriages after a valid marriage many
years ago in the church to a Catholic lady who bore him three
children raises many questions in the eyes of Catholics and
non-Catholics alike," wrote one Joseph M. Kelly. "Did his
power and influence play a role in this unusual annulment?
To that extent, it is our business."

"The annulment was very embarrassing for Nancy, Sr.,"
said her close friend, Kitty Kallen. "She wishes she knew
more about it. She doesn't understand how [Frank got it] and
people are saying terrible things, that she got paid off, which
isn't true at all. I know that for a fact!"

"I think he did it for his mother," said Edie Goetz. "He
got that annulment to honor her memory."

32

Palm Springs, the lush desert oasis nestled at the base of the San Jacinto Mountains, is a citadel of organized crime. Nowhere in America is the Mafia's presence more blatant than in this resort, which is home to more than one hundred gangsters, including Anthony "Big Tuna" Accardo, Chicago's Mafia boss, who oversees his family's business interests in Las Vegas from his condominium a few miles from the Sinatra compound.

For years the sheriff's department kept track of organized crime figures and their friends and associates in the area. Heading the sheriff's list was the honorary mayor of Cathedral City, Francis Albert Sinatra, of 70588 Frank Sinatra Drive, Rancho Mirage. Also on the list were Chicago syndicate member John Lardino, identified in law enforcement intelligence files as a "former syndicate gunman who posed as a respectable union official"; Frank Calabrese, another Chicago hoodlum; Rene "The Painter" Piccarreto, a former lieutenant in the Rochester, New York mob, a man California investigators believe is an important conduit for laundering profits from New York rackets; Vincent Dominic Caci of the Buffalo Mafia family, who moved to Palm Springs after his release from prison.

The most prevalent criminal activity in the area is conspiracy, but according to prosecutors it is one of the most difficult crimes to prove.

"Some big hoodlums may put their heads together in the Coachella Valley and plan a crime," said Riverside County Sheriff Ben Clark, "but the actual crime they're planning won't occur here; it may happen in Chicago, Detroit, Kansas City, New York, or New Jersey."

In 1976, such a crime occurred in Tarrytown, New York. The mob built the Westchester Premier Theater, a seven-million-dollar, thirty-five-hundred-seat facility for live entertainment that went bankrupt within a year after the Mafia reaped millions by illicitly skimming profits. With shows featuring Frank Sinatra, Dean Martin, and Steve Lawrence and Eydie Gorme, the promoters packed the house. First-year revenues alone amounted to $5.3 million. Yet by December 1976 the Westchester Premier Theater was near bankruptcy. Only Frank's concerts in May 1977, for which he was paid $800,000, delayed the theater's closing.

Federal agents, who were investigating another matter, tapped the phone of Sinatra's friend Tommy Marson in Palm Springs and heard him talking to Gregory DePalma, who was linked to the Carlo Gambino crime family in New York and was running the Westchester theater. The two men discussed a plan "to siphon off money from an upcoming Frank Sinatra appearance at the Westchester theater in New York to keep [the money] from bankruptcy officials."

This conversation triggered a massive investigation into the theater's affairs. The result was the ten indictments handed down by a New York federal grand jury in June 1978, charging that racketeers defrauded the theater's investors, stole the assets by illegally skimming receipts, and threw the company into bankruptcy.

Throughout the investigation and trial, Frank's name dominated the headlines, beginning with reports that Mafia chieftain Carlo Gambino had helped finance the theater with a $100,000 investment on condition that Frank be signed up to perform. Before the proceedings were over, the federal prosecutor, Nathaniel H. Akerman, disclosed in court documents that an unnamed accomplice witness said that Frank had received $50,000 in cash "under the table" from one of the first two series of concerts. Frank was never charged.

On June 1, 1977, Gregory DePalma was talking to Salvadore Cannatella about a concession at the theater, the "T-shirt money."

DePalma said, "I took care of Louie out of that, Eliot, Ritchie, me, you, Mickey, Tom, and Jilly."

"Who Mickey?" said Cannatella.

"Mickey Rudin," said DePalma.

"Oh. He gets picked oh wha [sic] his—his cut from the thing right?"

"Yeah," said DePalma. "Well, I gave him my, er, I gave him five thousand dollars for the books." (The books referred to Frank Sinatra program books that were printed and sold by Sinatra's organization, not the theater.)

On April 15, 1977, William Marchiondo, a New Mexico lawyer, called Tommy Marson, asking for twenty tickets to the Sinatra show. Marson said this was a problem because he held back three hundred for each of New York's five (Mafia) families and Sinatra got five hundred tickets a night.

On May 7, 1977, DePalma and Louis Pacella discussed the T-shirts for the Sinatra–Dean Martin concert. They also discussed their difficulties in fending off Mickey Rudin's requests for additional seats. The government later claimed that Mickey Rudin's demand for these additional seats revealed his authority in handling the financial affairs of a Sinatra concert and might shed light on subsequent skimming and ticket scalping that led to the bankruptcy, but testimony concerning Rudin was ruled inadmissible.

Frank's first appearance at the Westchester Premier Theater was in April 1976, when he was moving from the soigné world of dinners with Governor Hugh Carey at "21" to meetings with "made" men at Sepret Tables, a Mafia restaurant on Third Avenue owned by Louis Pacella, also known as "The Dome" or "Louie Dones." Pacella, a capo in the organized crime family of "Funzy" Tieri, was identified by the Drug Enforcement Administration as dealing in heroin and cocaine. His lawyer said that he and Frank were "very, very, very close and dear friends . . . they were brothers, not because they share the same mother and father but because they shared love, admiration, and friendship for many, many years."

It was Louie Pacella who booked Frank into the Westchester Premier Theater in April and September 1976, and who persuaded him to come back in September 1977 for another performance, which would stave off bankruptcy proceedings for several months.

During his first engagement at the Westchester Premier

Theater, Frank posed for pictures with New York Mayor Abe Beame and then sang for an audience that included the Mafia hierarchy of Jimmy "The Weasel" Fratianno, Mike Rizzitello of Los Angeles, Tony Spilotro of Las Vegas, Russell Bufalino of Scranton, Pennsylvania, and several associates of Philadelphia boss Angelo Bruno. On April 10, 1976, he met Jackie Kennedy Onassis and the Peter Duchins at P. J. Clarke's in Manhattan after his evening show. The next night backstage in his dressing room, he put his arms around Greg DePalma and Tommy Marson and posed for a picture with Carlo Gambino, Jimmy Fratianno, Paul Castellano, Gambino's successor, Joseph Gambino, Carlo's nephew, and Ritchie "Nerves" Fusco. The prosecution introduced this photograph into the trial, which was reprinted in newspapers around the world. When Lee Solters, Frank's publicist since 1974, was asked to explain how the Mafia men managed to get so close to the singer, who was guarded at all times, he said, "I didn't hear a word you said." Pressed on the matter, he said, "I can't say anything."

The prosecution's major witness was Jimmy Fratianno, who cooperated with the government when he found out there was a Mafia contract on his life. He became the highest-ranking Cosa Nostra member to date to turn informer. Despite his record as an acting organized crime boss guilty of eleven gangland murders, the courts recognized him as an expert witness, and his testimony convicted more than twenty men since 1977.

Fratianno admitted to the Knights of Malta scam and claimed that after an informal induction ceremony in Palm Springs he took Frank aside and asked him for a favor. "Look, Frank, our [crime] family's in trouble," he said. "We've got people in jail and we've got to make some money, know what I mean?"

"Certainly," said Frank. "What can I do to help?"

"Number one, Frank, the Knights ain't got no money. The answer to both the Knights and our family could be solved if you did a benefit. Two days, four performances. I've talked to Greg DePalma, and you could do them at the Westchester Premier Theater. You know, add a couple of days to your next concert there. We've got a good working system over there. We're with the right people, you know. You understand what I mean, Frank?"

"Oh, absolutely," said Sinatra. "My pleasure, Jimmy.

Have Greg [DePalma] work out a schedule with Mickey.
Now, Jimmy, when you want to talk to me, work through
Mickey, he's my buffer. But if he bulls you, go to Jilly and
I'll straighten Mickey out. That way I don't have to [mess]
around with business deals."

Jimmy thanked Frank, saying, "The family will appreciate it, believe me, and if ever there's anything we can do for
you, just say the word and you've got it."

Fratianno claimed that the word came days later from Jilly
Rizzo, who said Frank wanted a Mafia contract on Andy
"Banjo" Celentano, a former bodyguard of Sinatra, who had
written a few articles for the *National Enquirer*.

"Now we hear this Banjo's writing a book about Frank,"
said Jilly, "and we want this stopped once and for all. Know
what I mean?"

"You want the guy clipped?"

"No, not right now. Just hurt this guy real bad. Break his
legs, put him in the hospital. Work him over real good, and
let's see if he gets the message."

"Where does he live?"

"That's the problem. I don't know. Burbank or Glendale,
but he ain't in the book. The best place to look for this guy's
at the racetracks. You can't miss him."

"Tell Frank we'll do it, but it might take some time,"
Jimmy said.

Unable to find the bodyguard, Fratianno said he soon
forgot about the request.

For the next three years of grand jury investigations,
indictments, and trials pertaining to the bankruptcy fraud of
the Westchester Premier Theater, Sinatra's name became
linked with the entangled Mafia scheme. Although never
charged with wrongdoing, Frank was later forced to explain
the grinning photograph of him taken backstage with the
lords of Cosa Nostra. Throughout the trial there were headlines like MOB HIT MAN IS TIED TO SINATRA (*New York Post*) and
HIT MAN SAYS HE HUDDLED WITH SINATRA (*Daily News*) and
POSSIBLE SINATRA TIE TO THEATER SCHEME IS STUDIED (*The New
York Times*) that kept his name entwined with corruption.
Rushing to his defense was columnist Pete Hamill, who
wrote in the *Daily News:* "This disgusting little cretiñ [Jimmy
Fratianno] has now been placed in a witness stand and put
under oath and asked to describe the inner workings of the

Mob. He spent all of his life lying and murdering, and we are supposed to believe what he says about Frank Sinatra. I'm sorry. But this is obscene."

On January 17, 1979, after a fourteen-week trial and seven days of deliberation, the jury was deadlocked, causing a mistrial.

In a separate trial, Frank's good friend Tommy Marson was convicted and sentenced to a year in prison and fined ten thousand dollars for his part in the bankruptcy fraud.

A new federal grand jury was impaneled to investigate allegations of criminal violations by certain people who were not defendants in the original case. It summoned Louis Pacella to testify. He was asked one question: "Do you know an individual by the name of Frank Sinatra?" He refused to answer. Offered immunity from prosecution, Pacella again refused to answer, was found guilty of contempt, and sent to jail for the duration of the jury's eighteen-month session.

Pacella appealed his sentence, and Assistant U.S. Attorney Nathaniel Akerman responded in April 1980 by filing papers in the U.S. Court of Appeals, charging that an unnamed witness knew that Frank Sinatra was involved "in the skimming of receipts at the theater." The prosecutor's papers stated: "The evidence developed at the trial of the Westchester Premier Theater case clearly provided several avenues of investigation . . . including the involvement of Frank Sinatra, Mickey Rudin, and Jilly Rizzo in skimming of receipts at the theater. Specifically, there was testimony that Jilly Rizzo, Sinatra's bodyguard and friend, received a portion of skimmed proceeds [from Sinatra's concerts] and there was tape-recorded evidence that showed that Mickey Rudin, Sinatra's manager and lawyer, also received five thousand dollars."

But no criminal charges were ever brought against Sinatra, Rudin, or Rizzo. Without the cooperation of Pacella, and without any additional evidence, the prosecutor was unable to prove the charges. As for Sinatra, he refused to comment on the federal inquiry as he wrapped himself in respectability, performing benefits for good causes at the bend of a knee.

Through marriage, the Sinatras had elevated themselves socially, so there were few traces left of the showgirl in a feathered headdress who danced her way across the Las Vegas stage, or the saloon singer with the grade school education. In their place stood a stunning wife bedecked with a queen's ransom in jewels and a husband hailed around the world as a humanitarian. Hand in hand, they chased the rainbow of respectability that had eluded Frank for so many years. While they were not embraced by the pedigreed elite, they were crowned by the rich and nouveau riche who go to nightclubs, winter in Palm Springs, and appear in Suzy's column.

As Mrs. Sinatra, Barbara began to do her part with charity work for the Desert Museum, the Desert Hospital, and the Sexually Abused Children Program in the Coachella Valley. She joined boards, volunteered her time, and contributed money, provided it was a considerable sum.

"We only deal in giving away millions," she said to a woman who requested a mere one thousand dollars.

Together, the Sinatras traveled to the south of France to attend galas for Princess Grace of Monaco and Baron Guy de Rothschild; they promoted and accompanied a caravan to the Holy Land for one hundred seventy people who paid twenty-five hundred dollars apiece; they sponsored charity balls for the World Mercy Fund, which ushered them into the lofty circles of Laurance Rockefeller and Barron Hilton. The world hailed them as Lord and Lady Bountiful.

In California, they waved to thousands as the grand marshals of the Rose Bowl Parade. In Philadelphia, Frank received the city's Freedom Medal while Barbara sparkled by his side. In New Jersey, he was hailed as a humanitarian for raising $600,000 for the Atlantic City Medical Center, and a wing was dedicated in his honor.

In New York, he helped raise one million dollars for Governor Hugh Carey's campaign expenses, and the governor immediately defended him to the press against charges of ties to organized crime.

"I have yet to see anyone lay any criticism against Frank Sinatra excepting he's very good to his friends," he said. "I admire and respect him, and I think it's a filthy assertion unworthy of comment."

In Denver, where Frank raised money for the Children's Diabetes Foundation, he was given the International Man of the Year award.

Italy presented him with its highest civilian honor—the *Grande Ufficiale Dell'Ordine Al Merito Della Republica Italiana*—calling him "a great and meritorious official of the Italian Republic."

In Egypt, he performed before the pyramids in a benefit

for President and Mrs. Anwar Sadat and received international press coverage for his generosity.

Caesars Palace staged a sixty-fourth birthday party for Frank, which also commemorated his fortieth anniversary in show business. The affair was videotaped by Sinatra's Bristol Productions and sold to NBC-TV for a two-hour show entitled *Sinatra—The First 40 Years*. In saluting Frank, Dionne Warwick presented him with a special Grammy from the recording industry; Jule Styne presented him with the Pied Piper Award from ASCAP; Caesars Palace announced that the fountain in front of the casino would be called the Frank Sinatra Fountain and the coins tossed in would go to the John Wayne Memorial Cancer Clinic at UCLA; the Egyptian ambassador read a message of congratulations from President Anwar Sadat; the Israeli Consul General read a similar one from Menachem Begin; and Dean Martin presented Frank with an honorary diploma from Hoboken High School to compensate for the one he never earned.

In Hollywood, the show was hailed as "the greatest event of the decade in the world of entertainment," but the East Coast wasn't so complimentary. The *Washington Star* published an editorial entitled "The King and His Court," which disparaged the spectacle and the "seemingly endless procession of sycophants who celebrated it for him, in a display of public groveling that would have embarrassed anyone except the gentleman in question, Mr. Frank Sinatra. . . .

"What was puzzling, as the festivities ground on and on, was the fear that seemed to quiver just beneath the gaiety. That wasn't love emanating from the TV set; it was obsequiousness. Some of the most celebrated men and women in entertainment marched across the stage—in Las Vegas, of course—in a parade of abjection. Has Mr. Sinatra really accumulated so much wealth and influence that he can reduce Orson Welles, once a great actor and film-maker, to a sycophantic blob?

"Even more puzzling than the groveling was all the blather about Mr. Sinatra's humanitarian enterprises. There were even emissaries from Israel and Egypt, in Camp David lockstep, on hand to present Mr. Sinatra with awards for his benevolence. Well, Mr. Sinatra's charities are rather like Mr. Rockefeller's dimes—good for the old blue-eyed image. They are not to be taken seriously by any except those who receive them."

Praising Frank as "the best singer of American popular music who ever walked down the pike," despite a voice "that may have lost much of its timbre," the *Washington Star* editorial expressed wonder and awe at his performance. "That such beautiful music should emerge from such vulgarity is one of the great mysteries of the age; but we must count our blessings, no matter how peculiar."

Then William Safire wrote a column in *The New York Times* about Frank's "lifelong gangland friendships." Having already called Safire "a goddamn liar," Frank now went on a rampage against all the press. He sent letters to President Jimmy Carter, to his Cabinet, to every member of the U.S. Senate and House of Representatives, every governor, to publishers, business leaders throughout the country, and deans of every journalism school in America, begging them to join him in a crusade to restrain the nation's "runaway press." He asked them to remind "the press that there is more to the Constitution of this great nation than the First Amendment it so frequently hides behind." Then he banned press coverage of him as the grand marshal in New York's Columbus Day parade.

Frank continued his association with Ronald Reagan, and campaigned for him in the 1980 presidential race. He sponsored the first major Reagan fund-raiser in the Northeast and raised more than $250,000 in Boston.

"Why do I support Governor Reagan? Because I think he's the proper man to be the president of the United States," said Frank. "It's so screwed up now, we need someone to straighten it out."

Appearing at a Reagan gala in Los Angeles and one in New Jersey with Raymond Donovan, he said, "I bring you regards from our President—the tooth fairy." He then assailed President Jimmy Carter. "Like Reagan, he was a movie star. Except then he worked under the name Mickey Mouse. He wants to be reelected. We should string him up."

Frank had used Reagan's name in 1980 as a character reference in applying for a Nevada gambling license as a "key employee." Frank's decision to apply for this license, which was not necessary for him as an entertainer, involved a full-scale investigation of his life. It would cost him $500,000, but he insisted that Caesars Palace submit the application so that he could cleanse his name once and for all.

"Mr. Sinatra wants to get his Nevada affairs in order," said Peter Echeverria, a member of the board of directors of Caesars Palace and the immediate past chairman of the Nevada Gaming Commission. "He wants to restore his reputation."

"It is very important to him," Mickey Rudin told the commission, saying that references to Sinatra over the years often mentioned that he had lost his gambling license because of entertaining Chicago Mafia boss Sam Giancana at Cal-Neva in 1963.

"Something happened sixteen and a half years ago that has left a shadow on his record," said the lawyer, who insisted that the commission consider Frank's case ahead of 200 other applicants who had been waiting more than a year for some kind of action, as well as 350 applicants for promotional licensing and 60 casino investors who needed approval.

Despite the bad publicity, the commission capitulated to Rudin's demand because he threatened to sue them to force compliance with the ninety-day limit on investigations. Ordinarily, applicants agreed to waive the ninety-day limitation, but Rudin wouldn't without some time control over the extent of the investigation into Frank's life. He knew that without some limitation they might spend two years investigating.

"He's one of the most investigated people in America," argued Rudin.

"It would be ludicrous to avoid calling him in," said Nevada Gaming Control Board Chairman Richard Bunker, who agreed to a time limit of nine months on the Sinatra investigation. He later declared that Frank's "worldwide prominence" made it "important" to act "as quickly as possible." He never explained why.

During those nine months, Frank burnished his image with good works and prestigious awards. His benefit for the Desert Hospital in Palm Springs raised $1.3 million. The district's grateful congressman, Jerry Lewis, addressed the House of Representatives and said Frank "as America's number one entertainer and philanthropist . . . has brought a song and a smile to the heart of a world that so needs a smile."

A week later, Sinatra's benefit for the University of Santa Clara raised $250,000, which the Catholic school announced would establish a Frank Sinatra chair in music and theater arts.

He hosted a benefit fund-raiser for Nazi-hunter Simon Wiesenthal and received the Humanitarian Award of the Year from Variety Clubs International. He was named national chairman for the Multiple Sclerosis Society's Hope Chest campaign. He volunteered to be the television spokesman for Chrysler for one dollar a year. He did a benefit at Carnegie Hall for the Police Athletic League and another in the Los Angeles Universal Amphitheater for St. Francis Medical Center. He performed for Danny Thomas's St. Jude Children's Research Center. He sang on the Jerry Lewis telethon for muscular dystrophy as well as for the Memorial Sloan-Kettering Cancer Center in New York.

By the end of the year his benefit performances had indebted to him politicians, educators, policemen, Catholics and Jews and Protestants, corporate America, the medical profession, and—on November 4, 1980—the fortieth president of the United States. Within days of his election Ronald Reagan showed his gratitude to the singer by naming him chairman of the inaugural gala.

"It's a big thrill," said Frank. "Somebody you love has made the big move. You don't say 'Hello, Ron' anymore. You say 'Hello, Mr. President.' . . . I promise I will try to make it the greatest gala in history—a night America and the world will remember."

The appointment drew worldwide coverage, setting off rumors that Reagan might appoint Sinatra U.S. ambassador to Italy—which drew scathing comment from Italian newspapers. Typical was that in *La Stampa*, the respected Turin daily: "Sinatra is welcome at any time for a singing engagement or to make a movie. But not in any other capacity. . . . If the American government thinks of Italy as the land of mandolins and La Cosa Nostra, then Sinatra would be the appropriate choice."

While Frank concentrated on the gala, Barbara Sinatra worked secretly with Jilly Rizzo to plan a party for her husband's sixty-fifth birthday on December 12, 1980.

"Please keep this under your Stetson, but I'm tossing a surprise birthday party for my blue-eyed cowboy," said the invitations she sent to more than one hundred people.

High on her list was William French Smith, named by Reagan to be attorney general. Months before, the Los Angeles lawyer had privately contacted the Nevada Gaming Con-

trol Board to assure them of Ronald Reagan's high opinion of
Frank, adding that he knew Frank only socially, not in a
business relationship, so he did not feel he could be a character reference. "However," said Smith, "Governor Reagan
finds him to be an honorable person who is extremely charitable and loyal."

The Smiths were delighted to receive their invitation
from Mrs. Sinatra, and flew to Palm Springs for the party at
which another guest was Sidney Korshak, the Los Angeles
labor lawyer linked to organized crime.

So the man scheduled to become the nation's highest law
enforcement officer shared a social evening with the Mafia's
lawyer at a party honoring a man with underworld connections. Puzzled, a reporter from *The Washington Post* called
Smith's office, where a spokesman said that the attorney
general–designate "had never met Korshak and wouldn't recognize him if he saw him on the street. . . . If he talked to
him [at the party], it was purely accidental."

William Safire of *The New York Times* was so revolted by
Smith's "rehabilitation of the reputation of a man obviously
proud to be close to notorious hoodlums" that he risked
Sinatra's wrath again in a column he wrote a few days later
saying the attorney general–designate had made "the first
deliberate affront to propriety of the Reagan administration."
Safire mentioned records in the Department of Justice that
contain "file after file on Sinatra's liaison with mobsters,
along with a vivid account of the first time the singer tried to
curry favor with a president-elect."

Years before, Safire had charged that Sinatra's introduction of Judith Campbell to Jack Kennedy and Sam Giancana
made "possible the first penetration of the White House by
organized crime." Now he wrote that Sinatra would be able
to use William French Smith's presence at his party to show
that he is respected by the law. "Let birthday-party goer
Smith review the FBI's Sinatra file. Then let him tell the
Senate to what extent he thinks it proper for a friend of
mobsters to profit from being a chum of the chief executive
and of the man who runs the Department of Justice."

Smith called the column "scurrilous" and "a cheap shot,"
saying through a spokesman that he was "totally unaware of
any allegations about Frank Sinatra's background."

The *Milwaukee Journal* found that reaction troubling. "Surely,
a lawyer chosen to be attorney general should understand

why his presence at the party was disturbing," said the newspaper's editorial.

During his confirmation hearings, the attorney general–designate surprised Senator William Proxmire (D-Wis.) by saying he was unaware of the FBI files mentioned in Safire's column that detailed Frank Sinatra's gangland associations. This made Smith sound either dumb or duplicitous.

"While I am aware of recent press reports setting forth such allegations," Smith told Proxmire, "I have never had access to any FBI files concerning any citizen. I have no basis for assuming that allegations reported in the press [about Sinatra] are true or false."

In a series of written questions, the senator asked: "When the Nevada Gaming Control Board checks Sinatra's reference by writing to President Reagan, how would you as attorney general suggest the president respond?"

Smith wrote, "As I am not familiar with all of the facts referenced by the question, I cannot say whether the matter is one on which it would be appropriate for the attorney general to render advice."

Senator Proxmire was annoyed. "Instead of telling us that he was not familiar with the facts, Mr. Smith's clear answer should have been that he had already been asked and made the response he made. [Smith's phone call for Reagan on behalf of Sinatra to the Nevada Gaming Board.] He was less than candid in his answer."

Casting the sole dissenting vote, Senator Proxmire voted against confirming the Los Angeles lawyer as attorney general.

Despite the controversy swirling around Frank, President Reagan remained loyal. This wasn't the first time that Sinatra's ties to organized crime had been brought to his attention. During the campaign, he had received a note from an outraged citizen about those gangland associations and had responded with a personal letter, saying: "I have known Frank Sinatra and Barbara Marx for a number of years; I'm aware of the incidents, highly publicized, quarrels with photographers, nightclub scrapes, etcetera and admit it is a life style I neither emulate nor approve. However, there is a less publicized side to Mr. Sinatra, which in simple justice must be recognized. It is a side he has worked very hard to keep hidden and unpublicized. I know of no one who has done more in the field of charity than Frank Sinatra. A few years ago a small town in the Midwest had suffered a terrible calamity; he went there on his own and staged a benefit to raise funds. All expenses were paid out of his pocket. He'd be very upset if he knew I'd told you these things. . . ."

The letter later sold at auction for $12,500, the highest price ever paid for a letter from a living person. The secret buyer? Frank Sinatra.

Days before the inauguration, the president-elect again was asked about Sinatra's involvement with gangsters. "We've heard those things about Frank for years," he said. "We just hope none of them are true."

Jubilant Republicans descended on Washington to stage the biggest and most expensive inaugural in history while the incumbent President from Plains, Georgia, tried frantically to negotiate for the release of the fifty-two Americans who had been held hostage in Iran by the followers of the Ayatollah Khomeni for 444 days after the seizure of the American embassy.

Columnist William F. Buckley, Jr., wrote that if the hostages were not released before Ronald Reagan took office on January 20, 1981, the new president should simply declare war on Iran. Frank Sinatra agreed, and immediately wired the editor of the *National Review:* DEAR BILL—BRAVO BRAVO BRAVO. IT IS THE MOST SENSIBLE SOLUTION I HAVE HEARD OR READ SINCE THE INCEPTION OF THE PROBLEM.

Wearing a Philadelphia Eagles warm-up jacket, a gift from owner Leonard Tose, Frank worked in an opulent gold-carpeted office in inaugural headquarters. Here he made his calls, persuading Johnny Carson to be master of ceremonies, and recruiting Bob Hope, Ethel Merman, Jimmy Stewart, Donnie and Marie Osmond, Charlton Heston, Robert Merrill, Mel Tillis, Debbie Boone, Charlie Pride, Ben Vereen, and the U.S. Naval Academy Glee Club. He called the line-up of performers "the greatest talents America could offer to any audience."

Intent on raising $5.5 million for the Reagan Inaugural Committee, Frank directed and produced a three-hour show for 20,000 people in the Capital Centre, which was edited for television. Before the show started, he took the spotlight in a $2,500 tuxedo to escort the Vice-President and his wife to their seats, and again to greet the Reagans, whom he had placed in thronelike chairs a few feet away from the stage.

He sang a lyrical revision of "Nancy with the Laughing

Face," retitled "Nancy with the Reagan Face." Turning to the President's wife, he said, "This is something special for our new first lady . . . I hope you like it, Nancy." Craning to read the lyrics from a card in his hand, he made love to the music: "I'm so proud that you're First Lady, Nancy, and so pleased that I'm sort of a chum/The next eight years will be fancy/as fancy as they come."

Nancy cried.

So did the critics. With the exception of Clive Barnes in the *New York Post*, who pronounced the Sinatra gala gay and grand, most were repelled by what they saw.

"It looked like a cross between Dial-A-Joke and *Hee Haw*," said Rex Reed in the New York *Daily News*. "I feel America is the greatest country in the world and the greatest talents in our country should have been up there proving it. Instead, we got a parade of jerks, clowns, and no-talent mediocrities that made you look forward to the brassiere and toilet-cleaner commercials. Except for the Metropolitan Opera's Grace Bumbry, the show had nothing to offer anyone with intelligence or a respect for quality."

"For a celebration and cross-section of American bad taste, it was not all-inclusive, but not for lack of trying," said Tom Shales in *The Washington Post*, dismissing the gala as "a tacky combination of a Hollywood awards show, a Kiwanis club talent contest, and a telethon stocked with fewer greats than near-greats and even more pure mediocrities."

Mike Royko of the *Chicago Sun-Times* was stunned by the performance of Ben Vereen, whose painted-on blackface and big white lips jolted 1981 sensibilities.

"For sophistication, it would be hard to top having a shuffling, grimacing, bulging-eyed black man in bum's clothing come out and do a minstrel routine in which he appeared to be brain-damaged," Royko wrote. "You just don't see that kind of sophisticated entertainment anymore—not since Stepin Fetchit died, and no other black actor came along who could so hilariously portray the dim-witted, gape-mouthed, obsequious black stereotype. It's possible that this performance offended some black viewers, but it probably made many of the rich Republicans in the audience yearn for the days when you could get good domestic help."

At the cocktail party before the show, Barbara Sinatra, wearing a black sequined flamenco dress, talked with her husband's lawyer, Mickey Rudin, and Albert "Cubby" Broccoli, producer of the James Bond movies, saying that she thought politicians and actors were alike. "They're both in a business under a lot of pressure," she said. "Politicians need actors to help raise money. And it's nice to be friends with somebody in office if there's a problem in your hometown, in case you need a stoplight."

The next day, wrapped in a new mink coat, Barbara, clutching her lawn ticket, took her designated place in front of the U.S. Capitol to watch the swearing-in ceremonies. Frank, enraged at being excluded from the chosen one hundred people given special passes by the Reagans, barged up the steps to take his place on the platform with members of the first family and select friends.

"Frank had not been invited to stand on the steps with the President and First Lady, but he bulldozed his way in anyway and took someone else's place," said a White House photographer. "He didn't have an authorized ticket, but he ballsed his way through, ramming past the Secret Service and the Capitol police. No one had the nerve to stop him. No one!"

33

From the beginning, Frank's gambling license seemed to be a sure thing, with the hearings in Las Vegas a mere formality. As early as December 8, 1980, Ned Day had written in the Las Vegas *Valley Times* that the license was "a lead-pipe cinch. You can tell by the pre-decision puffery which is starting to show up. . . ."

Variety had concurred on December 31, 1980: "Frank Sinatra's importance as adrenaline to the entire gambling industry here will probably offset disquieting allegations about ties to organized crime in his bid to become a key employee at Caesars Palace."

A week before the hearings, the *Los Angeles Times* headlined its story: SINATRA'S GAMING LICENSE SEEMS ASSURED. The *Las Vegas Sun* agreed: "It's absurd to think that [Frank Sinatra] wouldn't be licensed. It's naive to think that he shouldn't have special treatment."

"Approval is an eighty percent certainty," predicted George C. Swarts, former vice-chairman of the Nevada Gaming Commission. He pointed out that Las Vegas was losing too many gamblers to the new casinos in Atlantic City and needed Frank to bolster business. "When Sinatra's in town, the money's in town," he said.

Still, Mickey Rudin was not taking any chances. He wanted pictures of Frank and the Reagans in newspapers before the hearings and called the White House to ask why no photographs had been released of Sinatra with the President and First Lady. He was told that nothing could be released without the Reagans' approval.

"We had a lot of pictures with Frank, but Nancy had been so excited to see him that the veins on her neck stood out and she didn't want those photos released," said a White House photographer. "Rudin was quite upset about it."

The lawyer need not have worried. He had the assurance of Nevada's governor, Robert List, that things would be handled smoothly. In a secret meeting a few days before the hearings, the governor assured Frank that he would not be "kicked around or mutilated." When asked if it was not improper to meet secretly with a licensing applicant to give him that kind of assurance, the governor said he simply had wanted to reassure Frank that the hearings would not become "a three-ring circus."

Former Gaming Commissioner Clair Haycock criticized the governor for the secret meeting, saying that Frank did not deserve a Nevada gaming license. "From what's publicly known [about his ties to organized crime], I absolutely do not think he should be licensed," he said. The former district attorney, George Franklin, agreed. "The very most we have going for us in the state is the image of gambling control," he said. "If Sinatra, with his acknowledged background, can be approved for a license in Nevada, then even the image of control is destroyed. . . . It would sound the death knell for the gaming industry."

The governor took an active interest in the Sinatra case. Frank had raised more than five million dollars for athletic scholarships at the University of Nevada in Las Vegas and had been awarded an honorary doctorate in 1976 for "charitable endeavors."

When asked about Frank's friendship with the Chicago Mafia chief, Sam Giancana, chairman Richard Bunker had said, "I think it covers only one element of Mr. Sinatra's story. It has to be considered, along with all the things that have transpired since then."

But Bunker was apprehensive about the forthcoming publication of Aladena "Jimmy The Weasel" Fratianno's story, *The Last Mafioso*, by Ovid Demaris. He telephoned the author several times, asking to see the manuscript before publication, fearful that the Mafia informer would disclose damning material about Frank.

"If we gave Mr. Sinatra a license, would we be embarrassed when your book comes out?" he asked Demaris. "Are we going to be hurt by that book?"

Considering the licenses regularly granted unsavory characters, Demaris laughed. "How can one more hurt?" he asked.

Fratianno refused to cooperate with the board after Richard Bunker insulted the organized crime informer. So did Judith Campbell Exner, former girlfriend of President Kennedy and Sam Giancana. Having been introduced to both men by Frank Sinatra, she could have told investigators about their triangular relationship, but she refused because she felt that the hearings were a sham.

"What difference would it make?" she said later. "It was a foregone conclusion that Frank was going to get that license no matter what anybody said. They didn't want to believe how close he was to Sam."

The governor and Chairman Bunker had been apprised of the information turned up by five full-time investigators and three part-time assistants, who spent nine months looking into the allegations of Frank's links to organized crime. Not a law enforcement agency, the board was denied FBI cooperation, and so it lacked access to the surveillance reports, photographs and wiretaps that documented many of Frank's intimate associations with mobsters.

The Las Vegas Metropolitan Police Department also held back its investigative files from the board.

Without subpoena power, the Nevada Gaming investigators were unable to compel the interviews they needed to explore Frank's relationships to organized crime. They ended up getting a great deal of direction from Mickey Rudin, who arranged some of their interviews (Ava Gardner, Phyllis McGuire, Nancy Sinatra, Sr.) and discouraged others (Joe Fischetti and Mia Farrow). Because of these restrictions, the investigation was necessarily limited and could not possibly have been as far-reaching as promised. Relying primarily on newspaper stories, the agents traveled to Acapulco, to Miami, to Chicago, to Australia. They interviewed Miss Gardner in London, where she served them champagne and said how wonderful Frank was, without mentioning his close friendship with Sam Giancana, and the many times she had been with Frank and the Mafia chieftain in Las Vegas, Palm Springs,

New York, and New Jersey. In New Jersey, they discovered that Frank had lied on his license application by saying that he had never been arrested, but Mickey Rudin quickly took the blame, saying that Frank's 1938 arrest on a morals charge seemed so inconsequential that he didn't think it was worth mentioning.

While some of the agents worked on the personal investigation, others checked Frank's finances after he submitted a statement claiming a net worth of $14,107,137.29. In addition to $865,242.40 invested in publicly held companies, he listed $1,195,132.26 in his music companies* and the Budweiser (Anheuser-Busch, Inc.) distributorship he owned in Long Beach, California. His lawyer later testified under oath that the distributorship, a large company with thirty employees, grossed close to $30 million a year. Frank also listed $650,683.01 for other investments, including his trucking company, FAS Trucking, the aircraft hangar he owned in Palm Springs, a building in New York City, a wine distributorship, and a water well in Palm Springs.

His fixed assets totaled $4,591,431.33 for his houses in Rancho Mirage, Los Angeles, and Pinyon Crest. His New York property was in Mickey Rudin's name. Sinatra's other assets totalled $5,376,288.05 for cars, art, silver, china, office equipment, pension and profit sharing, and life insurance.†

A net worth of fourteen million dollars seemed extremely modest for a man who received about sixty thousand dollars a

*Sinatra listed the following privately held companies:

Somerset Distributors, Inc.	— $1,123,130.26
Artanis Productions, Inc.	— $10,000.00
Bristol Productions, Inc.	— $12,000.00
Sergeant Music Co.	— $1.00
Saloon Songs, Inc.	— $1.00
Frank & Nancy Music	— $14,000.00
Danny Stradella, Inc.	— $6,000.00
Affiliated Capital Corp.	— $30,000.00
Total	— $1,195,132.26

†In 1971, Frank sold his twelve-seat Grumman Gulfstream jet for three million dollars to Allen Dorfman's Chicago insurance company, a firm that the Chicago Crime Commission had listed as having syndicate connections. Dorfman, a good friend of Sinatra, had leased the luxurious jet, which bore the markings of 711-S (seven and eleven are a crapshooter's winning rolls; the "S" was for Sinatra), to the Teamsters Union Central States, Southeast, and Southwest Pension Fund for thirty thousand dollars a month. Dorfman paid Sinatra three million dollars for a used plane when a new one would have cost about the same amount.

month in royalties from Columbia Records, although he hadn't recorded for them in decades. Between 1953 and 1962, he had recorded at least twenty-five million dollars' worth for Capitol, and from 1961 to 1965, he recorded $14.4 million in albums and $1.5 million in singles for Reprise Records. He had earned one million dollars for each of his movies since 1963 as well as his television specials. He had sold his twenty-percent interest in Warner Bros.–Seven Arts to Kinney in 1969 for $22,500,000 in cash and convertible debentures. Mickey Rudin received $1.5 million for his services in negotiating the sale.

In 1970, Sinatra and Rudin had formed a company with Danny Schwartz (SSR Investment Co.) to buy 200,000 shares of National General Corporation (a giant conglomerate which included motion picture and book publishing subsidiaries), plus $2,200,000 principal value of NGC's four-percent debentures, which they sold in 1973 for about nineteen million dollars. In 1976, Sinatra had bought 420,000 shares of stock in Del Webb Corp., which owned four casinos in Nevada, for $2,139,294, and Mickey Rudin had bought 113,500 shares for $293,698. Together with Las Vegas publisher Hank Greenspun, the three men controlled eight percent of the company's common stock. They wanted the company to pay for the investigation necessary to license Frank—a matter of some $500,000—but when they saw Frank faced considerable political opposition to receiving a license, they sold their stock to Ramada Inns for ten million dollars.

Three years later, Frank still wanted to be licensed, so Caesars Palace agreed to submit his name for a "key employee" license, but the casino refused to pay the cost of the investigation. Frank assumed the burden himself and paid about $500,000 to have his background checked.

By 9:18 A.M. on February 11, 1981, the board was ready to take Sinatra's testimony in public hearing. He walked into city council chambers on East Stewart Avenue accompanied by his wife, his attorneys, his publicist, Jilly Rizzo, and his various character witnesses.. The first to testify was Peter Pitchess, the sheriff of Los Angeles County, who had given Frank a special deputy badge of the L.A. Police Department years before. Introducing himself as a "very good friend" of the applicant, the sheriff ended his testimony by stating: "If Mr. Sinatra is a member of the Mafia, then I am the godfather."

At the time Sheriff Pitchess made this remark, Ralph

Salerno, one of the county's leading experts on organized crime, was conducting a seminar in California for law enforcement officers. The next day Salerno addressed his class, many of whom worked for the sheriff: "When you see Pete Pitchess, tell him I say, 'Hello, Godfather!' " Six months later, Sinatra took Sheriff Pitchess and Mrs. Pitchess with him to South Africa.

The next character witness was an Episcopal priest, Father Herbert Ward, executive director of St. Jude's Ranch for Children in Las Vegas, who raved about Frank's generosity and the fact that he "gives glory to God." The priest was followed by the chancellor of the University of Nevada, for which Sinatra's benefits had raised more than five million dollars since 1974. He praised Frank's "many unheralded philanthropic endeavors."

Then came Hank Greenspun, who reminisced about the Cal-Neva incident in 1963, when Frank turned on Ed Olsen, chairman of the Nevada Gaming Board, for challenging him about having Sam Giancana on the premises. Mr. Greenspun revised history.

"It was nothing more than a shouting match [which] developed into a total character besmirchment, a hellish experience that this man has lived with for sixteen years," he said.

One of the star witnesses was Gregory Peck, who told the commission that Frank was a good citizen "who does more than anyone I know to serve his fellow man."

Kirk Douglas followed with an effusive recital of Frank's goodness and offered into testimony an article he had written for *The New York Times* which the paper had rejected. The article entitled "Virtue Is Not Photogenic" was filled with awe and admiration for Sinatra's generosity.

Sinatra's lawyer then addressed the commissioners, saying that under the Freedom of Information Act Frank had petitioned the government for all his files and had received "fourteen pounds" of FBI files and "another thirteen or so pounds" of IRS files, which he said he made available to the staff investigators. Dismissing most of the information as unsubstantiated and insignificant, the lawyer testified that the FBI was "out to get Mr. Sinatra" with "the net result [being] nothing." He read from an IRS report that said while "the taxpayer has openly consorted and traveled with Giancana, the evidence supporting a joint financial—financial or nominee interest between the taxpayer and Giancana is lacking."

In an affidavit, Bob Hope tried to put an acceptable face on the photograph of Frank with Carlo Gambino, saying that it was not fair "to draw conclusions about him from the fact that he may from time to time have been photographed with people who are not pillars of society." The comedian saluted Frank's "reputation for generosity" and said that because of his contributions to the entertainment industry in Nevada he should be given a gaming license.

The last witness called was Frank himself, who testified for almost an hour about his relationship with Sam Giancana.

Q: Did you ever discuss with Mr. Giancana the fact that you might be a front for him at the Cal-Neva or that he might have some type of a hidden interest there?

A: No, never.

The board did not have the FBI wiretaps that showed the December 1961 conversation between Giancana and Johnny Roselli in which they discussed the money Sam had put into Cal-Neva.

The chairman continued trying to ascertain how much Frank knew about Sam's presence on the property.

Q: There came a time in 1963, sometime between the nineteenth and twenty-seventh of July of that year, when Mr. Giancana was at the Cal-Neva Lodge. Did you have any prior knowledge or did you issue an invitation to Mr. Giancana to come to the lodge?

A: I never invited Mr. Giancana to come to the Cal-Neva Lodge. I never entertained him, and I never saw him.

Despite evidence to the contrary from an eyewitness, which was received by Ed Olsen in 1963 and is still in the Nevada Gaming Control Board's files, this lie went unchallenged. Even Phyllis McGuire had told the investigators that Frank had been on the premises when Giancana had visited her in July 1963, but when Frank denied it at this hearing, the commission said nothing.

Q: Do you recall going down to Miss [Phyllis] McGuire's bungalow and there walking into some type of an altercation with a gentleman and not an altercation that you were involved in, but seeing an altercation with a gentleman by the name of Collins?

A: How did I stay out of that one? No, I did not. I was not present. I was in Los Angeles when that happened. I got a phone call from one of my employees telling me there had been a problem.

The FBI agents who were following Giancana at the time knew of the fight between Sam and Phyllis McGuire's road manager, Victor LaCroix Collins, which Frank and George Jacobs broke up. Now, under oath, Frank was denying he took part in it. He got away with it because the FBI reports were unavailable to the commission's investigators, and Victor Collins was never contacted for his side of the story. Ed Olsen had a statement from Collins in 1963, but again no one bothered to present it as evidence at the hearing in 1981. When told of Sinatra's version of events, Victor Collins said, "He's lying under oath, but what do you expect?"

The chairman directed his next question to Mickey Rudin.

Q: When Miss McGuire was interviewed on January 27, 1981, she indicated to our investigators that it was her recollection that Mr. Giancana was there with her the first three to five days of her engagement, and that to her best recollection, she thought you were there at the same time. Now, you have certainly testified otherwise. Mr. Rudin, I wonder, are you in a position to have any recollection on that particular incident?

Rudin responded: "I would have to tell you it is my recollection that he was not there. I would also have to tell you that I don't have that much confidence in my recollection on the event. It may have been I have fixed my mind he wasn't there and that is now the story."

The chairman asked Frank if Giancana had ever been at Cal-Neva "while you were a licensee while he was included in the Book of Excluded Persons by the State of Nevada." Frank responded, "I haven't any knowledge of that."

The board apparently made no effort to interview any former employees of Cal-Neva who could have told them about Sinatra and Giancana playing golf together, the times they ate dinner together in the Cal-Neva dining room, the riotous parties they threw in the evenings in Miss McGuire's chalet.

Phyllis McGuire was enraged by Frank's dishonest testimony. "How could he say all those things?" she asked. "How could he deny his friendship with Sam? Frank adored the man, and then after his death Frank turned on him and denied their friendship just to get that damned license. . . . But Frank doesn't stand by his friends. Look at what he did to Jack Entratter, who had been his best friend for years. After Carl Cohen punched him out and Frank left the Sands,

Sinatra never spoke to Jack again. And Entratter lived next door to him in Palm Springs!"

Phyllis McGuire said that she had watched her career suffer as a result of loving Sam Giancana. Still, she had attended his funeral in 1975. Sinatra did not go to pay his last respects.

"That's the way Frank is," she said. "He cuts people out. I would hate to depend on that man's friendship. He would sooner help a rank stranger than come to the aid of a friend. He'll see a poor crippled man on the street corner and pay him to have surgery but turn his back on someone close to him [who is in trouble]. He'd give the prostitutes in Las Vegas five thousand dollars if they walked by, but he wouldn't be there for a friend in need. It just doesn't make sense.

"All the proof of Frank's friendship with Sam is in the FBI files. It's all there—the wiretaps and surveillance reports. Everything. I kept telling the gaming investigators who interviewed me to go to the Bureau's files. Why didn't they do it?"

The hearing continued:

Q: Mr. Sinatra, after purchasing the Cal-Neva, there came a time when you decided that you wanted to expand the facility there and enlarge the showroom, and you were out shopping for money and you had occasion to apply for some loans or at least a loan, is that true?

A: Well, Mr. Rudin, I think, can explain that a little better. We did apply for a loan but we were turned down.

The attorney said that he sent the loan application to the Teamsters Pension Fund in Chicago, which was the only institution other than a Nevada bank making loans for gaming in the state at that time.

Q: Did you and Mr. Sinatra at any time discuss this loan prior to applying or subsequent to applying and prior to their acting on it with Mr. Giancana?

Frank interrupted. "No, no," he said. The board did not have access to the FBI files on Sam Giancana, which contained wiretaps of the Mafia chieftain's complaints about being turned down for a similar loan believed to have been for expanding the Cal-Neva Lodge. ("There was a time when I could get all the money I wanted from the Hoffa union," Giancana said in a telephone conversation in 1963. "I got $1.75 million in just two days from the Central once [Central States Pension Fund]. Now all this heat comes on and I can't even get a favor out of him now. I can't do nothing for myself. Ten years ago I got all the fucking money I want from the guy and now they won't settle for anything.")

Q: Mr. Sinatra, while you were a licensee at the Cal-Neva Lodge, to your knowledge, was money ever illegally diverted by you or by any of your associates to Mr. Giancana?

A: No, sir.

Without the federal wiretaps that showed Paul "Skinny" D'Amato was the man the Mafia chief put at Cal-Neva to keep track of his investment and to collect his money, the board could not challenge Frank's statement to the contrary. Instead, the chairman took up the telephone conversation between Frank and Ed Olsen during which Sinatra used "vile and abusive language." Even seventeen and a half years later Frank resented being asked about it. Bristling, he said, "I wonder, sir, if there is a human alive who once in his life didn't lose his temper over a specific issue. If we are going to go on about this. . . ."

"If you want to ask for a show of hands here, we can do that," said the gaming board chairman soothingly.

"It was a four-minute conversation on the telephone, and we have now made it an international incident practically," said Frank.

Maintaining that the matter had to be explored, the chairman stated that Mr. Olsen, now deceased, was under the impression from his record that he was being threatened. "Was that your intention?" he asked.

"Not true, not true," said Frank. "It would be pretty absurd to threaten a man who is crippled, wouldn't you say so?"

"Well, I just am asking the questions."

"Wouldn't you say so?"

"Yes, it would appear to be."

"Fine," said Frank.

The chairman elected to take Sinatra's word for what happened instead of referring to the memorandum that Ed Olsen had written at the time of the incident, in which he quoted verbatim from his conversation with Frank: "Now, listen to me, Ed . . . Don't fuck with me . . . Just don't fuck with me, and you can tell that to your fucking board and that fucking commission too." Olsen also interviewed a witness who saw Frank break up the fight between Victor Collins and Giancana in the chalet. So he knew that Frank was not telling the truth when he said he was not on the premises. This was all part of the extensive oral history that Ed Olsen had given to the University of Nevada at Las Vegas before he died, but the Nevada Gaming Board agents did not make use of it in their investigation.

The chairman then asked Frank about his relationship with Willie Moretti, which Frank said was very vague in his mind. "He was a neighbor of mine when I bought a house in New Jersey, and the man from whom I bought the house, whose name I wish I could remember but I cannot, was a friend of Moretti's, or as I met him, Willie Moore. That is the man I met. He came over and visited my wife and daughter and myself and brought Willie Moore with him, introduced me to him."

Q: Did you know of Mr. Moore's background when he was introduced to you as Mr. Moore?

A: No. I never seen him before.

Q: Did he ever represent you as an agent in trying to book engagements or contracts through you at any time during that period of time?

A: Never.

Q: Was your career at that particular stage of your life ever a topic of discussion with Mr. Moretti, how he might be of some assistance to you?

A: Never.

Q: Did he ever introduce you to any nightclub owners who were booking entertainment at that particular time?

A: No, sir.

Yet on March 1, 1951, in his secret testimony to the Kefauver Committee, Sinatra had said, "Well, Moore, I mean Moretti, made some band dates for me when I first got started, but I have never had any business dealings with any of those men." Because the gaming investigators did not have a transcript of that testimony, they could not challenge Frank on his statements now.

Q: The allegation has been made, and I am sure you are not unfamiliar with it, that early in your career one of the reasons you progressed was due to the efforts of some members of organized crime. How would you respond to that allegation?

A: Simply. It is ridiculous.

Q: Did you at any time in those early years play night-clubs that, to your knowledge, were either owned or controlled by members or associates of what is called organized crime?

A: I could never prove that to you, never. . . . What I am trying to say, sir, there was always gossip as to who owned it or who ran it, but one would perjure oneself by saying, well, I am sure that so-and-so owned the club.

Asked about his relationship with Joe Fischetti, the cousin of Al Capone, Frank said that he was a very dear friend but that they had never had any type of business dealings. He said this unmindful of court papers in Florida that showed that Joe Fischetti was on retainer to the Fontainebleau Hotel in Miami and that for representing Frank there he received in excess of one thousand dollars a month.

Q: Did you have an occasion to travel with Mr. Fischetti at one time to Havana?

A: I happened to be on the same plane with him. I didn't travel with him.

Q: What was the purpose of your trip to Havana?

A: To find sunshine.

Q: And how long were you there?

A: About two days.

Q: Did Mr. Fischetti subsequent to your getting to Havana introduce you to Mr. Charles Luciano?

A: No, I was introduced to Mr. Luciano by a newspaperman named Nate Gross from Chicago.

Q: The allegation again is made that on that trip you conveyed by briefcase a sum of approximately two million dollars. How do you respond to that allegation?

A: If you can find me an attaché case that holds two million dollars, I will give you the two million dollars.

Q: Did you, subsequent to your meeting with Mr. Luciano in Havana, ever have occasion to meet Mr. Luciano again?

A: Never.

Q: You never came in contact with him?

A: Never.

Frank didn't mention the trip to Naples, Italy, with Hank Sanicola when the two men visited the crime lord, and the gold cigarette case Sinatra had had inscribed as a gift for Luciano.

Q: Could you offer any explanation as to why your name and address might have been in Mr. Luciano's possession when searched by Italian authorities?

A: I haven't the slightest idea.

Q: But your testimony is that save and except the time in Havana, you had had no contact at all with him?

A: I just met him in a bar and shook hands, as in many cases, and that was it.

The questioning turned to Frank's performance at the Villa Venice in a Chicago suburb in 1962. He was asked if he knew that Sam Giancana had a hidden interest in the ownership of the supper club.

"I don't know whether he had anything to do with the club and he never asked me to entertain there," said Frank. "An agent asked me to entertain there."

Neither Sinatra nor the commissioners seemed to be aware of the FBI wiretaps of Giancana's conversations about performing at the Villa Venice and Giancana's complaints about the demands Sinatra was making on him.

"That Frank, he wants more money, he wants this, he wants that, he wants more girls, he wants . . . I don't need that or him. I broke my ass when I was talking to him in New York," Giancana grumbled to an associate in the Armory Lounge on September 13, 1962.

Frank produced a contract showing that he had been paid fifteen thousand dollars for seven days of appearances at the Villa Venice, which was considerably short of the $100,000 a week he was making in Las Vegas at the time. Asked whether the $15,000 figure was commensurate with the other entertainers' Villa Venice contracts, an agent reported that it was and the board probed no further.

Q: Did you see Mr. Giancana while you were entertaining at the Villa Venice?

A: I might have.

Q: You don't recall?

A: No, but I might have. Just possible.

Giancana's daughter, Antoinette, was outraged by Frank's response.

"Just possible!" she said. "I couldn't believe my eyes when I read that any more than I could believe the other things that he said about my father. . . . We were at the Villa almost every night that Sinatra and his Rat Pack were there. Sam took us—friends, family members—to the dressing rooms of Sammy Davis, Jr. and Sinatra, which were upstairs. Sinatra and his group would be eating some bagels or some Italian food . . . [Frank] would give my father a hug, and so would Sammy Davis whenever Sam entered their rooms, and pictures were taken. Unfortunately, the photographs were confiscated by my sisters when my father died [in 1975], so I no longer have copies of pictures taken of Sinatra and Sam and me."

Miss Giancana was so upset by Frank's testimony that she called the Nevada Gaming Control Board to tell them what she knew and to show them the FBI documents that illustrated a much different relationship between her father and Frank than the one he attested to.

"The board people I talked with weren't very interested," she said. "They never bothered to come to see me to examine what documents I had."

The final matter covered in the hearings was Frank's involvement in the Westchester Premier Theater, but for this Mickey Rudin did most of the talking.

"Would you explain to us why Mr. Sinatra was not listed as a creditor in that bankruptcy when there was still money outstanding on that second contract?" asked the chairman.

Rudin said he didn't know why Frank was not listed. "From my standpoint, when they called me up and said they didn't want—they didn't want the embarrassment of listing the fact they hadn't paid Mr. Sinatra in full, I told them that was their problem and not mine because if they did not list the debt, it would not . . . be discharged by their being adjudicated bankrupt. The debt would survive against the entity if it ever reorganized and wouldn't be subject to the bankruptcy rules."

Q: Were you compensated for your services to Mr. Sinatra as pertaining to the Westchester contracts?

A: Yes, sir.

Q: How is that compensation? Is it a monthly retainer type?

A: Mr. Sinatra and I have had no written agreement over the twenty-five years. But generally I charge him on the basis of gross compensation or adjusted gross on a percentage basis.

Q: Did you personally receive any income from activities at the Westchester Theater other than the attorney fees that were paid to you by Mr. Sinatra.

A: No, sir.

Q: Mr. Sinatra, were you ever offered, prior to your going to the Westchester, a sum of fifty thousand dollars which unknown parties agreed to pay you outside of the reportable

income that a person would normally have? Were you ever
offered that amount of money to book the Westchester?

A: That is a negative.

Q: Did you ever discuss with a Mr. Thomas Marson, who
was one of the convicted defendants in the Westchester case,
a debt of fifty thousand dollars that he alleged the Westchester
might owe you?

A: No, I did not.

Q: From what you said to us, I would conclude that it
would be your testimony that you received then no illegal
money from any means. . . .

A: I have never in my life, sir, received any illegal moneys. I have had to work very hard for my money, thank you.

These questions and answers satisfied the board that Frank
had not taken fifty thousand dollars under the table as had
been alleged by a witness in the Westchester Theater case.
The commissioners had no knowledge of any large amounts
of cash Frank had access to. It might have been instructive to
hear him explain the briefcase full of money that he had
showed to Brad Dexter in 1964, saying, "There's more where
that came from." Or to learn why Barbara Sinatra carried in
her purse a ten-thousand-dollar packet of cash with the Caesars Palace wrapper still intact.

The board missed an opportunity to follow up Sinatra's
denials that he ever received any illegal moneys because it
did not have access to the August 3, 1962, memo prepared by
the Justice Department, which raised a number of questions
about Sinatra's relationship to the Fontainebleau Hotel. Allegations had been made by Ben Novak, owner of the Fontainebleau Hotel managing company, as well as others
interviewed by the FBI, that Sinatra refused payments for his
appearances at the Fontainebleau and received expensive
gifts of jewelry instead. Novak told FBI agents that he had
given Sinatra a $4,000 ring as a "token of his appreciation."
Joe Fischetti told FBI agents that he purchased "diamonds
and large pieces of jewelry" for Sinatra.

Based on these allegations, the Justice Department memo
speculated: "It seems incredible that Sinatra would perform
without charge for a commercial enterprise such as the Fontainebleau Hotel. And the above allegations give rise to a
number of questions: Did Sinatra report the $4,000 ring on
his federal income tax returns? What were the other gifts to
Sinatra from 'time to time'? Did Sinatra report these on his

federal income tax returns? Was there an agreement to compensate Sinatra for his services in 'gifts' to avoid the payment of federal income taxes? Does Joe Fischetti collect on his alleged 'piece' of Sinatra as a 'talent agent' for the Fontainebleau? Does Sinatra have a covert 'cash deal' arrangement with the Fontainebleau and does Joe Fischetti handle it? Does Fischetti get some of this income into Sinatra's hands by purchasing items such as diamonds and large pieces of jewelry for him?"

The report went on to question as to whether Sinatra had an "undisclosed interest" in the Fontainebleau Hotel. "If the total value of the 'gifts' received by Sinatra from Novak cannot be considered as reasonable compensation for his services at the Fontainebleau, does he increase his undisclosed capital investment in the hotel by performing there 'without charge'? Assuming that Sinatra actually performs at the Fontainebleau without charge and only for friendship, who are his friends in the hotel and why is he so generous with them?"

Despite the wiretap conversation of Tommy Marson saying that tickets were held back every night for Sinatra, Frank now denied ever receiving any complimentary tickets at the Westchester Premier Theater.

"I never had any tickets given to me, never," he said. Mickey Rudin corrected him. "Frank, not given you directly but given to us."

Sinatra refused to concede the point. "Not to me. I never had any tickets. That is what I wanted to have straight."

The questioning continued: Mr. Pacella on trial was asked by the assistant United States attorney, and I quote: "By way of background, do you know any individual by the name of Frank Sinatra?" Mr. Pacella invoked his Fifth Amendment rights at that question, and Mr. Pacella was subsequently granted immunity and notified his answer could not be used against him. But yet, he still stood on his Fifth Amendment privilege not to discuss that one particular question. He was asked the question by both the forelady of the grand jury and the U.S. District Court judge and still refused to answer, and because of that refusal to answer, was incarcerated. Do you have any knowledge, Mr. Rudin and Mr. Sinatra, why Mr. Pacella would take that position and refuse to answer that question?

Frank did not respond, and Mickey Rudin said that he did not know Mr. Pacella well enough to answer for him. The chairman then moved on to the chummy photograph of Frank, Carlo Gambino, and the other chieftains of Cosa Nostra.

Snapping with impatience, Frank said, "I was asked by one of the members of the theater—who he was doesn't come to me; I don't think it is that important—he told me Mr. Gambino had arrived with his granddaughter, whose name happened to be Sinatra, a doctor in New York, not related at all, and they'd like to take a picture. I said, 'Fine.' They came in and they took a picture of the little girl, and before I realized what happened, there were approximately eight or nine men standing around me and several other snapshots were made. That is the whole incident that took place."

Q: Did you have any information about any of the people that were in that photograph with you? Did you know any of them by sight?

A: Well, Mr. Marson, I think, was in the picture, whom I knew. He was one of the owners of the club, and I knew him. I later found out that I was introduced to somebody named Jimmy, and I found out later it was this fink, The Weasel.

Q: Subsequently, did you have an opportunity after this picture received some degree of notoriety to learn the background of some of those people?

A: No.

Q: When you were there?

A: No.

Q: As of today, you do not know what some of the background is?

A: I didn't even know their names, let alone their backgrounds. I didn't even know most of their names.

When Jimmy Fratianno, who had been accepted as "a very credible witness" in courtrooms across the country, heard Sinatra's account of the picture-taking session, he laughed.

"He said he was gonna take a picture with somebody's niece and he says all of a sudden eight men were around him. Well that's a lot of baloney. He wanted to take a picture with Gambino and he offered Gambino to come in the back, he wanted to meet him. And he goes to the Gaming Board and he just lied about these things. He said he didn't know who was there. He knows me, he knows Gambino, Tommy Marson, Paul Castellano. He [Frank] knows who they are. He knows just as much about this as I do. . . . He likes 'made' guys. He likes to be around them. He likes to have pictures taken with them. Look at all the publicity: Giancana, Lucky Luciano, the Fischettis, Gambino, myself! He thrives on the stuff, I'm telling you. Of course, he ain't gonna tell that to the President. I don't know how he covers that up."

Pearl Similly, a former politician from Staten Island, was not surprised to see the photograph of Frank standing near Paul Castellano and with his arm around Carlo Gambino. Castellano later succeeded Gambino as chief of the nation's most powerful Mafia family, and he and his top aide, Thomas Bilotti, ran the crime organization until they were gunned down gangland style outside a New York steak house.

"Tommy's brother, Jimmy Bilotti, told me he worked for Frank Sinatra for several years [70s and 80s]," said Pearl Similly. "Jimmy was a big gambler and the Bilottis and the Castellanos were very close with Sinatra, so I think Sinatra was doing them a favor to try to keep Jimmy a little busy so he wouldn't gamble so much. Jimmy told me that he traveled with Sinatra and made all his arrangements and when they went out to dinner he'd call and make the reservations at the restaurant. He was like a gofer, I guess. Jimmy didn't like Sinatra very much, but he thought Barbara was great."

Although known to "everybody in Staten Island," this connection of Frank Sinatra's was not known to the Nevada Gaming Control Board.

Frank tried to dismiss the Mafia photograph as one of millions taken backstage, by producing pictures of himself with a congressman, with the prime minister of Israel, with Gregory Peck, with the president of Egypt, with members of the San Francisco police department. "This represents a one thousandth maybe, a minimum amount of photographs that I have taken with people who come backstage," he said. The Nevada gaming chairman said he felt it was a sad commentary on our times that the decent people in Frank's photographs weren't as newsworthy as the disreputable ones, the "who's who of what's what . . . in organized crime."

Q: Again coming back to Mr. Fratianno, Mr. Sinatra, he alleges that in 1976 an associate of yours, Mr. Rizzo, contacted him about "breaking the legs of a former bodyguard" who was giving you problems. The man's name was Andrew Celentano, and I would just ask you for the record. Did you know Mr. Andrew Celentano?

A: For the record, I did not know this man of whom you speak, and also for the record, I wish that we didn't have to discuss Mr. Fratianno, because he is a confessed murderer, a perjurer, and I would rather not discuss him involved with my life. That is a fair enough request.

Q: Yes. Unfortunately, I can appreciate what you are saying. It is in the public record. . . . We are not suggesting that unsubstantiated allegations of Mr. Fratianno will go unchallenged here. But we do think it is necessary to put it on the record.

A: Well, it is now on the record. I never asked anybody to do anything like that, that kind of thing.

One of the board's agents stepped forward to say that he had developed information that Celentano had worked as a security officer at the Fontainebleau Hotel in Florida from 1968 to 1970 and while there was hired by Sinatra to be his personal security guard. He also worked on two movies with Frank in Florida, *Tony Rome* and *The Lady in Cement*. During those three years, Celentano accompanied Frank on an entertainment tour. His widow, Evelyn Celentano, said that her husband considered himself a friend of Frank and had sent him sixty long-stemmed roses on his sixtieth birthday in 1975, but that he had contributed to a series of articles on Sinatra in the *National Enquirer* that had been uncomplimentary. Despite all this, Frank maintained that he did not know Andy Celentano.

The chairman of the Nevada Gaming Board then turned to what he called Frank's "isolated incidents" of violence, his fights with Carl Cohen in 1967, Sanford Waterman in 1970, and Frank Weinstock in 1973. The chairman said nothing of Sinatra's 1966 fight with Frederick Weisman in the Polo Lounge of the Beverly Hills Hotel, which put Weisman in the hospital in critical condition. Frank dodged blame for any of the fights, so the chairman moved smoothly on to the subject of Australia, which Frank clearly evaded.

Q: Mr. Sinatra, would you explain to us what happened in Australia in 1974?

A: I don't remember.

Q: Were you in Australia in 1974?

A: I was there, but I don't remember what happened.

Q: You don't remember what happened?

A: No, I don't remember.

Q: At all?

A: Not at all.

Q: Or is it you just don't want to put it on the record?

A: No, it is just not a matter of putting anything on the record. I don't remember what happened. Some big uproar came out of Australia, and we became the scapegoat again . . . Mr. Rudin might be able to tell you some more about it. . . .

At Frank's bidding, Rudin jumped in to condemn the Australian press, whom Frank had called hookers and pimps, causing unions to go on strike in protest. Rudin said he was told that the strike would be called off once Sinatra apologized, but Rudin had refused to be conciliatory. "There will be no apologies. If you want to find a method of solving this situation, some kind of a joint meeting and statement, we will do it."

At the hearing, Frank denied having had all the trouble that was reported in the press. "We were never frozen out of food at the hotel and so on and so forth," he said. "It was blown up way out of proportion."

Q: You do remember it better now then?

A: No, not all of it. I really don't want to remember it.

Q: Mr. Sinatra, it would appear to me, given an opportunity to explain some of these things, you might take this as an opportunity.

A: I appreciate what you are saying to me, Mr. Bunker, but these things are age-old.

Q: But I do think if there is an explanation for some of these things, that this certainly is the appropriate time to make it.

A: Mr. Rudin made all the explanation that I can remember anyway.

"That's fine," said the chairman, accepting Frank's petulant response as the final explanation of his behavior. Moving on to the next question, he asked Frank about his $46,500 marker from Harrah's in Lake Tahoe which had been on the casino's books since 1978 and had never been collected. Frank said he didn't remember anything about it, so Mickey Rudin explained that it had been written off by Harrah's in 1980, and that he was still waiting for the necessary tax forms from them. Harrah's acknowledged it was their mistake. The board accepted the explanation.

The next question concerned an uncollected marker at Caesars Palace that had only recently been repaid. Rudin answered. "There again some dust fell through the cracks, and again, not my fault, and Mr. Wald runs generally a tight ship. . . . That's been straightened out."

Frank was asked about his close friendship with Eugene Cimorelli, an associate of the Chicago Mafia boss, Tony Spilotro, and a golfing partner of Tony "Big Tuna" Accardo at the Indian Wells Country Club near Palm Springs. Observers had expected the chairman to question Sinatra about whether he had exerted pressure on Caesars Palace to get Cimorelli a job as a casino host, but that line of questioning was never pursued. Instead, he asked Frank whether he had appeared on a local television show as a favor to Cimorelli. Frank said that it was possible.

Q: Are you acquainted with a man by the name of Matthew Ianello?

A: I don't think so. What is his alias?

Q: His alias is Matty the Horse.

A: No.

Q: Mr. Rudin, do you know Mr. Ianello?

A: Yes, I do.

It was not surprising that Frank was so vague testifying about his Mafia friendships considering that he had told Pete Hamill a few years before when they had discussed a possible collaboration on Sinatra's autobiography that he would never discuss his involvement with the mob. "Some things I can't ever talk about," he said. "Someone might come knockin' at my fucking door."

Continuing the questioning, Chairman Bunker asked Frank about his relationship to the Kennedys.

"Mr. Sinatra, it is well known that you were, I guess it would be correct to say, a friend of both the late John Kennedy and Robert Kennedy," he said. "And our question would be: Did you at any time ever attempt to intercede on behalf of Mr. Giancana with either one of those gentlemen?"

Despite wiretap evidence indicating that Frank had interceded with the Kennedys for the Mafia boss, he denied ever doing it.

"Negative," he said.

"Never at all?" asked the chairman.

"Never."

Robert Kennedy's appointment book as attorney general showing the date Peter Lawford came to see him at the Justice Department to plead Frank's case for Giancana was not available to the Nevada Gaming Control Board. Nor did they know of Lawford's intercession on Sinatra's behalf.

FBI wiretaps record Johnny Roselli telling Giancana that Frank had told him he had written Sam's name on a piece of paper and shown it to Bobby Kennedy, saying: "This is my buddy. This is my buddy. This is what I want you to know, Bob." But the Nevada Gaming Control Board did not have access to FBI wiretaps.

When Frank was asked by Bunker how he had first met Sam Giancana, Frank said he didn't remember.

"At Cal-Neva, were you ever in his presence at Cal-Neva?" asked one of the commissioners.

Frank denied that he ever was.

"There is an allegation that you were in Hawaii . . . Mr. Giancana was there at that particular time and you were together. Did you have a meeting over there?"

Frank said he couldn't remember, although he and his Mafia pal Giancana had made an indelible impression on the female flight attendants en route to Hawaii. The FBI agents following Giancana later told reporters that the flight attendants had complained bitterly about the harassment they had been subjected to by the two men.

Phyllis McGuire also recalled the trip to Hawaii because Sam was supposed to be with her in Belle Vernon, Pennsylvania, for her opening at the Twin Coaches. "Sam called me to say that he and 'The Canary,' his code name for Frank, were going to Hawaii," she said. "That night, Frank called me three times trying to get Sam out of the doghouse, but I refused to take any of his calls. They were gone for about a week on that trip."

Sinatra's hearing lasted five and one-half hours. One of the commissioners proposed that a gaming license be limited to six months to see just how deserving Frank really was. "He has indicated and his attorneys have advised us Mr. Sinatra is a changed man from seventeen years ago," said the commissioner. "Well, as I sit here today, there were a couple times that I hope[d] that Mr. Sinatra has changed some."

Chairman Bunker closed the proceeding. "I have reached the point in my life that I don't really care what anybody outside the state of Nevada thinks about gaming, the national media or anybody else. We have an economy here that is based on something that is illegal in every other jurisdiction but New Jersey, and people coming into this area, whether they be FBI, whether they be whoever they are, might come in here with different ideas than what some of us think that have lived here all of our lives."

Bunker moved that Frank be recommended to the Nevada Gaming Commission for license approval for six months on a limited basis; the three commissioners approved unanimously; Frank walked out of the room to thunderous applause.

That night, Johnny Carson, in his monologue on *The Tonight Show*, said, "I just got word that Gregory Peck was nominated for an Oscar for his performance at the Frank Sinatra hearing."

Next, Frank faced the five-member Gaming Control Commission, which had the final say in all licensing matters. That hearing, on February 19, 1981, lasted one hour and forty-five minutes. Again, Frank denied ever associating with members of organized crime. Rudin backed him up when asked whether he had any knowledge of Sinatra's association with people who might be considered unsuitable by Nevada gaming authorities.

"Absolutely not," said Mickey Rudin. Over the years many syndicate men had been Frank Sinatra's houseguests in Palm Springs. Men like Mickey Cohen, Sam Giancana, Joe Fischetti, Johnny Roselli, Johnny Formosa, Skinny D'Amato—and Doc Stacher, whom friends remember playing gin rummy at Frank's house for hours at a stretch.

The chairman, Harry Reid, asked Frank a few more perfunctory questions and then turned the hearing into a testimonial by reciting a poem he said he had received that morning:

Frank Sinatra is the subject, a gaming license he requests;
His life you'll review, his morals give tests.
I hope you'll consider all the good Frank has done,
In sharing and giving, many hearts he has won.

They claim he slipped once, he's paid for it dearly.
Must we condemn him more by bringing it up yearly?
It's your duty as commissioners to question and ask,
And to investigate the subject to get all the facts.

He's proved to Nevada his word he has kept.
Let's grant him a license with all due respect.
He's trustworthy, honest, a man of great pride.
As believers, as gamblers, let's let the bets ride.

This man you are reviewing, please keep him in mind.
He's given to the crippled, poor, and the blind.
He's known to have a heart of pure gold,
Never asking for thanks, nor wants his greatness told.

He's been brought to his knees, he's gave [sic] a clean fight.
To error [sic] is human, but Frank's proved he's right.

The chairman then extolled Frank for his generosity: "You have built orphanages, you have built orthopedic hospitals, you have built mental facilities for retarded people, you have built blind centers, you have helped build universities. . . . I believe that we only have one alternative in this thing. The only thing that we can do, contrary to what anybody thinks, and the fact that they're never going to stop writing about your association with Sam Giancana, they're never going to stop writing about the fact that . . . you gave Lucky Luciano a cigarette lighter [sic]; they're never going to stop talking about Fratianno . . . I don't know now what the commission is going to do, but I would certainly hope that one of the commissioners would make a motion to grant you a license, taking away the six-month limitation, and just give you the license."

The commissioners rushed to vindicate Frank.

"I am satisfied with Mr. Sinatra's responses," said one, "and I am satisfied with the investigation that was performed by our staff on the Cal-Neva incident. With regard to the other incident or incidents that allegedly happened, whether they did or not remains to be seen. . . ."

"I think we have heard testimony today and our investigation indicates that Mr. Sinatra was not on the premises at the time Mr. Giancana was at the Cal-Neva. Possibly that's right," said another.

"I am not suggesting that [Frank Sinatra] is a saint by any means," said a third, "but I am suggesting in the areas that we have investigated, we have not found any substantive reason that he should not be granted a gaming license. One other thing the people of our state need to know is that in the gaming business we aren't necessarily going to have a group of choir boys. There are going to be people that have had some types of associations."

Yet the Nevada statutes are very clear as to what type of person is eligible for a gaming license:

A person of good character, honesty and integrity, a person whose prior activities, criminal record, if any, reputation, habits, and associations do not pose a threat to the public interest of this state or to the effective regulation and control of gaming or create or enhance the dangers of unsuitable, unfair, or illegal practices, methods and activities in the conduct of gaming, or the carrying on of the business of financial arrangements incidental thereto.

By a four-to-one vote, the board removed the six-month limitation on Frank's license, and sent him out of City Hall with its seal of approval.

"We got that junk behind us," Frank said wearily. "We cleared the air."

34

By 1980, Frank Sinatra's movie career was over. He had made his first television film in 1977, *Contract on Cherry Street*, because it was his mother's favorite story about the mob, but the reviews had been disappointing. The *Los Angeles Times* called it "dreadful . . . tawdry, slow, and tacky."

The following year, he had played a tired detective in the movie of *The First Deadly Sin* after Marlon Brando rejected the role. The reviews were devastating. He had wanted to play the alcoholic lawyer in *The Verdict*, but the role went to Paul Newman. In 1983, he played only a cameo in *Cannonball Run II* with Sammy Davis, Jr., Dean Martin, and Shirley MacLaine, which the critics kindly ignored.

As much as Frank still wanted a good movie role, he refused to play any part that made him look old. Consequently, he turned down the role of the aging Kennedy patriarch in *Winter Kills*, by one of his favorite writers, Richard Condon.

"I went out to see Frank with the screenplay to ask him if he'd like to play Pa," said the novelist. "He read it seriously, but when I got back home, I had a letter from him saying that the part 'is just too old for me.' He didn't want to appear on the screen as a venerable elder."

Frank tried television again in 1981 with "Sinatra—The Man and His Music," but the special fared so poorly in the

Neilsens (forty-eighth out of sixty-five) that NBC refused to renew his option.

Yet, his voice, now darker, tougher, and loamier, swept him into his most successful period, bringing him greater financial rewards than he had ever known. In 1980, he released *Trilogy*, his first album in five years. The three-disc package with 500 musicians comprised his past, his present, and his future. In the album he sang hauntingly of making peace with his roots, of returning to Hoboken before his music ended.

The album sold for $20.95, turned "gold" (sold 500,000 units) within weeks, and was followed by *She Shot Me Down* in 1981, an album consisting of nothing but songs of lost love. In 1982, RCA Records released the complete Tommy Dorsey–Frank Sinatra sessions in three double-album sets. In 1983, Mobile Fidelity Sound Labs released a sixteen-album package from his Capitol years (1953–1962) entitled *Sinatra*, which sold for $350 and became a collector's item. In 1984, at the age of sixty-eight, he recorded another album, *L.A. Is My Lady*, with Quincy Jones. Reviews were mixed, sales modest. He followed with *The Best of Everything*.

Among serious collectors, the most prized Sinatra recordings are the private vinyls, the unreleased masters, and the recording session outtakes that have been pirated over the years, creating a lively underground market. The noncommercial material is fiercely guarded by collectors, including Frank himself, but occasionally some of it is broadcast by radio disc jockeys, much to Sinatra's dismay. New York radio host Jonathan Schwartz, a devoted Sinatra fan, frequently played material from his private collection, which included an outtake of Frank trying to sing "Lush Life," a difficult song that he never could master. After several starts and stops, Frank stormed out of the recording studio and slammed the door, all of which was captured on the pirated tape. For years, Frank had been seething about Schwartz's playing such noncommercial material, but when the disc jockey broke the release date for *Trilogy* and then criticized it as "narcissistic . . . subservient" and "a shocking embarrassment in poor taste," Sinatra called the owner of WNEW, saying: "Get him off!" The next day, Schwartz was put on an extended leave of absence.

New York *Daily News* columnist Liz Smith printed what

happened in her syndicated column, saying: "I don't care how fabulous the singer is . . . What kind of world is it when critics are not safe to criticize freely? And since when did criticism ever hurt Frank Sinatra one jot or tittle?"

The next day she received one of Frank's virulent telegrams: YOUR INFORMATION IN REGARD TO JONATHAN SCHWARTZ AND MYSELF STINKS. I NEVER AT ANY TIME ASKED ANY EXECUTIVE OF WNEW TO "GET RID OF HIM." WE DID NOTIFY SAID RADIO STATION THAT IF SCHWARTZ DID NOT STOP PIRATING AND PLAYING UNRELEASED RECORDS AND OUTTAKES, WHICH IS ILLEGAL, WE WOULD BRING A LAWSUIT AGAINST JONATHAN AND SAID RADIO STATION. IT IS ASTONISHING TO ME HOW YOU AND MOST OF YOUR COLLEAGUES CAN GET SO SCREWED UP WITH YOUR INFORMATION. He went on to say: MY WORK IN EVERY FIELD HAS BEEN CRITICIZED, GOOD AND BAD, FOR YEARS AND NONE OF IT EVER MEANT CRAP TO ME BECAUSE THE PEOPLE WHO CRITICIZE ME DO NOT HAVE THE CALIBRE OF MY MUSICIANSHIP OR MY PERFORMING KNOW-HOW. He signed the telegram: SINATRA, SINATRA, SINATRA.

Schwartz got his job back six weeks later, but Liz Smith had made a powerful enemy. She took Rona Barrett's place in Frank's monologues, and he viciously described her from concert stages across the country as being "so ugly she has to lie on the analyst's couch face down."

When he was singing, Frank continued to captivate audiences with his immutable magic. His baritone sometimes cracked, but the gliding intonations still aroused the same raptures of delight as they had at the Paramount Theater. Older and more affluent now, his loyal middle-aged fans paid dearly to watch him recapture a piece of their youth. In his sixties he had become a legend, an institution, a wonder to behold onstage.

He was paid two million dollars for four concerts in Argentina, and two million dollars for nine concerts in Sun City (South Africa). For every show he did at Resorts International in Atlantic City he was paid fifty thousand dollars. Then in 1982 he signed a three-year contract with the Golden Nugget casino for sixteen million dollars. In addition, he made $1,300,000 for the Showtime television rights to his "Concert for the Americas" in the Dominican Republic and $1,600,000 for his 1982 concert series at Carnegie Hall. He also made $250,000 for one evening of song at the ChicagoFest in 1982; two years later, he returned to Chicago and made $450,000 in six days at the Arie Crown.

"With that kind of income, Frank needs a lot of deductions, and he figures it's better to give to charity and get the good publicity, plus the tax write-offs, than to let the IRS have it," said a friend. "So a couple of times a year, Sonny [Nathan Golden, Frank's accountant] figures out how much he's got to unload, and Frank starts doing his charity bit with the donations and everything."

Frank's trip to Sun City in Bophuthatswana, South Africa, in 1981 tarred him with the racist apartheid policies of South Africa and subjected him to criticism from around the world.

"He is trying to pretend that he's going into a separate state, which it is not," said an official of the National Congress of South Africa (ANC). "We don't recognize Bophuthatswana as a separate state from South Africa, and our policy is the same as if he agreed to perform in South Africa. He is saying that the black people of South Africa should be living in thirteen percent of the land."

The Reverend Jesse Jackson also criticized Frank for accepting the Sun City engagement. "Sinatra gained respect when he came with us to Alabama in the sixties by identifying with the right cause, and he simply shouldn't be trading his birthright for a mess of money now," he said.

Frank's publicist, Lee Solters, tried to defend the trip by saying that Frank's contract forbade any type of segregation. "We think that the establishment of Bophuthatswana as an independent country is the right step for their future development . . . [but] . . . I couldn't give a shit about the African organizations' opinions." Mickey Rudin, who had traveled ahead to make sure that segregation was not practiced in Sun City, said that he found "more interracial harmony than can even be found in some of our American cities."

Reassured by his publicist and his lawyer, Frank accepted the engagement despite appeals by the United Nations, the African states, and some black people of South Africa to boycott the apartheid country. "I play to all," he said. "Any color, any creed, drunk or sober."

But those who remembered the young liberal singer from Tommy Dorsey's band were disheartened. They recalled the Frank Sinatra who flew into Gary, Indiana, in 1945 to preach racial tolerance to students who were objecting to Froebel High School's "pro-Negro" policies. They remembered how Frank, always an advocate of civil rights, had helped give Sammy Davis, Jr., his start in show business and how he had paid tribute to the Reverend Martin Luther King, Jr., in 1961 by performing at a benefit in Carnegie Hall to raise money for the Southern Christian Leadership Conference. The Frank Sinatra who condemned bigotry in *The House I Live In* in 1945 seemed light years away from the sixty-five-year-old singer who was now profiting from apartheid by appearing in the "homeland," founded in 1977 as a puppet of the racist South African government and not granted diplomatic recognition by any other country on earth.

On the trip, Frank was made an honorary tribal chief and presented the Order of the Leopard by the president of Bophuthatswana, who proclaimed him "the king of the entertainment world." He sang in the $33 million Sun City Hotel and Country Club and collected $2,000,000 from a country whose annual per capita income averages five hundred dollars.

In anti-apartheid eyes, the worst thing Frank did by this performance was to legitimize Sun City for other entertainers like Linda Ronstadt, Dolly Parton, Liza Minnelli, Paul Anka, Ray Charles, and Olivia Newton-John. But within two years, leading artists and athletes in the United States launched a campaign to refuse to perform in South Africa. The group, led by Harry Belafonte and Arthur Ashe, included stars like Paul Newman, Jane Fonda, Tony Bennett, Bill Cosby, Muhammad Ali, and Wilt Chamberlain.

"Word needs to get out loud and clear that Bophuthatswana is only a phony homeland," said Arthur Ashe. "Nobody should be fooled. If an actor or actress goes there, then they are going to South Africa and they are giving approval to a racist regime."

Singling out Frank for criticism, the United Nations Special Committee Against Apartheid released a register of 211 entertainers who performed in South Africa, saying that while some of the "collaborators" had perhaps visited the country because of ignorance of the situation, or the lure of exorbitant fees, others showed deliberate insensitivity or hostility to the legitimate aspirations of oppressed people. "Special mention must be made in this connection of Frank Sinatra, who performed in Sun City in . . . 1981 . . . and again went to South Africa in 1983 despite many appeals and protests by anti-apartheid groups. . . ." The U.N.'s celebrity register was compiled to facilitate boycott actions by governments, organizations, and individuals of those who supported Pretoria's dehumanizing policies.

"Their subsequent demonstrations, meetings, and resolutions to broaden the movement could be called 'Frank's contributions,' " said *The Village Voice*.

Nothing exemplified Sinatra's personal evolution more than this trip to South Africa. During the early years, when he was represented by George Evans, who had him making speeches about racial equality, such a trip would have been unthinkable, even for two million dollars. As a passionate liberal, Sinatra had spoken out fervently on the issue of race relations:

"We've got a hell of a long way to go in this racial situation. As long as most white men think of a Negro as a Negro first and a man second, we're in trouble. I don't know why we can't grow up. It took us long enough to get past the stage where we were calling all Italians 'wops' and 'dagos,' but if we don't drop this 'nigger' thing, we just won't be around much longer. Hell, actors have got to take a stand politically, even if we're afraid we'll get hurt at the box office." He said that in 1947.

In 1970, after aligning himself with Republicans like Ronald Reagan, Richard Nixon, and Spiro Agnew, Frank lost the impetus to speak out on issues like race relations. As part of the establishment now, he had become politically complacent and conservative. The only issue that continued to excite him was his hatred of the press, which found expression in all his performances.

Acknowledging applause at the Los Angeles Universal Amphitheater, he said, "I haven't heard that much clapping since NBC kicked Rona Barrett off the lot." While entertaining NBC affiliates at the Century Plaza Hotel in 1982, he described CBS-TV newsman Dan Rather as a "yccch." In Atlantic City, he disparaged Barbara Walters of ABC-TV as "Baba Wawa, a real bow-wow . . . a pain in the ass who has a lisp and should take diction lessons."

The next day, Liz Smith called him a pain in the ass for his gratuitous attack, and echoing the growing sentiments of his audiences, asked: "Why doesn't this great big bully just shut up and sing. . . . Here is one of the finest talents of our time, a real legend both from his long career and his many good works for friends and for charity. Why does he have to keep ruining it all the time by stooping onstage to the petty throwing of cow chips?"

The next night, Frank spewed his anger toward the columnist from the stage of Atlantic City's Resorts International.

"Gossip columnists are probably the lowest form of journalists," he said, "The latest one is old Liz in New York. She's now got a big thing going on because I said something about Barbara Wawa. Who in hell doesn't say something about Barbara Wawa? It's getting so that Ms. Smith is now being called in the trade the extra-strength Tylenol of the journalists. She's a dumpy, fat, ugly broad. . . . She really got teed off at the fact that I said Barbara Wawa was a pain in the ass. And she is. She's dangerous too. She's very dangerous.

"Do you know that Barbara Walters one time in an interview with Mrs. Lady Bird Johnson after President Johnson died—she had the gall and the *cojones* to say to this woman— she asked this question: How did you feel about your husband's extracurricular activities outside with other women? This is after he had died. She's talking to the widow. That's the kind of danger there is in people like that. Oh, if they were only guys, I'd . . . oh. . . .

"Now this fat broad in New York got sore about it and went to her defense. Barbara Wawa doesn't need defense. She needs diction lessons. Did you ever listen to her? She says 'too-too twain' and 'I wuv a wabbit.' Diction lessons, not defense. She doesn't need that. And a tuck here, and there, too, under the ear and under the nose. . . ."

Enraged by Liz Smith's comment that his wife had been embarrassed by his outbursts, Frank continued:

"She said in her column that the one who's the most upset about my attack on Barbara Wawa was my wife, Barbara. Now, my wife never gets mad at me. Did Juliet ever get mad at Romeo, for chrissakes? I'm her E.T. How could she get mad at me. . . . That dopey broad also said in her column that Barbara Wawa was considered persona grata at the White House. That makes sense, because the President has to deal with Castro and Qadhafi. Now, I don't know what the hell goes on at the White House. Ronnie's on his own at the White House. . . . Don't you yell at me, lady. This is my platform up here. I don't have a newspaper to publish me like they do."

Frank took every opportunity to berate his journalist enemies. Gleefully, he told Beverly Sills how he had approached Katharine Graham, chairman of the board of the Washington

Post Company, to say that her paper was a rag and her clothes were even worse.

"Who does your outfits? Edith Piaf's dressmaker?" he asked Mrs. Graham, referring to the fact that Edith Piaf, the "Little Sparrow," wore rags.

Horrified by the story, Beverly Sills said, "Tell me something, Frank. What do you get out of doing something like that?"

"Satisfaction," said the singer.

Provoked by a Paul Conrad cartoon that appeared in the *Los Angeles Times* portraying President Reagan with a hearing aid, Frank sent a letter to the editor, blaming the newspaper for publishing the "poison" of Conrad, who, he said, "is a disgrace to responsible journalism, an insult to anything that calls itself a newspaper and you all ought to be ashamed of yourselves for hiding behind the First Amendment, which was never intended for people like Conrad anyway."

Earlier, he had fulminated about an article in *People* magazine. In a two-page, single-spaced letter, he had said that the publication was "to accurate journalism what Preparation H is to advanced medicine. . . . Long after Anita Bryant has begun dating the head of the Gay Task Force, I will still have nothing to do with *Time, People,* or any of its illegitimate offspring or clones." He ended: "Good manners and the federal government still prevent me from sending your editor garbage through the mails, something postal inspectors seem to overlook when it comes to handling *People* magazine."

Not even the presence of the President and First Lady could stem his tirades. At a Kennedy Center concert attended by the Reagans in 1983, he offered a toast: "To the confusion of our enemies—the press in general and the gossip columnists in particular." Saying that Washington has "a little gossip now and then," he asked how anyone could be expected to live with "those idiots," and hoped that "they all break their typewriters or sew up their mouths."

Nancy Reagan, too, had felt persecuted, misunderstood, and threatened by probing journalists at the beginning of her husband's first term in office in Washington, D.C. Frank, in turn, had felt quite protective toward the First Lady when press coverage focused on her extensive wardrobe, the designer clothes she had accepted free and was forced by law to return, the $250,000 diamond necklace and earrings she had borrowed from Harry Winston for the inaugural and kept for six months, the $209,508 she spent for 220 place settings of new White House china, and the $822,641 she raised from private donors to redecorate the White House. Because of the First Lady's love of luxurious living, the Reagan administration soon became known as "millionaires on parade."

"She's had such a bum rap," said Frank. "The china was a terrible, terrible misrepresentation. The china was given by citizens. She didn't buy it with our . . . tax money. It was given to the White House, and what's wrong with having pretty china in the White House? What's wrong with having a White House that's the most wonderful capital building in the world? Nothing wrong with that at all. When she first came to town . . . she got a bad going over by the press, which doesn't surprise me . . . [Nancy] is a very classy lady. She's quite shy, contrary to what is said about her . . . she is warm and fun. She has a great sense of humor and giggles and . . . she's just great . . . just great."

Nancy, in turn, acted like a thrilled schoolgirl in Frank's presence. A special rapport developed between the First Lady and the singer, whose Secret Service code name was "Napoleon." Frank flew to Washington several times to have private luncheons with her in the White House solarium, where they chatted for hours. On his trips to Washington to see Nancy, Frank came unaccompanied by his wife, who was not close to Mrs. Reagan. Barbara seemed to resent her husband's fawning attentions to the First Lady. The feeling was mutual on Nancy Reagan's part.

"Even when the Sinatras were invited to a White House state dinner, Mrs. Reagan always wanted Frank seated next to her and Barbara . . . well, we had to seat Barbara in outer Mongolia," said a staff member.

After his private luncheons with the First Lady, Frank flew back to Palm Springs. The White House staff ushered him in and out of the family quarters so that he was never seen by the press. "We always knew better than to ever interrupt those luncheons," said a member of Mrs. Reagan's staff. "When she was with Sinatra, she was not to be disturbed. For anything."

As soon as Frank heard about the assassination attempt on President Reagan, he rushed to Washington to be at Nancy's side; he sat next to her on the Truman balcony watching the Fourth of July fireworks; he danced with her most of the night at the Annenbergs' New Year's Eve party, which so angered his wife that she stormed out and refused to attend the following year. Frank offered to buy Nancy Reagan the Bulgari jewels that she had borrowed to wear to the wedding of Prince Charles; he contributed ten thousand dollars to her White House redecoration project; he arranged for her to receive the Scopus Award from the American Friends of Hebrew University; he helped her promote the Foster Grandparents program by singing with her at the White House and then recording the song for Reprise Records, with all royalties going to Foster Grandparents. He even flew into Washington to be the surprise entertainer at a Congressional Club luncheon in her honor.

Bedazzled, Nancy relied on him for everything pertaining to White House entertainment, making him the unofficial czar in charge of performances for state dinners. The White House social staff soon learned to look to him for direction. He upgraded the lighting with colored filters in the East Room and suggested a new sound system, which the White House purchased and installed to his specification. He taught the resident staff—engineers, ushers, and the social office—how to maximize a performance with the placement of the stage, putting plantings in the acoustical dead zones and making the live zones technically correct.

Frank arranged for Zubin Mehta, conductor of the New York Philharmonic, to perform at the state dinner for Indian Prime Minister Indira Gandhi. When Mrs. Reagan wanted Mel Tillis to sing, Sinatra told the country singer to appear, informing him: "I've already checked your schedule and you are free."

The only friction to arise between Frank and the First Lady occurred during the queen of England's ten-day visit to the United States in March 1983. This was an important occasion for Nancy, who wanted to return the same kind of royal hospitality she and the President had received at Windsor Castle. She put Frank in charge of the dinner at the Twentieth Century Fox studios in Hollywood at which she would welcome the British monarch, hoping that he would produce a spectacular gala.

Unfortunately, Frank was not at his best for the occasion. He had learned that the queen was planning a dinner the following evening aboard her yacht, H.M.S. *Britannia*, in honor of the Reagans, to which he had not been invited.

Irate, he made his wife, Barbara, call the White House and talk to Mike Deaver about the royal slight. The presidential advisor said he could do little to accommodate the Sinatras because the guest list was the queen's, and the White House had nothing to do with it. At Barbara's insistence, though, Deaver reluctantly called Buckingham Palace.

"We have a very difficult situation here," said Deaver, "and I do hope you won't think us too presumptuous, but if it would be possible to receive Mr. Sinatra on the yacht, we'd be most grateful."

The palace politely took the matter under advisement, but declined to extend Frank an invitation. More than a week passed while Frank waited impatiently. Finally, he threatened to pull out as producer of Nancy's dinner for the queen unless he were included on the royal yacht. An appeal was quickly made to Walter Annenberg, the former U.S. ambassador to the Court of St. James, to intercede for Frank. Only then did the queen agree to include the Sinatras in her shipboard party.

As the architect of Nancy Reagan's regal welcoming party, Sinatra had hoped to impress the Hollywood aristocracy, but the social pressure of an evening dominated by the White House and Buckingham Palace seemed to be too much for him. He nervously stumbled over his lines and forgot the words to his songs. Committing a terrible faux pas, he neglected to welcome the queen from the stage and then compounded his mistake by throwing kisses to the First Lady. Torrential rains beat down on the tin roof of the sound stage, making a disconcerting racket throughout the dinner as Queen Elizabeth patiently listened to eighty-seven-year-old George Burns tell off-color jokes. Nancy Reagan winced with embarrassment as Reuters described the performers including Frank, sixty-seven, and Perry Como, seventy, as "old Hollywood."

"It was a disaster—an absolute disaster," said a White House secretary. "Frank put on the worst Las Vegas variety show, completely lacking in style and taste, and Mrs. Reagan was humiliated. She was very upset with him, very irritated, especially when he wanted the queen to take a tour of the studio, and became petulant when she declined. The menu was seafood, which the queen had expressly asked not to be served, plus sticky, cold chicken pot pies and sour wines. The valets ran out of umbrellas, and then Frank violated all protocol by leaving before the queen did. I guess he knew that he had blown it and just wanted to get away as fast as he could."

The British press was astounded by the evening, and reported in detail the American gaffes and repeated breaches of protocol.

QUEEN'S TRIP IN TURMOIL headlined the London *Evening Standard*.

SNUB FOR YANKS said the *Daily Star*, because the queen had not been introduced to guests like Bette Davis, Fred Astaire, and Jimmy Stewart.

Describing Sinatra's voice as "rasping and flat," the *Manchester Guardian* pronounced the evening extremely tedious: "Overall it was not exactly an exhilarating performance."

British stars agreed. "It was so boring, I almost fell asleep," said Elton John.

"A bit dour," said Julie Andrews.

"It was the usual Hollywood cattle call, rather dull in many ways," said society columnist Pamela Mason.

Though she did her husband's bidding at every turn, Barbara Sinatra occasionally chafed in her role as the subservient wife, for she had to tolerate public insults and scornful abuse during his black mood swings. In Frank's manic phase, she was "my beautiful bride"; in his depressive stage, she was "the dumbest broad I ever met."

"I was Sinatra's gofer at Caesars Palace for four years," said Gloria Massingill, "and whenever he and Lady Barbara went at it, I'd be buzzed on my beeper to get her luggage ready and get her to the plane to fly back to Palm Springs. This happened whenever he stayed in the casino all night drinking and gambling and wouldn't come to bed. She'd leave him and go home to the desert. Once they separated for several days and everyone thought for sure that they were going to get a divorce."

The public fights between the Sinatras grew coarse and crude, especially if Frank was drinking. He called her vicious names, which she returned in kind. So strong were the rumors of marital discord that in 1983 Frank felt compelled to say something during a barbecue given by Judy Green, widow of Frank's close friend Bill, in Southampton on New York's Long Island. Rising after dinner with a glass in his hand, he said, "You may have been hearing bad rumors about Barbara and me recently, but I'm telling you that we have been married for seven years. We also plan to be married for another seven years and after that for another seven years and on and on." Everyone smiled thinly.

Earlier that evening, Frank began drinking and nearly ruined the party when he inexplicably turned on New York socialite Pat Patterson as she approached him. Teasingly, she said that Frank owed her $750 for a dress that she had bought years before for a blind date they were supposed to have but which had been canceled at the last minute.

"Come with me," said Frank, and, in front of several guests, he escorted her to the door where his bodyguards were standing. "These men will see that you get home."

"What do you mean?"

"I mean I want you out of here," he said. "You're leaving—now."

"But . . . but . . . I have to get my purse."

"I'll get your purse," said one of the bodyguards. "When Mr. Sinatra says 'out,' he means 'out.'"

Frank had already returned to the party, where guests were speechless but much too frightened to object to his behavior. Later, they watched in horror as he assailed the head of Atlantic Records, Ahmet Ertegun, saying, "You ruined music with your rock and roll. It's your fault what's happened to the music business. You've destroyed music in this country. . . ." Without a word, the record executive moved away from Frank. Still, no one said anything for fear of drawing the abuse on himself.

"It's amazing that none of those very social people ever objected to Frank's bodyguards, but they never did," said Stephen Green. "I remember when he visited Dad [William Green] and Judy in Mt. Kisco and he arrived with two of his henchmen, Joe Tomatoes and Jerry The Crusher. At the end of the weekend, Joe Tomatoes was sitting with Frank at the pool and, winking at Dad, Sinatra said, 'Have you got your letter written yet?'

" 'Huh? What letter?' said Joe Tomatoes.

" 'Oh, God, Joe, how can I take you anywhere?' said Frank. 'Don't you know that at the end of a nice weekend like this you're supposed to write the hostess, in this case, Mrs. Green, a very nice letter telling her how happy you were to share her hospitality? I can't believe you haven't done that yet.' He shook his head in disgust, and Joe Tomatoes, a real gorilla, went back into the main house. He walked out three hours later with a letter that looked as if it had been written by a five-year-old in left-handed print. The note said: 'Thank you Mrs. Green for the good food and the nice time. Thank you. Joe Tomatoes.' Dad and Judy so loved that letter that they had it framed in gold and hung in the guest room for all future guests to see.

Introducing the bizarre into the privileged lives of his rich society friends was one of Frank's most memorable traits. He brought them a touch of vulgarity, a hint of the sinister. Though ordinarily they saw only the good Frank, who lavished presents upon them, sang at their benefits, and championed their charities, they occasionally glimpsed the bad Frank, who acted like a monster.

Sinatra gave the country a televised look at his schizoid self in the winter of 1983: the good Frank graciously accepted a major national tribute, but days later the bad Frank berated a woman blackjack dealer at the Golden Nugget in Atlantic City.

The national tribute came on December 4, 1983, when the President of the United States paid homage to Frank for his lifelong achievements in the performing arts. He was one of the five honorees saluted in *The Kennedy Center Honors: A Celebration of the Performing Arts*, televised by CBS. Quoting Henry James, the President said that "art is the shadow of humanity" as he slipped a rainbow-colored ribbon around Frank's shoulders, and he continued: "You have spent your life casting a magnificent and powerful shadow."

Standing alongside dancer-choreographer Katherine Dunham, director Elia Kazan, actor Jimmy Stewart, and composer-critic Virgil Thomson, Frank glowed in the grandeur of the occasion.

"For the country itself," Sinatra said, "it's an important thing to do, to honor the arts people. I suppose it's like the Oscars or the Tonys, but the biggest. But in any award, when you're honored by your peers, that's what really counts."

"And your government," said his wife, Barbara.

"And our government," Frank added.

Yet days later, the honoree was gambling at the Golden Nugget in Atlantic City with Barbara, Dean Martin, and Martin's manager, Mort Viner. Frank told Kyong Kim, the thirty-three-year-old blackjack dealer, to deal to him by hand, not from the legally required sealed plastic box, which is called a shoe. The dealer paused, saying she would have to check with her supervisor.

"You don't want to play one deck, you go back to China," snarled Frank.

Hearing the disturbance, the casino supervisor, Joyce Caparele, walked over.

"He said he wanted the single deck, or if he didn't get his way about it that he would not be putting on the show," she said. "I thought if I didn't go along . . . if I would have said anything to Mr. Sinatra about anything that might have ruffled his feathers, I was afraid I would get fired."

The pit boss, Maxwell Spinks, was summoned to tell Frank that it was out of his authority to allow the dealer to deal to him by hand.

"I can't make a decision on this," he said. "You would have to take it to higher authority."

"Just run along and get higher authority," said Frank.

Alarmed by what he had heard of Sinatra's volatile character, the shift manager, Robert Barnum, thought the singer should be accommodated. Fearing that violence might erupt any minute, the pit boss acquiesced to the demand. "[Sinatra] seemed to be pumping himself up into a very dictatorial-type attitude," he said.

The dealer, close to tears, began dealing by hand, more afraid of Frank than she was of breaking the law. The incident was videotaped by surveillance cameras and later shown on the *CBS Evening News*, giving Americans a disconcerting look at the petty tyrant within the man so recently honored at the Kennedy Center.

Months later, the New Jersey Casino Control Commission fined the Golden Nugget $25,000 for allowing the infraction and suspended four employees for three to fourteen days for breaking state gaming regulations. Joel R. Jacobson, vice-chairman of the commission, expressed outrage that the man responsible escaped without reprimand.

"When a folk hero like Frank Sinatra exhibits himself as an obnoxious bully, forcing working men and women to commit infractions which cause them to be reprimanded and to lose significant amounts of income, to fear the loss of their job, it may very well be time to reconsider the question of licensing entertainers."

Blaming the "merciless media," Golden Nugget chairman

Stephen Wynn defended Frank. "He's the only major entertainer who works more nights for charity than for money."

Jacobson retorted: "Mr. Sinatra's volatile temper and his intimidating, abusive behavior [showed] no evidence of compassion or humanitarianism. There was no charity [in his actions]."

Feeling insulted and demeaned, Frank slashed back in anger, calling Jacobson a parasite and vowing never to appear again in New Jersey.

Mickey Rudin made the announcement: "Mr. Sinatra has instructed me to limit the number of his performances and, therefore, has decided that he will not perform in a state where appointed officials feel the compulsion to use him as 'a punching bag.' . . . It is difficult to believe that Mr. Jacobson was not well aware of the fact that the obnoxious remarks he made for the benefit of the television cameras would result in headlines throughout the world."

The lawyer berated all New Jersey officials for not springing to Frank's defense and for not chastising Jacobson. Expressing outrage that Sinatra had not heard "from any of the prominent citizens of the State of New Jersey who have called upon him to render his services for charitable causes, or even from the board of governors of a hospital that has insisted on putting his name on one of their buildings," Rudin canceled Frank's coming engagement in Atlantic City with Dean Martin.

New Jersey Assemblyman Michael Adubato proposed that the state make an official apology to "our native son . . . for unwarranted and obnoxious criticism of him. . . . Let's plead with him to return to New Jersey, the home of your parents, Dolly and Marty Sinatra. Frank, come back to your roots. Come home to New Jersey. I love you."

When Adubato stood up with his resolution, Assembly members from the southern part of the state walked out of the chamber while others called him out of order and ended the discussion.

The New York *Daily News* expressed its sentiments in an editorial entitled "Old Sore Eyes" which said: "Sinatra is not only an arrogant, offensive bully, he is also a whiner. He can dish it out but he can't take it. He's a snob who has repudiated the people who paid his way to celebrityhood. Las Vegas can keep him."

35

Before he issued his edict against New Jersey, Frank made a pilgrimage to Hoboken to make peace with his Irish godfather, to whom he had not spoken for almost fifty years. The death of his mother had left him bereft of his past, his roots. All of his parents' relatives were dead, with the exception of a ninety-year-old aunt in a nursing home. There was no one left to connect him with his mother and father except for Frank Garrick, once Marty Sinatra's best friend and the man Dolly had chosen to be her son's godfather. But the two men had not spoken to each other since Garrick had fired Frank, when his teenage godson tried to preempt a dead reporter's newspaper job.

"Oh, the temper and the names he called me," Frank Garrick recalled. "Words you have never heard. That temper was something in those days. Murderous. He never spoke to me again and neither did Dolly. Marty still came around, but it was never the same. I wasn't invited to Frankie's wedding to Nancy Barbato. I never met his kids. I wasn't even asked to the fiftieth anniversary party he had for his folks in Jersey City. But a while after his mom died, he called me up and said he would like to come over. He never made it, though. Then he called a couple of times more, but he never showed up. I didn't think he ever would."

Finally, in June 1982, Frank returned to Hoboken to see his eighty-five-year-old godfather, but he didn't go alone.

Accompanied by his secretary, Dorothy Uhlmann, and his best friend, Jilly Rizzo, he knocked on the door of the Garricks' three-room apartment in a senior citizens' building on the edge of town.

"After all those times of him calling us and then not coming, I didn't believe he would ever show up," said Minnie Garrick, "but there he was at the door looking so sheepish and nervous. Frank was out on the little porch, so Frankie went out there and put his arms around him. They both started crying."

"He [Sinatra] said he was so sorry and he should have done this a long time ago, but he was scared," said Garrick. "I told him he should have done it a long time ago too. He sat down in here on the couch and gave us a big basket of fruit with a cellophane wrapper and an envelope with five one-hundred-dollar bills. 'And that's just the beginning,' he said when we opened the envelope. He told me we're all that he has left now, so he wanted to keep us close. He even wanted us to move to Palm Springs and live with him, but we couldn't do that. We have our own children and grandchildren here. . . . Frankie's so changed from the hard-charging kid he used to be. In the beginning, he was just like his mom. A real pusher and tough, tough, tough, but now he's like his old man. Real quiet and calm. That's Barbara that's done that. She's a real lady."

Two weeks later, Frank sent a limousine to Hoboken to bring the Garricks to Atlantic City, where he was performing for four days. Dorothy Uhlmann gave them a photograph of Frank in a tuxedo that he had signed: "To Frank and Minnie with much love and affection, Your godson, Francis." She then told them that Frank wanted to talk to Mr. Garrick alone, man to man.

"I went into his apartment in the hotel, and Barbara was getting ready to leave, but Frank told her she could stay because she didn't know what we were talking about. For the next hour and a half, we reminisced about Hoboken and what had happened so many years ago. He told me that after he had appeared at the Union Club once they booed him and he hated it. He said that he'd never come back again. He said that Hoboken hated him because of his mother, and I said, 'No, they don't, Frank. Not at all. They're proud of you. You're doing wrong by not coming back.' That's when he said that maybe he would go back one of these days, but . . .

He talked a lot about Dolly's death and how terrible it was. He said he saw the wreckage and how they found one arm here and another arm there and piles of her clothes twisted on the rocks. He wanted to know about his baptism and how the priest had made a mistake and named him after me instead of Marty. I told him the story and he laughed. 'Yeah, my mom told me all about it,' he said. I guess he wanted to hear it again.

"Barbara never said a word during the whole time we talked. She's perfect for Frank. She takes care of him and she knows her place. She's lovely."

A few months later, the Garricks received another photograph from Frank, this one a colored glossy of himself and Barbara sitting next to each other holding hands. The picture was framed in gold with a gold-painted plaque that read: "To Frank and Minnie. Love & XXX, Frank and Barbara, July 1982." For Christmas they both received Cartier tank watches, and anytime Frank performed at Carnegie Hall they received free tickets for themselves and their friends. The next year, Frank took them a painting he had done. They hung it with pride alongside their picture of the pope and the statue of the Infant of Prague.

Thrilled to be reconciled with his godson, Frank Garrick spoke glowingly of Sinatra's visit. The reporter who interviewed Garrick wrote a long story, which was picked up by Frank's clipping service.

"He was very, very upset," recalled Garrick later. "The next time I saw him he asked me if I had said all those things, and then he told me never ever to talk to anyone again like that. He's very bitter. He never was bitter before, but he's real bitter now about the press and we're not supposed to talk to anyone about anything."

Striving hard to control the flow of information around him, Frank held tightly to the secrets of his family. He had been stung by the stories of his son's three paternity suits,* and although he supported Frank, Jr., with lawyers to fight each case, Frank felt his family name had been tarnished by

---

*In 1970 Carol Sue Edmondston had filed suit charging Frank, Jr., with fathering her child, Victor Randolph. In 1980 Mary Wallner took him to court declaring him the father of her daughter, Francine. After an eight-month romance with Jr. in 1977, Mary Fleming gave birth to Francis Wayne Sinatra, Jr., and named Jr. as the father.

the press coverage. He also worried that the children might indeed be his grandchildren.

"He got real upset by that paternity business and wanted Frank, Jr., to take responsibility and act like a man," said Gloria Massingill. "As I recall, he made sure that Frank, Jr., paid each of the mothers a monthly allowance or something."

Little has been printed about Sinatra that wasn't first shaped and refined by his publicists. Over the years, writers had to cooperate with his press agents or they didn't get a story, and even then they rarely got a personal interview. If they did, they had to keep their questions general and not venture into difficult areas that might cause pain or embarrassment.

During an unguarded moment, Frank once said he would never allow the story of his life to be told.

"Never. That will never happen as long as I have any control over the project . . . there's too much about my life I'm not proud of."

When he was approaching seventy, he decided to tell the story he wanted told, and he planned to do it as a feature film.

"I want it done while I'm still alive," he said. "If they do my life story when I'm dead, they'll screw it up. I want to be around to see it's done right."

He had been trying for several years to write his autobiography but had not found a writer who would tell the story the way he wanted it told. So he decided to turn the film project over to his daughter, Tina, who planned to produce it as her first television miniseries.

Frank wanted the project to be presented with the kind of dignity befitting a close personal friend of the President of the United States. In the last few years the Reagans had made him part of their inner circle in the White House, and he reveled in the public perception of him as a Reagan insider. He was so comfortable in the role that he frequently joked about it. In a telegram to the Friars Club making excuses for his absence at a roast, he said: PRESIDENT REAGAN DOESN'T LIKE ME AND GEORGE SHULTZ [Secretary of State] TO BE ABSENT FROM THE WHITE HOUSE AT THE SAME TIME. He had been appointed to the President's Commission on the Arts and Humanities; he had performed at White House state dinners; he had been invited to the intimate birthday celebrations of both the President and First Lady.

In the summer of 1984, the President asked Frank for

help in his reelection campaign and made him the ambassador of fund-raising by sending him to seven cities for cocktail parties with selected Republicans who paid thousands of dollars for the privilege of being in his presence. Frank raised $500,000 for the Republican Victory '84 get-out-the-vote drive.

The hardest trip was the one that the President asked him to make in July, accompanying Reagan to the Festival of St. Ann in Hoboken. Running against the Mondale-Ferraro ticket, Reagan felt that he needed to ingratiate himself with blue-collar Italians, who traditionally voted Democratic. So a New Jersey campaign swing had been planned, including a stop in Sinatra's hometown for the church festival honoring the mother of the Blessed Virgin Mary, the patron saint of women. And Reagan wanted to arrive there with Hoboken's native son, the world's most famous Italian-American singer.

Since 1900, St. Ann's had been the parish church of the Italian community. The saint's feast day was celebrated around the world on July 26 and was dedicated to women, especially pregnant women. It was an appropriate time for President Reagan to deliver his message against abortion and for prayer in the public schools. He wanted to attend the traditional procession as women carried the 580-pound statue of St. Ann through the streets while parishioners rushed forward to pin money and flowers and jewelry to the cape hanging from her shoulders.

The President also wanted to stay for the spaghetti dinner and zeppole dessert with the archbishop in the church basement. Frank begged off the dinner and did not sit on the dais as the President condemned abortion in front of people who still remembered his mother as "Hat Pin Dolly."

Meeting the President in Newark, Frank flew by helicopter with him to Hoboken. They were driven in a presidential limousine to the church rectory at Seventh and Jefferson streets. Hundreds of people surged forward to greet Reagan, but hundreds more shouted to Frank, cheering his arrival and welcoming him back home.

"I can't believe he came back," said Margie LaGuardia, a lifelong Sinatra fan. "I felt like he would never be seen again in this city."

Shaking the outstretched hands like a veteran politician, Frank, once an infrequent boyhood parishioner of St. Ann's, smiled and laughed and greeted everyone amiably, but within twenty minutes he was back in the presidential limousine and heading for a concert in Hartford, Connecticut, while the President was inside the church pleading for the rights of the unborn.

New York Governor Mario Cuomo said he was disgusted by the sight of the President in Hoboken alongside Sinatra and the purple robes of the archbishop of Newark.

"It's just the most outrageous kind of pandering," he said. "Reagan probably thought, 'I'll get the Catholics, I'll put Frank Sinatra next to me, he's Italian,' that means all the Italians will vote for him."

The governor's criticism made no difference. Reagan won reelection by one of the largest landslides in history and he later repaid his Hoboken friend in full.

Once again, the President named him as director of entertainment and executive producer of the inaugural gala, despite an editorial in the New York *Daily News* that said, "Find Another Singer."

Reagan was inured to carping in the press about his friendship with Frank and dismissed it. He had ignored Joseph Kraft's column months before that had questioned his judgment in honoring Sinatra at the White House.

"The singer is not under indictment or anything of the kind," Kraft wrote. "But he is well known for alleged association with gangster elements. So holding him up for public admiration is the reverse of good taste. It is sleazy."

Nevertheless, the President was not prepared for the menacing encounter that occurred on the eve of his inaugural at the gala rehearsal. Frank had walked into the Convention Center after reading a profile about himself on the front page of *The Washington Post* Style section entitled: "The Rat Pack Is Back—Sinatra and his Sidekicks: A Cool for Modern Times?"

Barbara Howar, a reporter from *Entertainment Tonight*, approached him, saying: "Frank, I wonder if I could . . ."

Wheeling around before she could finish her question, Frank shook his gloved index finger. "Listen, I want to tell you something," he said. "You read the *Post* this afternoon? You're all dead, every one of you. You're all dead."

Television cameras and microphones captured the ferocious encounter and replayed it on the evening news, much to the consternation of the Reagans. Neither of them uttered a word in rebuke, though, for they, too, had been smarting from press coverage of Nancy's $46,000 inaugural wardrobe and insinuations that the streets of Washington were paved with idolatrous Republicans in mink coats and stretch limousines.

Sinatra continued seething about the *Post* article after the gala was over.

"You know why I get upset?" he said. "Did you see that thing in the paper? Geez! We're working eighteen hours a day trying to put together a show and every second counts, every second is important because we had so little time to put the show together, and then this thing comes out!

"I'm upset because the entire [entertainment] industry is performing like the Marine Corps. They come here from all parts of the world. Some stars gave up dates to come here. The show biz people are like the civilian Marine Corps, always ready to give our all. And then you see this story in print. It's a rehash of old stuff that was reprinted only because of the inaugural parties. . . . You see why I'm upset, because they don't use the First Amendment, they abuse it. They haven't earned the right to be called journalists and they give other journalists a bad name. . . . The show was a masterful job that came off as if we had been rehearsing for weeks. All the stars did great. Eva Gabor had to change an entire schedule to get here. It all jelled, like clockwork. They didn't write that, they had to dig up old stuff."

Frank's tirade did not embarrass the President or First Lady, but their son, Ron Reagan, Jr., confided to friends his shame and disgust over his parents' friendship with Sinatra. A few months later, on May 23, 1985, the President presented Sinatra with the nation's highest civilian award, the Presidential Medal of Freedom. His fellow recipients were Jimmy Stewart, the President's favorite movie star; marine explorer Jacques-Yves Cousteau; former secretary of the Smithsonian Institution S. Dillon Ripley II; retired Army General Albert Wedemeyer, a World War II hero in the Pacific Theater; retired Air Force General Charles E. "Chuck" Yeager, record-setting test pilot and first man to break the sound barrier; philosopher and educator Sidney Hook; former ambassador to the United Nations Jeanne J. Kirkpatrick; and Mother Teresa, the Roman Catholic nun who won the Nobel Prize for her work among the poor of Calcutta.

On the day of the presentation ceremony, the President addressed the honorees in the Blue Room of the White House.

"My guess is that probably as long as this nation lasts,

your descendants will speak with pride of the day you attended a White House ceremony and received this, the Medal of Freedom," he said. "Each of you has achieved the hardest of all things to achieve in life, something that will last and endure and take on a life of its own. And fifty years from now, a century from now, historians will know your names and your achievements. You have left humanity a legacy."

Placing the beribboned medal around Frank's neck, the President said: "His love of country, his generosity for those less fortunate, his distinctive art, and his winning and compassionate persona make him one of our most remarkable and distinguished Americans and one who truly did it his way."

There was to be still another award for Frank that day, this one back in Hoboken. Having ridiculed his hometown as a "sewer" for so many years, he was now returning in triumph to receive an honorary Doctor of Engineering degree from the Stevens Institute of Technology, the school his parents had prayed he would attend.

When the trustees had announced that they would confer this award on him, more than one hundred graduating seniors, one-third of the student body, signed a protest, citing his lack of educational credentials.

"The fact that Sinatra was born in Hoboken is a poor excuse for bestowing this honor," said the petitioners. "An honorary degree is awarded to someone who has distinguished himself in a particular field. Frank Sinatra is recognized in the area of entertainment, not engineering, not science, and not education. The stories say that Sinatra always wanted to go to Stevens when he was growing up in Hoboken. If he wanted it that badly, why didn't he bother to graduate from high school?"

The institute, though, stood behind its choice, saying that Frank was being honored as a humanitarian.

So on May 23, 1985, Sinatra went to Hoboken to receive an honor personally important to him. With the honorary doctorate he was finally making his parents' dreams of a college degree come true. He could stand up with pride to the memory of his mother and father.

Standing proudly in the black robes of a baccalaureate, he touched his tasseled graduation cap and beamed as the chairman of the Stevens board of trustees handed him the diploma and draped the red and gray engineer's hood over his shoulders. Walking to the center of the stage, he looked out on the stately campus that had always seemed like a king's paradise to him as a Depression child. The Italians who once knew his parents now gazed at him in awe. They were proud that one of their own had achieved such stunning success in the new world, and for a moment, Frank, too, seemed to recognize the wonder of his life.

"Today is quite a day for me . . . along with Jimmy Stewart, Jacques Cousteau, and others, I received a Medal of Freedom from the President of the United States," he said. "And now, here I am with you, at this institute of higher learning—the school I dreamed of attending when I was a kid." His face was flushed and his words, some garbled, came haltingly as he referred to the college as "the Stevens Institute of Humanities." He talked about his father who could not read or write. "My father was a great believer in education. . . . This is the school he had chosen for me to attend. My dad was—like all other dads I suppose—a wonderful man. . . . I must say I have that little bit of regret at all times at not having continued my education. . . . I am so honored . . . to be a small part of your day. This is more enjoyable than being at the White House. There nobody raised a fuss."

The crowd broke into cheers, as if their applause could wipe away the embarrassment of the student protest, but Sinatra was without rancor on that sunny afternoon at Castle Point. At peace with himself and his past, he told them how Stevens had helped him as a singer when he sprinted across the campus track trying to improve his lung capacity. Again the crowd cheered, happy to have been a part of this American dream. And Frank was grateful to them.

"I . . . I . . . hope you live to be four hundred years old," he said, "and may the last voice you hear be mine."

Then, just weeks after he had received his nation's highest accolade and the most coveted honor his hometown had to offer on one and the same day, his awards fell victim to the satirical pen of Garry B. Trudeau, the creator of "Doonesbury," one of America's most popular comic strips.

In a series of six strips, the artist depicted Frank's ties to the Mafia and mocked the values of a society that would honor such a man with a Medal of Freedom and a doctorate from the Stevens Institute of Technology. With scathing humor, Trudeau showed the President of the United States paying homage to a man who literally embraced the worst criminal elements of America, as Frank did when he posed for a picture with his arms around Carlo Gambino.

The prestige of the Medal of Freedom was tarnished by Trudeau's caricature of Frank shouting obscenities, bullying young women, and chasing after gangsters like a lovestruck teenager. Even sillier was the honorary degree, awarded to him for applying "his talents to the benefit of mankind," which in Trudeau's comic strip included trying to get a casino employee fired for refusing to break the law.

Sinatra responded to the stinging satire by issuing a statement: "Garry Trudeau makes his living by his attempts at humor without regard to fairness or decency. I don't know if he has made any effort on behalf of others or done anything to help the less fortunate in the country or elsewhere. I am happy to have the President and the people of the United States judge us by our respective track records."

Some newspapers, including the *Los Angeles Times*, refused to publish the strip because of a possible lawsuit from Sinatra. The letters to the editor of the *Times* about their refusal totaled 221. Two hundred and six letters criticized the decision and praised Trudeau; only fifteen letters praised Sinatra or criticized the cartoonist. That tally gave Frank a harsh barometer of public sentiment.

Still, bedecked in his ribbons, his awards, and his citations, he continued to present himself to the world as a great humanitarian, an inheritor of the American dream who had all that society could offer in terms of wealth and power and fame. Yet the honors of polite society and grateful politicians could never wipe out the stain of his Mafia associations or his ties to organized crime.

To those who had been touched by the magic of Frank Sinatra's music, his Mafia ties would never matter. For they had witnessed a peerless talent and that was enough. They had been moved by a performer who even at the age of seventy could still stir irrevocable longings. For fifty years, he had been interpreting the mood of his generation, taking people back to a time when love was young and life full of promise. With a catch in his voice betraying his own pain and loneliness, he reached into their souls, stoking their vulnerabilities. He soothed them and made them feel that their lost dreams were understood, their heartbreaks shared. His ballads became their anthems of romance—seductive, memorable, unique. More than any other popular singer, Frank Sinatra became the touchstone of his time.

DISCOGRAPHY

1940

SINGLES (VICTOR, *with Tommy Dorsey*)
  "I'll Never Smile Again"
  "Imagination"
  "Trade Winds"
  "Our Love Affair"
  "We Three"
  "Stardust"

NOTE: Only singles listed are those that made *Billboard* magazine's Top Ten.

1941

SINGLES (VICTOR, *with Tommy Dorsey*)
  "Oh, Look at Me Now"
  "Do I Worry?"
  "Dolores"
  "Everything Happens to Me"
  "Let's Get Away from It All"
  "This Love of Mine"
  "Two in Love"

1942

SINGLES (VICTOR, *with Tommy Dorsey*)

"Just As Though You Were Here"
"Take Me"
"Daybreak"
"There Are Such Things"

1943

SINGLES (VICTOR, *with Tommy Dorsey*)
"It Started All Over Again"
"In the Blue of the Evening"
"It's Always You"
"All or Nothing at All" (COLUMBIA, *with Harry James*, recorded and first released in 1939)
COLUMBIA
"You'll Never Know"
"Close to You"
"Sunday, Monday or Always"
"People Will Say We're in Love"

1944

SINGLES (COLUMBIA)
"I Couldn't Sleep a Wink Last Night"
"White Christmas" (released in 1946)

1945

SINGLES (COLUMBIA)
"I Dream of You"
"Saturday Night"
"Dream"
"Nancy"

1946

SINGLES (COLUMBIA)
"Oh! What It Seemed to Be"
"Day by Day"
"They Say It's Wonderful"
"Five Minutes More"
"The Coffee Song"

1947

SINGLE (COLUMBIA)
"Mam'selle"

1949

SINGLE (COLUMBIA)
"The Huckle Buck"

1954

SINGLES (CAPITOL)
"Young at Heart"
"Three Coins in the Fountain"
LPs (CAPITOL)
Songs for Young Lovers
Swing Easy

1955

SINGLES (CAPITOL)
"Learnin' the Blues"
"Love and Marriage"
LP (CAPITOL)
In the Wee Small Hours

1956

SINGLE (CAPITOL)
"Hey, Jealous Lover"
LP (CAPITOL)
Songs for Swingin' Lovers

1957

LPs (CAPITOL)
Close to You
A Swingin' Affair
Where Are You?
A Jolly Christmas from Frank Sinatra

1958

LPs (CAPITOL)
Come Fly with Me
Only the Lonely

1959

LPs (CAPITOL)
Come Dance with Me

Look to Your Heart
No One Cares

1960

LP (CAPITOL)
Nice 'n' Easy

1961

LPs (CAPITOL)
Sinatra's Swingin' Session
All the Way
Come Swing with Me
(REPRISE)
Ring-A-Ding-Ding
Sinatra Swings
I Remember Tommy

1962

LPs (CAPITOL)
Point of No Return
Sinatra Sings of Love and Things
(REPRISE)
Sinatra and Strings
Sinatra and Swingin' Brass
All Alone

1963

LPs (REPRISE)
Sinatra-Basie
The Concert Sinatra
Sinatra's Sinatra

1964

LPs (REPRISE)
Frank Sinatra Sings Days of Wine and Roses, Moon River and other Academy Award Winners
Sinatra-Basie: It Might as Well Be Swing
Softly, As I Leave You

1965

LPs (REPRISE)
Sinatra '65
September of My Years
A Man and His Music
My Kind of Broadway

1966

SINGLES (REPRISE)
"Strangers in the Night"
"That's Life"
LPs (REPRISE)
Moonlight Sinatra
Strangers in the Night
Sinatra-Basie: Sinatra at the Sands
That's Life

1967

SINGLE (REPRISE)
"Somethin' Stupid" (with Nancy Sinatra)
LPs (REPRISE)
Francis Albert Sinatra & Antonio Carlos Jobim
Frank Sinatra and Frank & Nancy

1968

LPs (REPRISE)
Francis A. & Edward K.
Cycles

1969

LPs (REPRISE)
My Way
A Man Alone

1970

LP (REPRISE)
Watertown

1971

LP (REPRISE)
Sinatra & Company

1973

LP (SINATRA)
   Ol' Blue Eyes Is Back

1974

LPs (REPRISE)
   Some Nice Things I've Missed
   The Main Event/Live from Madison Square Garden

1980

LPs (REPRISE)
   Trilogy (three-record album)

1981

LP (REPRISE)
   She Shot Me Down

1984

LP (QWEST)
   L.A. Is My Lady

FILMOGRAPHY

Las Vegas Nights (Paramount, 1941)
PRODUCER: William LeBaron. DIRECTOR: Ralph Murphy. SCREEN-
PLAY: Ernest Pagano and Harry Clork. CAST: Constance Moore,
Bert Wheeler. Tommy Dorsey and His Orchestra, with Frank
Sinatra as the male vocalist singing "I'll Never Smile Again."

Ship Ahoy (MGM, 1942)
PRODUCER: Jack Cummings. DIRECTOR: Edward Buzzell. SCREEN-
PLAY: Harry Clork. CAST: Eleanor Powell, Red Skelton, Bert
Lahr, Virginia O'Brien. Tommy Dorsey and His Orchestra, with
Frank Sinatra singing "The Last Call for Love" and "Poor You."

Reveille with Beverly (Columbia, 1943)
PRODUCER: Sam White. DIRECTOR: Charles Barton. SCREENPLAY:
Howard J. Green, Jack Henley, and Albert Duffy. CAST: Ann
Miller, William Wright, Dick Purcell, Franklin Pangborn, Tim
Ryan, Larry Parks, with Frank Sinatra singing "Night and Day."

Higher and Higher (RKO, 1943)
PRODUCER AND DIRECTOR: Tim Whelan. SCREENPLAY: Jay Dratler
and Ralph Spence. CAST: Michèle Morgan, Jack Haley, Frank
Sinatra.

Step Lively (RKO, 1944)
PRODUCER: Robert Fellows. DIRECTOR: Tim Whelan. SCREENPLAY:
Warren Duff and Peter Milne. CAST: Frank Sinatra, George
Murphy, Adolph Menjou, Gloria DeHaven, Walter Slezak.

Anchors Aweigh (MGM, 1945)
PRODUCER: Joe Pasternak. DIRECTOR: George Sidney. SCREEN-PLAY: Isobel Lennart. CAST: Frank Sinatra, Kathryn Grayson, Gene Kelly, Jose Iturbi.

The House I Live In (RKO, 1945)
PRODUCER: Frank Ross. DIRECTOR: Mervyn LeRoy. SCREENPLAY: Albert Maltz. CAST: Frank Sinatra
Note: *The House I Live In*, a ten-minute short, won a special award from the Academy of Motion Picture Arts and Sciences.

Till the Clouds Roll By (MGM, 1946)
PRODUCER: Arthur Freed. DIRECTOR: Richard Whorf. SCREENPLAY: Myles Connolly and Jean Holloway. Based on the life and music of Jerome Kern. CAST: June Allyson, Lucille Bremer, Judy Garland, Kathryn Grayson, Van Heflin, Lena Horne, Van Johnson, Angela Lansbury, Tony Martin, Virginia O'Brien, Dinah Shore, Frank Sinatra, Robert Walker.
With guest star Sinatra singing "Ol' Man River."

It Happened in Brooklyn (MGM, 1947)
PRODUCER: Jack Cummings. DIRECTOR: Richard Whorf. SCREEN-PLAY: Isobel Lennart. CAST: Frank Sinatra, Kathryn Grayson, Peter Lawford, Jimmy Durante.

The Miracle of the Bells (RKO, 1948)
PRODUCERS: Jesse L. Lasky and Walter MacEwen. DIRECTOR: Irving Pichel. SCREENPLAY: Ben Hecht and Quentin Reynolds. CAST: Fred MacMurray, Alida Valli, Frank Sinatra, Lee J. Cobb.

The Kissing Bandit (MGM, 1948)
PRODUCER: Joe Pasternak. DIRECTOR: Laslo Benedek. SCREEN-PLAY: Isobel Lennart and John Briard Harding. CAST: Frank Sinatra, Kathryn Grayson.

Take Me Out to the Ball Game (MGM, 1949)
PRODUCER: Arthur Freed. DIRECTOR: Busby Berkeley. SCREEN-PLAY: Harry Tugend and George Wells. CAST: Frank Sinatra, Esther Williams, Gene Kelly, Betty Garrett, Edward Arnold, Jules Munshin.

On the Town (MGM, 1949)
PRODUCER: Arthur Freed. DIRECTORS: Gene Kelly and Stanley Donen. SCREENPLAY: Adolph Green and Betty Comden from their musical play based on an idea by Jerome Robbins. CAST: Gene Kelly, Frank Sinatra, Betty Garrett, Ann Miller.

Double Dynamite (RKO, 1951)
PRODUCER: Irving Cummings, Jr. DIRECTOR: Irving Cummings. SCREENPLAY: Melville Shavelson. CAST: Jane Russell, Groucho Marx, Frank Sinatra.

Meet Danny Wilson (Universal-International, 1952)
PRODUCER: Leonard Goldstein. DIRECTOR: Joseph Pevney. SCREENPLAY: Don McGuire. CAST: Frank Sinatra, Shelley Winters, Alex Nicol.

From Here to Eternity (Columbia, 1953)
PRODUCER: Buddy Adler. DIRECTOR: Fred Zinnemann. SCREENPLAY: Daniel Taradash. CAST: Burt Lancaster, Montgomery Clift, Deborah Kerr, Donna Reed, Frank Sinatra, Ernest Borgnine.
Note: *From Here to Eternity* won eight Oscars in 1953: Best picture, direction, screenplay, photography, film editing, sound, supporting actress (Donna Reed), and supporting actor (Frank Sinatra).

Suddenly (A Libra Production, released by United Artists, 1954)
PRODUCER: Robert Bassler. DIRECTOR: Lewis Allen. SCREENPLAY: Richard Sale. CAST: Frank Sinatra, Sterling Hayden, James Gleason, Nancy Gates.

Young at Heart (An Arwin Production, released by Warner Bros., 1955)
PRODUCER: Henry Blanke. DIRECTOR: Gordon Douglas. SCREENPLAY: Adaptation by Liam O'Brien from the screenplay *Four Daughters* by Julius J. Epstein and Lenore Coffee. CAST: Doris Day, Frank Sinatra, Gig Young, Ethel Barrymore, Dorothy Malone.

Not as a Stranger (A Stanley Kramer Production, released by United Artists, 1955)
PRODUCER AND DIRECTOR: Stanley Kramer. SCREENPLAY: Edna and Edward Anhalt. CAST: Olivia de Havilland, Robert Mitchum, Frank Sinatra, Gloria Grahame, Broderick Crawford, Charles Bickford.

The Tender Trap (MGM, 1955)
PRODUCER: Lawrence Weingarten. DIRECTOR: Charles Walters. SCREENPLAY: Julius J. Epstein. CAST: Frank Sinatra, Debbie Reynolds, David Wayne, Celeste Holm, Jarma Lewis, Lola Albright, Carolyn Jones.

Guys and Dolls (A Samuel Goldwyn Production, released by MGM, 1955)
PRODUCER: Samuel Goldwyn. DIRECTOR AND SCREENPLAY: Jo-

seph L. Mankiewicz. CAST: Marlon Brando, Jean Simmons, Frank Sinatra, Vivian Blaine.

The Man with the Golden Arm (A Carlyle Production, released by United Artists, 1955)
PRODUCER AND DIRECTOR: Otto Preminger. SCREENPLAY: Walter Newman and Lewis Meltzer. CAST: Frank Sinatra, Eleanor Parker, Kim Novak.

Meet Me in Las Vegas (MGM, 1956)
PRODUCER: Joe Pasternak. DIRECTOR: Roy Rowland. SCREENPLAY: Isobel Lennart. CAST: Dan Dailey, Cyd Charisse, Jerry Colonna, Paul Henreid, Lena Horne, Frankie Laine, Mitsuko Sawamura. Note: Frank Sinatra appeared as an unbilled guest along with Debbie Reynolds, Tony Martin, Peter Lorre, Vic Damone, and Elaine Stewart.

Johnny Concho (A Kent Production, released by United Artists, 1956)
PRODUCER: Frank Sinatra. DIRECTOR: Don McGuire. SCREENPLAY: David P. Harmon and Don McGuire. CAST: Frank Sinatra, Keenan Wynn, William Conrad, Phyllis Kirk.

High Society (MGM, 1956)
PRODUCER: Sol C. Siegel. DIRECTOR: Charles Walters. SCREENPLAY: John Patrick. CAST: Bing Crosby, Grace Kelly, Frank Sinatra, Celeste Holm, John Lund, Louis Calhern.

Around the World in 80 Days (A Michael Todd Production, released by United Artists, 1956)
PRODUCER: Michael Todd. DIRECTOR: Michael Anderson. SCREENPLAY: James Poe, John Farrow, and S. J. Perelman. CAST: David Niven, Cantinflas, Shirley MacLaine, Robert Newton, Frank Sinatra in a cameo appearance as a drunk in a Barbary Coast saloon.

The Pride and the Passion (A Stanley Kramer Production, released by United Artists, 1957)
PRODUCER AND DIRECTOR: Stanley Kramer. SCREENPLAY: Edna and Edward Anhalt. CAST: Cary Grant, Frank Sinatra, Sophia Loren.

The Joker Is Wild (An M.B.L. Production, released by Paramount, 1957)
PRODUCER: Samuel J. Briskin. DIRECTOR: Charles Vidor. SCREENPLAY: Oscar Saul. CAST: Frank Sinatra, Mitzi Gaynor, Jeanne Crain, Eddie Albert.

Pal Joey (An Essex–George Sidney Production, released by Columbia, 1957)
PRODUCER: Fred Kohlmar. DIRECTOR: George Sidney. SCREENPLAY: Dorothy Kingsley. CAST: Rita Hayworth, Frank Sinatra, Kim Novak.

Kings Go Forth (A Frank Ross–Eton Production, released by United Artists, 1958)
PRODUCER: Frank Ross. DIRECTOR: Delmer Daves. SCREENPLAY: Merle Miller. CAST: Frank Sinatra, Tony Curtis, Natalie Wood.

Some Came Running (MGM, 1958)
PRODUCER: Sol C. Siegel. DIRECTOR: Vincente Minnelli. SCREENPLAY: John Patrick and Arthur Sheekman. CAST: Frank Sinatra, Dean Martin, Shirley MacLaine, Arthur Kennedy.

A Hole in the Head (A Sincap Production, released by United Artists, 1959)
PRODUCER AND DIRECTOR: Frank Capra. SCREENPLAY: Arnold Schulman. CAST: Frank Sinatra, Edward G. Robinson, Eleanor Parker, Carolyn Jones, Thelma Ritter, Keenan Wynn.

Never So Few (A Canterbury Production, released by MGM, 1959) PRODUCER: Edmund Grainger. DIRECTOR: John Sturges. SCREENPLAY: Millard Kaufman. CAST: Frank Sinatra, Gina Lollobrigida, Peter Lawford, Steve McQueen.

Can-Can (A Suffolk-Cummings Production, released by Twentieth Century Fox, 1960)
PRODUCER: Jack Cummings. DIRECTOR: Walter Lang. SCREENPLAY: Dorothy Kingsley and Charles Lederer. CAST: Frank Sinatra, Shirley MacLaine, Maurice Chevalier, Louis Jourdan.

Ocean's Eleven (A Dorchester Production, released by Warner Bros., 1960)
PRODUCER AND DIRECTOR: Lewis Milestone. SCREENPLAY: Harry Brown and Charles Lederer. CAST: Frank Sinatra, Dean Martin, Sammy Davis, Jr., Peter Lawford, Angie Dickinson, Richard Conte, Cesar Romero, Patrice Wymore, Joey Bishop, Akim Tamiroff, Henry Silva.

Pepe (A G.S.–Posa Films International Production, released by Columbia, 1960)
PRODUCER AND DIRECTOR: George Sidney. SCREENPLAY: Dorothy Kingsley and Claude Binyon. CAST: Cantinflas, Dan Dailey, Shirley Jones, Frank Sinatra in guest appearances.

The Devil at 4 O'Clock (Columbia, 1961)
PRODUCER: Fred Kohlmar. DIRECTOR: Mervyn LeRoy. SCREEN-PLAY: Liam O'Brien. CAST: Spencer Tracy, Frank Sinatra, Kerwin Matthews, Jean-Pierre Aumont.

Sergeants 3 (An Essex–Claude Production, released by United Artists, 1962)
PRODUCER: Frank Sinatra. DIRECTOR: John Sturges. SCREEN-PLAY: W. R. Burnett. CAST: Frank Sinatra, Dean Martin, Sammy Davis, Jr., Peter Lawford, Joey Bishop.

The Road to Hong Kong (A Melnor Films Production, released by United Artists, 1962)
PRODUCER: Melvin Frank. DIRECTOR: Norman Panama. SCREEN-PLAY: Norman Panama and Melvin Frank. CAST: Bing Crosby, Bob Hope, Joan Collins, Dorothy Lamour, Robert Morley, with Frank Sinatra, Jerry Colonna, Dean Martin, David Niven, and Peter Sellers as unbilled guest stars.

The Manchurian Candidate (An M.C. Production, released by United Artists, 1962)
PRODUCERS: George Axelrod and John Frankenheimer. DIRECTOR: John Frankenheimer. SCREENPLAY: George Axelrod. CAST: Frank Sinatra, Laurence Harvey, Janet Leigh, Angela Lansbury, Henry Silva.

Come Blow Your Horn (An Essex–Tandem Production, released by Paramount, 1963)
PRODUCERS: Norman Lear and Bud Yorkin. DIRECTOR: Bud Yorkin. SCREENPLAY: Norman Lear. CAST: Frank Sinatra, Lee J. Cobb, Molly Picon, Barbara Rush, Jill St. John, Tony Bill.

The List of Adrian Messenger (A Joel Production, released by Universal, 1963)
PRODUCER: Edward Lewis. DIRECTOR: John Huston. SCREENPLAY: Anthony Veiller. CAST: George C. Scott, Dana Wynter, Clive Brook, with Frank Sinatra, Tony Curtis, Kirk Douglas, Burt Lancaster, Robert Mitchum in guest appearances.

4 for Texas (A Sam Company Production, released by Warner Bros., 1964)
PRODUCER AND DIRECTOR: Robert Aldrich. SCREENPLAY: Teddi Sherman and Robert Aldrich. CAST: Frank Sinatra, Dean Martin, Anita Ekberg, Ursula Andress, Charles Bronson.

Robin and the Seven Hoods (A P-C Productions Picture, released by Warner Bros., 1964)

PRODUCER: Frank Sinatra. DIRECTOR: Gordon Douglas. SCREEN-PLAY: David R. Schwartz. CAST: Frank Sinatra, Dean Martin, Sammy Davis, Jr., Peter Falk.

None but the Brave (An Artanis Production, released by Warner Bros., 1965)
PRODUCER AND DIRECTOR: Frank Sinatra. SCREENPLAY: John Twist and Katsuya Susaki. CAST: Frank Sinatra, Clint Walker, Tommy Sands, Brad Dexter, Tony Bill.

Von Ryan's Express (A P-R Productions Picture, released by Twentieth Century Fox, 1965)
PRODUCER: Saul David. DIRECTOR: Mark Robson. SCREENPLAY: Wendell Mayes and Joseph Landon. CAST: Frank Sinatra, Trevor Howard, Raffaella Carra, Brad Dexter, Sergio Fantoni, John Leyton, Edward Mulhare.

Marriage on the Rocks (An A-C Productions Picture, released by Warner Bros., 1965)
PRODUCER: William H. Daniels. DIRECTOR: Jack Donohue. SCREENPLAY: Cy Howard. CAST: Frank Sinatra, Deborah Kerr, Dean Martin, Cesar Romero.

Cast a Giant Shadow (A Mirisch-Llenroc-Batjack Production, released by United Artists, 1966)
PRODUCER, DIRECTOR, AND SCREENPLAY: Melville Shavelson. CAST: Kirk Douglas, Senta Berger, Angie Dickinson, with Frank Sinatra, Yul Brynner, John Wayne in guest appearances.

The Oscar (A Greene-Rouse Production, released by Embassy Pictures, 1966)
PRODUCER: Clarence Greene. DIRECTOR: Russell Rouse. SCREEN-PLAY: Harlan Ellison. CAST: Stephen Boyd, Elke Sommer, Milton Berle, Eleanor Parker, Joseph Cotten, with Frank Sinatra in a guest appearance.

Assault on a Queen (A Sinatra Enterprises–Seven Arts Production, released by Paramount, 1966)
PRODUCER: William Goetz. DIRECTOR: Jack Donohue. SCREEN-PLAY: Rod Serling. CAST: Frank Sinatra, Virna Lisi, Tony Franciosa, Richard Conte.

The Naked Runner (A Sinatra Enterprises Production, released by Warner Bros., 1967)
PRODUCER: Brad Dexter. DIRECTOR: Sidney J. Furie. SCREEN-PLAY: Stanley Mann. CAST: Frank Sinatra, Peter Vaughan, Derren Nesbitt.

Tony Rome (An Arcola-Millfield Production, released by Twentieth Century Fox, 1967)
PRODUCER: Aaron Rosenberg. DIRECTOR: Gordon Douglas. SCREENPLAY: Richard L. Breen. CAST: Frank Sinatra, Jill St. John, Richard Conte, Gena Rowlands.

The Detective (An Arcola–Millfield Production, released by Twentieth Century Fox, 1968)
PRODUCER: Aaron Rosenberg. DIRECTOR: Gordon Douglas. SCREENPLAY: Abby Mann. CAST: Frank Sinatra, Lee Remick, Ralph Meeker, Jack Klugman.

Lady in Cement (An Arcola–Millfield Production, released by Twentieth Century Fox, 1968)
PRODUCER: Aaron Rosenberg. DIRECTOR: Gordon Douglas. SCREENPLAY: Marvin H. Albert and Jack Guss. CAST: Frank Sinatra, Raquel Welch, Dan Blocker, Richard Conte.

Dirty Dingus Magee (MGM, 1970)
PRODUCER AND DIRECTOR: Burt Kennedy. SCREENPLAY: Tom and Frank Waldman and Joseph Heller. CAST: Frank Sinatra, George Kennedy, Anne Jackson, Lois Nettleton.

Contract on Cherry Street (a television movie, Columbia, 1977)
EXECUTIVE PRODUCER: Renee Valente. PRODUCER: Hugh Benson. DIRECTOR: William A. Graham. TELEPLAY: Edward Anhalt, based on the book by Philip Rosenberg. CAST: Frank Sinatra, Jay Black, Martin Balsam, Martin Gabel, Harry Guardino, Henry Silva.

The First Deadly Sin (An Artanis–Cinema VII Production, released by Filmways, 1980)
PRODUCERS: George Pappas and Mark Shanker. DIRECTOR: Brian Hutton. SCREENPLAY: Mann Rubin. CAST: Frank Sinatra, Faye Dunaway, David Dukes, George Coe, Brenda Vaccaro.

Cannonball Run II (Warner Bros., 1984)
PRODUCER: Albert S. Ruddy. DIRECTOR: Hal Needham. SCREENPLAY: Hal Needham, Albert S. Ruddy, and Harvey Miller, based on characters created by Brock Yates. CAST: Burt Reynolds, Dom DeLuise, Dean Martin, Sammy Davis, Jr., Telly Savalas, Shirley MacLaine, Susan Anton. Frank Sinatra played himself.

AUTHOR'S CHAPTER NOTES

The following chapter notes indicate some of the sources used by the author in writing each chapter of the book, including the people interviewed, the documents examined, and the published sources consulted. It is by no means comprehensive, but it is intended to give the reader a general overview of some of the author's research.

CHAPTER 1

Information on Frank Sinatra's arrest and morals charges was obtained from arrest records and court files in Bergen County and Hudson County, New Jersey, courthouses. In addition, the author interviewed Toni Francke on March 8, 29, and June 12, 1983, and read the coverage of the episode in the *Hudson Dispatch*.

Among the books consulted on the history of Hoboken were: Procter, Mary and Bill Matuszeki, *Gritty Cities*, Philadelphia: Temple University Press, 1978; Miller, George Long, *The Hoboken of Yesterday*, Hoboken, New Jersey: Poggi Press, 1966; Clark, Geoffrey W., "An Interpretation of Hoboken's Population Trends, 1856–1970"; Fiel, John Perkins, *Halo over Hoboken*, New York: Exposition Press, 1955; Kenny, John Jr., *The Bicentennial Comes to Hoboken*, New Jersey Hoboken American Revolution Bicentennial Committee, 1976; Cunningham, Barbara, ed., *The New Jersey Ethnic Experience*, Union City, New Jersey: Wm. H. Wise & Co., 1977; Varacalli, Joseph A., *Ethnic Politics in New Jersey: The Changing Nature of Irish-Italian Relations, 1917–1983*, Department of Sociology, Nassau Community College, 1983.

Background on the Sinatra family was obtained from many sources, including the Hudson County Records Bureau, and interviews with Rosalie Garavante Blumberg on March 4, 1984; Steve Capiello, mayor of Hoboken, on January 24, 1983; Doris Corrado on January 20, 21, and 24, 1983; and Frank Garrick on January 20, 1983.

CHAPTER 2

The author obtained background information on Frank Sinatra's family from interviews with Rosalie Garavante Blumberg, Rose Bucino Carrier on February 18, June 13, and August 1, 1983, and August 4, 1984, Doris Corrado, Tony Macagnano on February 18, 1983, Adam Sciaria on February 16, 1983, Bob Anthony on January 17, 1983, Kathryn Buhan on January 24, 1983, Joan Crocco Schook on January 24, 25, and February 16, 1983, Joe Romano on January 21, 1983, and Agnes Carney Hannigan on January 25, February 18, and March 11, 1983.

In addition, the author consulted records in the Hudson County Courthouse, the Hoboken Fire Department, and articles published in magazines such as the *Jersey Journal, Look, Esquire,* and *Photoplay.*

CHAPTER 3

Material in this chapter comes primarily from the many interviews with the Sinatras' friends and neighbors in Hoboken, among them Tony Macagnano, Agnes Hannigan, Doris Corrado, Rose Carrier, Anna Spatolla Sinatra, and Frank Garrick. In addition, the author interviewed Nick Sevano on seventeen occasions in June and August 1983, March to September 1984, and in January 1985.

CHAPTER 4

Much of the material concerning the beginning of Sinatra's career was obtained from interviews with Fred "Tamby" Tamburro on February 7, 1983, Don Milo on January 22 and February 15, 1983, Tony "Skelly" Petrocelli on January 21, 1983, Marian Brush Schreiber on January 23 and 25 and February 20 and 28, 1983, Frank Capone Cipriello on February 16, 1983, Adeline Yacinda on March 10, 1983, and Sam Lefaso on February 21 and August 21 and 22, 1984. Among the other material consulted by the author were news articles in the *New York Journal-American, New York Post,* the *New Jersey Monthly, Bandleader,* and *Look.* The author also read *Beyond the Melting Pot,* Glazer, Nathan, and Moynihan, Daniel P., Cambridge, Mass.: The M.I.T. Press, 1963; Barzini, Luigi, *The Italians,* New York: Atheneum, 1981; and Tony Sciacca's book, *Sinatra,* New York: Pinnacle Books, 1976.

Information in this chapter on other aspects of this period in Sinatra's life was obtained from, among other places, records of the Hudson County Courthouse, other personal interviews, and news articles.

CHAPTER 5

Much of the material in this chapter comes from some of Sinatra's early associates, either in their own published memories or in personal interviews with the author. Among these are Simon, George T., *The Big Bands,* New York: Schirmer Books, 1981; Haines, Connie, *For Once in My Life,* New York: Warner Books, 1976; Herb Sanford's *Tommy and Jimmy: The Dorsey Years,* New York: Arlington House, 1972; Sammy Cahn's *I Should Care: The Sammy Cahn Story,* New York: Arbor House, 1974; and articles in the *New York Post,* New York *Daily News, American Mercury,*

Hollywood Citizen News, Los Angeles Herald Examiner, and the *Chicago Sun-Times.* The author also interviewed Nick Sevano, Herb Caen, on March 23, 1984, Al Algiro, Sammy Cahn on July 7, 1983, Rita Marrit on April 7, 11, and 18, 1984, Mary Lou Watts on July 12, 1984, Arthur Michaud on March 11, 1984, and N. Joseph Ross on October 2, 1984. Two previous books on Sinatra, Arnold Shaw's *Sinatra,* London: W.H. Allen, 1968, and Robin Douglas Home's *Sinatra,* New York: Grosset & Dunlap, 1962, as well as numerous newspaper interviews with Sinatra were also used. In addition, the author also examined arrest records in the Hudson County Courthouse.

CHAPTER 6

Among the sources consulted by the author were articles in the *Saturday Evening Post, New York Post, PM, Look,* New York *Daily News,* and the *New York Journal-American* as well as several books and personal interviews.

In George Burns's book, *Dr. Burns' Prescription for Happiness,* New York: G.P. Putnam & Sons, 1984, George Burns recounts that he once offered Sinatra $250 to sing on his radio show. He says, "I was about to sign him when I learned I could get an act called the Three Smoothies for the same money. Well, I wasn't born yesterday. If I could get three people for the same money, what would I want with that skinny kid? So I took the Smoothies. Frank has never forgotten that. Every Christmas I get a gift from him with a note thanking me for not doing for his career what I did for the Smoothies."

In one of two interviews with Mitch Miller in November 1983, Mr. Miller told the author, "Jimmy Van Heusen once canceled dinner with me by saying, 'I'm sorry, but I've got to eat with the Monster.' Everyone called Sinatra the Monster."

CHAPTER 7

Much of the material in this chapter comes from author interviews with, among others, Fred "Tamby" Tambarro, Nick Sevano, Ben Barton on July 8 and 13, 1983; Minnie Cardinale on February 19, 1983; Connie Cappadona on September 27, 1984; Richie Shirak on January 22, 1983, and Joey (GiGi) Lissa on January 21, 1983. The author also used several published news articles and books.

CHAPTER 8

The author gathered information on the early years of Sinatra's success from many sources, particularly interviews with Marian Brush Schreiber, Mary Lou Watts, and Tony Macagnano and articles in the *Los Angeles Times, Los Angeles Herald Examiner, PM, Look, Boston Post, New York World Telegram, Hollywood Reporter,* and *New York Post.*

CHAPTER 9

The story of Sinatra's war years was obtained from interviews with Phil Silvers on March 14, 1984, Jo-Carroll Silvers on March 15, 18, 19, 27,

1983, and Sammy Cahn. The author also had access to an oral history taped by Jack Keller. Several articles and books were also used.

CHAPTER 10

Material on Sinatra's early years at MGM was obtained from several sources, among them files at MGM examined by the author and many published accounts, including John Douglas Eames's *The MGM Story*, New York: Crown, 1979, and Earl Wilson's *Sinatra*, New York: New American Library, 1976, as well as other articles and interviews. Among the sources for Sinatra's friendship with Joe Fischetti, his trip to Havana and the resulting publicity were MGM files, Joe Fischetti's FBI files (obtained through a Freedom of Information Act request) in which Fischetti told agents in 1963 that he had known Sinatra for twenty-five years since they were "kids," and Jack Keller's oral history tapes as well as numerous books and newspaper articles. Among these were Ovid Demaris's *The Green Felt Jungle*, New York: Trident Press, 1963; David Hanna's *The Lucky Luciano Inheritance*, New York: Belmont Tower Books, 1975; Feder and Joesten's *The Luciano Story*, New York: Award Books, 1972; Eisenberg, Dan, Landau's *Meyer Lansky: Mogul of the Mob*, New York and London: Paddington Press, 1979; John Rockwell's *Sinatra: An American Classic*, New York: Rolling Stone Press, 1984; and articles in the *New York World Telegram*, *New York Post*, *New York Sun*, *Havana Post*, and *Los Angeles Times*.

As to MGM legal files, a daily production report is prepared by the assistant director and is a day-to-day report that tells who worked, both cast and crew, the period they worked, and any comments about the day's activities.

Other information in this chapter, including Sinatra's feud with Lee Mortimer, was documented by reference to Jack Keller's oral history tapes, interviews with John Hearst, Jr., on November 4, 1983, William Randolph Hearst on November 1, 1983, Anna Carroll, Hearst's secretary, on November 6, 1983, Mel Tormé on April 18, 1984, Anna Spatolla Sinatra, Phil Evans on January 31, 1986, and Betty Garrett on July 30, 1983. The author also used Bill Davidson's *The Real and The Unreal*, New York: Harper & Bros., 1957, Charles Higham's *Ava*, New York: Delacorte Press, 1974, and several articles about Ava Gardner. The author also examined arrest records in Hudson County Courthouse.

CHAPTER 11

Background information about Ava Gardner was obtained from Higham's book, *Ava*, as well as Flamini's book, also entitled *Ava*, New York: Coward, McCann, and Geoghegan, 1983, and John Daniell's *Ava Gardner*, New York: St. Martin's Press, 1982. Other information in this chapter on Sinatra and Gardner was obtained from many sources as well as these three books, among them, interviews with Nick Sevano, Betty Burns Paps on March 11 and April 18, 1984, Anita Colby Flagen on October 17, 1985, a relative of Jack Keller's on June 21, 1983, and Artie Shaw on December 17, 1983, and April 10, 1984. The author also had access to

Michael Thornton's interviews with Ava Gardner on November 17, 19, 20, and 28, 1982, an unpublished interview by Bill Martin of Budd Granoff on March 16, 1985, MGM legal files, and Justice Department files containing the Willie Moretti telegram to Sinatra.

On April 25, 1984, the author interviewed Corinne Entratter, who told the author, among other things, that Sinatra had nicknamed her husband, Jack, "Jew Feet" because of orthopedic shoes he wore due to the osteomyelitis he suffered as a child. "I have watches that Frank would give Jack, 'Stay on time to J.F.' meaning Jew Feet," said Corinne Entratter. "One leg of Jack's was shorter than the other and shriveled. Even though he was six feet two inches, he walked with a limp. He wore Space Shoes, so [Frank] called him Jew Feet."

The story of Sinatra's departure from MGM was obtained, in part, in interviews on March 25 and April 11, 1984, with a former MCA agent who requested anonymity and the MCA files in the Justice Department obtained by the author through the Freedom of Information Act.

Additional information about Sinatra's marriage and career was gathered from several sources, among them interviews with Kitty Kallen on July 18, 1983, Mitch Miller on October 24, November 1, 4, 1983, Irving Mansfield on October 26, 28, November 3, December 3, 12, 14, 1983, and April 4, 1984, and numerous newspaper and magazine articles.

Material on Sinatra's testimony before the Kefauver committee and questions about his Mafia connections generally were obtained from a variety of sources, including the transcript of Sinatra's testimony in executive session as well as the testimony of others called by the committee, interviews with Joseph L. Nellis on February 17, 18, 19, 1984, and several newspaper accounts of the committee's work. Books such as Vincent Teresa's (with Thomas Renner) *Vinnie Teresa's Mafia*, New York: Doubleday & Co., Inc., 1975, and Kefauver's *Crime in America*, New York: Doubleday & Co., Inc., 1951, were also consulted.

In 1961, Sinatra Enterprises came under scrutiny in the investigation of a Mafia-linked car dealer in Chicago. The Sterling-Harris Ford Agency declared bankruptcy after $80,000 disappeared from the agency's treasury and 359 cars vanished from the lot. The *Chicago Daily Tribune* called it a "gangland mystery" and reported that at a weekend sale, "buyers, including crime syndicate gangsters, plunked down cash for autos sold far below factory prices." Less than two weeks before the "gangland mystery," two of the cars, white Thunderbird coupes, were found in the possession of two executives of Sinatra Enterprises, more than 2,000 miles away in Los Angeles.

CHAPTER 12

Information in Chapter 12 was obtained from various sources, among them, interviews with Dorothy Manners on August 8, 1951, Rene Valente on July 25, 1983, and George Jacobs on June 15, 1983. A number of articles were consulted, including those in the *Los Angeles Herald Examiner*, *Los Angeles Daily News*, *New York World-Telegram*, *New York Post*, and

Modern Screen as well as Flamini's book on Ava Gardner and Shelley Winter's *Shelley Also Known as Shirley*, New York: William Morrow, 1980.

CHAPTER 13

Sinatra's tumultuous relationship with Ava Gardner has been well documented in numerous articles and books consulted by the author, including Richard Gehman, *Sinatra and His Rat Pack*, New York: Belmont Books, 1963; Lana Turner's *Lana*, New York: E. P. Dutton, Inc., 1983; Higham's biography of Ava Gardner, and articles in the *Los Angeles Herald Examiner*, *New York Post*, *Woman's Home Companion*, *Variety*, *Los Angeles Mirror*, *Los Angeles Times*, and Sinatra's own two-part series in the *American Weekly*. Material was also supplied in interviews on March 9, 10, 12, 22 and April 3, 16, 17, 1984, with a woman who lived with Jimmy Van Heusen. Also interviewed were Nick Sevano, Rita Maritt, Joan Cohn Harvey on July 11, 1983, and Michael Thornton's interviews with Ava Gardner were consulted. MGM legal files examined by the author provided additional information.

CHAPTER 14

The story of Sinatra and *From Here to Eternity* was obtained from the author's interviews with several people, among them, Abe Lastfogel on June 10, 1983, Corinne Entratter on April 25 and September 24, 1984, Joan Cohn Harvey, Eli Wallach on November 28 and December 5, 1984, Daniel Taradash on July 6, 1983, Walter Shenson on June 1, 1984, John J. Miller on December 12, 16, 1983, and law enforcement sources. Books including Shaw's and Wilson's on Sinatra, Flamini's on Gardner, Patricia Bosworth's *Montgomery Clift*, New York and London: Harcourt Brace Jovanovich, 1978; Robert Laguardia's *Monty*, New York: Arbor House, 1977; William Goldman's *Adventures in the Screen Trade*, New York: Warner Books, 1983; and Leonard Katz's *Uncle Frank: The Biography of Frank Costello*, New York: Drake, 1973, were also consulted. MGM legal files provided additional information.

Sinatra's letter to producer Leland Hayward signed "Maggio" is on file in the correspondence collection at the Performing Arts Research Center at the New York Public Library. It reads: "Dear Leland—my paisan Mr. Sinatra is still on cloud nine and the bum refuses to come down. . . . He's so thrilled, he's ridiculous. . . . I wish I had as many nice friends and relatives as he has—Thanks for making him happy. Maggio."

The author obtained FBI files on agent George Wood under the Freedom of Information Act that illustrate Wood's association with gangsters. One file showed that Wood visited Frank Costello in prison more than ten times.

CHAPTER 15

Some of the information in Chapter 15 comes from published sources such as *Billboard*, *Modern Screen*, *New York Post*, *Los Angeles Times*, *New York Journal-American*, *Los Angeles Herald Examiner*, Lee Israel's book,

Kilgallen, New York: Delacorte Press, 1979; Verita Thompson and Donald Shepherd's *Bogie and Me*, New York: St. Martin's Press, 1982; Sammy Davis, Jr.'s, *Hollywood in a Suitcase*, New York: Berkley Books, 1980; and Wilson's *Sinatra*. The author also interviewed Nick Sevano, Peter Lawford on May 15 and June 2, 1983, Marvin Moss on March 9, 1984, a girlfriend of Jimmy Van Heusen's on November 18, 1983, Abe Lastfogel, Nelson Riddle on July 15, 1983, Norma Ebberhart on March 15, 1985, Vanessa Brown on June 22, 1983, Ketti Frings on February 6, June 26, and December 27, 1980, Peter Darmanin on November 22, 1980, and Shecky Greene on August 4, 1983. In a December 1982 interview with Mike Douglas, the author was told that Douglas "went to look at Frank's house years ago and there was a shrine to Ava. So help me God, there was actually a statue of her in the backyard." A 1958 Walter Winchell column in the *Los Angeles Herald Examiner* also said, "We visited Sinatra's beautiful castle-in-the-air home on top of a movie town mountain. On the lawn is a statue of Ava Gardner."

CHAPTER 16

Material in Chapter 16 was obtained from a variety of sources. The author examined arrest records in the Hudson County Courthouse as well as local news articles relating to Sinatra's uncles Augustus Garavante and Lawrence Garavante. The author also obtained a copy of an August 3, 1962, Justice Department FBI report entitled "Francis Albert Sinatra, a/k/a Frank Sinatra." She examined the Oral History of Robbins E. Cahill at the University of Nevada at Las Vegas. Many published sources were also consulted, including the New York *Daily News*, *New York Post*, *New York Herald-Tribune*, *Los Angeles Times*, *Los Angeles Mirror News*, *Look*, and Sammy Davis, Jr.'s, *Yes I Can*, New York: Pocket Books, 1966.

In the late 1940s, Frank gambled at the Cove, an illegal club in Palm Springs run by Bobby Garcia. "At that time, I thought Frank Sinatra was one of the nicest guys I ever met," Garcia told Ovid Demaris in 1979. "He was gambling, and the way he was gambling he didn't have a prayer. . . . He used to come down on weekends. At that time he was married to Nancy. He owed the joint a marker for about $5,800. . . . One night Sinatra came in and he's telling me about Mickey Cohen. He'd met the top man in the state of California." Frank told Garcia that he had given Cohen $5,000 for a magazine called *Hollywood Nightlife*.

"Frank was so enthused about meeting Mickey Cohen, the bigshot of the underworld," said Garcia. A few weeks later, Sinatra told Garcia that Mickey Cohen wanted another $5,000 for his magazine, but Garcia advised him not to lend the money. "They are going to keep five-thousanding you to death, you stupid son of a bitch," he told Frank. "I'll tell you what I'll do. I'll tear up your marker if you quit gambling. Sinatra said, 'Can you do that?' I said, 'Never mind.' I got his markers and I tore them up. Frank quit gambling in the joint from then on."

In addition, the author interviewed Mel Tormé, Mrs. Lee J. Cobb on April 28, 1984, Mitch Miller, Lor-Ann Land, Beans Ponedel on July 15,

1983, Mrs. Ralph Greenson on April 27, 1984, and Charlotte Austin on March 20, 21, 28, 1984.

CHAPTER 17

In obtaining information about Sinatra's film career in the 1960s, the author interviewed a number of people, including Sam Spiegel on November 4, 1983, Jim Byron on October 8, 1985, Mitch Miller, Richard Condon on April 10, 1984, Beans Ponedel, Ketti Frings, Sam Shaw on April 3, 1984, Jeannie Sakol on December 12, 1984, Ronnie Cowan on June 23, July 13, 25, 1983, Jacqueline Park on May 8, 20, 1983, March 15, April 6, and May 20, 1985, and an assistant to Stanley Kramer who requested anonymity on December 13, 1984.

In an interview with Paul Chandler on April 10, 1984, Chandler, who once worked for Sinatra, told the author that "Swifty Lazar, one of Frank's houseguests, would not get out of bed without a towel on the floor."

In an interview with a friend of Sam Spiegel's on September 25, 1983, the author was told of this incident:

On March 27, 1958, the night before the Academy Awards, Spiegel and his wife, Betty, walked into Romanoff's in Hollywood with Billy and Audrey Wilder and Rita Hayworth and Jim Hill. Sitting on a banquette, Frank said hello to the group. Spiegel looked over. "Hello there," he said. A few minutes later, according to one of the Spiegel party, Sinatra said, "Hey, Sam."

"Yeah," said Spiegel.

"Good luck."

"Thanks."

"Hey, Sam."

"Yes, Frank?"

"You are going to sweep the boards." [Spiegel's film, *The Bridge on the River Kwai*, was nominated for and won the award for best movie of the year.]

"Thanks, Frank."

"Hey, Sam."

"Yes, Frank," said Spiegel, growing increasingly irritated.

"You deserve 'em. *Bridge* was a great film."

"Thank you very much."

"Hey, let me tell you something, pal. My name is Frank. Frank Sinatra. And when you see me, you say, 'Hello, Frank' or 'Hello, Mr. Sinatra. You just don't say, 'Hello there.' "

"Under the circumstance, you are lucky that I even bothered to speak to you at all," said the producer.

"Let me tell you something, you wise guy. The day you don't speak to me is the day you get your fucking teeth knocked in."

"Mr. Sinatra, if you don't mind, we are in the middle of dinner and you are disturbing my wife."

Frank glared at Betty Spiegel. "Look, doll," he said. "You got a pretty puss. You want to keep it that way and shut up."

"Frank, you were not invited and you are disturbing us," said Betty Spiegel.

"Well, you're stuck with him," said Frank. Turning to Spiegel, he yelled, "Hey, fat man."

Rita Hayworth sprung toward Sinatra. "Let me at him. Let me at him," she said. Audrey Wilder said, "Hey, Frank. Hey, Frank." Spiegel tried to restrain his rage. "Frank, if you have the guts to join me outside without your bodyguards, let's go."

Everyone waited for Frank to lunge, but he got up and left the restaurant without saying another word.

The author consulted articles in the *New York Post*, as well as several books, including Graham Payne and Sheridan Morley's *The Noel Coward Diaries*, New York: Little Brown and Co., 1982; Lauren Bacall's *By Myself*, New York: Alfred A. Knopf, 1979; Ezra Goodman's *The Fifty Year Decline and Fall of Hollywood*, New York: Simon and Schuster, 1961; and Gerald Frank's *Judy*, New York: Harper & Row, 1975. The author also examined documents in Stanley Kramer's papers in the Special Collections Department of the UCLA Library.

CHAPTER 18

Some of the information in this chapter was obtained from published sources, including the *New York World-Telegram and Sun*, *Los Angeles Times*, *Los Angeles Examiner*, *Chicago Sun-Times*, and *The Star*.

Lester Velie reported in the *Reader's Digest* that Capone gangster Charley "Cherry Nose" Gioe once introduced Sidney Korshak to Willie Bioff, panderer and labor racketeer, this way: "I want you to pay attention to Korshak. When he tells you something, he knows what he's talking about. Any message he might deliver to you is a message from us." Bioff testified to this introduction in a million-dollar movie shakedown trial of 1943 that sent seven Capone mobsters to jail.

The author also interviewed Richard Condon, Bill Davidson on May 23, June 12, 1983, and April 9, 1984, and the publicist on June 13, 1984. In an interview on August 4, 1984, Mrs. Griffin Dunne told the author: "It was at a party upstairs in the Bistro for the authors of *Is Paris Burning?* Frank was very drunk and insulting everyone. He told me to lose my husband [writer Dominick Dunne]; he called Gloria Romanoff "Miss Busybody" and told her to stay out of his life. Then Betty Bacall let him have it and he said, 'I never liked you anyway. I was never in love with you.' He was just awful."

CHAPTER 19

The author interviewed a number of people who contributed information in this chapter, among them Maurice Manson on July 14, 1983, Sandra Giles on July 12, 13, 20, 1983, Peter Lawford, Joseph Shimon on November 5, 6, 1984, and January 5, 1985, Doug Prestine on June 21,

1983, Rona Barrett on May 10, 1983, and George Jacobs. Articles in the *New York Post*, *Chicago Sun-Times*, *New York Times*, and *Variety* were also consulted, along with several books.

CHAPTER 20

The material concerning Sinatra's relationship with Sam Giancana and with the Kennedys was obtained from a wide variety of Justice Department and FBI files, surveillance records and wiretaps, interviews, and published books and sources.

The author obtained Sam Giancana's Justice Department file through a Freedom of Information Act request. She also read William Brashler's book, *The Don: The Life and Death of Sam Giancana*, New York: Harper & Row, 1977; Antoinette Giancana and Thomas C. Renner's *Mafia Princess*, New York: William Morrow and Co., Inc., 1984; *My Story* by Judith Exner as told to Ovid Demaris, New York: Grove Press, 1977; *The Boardwalk Jungle* by Paul "Skinny" d'Amato as told to Ovid Demaris, New York: Bantam Books, 1986; John Davis's *The Kennedys: Dynasty and Disaster*, New York: McGraw Hill Book Co., 1984; Michael Hillman and Thomas C. Renner's *Wall Street Swindler*, New York: Doubleday & Co., 1977; Collier and Horowitz's *The Kennedys: An American Drama*, New York: Summit Books, 1977; and Kenneth O'Donnell and David E. Powers's *Johnny, We Hardly Knew Ye*, New York: Pocket Books, 1973.

Transcripts of federal wiretaps and Justice Department files on John F. Kennedy were examined by the author as were oral histories of David McDonald, president of the Steelworkers Union, and Representative Tom Rees (both available at the John F. Kennedy Library in Boston, Mass.).

The author conducted extensive interviews with many people, including Peter Lawford, Victor LaCroix Collins on June 4, 1984, William Reed Woodfield on July 9, 10, 19, 1983, Joseph Shimon, Dave Powers on January 22, 1982, George Jacobs, former Senator George Smathers on February 22, 1978 (who told the author, "Jack used to tell me how much Frank liked making it with colored girls"), Judith Exner on June 5, 1983, Albert Maltz on May 9, 1983, Nick Sevano, John Sigenthaler on February 4, 1986, Paul Corbin on March 24, 1985, and Shelly Davis on July 5, 1983. In an interview on April 3, 1985, Professor Paul Blakey of Notre Dame told the author, "I was a trial attorney in Justice and defending a case in Reading, Pennsylvania, against another attorney from New Jersey, Angelo Melandra, who said during the recess: 'Tell the Attorney General [Robert Kennedy] hello for me. I was in West Virginia with him.' I asked Dave Walker about it and he said that Melandra had Sinatra's money in West Virginia and that it was mob money. Dave Walker knew it from electronic surveillance."

The author interviewed Mort Sahl on May 30, 1983, and his wife on June 5, 1983. Sahl told the author that he was not invited by Sinatra to participate in the Kennedy inaugural. "The Kennedys started ruling and I started attacking." In 1974, Sahl attacked Sinatra. "Once you get Sinatra on your side in politics, you're out of business." Sahl made jokes about the billing at Caesars Palace featuring Frank and his two singing children. "Coming attractions: the Daughter, The Son, The Father, and the Holy Ghost." Frank sued him for $10,000; he claimed Sahl still owed him part of an old $20,000 loan. "Frank used that lawsuit as a way to get back at Mort," Mrs. Sahl told the author. "Frank got Mort writing for the Kennedys and then there was trouble between the Kennedys and Mort. . . . Frank threatened Mort all over town. . . . I hate him. Frank Sinatra is scum of scum."

In an interview with Brad Dexter on June 12, 1985, Dexter related how Sinatra prevailed on his strong friendship with Harold Gibbons, Teamster vice-president, to get some carpeting for his Learjet removed from a ship during the 1964 longshoremen's strike. The ship carrying the carpeting from Hong Kong was stalled in Los Angeles harbor, closed because of the strike. "Frank told me to call Gibbons in St. Louis to get his carpeting off that ship so he could outfit his Learjet. I called, and Gibbons id he would take care of it. An hour later, Frank's carpeting was being removed from the ship and taken to the Air Research terminal in Santa Monica, where we picked it up."

Articles in *Variety*, the *New York Herald-Tribune*, the *New York Post*, *The Washington Post*, the *Sacramento Bee*, and the *Saturday Evening Post* were also consulted.

The Washington Post also reported:

Another copy of the private investigator's report disclosing Nixon's visits to a New York psychiatrist that Sinatra had tried to surface in 1960 was leaked to Drew Pearson in the closing days of the 1968 campaign, when Hubert Humphrey was running against Nixon. The psychiatrist, Dr. Arnold Hutschnecker, initially confirmed treating Nixon in the 1950s but after a call from a Nixon aide he amended his statement so the columnist killed the story, saying later: "It is true as some have pointed out that if this had been published before the election the outcome might have been different."

CHAPTER 21

Material in this chapter was derived from the author's interviews with Brad Dexter, a woman who lived with Jimmy Van Heusen, Dave Powers, Mort Janklow on March 12, 1982, Joseph Shimon, Anthony Quinn on March 21, 1985, Robert F. Kennedy's appointments secretary on February 4, 12, 1986, Judith Exner, Paul Chandler on April 11, 12, 20, 23, 24, 1984, Peter Lawford, a business associate of Sinatra's who requested anonymity, and Richard Condon. In the interview with Dave Powers, he mentioned the gold plaque that Sinatra put on the bedroom door about Kennedy's visit to his home. Powers said, "Jack never stayed with Sinatra when he was president. Never. He only stayed there as senator. Never as President or President-elect." The author also examined documents in the John F. Kennedy Library in Boston, Mass., as well as federal wiretaps from Justice Department files.

Numerous newspaper clips and books about Sam Giancana were also used.

CHAPTER 22

In this chapter the author relied on Justice Department files on Frank Sinatra, federal wiretaps, and numerous interviews, among them with G. Robert Blakey, Peter Lawford, Peter Maas on February 8, 1984 (Maas was in Attorney General Robert Kennedy's office when Kennedy received a phone call from Sinatra), Chuck Moses on July 24, 1983, Elizabeth Greenschpoon (the former Mrs. Mickey Rudin) on March 20, 21, April 4, 29, 1984, Joe Hyams on July 8, 1983, William Reed Woodfield on July 9, 10, 19, 1983, Mike Shore on March 9 and April 9, 1984, Kris Kristofferson on July 21, 1983, a White House employee who requested anonymity, Edmund (Pat) Brown on April 17, 1984, Al Algiro, Frank Sinatra's cousin Fred Tredy on May 21, 1983, Frank Garrick, and Sister Consilia on January 9, 20, 1983.

The author also interviewed a close friend of Sinatra's who requested anonymity and who told the author, "Frank was seeing Giancana, and Sam did a lot to help Kennedy get elected President with all that Teamster money. He bought Cook County for Jack, and Frank could never understand why Jack Kennedy wouldn't accept Giancana as a friend. Frank thought if politicians can take the money they need to get elected, why can't they consent to take the friendship that goes along with the money. Frank never understood that."

The author gained additional information from articles in *The New York Times*, *New York World-Telegram and Sun*, *New York Post*, *Time*, *Variety*, *Herald-Tribune*, *London Daily Mail*, *Jersey Journal*, and the *Sacramento Bee*.

The author also consulted G. Robert Blakey and Richard N. Billings's book, *The Plot to Kill the President*, New York: Times Books, 1981, among others.

Following the dedication of the Frank Sinatra Youth House in Israel, Frank's films and records were banned by one Arab League. He said, "I am deeply disappointed that statesmen anywhere should condemn anyone for aiding children of whatever faith or origin."

With regard to Sinatra's relationship with Ed Sullivan, in 1947, when Frank slugged Lee Mortimer, Sullivan defended Frank. "Basically, Sinatra is a warmhearted, decent person, and I think it's about time they stopped kicking him around," he wrote in his column. Frank was so grateful for the public support that he sent Sullivan a gold watch that was inscribed: "Ed, You can have my last drop of blood. Frankie." After Sinatra attacked Sullivan in 1955, protesting "newspaper personalities on TV" who use movie celebrities "without paying for their services," Sullivan bought a full-page ad in *The Hollywood Reporter* ridiculing Frank's television ratings. "P.S. Aside to Frankie Boy. Never mind that tremulous 1947 offer. . . . I don't wear wristwatches . . . furthermore, it's on its way back." The two men made up four months later when Sullivan was almost killed in a car accident. Robert Weitman of CBS-TV, the former manager of the Paramount, suggested to Frank that he call Ed to wish him well. Frank agreed. "I love Ed and I know he loves me," he said as reported in the *New York Post*. He then appeared on Sullivan's television show without payment.

On April 20, 1968, the Fontainebleau Hotel dropped its $10 million libel suit against the *Miami Herald* in which Sinatra was under threat of contempt for ignoring a subpoena. The *Herald* published a joint statement with the hotel in which the newspaper said its investigation had indicated that an insurance company was titleholder of record of the hotel land on Miami Beach and that Ben Novak was sole owner of the operating company. The *Herald* had challenged the hotel's ownership and had repeatedly subpoenaed Sinatra to testify after the hotel filed suit.

CHAPTER 23

The author obtained material on Sam Giancana and the Cal-Neva Lodge from the transcripts of federal wiretaps in FBI files, Edward A. Olsen's Oral History on file at the University of Nevada in Reno, and from Justice Department files, some of which were obtained through the Freedom of Information Act. In addition, she conducted extensive interviews with, among others, Chuck Moses; a business associate of Hank Sanicola; Peter Lawford; Herb Caen; Bethel Van Tassel on August 28, 29, September 6, and October 4, 1984, and April 5, 1985; Louise Anderson on August 29, 1984, and April 5, 1985; Phyllis McGuire on July 8, 1985; Victor LaCroix Collins; Jacqueline Park on May 20, 1983; Ben Barton; Nick Sevano; Joe Shimon; and law enforcement officials. She gained additional information from the newspaper files of the *Los Angeles Herald Examiner*, *The Wall Street Journal*, the *Chicago Sun-Times*, the *New York Post*, and the *Nevada State Journal*. Several books were also consulted.

CHAPTER 24

The kidnapping of Frank Sinatra, Jr., has been well documented in *The New York Times*, *Los Angeles Herald Examiner*, *New York Post*, *Herald-Tribune*, and *Daily News*. In addition, the author interviewed Frank Sinatra, Jr. on January 15, 1983, Peter Lawford, Ed Pucci on April 13, 1984, one of the federal agents who worked on the case and requested anonymity, Nelson Riddle, and Robert Carl Cohen on March 17, 1984, and also read the record of the trial of the kidnappers. Robert Carl Cohen wrote a screenplay about the episode entitled *I Kidnapped Frank Sinatra, Jr.: The Full Confession by the Perpetrator of One of the Century's Most Controversial Crimes*, a copy of which he allowed the author to read.

Other information in this chapter was obtained from interviews with Patricia Bosworth on December 15, 1983, Corinne Entratter, Chuck Moses, Brad Dexter on April 8, 9, 13, 25, May 25, June 28, 29, September 9, 21, December 11, 1984, and February 10, 1985.

In his autobiography, *An Open Book*, New York: Knopf, 1980, John Huston wrote: "Later, when I was editing a picture in Rome, I heard that [George C.] Scott broke into Ava's suite at the Savoy, which caused a scandal. When she came back to the United States, I think Frankie

Sinatra commissioned a couple of his lads to go around with her." At the same time, Frank was quoted in *Photoplay*, April 1965: "If there's one guy I don't tolerate, it's a guy who mistreats women. They are the real bullies in life and what they need is a real working over by a man their own size." Stories circulated that after beating up on Ava, Scott returned to his hotel room and found that all of his shirts and sweaters and suits had been cut off at the shoulders.

Among his friends, Frank was renowned for sending telegrams. On the day Lady Adélé Beatty, one of his former lovers, married Stanley Donen, Frank sent her an unsigned wire, saying: HOW COULD YOU?

CHAPTER 25

Sinatra's relationship with Mia Farrow has been widely discussed in, among other places, the *Ladies' Home Journal*, *New York Post*, *Life*, *Photoplay*, *Seventeen*, *Los Angeles Herald Examiner*, and the *New York Journal-American*. The *New York Post* reported that when Robert Vaughn was on the *$10,000 Pyramid* television game show, he wanted to give his partner a clue to the word "Sinatra." In the excitement he said, "Mia Farrow's father." His partner said, "Oh, sure, Frank Sinatra" and won!

Regarding Sinatra's physical fights with others, Richard Condon said, "Frank once told me that the only way to negotiate a dispute figuratively was to kick the disputant in the ankle and as he hopped on one foot, holding the injured foot, to belt him soundly across the chops."

Other material in this chapter was derived from, among other sources, interviews with Brad Dexter, Franklin Fox on April 18, 1984, Corinne Entratter, George Jacobs, Laurence Eisenberg on October 24 and November 1, 1983, Edith Mayer Goetz, and a member of Frederic Weisman's family who requested anonymity.

In an interview with Alan Horowitz on April 5, 1984, Horowitz told the author:

"Sammy Cahn and Jimmy Van Heusen originally wrote that song ['September of My Years'] that way for Frank but they got scared and changed it to "September of His Years" because the other way sounded like Frank was getting old. When Sammy went to play it for Sinatra, he changed it back."

Various other newspapers, magazines, files, and books were also consulted.

CHAPTER 26

Material in this chapter was obtained from interviews with a number of people, including Brad Dexter, a woman who lived with Jimmy Van Heusen, Jim Mahoney on June 22, 1983, Jackie Mason on December 20, 1983, Edmund (Pat) Brown, Sandi Grant Bennett on June 7 and July 7, 1983, Shecky Greene, David Susskind on February 2 and April 5, 1984, William Hundley on October 28, 1985, Joseph Shimon, and George Franklin on June 30, 1983.

The author also examined the Las Vegas Sheriff's office records and reports, Justice Department files on Joe Fischetti, and numerous newspaper articles and books.

Sinatra put his friends in the movie *Tony Rome*. In addition to Shecky Greene, he put his lawyer, Mickey Rudin, in as a pawnbroker, Jilly Rizzo played a bartender, and Mike Romanoff was listed as assistant to the producer. Girlfriends like Jill St. John, Deana Lund, and Tiffany Bolling were also given roles.

When Nancy Sinatra was writing a book about her father, she sent letters to her father's friends and associates seeking quotes and loving anecdotes "from all those who have had close contact" with him. Unamused by the letter, Ava Gardner refused to respond. "Close contact?" she snapped. "Doesn't she remember I married him?" (*Ladies' Home Journal*, July 1972.) Still steaming about the letter, Ava mentioned it to Michael Thornton in 1982. "Did you know that [she] wrote to me recently to say she was writing a book about Frank and that maybe I could help her with recollections as somebody once associated with him. As if I didn't have a rather closer relationship than that! I told her sorry, but no thank you." (Thornton's interview with Gardner, November 1982.) Nancy, in turn, exploded when Jacqueline Kennedy Onassis refused to contribute. "My father escorted, campaigned—he helped JFK in every way—and this is how Mrs. Onassis handles it," she said. "The late John Kennedy was a very big part of my father's life. How dare she be that cruel!" (*Los Angeles Times*, June 4, 1972.) Nancy's book, which was started in 1966, was not completed until 1985.

CHAPTER 27

In gathering information for Chapter 27, the author interviewed Norman Sherman on February 15, 1984, William Connell on December 14, 1984, Al Algiro, Michael Viner on September 8, 1981, Nancy Seidman on December 14, 1983, Mrs. Ted Allen on August 5, 1983, George Jacobs and Joseph L. Nellis. The author also examined documents in the Hubert Humphrey Archives at the University of Minnesota.

The author consulted articles in *McCall's*, *Cosmopolitan*, *The Star*, *Time*, *Photoplay*, *Miami Beach Sun*, *Ladies' Home Journal*, and numerous newspaper clips. In the *Bedside Book of Celebrity Gossip*, New York: Celebrity Research Group, 1984, Ruth Gordon was quoted:

"Did you ever try to tell a story to Frank Sinatra? If you do, he's apt to interrupt: 'Is this going to take long?' "

The New York Times reported on August 15, 1978, in an article headlined "Sinatra, Now a GOP Insider" that

"knowledgeable sources said here that at one point in 1968, a member of Mr. Humphrey's staff asked the Department of Justice, 'Are we going to be embarrassed by Sinatra if he participates in our campaign?' The answer was affirmative."

In a January 15, 1983, interview with Frank Sinatra, Jr., Sinatra, Jr., claimed to know what happened to Jimmy Hoffa. Jimmy Hoffa was pardoned by President Richard Nixon in 1971. Four years later, on July 31, 1975, Hoffa was abducted in Detroit and never seen again. Law enforcement officials assumed a Mafia murder to keep Hoffa from running against Frank E. Fitzsimmons for the presidency of the Teamsters Union in 1976. To date, the case has never been solved, although there are several theories. Yet Frank Sinatra, Jr., said:

> "I know what happened to Jimmy Hoffa. I know people—certain people . . . and they know me. . . . No, I can't tell you, but I do know what happened."

CHAPTER 28

The author interviewed Sister Consilia, Al Algiro, Nancy Siracusa, Peter Lawford, George Franklin, Ralph Salerno on December 16, 20, 1983, Steve Allen on March 22, 1984, and an IRS undercover agent who requested anonymity.

Sinatra was eager to keep his New Jersey State Crime Commission testimony confidential. Before he started testifying, he presented the commissioners with a piece of paper, saying:

> I want you to just familiarize yourself with it as your attorneys have. And very loosely paraphrasing it, it means what goes on in this room with respect to testimony or evidence is to remain in this room, as it's an executive session.

The next year Frank was negotiating with Tommy Thompson of *Life* magazine to photograph the Joe Frazier–Muhammad Ali fight in March. In an interview with Denny Walsh on March 7, 1984, Walsh told the author that after signing the *Life* contract, Sinatra heard that Walsh, also with *Life* at the time, and one of America's premier investigative reporters, was in New Jersey working on a story. Sinatra was convinced that the Pulitzer Prize–winning journalist was trying to get hold of the transcript of his secret testimony before the New Jersey State Crime Commission. He threatened to cancel his contract with *Life* unless the magazine "called off" Walsh. Tommy Thompson was beside himself and began trying to locate Walsh, calling him every hour until three in the morning. "When I told him I wasn't working on a Sinatra story, I never saw a man so relieved in all my life," said Denny Walsh.

Modern Screen, August 1969, reported this story as related by Dino Martin, Jr., who was dating Tina Sinatra:

> "He's quite a guy, that Frank," said Dino. "Tina and I have gone down to Palm Springs and stayed at Frank's house several times. The last time he flew us down on his own private jet, and he was aboard, too. Frank apparently learned there was a guy waiting for him at the airport terminal with a subpoena for his arrest. So we

swerved around the landing strip and instead of heading into the terminal, we headed across the desert, on the ground. The airplane stopped and the three of us got into a waiting helicopter and flew to his house. As we were landing on the heliport at Frank's house, the guy with the subpoena was still waiting to catch him at the airport."

In his biography, *Eddie: My Life and Loves* New York: Harper & Row, 1981, Eddie Fisher tells of this incident:

Frank wore his emotions on his sleeve, and I always thought his cocky tough-guy attitude was probably just a way of protecting himself from being hurt. He seemed to prefer respect to love and when he thought he had been insulted he was like a wild man. I saw his quick temper flare while we were together in London. All his friends used to hang out in his suite at Claridge's, and one morning I walked in and saw a young woman with a scarf around her head. I had no idea who she was and I said to Frank. "Good morning, Your Highness." "She" was the Highness, Princess Alexandra, and we all sat around and had a nice chat. But somehow the newspapers found out about her visit, and Frank blew his stack. He swore he was going to get the guy who told reporters, and one by one, he buttonholed his friends, including me, demanding to know who had betrayed him.

The night before he was to leave London, we all wound up in his suite again for drinks and a healthy dose of Sinatra tapes, a usual feature at his parties. "I've narrowed it down to two people," Frank announced, still playing detective, "the assistant manager of the hotel and the elevator operator, and I want everybody here tomorrow morning at 10:00."

"Frank," I said, "these things happen. Forget it. You've just come off this marvelous world tour, don't blow it now." I was worried about Sinatra's image.

"Who the fuck asked you?" he snarled.

I don't know what Frank thought he was going to do, but he left London the next morning without doing anything. Typical, I thought, a lot of energy and anger wasted.

The author also consulted numerous newspaper and magazine stories and several books, including Lou Cannon's *Reagan*, New York: Putnam's Sons, 1982, John Cooney's *The Annenbergs*, New York: Simon & Schuster, 1982, and Salerno and Tomkins's *Crime Confederation*, New York: Doubleday & Co., Inc., 1969.

CHAPTER 29

Information on the relationship between Sinatra and Vice-President Agnew was derived from many interviews, including ones with Vic Gold on January 24 and February 1, 1984, and Peter Malatesta on July 5, 25, 26, and 31, 1983, as well as numerous newspaper and magazine articles. The author also examined the transcript of the House of Representatives' Select Committee on Crime Hearings of July 18, 1972, the *Congressional*

Record, and interviewed Philip Nobile on November 10, December 14, 1983, February 12, 1984, and Elizabeth Greenschpoon (the former Mrs. Mickey Rudin).

In April 1976, the *Boston Globe* reported that on February 23, 1976, Sinatra met with CIA Director George Bush in New York and offered to keep the agency informed of his worldwide travels and meetings with foreign dignitaries. "It was a very sincere and generous offer," said Bush's brother, Jonathan, who also attended the meeting. "Sinatra said he was always flying around the world, and meeting with people like the Shah of Iran and the royal family of Great Britain," he said. "He emphasized time and again that his services were available and that he wanted to do his part for his country."

CHAPTER 30

Material in Chapter 30 was obtained from published articles in *The Washington Post, Evening Star, The New York Times, Chicago Tribune, Los Angeles Times,* New York *Daily News, Newsweek, Variety, Washington Star, Women's Wear Daily, Chicago Sun-Times,* and numerous Associated Press stories. In addition, the author consulted transcripts of Sinatra's remarks at Caesars Palace on January 25, 1974, and June 6, 1974, Rona Barrett's autobiography, *Miss Rona,* Los Angeles, Ca.: Nash Publishing, 1972, and interviews with Vic Gold, Rona Barrett, and Marvin Lewis on July 25, 26, 30, 1983. In an interview with Jim Mahoney, Mahoney said, "Do you know what death is? It's a phone call from Mickey Rudin." The author also reviewed the depositions and trial record in Frank Weinstock's lawsuit.

CHAPTER 31

The author interviewed Joan Cohn Harvey, Edith Mayer Goetz, Peter Malatesta, Mr. Blackwell on April 23, 1984, Arthur Marx on April 16, 18, 20, 1984, Frank Weinstock on December 6, 1985, Celia Pickwell on March 30, 1984, Gratsiella Maiellano on July 10, 1985, Joyce Haber on July 22, 1983, and March 9, 1984, Robert Pack on January 11, 1983, Frank Sinatra, Jr., Steven Green on January 21, 1984, Bahman Rooin on June 3, 1983, Sister Consilia, Phyllis McGuire on July 8, 1985, Richard Condon, Nick Sevano, Thomas F. X. Smith on January 25, 1983, and June 5, 1985, Anita Colby Flagen on October 17, 1985, and Kitty Kallen.

In an interview with Charles Blakely on March 31, 1984, the author was given the following information about Zeppo Marx's will:

When Zeppo died in November 1979, he left his diamond ring and gold belt buckles to his adopted son, Bobby Marx. He also left him $25,000 in trust to pay for his law school education. Shortly before he died, Zeppo changed his will and left his Rolls-Royce ($65,000) and interest in a Safeway store ($160,000) to Barbara's sister, Patricia Jo Welch. Barbara was so angry that her sister received what she felt belonged to her son, Bobby, that she never spoke to Pat again. "It breaks Irene's heart that Barbara and Pat don't speak," said Barbara's father, Charles Blakely, "but she can't do anything about it." The next month, December 1979, Frank offered to adopt Bobby, but his children reacted so negatively that he dropped the idea.

In an interview with Phyllis McGuire, she told the author that when Sinatra's mother died, she sent a plane to Texas for Dr. and Mrs. Michael DeBakey to come to Palm Springs to be with him. "Johnny Carson and I filled in for Frank at Caesars Palace and do you know that son of a bitch never even thanked us?"

The author also read numerous newspaper and magazine reports of the Sinatra-Marx marriage, including those in the *Ladies' Home Journal, Las Vegas Desert Sun, Modern Screen, Chicago Sun-Times, National Enquirer,* New York *Daily News,* and *The New York Times.*

In addition, the author consulted several books, among them Ovid Demaris's *The Last Mafioso.*

CHAPTER 32

In the Westchester Premier Theater case, the author read transcripts of wiretaps and depositions and reviewed trial and other court records as well as the news coverage in papers such as *The New York Times, The Wall Street Journal, New York Daily News, Riverside (Calif.) Press-Enterprise,* and *Newsday.* In addition, the author interviewed law enforcement officials, who requested anonymity.

Other material in this chapter was obtained from numerous other newspaper and magazine articles.

With respect to Sinatra's feuds with newspapers, he had previously forced hotels in Nevada not to advertise in the state's largest newspaper because of columns written about him that he did not like.

"He did it twice at the Sands Hotel before Howard Hughes took over, and now he forced Caesars to pull the advertising of his act," stated a 1969 editorial in the Las Vegas *Review-Journal.* "The balding, middle-aged crooner again sang the blues about the R-J and apparently thought he would stop the presses by dictating the advertising policy during his stay.

". . . To point out how childish Sinatra actually is, to order his ads out of the state's largest newspaper can only be compared to the way he idolizes underworld figures. He gave up a gambling license rather than break off a friendship with Chicago gangland Mafia boss Sam Giancana."

The *Sacramento Bee* published a story by Denny Walsh and Nancy Skelton entitled "Palm Springs, Where Stars, Pols—and Mobsters—Live in Style." Although not mentioned in the article, Peter Epsteen was referred to in a photo caption as an "automobile dealer financed by the Mafia." Represented by Sinatra's attorney, Mickey Rudin, Epsteen filed a $6 million libel suit against the newspaper. He denied any affiliation with the Mafia and demanded a retraction. The *Sacramento Bee* published a story reporting Epsteen's denial but did not retract the charge.

Lawyers representing the newspaper hired former FBI agent William Roemer to investigate the matter. Roemer is a lawyer with twenty-two years' experience investigating organized crime in Chicago. In an interview with the author on March 15, 1986, Roemer told her: "I flew to Chicago and sat down with a lower level Mafia boss at Crane's restaurant. I told the mobster that we were going to subpoena Gus Alex and Tony Accardo [two of Chicago's top Mafia chieftains] for depositions and bring them into the lawsuit as hostile witnesses in an effort to prove their connections with Peter Epsteen. I also said I would testify to that effect and this guy knew I could say plenty from my thirty years with the Bureau, most of it investigating organized crime. He told me he would get the word to Alex and Accardo by sundown that day. A few weeks later, Peter Epsteen dropped his lawsuit."

Iacocca by Lee Iacocca with William Novak, New York: Bantam Books, 1984, recounts that Sinatra offered to help Chrysler stay in business by doing television commercials for a well-publicized fee of one dollar a year. In addition to the one dollar, Frank received stock options which Iacocca said were valuable. "I hope Frank held on to them, because if he did, he made a bundle."

In 1979, Ford Motor Company stockholders brought a $50 million lawsuit against Henry Ford II and the company. The suit alleged in part that Ford had diverted company money for personal use. William Safire wrote a column stating that Ford had had a meeting with Frank Sinatra in hopes that Sinatra could use his influence with Roy Cohn, the stockholders' attorney, to "lay off." After reading the column, Frank sent Safire a telegram: YOU ARE A GODDAMN LIAR. This incident was reported in *New York* magazine in October 1984.

CHAPTER 33

The author consulted the transcripts of the Nevada Gaming Board's 1981 hearings and conducted extensive interviews with one of the Board's investigators, who requested anonymity, on June 6, 29, and September 1, 1983. Information on Sinatra's finances was taken from the financial statement submitted by Sinatra to the Board.

The author interviewed Ovid Demaris on March 21, 1984, Judith Exner, Ralph Salerno, Phyllis McGuire, and Victor LaCroix Collins, Robert Kennedy's appointments secretary on February 4 and 12, 1986, Pearl Similly on January 14, 1984, and consulted several magazines and newspapers, including *The Wall Street Journal*, *New York* magazine, the *Los Angeles Times*, and *Variety*. *Billboard* reported in June 1975 that Sinatra started adding an extra clause to his contract stipulating that no one, "no matter how famous," was to be allowed backstage or even to approach him.

In 1976, Judith Exner announced plans to write a book detailing her introduction to John F. Kennedy and Sam Giancana by Frank Sinatra, and her affairs with all three men. Sinatra's publicist wanted to issue a press release denying any Exner connection to Frank. Instead, they settled on a one-sentence press release drafted by Lee Solters: "Hell hath no fury like a woman with a literary agent." Sinatra scratched out "woman" and wrote "hooker." Rudin crossed out "hooker" and inserted "hustler," which is the way the release appeared.

After Kirk Douglas had submitted his article "Virtue Is Not Photogenic" to *The New York Times*, the newspaper's associate editor, Charlotte Curtis, returned the piece to the actor, saying: "Warm and affectionate as the piece is, it won't work either for Frank or for you, I'm afraid, and we are most hesitant to publish it."

Information on Sinatra's performances at the Fontainebleau Hotel was obtained from the Justice Department's August 3, 1962, report on Sinatra.

On February 16, 1981, columnist William Safire printed Norman Mailer's response to Sinatra's comments about the attaché case he was carrying in Havana. "I've been doing some calculations on how many one-hundred-dollar bills can be fitted into a Samsonite attaché case twelve inches by fifteen inches by five inches deep," he told Safire. "A one-hundred-dollar bill measures 6.2 inches by 2.6 inches. You can squeeze 350 bills down to one inch. That's thirty-five thousand dollars to a one-inch packet. You can lay six of those packets along the seventeen-inch axis and four others lengthwise into the space that is left on that first layer. And there is still overage. Let's see: ten packets per layer make $350,000. Multiplied by five one-inch layers that makes $1,750,000. . . . Make half-inch packets and tilt them sideways. I've worked it out: you can fit two million twelve thousand dollars into an attaché case."

During the author's interview with Phyllis McGuire, McGuire commented on how Frank's friendship with Jack Entratter ended. Frank had cast other friends aside as cruelly as Jack Entratter. Men like George Evans, Hank Sanicola, Nick Sevano, Joe DiMaggio, Brad Dexter, and Peter Lawford, who had loved Frank and stood loyally by his side suddenly found themselves frozen out of the Sinatra circle for some real or imagined slight. Some, like Brad Dexter, didn't let it bother them. Others, like Peter Lawford, never survived the hurt.

"I tried several times to apologize for whatever it was that I had done to Frank, but he has not spoken to me for over twenty years," said Lawford in 1983. "He wouldn't take my phone calls and wouldn't answer my letters. Wherever I saw him at a party or in a restaurant, he just cut me dead. Looked right through me with those cold blue eyes like I didn't exist. Friends of mine went to him to patch things up, but he'd always say, 'That fucking Englishman is a bum.' I even talked to his daughter, Tina, about it, saying what a waste it was to squander a good relationship on a misunderstanding. She agreed with me and said to write Frank again, so I did, but he never responded. . . . I don't want to go to my grave having been responsible for someone being so disturbed that he carried a grudge all his life."

On January 15, 1979, *Barron's National Business and Financial Weekly* published a letter to the editor from Mickey Rudin under the heading "Sinatra's Mouthpiece." Rudin sued for libel, saying it conjured up images of "shyster." The case went to trial in U.S. District Court in New York. Rudin lost.

CHAPTER 34

The author interviewed Richard Condon, Steven Green, Gloria Massingill on June 27, 1983, and a guest at Judy Green's 1983 Southhampton barbecue, who requested anonymity, on October 9, 1984. Various newspaper articles were also consulted. The author also obtained a copy of Sinatra's $16 million Golden Nugget contract, correspondence between Sinatra and the Golden Nugget's vice-president and general counsel, and a stock option agreement between Milton Rudin and the Golden Nugget. The author interviewed a friend of Sinatra's concerning his charitable deductions. This person also requested anonymity. Additional information on the Golden Nugget incident was obtained from the transcript of the August 1, 1984, hearing before the New Jersey Casino Control Commission, various newspaper articles, and Mickey Rudin's statements in an August 29, 1984, press release issued by Sinatra's publicists, Solters, Roskin/Friedman, Inc. In addition, the author interviewed a member of the Secret Service on January 3, 1986, and a member of the White House staff on June 3, 1984.

The author also consulted the United Nations Special Committee Against Apartheid's celebrity register, and various newspapers and magazines, including *People* magazine and *The Washington Post*.

Background on the President's tribute to Sinatra's achievements in the performing arts was obtained from television coverage and several newspaper articles.

CHAPTER 35

The material on Sinatra's participation in Reagan's 1984 reelection campaign was obtained from various articles in *The New York Times*, the *Washington Times*, the *Jersey Journal*, and the *Hudson Dispatch*. The author also interviewed a friend of Ronald Reagan, Jr., on December 7, 1985, who requested anonymity.

On February 10, 1985, *Star* magazine recounted reporter Barbara Howar's response to Sinatra's outburst over *The Washington Post*'s profile, "The Rat Pack Is Back": "The least I expected when I went up to him was to be recognized. I expected him to know who I am. It isn't like I didn't have dinner with him once—with Henry Kissinger. All the while we were eating, Sinatra kept bemoaning, 'I'm not associated with the Mafia. . . .' He kept beating that old horse to death. Then finally Kissinger looked at him and said, 'I'm very disappointed, Frank. Who is going to take care of my enemies?' "

Information on Sinatra's receipt of the Presidential Medal of Freedom and the honorary degree from the Stevens Institute was obtained from *The Washington Post*, *The New York Times*, the New York *Daily News*, *The Washington Post*, and the *Los Angeles Times*.

Background on Garry Trudeau's Doonesbury comic strip was obtained from several newspapers, including *The Washington Post* and the *Los Angeles Times*.

BIBLIOGRAPHY

Agnew, Spiro. *Go Quietly or Else*. New York: William Morrow, 1980.

Arnaz, Desi. *A Book*. New York: Warner Books, 1976.

Bacall, Lauren. *By Myself*. New York: Alfred A. Knopf, 1979.

Barrett, Rona. *Miss Rona: An Autobiography*. Los Angeles: Nash Publishing, 1974.

Barzini, Luigi. *The Italians*. New York: Atheneum, 1981.

Blakey, Robert G., and Richard N. Billings. *The Plot to Kill the President*. New York: Times Books, 1981.

Bosworth, Patricia. *Montgomery Clift*. New York: Harcourt Brace Jovanovich, 1978.

Bradford, Sarah. *Princess Grace*. New York: Stein and Day, 1984.

Bradlee, Benjamin C. *Conversations with Kennedy*. New York: Pocket Books, 1976.

Brashler, William. *The Don: The Life and Death of Sam Giancana*. New York: Harper and Row, 1977.

Cahn, Sammy. *I Should Care: The Sammy Cahn Story*. New York: Arbor House, 1975.

Cannon, Lou. *Reagan*. New York: G. P. Putnam's Sons, 1982.

Cheshire, Maxine, with John Greenya. *Maxine Cheshire, Reporter*. Boston: Houghton Mifflin Company, 1978.

Cohen, Mickey, as told to John Peer Nugent. *Mickey Cohen in My Own Words*. Englewood Cliffs, N.J.: Prentice-Hall, 1975.

Collier, Peter, and David Horowitz. *The Kennedys*. New York: Summit Books, 1984.

Cooney, John. *The Annenbergs*. New York: Simon and Schuster, 1982.

Cunningham, Barbara. *The New Jersey Ethnic Experience*. Union City, N.J.: Wm. H. Wise and Company, 1977.

David, Saul. *The Industry*. New York: Times Books, 1980.

Davidson, Bill. *The Real and the Unreal*. New York: Harper and Brothers, 1961.

Davis, John H. *The Kennedys: Dynasty and Disaster 1848–1983*. New York: McGraw-Hill, 1984.

Davis, Sammy, Jr., and Burt and Jane Boyar. *Yes I Can*. New York: Pocket Books, 1966.

Davis, Sammy, Jr. *Hollywood in a Suitcase*. New York: Berkley Books, 1980.

Demaris, Ovid, and Ed Reid. *The Green Felt Jungle*. New York: Trident Press, 1963.

Demaris, Ovid. *Captive City: Chicago in Chains*. New York: Lyle Stuart, 1969.

Demaris, Ovid. *The Last Mafioso*. New York: Bantam Books, 1981.

Demaris, Ovid. *The Boardwalk Jungle*. New York: Bantam Books, 1986.

Dexter, Dave, Jr. *Playback*. New York: Billboard Publications, 1976.

Douglas-Home, Robin. *Sinatra*. New York: Grosset & Dunlap, 1962.

Drosnin, Michael. *Citizen Hughes*. New York: Holt, Rinehart and Winston, 1985.

Eisenberg, Dan, Uri Dan, and Eli Landau. *Meyer Lansky: Mogul of the Mob*. New York and London: Paddington Press, 1979.

Exner, Judith, as told to Ovid Demaris. *My Story*. New York: Grove Press, 1977.

Feder, Sid, and Joachim Joesten. *The Luciano Story*. New York: Award Books, 1972.

Field, John Perkins. *Halo over Hoboken*. New York: Exposition Press, 1955.

Fisher, Eddie. *Eddie: My Life, My Loves*. New York: Harper and Row, 1981.

Flamini, Roland. *Ava*. New York: Coward, McCann and Geoghegan, 1983.

Frank, Gerold. *Judy*. New York: Harper and Row, 1975.

Gage, Nicholas, ed. *Mafia, U.S.A.* Chicago: Playboy Press, 1972.

Gehman, Richard. *Sinatra and His Rat Pack*. New York: Belmont Books, 1963.

Giancana, Antoinette, and Thomas C. Renner. *Mafia Princess*. New York: William Morrow, 1984.

Glazer, Nathan, and Daniel P. Moynihan. *Beyond the Melting Pot*. Cambridge, Mass.: M.I.T. Press, 1963.

Goldman, Albert. *Elvis*. New York: McGraw-Hill, 1981.

Goldman, William. *Adventures in the Screen Trade*. New York: Warner Books, 1983.

Goodman, Ezra. *The Fifty-Year Decline and Fall of Hollywood*. New York: Simon and Schuster, 1961.

Graham, Sheilah. *Confessions of a Hollywood Columnist*. New York: William Morrow, 1969.

Haines, Connie, as told to Robert B. Stone. *For Once in My Life*. New York: Warner Books, 1976.

Hammer, Richard. *Playboy's Illustrated History of Organized Crime*. Chicago: Playboy Press, 1975.

Hanna, David. *The Lucky Luciano Inheritance*. New York: Belmont Tower Books, 1975.

Heaney, John J. *The Bicentennial Comes to Hoboken*. Hoboken, N.J.: Hoboken American Revolution Bicentennial Committee, 1976.

Hellerman, Michael, with Thomas C. Renner. *Wall Street Swindler*. Garden City, N.Y.: Doubleday and Company, 1977.

Higham, Charles. *Ava*. New York: Delacorte Press, 1974.

Hopper, Hedda, with James Brough. *The Whole Truth and Nothing But*. New York: Doubleday and Company, 1963.

Hotchner, A. E. *Choice People*. New York: William Morrow, 1984.

Howlett, John. *Frank Sinatra*. New York: Wallaby Books, 1980.

Huston, John. *An Open Book*. New York: Alfred A. Knopf, 1980.

Iacocca, Lee, with William Novak. *Iacocca: An Autobiography*. New York: Bantam Books, 1984.

Kahn, E. J. *The Voice*. New York: Harper and Brothers, 1946.

Kefauver, Estes. *Crime in America*. Garden City, N.Y.: Doubleday and Company, 1951.

Kelley, Kitty. *Elizabeth Taylor: The Last Star*. New York: Simon & Schuster, 1981.

La Guardia, Robert. *Monty*. New York: Arbor House, 1977.

Lasky, Victor. *J.F.K.: The Man and the Myth*. New York: Dell Books, 1966.

Lonstein, Albert I., and Vito R. Marino. *The Compleat Sinatra*. Ellenville, N.Y.: Cameron Publications, 1970.

Lonstein, Albert I., and Vito R. Marino. *The Revised Compleat Sinatra*. Ellenville, N.Y.: Cameron Publications, 1970.

Malatesta, Peter. *Party Politics*. Englewood Cliffs, N.J.: Prentice-Hall, 1982.

Manchester, William. *The Glory and the Dream*. New York: Bantam Books, 1974.

Mansfield, Irving, with Jean Libman Block. *Life with Jackie*. New York: Bantam Books, 1983.

Maritt, Rita, with Gioco Sfrenata. *Adventure Di Un Sex Symbol*. Milano: Gianglacomo Feltrinilli Editore, 1980.

Marx, Arthur. *Everybody Loves Somebody Sometime*. New York: Hawthorn Books, 1974.

Messick, Hank, and Joseph Nellis. *The Private Lives of Public Enemies*. New York: Peter Wyden, 1974.

Messick, Hank. *The Beauties and the Beasts*. New York: David McKay Company, 1973.

Miller, George Long. *The Hoboken of Yesterday*. Hoboken, N.J.: Poggi Press, 1966.

O'Donnell, Kenneth P., and David E. Powers, with Joe McCarthy. *Johnny, We Hardly Knew Ye*. New York: Pocket Books, 1973.

Otash, Fred. *Investigation Hollywood!* Chicago: Henry Regnery Company, 1976.

Pack, Robert. *Edward Bennett Williams for the Defense*. New York: Harper and Row, 1983.

Parmet, Herbert S. *JFK: The Presidency of John F. Kennedy*. New York: Penguin Books, 1983.

Payne, Graham, and Sheridan Morley. *The Noel Coward Diaries*. Boston: Little Brown and Company, 1982.

Pilat, Oliver. *Drew Pearson: An Unauthorized Biography*. New York: Harper's Magazine Press, 1973.

Pleasants, Henry. *The Great American Popular Singers*. London: Victor Gollancz, 1974.

Procter, Mary, and Bill Matuszeki. *Gritty Cities*. Philadelphia: Temple University Press, 1978.

Puzo. Mario. *The Godfather*. New York: New American Library, 1969.

Puzo, Mario. *Inside Las Vegas*. New York: Charter Books, 1977.

Reid, Ed. *Mafia*. New York: Random House, 1950.

Ringold, Gene, and Clifford McCarthy. *The Films of Frank Sinatra*. Secaucus, N.J.: The Citadel Press, 1980.

Rockwell, John. *Sinatra: An American Classic*. New York: Rolling Stone Press, 1984.

Rogers, Henry C. *Walking the Tightrope: The Private Confessions of a Public Relations Man*. New York: Berkley Books, 1982.

Salerno, Ralph, and John S. Tompkins. *The Crime Confederation*. Garden City, N.Y.: Doubleday and Company, 1969.

Salinger, Pierre. *With Kennedy*. Garden City, N.Y.: Doubleday and Company, 1966.

Sanford, Herb. *Tommy and Jimmy: The Dorsey Years*. New Rochelle, N.Y.: Arlington House, 1972.

Saunders, Frank, with James Southwood. *Torn Lace Curtain*. New York: Holt, Rinehart, and Winston, 1982.

Scheim, David E. *Contract on America*. Silver Spring, Md.: Argyle Press, 1983.

Sciacca, Tony. *Sinatra*. New York: Pinnacle Books, 1976.

Shaw, Arnold. *Sinatra: A Biography*. London: W. H. Allen, 1968.

Short, Martin. *Crime, Inc*. London: Thames Methuen, 1984.

Silvers, Phil, with Robert Saffron. *This Laugh Is on Me*. Englewood Cliffs, N.J.: Prentice-Hall, 1973.

Simon, George T. *The Big Bands*. New York: Schirmer Books, 1967.

Simon, George T. *Simon Says: The Sights and Sounds of the Swing Era 1935–1955*. New Rochelle, N.Y.: Arlington House, 1971.

Singer, Robert. *The Bad Guys' Quote Book*. New York: Avon Books, 1984.

Smith, Thomas F. X. *The Powerticians*. Secaucus, N.J.: Lyle Stuart, 1982.

Sorenson, Theodore C. *Kennedy*. New York: Bantam Books, 1966.

Stine, Whitney. *Stars and Star Handlers*. Santa Monica, Calif.: Roundtable Publishing, 1985.

Talese, Gay. *Fame and Obscurity*. New York and Cleveland: World Publishing Company, 1970.

Taylor, Theodore. *Jule: The Story of Composer Jule Styne*. New York: Random House, 1979.

Teresa, Vincent, with Thomas C. Renner. *Vinnie Teresa's Mafia*. Garden City, N.Y.: Doubleday and Company, 1975.

This Fabulous Century. New York: Time-Life Books, 1969.

Thomas, Bob. *King Cohn*. London: Barrie and Rockliff, 1967.

Thompson, Verita, with Donald Shepherd. *Bogie and Me*. New York: St. Martin's Press, 1982.

Todd, Michael, Jr., and Susan McCarthy Todd. *A Valuable Property*. New York: Arbor House, 1983.

Turner, Lana. *Lana*. New York: E. P. Dutton, 1982.

Varacalli, Joseph A. "Ethnic Politics in Jersey City: The Changing Nature of Irish-Italian Relations, 1917–1983." Garden City, N.Y.: Nassau Community College, Department of Sociology, 1983.

White, Theodore H. *The Making of the President: 1960*. New York: Atheneum, 1961.

Wilson, Earl. *Sinatra: An Unauthorized Biography*. New York: New American Library, 1976.

Winters, Shelley. *Shelley Also Known as Shirley*. New York: William Morrow, 1980.

INDEX

About the Author

KITTY KELLEY left her job with *The Washington Post* in 1971 to pursue free-lance writing. She has written for *The New York Times*, *Newsweek*, the *Los Angeles Times*, and the *Chicago Tribune*, as well as *Ladies' Home Journal*, *Good Housekeeping*, and other women's magazines. Her previous books, *Jackie Oh!* and *Elizabeth Taylor: The Last Star*, were both national bestsellers.

SPECTACULAR ENTERTAINMENT ALL SUMMER LONG!
SUMMER SPECTACULAR FREQUENT READERS SWEEPSTAKES
WIN *A 1988 Cadillac Cimarron* Automobile or
12 other Fabulous Prizes

IT'S EASY TO ENTER. HERE'S HOW IT WORKS:

1. Enter *one* individual book sweepstakes, by completing and submitting the Official Entry form found in the back of that Summer Spectacular book, and you qualify for that book's prize drawing.

2. Enter *two* individual book sweepstakes, by completing and submitting two Official Entry Forms found in the back of those two Summer Spectacular books, and you qualify for the prize drawings for those two individual books.

3. Enter *three or more* individual book sweepstakes, by completing and submitting—in one envelope—three or more Official Entry forms found in the back of three or more individual Summer Spectacular books, and you qualify not only for those three or more individual books but also for THE BONUS PRIZE of a brand new Cadillac Cimarron Automobile!

Be sure to fill in the Bantam bookseller where you learned about this Sweepstakes . . . because if you win one of the twelve Sweepstakes prizes . . . your bookseller wins too!

SEE OFFICIAL RULES BELOW FOR DETAILS including alternate means of entry.

No Purchase Necessary.

Here are the Summer Spectacular Sweepstakes Books and Prizes!

BOOK TITLE

On Sale May 20, 1987

ACT OF WILL

MEN WHO HATE
WOMEN & THE WOMEN
WHO LOVE THEM

VENDETTA

On Sale June 17, 1987

LAST OF THE BREED

PRIZE

A luxurious weekend for two (3 days/2 nights) at first class hotel, MAP meals—(transportation not included)
Approximate value: $750.00

Gourmet food of the month for 6 months N.Y. Gourmet Co.
Approximate value: $750.00

Schrade Collector's Knife set
Approximate value: $750.00

Sharp Video Camera and VCR
Approximate value: $1,600.00

| WHITE DOVE (available in US only) THE MOTH (available in Canada only) | Lenox China white coffee service Approximate value: $750.00 |

WHITE DOVE (available
in US only)
THE MOTH (available
in Canada only)

Lenox China white coffee service
Approximate value: $750.00

THE BE (HAPPY)
ATTITUDES

Set of DP workout equipment
Approximate value: $1,000.00

On Sale July 15, 1987

THE UNWANTED

Bug Zapper and Samsonite Chairs—
Table—Umbrella—Outdoor Furniture
Approximate value: $1,300.00

A GRAND PASSION

Cake of the month plan
Approximate value: $800.00

110 SHANGHAI ROAD

$1,000 American Express Gift
Certificates
Value: $1,000.00

On Sale August 12, 1987

HIS WAY

Disc Player with library of
Sinatra discs
Approximate value: $1,000.00

SUSPECTS

Home Security System
Approximate value: $1,000.00

PORTRAIT OF A
MARRIED WOMAN

Minolta Auto-Focus Camera Kit
Approximate value: $750.00

OFFICIAL RULES

1. There are twelve individual sweepstakes, each with its own prize award. There will be twelve separate sweepstakes drawings. You will be entered into the drawing for the prize corresponding to the book(s) from which you have obtained your entry blank, any one or up to all twelve. Submit your completed entry on the Official Entry Form found in this book and any of the other participating books ... mail one or up to all twelve completed sweepstakes entries *in one envelope* to:

Frequent Readers Sweepstakes
PO Box 43 New York, New York 10046

2. NO PURCHASE NECESSARY TO ENTER OR WIN A PRIZE: Residents of Ohio and those wishing to obtain an Official Entry Form (covering all 12 sweepstakes) and the Official Rules send a self-addressed stamped envelope to: Frequent Reader Sweepstakes, P.O. Box 549, Sayreville, NJ 08872. One Official Entry Form per request. Requests must be received by August 14, 1987. Residents of Washington and Vermont need not include return postage.

3. Winners for each of the 12 sweepstakes will be selected in a random drawing to be conducted on or about October 19, 1987, from all completed entries received, under the supervision of Marden-Kane, Inc. an independent judging organization. If any of the 12 consumer winners selected have included completed Official Entry Forms from three or more books, or have included completed Official Entry Forms from three or more books, or have entered 3 or more sweepstakes on the Alternate Mail-In Official Entry Form (See Rule #2) they are qualified to participate in a separate BONUS DRAWING to be conducted on or about Oct. 19, 1987 for a 1988 Cadillac Cimarron. In the event that none of the twelve individual sweepstake prize winners qualify for the BONUS PRIZE, the bonus prize will be selected from all completed sweepstakes entries received. No mechanically reproduced entries accepted. All entries must be received by September 30, 1987 to be eligible. Not responsible for late, lost or misdirected mail or printing errors.

4. By entering this Sweepstakes, each entrant accepts and agrees to be bound by these rules and the decision of the judges which shall be final. Winners will be notified by mail and may be required to execute an Affidavit of Eligibility and Release which must be returned within 14 days of receipt. In the event of non-compliance within this time period, alternate winners will be selected. Winner(s) consent to the use of his/her name and/or photograph for advertising and publicity purposes without additional compensation. No substitution or transfer of prizes allowed (vacation prize subject to availability, and must be taken within one year of notification). Taxes, License and Title Fees are the sole responsibility of the prize winners. One prize (except for Bonus Prize) per family or household. Retailer named on winning twelve blanks will win duplicate sweepstakes prize. (Retailers are not eligible for bonus prize.)

5. Sweepstakes open to residents of the United States and Canada except employees and their families of Bantam Books, its affiliates and subsidiaries, advertising and production agencies and Marden-Kane, Inc. Void in the Province of Quebec and wherever else prohibited or restricted by law. Canadian residents will be required to answer a skill testing question in order to be eligible to receive a prize. All federal, state and local laws apply. Odds of winning a prize in each sweepstake depend upon the total number of completed entries received for that sweepstake. (All prizes will be awarded)

6. For a list of major prize winners, send a stamped, self-addressed envelope to: Frequent Readers Sweepstakes, c/o Marden-Kane, Inc., P.O. Box 711, Sayreville, NJ 08872.

HIS WAY: THE UNAUTHORIZED BIOGRAPHY OF FRANK SINATRA
OFFICIAL ENTRY FORM

Please complete by entering all the information requested and

Mail to: Frequent Readers Sweepstakes
P.O. Box 43
New York, N.Y. 10046

NAME _____

ADDRESS _____

CITY _____ STATE _____ ZIP _____

BANTAM BOOK RETAILER WHERE YOU LEARNED ABOUT THIS SWEEPSTAKES

NAME _____

ADDRESS _____

CITY _____ STATE _____ ZIP _____

Completed entries must be received by September 30, 1987 in order to be eligible.

ISBN-0553-26515-6

BANTAM
SHOP·AT·HOME
C·A·T·A·L·O·G

Special Offer
Buy a Bantam Book
for only 50¢.

Now you can have Bantam's catalog filled with hundreds of titles plus take advantage of our unique and exciting bonus book offer. A special offer which gives you the opportunity to purchase a Bantam book for only 50¢. Here's how!

By ordering any five books at the regular price per order, you can also choose any other single book listed (up to a $4.95 value) for just 50¢. Some restrictions do apply, but for further details why not send for Bantam's catalog of titles today!

Just send us your name and address and we will send you a catalog!